Psychology of Adjustment

KAPLAN & STEIN

Paul S. Kaplan
Suffolk County Community College

Jean Stein

Psychology
of Adjustment

Wadsworth Publishing Company
Belmont, California
A Division of Wadsworth, Inc.

A Study Guide is available to help students master the concepts presented in this book. Order from your bookstore.

Psychology Editor: Kenneth King
Production Editor: Hal Humphrey
Designer: Cynthia Bassett
Copy Editor: Susan Caney-Peterson
Illustrator: Mary Burkhardt

Printed in the United States of America

1 2 3 4 5 6 7 8 9 10—88 87 86 85 84

ISBN 0-534-01031-8

Library of Congress Cataloging in Publication Data
Kaplan, Paul.
    Psychology of adjustment.
    Bibliography: p.
    Includes index.
    1. Adjustment (Psychology)   I. Stein, Jean,
1947–   II. Title.
BF335.K33   1984   155.2′4   83-6565
ISBN 0-534-01031-8

Photo credits appear on p. 429.

To Rebecca Kaplan
& in memory of Abraham Kaplan

To Rose & Norman Ishler

- "I didn't adjust to the divorce for two years."

- "She adjusted to college very quickly—as if she'd never lived any other kind of life."

- "He did well in his job, until the company relocated. He never did adjust after the move, though."

We've all heard statements like these before; most of us have made similar comments ourselves. Yet each of these statements reflects a common misconception: that adjustment is a state—a goal at which people can "arrive." Actually, people never stop adjusting. Adjustment is a dynamic, lifelong process of acting and reacting; of coping, mastering, and often transcending certain challenges of life—only to be challenged anew.

It is just this dynamic quality of adjustment that we hope to convey in this text. We see adjustment as an active process, in which individuals have considerable control over their destiny. The more they understand about both the processes involved in adjustment and the many techniques of adjustment, the easier it can be to meet daily challenges. Thus, learning about the psychology of adjustment can have a great deal of practical significance.

About This Book

There are many different approaches to studying adjustment, and there are textbooks to represent each approach. Some texts are comprehensive and academically oriented; others take a practical, self-help approach. Still others talk directly to the personal experiences and social milieu of students. *Psychology of Adjustment* tries to combine the

strengths of all of these approaches. Its scholarship, we believe, is as thorough as that of any major text today; yet it speaks to the interests, questions, and problems that the diverse students of today are likely to share. We'd like to point out some of the strengths that we feel set this text apart.

Organization   The book's organization provides a logical and practical approach to learning about adjustment. We begin with the basics: adjustment and personality, motivation, learning, and development. Part I includes a chapter on each of these four *fundamentals of adjustment,* explaining these processes in a personal way that lays the foundation for understanding adjustment. Part II discusses *safety needs* and factors such as stress, anger, and guilt that pose threats to our sense of security as individuals. *Belongingness needs*—including social roles and sex roles, relationships, love commitments, and sexual adjustment—are the topic of Part III. Part IV deals with the self-concept and with issues related to *esteem needs.* Finally, the last two chapters on consciousness and values are grouped under the heading *self-actualization.* These two chapters also deal with people's strivings toward higher levels of adjustment and understanding.

You may have noticed a resemblance between the organization we've just described and Abraham Maslow's well-known hierarchy of needs. This structure does *not* imply any specific endorsement of Maslow. Indeed, throughout the text we have tried to give "equal time" to each of the major psychological approaches. We chose this organization because it lends itself to teaching adjustment. Its logical progression, from questions such as, "How did I get to be the way I am?" or, "What's the best way to manage stress?" on up to, "How can I make the most of myself?" provides a step-by-step look at the kinds of adjustment issues real people face in daily life.

Comprehensiveness   Comprehensiveness is a second strength of this text. We cover all the topics traditionally found in adjustment textbooks. However, there are many new developments and issues that affect the field of adjustment, and our text tries to present the most relevant of these, including:

- Discussions of many of the newer cognitive positions along with the behavioral, psychoanalytic, and humanistic approaches

- Discussions of many topics that receive little coverage in most other adjustment texts, including guilt, memory, assertiveness training, the process behind encounter groups, communication (both verbal and nonverbal) in relationships, and the way in which disabilities affect the self-concept

- A chapter-length treatment of social roles and sex roles that encourages readers to think about their own stereotypes

- A realistic look at the process of making vocational choices that includes not only suggestions for decision making, but also information about how the job market is changing

- A broad look at sexual adjustment that should be just as relevant to students returning to college in mid-life as it is to young people

Practical Orientation   A practical orientation is a third strength of this book. Psychology of adjustment is a practical course. We recognize its practical value and suggest directions that can help readers put psychological principles to use in a variety of areas, from reducing life stress, to losing weight, to "fighting fair" in arguments. We've also drawn from numerous current sources to provide ideas for the kinds of decisions students are likely

to face: dealing with someone who drinks too much, establishing personal ideals that are realistic, evaluating self-help books in a bookstore, and even applying common-sense consumer principles in choosing (or firing) a therapist.

Sound Scholarship and Personal Presentation This is still another strength. While our research is thorough and up-to-date, it is presented in clear language that is easy to understand—without talking down to readers. Examples have been selected to introduce psychological concepts in a way that will be particularly relevant to readers. For instance, our chapter on stress opens with a look at Elvis Presley—a case study that illustrates the point that even success can be a source of stress that requires vital coping skills.

Special Features

In addition to the elements we've just described, this text also has a number of special features that enhance its value as a teaching aid.

Boxes   A "three-dimensional" box program draws upon many valuable sources to amplify discussions in the text. We include three different types of boxes to provide a diverse and interesting supplement to text discussions:

- *Adjustment and You.* These boxes provide both personal guidance and "hands-on" applications for readers. Included are self-evaluation scales as well as many practical models for adjustment.

- *Focus on Research.* We present certain research studies in more detail to show how psychologists pose and go about answering questions related to human behavior. Thus, psychology as science is not slighted, in spite of our applied emphasis. These research boxes explore questions of particular emphasis. When will flattery get you nowhere (and why)? How do various discipline styles affect children? How does alcohol affect aggression?

- *Perspectives on Adjustment.* These boxes look at current adjustment issues from several perspectives—summarizing the controversy on sex education in the schools, for instance, or presenting vignettes from the lives of real people, from Patty Hearst to a flight attendant who became a "prescription junkie."

Key Terms Key terms are listed at the end of each chapter, in order of appearance in the chapter discussion. Definitions are easy to find because they are listed not only in the combination glossary-index at the end of the book, but also in a "running glossary" that is set off from the text on each page where a term is introduced.

Chapter Summaries Chapter summaries provide a sequential overview of the ground covered in each chapter. We have used a simple format for these summaries, numbering each short paragraph. Combined with the key term listings, these short summaries will serve as useful study aids for readers.

Ancillaries An excellent *Study Guide* for students that features personal applications and cases to better enable students to understand concepts has been prepared by Gary King of Rose State College. Additionally, there is a very detailed *Instructor's Manual* that outlines and summarizes the book's chapters and features numerous classroom demonstrations, as well as providing bountiful multiple choice and discussion questions. The multiple choice questions are unique in that many of them test students' understanding through the application of concepts to cases.

Acknowledgments

A number of people have contributed to this book in many ways, and we'd like to thank them here. First, the team at Wadsworth: psychology editor Ken King for his helpful guidance and his belief in this book; production editor Hal Humphrey for his professionalism in dealing with the incredibly detailed process of transforming a manuscript into a book (all the way down to tracking down the best photo of a laboratory rat!); special projects editor Mary Arbogast for her patience and good humor in helping us through the week-by-week revision process; and assistant art director Cynthia Bassett for the handsome design of this textbook. Thanks also to permissions editor Peggy Meehan, copy editor Susan Caney-Peterson, and editorial assistant Dina Bensen for their considerable know-how and assistance.

We would also like to thank the reviewers whose constructive criticism has provided invaluable guidance: Dr. Ronald G. Evans, Washburn University; Dr. Carol Grams, Orange Coast College; Dr. Mitzi G. Jones, Alabama A & M University; Dr. Joanne L. Roberts, El Camino College; Dr. Sidney Hochman, Nassau Community College; Dr. Michael M. Levine, Bloomsburg State College; Dr. David G. Weight, Brigham Young University; Dr. James N. Greene, South Dakota State University; Dr. Ron Ponsford, Northwest Nazarene College; Dr. Don Stephenson, College of Southern Idaho; Dr. William Ray, Pennsylvania State University; Dr. John Altrocchi, University of Nevada, Reno; Dr. Dale Simmons, Oregon State University; Dr. Gary King, Rose State College; Dr. Robert A. Osterhouse, Prince George's Community College; Dr. Norman L. Kellett, Fisher Junior College; Dr. Anna M. Nemec, Macon Junior College; Dr. Keith Trasher, Rose State College; Dr. Myree Hayes, East Carolina University; Dr. Robert M. Petty, The University of Santa Clara; and Dr. Louis A. Martone, Miami Dade Community College.

Finally, both of our families deserve mention for putting up with the late nights, variable moods, and demands for peace and quiet that are all part of writing a book. Thanks to our spouses, Leslie and Phil, and our children—Stacey, Amy, Jodi, and Laurie Kaplan and Rebecca and Adam Stein—for contributing to our effort in their own highly individual ways.

CONTENTS IN BRIEF

C O N T E N T S

*Part One
Fundamentals
of Adjustment 1*

Chapter Six/Anxiety, Guilt, and Depression 127

Chapter Seven/Anger and Aggression 156

*Part Three
Belongingness
Needs 175*

***Part Four
Esteem Needs
275***

Chapter Twelve/The Self 276

Chapter Thirteen/Work and Leisure 298

Chapter Fourteen/Therapy and the Human Potentials Movement 326

supplemental materials

*Part Five
Self-
Actualization
351*

Contents

*Fundamentals
of Adjustment*

Joan wants a divorce but is frightened at the prospect of fending for herself. With two small children to care for, she wonders whether it would not be better to tolerate the unhappy home situation. Although there have been few violent quarrels, petty bickering continues around the clock and neither spouse is happy. The couple often spends entire evenings without speaking to each other, and neither passes up an opportunity to hurt the other. Marriage counseling has accomplished little, and the home situation has deteriorated to a point where Joan feels it is harming the children.

Adjustment and Personality

Joan's decision would be easy if she knew that a divorce would end her troubles, and that she could support herself and her two children. Yet doubts overwhelm her. What if she can't support herself and her husband won't pay support? What if she becomes more miserable and lonely without him?

Joan's dilemma points to a painful but well-known fact: few issues in life are black-and-white. Whichever decision Joan ends up making, it is likely to be years before she is able to judge its true consequences. Even then, those consequences may appear to her as a sum of positive as well as negative outcomes. Adjustments are rarely radically positive or negative, but stand somewhere in between.

This chapter is about adjustment, the types of strategies we use to cope with and master the challenges we face. These patterns of adjustment, along with our attitudes toward them, comprise a major portion of what we call personality. The study of adjustment looks at issues such as that confronting Joan. It also looks at the hundreds of less momentous decisions that people make (or allow to slip by) each day.

The field of adjustment has a unique and particularly relevant domain in **psychology,** the study of human and animal behavior. It deals with the choices, strategies, motivations, and goals, as well as the actual consequences of behavior. We will explore the question of how individuals respond to the challenges that arise throughout life, looking for ways to improve these strategies in a changing world. We explore personality as well as adjustment in this chapter, because knowing *who* we are is essential to understanding *what* we do.

What Is Adjustment?

Each day, we are faced with new situations that demand decisions. These situations involve changes in both our *internal state* (as when a person discovers that the same job or relationship is no longer satisfying) and in our *external environment* (as when a person moves to a new town or a parent dies). The process of **adjustment** involves a person's attempt to cope with, master, and transcend such challenges.

This working definition provides a starting point for understanding adjustment. As the opening example pointed out, however, adjustments themselves aren't always definite, nor do we always know if they are "right" or "wrong," nor do they necessarily have clear starting points or endings. This combination of qualities can make the concept of adjustment a difficult one to grasp. It may be helpful, therefore, to devote a little more space to two important qualities of adjustment. First, adjustment is a process, in that it involves continuous change. The second important quality is that people develop consistent patterns of adjusting to these constant changes.

Adjustment as a Process

Adjustment is a *process:* it is a means, rather than an end product. Life is a series of changes and challenges, and as a result, people are always in the process of changing. They adopt new techniques and strategies for adjusting to their world. Such changes are an integral part of growth and development.

It is difficult to view adjustment as a process, however. People are raised to think in terms of end products and consequences. End products such as winning and losing, success and failure seem to attract much more attention than does the long path we take to reach those states. Yet, it isn't always possible to define the end product as distinctly positive or negative. Nor, as happened to Joan, can you always foresee the final consequences of the adjustments you are making. Later in life, Joan may see her decision as having created a series of challenges and confrontations, each of which had to be handled individually.

> **Psychology** The study of human and animal behavior.
>
> **Adjustment** The process by which an individual attempts to cope with, master, and transcend the challenges of life by utilizing a variety of techniques and strategies.

The rule of existence, then, seems to be one of continuous change. A student finally pays off all her credit card charges from Christmas, only to find her 1966 Ford with 100,000 miles breaking down. Just when working parents find a good childcare facility that allows them to return to their careers, their child becomes ill, forcing one or the other to take time off.

This dynamic quality of life forces people to live in a constant state of flux. You either change, or you sadly find yourself out of step with the environment. Yet, change also forces people to use certain coping strategies consistently in similar situations.

Patterns of Adjustment

It is virtually impossible to stop and consider how we want to react to each minor change in ourselves or our environment. Most of the time, we respond more-or-less automatically—by going out to the grocery store when supplies are low, or by spending less time with a boy or girlfriend we no longer get along with, or by studying late at night to prepare for an upcoming exam.

You might use the term "thermostat effect" to label these automatic adjustments. Just as the ups and downs of your house's temperature cause the thermostatic heating system to click off and on, so also do our behaviors, our pace of life, and our attitudes shift in response to environmental or bodily needs. "Click"—time to re-stock supplies. "Click"—time to cool down that relationship. "Click"—time to catch up on studying.

Moving toward, away, or against challenges   Karen Horney described three possible reactions to problems that one encounters beginning with early parent-child conflicts. *Moving toward* involves behaviors such as ingratiating oneself to others, *moving away* relates to escaping, and *moving against* involves protest and perhaps aggression.

This analogy carries us only so far, however, for while thermostats have only a limited number of responses (two, in fact—"on" or "off"), we "human thermostats" work in much more individual ways. Each of us is different from the next. Some people can't seem to pull themselves out of a relationship even if it is unrewarding; some refuse to prepare for exams, or they do their studying way ahead of time; still others almost never visit a grocery store at all, leaving that task for someone else in the household. In every situation, each individual develops characteristic patterns of response or adjustment.

Psychologist Karen Horney (1945)* classified these adjustment patterns in terms of three very broad types of responses. She suggests that people tend to deal with problems by either **moving toward** them, **away** from them, **or against** them. Horney believed that each of these strategies demonstrates an important individual need. Thus, the person who always solves problems by escaping (moving away from them) may be afraid of becoming too involved and dependent on others. People who always move toward others, by ingratiating themselves to others or seeking advice, may be demonstrating an excessive need for love, while those who move against problems by reacting aggressively may be demonstrating an excessive need for power. In Horney's view, a person needs to use all three of these strategies in order to reach a healthy adjustment. The overuse of any one strategy is inherently unhealthy.

What Is Healthy Adjustment?

Horney's analysis raises an important question, in our understanding of adjustment. We all adjust to problems and changes in one way or another. But which adjustments are healthy, and which kinds

---

*In this text, we will be using the short reference form common to psychological or scientific works. The bibliography at the end of the book provides the complete title and publication information for each reference cited.

of behaviors represent unhealthy adjustments? There are a number of answers to this question, but two elements seem especially important. These are an understanding of your own needs, and a healthy respect for others.

Understanding Your Own Needs

You probably know people who continually use one response to cope with their problems. They seem to be unaware of alternatives to their actions. This is unfortunate, since flexibility is an important aspect of healthy adjustment. As Karen Horney noted, it is unhealthy to overrely on any single method of dealing with problems. Thus, while it may be appropriate to deal with some arguments by going out for a walk to give yourself a chance to "cool off," you can't escape all problems by getting away from them.

Instead of relying on habitual responses, an important part of healthy adjustment is the ability to take problems as they arise—to analyze and respond to them according to your needs. This isn't always easy. It takes special will and awareness to admit that the strategy you have been using is not working, and to switch to a different one. Thus, if you are constantly arguing with your boss, it may be time to seek out a different strategy. In order to do this, though, you must go through a three-part "soul-searching" process. You must:

- become aware of what you are doing;
- understand that it has failed to satisfy your needs; and
- be willing to seek out and experiment with different strategies.

A Healthy Respect for Others

A second quality of healthy adjustment is a respect for the needs of others. As an example of this criterion, imagine that you are in a rush to exchange some jeans you've purchased. There are two people ahead of you in line, and you are impatiently awaiting your turn when someone walks up from the back of the line and begins a transaction. She looks at you and says, "You don't mind—do you?" then turns around and continues her exchange before you have a chance to reply.

If healthy adjustment merely meant satisfying one's own needs, this approach would seem sound. However, this person has trampled on the rights of everyone else. Eventually, she will run into a situation in which people do not tolerate such conduct. In addition, such behavior is certain to have rather dire social consequences. Very few people will want to have much to do with her.

Healthy adjustment requires taking the rights and feelings of others into consideration. People who only consider their own needs in any situation are likely to be seen as selfish and crude. They might obtain short-term satisfaction for their immediate needs, but only at the expense of their relationships with others. In the long run, such individuals are often isolated, or are merely tolerated by others.

Being "Healthy" vs. Being "Normal"

A third point is important in understanding healthy adjustment, and this is the distinction between "normal" and "healthy." The two terms are often confused. Consider the following dialogue:

Burt: I just feel so strange around him because he's—you know what.

Mark: You mean he's gay—a homosexual.

Burt: Yes—it gives me the creeps just thinking about it. It's so unnatural, abnormal. I don't know—I just don't know what to say around him. I get tongue-tied.

Mark: How does being gay affect him as a person though?

Burt (*ignoring Mark's comment*)*:* He must be sick.

Mark: Why?

Burt: If it's abnormal it's sick, and if it's sick then it must be unhealthy.

You've come a long way, baby.

VIRGINIA SLIMS *Lights*

Warning: The Surgeon General Has Determined That Cigarette Smoking Is Dangerous to Your Health.

9 mg "tar," 0.7 mg nicotine
av. per cigarette by FTC method.

Acceptable behavior changes over time. One example of this is the changing concept of where "a woman's place" should be.

Many people, like Burt, make no distinction between abnormal and unhealthy adjustment. Yet this distinction is vital. The terms *normal* and *abnormal* and *healthy* and *unhealthy* are often confused, although they have different meanings.

Normality The broad range of statistically usual or accepted behaviors within a particular society.

Abnormality Behaviors that are statistically unusual within a society.

Normality and **abnormality** are statistical concepts: they refer to the broad numerical range of common or uncommon behaviors within a particular society. But what is "abnormal" need not be "unhealthy." For example, few people in the United States vote in every election. It is statistically unusual for someone to vote, in other words. Yet no one would call such behavior unhealthy.

What is considered normal or abnormal is determined by the time, the society, and the situation. Without taking all three into account, it is easy to misunderstand the concept of normality.

The Time Period "Acceptable behavior" often changes over time. In 1914, the idea of infants touching their genitals was so distasteful that parents took drastic measures to prevent this in homes all over the United States. The acceptable "treatment" for this behavior was to tie the infant's arms and legs to the crib posts. Such behavior would today be considered not only abnormal but child abuse.

The Society Normality and abnormality are also defined by the society. Practices common to one culture are often not tolerated in another. Consider your own reactions, for instance, if your grandparents wandered off into a blizzard, never to be seen again, shortly after they retired. You would probably respond with shock and grief. Yet in some Eskimo societies (particularly in times of famine) it is normal for older people to turn themselves out to the elements after they can no longer make an economic contribution to society.

Again, in the Melanesian Trobriand culture, each young adult was traditionally expected to engage in sexual intercourse before marriage. Sexual behavior was considered normal, and much of it occurred in public (Malinowski, 1929). Our culture has traditionally discouraged premarital sex (although this area is admittedly undergoing some change), and even the most "liberated" of us tend to think twice about what we practice in public. In sum, then, every human behavior is open to the interpretation of society. And it is the society which establishes criteria for what is to be considered normal and abnormal behavior.

The Situation   A third factor that determines "normal" patterns of behavior is the situation itself. Cheering at a football game is acceptable, but a rousing cheer upon being told you just failed your driving test for the sixth time would be considered rather odd. Being depressed at the loss of a friend is usual, but few people feel dejected at winning a lottery (although as we'll see in Chapter 5, even sudden wealth is not entirely without stress). Our behavior changes with our view of the circumstances.

Healthy Adjustment: A Working Definition

In all, then, there are a number of standards for determining what is healthy adjustment. Our own working definition can be drawn from the guidelines just described:

- First, healthy adjustment includes an understanding of our own individual needs.

- Second, healthy adjustment includes a respect for human life and an awareness of the rights of others.

- Finally, healthy adjustment is flexible and tolerant, and it represents choices made from options rather than simply responding in "acceptable" or "normal" ways (although a person need not always be a pioneer in order to be healthy).

Although flexibility is important, we each respond and behave according to distinctive and consistent patterns. These patterns include thoughts and feelings as well as behaviors, and collectively they form our personalities (Mischel, 1976). If we could understand these patterns of behavior, we might be able to understand and improve our own adjustments.

What Is Personality?

"If I went home and told my mother that I was going to spend the weekend with my boyfriend, I know exactly what she'd do. She'd look up to heaven and cry, 'What did I do wrong?' I call that 'guilt trip number one.' Then she would proceed to 'guilt trip number two.' She'd talk to my father and he'd sit down and give me a lecture. Every now and then he'd ask me if I agree. If I dare to say no, it's two more hours, so I usually just sit there and nod."

Sound familiar? We are all well aware of how those around us will behave given a set of circumstances. We can predict what will make them happy, sad, frustrated, proud, and angry. After a while, their characteristics seem rather set, almost unchanging. The fact that one person is habitually the life of the party while another sits around seriously discussing politics makes the world predictable, and it provides us with a sense of security. If our behaviors weren't so stable, predicting other people's reactions would be impossible. Life itself might prove one long suspicion after another.

Predictability not only enhances security, it also helps us deal effectively with others. If a friend prides himself on his honesty, you can predict that he will return excess change at a restaurant or that he will give you a fair price if he's selling his old calculator. If another friend tends to get out of trouble by blaming others, you might be less inclined to work together with her on a project. It is this predictable aspect of human behavior that is usually called **personality.** When people say that "Glenn has a great personality," they are basically approving of his particular set of attitudes, beliefs, and behavior patterns.

The degree to which personality is predictable, however, is open to debate. As in any area of

> **Personality**   An individual's distinctive and predictable behavior patterns that may include thoughts, attitudes, feelings, values.

People react to situations in a characteristic fashion—a fact that helps provide us with a sense of security. How would you feel if you watched a movie in which Laurel and Hardy's roles were reversed?

human behavior, there are broad regions of *un-predictability* that make the science of psychology far less precise than any laboratory science. Two factors may be especially relevant here: stability in different situations, and stability over time.

Stability in Different Situations

For one, we may all agree that Glenn has a "great personality." But such a behavioral assessment is probably based on common day-to-day situations.

What happens in an abnormal, uncommon, highly stressful situation? How would witty, charming, considerate Glenn respond when faced with an emergency? He just might startle you by avoiding the situation, or becoming upset and angry, or being at loss for a solution. Perhaps those 30s and 40s movies—where the leading actress tells her erstwhile boyfriend that "I never really knew you 'til now"—were actually making a scientifically accurate statement about the psychology of personality.

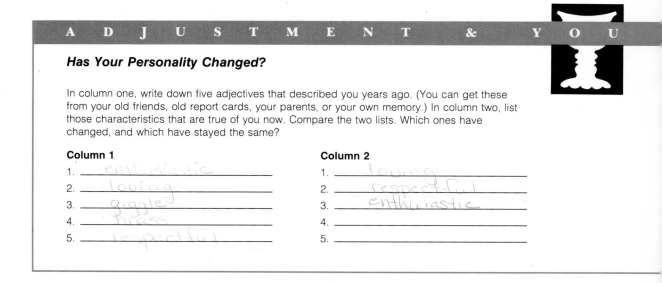

Has Your Personality Changed?

In column one, write down five adjectives that described you years ago. (You can get these from your old friends, old report cards, your parents, or your own memory.) In column two, list those characteristics that are true of you now. Compare the two lists. Which ones have changed, and which have stayed the same?

Column 1

1. _enthusiastic_
2. _loving_
3. _giggled_
4. _brass_
5. _respectful_

Column 2

1. _loving_
2. _respectful_
3. _enthusiastic_
4. _____
5. _____

Stability over Time

A second factor in predicting personality is change over time. Admittedly, a person who likes adventure and who sees herself as a "daredevil" will probably have a different attitude toward sky diving than another person who avoids danger and finds more than enough thrills playing arcade games. While these two individuals react differently to risky situations, will they always respond in the same fashion? How many aspiring adventurers actually grow up to become Evel Knievels,* Annie Oakleys, or 007s? Alternatively, what are the odds that a cautious, conservative person will take up hang-gliding or auto racing later in life? We hear a lot about midlife crises and personality change over time, and this area of development has fascinated psychologists for some time. You may not have passed through a midlife crisis yet, but the exercise in the box *Has Your Personality*

*On the other hand, how many would want to? According to the *Guinness Book of World Records* (1981, p. 471), one record held by Knievel is for broken bones—433 of them!

Changed? may give you some insight into how consistent your own personality has been over time.

Many researchers have tried to measure just how much or how little personality changes over time. The findings of these studies are still rather controversial. However, the results indicate that most people are moderately stable in such areas as *activity level*, *values*, and *vocational interests*, at least from adolescence through middle adulthood. Especially stable is the way most people see themselves throughout life (Mischel, 1968). Your sense that you are the same person you always were seems to continue throughout the years—although there is much less stability in the way others see you. Changes, however, are usually gradual, and although you aren't exactly the same individual you once were, you are still easily recognizable.

The questions of how our self-perceptions and behavior patterns arise, what they mean, and how they change over time have been studied at length, and they have been answered in several different ways. We'll look at three of the most important answers, or theories of personality, in the remainder of this chapter.

How Do You View Personality?

Each one of the following series of statements describes a distinct personality theory. Which one statement in each group best describes your own view?

1. **a.** All behavior is determined by powerful biological drives and instincts.

    b. Infants are basically "blank slates" whose personalities are molded by their environment, not by internal drives.

    c. People are motivated by an innate tendency toward self-fulfillment.

2. **a.** People are basically irrational in their actions, and are often unaware of why they act in a certain way.

    b. We know why people act as they do: their behavior is learned. Thus, scientific method and controlled studies of learning—even animal experimentation—can lead to a greater understanding of human behavior.

    c. People are so fundamentally different from animals that animal research is of little value in understanding human behavior. People's subjective experience is a critical mediator of behavior.

3. **a.** In order to change, people must first gain insight into why they act as they do.

    b. In order to change, a person must unlearn old behaviors and relearn new ones.

    c. People have the ability to transcend their own problems and live fulfilling lives; unlearning or insight experiences may not be necessary.

An evaluation will be provided later in the chapter.

Personality: Three Views

There are so many ways to approach the study of personality that it would be impossible to outline them all. The same behavior can be explained according to several different theories, and different schools of psychology consider one factor more important than another. The three primary orientations—the psychoanalytic, the behaviorist, and the humanistic views—take very different perspectives, and debates among their supporters can become quite heated. (The boxed questionnaire, *How Do You View Personality?*, provides you with an opportunity to see whether you lean toward one or another of these schools of thought.)

Taken together, these various explanations provide us with a coherent framework for understanding personality. We will look at each theory in turn, beginning with one of the least understood: the psychoanalytic theory of Sigmund Freud.

Freud's Psychoanalytic View

Although Sigmund Freud's name is a household word, most people have little understanding of his theories (Fine, 1973). Because his theory seems difficult to understand, his complex system is often oversimplified. For instance, the words "Freud" and "sex" are universally linked, yet few

Sigmund Freud. His theory stresses the importance of the unconscious in determining human behavior. Right: The Nightmare, *by Henri Fuseli, is one artist's depiction of such forces.*

people really appreciate what Freud meant by human sexuality. (This will be discussed more fully in Chapter 4.) Although not many people in the world today would consider themselves to be orthodox Freudians, his influence is pervasive. Often, people agree with many of his basic premises without realizing they are part of Freud's psychoanalytic theory.

The term **psychoanalytic** describes the theory of personality and motivation that involves describing and analyzing the unconscious forces of the mind. Freud's theory views many of our personality attributes as reflecting early childhood experiences, as illustrated in the boxed material *Felix, Oscar, and the Importance of Early Experience.* Often, such experiences have been long forgotten, and indeed, one of the central elements in Freudian theory is the importance of "what you don't know." We'll look at two basic parts of this theory: Freud's levels of consciousness, and his three constructs of the mind.

Levels of Consciousness   Have you ever taken an instant dislike to someone without knowing why? Have you ever done something and not been satisfied by your own explanation? Have you ever said something that "just slipped out"? If your answer to any of these questions is yes, then Freud's view of the unconscious may be of interest to you.

Freud posited three levels of consciousness or awareness (see Figure 1.1). The **conscious** mind is composed of "the portion of mind that is aware of

Psychoanalytic theory   The theoretical position of Sigmund Freud and his followers. Psychoanalytic theory looks to the unconscious forces within the mind to explain personality and motivation.

Conscious   A Freudian term used to denote the thoughts and emotions that any individual is aware of at a particular moment.

Felix, Oscar, and the Importance of Early Experience

Can two totally different individuals who have been tossed out by their wives live together without driving each other crazy?

This question is asked in the television adaptation of Neil Simon's *The Odd Couple*. Oscar Madison's sloppiness is legendary. He is so disorganized and messy that his room is considered ready to be condemned by the health department. He often eats salami and jelly sandwiches in bed, and uses a dart board to hang his clothing. Felix Unger is fastidiously clean and a creature of habit, routinized, inflexible, and compulsively neat. He is such a critic and perfectionist that in ulcer language, as one comedian noted, he is called a "carrier."

Glimpses of Felix and Oscar's childhoods clearly indicate that these traits were developed early. The influence of early childhood on personality is an important concept in psychoanalytic thought. Freud felt that ingrained behavior patterns and personality characteristics were the consequence of parents' early handling of their children's needs and drives, as well as the demands they made on their children. Thus, too strict a toilet-training program could produce a compulsively neat, rigid personality (enter Felix!); an infant who was denied the chance to suck and chew might become a chain smoker, and so forth. (Freud's explanation of why this happens will be discussed in Chapter 4.)

Felix Unger (left) and Oscar Madison.

Level I: The Conscious
"I smell smoke...I like the way the artist drew this picture...I'm hungry."

Level II: The Preconscious
"Last night's dinner was awful...Susan's parents couldn't believe it when we told them we didn't want a big wedding."

Level III: The Unconscious
"I don't want to get married at all!...My parents weren't happy together...I wish I had John's money."

Figure 1.1   Levels of Consciousness

the immediate environment" (Chaplin, 1975, p. 110). Perhaps at this moment you are aware not only of the printed page before you, but also of the smell of your dinner in the oven and the sound of the TV set in the apartment next door.

Memories that can easily be brought to awareness comprise the second level of consciousness, called the **preconscious** or **foreconscious** (Eidelberg, 1968). The name of your psychology professor, what you saw at the movies last Thursday evening, and the make and year of your car are examples of material that is easily brought back into awareness.

For most people, the concept of consciousness ends here, but Freud takes the idea one step further. He saw still another level, and this one was by far the most important in determining behavior, he believed. He called this level the unconscious. The **unconscious** consists of experiences, feelings, and urges that may be too anxiety-provoking to be placed into awareness. Deep, instinctual, primitive wishes and urges are also contained in the unconscious (Cartwright & Cartwright, 1971), and they motivate much of human behavior.

The three levels of consciousness are often likened to an iceberg: only a small fraction is visible. To the Freudian, we are unaware of the true nature of our motivations, wishes, and feelings: most of these dynamic forces lie underneath the surface, deep within the unconscious.

> **Preconscious (foreconscious)** A Freudian concept describing the construct of the mind that contains memories and feelings that can easily be brought into the consciousness if the individual focuses upon the material.
>
> **Unconscious** One of Freud's three levels of conscious awareness; consists of the thoughts, impulses, and feelings of which an individual is not aware. According to psychoanalytic theory, these feelings, thoughts, and impulses that lie below the level of awareness are basic to understanding motivation.

Although we may not be aware of it, manifestations of the unconscious are everywhere, and they play a vital role in our responses to all kinds of situations. For example, Tom has spent the last three months trying to convince the Board of Directors to hear his plan for a new advertising campaign. Finally he receives an invitation to address the Board. The following morning he "forgets" to set the alarm clock and sleeps through the meeting. Now there are a number of plausible explanations for Tom's behavior. However, it is just possible that Tom was afraid that he would be turned down and, in order to spare himself the rejection, he slept through it. He is consciously unaware of this motivation. This can be the case with a final examination, a date, or a job interview. Placing some anxiety-producing event out of your conscious mind is called **repression,** and it is one way of defending yourself from anxiety. (We will discuss repression and several other defense mechanisms later on in Chapter 6.)

According to Freud, your real motives and feelings are often hidden from your conscious mind. Only by using special techniques to develop insight into the unconscious can a person become aware of these underlying forces. But how do these unconscious forces interact? Freud's theory was very complex, but we'll look at one of the best-known elements of his explanation below: his conception of the id, the ego, and the superego.

The Id, Ego, and Superego   Freud explained the workings of the mind by creating a model consisting of three constructs: the id, the ego, and the superego.

The **id** is the repository for each person's instinctual desires and motivations. The id knows only its own desires. It seeks immediate gratification, always crying "I want" or "I must have." Food, sex, comfort, pain reduction, and pleasure are all constantly sought. The workings of the id are unconscious, for the true nature of the desires are screened from the individual's conscious mind. (A newborn infant might be called "all id," for it demands immediate relief for each need.)

With maturation, the influence of the id is gradually tamed by the conscious portion of the mind, the **ego.** The ego interprets reality. It is responsible for mediating between the desires of the id and the realities of the environment. For example, suppose your id wants the hero sandwich that your friend just bought. You probably wouldn't take it out of her hands and eat it. Your id may not care how you get your nourishment, but your ego understands the social consequences of such behavior. Your ego demands that you dig down into your pocket, wait in line, and purchase your own hero. Not only that, but it dominates your consciousness to the extent that you will probably not even be aware that the id desired your friend's hero! A compromise has taken place, without your even knowing it, to satisfy the id's desires in a socially approved manner.

A strong ego is one that can deal realistically with the environment, satisfying the individual's needs in a reasonable manner by using a variety of strategies. But the ego also has to deal with the third construct, the superego.

While the id is present at birth and the ego develops soon thereafter, the **superego** does not

---

Repression   A defense mechanism by which unacceptable or anxiety-producing impulses, thoughts, or feelings are not allowed to enter consciousness.

Id   The construct of the mind that Freud viewed as the focus of all the instinctual desires and needs.

Ego   The term used to describe the conscious portion of the mind in psychoanalytic thought. The ego mediates between the individual's wishes and desires and the realities of the environment.

Superego   The construct of the mind in psychoanalytic theory that includes societal and parental morals and values that have become internalized. Violations of the superego's standards lead to feelings of guilt.

really begin forming until early childhood. It consists of parental and societal mores and ethics. "Don't lie, don't steal, don't cheat" are all examples of the superego's rules. When you act in a way that is contrary to these rules, the superego is responsible for the guilt that you feel. For example, society expects you to unconditionally love and respect your parents. You know, logically, that such an expectation is impossible *all* of the time—yet you still feel guilty when you fail to live up to that standard.

Freud's conceptions of the importance of early experience, the levels of consciousness, and the three constructs of the mind provide a comprehensive explanation of personality. (We'll return to other aspects of his theory at later points in this text.) Despite his wide influence, however, few people today are orthodox or hard-line Freudians. Many elements of his theory were always controversial, even among those who followed him.

A Neo-Freudian Interpretation   A group of theorists have accepted some of Freud's ideas while rejecting others. Commonly these **neo-Freudians** (new Freudians) downplay the importance of sexuality and the unconscious, emphasizing instead the functioning of the ego.

One of the outstanding neo-Freudian theorists was Alfred Adler, a contemporary of Freud who replaced Freud's emphasis on a sexual drive with one of human striving for superiority—a drive to master one's environment. One element of Adler's theory is especially relevant to our understanding of personality and adjustment. This is the idea of *compensation*.

According to Adler, people are motivated by social experiences and subjective feelings of inferiority. A person may attempt to compensate for these inferiorities by choosing a uniquely personal lifestyle (Papanek, 1971). The compensation may be direct, or it may be indirect. Theodore Roosevelt provides an example of **direct compensation.** A slight, weak, sickly child, he exercised at a strenuous, sustained pace until he became quite an

Should I or shouldn't I? Freud sees behavior in terms of conflict between what we want to do and the prohibitions placed on us by the environment.

Neo-Freudian   Literally, "new Freudian." Psychologists of this orientation tend to downplay Freud's original emphasis on sexuality and the unconscious, emphasizing the ego's functioning and the influence of sociocultural factors.

Direct compensation   A form of compensation in which an individual attempts to overcome or make up for a real or imagined deficiency or failure by achieving in this area.

athlete and sportsman. **Indirect compensation** occurs when a person makes up for a sense of inferiority by becoming proficient in another field, as when a boy who has never been chosen for the punchball game compensates by studying and becoming a great engineer or tropical fish expert.

To Adler, each individual has a unique method of achieving mastery over the environment by engaging in a particular style of life. This lifestyle reflects not only subjective feelings of inferiority or superiority, but also the social realities of each person's own circumstances. Thus, a person who lives in an urban ghetto may find the only way to gain power in a group is by becoming physically stronger and more streetwise than all the others. A wealthy person who desires the same power, in contrast, may need other social skills. The goals are similar, but the manner in which each attains mastery is different.

It is easy to see how different skills and adjustments would be needed by an inner-city youth and a well-to-do suburbanite. But environment and expectations also influence personality in far more subtle ways. Some elements of Adler's theory of birth order described in the box *First, Second, or Third...and Does It Matter?* may surprise you.

Thus, social forces and cultural environment are important factors in understanding personality. Adler emphasized social interest and the striving for superiority (Feshbach & Weiner, 1982); other neo-Freudians, including Karen

Horney, Erich Fromm, Harry Stack Sullivan, and Erik Erikson, also used Freudian thought as a point of departure in developing their own theories. While their theories cannot be reviewed fully here, some of their views on specific topics can be found throughout the text.

Yet many psychologists have become dissatisfied with Freudian and neo-Freudian theories. They argue that psychoanalytic theory is based on data that are unreliable and hypotheses that can't be tested (Lundin, 1974). Some of these psychologists have searched for a theory that could deal with behavior without resorting to guesswork about the unconscious (Skinner, 1974). Ideally, such a theory should be based on data that can be easily tested in a laboratory. These criteria are satisfied by the second major school of thought, learning theory.

Learning Theory and Personality

If a rat is run through a maze, its behavior can be predicted by manipulating where and when it gets a reward. As long as the environmental rewards, the punishments, and the learning history of the animal are known, it is possible to predict its behavior.

Just as a rat travels through a maze, suggest learning theorists, or **behaviorists,** so do humans travel through life. This analogy is important. It means that if the exact rewards and punishments are known along with the background of the person, that individual's behavior can be predicted, controlled, and modified.

Behaviorists, then, emphasize the importance of learning in determining the behavior of an organism. Learning theory does not deal with internal processes such as awareness, self-fulfillment, or nonobservable events. It emphasizes the observable and measurable. Mental events like thinking, intuition, and imagination are not denied, but they are considered unnecessary for predicting behavior (Skinner, 1974). Thus, learning

---

Indirect compensation A form of compensation in which an individual attempts to overcome a real or imagined deficiency by achieving in another unrelated area.

Behaviorism (learning theory) A school of psychology that rejects the study of consciousness and internal phenomena in favor of techniques that measure overt, observable behavior patterns.

First, Second, or Third . . . and Does It Matter?

- Did your parents take more pictures of you than they did of your siblings? No
- Do you show greater leadership ability than your siblings? yes
- Are you more serious than your siblings? yes
- Do your parents have greater expectations for you than your siblings? No

If your answer to most or all of these questions is "yes," you are probably the first-born in your family. Some of neo-Freudian psychologist Alfred Adler's most interesting work relates birth order to personality and lifestyle. An avalanche of studies have explored this subject, many of them generally supporting Adler's ideas. (It should be remembered, however, that these generalizations do not hold true for every individual or every cultural group.)

Many of the greatest names in history and in the arts have been first-born. These include a number of political figures. Of the seven original astronauts, all were either first-born or only children (thus, first-born). First-borns predominate in Ivy League schools and they also outnumber later-borns in *Who's Who*. Yet proportionally, later-borns outnumber first-borns in the general population by a considerable margin. Why the difference in achievement?

The first child, according to Adler, is usually the most wanted child. This does not mean that later-born children are loved any less, but that the experience of being a parent is new and more exciting with the first. Parents of the first child tend to vow not to make the same mistakes their parents made. (They'll make others.) They are more likely to be strict; they will probably consult child-rearing manuals currently in vogue; and since the child is a novelty, plenty of attention is often showered upon her or him. This combination of strictness and additional attention gives the first-born a head start on the way to achievement in life.

Second-born status is often considered a more uncomfortable position. The child gets none of the push that the first-born child receives, and little of the babyish attention that is lavished upon the last child. Yet, this position also has advantages. Second-born children often learn to deal effectively with older and younger children, and they are often rather persuasive. They may show opposite interests when compared to the first-born: for instance, if the older sibling is intellectual and hard-driving, the second may become athletic and lackadaisical about schoolwork.

The third-born is supposedly spoiled. The parents are either worn down or worn out. These thirds are able to get around their parents and learn the ropes from their older siblings. Manipulation is often used in an attempt to get what they want. Perhaps due to slackening discipline, later-born children may tend to be more radical and take on responsibility at a later age than their older siblings.

theory is essentially a laboratory theory based strictly upon the scientific method: People act according to rules that can be discovered through laboratory experimentation and then used to predict future behavior.

Learning theorists argue that personality is really no different from any other set of behaviors. It, too, is a product of learning. If Jerry reacts aggressively every time his mother says "no," it may be because his screaming and yelling have always succeeded in changing his mother's mind. Jerry reacts in this manner because he has *learned* to do so. Faced with the same or similar situations, he will continue to react aggressively, unless he learns otherwise. This way of learning is known as operant conditioning, and it is one of the three most important learning processes.

Three Learning Processes   The three processes of learning will be discussed in detail in Chapter 3, but a brief summary here can help demonstrate how they relate to personality. In **classical conditioning,** a *neutral stimulus* is paired with a stimulus that brings a certain response on its own (called an *unconditioned stimulus*), until the person learns to react to the neutral stimulus as if it were the unconditioned stimulus. If this sounds complicated, an example may help.

Let's say you're driving your '67 Buick when you begin hearing strange engine noises. As you are accustomed to a variety of engine noises, and they normally mean nothing to you, they are a neutral stimulus. You continue on your way. After a few minutes, all the warning lights go on and your car comes to a halt right in the middle of a busy intersection. This, most definitely, brings an *unconditioned response:* you become anxious and

upset and have the unpleasant feeling that the world is out of your control. After just one or two of these occurrences, you may find that you have been conditioned: you react to these and other engine noises with anxiety and fear.

Operant conditioning is another learning process. It involves the development of behavior patterns that "are controlled by what follows them, not what precedes them" (Salkind, 1981, p. 129). The individual acts in a certain way, receives a pleasant consequence, and this consequence strengthens, or *reinforces,* the behavior. If a child in a supermarket, for example, throws a temper tantrum because he wants a candy bar, and his father gives in to keep him quiet, this type of behavior is reinforced and is likely to be repeated. Many personality traits are formed through this **reinforcement** process.

A third learning process is *imitation,* learning by observing those around you. Whether or not observation learning is innate (that is, an inborn characteristic) is a subject of controversy, but its potency is unquestioned. If your parents give generously to others, you may follow their example so that generosity becomes part of your personality, also. In the same way, behaviors such as withdrawal and aggression can also be learned by observing other people.

Many studies have demonstrated that children imitate aggressive models (Bandura, 1973). In some of these studies, children first observe an adult playing violently with a doll, then are given an opportunity to play with the doll themselves (Bandura, Ross, & Ross, 1961). The results show that children who have observed violent behavior are themselves less inhibited against violence; they also learn new ways of aggressing.

Generalization and Discrimination   In the behaviorists' view, the three learning processes just described are basic in developing the consistent behavior patterns we call personality. In order to mold personality in this way, however, two phenomena must also take place. These are generalization and discrimination. **Generalization** is the

---

Classical conditioning   A learning process in which a neutral stimulus is paired with a stimulus that elicits a response until the originally neutral stimulus itself produces the response.

Operant conditioning   In learning theory, the process in which behavior is altered because of the consequences it produces.

Reinforcement   The presentation of a stimulus following a behavior in order to increase the likelihood that the behavior will reoccur.

Generalization   A term used in learning theory to denote the process by which a specific response to one situation becomes a consistent response to similar situations.

Part One / Fundamentals of Adjustment

process by which a specific response to one situation (such as throwing a tantrum in the supermarket) becomes a consistent response to similar situations (tantrums every time the child wants something). The greater the similarity between situations, the greater the chance that generalization will take place.

Generalization, of course, may not always be appropriate. There is a big difference between yelling at your younger brother and berating a police officer who has just stopped you for speeding. The characteristics of the situations are important as well. As people encounter more and more experiences, they learn to differentiate, or *discriminate* (**discrimination**), one from the other. You might yell at your little brother, but you would try a different strategy on the policeman. This explains why a person may act domineering in one situation and submissive in another.

The Cognitive Learning Approach   Learning theory is an elegant, straightforward attempt to use logical rules to explain human behavior. Yet learning theory seems oddly mechanistic to some people, for it is difficult to think of humans without also considering such factors as their state of well-being, their thought processes, or their feelings. In recent years, a group of behaviorists have been modifying learning theory to include these human elements (Mahoney, 1977a). Factors such as the state of the organism, as well as expectations, beliefs, thoughts, and feelings, are called *cognitive* factors, and they are all seen by this group of **cognitive-behavior theorists** as mediating between the stimulus-response relationship envisioned by behaviorists.

The box *The Importance of Talking to Yourself* illustrates one aspect of the mediating role of cognitive factors: doing things hastily, without thinking, produces different effects than does careful "self-talk." Another element has been pointed out by the cognitive theorist Albert Ellis, who notes that "people invariably talk to themselves (and others) and the kinds of things [people] say to themselves, as well as the form in which they say

these things, significantly affect their emotions and behavior and sometimes lead them to feel emotionally distressed" (1977, p. 4). If these self-statements are irrational and perfectionistic, they can lead to emotional disturbances and unhappiness. Ellis identifies ten irrational self-statements, which are listed in Table 1.1. It is easy to see how such attitudes could produce a great deal of anxiety in a person's life.

Cognitive theory focuses on an aspect of behavior that separates humans from lower animals—a quality that helps us appreciate the unique attributes and characteristics of each person. It is just this celebration of "humanness" that has prompted the growth of what is called the "third force" in psychology: humanistic psychology.

Humanistic Psychology

Humanistic psychology emphasizes a positive approach to studying people's inner nature and understanding how they may realize their creative potential (Nordby & Hall, 1974). Humanistic psychologists consider each human unique, and they accord people a position of honor and privilege that sets them apart from other animals (Matson, 1971).

Discrimination In learning theory, the process by which an individual learns to differentiate between stimuli.

Cognitive-behavioral approach The modification of the learning or behavioral model to include such cognitive factors as the state of the organism, expectations, beliefs, and thought patterns.

Humanistic psychology The branch of psychology focusing upon the basic qualities and inner nature of human beings in order to understand how they may reach their potential.

The Importance of Talking to Yourself

Have you ever approached a task and found yourself thinking, "O.K., now slow down, get it right, you're doing just fine, just a little more ... good, that was perfect!" We often talk to ourselves, and self-talk can be helpful in controlling our behavior.

In the past decade or so, there has been considerable interest in the cognitive viewpoint, which stresses the importance of such factors as beliefs, thoughts, and perceptions. People are thinking and planning beings, and it stands to reason that altering a person's thought patterns can cause changes in overt behaviors.

Donald Meichenbaum and Joseph Goodman decided to test this premise, examining the possibility of altering the behavior of impulsive children by teaching them to use self-instructional statements. Fifteen second-grade children, ages 7 to 9, who had behavior problems were assigned to one of three treatment groups. The first group, the *cognitive training group,* received four half-hour training sessions that taught the children to verbalize particular statements as they carried out a task. These statements had to do with analyzing the nature of the task and which strategies should be used, as well as using self-guidance instructions and reinforcing statements.

The second group, called the *attention control group,* had the same number of training sessions, performing the same kinds of tasks as the first group, but they received no training in the use of self-statements. The last group, the *assessment control group,* received the same evaluative instruments. However, they did not meet with the experimenter as had the other two groups.

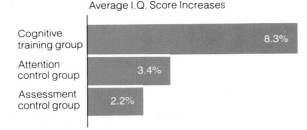

Average I.Q. Score Increases

Cognitive training group — 8.3%
Attention control group — 3.4%
Assessment control group — 2.2%

The results clearly demonstrated that the cognitive training group had profited from the experience. Their intelligence scores on the nonverbal test increased an average of 8.3 points, compared with only 3.4 points for the attention control group and 2.2 points for the assessment control group. In addition, the total time these students used to make their decisions increased, thus demonstrating reduced impulsiveness. The accuracy of their work on the motor task also improved as the investigators found that the students in the cognitive training group made fewer errors. Unfortunately, there were no significant differences reported in classroom behavior, but this was probably due to the brevity of the treatment.

From this study, we can conclude that teaching impulsive children to "talk to themselves" is an effective strategy for improving their performance on a variety of psychological tests. Teaching children to regulate and use their internal speech can result in greater self-control. The experimenters believe that this procedure can be very useful in altering people's behavior in a variety of settings.

Source: Meichenbaum & Goodman, 1971.

Table 1.1   Ten Irrational Self-Statements

1. You need love or approval from all the significant people in your life.
2. You must prove thoroughly competent, adequate, and achieving in everything in order to consider yourself worthwhile.
3. When people act obnoxiously, you should blame them and view them as bad or wicked.
4. Things are terrible or catastrophic if they are not the way you wish them to be.
5. Unhappiness comes from external sources, and you are powerless to control or change your feelings.
6. If something seems dangerous or fearsome, you should keep worrying about it.
7. It is easier to avoid life's difficulties and responsibilities than to solve them.
8. Your past is an all-important determinant of your present behavior: if something once strongly influenced your life, it always will.
9. People and things should turn out better than they do; it's a shame that you can't find good solutions to life's problems.
10. You can achieve happiness by inaction or passivity.

Source: Adapted from Ellis & Harper, 1975.

Because of its emphasis on the uniquely human ability to strive and grow, some of the central tenets of the humanistic view provide a helpful framework for studying adjustment. Below, we'll describe Abraham Maslow's hierarchy of needs and see the various levels of adjustment that form the broad structure of this text. Carl Rogers' humanistic theory is similar in many respects to that of Maslow, and we'll look briefly at his concept of the self.

Maslow's Humanistic Theory   Maslow's view of human behavior presents a sharp contrast to both the Freudian and the learning theory approaches. One reason for this is the humanist emphasis on **holism,** the understanding of human behavior in the context of the individual's total experience. The humanist recognizes, for instance, that peo-

ple will behave differently when they are tired or distressed than they will when they are relaxed.

Maslow also criticizes behaviorists for using animals to deduce basic truths about human behavior. In his view, the development of art, humor, poetry, and science bear testimony to each person's unique potential for creativity. People can experience a full range of complicated and, at times, conflicting emotions that are unique to the animal kingdom. No laboratory experiment on a monkey or rat can tell us about these dimensions of personality.

A third distinction of humanism is its basic optimism. Maslow disagrees with the Freudian practice of basing theory upon the dark side of human nature and on psychological disturbances. To Maslow, theories built upon these foundations will yield a "crippled" psychology—one that ignores the positive aspects of human functioning. In contrast, he sees humans as basically good. It isn't always easy, of course, to look at people in this light. As Hjelle and Ziegler point out, "One might not be able to appreciate this view while being mugged in Central Park. However, from the humanistic perspective, evil, destructive and violent forces in the behavior of muggers arise from a bad environment rather than from any inherent rottenness on their part" (1976, p. 255).

In Maslow's view, people are motivated by two separate sets of needs. The first type is called **deficiency needs,** or **D-needs.** These include food, air, and security—needs that breed discomfort or even illness in their absence (Maslow,

Holism   An approach to studying behavior whose central position is that human beings can only be understood by looking at the whole individual rather than one specific element.

D-needs (deficiency needs)   Needs such as food, air, security, and even possibly love, whose absence motivates the individual to search relentlessly until they are satisfied. See also *B-needs.*

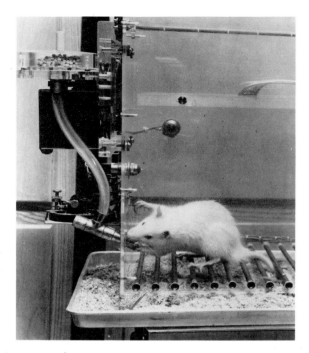

Two examples of observable behaviors. According to behaviorists, we can learn much about our own behavior by studying how this rat earns rewards. Humanists argue, however, that laboratory animals can never tell us about dimensions of human behavior such as those shown at left.

B-needs (being needs or metaneeds) A group of needs that involve a striving after the attainment of a higher goal associated with the development of one's potential. B-needs find their greatest expression in the drive towards self-actualization.

Biological needs (physiological needs) Those needs that arise from tissue deficiencies, such as needs for food, pain reduction, and warmth. Most biological needs are necessary for the survival of the organism. Biological, or physiological, needs form the first level of Maslow's need hierarchy.

1968). People can also be motivated by **being needs (B-needs)**, which are also called *metaneeds*. These metaneeds are associated with the fulfillment of each person's unique potential. These needs are also innate, but they do not result from deficiencies. *B*-needs become prominent only after *D*-needs are largely satisfied. They involve the attainment of goals such as beauty, justice, and self-fulfillment. *B*-needs find their greatest expression in the drive to develop our potential and become all we can be, the drive Maslow calls self-actualization.

Maslow argued that these needs could be arranged in a more elaborately graduated hierarchy, as Figure 1.2 shows. At the bottom are the basic **physiological needs,** including food, pain

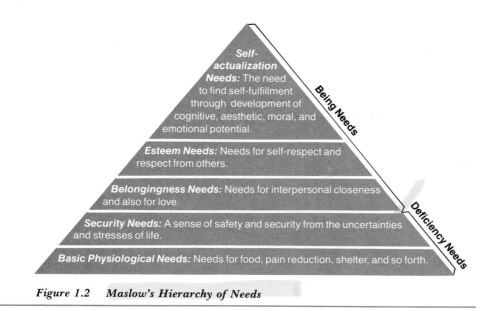

Figure 1.2 Maslow's Hierarchy of Needs

reduction, and warmth. As these are satisfied, the next level begins to exert its influence on the individual.

This second level of needs involves **security** and orderliness. These needs are easy to recognize. Children's worst fear is abandonment; later, adults also look for safety and security from the stresses and uncertainties of life. Since few people in the United States need be overly concerned about biological needs, these safety needs seem to be dominant for most of us. The unwillingness to change, take a chance, or do something different can often lead to a life of boredom and limited productivity. If safety is truly attainable, its price is high.

When safety needs are relatively satisfied, the third level of needs—those of **belongingness** and love—become apparent. The need for interpersonal closeness, a feeling of belonging, as well as the desire for love may sometimes be difficult to gratify in a technological society. Where people move quickly from job to job and town to town, development of interpersonal relationships can

be difficult. As a result, some people have a fairly steady stream of acquaintances, which only partially satisfies their third-level needs.

The fourth level consists of **esteem needs:** such needs as self-respect and recognition from others. In Maslow's words, "satisfaction of the self-esteem need leads to feelings of self-confidence, worth, strength, capability, and ade-

> **Security needs** The second level of needs in Maslow's need hierarchy, involving the need for safety and order.
>
> **Belongingness needs** The third level of needs in Maslow's need hierarchy, involving a striving for love, interpersonal intimacy, and a feeling of belonging.
>
> **Esteem needs** The fourth level of Maslow's need hierarchy; such needs as recognition and praise for one's achievements. Maslow emphasizes the importance of both receiving esteem from others and attaining a measure of self-esteem.

quacy of being useful and necessary in the world" (1970, p. 45). Earning esteem from others is just as important. This includes recognition of your activities in all spheres of life.

Even if all these needs are somewhat satisfied, Maslow notes that "we may still often (if not always) expect that a new discontent and restlessness will soon develop, unless the individual is doing what he, individually, is fitted for" (1970, p. 46). The satisfaction of a fifth level of needs, the **self-actualization** needs, involves the full development of all a person's abilities and potentials in a creative manner. Self-actualization is not synonymous with exceptional talent or creativity. People need not be great musicians in order to appreciate music to its fullest, nor do they need to be great physicists to be the best that they can. After studying a number of individuals considered to be self-actualized, Maslow noted a total of 15 characteristics that describe these individuals, as listed in Table 1.2. You may wish to consider how many of these describe you at the present time, and which ones you feel you could develop with time and effort.

Maslow's concept of self-actualization as the driving force in life may seem a bit far-fetched. After all, few people seem to be self-actualized—less than 1 percent according to Maslow! One reason for this is the crippling effects of stereotypes, prejudices, and racism that prevent people from developing their abilities. In addition, according to Maslow, lower needs must be satisfied before a person can reach self-actualization. Thus, a young doctor found he could not speak to his parents. The gulf between them seemed to be widening every day. His father spoke in terms of prestige and financial security while he was more interested in doing something for society. He decided not to open a practice in a rich suburban section

Self-actualization The fifth and highest level of needs in Maslow's need hierarchy, involving the full development of one's abilities and the reaching of one's potential.

Maslows Self-Actualization

Table 1.2 Characteristics of Self-Actualized Individuals

1. A realistic perception of other people and the world.
2. A true acceptance of oneself, others, and nature.
3. Self-actualized people are spontaneous and their behavior is marked by simplicity and naturalness.
4. A commitment to a duty, vocation, or cause.
5. A respect for, and a need for, privacy.
6. A dependence on their inner sense rather than the environment. (conscience or value structure)
7. An ability to appreciate and enjoy everyday life. (Highly motivated)
8. An ability to experience and appreciate peak moments in life.
9. A genuine desire to help other human beings develop their potential.
10. An ability to form deeply satisfying interpersonal relationships.
11. A democratic character structure that includes a respect for each individual and a feeling that one can learn from every human being.
12. A highly personal sense of right and wrong.
13. A philosophical, unhostile sense of humor.
14. A creative lifestyle in which their talents and abilities can develop.
15. The self-actualized individual is neither totally submissive to the culture nor completely detached from it. A satisfying compromise is reached.

Source: Adapted from Maslow, 1970.

of town, but instead to work for less in an inner-city clinic. He could not understand his father's feelings. Growing up in the Depression, his father felt that financial security was most important. His son, who had known such financial security all his life, had gone beyond this monetary perspective.

Rogers' Concept of the Self Carl Rogers' humanistic theory has much in common with Maslow's, stressing the importance of the human drive toward self-actualization. We mention Rogers here because his definition of the self provides a useful perspective for understanding personality, and thus helps lay our own groundwork for discussing adjustment in this text.

To Rogers, the chief organizer of each person's subjective experience is the *self:* the collection of feelings, attitudes, concepts, values, goals, and ideals that influences the way we all behave. In short, the self might be seen as your own picture of you. It develops from birth, combining your own subjective experience with those values and attitudes of your parents that you have accepted. Experiences that are consistent with your perception of yourself are acceptable and fill you with a sense of warmth and security. But experiences that are at odds with your self-concept may cause you to feel threatened and uneasy (Rogers, 1959).

For example, you will be troubled if you cheat on an exam despite your strong belief that it is wrong to cheat. Your subjective experience of cheating is not consistent with your self-concept of being honest. This conflict engenders feelings of uneasiness and may cause you to defend yourself by making excuses for your behavior ("All I did was check my answers"), or simply deny to yourself the experience of having cheated ("I didn't cheat"). Rogers sees personal adjustments as directed toward reducing conflicts between our self-concepts and our behaviors—a process, he believes, that takes place through conscious striving.

Adjustment and Personality

At this point, you may wish to go back and evaluate the statements you agreed with in the box *How Do You View Personality?* on page 10. "A" answers show a preference for the Freudian view; "B" for learning theory; and "C" for the humanistic view of personality. Perhaps your answers have changed after reading about these views; or perhaps you have found it difficult to choose any one theory as a basis for interpreting all behavior.

Often, people claim to be **eclectic**. That is, they choose the best from each perspective. Certainly, every one of the theories described in this chapter has something to offer. The psychoanalytic theory demonstrates the importance of unconscious motives and biological drives. Learning theory stresses the importance of environmental factors. And the humanistic perspective contributes a philosophy of self-actualization, while stressing the importance of the self and subjective experience. You need not commit yourself to any one theory to appreciate the contributions each has made to our understanding of human behavior.

This appreciation for each contribution can help us understand how and why people adjust to changes in the manner they do. By taking into account both internal and external processes, biological motivations, and the drive toward self-actualization, we can begin to understand the immense variety of factors that influence our behaviors.

Eclectic Choosing aspects of many different theories as opposed to embracing the principles or techniques from only one. A therapist is eclectic if she or he uses techniques from more than one therapeutic approach.

Throughout this text, we will try to present an active and flexible view of adjustment. People are all subject to biological drives and environmental influences, but also important are the self and the ability of each individual to make choices. You need not react in the same old way: you can change. The ability to become a happier, more fulfilled individual lies within each and every person.

A Look Ahead

To understand human behavior, we must begin with the basic motivations of humans. Likewise, to understand the process of adjustment, we believe the best place to begin is with the four basic areas of psychological knowledge: personality, motivation, learning, and development.

These basic elements of human behavior are the subject of Part I of this text. In this chapter, we introduced the process of adjustment as well as the concept of personality. Chapter 2 carries us one step further. It deals with various types of motivation, exploring the question of why we behave as we do. Topics include sleeping and insomnia; eating and obesity; boredom and novelty; achievement and affiliation. Chapter 3 introduces the basic processes of learning, and the ways people can use learning theory to improve themselves and their environments. Finally, Chapter 4 explores human development. How does genetics affect our lives? How important is early experience?

Each of these basic areas of psychological concern affect our day-to-day behaviors, and they are also useful tools for understanding and predicting behavior. Just as the satisfaction of basic needs, according to Maslow's theory, opens each person up to new needs and opportunities, we hope that the understanding of these basic areas will help you be open to new discoveries about yourself and the world around you.

Summary

1. The process of adjustment involves people's attempts to cope with, master, and transcend the challenges of life by using a variety of techniques and strategies. Adjustment is viewed as a process, not an end state.

2. The field of adjustment includes the study of choices, strategies, motivations, and goals as well as the consequences of behavior.

3. People are predisposed to react to situations in the same way in which they reacted in the past. In order to alter this pattern of behavior it is necessary to become aware of it, understand that it has failed to achieve our goals, and seek out and experiment with new and different strategies. People may react to a problem by moving toward, away from, or against the object of concern. Healthy adjustment requires the balanced and coordinated use of all three strategies.

4. Normal behavior can only be understood in terms of a broad range of accepted behaviors within a particular society. The time period, situation, and society determine normal and abnormal behavior.

5. The term *personality* describes an individual's distinctive patterns of behaviors used to cope with the challenges of life, as well as characteristic thoughts and feelings. Your reaction to any situation will depend upon your perception of the situation and your personality.

6. Freud divided consciousness into three levels—the conscious, preconscious, and unconscious. Unconscious feelings and thoughts, he believed, were the chief motivators of human behavior. Freud's three constructs of the mind included the id (primitive desires), the superego (morals and ethics of the society), and the ego, which mediates between the id and the environment.

7. Many psychologists who came after Freud accepted some of his principles but rejected others. One of these neo-Freudians, Alfred Adler, saw a striving for superiority and a drive to master the environment as the primary motivators of behavior.

8. Learning theorists or behaviorists view personality in terms of behavioral patterns that have been learned. These theorists emphasize the learning processes of classical conditioning, operant conditioning, and imitation, and they see generalization and discrimination as influencing how people behave in specific situations.

9. Some psychologists have modified the learning theory approach to personality by introducing cognitive (mental) factors such as attitudes and perception. They stress the importance of people's thoughts on their behaviors.

10. The humanistic school of personality stresses the uniqueness of humanity, freedom of choice, and the importance of subjective experiences. According to Abraham Maslow, human beings are motivated by both D or deficiency needs and by B or being needs, which are also called metaneeds. These needs are arranged into a hierarchy from physiological needs, to security needs, to belongingness needs, to esteem needs, to self-actualization.

11. Another humanistic psychologist, Carl Rogers, emphasized the importance of self-concept—the view each of us holds of our self.

Key Terms and Concepts

adjustment

psychology

moving toward, away from, and against challenges

normality

abnormality

personality

psychoanalytic theory

conscious

preconscious or foreconscious

unconscious

repression

id

ego

superego

neo-Freudian

direct compensation

indirect compensation

behaviorism

classical conditioning

operant conditioning

reinforcement

generalization

discrimination

cognitive-behavior theory

humanistic psychology

holism

D-(deficiency) needs

B-(being) needs

physiological needs

security needs

belongingness needs

esteem needs

self-actualization

eclectic

Have you heard of tiny Melinda Mae,
Who ate a monstrous whale?
She thought she could,
She said she would,
So she started right at the tail.
And everyone said "You're much too
    small,"
But that didn't bother Melinda at all.
She took little bites and chewed very
    slow.
Just like a good girl should ...
And in eighty-nine years she ate that
    whale
Because she said she would!
               —Shel Silverstein*

Motivation

*"Melinda Mae" from *Where the Sidewalk Ends* by
Shel Silverstein. Copyright © 1974 by Shel Silver-
stein. Reprinted by permission of Harper & Row,
Publishers, Inc.

We all know people who are driven—perhaps not to the extent that Melinda Mae was (or perhaps with more pragmatic goals!). What causes people to set their sights on something, then spend days, years, or even a lifetime achieving it?

This is one question psychologists ask about motivation, but there are many other questions that are equally relevant. Why do we eat when we're not hungry? What makes a person spend hours fiddling with a Rubik's cube? Why can't we get to sleep some nights—and why do we need sleep anyway?

Such questions, like the questions about personality and adjustment we explored in Chapter 1, are basic to understanding ourselves and others. Motivation is a complex topic and the answers aren't always clear, even to psychologists; but we will begin to explore them in this chapter as we look at needs, drives, and some important types of motivation.

Motivation

Psychologists use the term **motivation** to describe the reasons behind people's behavior. The different schools of psychology view motivation in different ways, however. Personality theorists such as Freud and Maslow consider the study of motivation crucial to an understanding of human behavior. As we saw in Chapter 1, Freud looked to the unconscious mind to explain virtually all of our behaviors. The humanist Maslow also saw motivation as highly important, building his need hierarchy around the basic deficiency needs and being needs. And the learning theorists, while they do not start with motivation per se in explaining behavior, do recognize motivation in terms of learned responses to acquired or innate needs or desires.

In studying motivation, psychologists use terminology that may sometimes confuse the layperson. Therefore, it is important to start with some clear definitions. In everyday language, most of us use words such as *motive, need,* and *drive* interchangeably. Psychologists make important distinctions:

- A **motive** is any force, internal or external, that is involved in accounting for the instigation, direction, and termination of behavior (LeFrancois, 1980). It is a very general term.

- A **need** is a specific deficit in an organism which, when satisfied, improves the individual's welfare. (For example, we all share basic needs for food, oxygen, and warmth; and when we lack any of these, we respond by looking for ways to satisfy the need.) A need gives rise to a drive.

- A **drive** is a state of arousal within an organism that leads to behaviors that will satisfy a need. A person who lacks food will probably experience a hunger drive, which causes her to search for that turkey leg left over from the previous night's dinner.

Our understanding of motivation in this chapter begins with exploring the relationship between needs, drives, and behavior.

The Drive Theory and Need Reduction

The great learning theorist Clark Hull drew the first comprehensive picture of motivation. His

---

Motivation An inferred condition that arouses behavior directed towards some goal. The study of motivation focuses on the complex factors that underlie behavior.

Motive Any force, internal or external, that is involved in the instigation, direction, or termination of behavior.

Need A specific deficit that when satisfied, improves the welfare of the individual.

Drive A state of arousal within an organism that leads to behaviors that will satisfy a need.

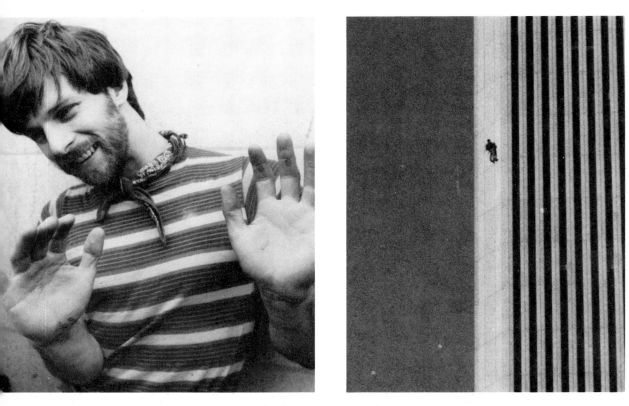

The study of motivation seeks to discover the "whys" behind human behavior. It isn't always easy, as in the case of "Spiderman" (George Willig), who enjoys conquering skyscrapers in his spare time, as shown at right.

drive theory argued that internal needs which result from tissue deprivation give rise to drives—the energy we direct toward satisfying these needs. Hull recognized that external cues can also be associated with a need. Watching a friend eat potato chips can give rise to a drive to eat some, even though no tissue deprivation or other internal need exists.

Of course, watching a friend eat potato chips may also have no effect on a person. Not everyone likes potato chips; and even if we like them, we might not feel like going out to buy them. Thus, there must be some mediating factors that determine how a need will translate into a drive and a drive into a particular behavior. Modern psychol-

ogists recognize two major cognitive factors that determine the strength of a person's goal-seeking behavior: the value of the goal, and the person's expectation that the goal can be attained.

The Value of the Goal   One important factor in determining behavior is which goals we value. The goal of potato chips is an unlikely motivation for a person who doesn't like them. In the same way, many of our behaviors are influenced by the goals we want or don't want to attain.

As an example, suppose you want to be a doctor but are aware of the difficulty of getting into medical school. The process of applying, then studying for several years if you are admit-

Part One / Fundamentals of Adjustment

Two major cognitive factors determine a person's goal-seeking behavior:

① The value of the goal, and…   ② The attainability of that goal.

You might be motivated to reach the goal shown in the first picture, but would you change your mind if you saw what the viewer sees in the second?

ted, is competitive and costly. Just how wholeheartedly you will enter this ordeal is determined, in part, by the degree to which you value the goal of being a doctor. Perhaps you have always wanted to be a doctor. This will probably give rise to a strong drive. On the other hand, perhaps your parents have always wanted you to be a doctor, but you're not sure that that's what *you* want for yourself. If this is the case, you may find that you don't have much drive; that your behaviors are not very goal-directed; and that you aren't very inspired as you write your application essays.

Attainability of the Goal   It is clear that the value of your goals is important in determining behav-

ior. A second factor is also important, however: your expectation that you can attain the goal. To return to the potato chip example, no matter how strong your craving, you will not go out to the store to buy chips if it's midnight and the stores are closed. Or, if your grades have been consistently low in high school and college, it's possible that you will give up on the idea of medical school because it simply seems beyond your reach.

Another factor in the attainability of a goal is your knowledge of how to go about pursuing it. Even if you have a realistic goal, you may spin your wheels and get nowhere if you don't know how to attain it. If you believe your path is right, however, and think your actions are bringing you closer to the goal you value, then your goal-seeking behaviors will be strengthened.

As an example, you may have a certain career in mind, such as becoming a cinematographer. Where do you go from here? Without advice and guidance from resources such as counselors, acquaintances in the field, or reading materials, you will probably have trouble channeling your behaviors toward your goal. If you do connect with the right resources, however, and begin to feel you are making progress toward your goal, then your drive will become strengthened and your behaviors more and more directed.

The concept of drive as an effort to reduce needs is a useful starting point in understanding motivation. Of course, motivation is not determined only by the factors of value, attainability, and knowledge. (Otherwise, all of us would be able to rationally explain why we do everything we do.) We'll be considering some of the complexities of motivation and behavior as we examine the various types of motivation.

The three types of motivation (left to right): primary motives, stimulus motives, and secondary motives.

Three Types of Motivation

Psychologists usually divide motivation into three categories or types. **Primary drives** occur in every person; they are based upon innate body needs for food, temperature control, elimination, and so forth. **Stimulus motives** include people's needs for stimulation, manipulation, and exploration. Lastly, **secondary** (or **learned**) **motives** have goals such as affiliation, achievement, and power. These motives are solely determined by culture, and they are acquired through various processes of learning.

While this broad distinction exists between types of motivation, we should note that the divisions are not always clear-cut. The primary hunger drive is innate, for instance, but the way in which we satisfy it is partly learned. Most Americans don't regard raw squid as a delicacy, yet it is a common food in Japan, served in most *sushi* bars. Stimulus motives also have a strong learned component, as we shall see. Thus, the three categories of primary, stimulus, and secondary motives represent real but sometimes overlapping distinctions.

> **Primary drives** Drives that occur in every human being and are based upon innate biological needs.
>
> **Stimulus motive** A motive that involves exploration, manipulation, curiosity, or stimulation.
>
> **Secondary (learned) motive** A motive, such as the achievement motive, which is determined largely by the culture and is acquired through the various processes of learning.

Primary Drives

Primary drives are based on innate needs to eat, drink, and eliminate; to sleep; to maintain a comfortable body temperature; and to reproduce. These needs are common to all people in all cultures, for they are necessary to the survival of the individual or the group. As we've seen, however, the environment has a strong influence on the way in which we satisfy primary drives; so also may psychological factors, such as anxiety or a sense of well-being. We can see what role these external and internal factors play by looking more closely at two primary drives: hunger and sleep.

The Hunger Drive

At first glance, the hunger drive seems simple enough: your body craves food and you answer its needs, in a clear replica of Hull's drive theory. Physiologically, the hunger mechanism involves the brain, the bloodstream, and various parts of the body including the stomach. A part of the brain called the *hypothalamus* tests for various substances in the bloodstream, including sugar and fat levels, rousing the body if these levels seem low. Stomach contractions are also often involved in the feeling of hunger.

However, the physiological explanation of the hunger drive does not in itself explain why so many people are overweight. Most Americans eat

Confessions of a Binger

John is a member of Overeaters Anonymous, a national organization modeled after Alcoholics Anonymous. Here, he remembers one binge from his youth:

When I was twelve or thirteen my parents had a 25th anniversary party and I brought home half of a huge cake. . . . At first I was cutting the cake from an angle to disguise that I was eating it. But then I kept on eating. When there was only a little left, I purposely dropped it on the floor, picked it up and ate it. Then I gave one crumb to the dog. Then I called my mother at work and told her that while I was trying to get a glass of milk from the refrigerator I knocked the cake on the floor and so I gave it to the dog (p. 45).

John's binges persisted, and he grew into an adult with a serious weight problem. But his episode of loss of control may be familiar to many of us who are within the normal weight range.

Source: Millman, Marcia, *Such a Pretty Face: Being Fat in America* (New York, W. W. Norton, 1980).

---

more food than their bodies need; in fact, some 25 to 40 percent of American adults have problems with excessive weight. Clearly, the hypothalamus does not always directly determine how much people eat. There are rare instances of glandular imbalances, low blood sugar, unusual metabolic rates, or brain dysfunction. Yet for most obese people, the cause revolves around psychological or environmental factors.

Obesity and Eating Patterns   Most obese people eat differently than people who do not have weight problems—a fact that has been researched rather thoroughly and is basic to an understanding of the problem of overeating. Several patterns have emerged.

One of the clearest patterns is that obese people often do not differentiate between when they are hungry and when they are not hungry. The quote in the box *Confessions of a Binger* illustrates this. One experiment compared subjects' verbal expressions of hunger to the physiological indicator of stomach contractions. Among thin people, there was a clear relationship between contractions and expressions of hunger, while this relationship was insignificant in obese people

(Stunkard, 1959). Simply stated, the obese subjects were unaware that they weren't really hungry. In another study, subjects were given a full meal and sent into a room where their task was to rate crackers for qualities such as flavor. The thin subjects ate only a few crackers, while the overweight subjects ate much more than they had to. Even when full, they continued to eat as long as there was a cracker in sight (Schachter et al., 1968).

Other studies have demonstrated other relationships. While thin people eat less when they are under stress, for instance, overweight people tend to eat more (Bruch, 1961). Their eating habits are also more affected by the taste of food (Schachter et al., 1968) and by the time element (Schachter & Grose, 1968). Heavy people eat more quickly than do people who are not overweight, and external cues, such as advertisements, have more of an effect on them.

These relationships have all been documented by research, but what causes them to be established in the first place? Here, the picture becomes more complicated, and clues seem to point towards factors such as childhood eating patterns, heredity, and learning.

Causes of Obesity Some researchers have argued that some people inherit a tendency to be overweight since the hypothalamus sets a higher level for fat in their bodies (Nisbett, 1972). In addition, early feeding habits may play a part in obesity (Knittle, 1972). Fat cells that are produced very early in life, before the age of two, stay with a person throughout life. Dieting may simply liberate fat from these cells, but the cells themselves stay right where they are. Obese individuals have more fat cells than do nonobese individuals. This explains why people who were once fat often still fight a daily battle to keep off the weight they have lost. A little ice cream here, a few pancakes there, and the problem returns. In addition, once an individual is overweight there is a tendency to stay that way. Judith Rodin (1981) argued that due to changes in the individual's metabolism, body chemistry, and activity level, it takes fewer calories to keep the person fat than it took to become so in the first place.

If early eating patterns play a role, hereditary factors also seem to be involved in obesity. These factors, however, are neither consistent nor easy to isolate. In a family where both parents and children are very heavy, it may seem easy to point toward heredity as the cause, until the family's eating patterns and attitudes toward eating are examined. If mealtime and snacktime are the most important times of the day, and the child is encouraged to eat to "lift the spirit" in times of stress, learning also plays a clear role in establishing overeating habits.

In all, then, some overweight persons may have legitimate cause to blame their condition on "fate" (which takes form either as the early formation of fat cells or their family's poor eating habits). However, the fact is that whether or not the stage has been set for obesity, it is the individual who chooses to overeat or not. It is also true that a person doesn't need to overeat a great deal in order to have a weight problem. If your input exceeds your output by just 35 calories a day for a year, you will gain 3 pounds in that year. The constant yearly "creeping" weight gain, especially prevalent among middle age people, is a serious

Both heredity and learned eating habits seem to be involved in obesity.

health problem in our society.

Since learning plays such a large part in eating habits, it would seem that the best way to control weight is to unlearn these overeating behaviors and to learn new ones. The four steps of the box *A Weight Program That Works* outline an approach to calorie control that uses eating patterns as a starting point.

It is clear that while hunger is a primary drive, eating is also much more than a physiological necessity. It is also affected by cultural, environmental, and psychological factors. The same relationship is also seen in another primary drive, the need for sleep.

A Weight Control Program That Works

Here is a four-step weight control program that stays away from radical weight loss that may quickly be regained. This program relies instead on informed behavior modification. As with any diet, your doctor should be consulted before you begin.

Step 1: Record-keeping

A vital, basic first step is to become aware of what, how much, and under what circumstances you are eating. Whether or not you are overweight, keeping a log of everything you eat for two weeks will tell you a great deal about your eating habits. Here is a suggested format:

Date (weight today: _____)*	Time	Place	Food Consumed	Emotional State	Alone? With Company?	Other Information

*Weighing yourself each day is recommended, always at the same time and on the same scale.

Step 2: Set Goals and Select a Diet

The next step is to establish goals for both the total number of pounds to be lost and a reasonable weekly goal, such as one or two pounds.

The selection of the diet itself is based on many factors. It should not be so restrictive as to be unrealistic; nor should it be a crash diet that causes too sudden weight loss or restricts vital nutrients. Stuart (1971) recommends a *food exchange* program: many foods of like calories are grouped into general categories, and the individual chooses foods from the appropriate group. Nutritional information about food choices is also necessary.

Sleep

One third of our lives is spent in sleep. There are wide variations in sleep needs, with some people requiring only 4 hours and others as much as 10 or more. On the average, though, most of us spend 5 to 9 hours of each 24-hour cycle asleep.

The drive for sleep is so strong that even one night without sleep clearly affects a person's efficiency. During World War II, Japanese forces on Guadalcanal used to send a pilot over American lines, with his engines carefully out of synchronization in order to keep the marines awake. The theory was basically sound: people who have inadequate sleep are fatigued and irritable, and this condition progressively worsens. In severe cases, the individual may actually begin to hallucinate.

An extreme example of sleeplessness is a voluntary case, done as part of a charity promotion, but it is interesting from a scientific standpoint. Peter Tripp, a New York disc jockey, stayed awake

Step 3: Self-control

The next step is to combine your goals, your diet plan, and your knowledge of your own eating patterns. You can then restructure your eating habits. For instance:

- Your records may show you snack on ready-made foods that take no time to prepare. Keeping these foods out of the house can save literally hundreds of calories each week.

- Perhaps you eat too quickly. It may help to place your fork down until each bite has been chewed and swallowed. Or, you might try waiting five minutes between courses. Both of these techniques will allow you to feel full well before you would if you had gulped your food.

- Do you eat in front of the TV, or at your desk as you study? If you eat while you're doing something else, you probably don't think about what you're eating; in addition, the TV or the books may become a stimulus for eating. Limiting the number of rooms in which you can eat can eliminate this problem (Ubell, 1973).

- If you are ashamed to overeat when you're with friends, you may find it helpful to plan social lunches more often.

Step 4: Reinforce Your Success

Success deserves reward. If you succeed in eating smaller portions, having leftover food on your plate, or passing an important milestone, treat yourself! An ice cream sundae may not be a good reward, but other nonfood treats such as new clothing, a trip, or going to a play are good. Comments from friends are also rewarding.

There are many other techniques for a successful weight control program, but this one illustrates a basic approach that works. The combination of behavior modification and reduced calorie intake, especially if it is combined with a sensible exercise program, can be not only effective, but an easy program to live with.

for 200 hours. The results showed clearly: irritability, hallucinations, memory lapses, and a certain amount of personality disorganization all occurred. Interestingly, though, the effects were quickly erased. Tripp concluded his adventure by sleeping for 13 hours; the only residual effect was a slight depression that lasted about 3 months (Smith, et al., 1978).

Tripp's experience was surprising in some ways, for it points up the fact that the effects of sleep deprivation can be easily undone. Why then do we need regular sleep? The question has been studied by many scientists.

Why Do We Need Sleep?   We know that sleep is necessary, but we still aren't sure *why* we need it. It seems clear that the sleep drive has something to do with the body's need to prepare itself for another day—but what needs preparation and how it all works are open to debate.

One theory suggests that our systems use sleep as a time for repairing themselves. For instance, the body might use sleep as a time to produce *neurotransmitters* (substances that carry nerve impulses from one nerve cell to another) that have been used up during the previous day (Stern & Morgane, 1974; Hartmann, 1973). However, some such restorations also seem to take place during the day; and in addition, our hours of sleep don't necessarily coincide with those times when our systems need to rest and repair themselves. If they did, most of us would fall asleep during the 6 o'clock news and sleep right through the dinner hour.

Another explanation of why we sleep is an evolutionary theory. According to this view, humans, like other animals, have evolved sleeping patterns that let them be most efficient. They find food and complete other life processes during the hours when they can function best, and they "shut down" temporarily when they can function least efficiently. Since our senses are not very acute at night, we might say that nature meant for us to be day creatures. If we had a sharp sense of smell and acute night vision, perhaps we would be nocturnal instead.

A third theory sees sleep as a way of conserving energy. No organism can last long under constant stress, and sleep provides a period of inactivity that allows the body to come down from everyday demands.

Electroencephalograph   A machine that measures and records electrical impulses in the brain.

Hypnogogic sleep   A term used to describe the boundary between sleep and wakefulness.

Rapid Eye Movement (REM)   Eye movements during sleep that are indicative of dreaming.

Insomnia   A general term used to describe the inability to get to sleep, stay asleep, or wake up refreshed in the morning.

Stages of Sleep   Whether any of these theories of sleep is valid is an intriguing question. What we know about the varying levels of light and deep sleep makes the picture more complicated, however. If sleep is a time for conserving energy and making repairs, it is certainly not a time when the brain turns off. Using an **electroencephalograph,** a machine used to measure brain waves, scientists have found that there are actually four stages of sleep. Figure 2.1 illustrates the brain wave patterns of each stage.

The slowing-down process actually begins before a person falls asleep. During **hypnogogic sleep,** that floating period between sleep and wakefulness, the heart rate slows, blood pressure lowers, and muscles become deeply relaxed. *Stage 1* sleep is the first stage of sleep; it is marked by rather irregular breathing and more muscle relaxation. It is followed by *stage 2, stage 3,* and *stage 4,* progressively deeper stages of sleep. As the figure shows, brain waves become longer and longer as they are emitted at slower intervals during these stages. Once stage 4 sleep has been reached (by about 1 to $1\frac{1}{2}$ hours after falling asleep), the sleeper passes back and forth between lighter and heavier stages throughout the night. **REM (rapid eye movement)** sleep occurs during later stage 1 phases, after the sleeper has already passed through stages 2 through 4. Most of our vivid dreaming has been found to take place during this stage (Aserinsky & Kleitman,1953).

Insomnia   The patterns of sleep just described may all be disturbed by environmental factors such as noises or lights. Another source of disruption is psychological. Sleep, like hunger, is a primary drive; but as with hunger, emotional or psychological factors influence the way in which it is carried out. One result can be **insomnia**—the inability to get to sleep, stay asleep, and wake up refreshed in the morning.

Insomnia has disrupted people's careers, their social lives, and even some marriages. According to conventional wisdom, tension and anxiety are its principal causes. Worries about exams, career choices, or love lives can all cause a person to toss and turn instead of getting needed rest.

If this is entirely the case, however, why does insomnia still plague some people *after* a crisis has passed—after the exam is over, the career decision made, or the relationship problem solved? Some sleep disturbances seem to be conditioned. In other words, after many anxious nights of trying to sleep in bed, the bed itself can become a source of anxiety even though the original cause of worry is gone. Where insomnia is related to psychological causes, people can often overcome their own sleep problems. The box *Coping with Insomnia* outlines a few strategies that may be helpful.

Another possible reason why insomnia sometimes outlives its original source can be sleeping pills. Sometimes, drugs that were originally taken to *relieve* insomnia may actually cause even greater sleeping problems (Wykert, 1976). People may build up a tolerance to a particular sleeping drug, requiring larger and larger doses for it to be effective. Some persons may eventually need several pills in order to get the same small amount of sleep they originally were able to get without pills. The number of prescriptions for sleeping pills totals well into the millions each year; and though some nonaddictive pills are being developed, the problem of drug-related insomnia is still a big one.

Primary drives help explain some of our behaviors. There is a separate class of behaviors, however, that are impossible to explain in terms of bodily needs. These behaviors are based on stimulus motives, such as manipulation, exploration, and curiosity.

Stimulus Motives

The experiment looked easy. Simply sleep, rest, and do nothing for as long as you can—and get

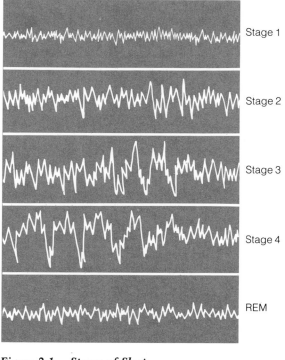

Figure 2.1   Stages of Sleep
Source: Adapted from records provided by T. E. LeVere.

paid, as well! It seemed like a college student's dream. It was actually an experiment to find out what happens when all external stimulation is blocked (Heron, 1957). Volunteer students wore thick protective garb on their hands so they couldn't touch anything, had a blindfold fitted over their eyes, and remained in a quiet room. A college student's dream, did we say? Within a day or two many students asked to stop the experiment. Some reported wild sensations and hallucinations, such as seeing eyeglasses parading before them. The effects didn't end with the experiment. Even afterwards, their perceptions of the world seemed strangely distorted, and many found simple motor tasks difficult to do.

Coping with Insomnia

Many factors can interfere with getting a good night's sleep, but some of these factors can be brought under control. If you have trouble sleeping, the following checklist may be helpful.

Does your evening routine keep you from relaxing?

The things you do before bedtime may interfere with your sleep. Do you:

- Have late-night coffee or tea? (Or do you drink these throughout the day? Caffeine may have a cumulative effect.)
- Exercise before bedtime?
- Study intensely or have "heavy" discussions late at night with friends?

Cutting down on stimulants and relaxing with quiet activities like reading before bedtime may make it easier to fall asleep. The *substitution approach* may also help: try clearing your mind of everything and visualizing a repetitive or boring scene instead.

Do you use your bed only as a place to relax?

Don't misuse your bed. If you have a tough math problem to solve, get out of bed to do it. Train yourself to think of your bed as a relaxing place, not a place to work through problems.

Do you do things "on schedule," or do you follow a different pattern each day?

The familiar "jet lag" effect shows how changes in our waking schedule can interfere with sleep. You may not start your days in one time zone and end them in another, but it is possible that you are creating the same effect by other means. Do you eat your meals at different times each day? Do you have one schedule for weekdays, and another for weekends? Regularizing your schedule may help make sleeping easier.

Are you troubled by daytime tensions or depression?

Depression and insomnia are often related. You may be surprised how quickly your sleeping problems clear up once you feel happy about life in general. If you can't seem to make headway on your own, professional help may be required, if only for a short time.

The stimulus motive isn't a primary drive, as are hunger and sleep. Unlike hunger and sleep, our drive for stimulation, exploration, and manipulation goes far beyond our survival, involving instead the exploration of our environment (Morris, 1982). In addition, when we satisfy drives like hunger and sleep we return to a less stimulated state—while exploring the environment often increases our state of arousal.

We all require stimulation that is constant and varied, however, and each of us has different needs for stimulation from the next person. Some of us require more stimulation than others, a motive that may be innate. We also seem to need more stimulation as children than as adults: the need to explore and to interact with the environment is almost the essence of childhood. This need remains with us as adults, to some extent—a point that hit home with one of the authors when his six-year-old daughter caught him playing with a yo-yo and asked him why he was doing it. Stuck for a good answer, he realized that motivations such as curiosity, manipulation, and exploration are part of human nature.

Society provides channels to satisfy our varying needs for stimulation, and the more complex the society, the more complex these channels become. Our own society, if we stop to think about it, is incredibly stimulus-oriented. Newspapers and magazines, movies, athletic competitions, live entertainment ranging from classical opera to male striptease acts, and even learning programs that are tailored for three-month-old infants only hint at the range of stimuli available.

Shaping Stimulus Motives

While we all need stimulation, two important factors are crucial in understanding how we satisfy this requirement. First, the stimulus motive is shaped and limited by our environment; and second, we have our own internal constraints. We'll look briefly at each.

Social Constraints   Watching children tells us a lot about the human motives of curiosity, exploration, and manipulation. A toddler in a high chair experiences and tests the physical properties of a banana, for instance, in a way that out-does even the most thorough research chemist. Something happens to this singleminded need to explore, however, as we grow up. Where does it go?

There are a few answers. One, of course, is that as we learn about certain everyday things (like bananas), we outgrow our need to perform experiments on them. Another significant answer concerns the way society shapes the stimulus mo-

tive. It is an interesting paradox that the same society that presents us with seemingly endless modes of entertainment also restricts our ways of satisfying stimulation needs.

As an example, consider what happens at school. Most often, students are rewarded for sitting still and repeating back to the teacher what they have heard. Active participation, manipulation, and curiosity are often discouraged, or at least clearly restricted. The same thing happens at home in some families. Children are trained not to touch things, nor to explore or change their environment. In the long run, this **socialization,** or channeling of behaviors to fit society's norms, restricts people's stimulus behaviors.

Internal Filters   While society works to curb stimulus motives, there also seems to be an innate need for each of us to limit the stimuli we experience.

This need is best understood by an analogy. A computer that receives too many commands will be overloaded and will not function efficiently. The same thing happens to humans who are "overloaded." Your three favorite pasttimes may be listening to music, watching TV football, and talking politics, but you won't want to do them all at once. If you do attempt such an endeavor, you'll probably find that you're not really tuning in on all three. This tendency to block out certain stimuli has led some scientists to suggest there may be a sort of mechanism in the brain—a "sensoristat"—that prevents overstimulation and allows us to choose a desirable stimulus level.

We know that we somehow tune out irrelevant stimuli in order to prevent overload from too many signals. How do we cope with just the opposite problem—too little variation in stimuli? All of us experience occasional bouts with boredom.

Socialization   The process by which the individual learns which roles are appropriate in a particular society.

The Great Escape

Late in the 1950s, a New York City bus driver kissed his family good-bye and went to work. The day started no differently than thousands of other workdays; only this time, he picked up his bus and drove it straight to Florida. Obviously, a large green-and-white bus with New York Transit Authority markings is not the best get-away transportation, especially in the South. He was picked up and extradicted to New York.

A huge crowd waited at the train station and the police were edgy. Were people really so angry at this man for pilfering public property? As the bus driver appeared in handcuffs, a huge cheer racked the station. The crowd surged forward seeking to pat the man on the shoulder and communicate understanding and encouragement.

What was the crowd cheering about? The bus driver's actions obviously hit a familiar chord among a great number of people. The "I wish I could . . . " daydream is a common response to being in a rut, and we feel empathy for the few who dare to act out their fantasies. The box *Becoming Unbored* offers some more pragmatic (if less exciting!) solutions to humdrum.

Boredom

Boredom is not caused by a total lack of stimulation. If it were, we would have to duplicate Heron's college student experiment in order to feel bored. Instead, the sense of weariness we experience in **boredom** is caused by a lack of change. Most activities become tedious and boring if they are continued too long. The factory worker doing the same job week after week; the dentist performing the same routine procedures year after year; or even the college student who has relaxed too much over summer vacation—all have shared the experience of being in a rut. And at one time most of us have probably felt tempted to do as the bus driver described in the box *The Great Escape*.

Being bored is no fun. But it has other, more damaging effects as well. A person who is in a rut may lose interest in getting him or herself out of it. It is easy to become more and more passive, relying on external suggestions rather than one's own initiative. Television is one of the most visible sources of passive stimulation in our society. It provides an easy way to spend a few hours without actively planning how to use one's time. Nielsen's Television Index Audience Estimates find an average weekly usage, per person in the United States, of 29 hours and 46 minutes (see Figure 2.2). For people who work for 35 hours each week and then put in another twenty-odd hours viewing TV, it's easy to see how there might not be much time left for planning other activities. This

> **Boredom** A feeling of weariness due to constant repetition or exposure to monotonous stimuli.

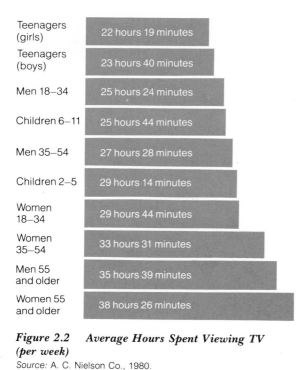

Teenagers (girls)	22 hours 19 minutes
Teenagers (boys)	23 hours 40 minutes
Men 18–34	25 hours 24 minutes
Children 6–11	25 hours 44 minutes
Men 35–54	27 hours 28 minutes
Children 2–5	29 hours 14 minutes
Women 18–34	29 hours 44 minutes
Women 35–54	33 hours 31 minutes
Men 55 and older	35 hours 39 minutes
Women 55 and older	38 hours 26 minutes

Figure 2.2   *Average Hours Spent Viewing TV (per week)*

Source: A. C. Nielson Co., 1980.

kind of eroding of initiative is one process that is both a cause and effect of boredom, and it contributes to a loss of satisfaction with life.

Another common facet of boredom is the vocational rut. Boredom on the job brings problems of great magnitude, including worker dissatisfaction, poor workmanship, and chronic absenteeism. Assembly-line jobs have rapid turnover rates that consume millions of dollars each year in retraining costs. The "assembly-line blues" have probably received the most media publicity as they relate to the auto industry and other repetitive jobs. The problem has received considerable attention and study in recent years, and many corporations have developed strategies to overcome it. These include job rotation, where workers rotate their positions on a regular basis; flextime, where hours of work are varied from the traditional nine-to-five; providing more social

outlets for workers; and training workers to see how their roles fit into the production process as a whole.

The blues also affect people in all vocations—from lawyers, to scientists, to college professors. Chapter 13 will look more closely at worker dissatisfaction and ways to overcome it. The tips in the box *Becoming Unbored* can be more broadly applied to the ruts or slumps most of us experience in vocations, relationships, or life in general.

Boredom is also related to a number of undesirable behaviors. A bored child may disturb other students in the classroom. Some people will indulge in aggressive behavior just to experience a new and different feeling and lessen their feelings of boredom (Cirese, 1977). In a society where many jobs are passive, some people may satisfy their need for stimulation by creating outbursts of their own.

Boredom is a stimulus problem, but learning plays a part in both falling into a rut and getting out of it. The way in which people's stimulus needs are satisfied is somewhat determined by what they have learned in their childhood. If people have learned creative and responsible ways to deal with boredom, they will cope with it by seeking new experiences that can further their own personal development. Thus, again learning plays a part in the satisfaction of our needs.

There is another group of motives that we have not yet discussed. Unlike primary or stimulus motives, these motives are entirely learned. We will turn to these next.

Learned Motives

Primary drives and stimulus motivation account for many aspects of behavior, but they do not explain all of our actions. Why do some people seem driven to seek political office, or to get top grades; why do others have "chips on their shoulders"; why are still others only happy when they keep in close touch with a network of friends?

Becoming Unbored

Diet books, parent training manuals, and self-help groups abound in our society, but few people have been trained to cope with boredom. If you're in a rut, how can you learn to get out of it? Here are a few tips:

Tip #1

Find ways of varying your stimulation. TV programmers and advertisers know how to do this, and you can take a hint from their strategy. For instance:

Change stations. How many TV shows last four or five hours? None, except for an occasional sportscast that runs into overtime. Our attention spans peak well before four or five hours. Thus, performing the same task, be it working, reading, or studying, is likely to become boring after a long spell, even if it's a task we enjoy. It helps to "change stations" during the day, so that you can move from one task to another as soon as your interest starts to lag.

Take a commercial break. If you have time or job constraints that keep you at one task most of the day, take a "commercial break." Dr. Lawrence Peter (1972) suggests taking regular "vacations" of about 15 minutes at certain times each day. Walk around the block, or move to another room of the house, or call up a friend you've been meaning to contact. You'll return to your task with a fresher perspective.

Tip #2

Small life changes are often easier to make than big ones. If you're in a rut, but feel stymied at the thought of doing something completely new, it may be easier to turn to something just a little different.

Studies have found that children choose toys and situations that are somewhat novel but not completely unfamiliar (Sarafino & Armstrong, 1980). Doing the same thing all the time may be boring, but a totally new situation can be frightening. Adults share the same feelings. If you need change, then, it may be easiest to take one small step at a time, allowing yourself to feel at ease before you progress to the next step. The adjustment will also be easier if you choose activities that relate to your own knowledge or background.

Tip #3

Try to find satisfaction in several areas of your life. If you're unhappy with your work, or school, or home life and you can't change it right now, build satisfying experiences in other areas of your life. Many people can tolerate a repetitive job if their home life is rewarding, or if they are taking a course about a topic that fascinates them.

Tip #4

If a marriage relationship seems to be losing its spontaneity, it is important for both partners to recognize they are in a rut. A conscious effort to "spice up" life together may be able to help. Getting away for a weekend, or taking a day trip to an interesting spot, or taking off an afternoon to go to the movies may help to revitalize a relationship by renewing a sense of fun.

Above all, it is important to realize that the solution to boredom lies within yourself. We may be conditioned to expect others to pull us out of our ruts and supply excitement for us. But boredom can be broken only by the person who is bored.

These motives are all *secondary* or *learned motives:* motives that are largely determined by the society in which a person lives. Although they are not necessary for existence, they dominate a good portion of our lives. Many learned motives have been identified, including achievement, affiliation, aggression, autonomy, and dominance. Such learned motives are conditioned by our families, peers, school, and society in general. We'll look more closely at two of these motives: achievement and affiliation.

Achievement

Psychologists define **achievement** as performing up to internal standards of excellence—or simply as striving for success (McClelland et al., 1953). Notice that the definition does not include basic societal standards for success, such as money or power. People who have high achievement motivations do not value these external trappings for their own sakes; their value lies instead in the success they symbolize.

Highly motivated people are often found in positions that allow unlimited growth and involvement. There are numerous famous examples of very wealthy people who, despite amassing tremendous wealth and power, continue to work and achieve.

Like anything else, there are gradations in the need to achieve. It is not an either-or motive. The person who strives for more and more and gives up everything else is at one end of the spectrum; the person who is so passive as to have no life goals is on the other end. Most of us are somewhere in the middle, showing moderate needs for achievement.

People who have high achievement motives will not respond to every task differently from those with low motivation. The two groups are likely to perform similarly, in fact, on tasks that offer little challenge. But if a problem or task presents the right challenge, the two groups are likely to respond differently. The achievers are usually attracted to tasks that are moderately challenging. Even where the outcome is in doubt, they feel that *they* can make the difference. People with lower achievement motivation, in contrast, are less likely to accelerate their efforts to the same extent.

Does a high achievement motivation ensure that a person will keep on striving for success? The answer is no. Some achievers do not seem to choose fields or tasks that challenge their abilities, and thus they never seem to "take off." Other people who have the potential to achieve seem to set up their own roadblocks, as if they actually feared success. We'll look at both of these paradoxes.

Fear of Failure   John stood out in high school. He was bright, polished, earned good grades, and also showed leadership abilities. As a senior, he was voted most likely to succeed. Ironically, 10 years later the prophecy seemed almost unbelievable. John is stuck in a dead-end job which offers little challenge, and he doesn't seem inspired to change for the better.

What happened? There are two opposing components of the need to achieve. The first is the need to accomplish and succeed, while the second is a desire to avoid failure (Atkinson, 1964; Birney, 1968). In some cases, as in John's, the **fear of failure** may outweigh the motivation to succeed. John responded to this fear by taking the easy way out: taking the easiest courses in college and later finding jobs in which he couldn't help but suc-

---

Achievement motive   The learned motive to excel, to succeed, or to perform up to high standards often set by oneself.

Fear of failure   One of the important elements involved in achievement motivation. Individuals with a need to achieve but a high fear of failure tend to avoid challenging problems, opting for very easy or almost impossibly difficult ones.

ceed. Fear of failure, like the achievement motive, is learned. The box *Trained to Fail?* suggests how this learning process might take place.

There is another response to fear of failure that may help to explain related kinds of behavior. Some people with great fear of failure may take on almost impossible tasks. Even if they fail, they can't be criticized because "nobody could do that anyway." Or, as one study of chronic procrastinators suggests, some people may respond to a fear of failure by putting off tasks until the very last minute. In the twelfth-hour scramble, their performance will no longer reflect their true ability, but instead how well the person can "pull things together at the last minute" (Burka & Yuen, 1982).

Fear of Success   The "fear of failure" theory explains some instances in which bright people fail to achieve, but there are other cases of underachievement that this theory doesn't explain. Some people, most often women, seem motivated by a desire not to achieve to their fullest.

The most famous piece of research on this topic provides an illustration of the **fear of success** motivation. In her now classic study, Matina Horner (1969) asked male and female college students to write essays. The women's essays began: "After first-term finals, Anne finds herself at the top of her class"; the men's lead-off sentence was identical, except for the substitution of the name "John" and the pronoun "his." The results? Most of the men's essays (91 percent) depicted a rosy future for John, but fully 66 percent of the women's essays showed ambivalence and concern for Anne. There was a strong theme that success

> **Fear of success**   Matina Horner's explanation for some people's (most often women's) seeming hesitancy to achieve. According to this theory, an individual feels that achievement in a particular area may bring social sanctions.

HERMAN

"How come you don't go fishing anymore?"

in male-stereotyped occupations, and in competing with men in general, often brings a woman into conflict with society's demands.

Is there a "sex-linked" fear of success that is not inborn, but ingrained in women by our society? Certainly, many changes have occurred since the Horner study. More women are now entering the professions, competing in formerly maledominated fields. And on a broader scale, social attitudes are changing perceptibly, so that success, achievement, and femininity are no longer mutually exclusive (Gardner, 1978). At the same time, more men seem to be questioning the meaning of achievement, thinking in terms of broad

Trained to Fail?

Are some people destined to fear failure? As this chapter discusses, two factors must be taken into account when discussing achievement motivation. The flip side of a desire to succeed is the fear of failing. People who have a high fear of failure will shy away from truly challenging assignments, choosing either the very safe and secure course or the impossible task. In the first choice, there is no doubt of their success, while in the second they can't be criticized for failing.

What causes some people to fear failure? Psychologists Richard Teevan and Paul McGhee investigated the theory that some parent-child interactions might lead to this fear. Forty-one mothers of male high school juniors and seniors were questioned about their interactions with their sons. Of these mothers, 20 had sons who were rated as possessing a high fear of failure, while 21 had sons with a low fear of failure.

The results of the questionnaire showed some interesting differences. Both groups of mothers expected independence and achievement-oriented behaviors early in their sons' lives. The high-fear mothers, however, gave neutral responses for their sons' achievements and punished their sons for unsatisfactory behavior. Mothers of low-fear students, on the other hand, rewarded achievements but were less critical of failures.

The authors concluded that it is not the early demand for achievement that determines fear of failure, but rather the reinforcements and punishments that are given. In patterns where positive achievement receives little response, but failures are directly punished, children learn to fear the consequences of failure, without feeling good about their successes.

From the results of this study, it seems clear that if we want children to show a positive attitude toward achievement and not failure, we should reward them for efforts and achievements, but tone down the criticisms for their failures.

Source: Teevan & McGhee, 1972.

---

lifestyles and investigating alternative value systems. Where these changes are leading us, no one knows. Times are changing, however, and these changes will affect your life.

Affiliation

A second learned motive is **affiliation**—the desire to associate oneself with other people. Affiliation, like achievement, varies from one person to the next. For some of us, deep relationships with friends are one of the most important parts of life. Given a good social environment, these people can be happy at virtually any job. Others are more task-oriented. They are likely to regard too much "gab" as an interruption, preferring to accomplish personal goals instead of sharing thoughts with friends.

Just as affiliation needs vary from person to person, they also vary according to the situation. You have probably found that in some circumstances—such as waiting for a very late bus, or sitting in a waiting room of a hospital—you are more likely to talk to the stranger next to you than

> **Affiliation motive** The desire to be in the company of, and associate with, other people.

in other situations. This phenomenon has been studied by psychologists such as Schachter (1959), who noted that affiliation increases when people are under stress.

Affiliation and Stress In one experiment, Schachter had extensive shock equipment shown to two groups of subjects (see Figure 2.3). The first group was shown the equipment and told they were in for a painful experience. They were then asked if they wanted to wait in separate waiting rooms or together in the same room. The second group received almost the same treatment. They were assured, however, that though the equipment looked imposing, the shocks it gave were mild and caused no pain. (Of course, no shocks were ever actually contemplated.) The first group, not surprisingly, was more anxious than the second group. They also showed a greater tendency to affiliate, with more of them asking to sit together in the same waiting room.

Schachter's experiment showed clearly that people respond to stress by seeking bonds. Just why this is so is an intriguing question. One answer is that we can obtain sympathy and support from people who are experiencing the same discomfort that we are. Somehow, they are talking the same language: conversation is easier because there is an automatic common ground. There is a greater possibility of reassurance and understanding.

Another answer is that we might have a greater need for positive social evaluations when we are under stress. If others who are going through the same thing are just as anxious as we are, we are reassured that our own feelings are appropriate. The more ambiguous the situation, the more we will want to compare notes with others.

There are times when this rule may not hold, of course. In a true emergency, people are more likely to seek out an authority figure than to look for others who are confused and insecure. In these instances—as in a fire or an auto accident—people need immediate help to get out of their predicament. Interestingly, though, there are likely to be strong bonds formed in the aftermath of a flood, or fire, or earthquake, as people who were once strangers share a common, highly stressful experience.

Affiliation and Privacy Almost all people are motivated to form bonds with others. Even those of us who thrive on companionship, however, also need privacy once in a while. In fact, Maslow (1970) in his study of self-actualized individuals found that these persons enjoyed periods of solitude.

Sometimes, we take privacy so much for granted that we don't realize how much we need it. Marriage counselors often hear young couples complain that before they were married, they always seemed to want to be together, while now they often want to be alone. Of course, they might not realize that before they married there were periods of enforced privacy, and that these periods no longer exist. The expectation that marriage somehow means constant company is unrealistic. Few people, no matter how much they love each other, want to be together all the time. Allowing partners the opportunity to be alone as well as together is necessary if both partners are to grow within a relationship.

Balancing Motives

If there is a moral to this chapter, it might be that too much or too little of anything can cause adjustment problems. Whether it be curiosity, achievement, or affiliation, eating or sleeping, an excess or deficit can be related to narrow development, so that the person does not experience life as fully as possible.

Each person has a highly individual balance of motives. As you become more aware of your own needs and motivations, you may desire to change some aspect of your behavior. This can be done, but it takes effort and knowledge. Change is never easy. But, as you will see, techniques have been developed that can help bring about changes.

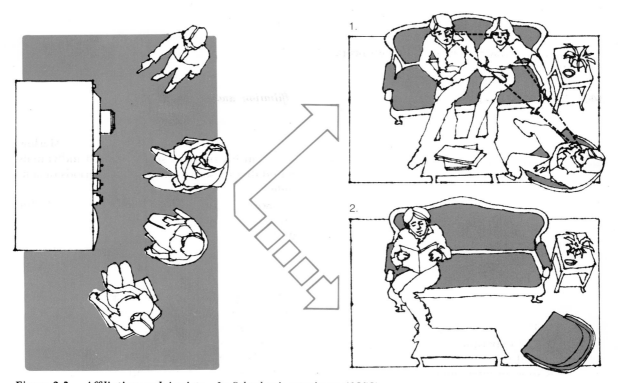

Figure 2.3   Affiliation and Anxiety   *In Schachter's experiment (1959), the first group was shown shock equipment and then ushered into the waiting room. They showed a strong tendency to affiliate. The second group, told that the equipment wasn't harmful, showed little need to interact.*

As you look back on this chapter, one striking theme has been the extent to which primary, stimulus, and secondary motives were all modified through learning. The environment operates in even the most basic of drives. To better understand how the environment affects behavior, it is necessary to understand learning. The basic principles by which we learn behavior, as well as change behavior, are discussed in the next chapter.

Summary

1.   Motivation involves the study of the reasons behind behavior. The terms *motive, need,* and *drive* are often confused. The term motive refers to all internal and external forces that instigate, direct, or terminate behavior. A need refers to a specific deficit in an organism, while a drive is a state of arousal that leads an individual to behave in a particular manner when faced with a need.

2.   According to Hull's drive theory, a need gives rise to a drive. When the goal is reached the need is satisfied.

3.   The strength of the goal-seeking behavior depends upon the value of the goal and the expectation that a particular set of behaviors will achieve it.

4.   Primary drives are defined as energy directed at satisfying innate physiological needs. Stimulus motives satisfy needs for stimulation, manipulation, and exploration, while secondary motives such as affiliation and achievement satisfy needs that are essentially learned.

5. The physiological explanation for the hunger drive does not explain the great incidence of obesity in our society. Overweight people have eating patterns that contribute to their condition: they are less likely to differentiate between being hungry and being full; they are more sensitive to external cues like advertisements; they tend to eat more when under stress; and they are less active. One way to lose weight is to start with an awareness of eating habits.

6. There are many theories to explain why humans require sleep. The body may use sleep as a time to make repairs, or to conserve energy. Our sleep patterns may be determined by evolutionary factors. In any case, sleep deprivation causes irritability and fatigue. Insomnia is largely caused by psychological factors, although sleeping pills may also contribute to insomniac patterns.

7. People have an innate need for stimulation. If deprived of all stimulation, they may experience severe side effects, including hallucinations. Boredom is usually caused by lack of change. Coping with boredom involves varying the amount of stimulation by alternating tasks, creating a pleasant social environment, and developing active interests such as hobbies.

8. Secondary or learned motives such as power, affiliation, or achievement are not innate, but reflect what we learn from the social environment. People with high achievement motives want to achieve for its own sake, not for money or power. They usually undertake challenging tasks, feeling confident that they can control the outcome. A person with a high achievement motivation but a great fear of failure will tend to undertake tasks that are either very easy (thus assuring success) or so difficult that success is highly unlikely. A person with high fear of success, in contrast, feels ambivalent about succeeding. This kind of fear has been more common among women.

9. The tendency to affiliate increases when a person is under stress. People affiliate in order to gain support from one another as well as to exchange information.

10. A balance of motives seems to be preferable to extremely high motivation in any one area. High motivation—in achievement, or stimulus motivation, or any other single area—seems to be associated with narrow development.

Key Terms and Concepts

motivation	REM (rapid eye movement)
motive	insomnia
need	socialization
drive	boredom
primary drive	achievement motive
stimulus motive	fear of failure
secondary (learned) motive	fear of success
electroencephalograph	affiliation motive
hypnogogic sleep	

Before dawn on January 9, 1800, a remarkable creature came out of the woods near the village of Saint-Sernin in southern France . . . . He was human in bodily form and walked erect. Everything else about him suggested an animal. He was naked except for the tatters of a shirt and showed no modesty, no awareness of himself as a human person related in any way to the people who had captured him. He could not speak and made only weird, meaningless cries. Though very short, he appeared to be a boy of about eleven or twelve, with a round face under dark matted hair (Shattuck, 1980, p. 5).

Learning

The 11-year-old "Wild Boy of Aveyron" —presumed to have been living alone in the woods for as long as eight years—was remarkable for the things he had never learned. He ran out in the snow almost naked; he put his hands into hot coals; he showed no response to verbal communication (for a time, he was presumed to be deaf). He never did learn to talk, although he became socialized in many ways.

The significance of this story for us lies in the overwhelming relationship between *what* we learn and *who* we are. Like the "Wild Boy," we are, in many respects, the product of what we learn from our experiences. As we explore the basic components of adjustment in Part I, it would be impossible not to include the topic of learning.

This chapter examines **learning,** defined as relatively permanent changes in behavior due to experience, as well as the related topics of memory and problem solving. In the following pages we will look at several ways in which learning takes place, exploring classical conditioning, operant conditioning, and social learning or imitation. These processes are particularly relevant to the study of adjustment, because understanding how we learned our own behaviors can help us to control these behaviors. We can also use these principles of learning to change those behaviors that are counterproductive. We will also look at the ways in which a person learns motor skills (such as playing billiards or swimming), as well as ways of improving verbal skills.

Classical Conditioning

Much of our learning seems to take place through classical conditioning, a process we introduced briefly in Chapter 1. To review, *classical conditioning* involves the pairing of a neutral stimulus with a stimulus that elicits a response, until the

Learning Relatively permanent changes in behavior due to experiences.

neutral stimulus itself produces that same response. The response is often physiological or reflexive in nature.

Classical conditioning sometimes takes place without our knowing it, occasionally with baffling results. The following hypothetical situation, based on an actual case that stymied a few doctors for a while, is a case in point. Suppose you've moved out of the Northeast because of your allergies to pollen. You settle in a southwestern community, where the sweet, warm air never carries any dust and people never call the local hospital to find out the daily pollen count. You find yourself in excellent physical shape—until you enter your fiance's house. Then your eye's water, you wheeze, and it's New Jersey all over again. What happened?

It seems that your fiance's house is decorated with artificial flowers, some of which look exactly like ragweed. The sight of the ragweed, even though artificial, was enough to cause an allergic reaction. You have been classically conditioned.

Far-fetched as this case may seem, it is but one of countless real examples of such conditioning associations. For instance, Dekker and Groen (1956) found that the sight of dust or goldfish, the smell of perfume, and even the singing of the national anthem could bring about asthmatic attacks in a group of sufferers that they studied. Once they had discovered which particular stimulus brought on an asthma attack in a person, they could elicit attacks at will—sometimes with only pictures of the stimulus. Theoretically, a stimulus that causes a reaction can be associated in this way with any other neutral stimulus, so that after repeated pairings it will cause the reaction itself. The shorter the interval between the conditioned and unconditioned stimulus, the more effective the conditioning process. The optimum interval is one-half second for human beings and most animals.

One question students often ask is how many pairings are necessary to establish conditioning. Years ago, some texts denied that one or two pairings were sufficient to cause conditioning to take place. Psychologists today realize that in some cir-

Save the Coyote: A Tale of Conditioning

Coyotes have always been a problem in ranching areas because they kill livestock. Ranchers have dealt with them in a way that is undeniably effective: they kill the coyotes. In some areas, however, this slaughter brought the wild coyote population close to extinction by the early 1970s.

An obvious conflict existed. On the one hand, a native species was in danger of extinction, and it had to be protected. On the other hand, ranchers rightly demanded that their livestock also needed protection.

In the end, the problem was solved by simple classical conditioning techniques. Gustavson and his colleagues (1974) treated lamb flesh with a chemical. When the coyotes ate it, they felt temporarily sick (then recovered completely). It took only one or two experiences with the treated lamb to convince the coyotes to look for another source of food. They preyed upon other animals in the environment, leaving the lambs for the ranchers.

cumstances, even a single pairing of the conditioned and unconditioned stimulus may be sufficient, especially if the consequences are powerful enough. The box *Save the Coyote: A Tale of Conditioning* illustrates one instance in which this fact proved to be highly beneficial.

There are other examples of single, powerful experiences that have caused conditioning to take place. **Phobias,** defined as "excessive or inappropriate fear(s) of some particular object or situation which is not in fact dangerous" (Sarason & Sarason, 1980, p. 520), are sometimes learned through classical conditioning. People can develop phobias about virtually anything, from being touched (haptephobia), to being trapped in a closed space (claustrophobia), to taking examinations. For example, if lightning flashed just as you heard a loud scream, you might later show a fear of lightning. Being trapped for hours in an elevator might cause a person to develop claustrophobia, fearing all enclosed spaces. Or the witnessing of a terrible accident downtown might be associated with *agoraphobia,* a fear of open places. Even a single pairing with such a powerful stimulus can sometimes be enough to cause conditioning to take place.

Stimulus Generalization

In the last two examples mentioned, you may have noticed that conditioned responses may sometimes become associated not just with the conditioned stimulus, but also with similar stimuli. You may fear not just elevators, but all enclosed places; or you may extend your fear of busy streets to venturing outside at all. This phenomenon is called **stimulus generalization.**

One very famous conditioning experiment illustrates how stimulus generalization may take place (see Figure 3.1). The experiment was performed many years ago, and it involved an 11-month-old named Albert (Watson & Raynor, 1920). At the outset, the experimenters placed a

> **Phobia** A fear that is either irrational or out of proportion to the danger presented by a particular object or situation.
>
> **Stimulus generalization** A term used in learning theory to denote an individual's response to stimuli that resemble the originally conditioned stimulus.

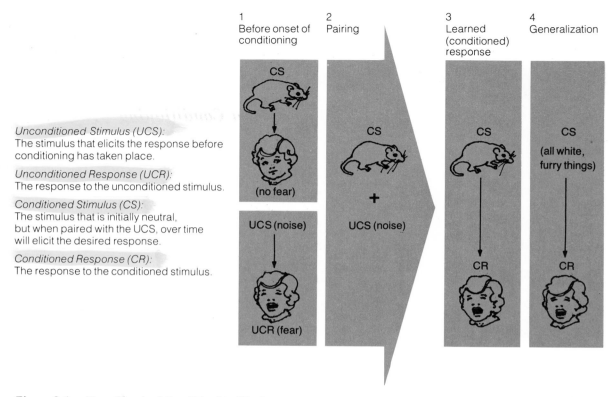

| 1
Before onset of
conditioning | 2
Pairing | 3
Learned
(conditioned)
response | 4
Generalization |

Unconditioned Stimulus (UCS):
The stimulus that elicits the response before conditioning has taken place.

Unconditioned Response (UCR):
The response to the unconditioned stimulus.

Conditioned Stimulus (CS):
The stimulus that is initially neutral, but when paired with the UCS, over time will elicit the desired response.

Conditioned Response (CR):
The response to the conditioned stimulus.

Figure 3.1   How Classical Conditioning Works

small white rat in Albert's crib, to test his reaction. He showed no fear, demonstrating curiosity and interest instead. Soon, though, each appearance of the animal in Albert's crib was paired with a loud noise, which startled and scared Albert. After a number of such pairings, Albert was conditioned to fear the rat. The fear response was elicited not only by the rat, but also by a dog, a cat, a fur coat, and virtually anything furry—even Santa Claus' beard.

Stimulus generalization is a daily phenomenon. For instance, the smell of your boyfriend's aftershave lotion might predispose you to feel friendly toward a total stranger who happened to be wearing it. Or, you may decide to stop going to all fast-food burger joints because you've had a bad burger at one food chain.

Of course, you know from your own experience that generalizations such as these do not always take place to this extent. You may like the smell of your boyfriend's aftershave on anyone, but you won't feel the same familiarity with everyone who wears it. Again, you may decide to boycott Macburgers while you continue to patronize all the other fast-food chains. This is because we learn to discriminate between different stimuli.

Stimulus Discrimination

In Chapter 1, we saw how classical conditioning can cause a person to feel anxious about engine sounds in a running car, especially if those sounds were once paired with a breakdown. But every engine makes some sounds, and most drivers learn to tell which ones predict trouble and which do not. They can *discriminate,* or differentiate between stimuli.

Stimulus discrimination can be defined as the "process of differentiating among stimuli" (Marx & Bunch, 1977, p. 495). Such discriminations can be seen in everyday life. You learn to differentiate the sound of the footsteps of each member of your household, for example, or you learn that you can sleep through your roommate's morning alarm because your classes don't start until several hours later.

Although you might learn to ignore the ringing of a roommate's alarm, it is possible that after a few weeks' vacation, you might wake abruptly the first time you heard it again. That is because the learning that takes place through conditioning can also be unlearned. We call this "un"-conditioning **extinction.**

Extinction

Extinction can often take place when the conditioned stimulus (for instance, Albert's rat) is presented *without* being paired with the unconditioned stimulus (the loud noise).* After repeated presentations like this, the person no longer responds as if a certain consequence were expected. The number of such trials needed to extinguish a particular response varies greatly, depending on a number of personal variables. Some phobias are very difficult to extinguish. Sometimes, too, a conditioned response seems to be extinguished, but then returns after a rest period. This is referred to as **spontaneous recovery.** When this happens, however, the response is usually easier to extinguish this second time.

Classical conditioning influences the way in which we react to our environment, at the level of stimulus and response. Learning also takes place

*Unfortunately, Watson never bothered to extinguish little Albert's fear of rats (Harris, 1979).

in many other ways, though, and these other processes play an even greater role in shaping who we are. We'll look next at a second form of learning, operant conditioning.

Operant Conditioning

Your history teacher asks a question and you think you know the answer; you proudly announce "Rutherford B. Hayes." The teacher looks at you, shakes her head, dismisses your answer with a gesture of disgust, and asks whether anyone has a serious answer. Angry and embarrassed, you secretly dream about revenge, or visualize her tripping over her attaché case. The next time she asks a question, you sit mute, looking bored.

The situation is different in your English class. When you answer a question incorrectly, this teacher replies "perhaps," or "there might be a better answer," or asks you to elaborate. Although he corrects your answer, somehow you don't feel like an idiot for making a mistake. You volunteer in his class, and you're willing to take the chance of being wrong.

These two classrooms illustrate different aspects of a second form of learning. **Operant conditioning** is the "process by which behavior is changed because of the consequences of that

---

Stimulus discrimination In learning theory, the process by which an individual learns to differentiate between stimuli.

Extinction The gradual decrease in a response that occurs due to a lack of reinforcement.

Spontaneous recovery The return of a learned response with rest after extinction.

Operant conditioning The learning process in which behavior is altered because of the consequences it has on the environment.

behavior" (Sarafino & Armstrong, 1980, p. 544). If we look at your behavior in both of your classes, we find that it was the consequences of your participation (in the form of the teachers' reactions) that determined whether or not you would continue to raise your hand in class. The principle behind operant conditioning is deceptively simple: behaviors that are reinforced tend to recur; those that are not reinforced tend to disappear. We will look at both reinforcement and the opposite process, punishment.

Reinforcement

The term *reinforcement* is often misunderstood. A reinforcement doesn't have to be a material reward, like a candy bar or a blue ribbon (although these may be reinforcements). Instead, anything that increases the frequency of a response that precedes it is a reinforcement. It can be anything from praise, to sex, to attention. Because reinforcements are so individual and variable, they can sometimes fool us: a particular reinforcement may be effective with one person, but completely ineffective with someone else.

An example of this is the mother who came to the psychologist with a problem. "Frankly, I am bewildered. As soon as my 8-year-old comes home from school, he knocks over lamps. He has broken three in the last two months." The psychologist naturally asked the mother how she reacted. "I scream at him and chase him upstairs," came the expected reply. After a bit of digging, the psychologist found that the mother was always on the telephone when her son came home from school, and that only after the lamps were tipped over would she hang up. The only way the child knew to get his mother off the phone was to tip over the lamps. She rewarded his behavior with attention. The answer was simply to meet him at the door before the behavior had a chance to be shown.

We all are reinforced for our behaviors in everyday life, and these reinforcements are often in conflict. A parent may reinforce a child for one behavior, such as honesty, while her peer group might reinforce just the opposite behavior, such as shoplifting. Such conflicts are inevitable, and the behavior exhibited will always be in the direction of the greater reinforcement. This is illustrated by the seemingly paradoxical outcome of one school's policy. In an effort to provide more positive reinforcement, pupils were given daily behavior reports. Those who were good in class had an angel stamped on the card they brought home to their parents each day; those who were bad received a devil. Within three weeks, the situation in school became chaotic. The well-behaved students improved—but the misbehaving students became even worse. The cause was the conflicting reinforcements of the school officials and peers. Members of "rough" peer groups saw the angel cards as signs of weakness; in these groups, the more devils a person received, the more reinforcement was provided by friends. Since school-age children put great stock in the evaluations of their friends, school officials had little chance of changing behavior through this strategy.

Conflicting reinforcements affect us in daily decisions, also. For instance, many women feel torn between the satisfactions of a promising career and those of motherhood, especially in the first years when infants grow and change rapidly. In some cases of conflicting reinforcements, it may be possible to work out a compromise that partially satisfies both sides of the conflict.

Using Reinforcement to Shape Behavior

The earlier story of the "angel" and "devil" cards describes an effort—albeit an unsuccessful one—to shape or change behavior through a planned reinforcement program. The use of reinforcers to encourage wanted behaviors is one of the primary techniques in behavior modification. As the story showed, however, the *mis*use of reinforcement may cause behavior changes that aren't wanted.

How can reinforcement be used effectively? Because we often want to improve our own habits

Table 3.1　Partial Reinforcement Schedules

Type	Definition	Example
Fixed ratio reinforcement	Reinforcement is delivered according to a fixed number of correct responses.	Your boss pats you on the back every second time you sell a suit at the men's wear shop where you work. If you sell ten suits, you will be reinforced for the second, fourth, sixth, eighth, and tenth suits sold.
Variable ratio reinforcement	Reinforcement is delivered in response to a variable number of correct responses.	If you sold ten suits, your boss might pat you on the back the first, fourth, eighth, ninth, and tenth times you succeeded in selling a suit. You never know when the reinforcement is coming.
Fixed interval reinforcement	Reinforcement is delivered after a fixed time interval, providing the correct response is given.	You receive your allowance every Friday after 3:00, if you ask for it.
Variable interval reinforcement	Reinforcement is delivered when the correct response occurs after various lengths of time.	You are interested in a certain girl in your class, but she is more interested in the football captain than in you. She will accept a date with you, but only if "Muscles" hasn't asked her first. Since you never know when he will decide to call her, you keep asking. Sometimes she accepts, but other times she doesn't.

or modify the behaviors of people we live or work with, it is useful to know the principles of reinforcement. (As students, in fact, we might even want to modify the behaviors of our teachers. The box *Turning the Tables on the Teachers* tells how this happened in one group.) We'll look quickly at these reinforcement principles in the next few pages.

Partial vs. Continuous Reinforcement　A reinforcement program may use either partial or continuous reinforcement. **Continuous reinforcement** involves rewarding each instance of the wanted behavior—for example, giving children a cookie each time they clean their room. **Partial reinforcement** relies on rewards also, but not every time the desired behavior takes place. Partial reinforcement may be based on either the number of correct responses (called a *ratio reinforcement*

schedule) or the time between correct responses (*interval reinforcement schedule*), and each of these may be either fixed or variable. Table 3.1 outlines the differences among these various approaches to reinforcement.

The choice of a reinforcement schedule is very important to the success of a particular type of behavior change program. Each approach offers its own advantages, but each also has disad-

---

Continuous reinforcement　A reinforcement schedule that involves rewarding each instance of the desired behavior. See, by contrast, *partial reinforcement*.

Partial reinforcement　Reinforcement that is not delivered on a continuous one-to-one, behavior-reinforcement basis. If partial reinforcement is used, only a portion of the desired responses will receive reinforcement.

Turning the Tables on the Teacher

Behavior modification—the use of the principles of learning to change behavior—is usually thought of as a tool of teachers and other trained professionals to change "undesirable" behaviors in their students. As such, it has had the reputation as a tool of the establishment. Like any other tool, however, it can be used by anyone who learns how to use it. For example, why not teach students to use these techniques to change their teachers' attitudes and behaviors towards them? This is exactly what was accomplished in Visalia, California, as reported by Farnum Gray and his colleagues.

The Director of Special Education for the Visalia school district designed a behavior modification program that taught a selected group of students how to change their teachers' attitudes and behaviors. The school official, together with a special consultant, decided to try their ideas at a local junior high school with a high percentage of troubled children. They chose seven students who were considered to be "incorrigible," instructing them in behavior modification techniques. Then, they moved these students into regular classes.

For the first two weeks the students were told to keep records of the positive and negative interactions with their teachers. However, an unexpected problem arose. It seems that these students easily recognized the negative interactions but seemed unaware of any positive ones. To counter this, students were educated, using role playing and videotapes, to identify positive interactions.

After this training, the students were ready to begin the reinforcement phase. They consciously smiled, increased their eye contact with teachers, and even praised their teachers. They also learned how to deal with negative teacher evaluations. During the five weeks of recording, the number of positive interactions increased dramatically and the number of negative ones decreased.

In the final stage of the program, the students stopped using behavior modification techniques. The result? Teachers again began giving more negative comments—showing that teachers, like everyone else, require periodic reinforcement. After this extinction phase ended, the students once again used their conditioning techniques. Although they kept no formal records, they reported great successes.

The idea of teaching students behavior modification techniques has been extended to instructing youngsters on how to influence their parents and peers. However, one word of caution should be noted. The reinforcement techniques must be used correctly—and the compliments must be sincere to be effective.

So, it seems that behavior modification techniques can be utilized in a number of ways. Teaching children how to reinforce their teachers and parents opens up new opportunities for improving teacher-child and parent-child interactions. These students now have positive behavioral alternatives that are useful and effective both inside and outside of the classroom. They have less need to misbehave since they have the power to influence the behavior of others. They have, in short, joined the ranks of the behavior shapers.

Source: Gray et al., 1974.

vantages in certain situations. For instance, continuous reinforcement usually results in quicker learning, because the person quickly associates the desired behavior with the reward. However, behaviors learned in this way are also extin- guished more rapidly once the reinforcers are no longer supplied.

It may take longer for a person to learn under a partial reinforcement schedule, but the behavior will be more resistant to extinction. Of the

An example of variable reinforcement. Because reinforcement always seems to be "just around the corner," many people find it very hard to stop.

various types of partial reinforcement, both fixed interval and fixed ratio schedules are highly predictable. As a result, their behaviors may be extinguished relatively easily. If your paychecks stop coming every Friday, you may quickly stop coming to work. A variable reinforcement schedule is even more effective. Because the person never knows when reinforcement will come, there is more willingness to keep on trying, and the behavior is not so easily extinguished.

This very fact explains a great deal about some seemingly illogical behaviors such as gambling or betting. It explains why many of us automatically check the coin return at public telephones. It also helps to explain why people get "hooked" on numbers rackets, or race track betting, or "slot machine syndrome," or other addictive gambling behaviors where the odds are overwhelmingly against winning in the long run. The attraction of all of these pastimes is the same: sooner or later the gambler will have a winning day (maybe even two in a row!). Since the person never knows when that day will come, winning seems always to be just around the corner. As a result, the behavior is extremely resistant to extinction.

The same principle works in reverse, by the way. Suppose your teacher told you to expect six quizzes during the semester, on a random (variable interval) basis rather than every two weeks. If you are like most students, you would keep up with your studies rather than waiting until the last minute—you never would know when the "last" minute was coming! (However, you might not enjoy the class very much, since your anxiety level would be high.)

Both continuous and partial reinforcement schedules offer advantages, with one offering faster learning and the other, more resistance to extinction. Perhaps the optimal method lies somewhere in between, beginning the conditioning process using continuous reinforcement and then switching to partial reinforcement. Reinforcement techniques are quite useful. Two interesting applications that are often used are token reinforcement and successive approximations.

Token Reinforcement **Token reinforcement procedures** (Hamblin et al., 1969) combine the advantages of full reinforcement and partial reinforcement. The technique works as follows:

■ First, desired behaviors are clearly defined, and an "economy" is established whereby those behaviors have a stated value in tokens.

Token reinforcement procedures (token economies) A technique used in operant conditioning in which an individual receives a token for performing some desired behavior and may either save the tokens and combine them with others or redeem them for some object or privilege.

Successive approximations (shaping) A technique used to train elaborate new behaviors in both humans and animals. The trainer first finds a behavior the organism can do and then reinforces slight changes in this behavior until it approximates the desired activity.

For instance, John's desired behavior is a clean room, which is defined as having *no* clothes behind the toy box, books on the floor, and so forth. (This definition is important, for cleanliness is often in the eye of the beholder!) John knows he will get a token each weekday his room is clean by 8:30 A.M. and each weekend morning by 10:00 A.M.

■ Next, tokens may be traded in for rewards at fixed intervals of time, and the reward varies according to the number of tokens earned. John may turn in his tokens each Sunday, for instance. Seven tokens earns him one treat; six, a lesser treat; and five, still less. An infinite number of variations are possible, and the system can be used in many settings, from prisons, to schools, to the home.

In designing any token system (or any other reinforcement system for that matter), it is important that the goals are attainable. Expecting a 70 percent student to get straight A's is asking too much in a short period of time, and the impossibility of it all might be so discouraging that the student will give up entirely. A better idea is to make the goal attainable. This can be done by setting "stepping stone" goals, using smaller rewards at the beginning but working step-by-step toward better and better goals. This is the basic principle behind successive approximation programs.

Successive Approximations **Successive approximations,** or **shaping,** is a technique used to train elaborate new behaviors (that is, behaviors that are beyond the subject's abilities at the beginning of the training program). It is a common technique that has been used for both humans and animals, and it has had some success with some seemingly impossible cases.

Autistic children, for instance, seem totally wrapped up in their inner world, often not even acknowledging the presence of other people. Teaching even basic language skills is beyond reach at the beginning of a training program. By setting small goals, however—such as first getting the child's attention, then making an "m" sound, then a "ma"—some skills can often be gradually taught. Rewards are used to reinforce each small success (a spoonful of ice cream is often used, as it can be repeated without being too filling), and a great deal of skill and patience are required of the trainers.

Autism is an extreme case, of course. The same techniques can be applied in coaxing changes out of yourself and others. To see how this can work, notice the role of successive approximations in the *Do-It-Yourself Behavior Modification* box. Making changes one step at a time allows you to see progress more clearly, and to reinforce each step in the right direction.

Up to this point, we have been discussing reinforcements as ways of encouraging wanted behavior. There is another method of getting others to change their behavior patterns, however—and this technique probably brings more vivid memories from most of our own childhood "behavior shaping" experiences. We'll look briefly at punishment next.

According to conventional wisdom, punishment is more effective than rewards. But is it?

Punishment

Punishment can be defined as the process by which undesirable behavior is followed by an aversive (negative) consequence. The goal of punishment is to lessen or completely eliminate the unwanted behavior. This may be accomplished in two ways (Karen, 1974). First, a positive reinforcer may be removed. For example, a parent seeing his child misbehave might turn off the television set. The second procedure involves following the undesirable behavior with a negative sanction, such as a spanking.

According to conventional wisdom, punishment is both easier to give and more effective than rewards. But is it? True, punishment can be effective when it is moderate, swift, certain, and combined with rewards for the desired behavior (Altrocchi, 1980). It is frequently overused, however, or used inconsistently, and there is often

little thought for reinforcing the desired behavior. Other problems can be caused by relying on threats that can't really be carried out, or punishing a person without communicating clearly what the punishment is for. Punishment can also interfere with communication in general, especially if it is harsh, frequent, and not balanced by positive reinforcement. A person who lives in fear of being punished is less likely to consult the

Autism (infantile) A condition involving a lack of responsiveness to others, impairments of communication, and bizarre responses to the environment. It develops before the age of 30 months.

Punishment An aversive consequence following a behavior that reduces the probability that the behavior will reoccur. Punishment is used to reduce or eliminate an undesirable behavior.

Do-It-Yourself Behavior Modification

Several behavior modification procedures are outlined in this chapter, as they apply to changing the behaviors of others. These same approaches can also be used to change our own behaviors. If you have made up your mind, for whatever reason, that you want to change a behavior pattern, the followng procedure can be helpful.

Step 1

Define your goals in a clear, concise manner. Just saying you want to stop smoking, improve your grades, or lose weight is too vague to be useful. Instead, set a specific target, for instance, to study two hours each weekday or lose 20 pounds. Part of defining your goals is differentiating between the long and the short term. Instead of planning to quit smoking cold turkey, you may need to set progressive goals: to cut down to 20 cigarettes a day in the first week, 15 in the second, and so forth. This use of successive approximations also works for losing weight or changing study habits.

Step 2

Start record-keeping before you begin your behavior modification. Monitor your own behavior for two weeks; record every relevant behavior after it happens—each time you reach for a cigarette, each time you study or put off studying, and so forth. Note the circumstances under which the behavior occurred: Were you feeling frustrated? Did you light up after class each day? **Self-monitoring,** systematically observing and recording your own behavior, will provide you with a baseline for measuring how your behavior changes.

Step 3

Choose a reinforcement that will be a meaningful reward to you. Such a reinforcement should be self-administered and something you can do on your own (for instance, buying a new tape instead of going out with the gang—they might not be available). The reinforcement should also be different from the behavior you are trying to modify: thus, don't treat yourself to a cigarette if you are trying to quit smoking. Finally, use the **Premack Principle** in choosing an appropriate behavior (Marx & Bunch, 1977). According to this rule, a common behavior is an effective reinforcer for behavior you want to encourage. If you drink coffee every day, make it dependent upon getting to work on time, or skipping the toast and jam for breakfast.

Step 4

Begin your behavior modification program, making extensive use of your self-monitoring records. (If you usually smoke while you are studying, move to the library where you can't smoke.) Since your short-term goals are easy to attain, you may find it less difficult than you expected to continue on the program until you reach your long-term goals. One word of caution: if you are trying to lose weight, stop smoking, or begin a new exercise regimen, you should consult a physician before starting your program.

Step 5

Constantly monitor your progress. Charts, tables, and graphs may help you visualize what is happening. They will also provide a reinforcement in themselves, for they enable you to see long-term changes.

punisher with personal problems for fear of even more reprisals.

One form of punishment is especially effective for some problems, however, such as sibling rivalry or temper tantrums. In **time-out procedures,** offenders are simply placed by themselves until the undesirable behavior ceases. Children who don't stop throwing tantrums, for instance, are sent to their rooms each time they do. They may return as soon as the behavior ceases.

This "time out" system may not bring magical changes at once. It is not unusual for the screaming to seem to grow worse for a time—simply because the child has already learned to expect tantrums to produce action. However, once the child learns that tantrums will no longer be reinforced with attention, a change in behavior should take place. (Sometimes, an adult may need professional help to carry out such a program, especially if the punishment is inconsistent or if appropriate reinforcements aren't used.)

In all, punishment can be effective when it fits the behavior, is consistent, and when it is accompanied by rewards for correct behaviors. If you find it difficult to tell whether or not your use of punishment can be more effective, the checklist in Table 3.2 may be helpful.

The processes of operant and classical conditioning are basic to understanding human and animal behavior. But one other process is also important; it is described by **social learning theory,** which emphasizes the importance of imitation in our daily lives.

Social Learning Theory

One family has two boys, a 3-year-old and a 16-year-old, and they spend a great deal of time together. The older boy habitually rises about five minutes before school starts, and looking through his sock drawer curses until he finds the correct shade to match his clothing. One day, big brother gets up a little earlier, finds the right socks waiting

---

Table 3.2   A Checklist for Effective Punishment

1. Does the punishment fit the crime? If it is too great, the person will remember the unfairness of the punishment but forget why he or she was being punished.
2. Are you being consistent?
3. Did you make a threat that you wouldn't carry out?
4. Did you listen to the other side of the story?
5. Before progressing to severe punishments for minor infractions, have you tried simple, smaller punishments?
6. Does the person understand why he or she is being punished?
7. Are you rewarding desirable behavior as well as punishing undesirable actions?
8. Is this a first-time offense, or one that has occurred often in the past? (If the offense isn't grave and it is the first time it has occurred, softer punishments might be in order.)
9. Will this have a tremendously negative effect on communication? If it does, there should be an alternative that is more acceptable.

Self-monitoring   One of the important steps to be taken in an attempt to alter one's own behavior. Individuals note the extent to which they indulge in a particular behavior, as well as the circumstances that surround it. This material is then used as a basis for a program of behavior change.

Premack Principle   A principle of learning that states that a common behavior can be used to reinforce a less-common behavior. For example, you might allow yourself to drink coffee only on days when you make it to work on time.

Time-out procedures   Any of a number of procedures used in operant conditioning to reduce the frequency of a particular behavior. For example, a child who jumps on the couch is placed in another room for a time.

Social learning theory   The theory of learning that stresses the importance of imitation in the learning and production of new behaviors.

---

for him at the top of the pile, and starts to close the sock drawer. The little one grabs hold of his brother's arm to stop him, yelling "Wait! You forgot to say _____ [expletive deleted]!" You see, according to the younger brother, the sock drawer can't be closed until the correct phrase is recited.

The lesson learned by this 3-year-old represents a different learning process than the operant and classical conditioning we have been discussing: he has learned by observing. We can see examples of observation and imitation—what we call *social learning*—all around us. Gestures, eating habits, values and attitudes, and traditions are all imitated.

Keeping up with yearly fashion and slang changes helps point out how powerful a force imitation is. In the late 70s and early 80s, young people often used the salutation "May the Force be with you," imitating one of the famous bywords from the movie *Star Wars*. A few decades ago, many women tried drastic diets in an effort to imitate the skinny look made popular by a famous model named Twiggy, while boys routinely wore their hair in "Beatle" cuts.

Many psychologists are quite concerned about the problem of providing adequate role models for children to imitate. Considering what we know about both the power of observation and the power of the mass media in our society, there may well be cause for alarm. The "shoot now, talk later" ideal and the frequent stereotypes of the macho male and either the emotional woman or the cold, sexless career woman—cannot help children set their own goals for meaningful personal fulfillment or self-actualization.

Imitation is often clearest in children, but as one of the primary forces in the long socialization process, it affects our behavior throughout our lives. As adults, we usually imitate our parents' voting habits and adopt many of their values, for instance. We may even imitate the things we dislike or fear the most about our parents. Some studies show a vicious cycle of child abuse, in that many abusing parents were themselves abused or neglected as children.

The choices we make even as older adults are also heavily influenced by what we see others doing. If you are approaching retirement and have a good friend who has just begun taking classes at the local university, this may well play a role in your own decision to set educational goals for your retirement years.

We have been looking at some of the effects of imitation, but how does imitation take place? Psychologists who study the process of imitation, or modeling, are *social learning theorists*. The most famous representative of this viewpoint is Albert Bandura. Bandura helped perform some pioneering studies that demonstrated the link between watching and doing.

Social learning theorists stress a **four-step process** that they say is necessary for imitation to occur (Bandura, 1977). The first factor, *attention*, is a factor in any learning situation. If you do not notice what someone is doing, you obviously can't imitate their actions. The second factor is *memory:* your ability to remember what you have seen. If you don't remember what happened, you can't enter the third phase of *behavioral reproduction* of the action. The reproduction is not necessarily exact. You may imitate just what you've seen, but you might also change it in some personal way or combine the actions of two or more models. The last phase of the imitation process is *reinforcement*. The reinforcement can be anything that motivates you to imitate. It could be praise from your peers; it could be avoiding censure from an authority figure; or it could be feeling like *Star Wars'* Han Solo because you've behaved in a way that reminds you of him.

> **Four-step process for social learning** In order for imitation, or modeling, to occur, four separate steps are necessary: attention, memory, behavioral reproduction, and reinforcement.

Part One / Fundamentals of Adjustment

Motor and Verbal Learning

Some learning, known as **verbal learning,** involves gaining information through the medium of language. We learn a great deal in the way of information, know-how, and even personal goals from what we read or hear from others. This verbal learning is essential in a technological society where we need to know about so many things that we may never actually experience.

The other important form of learning is **motor learning.** This is one of the most persistent forms of learning. Can you ever forget how to swim or how to ride a bicycle? Even if you haven't done either of these for several years, these abilities are probably still with you, even if they are a little bit rusty. Compare this motor skill memory to your childhood verbal memory of some fact you learned in Social Studies or English. (How many state capitals can you still remember?)

In general, motor learning tends to stay with us longer than verbal learning. However, all learning situations contain some important similarities, and the same kinds of factors affect both how quickly we learn and how well we retain both verbal and motor learning.

Factors That Affect Learning

Attention   The most important factor in learning is *attention,* the ability to focus on one portion of the environment. Whether you are remembering the name of the person just introduced to you or learning how to drive a car, little learning takes place without attention.

Everyone has had the experience of attending to one thing and still picking up a bit of another. But this incidental learning is slight compared to purposeful, attentive learning. If you've come upon the scene of a mugging and you are concentrating on the victim's broken arm, you may miss what he is saying about his stolen wallet.

Or if you are shivering next to an open window at a dinner party, you may lose track of the conversation going on around you. As we saw in Chapter 2, the mind filters out extraneous environmental information, so that if our attention is focused on one sensation or thought, we may be distracted from other things that are happening.

Meaningfulness   The more meaningful and relevant the information or skill, the more quickly we acquire it and the more likely we are to remember it. Consider, for example, an assignment to learn the jargon of microcomputers: RAM, ROM, floppy disks, bytes and kilobytes, and so forth. These terms would be easier to learn if you had seen a computer and already knew something about what it did. They would probably not be so easy to learn if you had no opportunity to put them to use.

Motivation   A third factor in learning is *motivation.* Common sense indicates that the more motivated we are, the more quickly we will learn. It is still controversial whether motivation directly affects learning, or whether it merely leads to an increase in the time you spend trying to learn about something. It has been found that students with both low and high motivation seem to score equally well on achievement tests, if they spend

---

Verbal learning   One form of learning (as opposed to *motor learning*), verbal learning involves the information we gain through the medium of language, as we read or hear about things from others.

Motor learning   One of the most persistent forms of learning, motor skills, like riding a bike or roller skating, tend to stay with us virtually throughout our lives, even if we make little use of them.

the same amount of time studying. Still, motivation, whether it affects learning directly or indirectly, is a key factor in acquiring both verbal and motor skills.

Feedback   Little improvement takes place if we can't evaluate how well we are doing. Some of the clearest examples of this come from motor learning. Consider the constant **feedback** (information received back from the environment concerning your behavior) needed in learning to drive. If you couldn't see that you were on the right side of the street or traveling at the same speed as the rest of the traffic, the task would be impossible. The same need is obvious in learning to bowl: you can't correct gutter balls if you don't know you've thrown them. Feedback is also important in verbal learning. Without quizzes, midterms, and homework grades, it is difficult to gauge what areas need the most preparation for finals.

Practice   A final factor in learning is *practice*. Practice is not only necessary for acquiring new skills, but for retaining them. Although we don't forget motor skills as readily as verbal skills, we still need practice in order to keep them from getting rusty.

In learning things in the first place, people often wonder if it is more effective to practice for several hours at a time, or for frequent, short periods. For most verbal and motor activities, the latter process seems more effective than the former. If you study a little each night, your performance will probably be better than if you spend three nights cramming for your final exam. After a certain period of time, we tend to fatigue, and our learning ability decreases sharply.

This does not mean that too much practice is harmful. To the contrary, one of the best ways to improve your learning is to overlearn it. **Overlearning** involves continuing to practice a skill even after it has been performed correctly. Overlearning is probably less satisfying, however, for after the initial phase of learning a new skill, things seem to be at a standstill. This is discussed in the box *The Learning Plateau: Is It a Myth?*

Throughout this chapter, we have been talking about the learning process itself. We have looked at conditioning and imitation and noted some factors that affect verbal and motor learning. Two additional processes relate very closely to this broad subject area, and we will look briefly at them in the remaining pages of this chapter. These are memory and problem solving.

Memory

Memory, or the retention of what we learn, actually involves three separate processes: encoding, storage, and retrieval. We'll discuss each of these phases.

Encoding

Encoding refers to the process by which new memories are coded in the brain. We tend to encode the meaning of what people say rather than their exact words (Bransford, 1979). One important factor necessary for encoding appears to be attention. We don't notice everything that happens around us and we don't encode everything.

Feedback   Information that is received concerning one's behavior or the behavior of others. In learning, feedback is used to guide and correct behavior.

Overlearning   Continuous practice of a skill even after it has been performed correctly. Overlearning is a good way of improving learning, even though it may be less satisfying than mastering a new skill.

Encoding   The process by which new information is initially coded for memory in the brain.

The Learning Plateau: Is It a Myth?

Imagine that you have been given a difficult homework assignment. You need to learn 100 Russian vocabulary words by your next class. At first, you seem to be meeting the challenge easily. But as you proceed, your progress becomes much slower, until you come to a standstill somewhere around 85 percent. No matter how often you test yourself, there are always about 15 words that elude you.

If you're like many people, you might give up at this point, writing yourself off as a solid "B" student. If you do, you've been victimized by the learning plateau. The *learning plateau* describes a familiar phenomenon: we often make rapid progress when we begin to learn a new skill, but this progress soon slows down and seems to come to a standstill. The phenomenon affects both motor and verbal learning—be it trying to improve your tennis beyond the "intermediate" class or practicing and learning a new language. It is a discouraging experience, for learning is far less satisfying when we can't see the results.

Amount of practice

The learning plateau need not be a source of frustration, however, as long as people understand why it happens. According to *Fitt's Law,* the learning plateau is a myth (Mussen & Rosenzweig, 1973). You see, at first, learning takes place rapidly because there is so much room for improvement. Then as your score rises, it becomes harder and harder to improve. There is much less room for improvement. The slower acquisition of learning occurs because there is so much less material left to master.

Understanding Fitt's Law can make a big difference in how we feel about learning—the difference, in fact, between continuing to try or simply giving up. If you know it will take longer to master the last 15 percent of what you learn, you may show more patience and experience less frustration.

Attention helps us screen the important from the not so vital in our environment. (This screening process sometimes surprises us, however. For instance, we may remember that there was a sound of water running in the background as we were talking with a friend, even though we didn't consciously notice it at the time.)

We also know that most of us can't remember everything we'd like to. There are a few famous cases of people with remarkable memories. For instance, there is one case of a 24-year-old (with a mental age of 7, incidentally—memory isn't always linked with intelligence) who learned the day of the week of each date during 13 centuries. When asked what day July 7, 1409 had been, he gave the correct answer without hesitation (Piaget, 1968). Of course, there's a good chance that you have little desire to remember this many details. However, it *is* useful to remember practical information, and it's annoying to forget a person's name or an important phone number.

There are many **mnemonic** (the "m" is silent) **devices**—that is, ways of remembering things more easily—and many have to do with the encoding phase of memory. Chunking, finding a central theme or logic, and visual imaging are among these devices. The discussion in the box *What Was That Word Again? . . . Mnemonic* describes these and some other devices.

Storage

Once information is encoded, it must be *stored,* or retained in our memories, for future use. We don't store everything we learn forever. Some memories are still vivid after several years; others (such as the phone number you've just looked up) seem to slip away in no time at all; still others seem to go through the encoding process, but then disappear. Psychologists who study memory distinguish two kinds of storage: short-term memory and long-term memory.

Short-term Memory   One type of memory is called **short-term memory.** Short-term memories are stored for only 30 seconds or so, and then lost forever. As an example, you've probably had the experience of calling information for a telephone number, then being interrupted just as you're about to make the call. When the interruption is

---

Mnemonic device   Any device that facilitates memorization.

Short-term memory   The limited memory that can store material for only about thirty seconds. If not rehearsed, such memories are forgotten.

What Was That Word Again? . . . Mnemonic

Mnemonic devices are memory aids. Most are based on our fundamental knowledge of how memories are encoded and stored in the brain. Memories are not independent of one another, and often one is the key for another. Here are some coding devices that can help make memory storage and retrieval easier.

Chunking

Memorize the following digits:

3 7 5 6 2 9 1 8 5 2 3

Difficult? The task will be easier if you group or *chunk* the numbers, as so:

375-629-18-523

The reason the task is easier now is because fewer units of information are being processed. As a general rule, processing up to five units of information is simple; seven can still be memorized; but nine is at the outside limit for many of us. Thus, reducing the original list of ten numbers to a more manageable list of four groups makes memorization far easier.

Acrostic Tricks

Here is another list to memorize:

Iceland	India
Lapland	Canada
Oman	Kenya
Volta	Israel
Ethiopia	England
Venezuela	

If it seems too difficult, look at the first letter of each country in the list. The letters spell I LOVE VICKIE. With cues that enable you to group words into a memorizable sequence, lists are easier to remember.

Visual Imaging

Here is yet another list to memorize—this one a shopping list:

cereal	celery
eggs	chocolate chips
milk	bread

The trick to visual imaging is to devise a single "mental picture" that portrays everything you want to remember. For the list above, you might set the following scene in your mind: your kitchen, with milk and cereal on the table, bread sitting on top of the toaster, and a chocolate-chip and celery omelette on a plate. The last of this group may be the easiest to remember, for the most bizarre images are often more memorable than everyday scenes. Visual images can also help in remembering people's names. If you meet five new people at a party, it will be easier to keep track of names if you visualize each person's face while rehearsing their names.

Understanding Themes or Logic

Another way to improve memory is to make sense out of whatever you need to memorize. Instead of memorizing all the details of a play, for instance, try learning the plot and central characters. From there, the details will be easier to remember since they will now have a memorable frame of reference.

over, you find you no longer remember the number. In order for short-term memories to stay with us longer, they seem to need to be stored in long-term memory. Rehearsing is helpful in transferring information from short to long term.

Long-term Memory **Long-term memory** includes all the information we retain for long periods of time, perhaps throughout our entire lifespan. Some information, events, or emotions are automatically stored in long-term memory. For example, you may always remember how you felt when you received socks from three different people at your fifth birthday party. Other information, such as your new automobile license number, may not be stored in long-term memory without rehearsal. Practice, rehearsal, and repetition seem to strengthen the memory and aid in storage. When we are prevented from rehearsing, rote memorization may be next to impossible.

Retrieval

Once information is encoded and stored in either long-term or short-term memory, it must be retrieved in order to be used. Sometimes, our retrieval systems don't work as well as we'd like them

to. If we asked you who ran for the winning touchdown in last year's Super Bowl, you might very well have encoded it and stored it in memory, but find you can't deliver the information.

It's frustrating to *almost* remember something, but the efforts we go through as we try to dredge up faded memories tell us something about the retrieval process. You may fumble around giving sounds that seem to make no sense. For instance, if you're trying to remember Robert Redford's name, you may stutter "Ruh . . . R-R-R . . . Richards . . ." and so forth—clearly circling in on names that start with the same sound (thus the expression "on the tip of the tongue"). It seems that much information is encoded by sound.

Another pattern shows up when we try to retrieve lists we have memorized. Psychologists have found that we tend to remember the beginnings and ends of lists better than the material in the middle. In addition, we often recall meaningful groups or clusters, rather than random items (Anderson, 1975). As an example, try to remember this list: staples, arm, leg, book, page, chest, picture, ankle, lungs, desk, flowers. If you work on this, you may find that you have constructed your own cues by grouping the words into two categories: body parts and office equipment. Even if the words are not given together, we recall them in meaningful groups.

How well you retrieve information often depends on how the question is asked. If you were asked to name the thirteenth president of the United States, you might be at a loss. After all, Millard Fillmore is not exactly a household word. Yet, if you were asked to pick the thirteenth president out of a list of names (a process known as **recognition**), you might be able to choose correctly. Most of us find it easier to recognize the correct answer when we see it than to pluck it out of the blue (Dodd & White, 1980)—the reason why multiple choice questions are, theoretically at least, easier than fill-in-the-blanks or essay questions on an exam. Essay questions test **recall,** which involves giving the correct answer when few if any cues are present. Of course, some infor-

Long-term memory Memory storage that is relatively resistant to forgetting. Long-term memory includes all the information we retain for long periods of time, perhaps throughout our entire life-span.

Recognition A measurement of memory in which an individual is asked to identify information to which he or she has been exposed in the past. Recognition is tested in multiple-choice examinations.

Recall The process of remembering something when few if any meaningful cues are provided.

mation seems to be lost forever, no matter how many cues we receive. Why we forget is a fascinating question that hasn't yet been answered adequately.

Why We Forget

The phrase "I forgot" is usually associated with letting people down, failure on tests, or being unable to manage your own life. We have probably all had the experience of forgetting something at some time or another. What causes it to happen? There is no one theory that can explain all instances of forgetting, but three theories may help in understanding what happens.

Fading of the Memory Trace   A common-sense theory of forgetting states that information **fades from the memory trace** because we haven't used it in a long time. For instance, you remember your current phone number, and perhaps the last phone number you had; but do you remember your first number?

This theory of fading seems logical in many cases, but it leaves some questions unanswered. Why does motor learning seem to stay with us longer than verbal learning, even when we don't use skills (such as bike riding or hitting a baseball) for years? And why do we remember some inconsequential facts, events, or images from years ago, while others seem totally lost? The fading explanation can't account for these phenomena.

Repression   A second explanation is that we *repress* some unpleasant material, putting it out of our minds. This seems to happen in some cases—as when your dental appointment slips your mind, or your parking ticket lies on your dresser for months because you keep forgetting to pay it. There are instances where anxiety, annoyance, fear, or some other negative feeling is associated with forgetting. But telephone numbers, names,

and most of the things we forget usually aren't negative. Thus, this theory, too, cannot explain most forgetting.

Interference   A third explanation of forgetting has become popular recently. In this theory, new information **interferes** with already learned material, or old information interferes with the learning of new material (Underwood, 1964). Thus, if you memorize one new phone number, and then a bit later must learn another number similar to the first one, the odds are that the phone number will be lost. Or if you study Psychology of Adjustment for an hour, then switch to Sociology, the theory predicts you would confuse the two subjects, perhaps forgetting much that you learned. The more similar the subjects, the more likely you would be to confuse them.

Problem Solving

It is difficult to approach the topics of learning and remembering, both basic elements in shaping our behaviors and our adjustments, without also talking about problem solving. We, the species *homo sapiens*, modestly think of problem solving as an (almost) uniquely human activity, at least to the degree to which we rise to challenges. What other species can plan cities, do crossword puzzles, or compute the distance between two stars?

Fading of the memory trace   An explanation that views forgetting as a result of lack of use of certain information or know-how. The theory has recently been de-emphasized.

Interference theory of forgetting   The theory that forgetting occurs because one bit of information learned either at an earlier or a later time interferes with the information already stored.

Problem Solving Styles

We all use information that we have learned in solving problems, and each of us approaches problems in what seems to be a unique fashion. In fact, there are a few general, very broad ways of approaching problems. Consider the following case as an example.

You are being held in a room by a gunman who is nervous and clearly excitable. The 20 people in the room know that the gun is loaded. The gunman screams that he is going to kill all of you. What action would you recommend to the group?

Psychologists James McKenney and Peter Keen have given this problem to many classes in an attempt to discover what problem solving styles are used. To date, two seem fairly well established (Ewing, 1977).

The first involves a systematic attack. In this style, you size up the situation by gathering information, defining the problem as accurately as possible. You find some method of solving the problem, and finally, painstakingly, you put the solution into a step-by-step behavioral sequence. People who solve problems in this manner often consider what they have read in the newspapers about hostage situations and try to get the gunman to talk about himself.

The second style involves an intuitive approach. This approach involves coming up with a myriad of alternative solutions and constantly redefining the problem as you go along. Individuals who use this approach don't commit themselves to a final situation but follow their hunches. One individual suggested that the group sneak around the gunman, turn off the lights, and jump him. Other plans included throwing their shoes at the gunman before rushing him.

On the surface, you might believe that there is an obvious advantage to the first approach. Certainly, systematic analysis is usually desirable. However, it has been found that for some problems that are difficult to define, intuitive thinking may be superior.

How Do We Solve Problems?

The example we've been discussing illustrates one subject that has interested psychologists: individual styles of problem solving. Another, even more fascinating question is how we solve problems—what happens inside our heads, so to speak. Two theories provide at least partial explanations. These are the **Gestalt theory** (*Gestalt* is the German word for "form" or "shape," implying that we look at the whole rather than its parts) and the **trial-and-error** explanation.

The Gestalt Theory Figure 3.2 presents a challenge: can you connect the nine dots, using four straight lines, without taking your pencil off the paper? Many of us could work on this problem all day without finding the solution. The answer is easier if you change your perception of the problem. When you realize you can extend the line beyond the dots, the solution becomes simple, as is shown on p. 74.

The essence of the Gestalt theory lies in people's ability to look at problems from a different perspective. Often, a new perception of a problem suddenly brings the answer—like a light bulb flashing on in your head. Psychologists call this sudden insight the **aha phenomenon.** Often,

---

Gestalt theory of problem solving An explanation of one process by which people solve problems by looking at a problem from a new perspective.

Trial-and-error An approach to problem solving in which a number of alternatives are tried until one succeeds.

Aha phenomenon The sudden realization of the correct solution to a problem.

---

too, you may find that a complicated problem becomes easier if you do something else for a while. When you come back to it, you may suddenly see it from a different viewpoint. This sudden insight also comes from changing your perception of the problem.

The role of past experience in this type of problem solving is uncertain. It does take an agile and free mind to look at problems from different vantage points. It seems, however, that people can be taught to look at situations from different perceptual viewpoints. But some of us seem to be more inclined to take a less flexible approach to problem solving.

Fixity   When people are *fixed* in their approach to a problem, they never question their assumptions. In the nine-dot problem, for instance, you may have assumed rules that were simply not there. Only after realizing there was no rule against extending lines beyond the dots could you solve the problem. Another example of **fixity** involves the habitual manner of responding to a certain problem. "It's always been done this way" is an excuse for never trying out a different solution.

Still another example of fixity might be a person's inability to take apart a broken chair because a screwdriver isn't handy. The assumption that only a screwdriver can act as a tool can prevent a person from trying a dime, or a knife blade, or some other household object that might work as well. Questioning basic assumptions like this can be of enormous help in solving difficult problems.

Trial and Error   Some problems, of course, cannot be approached so inventively. Suppose you're handed a keychain with 20 keys on it, and told to let yourself in to your boss's office while she's gone over the weekend. The only way to find which key fits (provided no one else can tell you) is to keep on trying until you've found it. You'll eliminate several, of course, just by their appearance. But

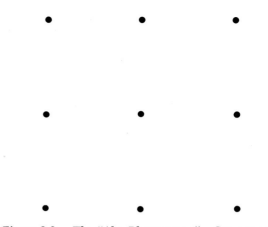

Figure 3.2   The "Aha Phenomenon"   *Can you connect the dots without lifting your pencil, using only four straight lines?*

the basic trial-and-error approach will have to guide you from there.

This trial-and-error approach, with certain variations, was for many years regarded as the only way people solved problems. Its systematic, logical, step-by-step approach, however, is quite different from (and in many ways directly opposite to) the Gestalt theory. Thus, while flexibility is important in effective problem solving, we seem to need both kinds of problem-solving approaches in our own personal repertoires.

We have come a long way in this chapter since the "Wild Boy's" emergence from the woods of southern France. Learning, remembering, and solving problems are tremendously complex topics; they are also basic elements in personality and adjustment. One more topic is also fundamental to our study of adjustment. We turn to development in the next chapter.

Fixity   A term used in problem solving to describe an individual's tendency to approach a problem in the same way.

Summary

1. Learning is defined as relatively permanent changes in behavior due to experience with the environment.

2. Classical conditioning is a process by which a neutral stimulus is paired with a stimulus that elicits a response until the first stimulus itself produces that response.

3. In operant conditioning, the individual's response is followed by reinforcement, which increases the frequency of the response. Behaviors that are reinforced tend to recur, while those that are not reinforced tend to disappear or be extinguished. When there are conflicting reinforcements, the behavior shown will be in the direction of the greater reinforcement.

4. Reinforcement can be delivered every time the correct behavior is shown (continuous reinforcement), or only some of the time (partial reinforcement). The latter can be delivered on a ratio schedule or an interval schedule. Partial reinforcement leads to slower learning, but the material is more resistant to extinction than it is if learned through continuous reinforcement.

5. In token reinforcement, the token you receive for the correct response can be traded in for a greater reward at the end of a stipulated time period.

6. The technique of successive approximations involves expecting more and more correct behaviors for a particular reward.

7. In punishment, an undesirable behavior is followed by a negative consequence, in the effort to diminish the unwanted behavior. Punishment is often incorrectly administered, but it can be effective when the punishment is fair and when it is combined with rewards for desired behavior.

8. Social learning theory describes a third important kind of learning. People often imitate what they see around them. Imitation is a four-step process, involving attention, retention, behavior, and reinforcement.

9. Many factors affect both verbal and motor learning: the relevance of the material to be learned, motivation, feedback, internal and external factors, attention, and the amount of timing and practice.

10. The three phases of memory are encoding, storage, and retrieval. The process by which new information is placed in memory is called encoding. Memory storage involves short-term memory (approximately 30 seconds) and long-term memory. We use cues to help us retrieve information from memory. This is why multiple choice exams are, theoretically at least, easier than point-blank questions or essay exams.

11. There are two main explanations of the process of problem solving. The trial-and-error school emphasizes attempting various solutions, then using experience to come to some type of solution. The Gestalt school looks at problem solving as essentially a creative activity involving altering one's perception of a problem, to "see it in a new light."

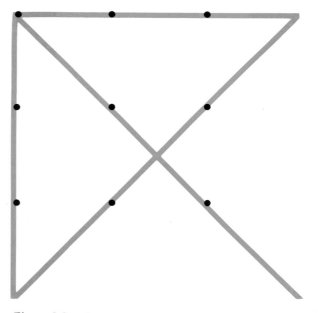

Figure 3.3   Answer to Figure 3.2 Problem

Key Terms and Concepts

learning

phobia

stimulus generalization

stimulus discrimination

extinction

spontaneous recovery

operant conditioning

continuous reinforcement

partial reinforcement

fixed interval reinforcement schedule

fixed ratio reinforcement schedule

variable ratio reinforcement schedule

token reinforcement procedures

successive approximations (shaping)

autism

punishment

self-monitoring

Premack Principle

time-out procedures

social learning theory

four-step process for social learning

verbal learning

motor learning

feedback

overlearning

encoding

mnemonic device

short-term memory

long-term memory

recognition

recall

fading of the memory trace

interference

Gestalt theory

trial and error

aha phenomenon

fixity

Have you ever been to a party where everyone else was either older or younger than you? Certain topics of conversation such as current events, baseball scores, or the old clichés about the weather provide a common footing for a while. When the conversation shifts to more personal subjects, however, you might have felt your interest wandering. It may be hard to relate to conversations about potty training if you have no children yourself or to become really involved in a discussion of social security benefits, tax shelters, or high school proms, if these topics aren't part of your current frame of reference.

Development

Developmental Psychology

Experiences such as this point toward a fact that has been studied by psychologists for only a relatively short period of time. Our concerns change over time, as individuals pass from infancy to old age. People's personalities may change, as do their physical, cognitive (intellectual), social, and vocational abilities, and all of these developments interact to make each of us a different person at age 20 from the person we were at 10—and a still different person at 50, in many ways, from the person we were at 20. The study of these changes, especially of how they affect behavior, is known as **developmental psychology.**

Understanding development is basic to adjustment, for a few reasons. For one, it gives us a window for seeing where we are in life. Each of us is an individual, but we share many common tasks, struggles, needs, and achievements over the course of a lifetime. Understanding what has happened in the past may make it easier to resolve current conflicts, and knowing what to expect in the future may help us set realistic goals.

A better understanding of development may also help in dealing with others. Seeing a troubled child, for example, from the perspective of her need to resolve a particular developmental task may provide you with insight that can help you to provide guidance or to know when professional advice is needed. The same is true for helping you understand a parent's needs at retirement, or a spouse's sudden urge to find a different direction in life.

This chapter doesn't answer all our questions about development and the life cycle. It does attempt to provide a broad overview, however. We will first look very generally at developmental trends over the life cycle, particularly at Erik Erikson's conception of eight common developmental conflicts or turning points. Each individual's experiences and adjustments are different from those of every other person, however, and we will also explore the genetic and environ- mental factors that make development a unique and highly personal adventure.

Developmental Trends

Human development is directional. That is, it follows a fairly consistent path from one point (infancy) to another (old age). We take this principle for granted, not even stopping to think about it unless we notice someone who is *not* following that path. Thus, if a 3-year-old suddenly stops walking but begins to crawl, we take notice and try to assess what happened; the same is true if a 40-year-old loses interest in work and becomes depressed and isolated.

Heinz Werner (1957) labeled this directional tendency in development the **orthogenetic principle** (the Greek root *ortho* meaning straight or true). According to Werner, development proceeds from a lack of differentiation to a state of increased differentiation, articulation, and integration (ibid., p. 125). We'll explore what this means more specifically, in terms of three developmental trends: from involuntary to voluntary control; from mass to specific control; and from external to internal control.

From Involuntary to Voluntary Control

Human infants are governed by reflexes: involuntary, stereotyped patterns of reacting to

---

Developmental psychology The branch of psychology that studies how organisms change qualitatively and quantitatively over time.

Orthogenetic principle Heinz Werner's concept that development is directional, proceeding from an undifferentiated and global state to a more integrated and differentiated one.

specific stimuli. Infants have many such patterns. Put something in their mouths, and they involuntarily suck; stroke the side of their cheeks, and they turn toward the stimulus. As they develop, these reflexes disappear and are replaced by movements that the older infant or child can voluntarily control. Thus, a young child who picks up a hot coffee cup may drop it in pain and surprise, while an adult (most times, at least!) will carry it over to a table and place it down gently despite the burning sensation. The analogy can be carried even further if we compare the rather imperfect movements of the average person-on-the-street to the finely tuned control of a Mikhail Baryshnikov, a Chrissie Evert, or a Dr. J. on the basketball court. This kind of skill and control, of course, results from years of practice and maturation, as well as a certain amount of natural talent.

From Mass to Specific Control

Another element in directional development is the increasing ability to use our muscles to perform rather intricate movements. If you take a piece of paper and write your name and address on it, notice the way you hold your pen, the slight changes in pressure you use to write legibly, and the slow and controlled movement of your hand. Such coordination takes years of practice. Ask a 3-year-old to draw something, and you'll notice that the control seems to come from the wrist, not the fingers. This is why children often have difficulty with a thin pencil or pen, but do better with a thick crayon (Kellogg, 1970).

> **Developmental tasks**   Specific tasks that individuals in a particular society are expected to master at a certain stage in their lives. For example, children are expected to talk in early childhood and to attain some measure of emotional independence in adolescence.

From External to Internal Control

Development also proceeds from external to internal control. In childhood, we depend upon others to give us information concerning what is right and wrong. Kohlberg (1973) notes that as children grow they begin to control their own behavior. They also increase their reasoning power so they are capable of making personal moral decisions on the basis of principle. Thus, an adolescent may invoke the right to privacy as she explains why she doesn't want her locker to be searched. A 6- or 7-year-old, in contrast, may express the same feelings, but without the reasoned argument based on universal principles.

The broad trends we have just explored take place primarily in the early years of life: they are mostly complete by the time we reach adulthood. Indeed, the most striking and critical developmental changes take place between birth and adolescence. And until recently, the field of developmental psychology focused almost entirely on childhood. One of the most famous—and controversial—of the theories of childhood development was Freud's theory of psychosexual development, outlined in the box *Freud's View of Development.*

There is still a great interest in childhood as the most crucial period of personality development. But we also recognize that development doesn't stop with adulthood. Theories of lifelong development carry us beyond the early development of control or the emergence of sexuality. What kinds of developmental challenges face us now, as adults, and what new challenges should we be preparing for? Will it make a difference if we resolve a conflict one way or another? We turn next to these questions.

Life-long Developmental Tasks

Several theorists have explained the life cycle in terms of **developmental tasks,** or age-related challenges that each person faces at different points in life. Havighurst's theory (1972, 1953) is an example. He sees the task of infants as learning to take solid foods, walk, talk, and toilet train. Children in middle childhood must make friends, develop fundamental skills in reading and writing, develop a conscience, and attain positive attitudes towards themselves and their society. Adolescent tasks include accepting one's body and sexuality, attaining emotional independence, and choosing a career.

Some of Havighurst's tasks may be considered controversial today. Among the developmental tasks of early adulthood, for instance, is the task of selecting a mate. While many people will certainly marry within this period in their lives (20–40 years), some will not. In addition, many people who never marry will lead happy, healthy, productive lives. We are faced with many more choices and alternatives in our lives than were past generations. There are many paths to happiness, especially in adulthood, and we must interpret the entire concept of adult developmental tasks with extreme care.

Erikson's Eight Challenges

Another, more well-known view of development is the **psychosocial theory** (combining psychological and social factors) of psychologist Erik Erikson (1968). Erikson presents eight choices or challenges that each person must face in developing from infancy to old age. Each choice has a cumulative effect, becoming a developmental "building block" upon which subsequent growth is based. These crises, outlined in Figure 4.1, take place at roughly the same age for each of us; and they result from a combination of psychological readiness, experience, intellectual growth, and social expectations. We'll look at Erikson's stages below, for they provide us with a useful framework for understanding the turning points in our own lives.

According to the orthogenetic principle, development proceeds from mass (whole body) control to specific control—permitting highly specialized adult behaviors in some cases.

Psychosocial theory Erik Erikson's theory of psychological development within a cultural or social framework. Each individual, says Erikson, travels through eight stages beginning at birth and ending in old age. Each stage has its positive as well as its negative outcomes.

Freud's View of Development

There are many theories of development. This chapter follows the lifelong course of development through eight stages or challenges proposed by Erik Erikson. Quite a different view is the controversial psychosexual theory of Sigmund Freud, who saw personality development in terms of the gradual emergence of constructive sexual energy or **libido.** His five stages carry the individual from infancy through adolescence.

The Oral Stage (Birth–18 months)

Sexual energy and activity are focused in the oral cavity, as infants seek gratification through sucking. If this need isn't gratified (or if it is *over* gratified), **fixation** may occur. The individual will continue to try to compensate for oral needs, through behaviors such as nail biting, smoking, excessive eating or drinking, or excessive talking.

The Anal Stage (18 months–4 years)

At about the age of 18 months, the libido becomes focused around the anal cavity. The child gradually gains the ability to control the process of elimination. Children who get extreme pleasure from expelling feces may become fixated at an anal aggressive stage; the result is a spontaneous, careless, ebullient personality. Children who respond to overly strict toilet training with either guilt or a power struggle may be fixated at the anal retentive stage, becoming regimented, miserly, and compulsively neat (Hjelle & Ziegler, 1976).

The Phallic Stage (4–6 years)

At around the age of 5, another shift takes place in the focus of the libido. This shift is qualitatively different from the earlier ones, for as pleasure becomes focused around the sexual organs (the penis in boys and the clitoris in girls), psychosexual development follows a different course for the two sexes.

The **Oedipal situation** is the most controversial of all Freud's concepts. He sees young boys as developing a sexual attachment to their mothers—an attachment that is fraught with anxiety, because the boy fears his father. Girls originally want their mothers, too; but they soon turn their attention to their fathers, who have a penis while they do not. This leads the daughter to desire to possess the father in the same way the boy desires his mother (Mullahy, 1948). By the end of the phallic stage, both boys and girls resolve these conflicts as they learn to identify with the same-sexed parent.

The Latency Stage (7–12 years)

The conflicts of the phallic stage are so powerful, Freud proposes, that the child soon enters a latency phase that provides a time of reassessment. Sexuality is quiescent during this interlude between the phallic and genital stages. The repression of attachments so evident during the phallic stage also extends to members of the opposite sex—leading to characteristic "I hate girls" clubs and other highly sex-segregated behavior. For both sexes, this stage is important in learning appropriate social roles.

The Genital Stage (12 years and up)

This final stage builds from the earlier stages of development. As the youngster enters into adolescence, attention is once more turned toward the opposite sex—this time, toward peers rather than parents. With this last shift, the individual will be ready to experience more mature relationships with opposite-sex partners.

Trust vs. Mistrust   The first psychosocial challenge is also the most important, for it serves as a major basis for people's later relationships with others. Erikson calls this conflict **trust versus mistrust,** and he sees its resolution as the primary challenge of infancy. A trusting person sees the world as a warm, safe place in which to live, filled with basically well-meaning individuals. If a sense of mistrust is developed, the person will have difficulty forming intimate relationships later on, and may be suspicious of others.

In this stage, as well as later stages, the role of other people is evident in determining how individuals resolve their conflicts. During this period of development, the most important part of the social environment is usually the parents. If they are loving, reasonably at ease with their role, and consistent, the child learns trust. Parents who are unhappy and anxiety-ridden, who resent parenthood or feel conflict about their responsibilities, may produce a sense of mistrust and insecurity in the child. Whichever way the trust versus mistrust conflict is resolved, it will influence the child's attitude throughout later stages of development.

Autonomy vs. Doubt   By the age of two, children have developed some important abilities. They can walk, talk (with widely varying degrees of success), manipulate objects on their own, and occasionally amuse themselves independently—if not always in the way their parents would choose! In the course of growing up, they no longer need the full-time care they required in the earliest months. They are now more independent, and this new freedom brings with it a second conflict: **autonomy versus doubt.**

As in the first stage, parents play a very important role in their children's resolution of this conflict. They must permit children to express *autonomy* or independence, expecting neither too much nor too little from them. For instance, if 2-year-old John wants to help with his own breakfast, the parent would be wise to let him set the table and perhaps pour his cornflakes into his bowl. Handling a gallon container of milk is probably beyond him, however: he needs to be protected from this until he is ready for the task.

If parents don't permit children to do these things on their own, or if they are insensitive to the child's desires, then the negative outcome, *doubt,* will arise. The child will feel a lack of confidence both in his relationships with others

---

Libido   Freud's term for the life force and sexual energy. As an individual develops, the libido attaches itself to different parts of the body in a sequence of stages Freud called *psychosexual.*

Fixation   A behavior pattern that results from the over- or under-gratification of the needs of an individual during a particular psychosexual stage, according to Freudian theory. For instance, a person fixated at the anal stage might be obstinate and miserly.

Oedipal situation   According to Freud, during the phallic stage the male child develops a sexual attraction towards his mother and wishes to do away with his father. (In females, a similar conflict arises called the Electra situation, in which the girl develops a sexual attraction toward the father.)

Trust versus mistrust   The first of Erik Erikson's eight psychosocial stages, this one occurring from birth to about eighteen months. The positive outcome, trust, relates to a feeling that one lives in a friendly, compassionate environment; the negative outcome, mistrust, refers to a basic attitude of suspicion and fear toward others.

Autonomy versus doubt   The second of Erik Erikson's eight psychosocial stages, this one occurring between the ages of about one-and-a-half and three. The positive outcome, autonomy, relates to the child's sense of independence; the negative outcome, doubt, refers to a state of heightened dependency.

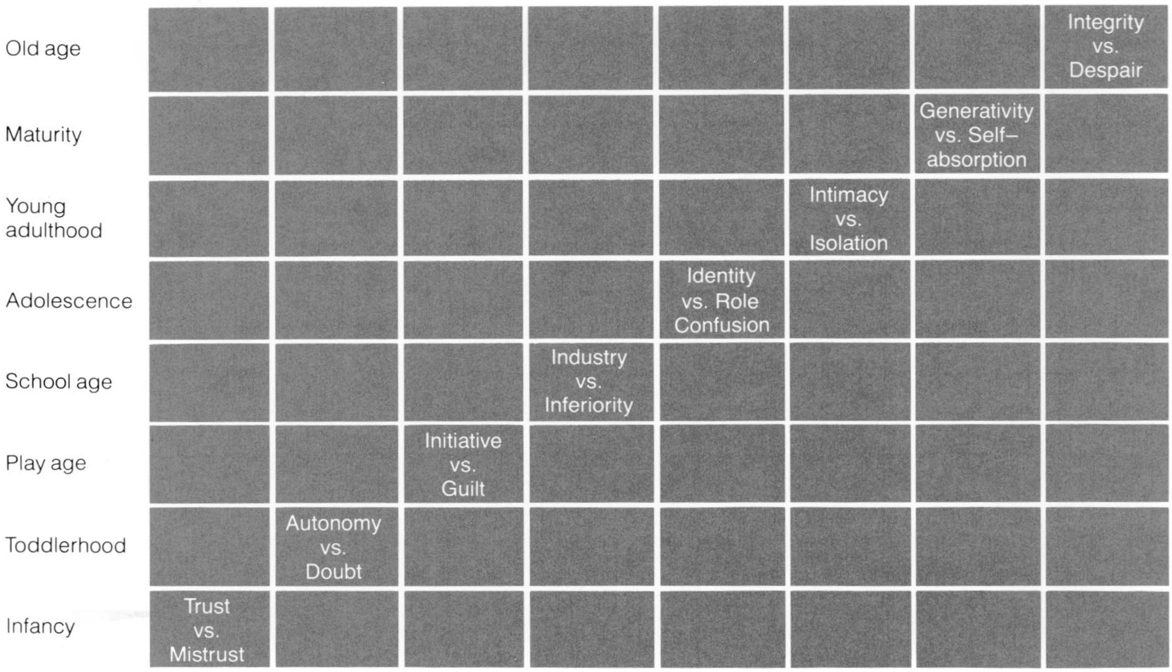

Old age								Integrity vs. Despair
Maturity							Generativity vs. Self-absorption	
Young adulthood						Intimacy vs. Isolation		
Adolescence					Identity vs. Role Confusion			
School age				Industry vs. Inferiority				
Play age			Initiative vs. Guilt					
Toddlerhood		Autonomy vs. Doubt						
Infancy	Trust vs. Mistrust							

Figure 4.1 Erikson's Eight Challenges

Source: Adapted from "Reflections on Dr. Borg's Life Cycle" by Erik H. Erikson from *Adulthood*, edited by Erik H. Erikson, by permission of W.W. Norton & Company, Inc. Copyright © 1978, 1976 by The American Academy of Arts and Sciences.

and in his ability to control the environment. Instead of confidence, there may be a pervading sense of helplessness. This, in turn, makes the next life conflict more difficult to resolve.

Initiative vs. Guilt The ages of four and five bring on new challenges. Children are well able to get around by themselves, to make their wishes

> **Initiative versus guilt** The third stage in Erik Erikson's theory of psychosocial development, this one encompasses much of early childhood. The positive outcome, initiative, relates to the child's ability to originate behavior patterns on his or her own; the negative outcome, guilt, involves the child's feeling that his or her own wishes are bad.

known through language, and to think for themselves. They can plan rather involved activities, attaining new heights in self-direction. Here, as in the earlier stages, the parents play a crucial role. If their self-direction is reinforced by their parents, children gain a sense of **initiative.** If, on the other hand, those efforts are discouraged by ridicule or excessive punishment, they may instead feel a sense of **guilt.** In later life, they may not be self-sufficient, but will instead be hesitant about making decisions for themselves. The discussion in the box *Discipline Styles: How Do They Affect Children?* reports some specific findings that suggest the crucial role of parents in developing either initiative or guilt.

Industry vs. Inferiority By the age of about seven, two important developments are taking

Erikson's first life challenge, that of establishing trust, lays the foundation for later relationships with others.

place. Parents begin to play a less influential role in their children's development, as people outside the home (especially peers) become important social forces. At the same time that outside forces begin to take on a greater meaning, children are also expected to take on more outside responsibilities. During the school years, from ages 7–12, academic learning and social skills become very important. The child's response to these new demands can take one of two directions, toward industry or toward inferiority.

Successes in both academic work and social and other skills all contribute to a sense of **industry** in the child. This sense builds an aura of confidence and mastery, which helps the child fit productively into society. In contrast, children who feel they can't do things well, or that their efforts don't lead to self-improvement, or that they aren't as "good" as other children develop a sense of **inferiority.**

It is important to note here how critical the role of the social environment can still be at the middle childhood stage. A child is singled out because of racial prejudice, or is subjected to sexist attitudes, or is overshadowed by an exceptional sibling may *feel* inferior without being any less

> **Industry versus inferiority** The fourth stage in Erik Erikson's theory of psychosocial development, this one takes place around ages 7–12. The positive outcome, industry, relates to a feeling of pride and satisfaction in one's work; while the negative outcome, inferiority, involves a feeling of not being as good as others.

Discipline Styles: How Do They Affect Children?

Most parents realize the need to set limits for their children; yet at one time or another, many wonder just where or how the line should be drawn. Will too much discipline discourage development? Can too little discipline hurt, or does it encourage independence?

Psychologist Diana Baumrind spent many years analyzing child-rearing patterns, and she drew some conclusions from what she learned about discipline. Baumrind identified three separate styles of parenting:

■ **Authoritarian** parents tend to control and establish absolute standards of conduct for their children. Obedience is prized, and there is little opportunity given for children to question or criticize. Punishment is used liberally.

■ **Permissive** or laissez-faire parents make few demands of their offspring, depending upon the children to control their own behavior. There are few arbitrary limits placed upon the children, and family policies are often discussed openly.

■ **Authoritative** parents guide their children's activities but give them freedom to act within clearly defined limits. Their control is flexible, and parents often explain family policies to their children. Verbal discussions are common and feelings are often expressed.

Do these different styles have different effects upon the children? Baumrind set out to find the answer to this question in a white middle-class nursery school, by studying a number of children who came from similar backgrounds. Each style of parenting seemed indeed to produce a different outcome. Children of *authoritarian* parents were often discontented, suspicious, and distrustful. Those of *permissive* parents were the least happy and self-reliant, showing little self-control. Those children raised in *authoritative* homes showed self-control and independence, and were cooperative.

The results are not difficult to explain. Authoritarian-raised children might well be hostile and distrustful, since they have had little practice in discussing their own needs or in openly expressing their anger. Children raised in permissive environments lack the guidance that may be necessary for successful development. Self-control has not had a chance to develop, since little was ever denied to these children, and they had no responsibilities. The lack of self-reliance among these children may indicate a tendency to look for structure elsewhere.

In contrast, the third group of authoritatively raised children may offer the best of both worlds. Children require both structure and freedom, both guidance and the opportunity to discuss feelings and make decisions. Such child-rearing procedures seem to lead to the development of happy, contented, responsible youngsters.

Source: Baumrind, D., 1971 and 1967.

capable than others. This sense of inferiority can carry over into adult personality and adjustment patterns.

Kevin's story shows the importance of social context. Kevin's brother, three years older, had the same teachers, football coach, and musical instructor as he did. While his brother was an A-student, won a football scholarship, and played in the all-state orchestra, Kevin was only mediocre in all of these areas. His parents seemed to constantly compare the two boys, and Kevin was acutely aware that he didn't measure up. At last, he simply stopped trying and developed behavior problems that interfered with class work. His parents reacted with punishment and threats.

Kevin's parents had refused to consider that they might play a role in their son's behavior problems, until Kevin saw a counselor. The counselor opened up communication between the boy and his parents, and at the same time encouraged Kevin to try new activities. Kevin found he was skilled in mechanics, shop, and some crafts (skills that his brother did not possess), and he began to feel better about himself and his abilities. He still tends to give up on himself too early, and he still feels inferior to his brother. However, he is developing a sense of industry, and because he now accepts himself, he will be better able to face the next challenge, identity versus role confusion.

Identity vs. Role Confusion Erikson suggested that the "crisis" of adolescence can be expressed as **identity versus role confusion.** This does not mean that your identity is completed in adolescence. However, substantial progress is usually made during this period. Answers to such questions as "who am I?", "where am I going?", and "where do I belong?" are crucial to the adolescent's transformation into a fully functioning adult. These questions are easier to ask than to answer, as Chapter 12 will explore in greater detail. There is a strong sense of ambivalence: the adolescent wants to break away, but still yearns for the safety of home; he or she fears growing, but also fears remaining a child. All of this ambivalence is not easy to work through—and so dealing with adolescents requires patience and understanding.

Some adolescents try to short-circuit this difficult problem of finding independence by overidentifying with a cause or ideology, or by identifying totally with their peer group. There is certainly more security in this solution. However, there is also less growth and development.

The failure to at least partially solve the riddle of one's identity produces the negative outcome of *role confusion.* This results in an inability to

In Erikson's fifth stage, identity vs. role confusion, the adolescent tries to work through the transition from childhood to adulthood.

make choices and a sense of alienation, which in turn makes the next stage, the attainment of intimacy, harder to achieve.

Intimacy vs. Isolation Once people have developed a sense of identity, they are ready to share in an intimate relationship with someone else. Erikson sees the identity stage as preparing people for intimacy: the reasoning is that unless you have a

> **Identity versus role confusion** The positive and negative outcomes of adolescence, according to Erik Erikson. The positive outcome, identity, relates to knowing who one is; the negative outcome, role confusion, involves not having developed a coherent self-concept.

strong sense of self, you will not be able to give and receive fully on an equal basis with a partner. Unless the previous conflict is resolved in a positive way, a person will either become submerged in a relationship or need to dominate it.

The conflict of **intimacy versus isolation** is common in young adulthood. Most people in their 20s and 30s experience one or more intimate relationships; many of them marry. A sexual relationship is one way of achieving intimacy (although a deep personal commitment is not always present); close friendships represent another form of commitment. Persons who choose isolation avoid intimate relationships, either with a sexual partner or with close friends. As a result, says Erikson, they do not experience this meaningful dimension of life—a factor that deeply affects subsequent life experiences.

Generativity vs. Self-Absorption   Erikson's belief that development continues throughout the entire life cycle often meets with student cynicism.

> **Intimacy versus isolation**   The fifth developmental conflict in Erik Erikson's theory, this one typical of early adulthood. The positive outcome, intimacy, relates to an ability to share and care for another individual; the negative outcome, isolation, involves the avoidance of close experiences with others.
>
> **Generativity versus self-absorption**   Erik Erikson's description of the psychosocial crisis of middle age. The positive outcome, generativity, relates to the act of sharing the benefits of one's life experiences; the negative outcome indicates an increasingly narrow focus on one's self.
>
> **Integrity versus despair**   The positive and negative outcomes of later maturity, according to Erik Erikson. The positive outcome, integrity, relates to a feeling of satisfaction with one's life; despair, the negative outcome, involves feelings of bitterness and missed opportunities.

All around them are patterns of self-absorption and stagnation, some of which are quite pronounced. "Dad just sits around every night drinking beer and watching television," a student recently complained. "It's hard to think of him as developing."

She had a point. The patterns of behavior exhibited by many middle-aged people, including her father, illustrate Erikson's negative outcome of **self-absorption.** Self-absorption leads to pervasive feelings of meaninglessness, lack of purpose in life, boredom, and depression. In contrast, some middle-aged people react in a very different way. With their children grown and their earning power at its zenith, there are rich opportunities for many middle-aged people to be creative. Some people respond to these opportunities by returning to school, performing volunteer work, spending more time with children, and taking an active role in their communities in other ways. **Generativity,** as Erikson calls it, becomes an important positive step in their development toward the next and final conflict.

Integrity vs. Despair   Erikson's final stage of development is described in terms of **integrity versus despair.** Erikson sees the older person as bringing personal knowledge and experience into an integrated whole. Those who achieve integrity are able to reflect on the past while accepting the present; they are better able to adapt to declining health, the death of companions, and life's other tragedies. They can also remain vital, sharing their wisdom and experiences with others.

The cumulative nature of Erikson's stages shows most clearly in this last challenge. A basic part of integrity is the ability to look back on a long life and be satisfied with what has been accomplished. The negative outcome, despair, arises from the feeling that life has somehow passed one by and it is too late to start all over again. The missed opportunities, neglected relationships, and the emphasis on the unimportant all combine to make the last years bitter and depressed.

Evaluating Ages and Stages: Norms and You

Any theory of lifelong development may leave readers with uneasy questions. How do I measure up? If my daughter isn't self-directed by age 5, is she in trouble? If I don't lead a creative life in my 40s, will I never experience the stage of generativity?

In assessing any timetable such as Erikson's, it is important to understand the exact nature of norms. In developmental psychology, **norms** indicate statistical averages, based upon a large representative sample of a population (Stassen-Berger, 1980). Norms should not be considered to represent ideal development. For example, the average 6-month-old may place his feet in his mouth and be capable of sitting. Yet, one baby may do this at seven months and another at five months. At times, even substantial deviations from the norm may not mean anything is wrong. However, it is often a good idea to investigate large deviations. Suppose that your 3-year-old hasn't uttered a sound since she was 6 months old. The average 3-year-old is already speaking simple sentences such as "Mommy go store." At this stage you would be wise to check her hearing.

Age-related norms are more rigidly applied to infants than to older children and adults. Babies normally can lift their heads at about two months when placed on their stomachs. An infant who does not accomplish this until five months may have some problem that ought to be investigated. On the other hand, five or ten year ranges are not unusual when we speak of marriage or retirement.

Slow development, it should be pointed out, does not necessarily mean that a child will always be behind. Many brilliant people did not walk or talk early. In fact, Einstein was a disappointment to his parents, who interpreted his rather slow start as a sign of dullness (Goertzel & Goertzel, 1962). Furthermore, it is not always an advantage to be above or ahead of the norm. People may react differently to children who are reading be-

The cumulative nature of Erikson's life challenges shows most clearly in the last stage, integrity vs. despair.

Norms In reference to development, the term "norms" refers to statistically usual behavior shown at various ages and stages.

fore kindergarten, playing the piano at four, or solving algebraic equations at six, treating them as if all their skills were as far ahead. In fact, emotional and social maturity may lag well behind intellectual development—a factor that many educators now recognize can cause personal confusion for children who skip a grade in school or enter clubs or study groups with older children.

In all, there is a danger to any rigid belief in norms. It is a mistake to expect all people to develop according to some statistical formula. In some cases, in fact, an overreaction to one person's perceived lag may create more problems than does the slow development itself. Thus, a 16-year-old boy may cause his parents concern because he doesn't show any interest in girls. His lack of interest may not necessarily be a problem, however. He might have been rejected earlier in his teenage years, or he may be developing a bit later than most. There *may* be problems, though, if parents, siblings, or friends overreact to the situation and cause him to feel pressured or "odd."

Norms, then, can be helpful in giving us a rough approximation of age-related sequences. Any excessive deviation may alert us to the possibility of a problem. But each case must be evaluated on its own merits, for development is a highly personal process.

This point—the highly individual nature of development—leads us to a new, important question. We've been looking at the common, very general stages of the human life cycle. What causes each one of us to develop along a slightly different course from every other person? We will explore this question in the remainder of this chapter.

Development as an Individual Process

"You are old, Father William," the young man said,
"And your hair has become very white;
Yet you incessantly stand on your head—
Do you think, at your age, it is right?"
—Lewis Carroll, "Father William"

We all have certain age-and-stage expectations about the way people (including ourselves) should behave. Yet, like Father William, there are always exceptions to these rules. Some people wait to marry until they are in their 60s or 70s; others can't seem to settle on a vocation until they reach their 40s or later; others—including some familiar figures such as Erikson, Chagall, Picasso, and Piaget—produce creative works well into their later years. The variation is also striking among children, who talk, teethe, read, and develop consciences at different ages.

Developmental psychologists are interested in the highly individual nature of people's timetables for growth and change. In explaining these personal differences, they look especially to two factors: genetics and environment. We will explore each of these in the next few pages.

Biology and Genetics

We are used to thinking of human beings as sharing a common biological structure, with a few rather notable differences between females and males. We might say that the "standard model" human has two eyes, two ears, one stomach, one thyroid, and so forth, with an exception here or there.

This is true, of course. In another sense, however, there is no such thing as a "standard model." Our brains are different in many subtle ways. As an example, the normal variation in weight is quite considerable: between 1,200 and 1,400 grams; and intellectual strengths and capacities vary greatly. (The weight of the brain is *not* directly related to a person's intelligence, by the way, at least in the normal range.) The weight and size of our muscles, skeletal structures, glands, and so on are also different from one person to another. Each one of us has our own biological balance. These differences combine to make us physiologically different from every other person, to develop in different ways and at our own pace, and also to think of ourselves as different. In great part, these differences are due to genetics.

Genetic Traits   Ever since the nineteenth century monk Gregor Mendel explored the laws of genetics with his hybridization of peas, we have known that genetics is associated with certain physical traits. In humans, genes control such traits as hair color, skin color, and height. Almost all of us know of at least one family in which a child looks strikingly like a parent, and there is plenty more evidence of genetic influence on physical traits.

Genetics influences personality as well as physical traits, although the degree to which this is so is harder to pinpoint. We know of some extreme cases in which the role of genetics seems quite important. An example is the development of the mental disorder **schizophrenia,** a condition marked by disordered thought processes, major disturbances of emotion and behavior, and the experiencing of hallucinations and delusions (Rosenthal, 1970). Various studies have demonstrated that when one identical twin shows schizophrenic behavior, there is a good probability that it will also occur in the other. There is also a greater likelihood of similar disorders among fraternal twins or siblings than among the general population. Even in identical twins, however, this correlation is far from perfect. Thus, many psychologists argue that it is the predisposition or vulnerability to schizophrenia that is inherited, not the disorder itself. The breakdown itself must be triggered by certain experiences or environmental influences.

Schizophrenia is a rather exceptional case, though; what about other personality traits? Is it true that "the apple never falls far from the tree"—that a talkative and domineering parent will have a talkative, domineering child, or that characteristics such as stubbornness, humor, and intelligence can be family traits? (And if so, is this due to one's genes, or to the environment in which one is raised?)

Some researchers have tried to isolate the role of genetics by studying identical twins who have been separated since birth. Since environmental factors are quite different, the reasoning is that common personality traits can be traced to genetics. Since the number of such twin pairs is often small, there is some controversy surrounding the results. Still, such twin studies suggest at least a probable genetic factor in personality.

Dworkin and his colleagues (1976) conducted a study that compared identical and fraternal twins through adolescence and well into adulthood on a number of characteristics. They found evidence that such traits as anxiety, dependence, dominance, and self-control seemed to have a genetic component that continued to show itself far into the adulthood years. Vandenberg (1967) argues that activity level, impulsiveness, and sociability have an inherited basis as well. Gottesman (1965) claims that introversion and extroversion are at least partially determined by one's genes. Note that these researchers do not claim total genetic control over behavior or personality traits, but rather a genetic predisposition toward a behavior pattern.

The Master Plan   If personality traits seem to be somewhat influenced by genetics, the developmental timetable is also predetermined to a large degree by a genetic master plan, especially in the very early months and years.

Genetic influences help determine the rate of development as well as influencing the content (McClearn, 1970). We all develop at our own individual rate. Some children develop hand-eye coordination faster, walk at an earlier age, and focus their eyes better than other children of the same chronological age. This does not mean that the environment has nothing to do with it at all. However, many skills such as walking, talking, and climbing are largely ordained by the master plan laid out by our genes.

To a degree, this master plan affects the age at which we acquire certain skills. Consider reading, for example. In order to read, children need

---

Schizophrenia   A serious mental disorder often marked by hallucinations, delusions, and disorders in thinking.

certain abilities. They need to focus their eyes on the printed word, to understand what words mean, and to differentiate the sounds of each letter; they also need a reasonably positive attitude towards reading and an ability to attend to instruction (Heilman, 1967). In fact, there are tests called (appropriately) reading readiness tests that are useful in predicting whether children will succeed or have difficulty learning to read. Children who don't have these skills or abilities may require special training. Or they may simply need more time to mature, as in some cases where there is a physical problem relating to the eye (Moore & Moore, 1978).

The same concept of readiness applies broadly to skills, intellectual situations, and emotional experiences (Anderson & Faust, 1973). Simply stated, **readiness** relates to the "degree to which the level of development of the individual matches the learning experiences provided for him/her" (Bergan & Henderson, 1979). Just as children cannot learn to perform new tasks until they have the appropriate abilities, the same concept can be applied to social skills as well.

Some Readiness Issues　The question of social readiness leads to some very practical questions for many people, especially in a society that seems to have trouble defining where childhood ends and adulthood begins. Do most young teenagers have the experience or strength to make responsible decisions about drugs, or sex, or drinking? This question takes on importance if one thinks of adolescence in Erikson's terms, as a time when individuals are struggling to form an identity for themselves.

> **Readiness**　A developmental state in which an individual has the psychological and physical abilities to cope with a particular task. For instance, children can begin to learn to read when they demonstrate reading readiness.

Another intriguing question that many of us deal with at one time is how to tell if we are ready for marriage. When one of the authors asked his class how many thought they were ready to get married irrespective of whether they had met the "right" person, very few raised their hands. (Even some of the married students didn't.) It is difficult to think of readiness in this regard, for people often tell each other that when they meet the right person they will "get ready." Yet, many students had their doubts.

Some plainly stated that they lacked the abilities and skills necessary to begin a successful marriage. These qualities included the willingness to share, the ability to be self-supporting, the possession of a strong personal identity, and the desire to settle down. One student remarked that if people had to have all of these qualities, they wouldn't get married until well into their forties! Of course, this is an extreme position, but most students seem to believe that more than love is necessary for a successful marriage.

The same kinds of apprehensions, it might be noted, surround other major life changes to one degree or another. Many couples don't know if they're *really* ready to take the responsibility when they first become parents. Even if they have wanted children, the responsibility is awesome. Again, many older adults feel apprehensive about retirement, feeling too young to give up the role they have held for so many years.

It is easy to see how genetics may affect such skills as walking, talking, or reading. It is much more difficult to see how one's genes affect such adult decisions as getting married, drug taking, or having sex. It is incorrect, however, to believe that heredity is only important during childhood. In reality, heredity affects development throughout life. For example, the rate at which you age is partially determined by your genes. On the other hand, aging can also be affected by environmental factors such as health habits, disease, and lifestyle. It is thus impossible to understand the complexities of human behavior without a full appreciation of the importance of the environment.

Environmental Influences

The fact that your environment can affect your development is so obvious that it is often stated as a matter of fact and left at that. Chapter 3 pointed out the importance of learning in virtually every area of human behavior. In discussing environment, we should stress that we are referring not only to the house you live in or the school classroom, but all the influences to which you are exposed.

No two individuals ever experience the exact same environment. If you have siblings, you were born at a different time than they were, and your family circumstances may have changed. If you are a fraternal twin, there are personality differences that cause your interactions and interests to be different from those of your sibling. The nature of your environment affects your behavior and outlook from the day of your birth. Think how different your life would have been if you had been born into the Rockefeller family. Your entire life, including your friends, schools attended, travels, and outlook on the world would probably be very different from those you presently hold.

It is easiest to explore the effects of environment if we look separately at the four most influential elements: the culture, family, peers, and educational influences.

Culture   Culture plays a crucial role in the behaviors and attitudes we learn, from the way we dress to the religious beliefs we hold. Culture also has an overriding influence on development. On a broad scale, we can see this effect when we compare one society with another. When Margaret Mead visited the Pacific island of Samoa in the 1920s, for instance, she observed that children grew up viewing all aspects of life—birth, sexual experiences, and death—as everyday events that were not hidden from them (Mead, 1928). Mead's observations have recently been contested. Still, her writings point to a society in which many aspects of development were treated differently than in western society.

Culture affects development in myriad other ways, too. Toddlers who are carried or kept confined most of the day, for instance, may develop independence in a different way from the 2-year-old in Erikson's western timetable; the same is true of the development of industriousness in a culture that, unlike our modern culture, expects children to perform economic chores that are vital to the family. We could provide many other examples of ways in which culture influences development.

Subcultural differences also exist within a society. Different ethnic, religious, and socioeconomic groups have their own traditions about raising infants, how much responsibility to give young children, at what age children should leave home and marry, and so forth. All of these beliefs and practices influence each individual's development.

Family Interactions   Another influence that is quite important in early development is the family environment. As we saw in Chapter 3, parents influence learning in many ways—by acting as role models, by delivering reinforcements and punishments, and by explaining concepts. The net effect of all these interactions is all-important in shaping not only our behavior patterns, but also our self-concepts: the way we view ourselves. We know, for instance, that youngsters who are raised in affectionate environments, experience praise, and are given responsibility tend to develop high self-esteem (Coopersmith, 1967). Even within the same family, each child experiences differences in the environment that reflect birth order, personality differences, and economic or structural circumstances (as when a mother stays home with the first infant, then returns to work after the second child is born). In these ways, the family creates a highly individual environment for each developing child.

Peer Influences   A third important influence is friends or acquaintances. The relationships we have with our peers are qualitatively different from those we share with our parents (Hetherington & Parke, 1979). We meet them on common ground and they share many experiences that our parents do not. Since they are in the same developmental stage, we tend to confide in them. Peers do not "replace" parents, as is often thought. Many of the values held by parents are shared by one's peers.

We learn from our peers and often imitate them. At times, they help us break away from the domination of parents. We prefer to be with our peers, especially in our early teenage years when we are striving toward self-definition and independence. It is a common experience for young teenagers to complain that they don't want to go shopping with their parents. Yet, this may not be the case as the teenage years come to a close. By the age of nineteen or so, most people are secure enough once again to enjoy their parents' company.

We typically value the opinions of our peers, especially regarding "surface" characteristics such as dress and music. In fact, it is often a waste of energy for parents to insist on outward conformity in these areas. This does not mean, however, that deeper values naturally flow from the peer group. The evidence indicates that adult, especially parental, influences may be as great or even greater than those of the peer group with respect to values, vocational choices, and religious and political orientations (Stassen-Berger, 1980).

Educational Influences   A fourth important influence on development is educational experience. Those of us who attend two years or more of college will spend a good part of 15 years in school—not counting preschool experiences, extracurricular lessons, or even further education. These experiences provide formal tutorial training, but they also are a highly important social training ground. At school, we learn many of our attitudes toward authority figures; toward social institutions and how to survive in them; and toward ourselves as industrious or lazy, good or bad, and bright or slow.

The Interactive Viewpoint

When we add together the various influences of heredity, culture, family, peers, and educational experiences, we can see that each person's development is a combination of various individual factors. In other words, both environment and genetics interact to shape each person's personality and development.

Exactly how this interaction takes place is open to question. Rather than assuming that genes for a certain trait—be it stubbornness, affiliation, or intelligence—can show themselves only in one manner, we realize that they can display themselves to varying degrees, depending upon the environment (Dobzhansky, 1973). Rather than asking what percentage of any trait is determined by genetics and what is due to environment, it might be more pertinent to ask *how* various factors interact to form a person's character (Anastasi, 1958). At this point in time, we are only beginning to understand the many subtle ways in which our genetic endowment interacts with our experiences and environment to produce our own individual behavior and personality.

How Important Is Early Experience?

We have seen in this chapter that our early conflicts and choices all influence our later adjustments to life. Erikson's eight lifelong challenges are based on this conception, and the idea has been integral to many psychological theories.

Freud believed that most adult problems could be linked to childhood difficulties. The behaviorists also view early experiences as important, since these experiences may determine later behavior patterns.

It is easy to see the tragic effects of early deprivation on some children. Indeed, many researchers have found that an infant's separation from a mother or caretaker can be linked to fearfulness, anxiety, depression, and the inability to relate to others (Bowlby, 1960; Spitz, 1945). Many of the early studies argued that once this pattern was established, its effects would be permanent.

It certainly happens that early experiences have a crippling, lifelong effect on some people. That is why the Joint Commission on the Mental Health of Children issued a listing of children's rights, as shown in the box *Children's Rights*. But it is revealing to look more closely at some of the reasons why this is so. Part of the cause for adulthood problems seems to lie in the fact that poor early experiences do not magically end with the first five years of life (Clarke & Clarke, 1976). Most young children who don't have the chance to develop trust, autonomy, or other of Erikson's qualities early in life are not going to find their lot radically changed later on. Their parents don't suddenly change for the better; their social environment doesn't drastically improve in most cases. Thus, adulthood problems may also result from a lifetime of negative experiences—not just a difficult childhood.

A second reason why negative early experiences may sometimes lead to lifelong problems is a concept that some readers may have heard of: the **self-fulfilling prophecy.** Defined briefly, this is the notion that "the expectation of some reality may influence the fulfillment of that reality" (Wrightsman, 1972, p. 610). In plainer language, once people learn to expect certain things of themselves, they sometimes give up trying to change. Just as a series of nasty falls may cause you to put away your skateboard for good, people may also decide that they're uncomfortable showing affection, or that they can't make decisions well, or that they won't succeed because they aren't as good as other people. Because they give up, they set up their own roadblocks that prevent growth.

We are also affected by the expectations significant others in our lives have for us. Our parents and teachers may expect certain behaviors, and their expectations can affect how we see ourselves and how we act. This was nicely demonstrated by a study performed by Rosenthal and Jacobson (1968).

These researchers informed elementary school teachers that certain of their students (who had been randomly selected) had scored very high on the Harvard Test of Inflected Acquisitions (a nonexistent test), designated these students as "late bloomers," then waited to see what would happen. The self-fulfilling prophecy seemed to work. "Bloomers" showed impressive intellectual gains and were seen by their teachers as happier, more interesting, and better adjusted than the other students in the class.

This study strongly suggests that students respond positively when teachers believe in them and expect them to succeed. The opposite is also true, and not only in school situations. Children who are expected to be poor students or to misbehave are likely to integrate these expectations into their own self-images. The school classroom is often a fertile ground for such image building, and the self-fulfilling prophecy seems to be a powerful force in determining people's behavior.

Both of these situations—the cumulative lifetime experiences and the self-fulfilling prophecy—may be reason enough to support the developmental task theory that each of life's stages prepares the way for the next. This is not to say, however, that a wrong turn at one point cannot be corrected later on. Most researchers now recog-

---

Self-fulfilling prophecy The concept that one's expectations concerning some event affect the probability of its occurrence.

Children's Rights

Early experience is very important in influencing the direction and momentum of each person's development. Recognizing this, the Joint Commission on the Mental Health of Children issued a report in 1969, listing rights that each child should enjoy—and which should be protected by law wherever possible (Shore, 1979). Here is a brief version of that list of rights, regrouped in order to simplify the categories:

The Right to Be Born Healthy

Every year, thousands of children are born with serious mental and physical handicaps that could have been prevented if their parents had taken adequate precautions. Causes include the pregnant woman's ingestion of drugs or alcohol; the lack of prenatal care, including poor maternal nutrition; X-rays; and smoking (Stechler & Halton, 1982); as well as maternal illnesses such as rubella and syphilis.

Education can often prevent some of these problems from arising. One of the difficulties, however, involves the simple fact that a woman may not know she is pregnant during the crucial early months of pregnancy, when the developing embryo is so vulnerable to the effects of disease or drugs.

The Right to a Safe and Stimulating Physical Environment

Children have the right to a safe, well ventilated, physically healthy environment. They need to be protected from traffic, poisonous substances, or other dangers; they also need play space and human interaction that can provide stimulation.

The right to a safe physical environment also includes the right to adequate nutrition. For children whose mothers were malnourished during pregnancy, this is especially important, for some cases of mental deficiency seem to be linked to malnutrition during pregnancy and the first few years of life (Richardson, 1980). Most people, unfortunately, do not make food choices based upon solid nutritional considerations (Hamilton & Whitney, 1979)—a fact that the popularity of junk food attests to. Children in the western world may get enough calories but still suffer from a lack of important vitamins and minerals.

---

nize that not all cases of early deprivation result in later abnormal behavior (Endler et al., 1976). When it does affect the child, these conditions can be treated and often reversed, as is illustrated in the box *Early Malnutrition: Is the Damage Permanent?* In the words of Clarke and Clarke, "It appears that there is virtually no psychosocial adversity to which some children have not been subjected, yet later recovered, granted a radical change of circumstances" (1976, p. 268).

Further than this, some children seem simply to be invulnerable to their surroundings. Here is one example:

The ten-year-old had everything against him: extreme poverty, an ex-convict father who was dying of a chronic disease, an illiterate mother who sometimes abused him, two mentally retarded siblings. Yet his teachers described him as a charming boy, loved by everyone in the school, a good student and a natural leader. (Pines, 1975, p. 164)

The Right to a Secure and Loving Emotional Environment

The right to an emotional environment that will encourage healthy development is based upon two important factors, love and discipline. We all need love, as Chapter 7 will discuss. In the context of child-rearing, love relates to a number of behaviors which include stimulation and affection. There is no such thing as "too much" love, as long as a child is also given limits through discipline. Children require guidance. When the limits are reasonable, guidance is rational, and punishments—where necessary—are delivered fairly and consistently and are balanced by reinforcement for the desired behavior, children seem to thrive.

The Right to Intellectual Development

Children require the stimulation of all their senses. Such stimulation begins at birth when parents fondle, laugh, and play with their child. When children from stimulating home environments reach school age, they arrive with superior skills and have a better chance of academic success in school (Pines, 1975).

All children also have the right to attend schools in which resources can provide them with an opportunity to achieve. Children's needs for these resources may vary. Some may need extra help in reading; others may have learning disabilities that require remediation; still others may be gifted, and they also have special needs if they are to reach their potential. Only when these special services are made available do all children gain an equal opportunity to learn.

The Right to Treatment

Troubled children also have the right to receive adequate medical and psychological help as early as possible, in a convenient setting. The closer children are to home, the easier it is for the child to live as normal a life as possible, and the easier for the entire family to adjust to new circumstances.

Providing the best possible physical and emotional environment increases children's chances of becoming independent, self-sufficient members of society. It also gives children an opportunity to enjoy life and to develop their potential.

We all know people who have risen above an unhealthy environment to lead outstanding lives. There are families in which one child has a police record that includes assault, robbery, and burglary charges while the other has never seen the inside of a police station. Garmezy (1976) studied children who were raised in schizophrenic environments and yet did not suffer from the disorder. In fact, many were showing signs of very healthy development.

Such **invulnerables,** children who seem to cope well despite poor environments, are more the rule than the exception. Perhaps scientists should take a closer look at these children who

Invulnerables   A term used to describe children who are raised in very bad environments and yet show little or no emotional disturbance.

Early Malnutrition: Is the Damage Permanent?

One of the greatest dangers to the world's children comes from malnutrition. A number of studies show that early malnutrition leads to fewer brain cells and retarded mental development, a condition that is often complicated by the fact that many malnourished children are also deprived of a stimulating environment. It is difficult to separate these two factors, and many psychologists believe that they work together to produce a deadly effect of retarded mental and physical growth. When malnourished children are raised in stimulating environments, however, the effects often seem less drastic.

Since the environment is an important contributor to damage caused by malnutrition, could this damage be reversed by a more enriched environment? This question prompted one team of scientists to look for a population of children who had been victimized by malnutrition, then experienced substantial change for the better in their environment. They found such a population among a group of Korean orphans who had been adopted by American parents by the age of 3.

The investigators examined the records of 908 female orphans whose developmental histories were complete. After controlling for physical defects and wrestling with a number of practical considerations, they ended up with a sample of 141 children. This sample was divided into three distinct groups—malnourished, moderately nourished, and well-nourished—on the basis of their height and weight when they entered the Korean orphanage. The children's adopted families were contacted, and permission was obtained to gather data on the children's height, weight, intelligence scores, and achievement. The results of the study are heartening.

The children in all three groups had improved significantly in height and weight, so that they were all above the mean for Korean children on these measures. (They were not up to the level expected of American children, but this might be attributable to genetic differences between national groups.) Each of the groups had reached or exceeded the average intelligence scores for native born, well-nourished Americans. The children in all three groups were also doing well in school. It should be noted that although all the groups had developed well, the group of malnourished children was still behind the well-nourished group.

In all, however, this study suggests that if malnourished children are adopted at an early age and their environment is permanently changed for the better, the effects of malnutrition can be reduced and even reversed. People are resilient, and one should be wary about making overly pessimistic statements about the disabling effects of early experience. In most cases, the results of poor early experiences, if countered early enough with sufficient force, can be substantially reduced and even overcome.

Source: Winick et al., 1975.

seem to be able to transcend their circumstances. Maslow suggested that psychologists study the essentially healthy individual rather than those who are considered unstable and unhealthy. If mental health is indeed a matter of transcending one's environment (Maslow, 1961), then these children's success ought to be investigated to learn how they achieved their level of functioning.

Postscript: What Does This All Mean to Us?

What can we learn from developmental psychology that may be important to our own adjustments? First, developmental psychologists stress that we are not genetically programmed or predestined to be the way we are. Genetics may indeed give us certain potentialities and limitations, but our genetic endowment interacts with the environment to produce our behavior and personality. Since we have the power to change our environment and release our potential, we are not merely helpless pawns in the development process. Rather, we can participate in it.

Secondly, modern developmental psychology has finally come to realize that people can change, that they are not merely the products of their early experiences. We need not continue to blame our unhappy childhoods for our present difficulties. The effects of early experience are reversible. This book takes the viewpoint that people can change, and that the techniques for doing so are available.

Third, each age or stage brings us different tasks and crises that we all must face. These tasks can be viewed as challenges that we have the power to meet, analyze, cope with, and master.

Finally, development continues throughout life. It does not end at the age of 5, in adolescence, or during middle age. We may have to alter our thinking patterns to allow for continuous development throughout life.

It is clear, then, that we cannot view ourselves as end products. We are constantly in the process of becoming, and we have the power to influence this process.

Summary

1. People develop in a recognizable progression, from involuntary to voluntary control, from mass to specific muscular control, from external to internal control, and from dependence to independence. This directional development is called the orthogenetic principle by Heinz Werner.

2. Each stage of life has its special potential for joy, and it also presents us with particular challenges or trials. Age-related challenges that almost everyone experiences are called developmental tasks. If a person does not successfully cope with these tasks, the person's development may be adversely affected in some sense.

3. Erik Erikson described the life cycle in terms of eight stages, each of which can be expressed in terms of a positive and a negative outcome. From infancy to old age, these include trust versus mistrust; autonomy versus doubt; initiative versus guilt; industry versus inferiority; identity versus role confusion; intimacy versus isolation; generativity versus self-absorption; and finally, integrity versus despair.

4. Norms are statistical averages that are based upon a large representative sample of a population. They should not be considered to reflect ideal development. Even substantial deviations from the norm may not be meaningful. However, such deviations should alert one to the possibility of a problem.

5. Most psychologists today see personality and behavior as a result of both genetics and environment. Genetic influences are important throughout life. They influence physical traits, predispositions toward diseases and personality traits, and one's rate of development.

6. The concept of readiness relates to the match between the level of development of the individual and the learning experiences provided for the child. A child requires certain skills and abilities before he or she is able to master other skills. The concept of readiness may be applied to social as well as intellectual tasks.

7. One's cultural background, family environment, peers, and educational experiences influence development.

8. The importance of the first years of life was emphasized by Freud as well as many other theorists. The recognition that these years are important is basic to the list of children's rights put forth by the Joint Commission on the Mental Health of Children.

Some children may show no major emotional problems, despite being raised in a poor environment.

9. When the expectation that something will occur actually increases the likelihood that it will happen, the self-fulfilling prophecy is said to be operating.

10. Baumrind has identified three parenting styles, the *authoritarian,* the *permissive,* and the *authoritative.* Baumrind found children raised under authoritative guidance to be the best adjusted of these three groups.

11. This chapter comes to four conclusions. First, people are not predestined to be one way or another: they have the power to change their environment and participate actively in their own development. Secondly, the effects of early experience are reversible. Thirdly, each stage or age brings with it distinctive tasks and crises that may be viewed as challenges. Finally, development continues throughout the entire life span.

Key Terms and Concepts

developmental psychology

orthogenetic principle

developmental tasks

psychosocial theory

libido

fixation

Oedipal situation

trust versus mistrust

autonomy versus doubt

initiative versus guilt

industry versus inferiority

authoritarian parents

permissive parents

authoritative parents

identity versus role confusion

intimacy versus isolation

generativity versus self-absorption

integrity versus despair

norms

schizophrenia

readiness

self-fulfilling prophecy

invulnerables

Safety Needs

"On the night of July 30, 1954, Elvis Presley made his real debut as a public performer. . . . No sooner did he start singing, than he began to hear a lot of shouting and screeching from the audience. . . . He kept on singing and banging his guitar till he got through the tune. Then, after the applause, he launched into 'Blue Moon.' Again, there was a lot of unexplained noise from the crowd. When Elvis finished this time, he discovered that he had stopped the show cold. The audience was demanding an encore. As Elvis huddled with the band, he demanded: 'What's making 'em holler so

Stress

much?' 'It was your leg, man!' Scotty and Bill told him, laughing. 'It was the way you were shakin' your left leg. That's what got 'em screamin'.'" (Goldman, 1981, p. 120)*

The rest, of course, was history.

*Reprinted by permission of McGraw-Hill Book Company.

Why begin a chapter on stress with the first "leg" (the left leg!) of Elvis's journey down the road to success? After all, it would be hard to name another person who epitomizes the rags-to-riches success story more than Elvis. In one sense, if anyone *didn't* live a stressful life, you might think it was Elvis.

In another sense, however, Elvis's story captures the eye because of the startling chronology it presents. Look at the facts:

Birth: 1935
Stardom: 1954 (age 19)
Death: 1977 (age 42)

In terms of statistics, the story is one of a quick rise and fall—a common theme that has had many familiar variations among the very famous and also among not-so-famous persons who have pursued success in other areas.

The point of all this is that stress is far broader than the kinds of experiences with which we usually associate it. True, stress includes the tensions that arise from being stuck in a traffic jam, worrying about an exam, arguing with your parents, or having a death in the family. But stress also includes many experiences that we consider to be positive. Becoming a superstar may not be among the forms of stress you will have to face during your lifetime, but other experiences such as winning a race, getting married, taking a vacation (the list could go on) also impose stress on many of us.

We tend to think of stress as it relates to unpleasant pressures and events. But sudden and meteoric success, as Elvis Presley experienced, can also cause tremendous stress.

What Is Stress?

The very fact that stress includes such a broad range of experiences presents psychologists with somewhat of a dilemma. How can the term be defined? Actually, there is no single accepted definition for the term *stress*—although many have been suggested. For our purposes, we can define **stress** as "a state of physiological and psychological tension resulting from threatening . . . demands from the environment" (Darley et al., 1981, p. 612). Or, in plainer language, stress can be described simply as any situation in which an individual is forced to cope.

> **Stress** A condition of physiological or psychological tension resulting from demands in the environment that the individual perceives as threatening. More simply put, any situation in which the individual is forced to cope.

This chapter deals specifically with stress, but each of the chapters in Part II relates closely to the broad concept of stress we present here. That is because any situation or emotional state that interferes with security or safety—including conflict, frustration, anxiety, fear, and anger—presents a form of stress with which the individual must cope. Learning to cope with these states is an important step in making personal adjustments.

Just as there are many definitions of stress, there are also many ways of studying stress. Cox (1978) argues that the study of stress may be approached from three different directions. One approach looks at the nature of **stressors,** the external events and conditions that cause stress. A second approach looks at the individual's physiological and psychological responses to stress. Much research has studied how people react to the demands of the environment, and predictable physiological response patterns have been discovered. The third approach investigates stress in terms of a "lack of fit" between the individual's ability to cope and the demands that are imposed by the environment. An imbalance between these two factors leads to the subjective experience of stress.

We will take all three approaches as we explore stress in this chapter, starting with a look at the kinds of situations and circumstances that produce stress in our lives; then at the physiological and psychological dynamics of stress; and finally, at the relationship between the individual and the environment, and ways that we can improve our abilities to cope with stress.

What Causes Stress?

If you were asked to recall your most stressful experiences, they would probably involve some negative events—a death in the family, an accident or illness, a failure of some kind, or a rejection. These situations can certainly all be identified as stressors. However, we have also seen that positive experiences often act as stressors. Whether stress is experienced as positive or negative depends not only on the circumstances that cause the stress, but also on another very important factor: the individual. We'll look first at the individual and then at several types of stressors.

The Individual Ingredient

It is easy to assume that stressors have the same effect on everyone. A lost wallet, a serious illness, or losing a job, for instance, would be upsetting to virtually anyone—or so it might seem.

This is not always the case, however, for *we* ourselves are important factors in the amount of stress we experience. An example of this is public speaking. You may enjoy a sense of excitement and arousal when you speak before a large crowd of people, while your friend may find public speaking an almost unbearable ordeal. Again, you might be able to think of few experiences more trying than spending 5 hours with a 1-year-old—but you may have friends who have their own children and find the experience rewarding. Even in highly stressful situations, individual interpretation is an important factor. A person who has had emergency training (a firefighter, for instance) will experience far less stress than the average layperson when faced with disaster.

Factors such as training, self-concept, past experiences, and physical and emotional stamina all influence both the outlook and resources each of us uses in dealing with stressful situations. These factors can all be changed to one degree or another, and at the end of the chapter we'll see how we can learn to cope better with some forms of stress. For the moment, we'll turn our attention to some of the most common sources of stress, including life changes, stressors in the home, and stressors at the workplace.

Stressors Events or conditions that cause stress.

Life Changes as Stressors

Any life change acts to "throw us off balance" for a time, forcing us to cope. Thus, life changes comprise one major group of stressors. Marriage, starting a new job, moving to a new town are all included in this grouping; so are divorces, illnesses, deaths of friends or family, and many other changes in status, routine, or social networks. In most cases, we can bounce back from these situations, making an adjustment within either a short or a somewhat longer period of time. Sometimes, however, several stressful events occur within a relatively short time period. What happens then?

This question was partially answered by psychologists Holmes and Rahe (1967). They compiled a "life events scale," listed in Table 5.1, which rates 43 life events according to the degree of stress they impose upon a person (measured by the units in the right-hand column). According to Holmes and Rahe, several life changes within a short time can have profound effects on a person—a much greater effect than if the same changes were to occur over several years. In such cases, the researchers see not only psychological effects of stress (for instance, tenseness, inability to sleep, or depression), but also an increased likelihood of disease.

The life events scale is used as a means of predicting this likelihood of disease (Holmes and Masuda, 1972). The researchers suggest that exposure to 300 units of stress within a year is extreme, bringing about an 80 percent chance that the individual will develop some major physical ailment. (We'll discuss physical responses to stress later in the chapter.) Any stress levels between 150-300 units make the person more vulnerable to illness. The disorder may take psychological rather than physical form, through deep depression or some other reaction.

Holmes's work has been reported in literally hundreds of books and magazine articles about stress, and the correlations between events such as those listed and stress reactions is quite high.

Table 5.1 Life Events Scale

Event	Scale of Impact
Death of spouse	100
Divorce	73
Marital separation	65
Jail term	63
Death of close family member	63
Personal injury or illness	53
Marriage	50
Fired at work	47
Marital reconciliation	45
Retirement	45
Change in health of family member	44
Pregnancy	40
Sex difficulties	39
Gain of new family member	39
Business readjustment	39
Change in financial state	38
Death of close friend	37
Change to different line of work	36
Change in number of arguments with spouse	35
Mortgage over $10,000	31
Foreclosure of mortgage or loan	30
Change in responsibilities at work	29
Son or daughter leaving home	29
Trouble with in-laws	29
Outstanding personal achievement	28
Wife begins or stops work	26
Begin or end school	26
Change in living conditions	25
Revision of personal habits	24
Trouble with boss	23
Change in work hours or conditions	20
Change in residence	20
Change in schools	20
Change in recreation	19
Change in church activities	19
Change in social activities	18
Mortgage or loan less than $10,000	17
Change in sleeping habits	16
Change in number of family get-togethers	15
Change in eating habits	15
Vacation	13
Christmas	12
Minor violation of the law	11

Reprinted from *U.S. News & World Report,* September 24, 1973. Copyright 1973 U.S. News & World Report, Inc.

However, we should be careful in considering this scale. Certainly, not all people exposed to multiple changes will develop illness or experience severe psychological reactions; and many persons may show signs of breakdown after undergoing only slight alterations. In other words, the individual's response to stress is quite personal.

In addition, the scale itself should be taken only as a general guideline. Some of the events it lists may need updating—the $10,000 mortgage, for example, reflects an economy that makes some of us misty-eyed with nostalgia. In addition, the scale represents only one class of stressors. It does not list many daily sources of stress, such as a complicated schedule of work and classes, or a living environment that is noisy or tension-filled. These day-by-day situations also act as stressors.

Stressors in the Home

Wherever two or more people live together, at least some disagreements are inevitable. Every member of a household has his or her own needs and desires, and these needs may conflict with those of another member. This is true of marital partnerships, parent-child relationships, and certainly of roommate arrangements.

Getting along in any relationship often entails a measure of self-sacrifice, or at least the ability to delay gratification. A wife or husband may come home from work ready to kick off the shoes, collapse, and spend the rest of the evening curled up with a good book. Or one member of the household may feel like partying at 10 P.M. or jazzercizing at 6 in the morning. A fact of life, however, is that to maintain peace in a household, you can't do everything you feel like doing. There may be responsibilities that keep the husband or wife from relaxing. If there are children at home, they will need to switch roles completely and start a whole new round of interactions the minute they walk in the front door—a far cry from curling up with a book. Again, the would-be late-night party-giver or early-morning jazzercizer will probably need to put off their plans out of consideration for the other folks they live with. While all of us might prefer to follow our own whimsies, a failure to compromise is likely to produce tension, ill-feelings, and a certain degree of stress in the household.

There are hundreds of stressors around the house. Unpaid bills, broken appliances, burned suppers, and competing demands for your time and attention can all cause stress. Some home environments tend to be more stressful than others, however. Homes that are noisy, tense, overcrowded, and filled with discord tend to be particularly stressful. In addition, the domestic roles of wife, husband, mother, father (or the in-between role of the adolescent in most American families) all put pressures on us that can cause stress, especially when the demands of these roles conflict. The box *Home Stress Checklist* provides a rough indication of some factors in the home environment that can produce stress. It is meant as a general awareness exercise rather than a specific measuring instrument. Therefore, no scoring guidelines are provided.

Another factor in evaluating home stress levels is the emotional state of the person undergoing stress. For all of us, it is easier to cope with the neighbor's dogs barking, or with demanding children, or with any other pressure, if we are relaxed.

Feelings of tension and anxiety tend to cloud our sense of perspective, making it all the more difficult to cope with stress. This all relates back, of course, to the cumulative nature of stress noted by Holmes and Rahe. If you are ill, or have had a rough day, or are experiencing real worries about another matter, you may find that even a minor irritation is the proverbial straw that breaks the camel's back. This is the very reason why item #4 is one of the most important questions in the checklist, for a daily chance to escape from the pressures of family roles, jobs, and the hubbub of everyday activities helps to reduce the accumulation of stress.

Home Stress Checklist

A precise gauge of home stress is impossible. This checklist can act as a rough guideline, however. Check the appropriate answers to evaluate the stress levels in your home life.

1. **Roles:** How many "hats" do you wear?
   breadwinner _____
   mother/father _____
   husband/wife _____
   other contributor _____
   bill payer _____
   gardener _____
   housekeeper _____
   menu planner _____
   cook _____
   dishwasher _____
   home repair expert _____
   other _____

2. **Environmental Stress:** Are there physical factors in your household that bother you?
   noise _____
   crowding _____
   disorganization, messiness _____
   leaks, drips, or other nagging repair jobs _____
   lack of storage space _____
   other _____

3. **Interpersonal Stress:** How do you rate your household's tension level?
   low (little interpersonal discord, and when there is, you can talk it out) _____
   moderate (some tension, but it's usually tolerable) _____
   high (@#*!) _____

4. **Time Out:** How often do you have a chance to be alone and do something relaxing and pleasurable?
   each day _____
   several times a week _____
   a few times a week _____
   rarely _____

Stressors at Work

For most adults, weekdays can be divided between household hours and work hours. (The two need not take place in different locations.) Besides life changes and home stressors, work is a third major source of stress in many people's lives.

A great deal of research has explored stressors in the work environment and their effect upon employees. Does work have to be stressful? In answer to this question, one student replied that that was why they call it work! Yet the question remains. How much stress is necessary and desirable in the work place?

How Much Is Too Much?   Some of us seem to work better under stress. That is one reason why it's often easier to sit down and write a term paper when it is due in a few days than when the deadline is three months off. Yet there is little doubt that excessive stress has a negative effect on the quality and quantity of work (Poulton, 1971).

In other words, there seems to be an optimum level for stress, and this level varies with the task. The more complicated the task, the less arousal is required and the more damaging stress is likely to be to the final product. Stress has less effect upon a well-practiced skill since less thought and concentration is needed to perform it. However, when learning or practicing a new skill, stress is likely to be counterproductive. For example, a number of studies using noise as a stressor have demonstrated that a noisy environment increases the number of errors when the task is complex (Poulton, 1971). Although a moderate amount of stress may be necessary to maintain arousal, teachers and employers should be wary of creating an environment that contains

> **Role ambiguity** Work situations in which workers are uncertain of the exact nature of their responsibilities.

excessive stress, especially if the work is complicated or requires complete concentration. Both on the job and in the school, the accuracy of the work will suffer if the amount of stress becomes too great for the individual to handle.

Stress by Design   Most of us would agree that certain jobs seem more stressful than others. Air traffic controllers who must make critical decisions—and who are well aware of the meaning of failure—tend to suffer a variety of stress-related disorders (Arehart-Treichel, 1976). Yet, you do not have to be in a job where life-and-death decisions are made in order to experience stress. Any job can be stressful if it carries elements of frustration, pressure, anxiety, and conflict—and what job doesn't?

Psychologists have found that certain jobs seem to have more stress structured into them than do others. Kahn and Quinn (1969) argue that if your job contains role ambiguity, conflict, or overload, its very structure will cause stress. Much of the stress in the world of work could be reduced, or even eliminated, if these elements had been considered when the job was created.

Role ambiguity refers to a lack of understanding about what your job entails. Do you know exactly what is expected of you on your job? If you and your supervisor independently wrote a list of your responsibilities, would these lists be identical? For many people, the answer is no. A person who is hired as a checker in a supermarket will be likely to feel tense and irritated about cleaning the floor in front of the market, especially if that responsibility wasn't defined at the time of hiring. Likewise, students experience more stress when they don't know what is expected of them. If the instructor says "read the material when you get a chance," is the material assigned or not? Will it appear on the midterm? Specifically outlining the responsibilities of each worker can reduce role ambiguity, thus alleviating one potential source of stress.

A second source of stress on the job is **role conflict.** As it applies to the work situation, role conflict describes the different expectations communicated to you by various supervisors. These expectations may not always be the same. One supervisor may expect a job to be done one way, while the other wants it done another way. How can you respond?

Most people experiencing role conflict try to reach some sort of compromise. Knowing which supervisor is most important to their position, they tend to perform the job closest to that person's specifications. This may not work, however. If both supervisors have authority over different aspects of your work, quite a stressful situation can arise.

A third source of stress is **role overload.** Many of us have jobs in which it is simply impossible to do everything expected of us, even if we are fully aware of the behaviors required. We choose what we think is most important and leave the lower priorities for last. Thus, the mail waits while the work schedule for next week is designed. But what if we cannot assign priorities to our tasks, either because we can't establish priorities or because different supervisors demand different chores to be performed first? This is almost certain to lead to pressure, which gives rise to stress.

How extensive are role ambiguity, role conflict, and role overload in the workplace? These problems seem to be common. In one survey, Kahn et al. (1964) found that 35 percent of the workers questioned complained of a lack of clarity in their job descriptions, 30 percent weren't certain what was expected of them, and 48 percent felt that they had little idea of the priorities of their jobs.

The Work Atmosphere   In addition to the structure of the job role itself, other factors at the workplace may also lead to stress. Like every other interpersonal situation, disagreements and arguments happen, causing tension. It's difficult to share an office with a person who wants to gossip while you want to work, or to have a supervisor who takes credit for something you worked very hard to produce. Each place of business has its own atmosphere: some are relaxed and happy, while others inspire no sense of belonging or support. A relatively friendly atmosphere with good interpersonal relations can act as a buffer against work stress, just as a secure home situation can become a critical mediator of stress (Lowenthal & Weiss, 1976). It would seem reasonable, however, that much stress could be eliminated by examining the design of the job itself and structuring it to reduce ambiguity, conflict, and overload as much as possible.

Environmental Stressors

A fourth group of stressors can relate to either work or home, although they are not necessarily associated with either. Environmental stressors are actual physical conditions, such as heat or cold, noise, or crowding, that cause stress. Even visual conditions can act as stressors. If a skyscraper were being erected between your apartment and a spectacular city view, you might find yourself tense and angry each time you looked out

Role conflict   A situation in which the demands of two or more roles assumed by an individual are to some extent contradictory. In the workplace, role conflict may refer to a situation in which two or more supervisors expect different, inconsistent, and incompatible behaviors from a worker.

Role overload   A situation in which individuals cannot accomplish everything expected of them and thus must assign priorities to various tasks. Like role ambiguity and role conflict, this situation causes stress in the workplace.

your window. Environmental stress does not always need to be immediately obvious. People living near a nuclear reactor, or in areas of the country where chemical wastes were once disposed of, may experience environmental stress so severe that it forces them to make major life changes.

Psychological Dynamics of Stress

We have seen how life events, environmental factors, and work and home situations can act as stressors. How do they produce stress? Most often, these factors set in motion certain psychological dynamics that produce unpleasant sensations or emotions. A complete list of these psychological forces is impossible, but we'll look below at some of the more common ones: frustration, conflict, pressure, and deprivation. (Anxiety, guilt, depression, anger, and aggression are also included in this list. They are the subjects of Chapters 6 and 7.)

Frustration

One of the most common elements in stress is **frustration,** which can be defined as "the interference with, or blocking of, the attainment of some goal" (Vander Zanden, 1977, p. 240). We all encounter frustrations each day. The slow checker at the supermarket, the teacher who won't listen to reason, and the traffic jam that causes you to be late to a meeting are all frustrating in that they keep you from reaching a goal. Certain broad environmental situations also cause frustration: examples are urban strikes that cause public transportation to come to a standstill; high national unemployment levels that keep people out of jobs; or racial prejudice that blocks the ambitions of many capable people.

Consequences of Frustration Frustration is an unpleasant or negative experience, but it does not necessarily cause people to behave in negative ways. True, frustration can have unpleasant consequences: it often leads to anger, which may in turn lead to aggression (although this isn't necessarily the case, as we'll see in Chapter 7). Frustrations that affect large groups of people may lead to political instability or rioting, as in the race riots of the 1960s in our country. The broken windows, stripped cars, and pointless graffiti that can be found in virtually every American inner city area stand as mute testimony to the frustration of ghetto life.

Frustration may also have positive consequences, however. As evidence, consider your own responses to frustration. If you're a fairly good tennis player, but you just can't seem to beat your friend, your response will probably not be aggression, or depression (at least not at first!), but perseverance. The most common response to frustration is to "try, try, try again"—to rise to the challenge. Thus, frustration is a motivating force that often impels people toward greater efforts.

The power of this kind of positive response can be seen in many cases in which people distinguish themselves by putting forth an all-out effort to overcome physical, economic, or other barriers. One of the most famous examples of this is Teddy Roosevelt, a skinny, asthmatic child who spent much of his boyhood sick in bed. Determined to "make his own body"—since nature hadn't supplied him with much of one—he began exercising at the age of 12. He went on to become a mountain climber (he climbed the Matterhorn), a cowboy, a big game hunter, and a war hero as the leader of the famous Rough Riders in Cuba—as well as a political leader. "T.R." responded to his frustrating situation by compensating for it. But not all people respond in this way. What determines whether a person will try to overcome frustrations, or will respond instead by becoming destructive or depressed?

> **Frustration** Any interference with, or blocking of, the attainment of a goal.

Inner city scenes such as this stand as mute testimony to the frustration of ghetto life.

Frustration Tolerance   A number of factors influence *frustration tolerance,* the capacity to continue functioning during times of frustration (Allport, 1961).

One factor is our own goals and perceptions. As with other elements of stress, situations that are frustrating to you may not be seen in the same way by someone else. If you are a punctual person who hates to be late, a traffic jam will be much more frustrating to you than it is to someone who doesn't mind listening to the car radio and who isn't in a hurry.

A second important factor in frustration tolerance is thought patterns: can you put frustrations into perspective, or are you so annoyed that you focus all your thoughts on nothing else? Your cognitive patterns have a great deal to do with your emotional responses to frustration, and changing these patterns can be an important step in learning to cope with frustration. The box *Three Questions for Dealing with Frustration* presents some thoughts that may help you to use cognitive techniques to keep frustration in perspective.

A third factor in frustration tolerance is the accumulated experiences of the past several hours or days. If you've had several frustrating experiences already, you may find that even a minor incident is enough to make you lose control. This

Three Questions for Dealing with Frustration

We've all heard of counting to 10 when we are frustrated or angry. It is helpful to use a tactic like this to give a situation time to "defuse." Even more helpful, in frustrating situations, is to use a cognitive technique. Before you react, ask youself some questions:

- Why am I feeling frustrated? What is my goal and what is the obstacle?
- Is my feeling appropriate for the level of frustration found in this situation? Am I reacting to this situation or to prior frustrations?
- Are there alternative solutions? How can I reduce my frustration?

Can it really make a difference if you stop and consider these questions? Many students assume that such an exercise is too impractical, or that it won't make a difference even if they do go through with it. It does work, however. We can learn to change our thought patterns, just as we may have learned ineffective thought patterns as children. And changing thought patterns can help in dealing with frustration—for precisely the reason that cognitive psychologists tell us. Our responses to frustration are based on the way we perceive and interpret them.

phenomenon was noted by Freud, and it is often called the **hydraulic principle.** It describes situations where the combined frustrations of the day build up to a point where they finally erupt in angry release.

A fourth variable in frustration tolerance is partly a product of your upbringing. Can you remember how your parents or siblings handled their frustrations? As was pointed out in Chapter 3's discussion of the vicious cycle of child abuse, children often imitate the coping techniques of those around them, even in cases where they consciously don't want to.

> **Hydraulic principle** A principle that states that frustrations and pressure build up until they finally reach a point at which the individual must release them through anger. The final frustration may be mild, but because it is added to the pressures already accumulated, the reaction may seem out of proportion.

Your own childhood experiences, and not just the behaviors you observed in others, are also involved in frustration tolerance. People who face constant frustration during childhood may be discouraged or angry as a result; but too little frustration may also be harmful, for the child never has a chance to learn how to cope. It seems that some frustration is an important part of growing up, for it allows children to develop an emotional tolerance, an "ability to withstand the effects of negative emotions" (Hurlock, 1978).

Still other factors affect our ability to cope with frustration (Jourard & Landsman, 1980). Physical health is one: a headache, fatigue, or other aches and pains may make it much more difficult to tolerate frustration. An overall sense of competence and independence is also important: that is why it's so frustrating for many of us to be at the mercy of an auto mechanic when something is wrong with the car. A sense of meaning in life can also make a difference in the degree to which frustrations get us down, perhaps because the major goals seem so much more important than the kinds of situations that may be blocking them. One other factor in dealing with frustration is the ability to find a release for pent-up feelings. This factor will be discussed later in this chapter, as we explore ways of coping with stress.

Conflict

A second common element in stress is conflict. **Conflict** occurs when people are faced with two or more alternatives and must choose between them. We are called upon to make hundreds of decisions daily, and while we negotiate many of them easily, the cumulative effects can be great.

Kurt Lewin (1951) described three different types of conflict, each of which produces stress. These are the approach-approach situation, the avoidance-avoidance conflict, and the approach-avoidance situation (see Figure 5.1).

Approach-Approach Conflict   In the **approach-approach situation,** the person must choose between two pleasant situations. Should you treat yourself to the eclair on the menu, or to the world-reknowned mousse au chocolat? Or, let's see, a vacation in Tahiti, or should it be the French Riviera this year? (Or read another chapter of this book, or listen to your favorite tape?) Such decisions tend to be rather delightful, and therefore we may not take them very seriously. They can be stressful, however, since only one alternative can be chosen. This is one reason why many marital arguments center around the issue of how money is to be spent.

Avoidance-Avoidance Conflict   Far more conflict is likely to arise when both alternatives are unpleasant. The proverbial "frying pan or the fire" situation is the classic example of the **avoidance-avoidance situation,** but it takes form in many everyday choices. Should you stay home alone during the holidays, or spend them with people you don't like? Should you study for your math

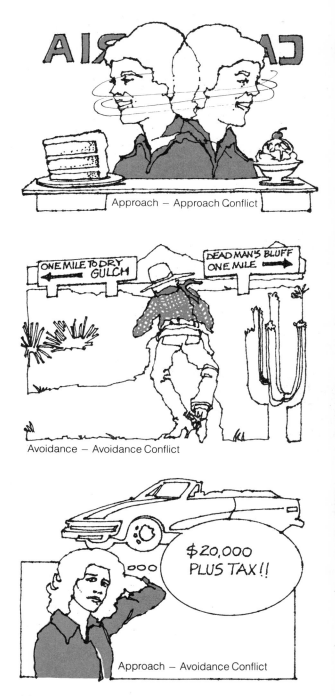

Approach – Approach Conflict

Avoidance – Avoidance Conflict

Approach – Avoidance Conflict

Figure 5.1   Three Classical Conflict Situations

test or do your household chores? In either case, a decision has to be made . . . even though there is a tendency to avoid the moment of truth until the very last minute. At that point, things are no easier, however—for the greater the time pressure, the more stressful are decisions.

Approach-Avoidance Conflict   It is unusual for alternatives to be either completely positive or completely negative. More often, they are a combination of both. These situations, called **approach-avoidance situations,** cause us quite a bit of consternation, and that is because this type of conflict includes a new element that is not present in the other two conflict situations. The same goal has both positive and negative qualities, and that makes the decision even more difficult.

Should you take a job in the photography studio? On the one hand, it's just what you've always wanted to do, and you think it will help you get a start toward your career. On the other hand, the pay is pretty bad, and the hours are inconvenient. Should you ask your friend for a cigarette? You want one so desperately you can taste it—yet you've resolved to quit smoking and you haven't had a cigarette for a week. In cases like this last one, the battle may be almost visible as your hand starts to reach out for the pack, then is consciously withdrawn.

A variation of the approach-avoidance situation is the **double approach-avoidance conflict.** This typically involves an either/or choice between two alternatives, each of which has both advantages and disadvantages. When you are offered that photography job, you may also have the opportunity to enter the family business. One has glamour and interest, but pays poorly; the other is not what you really want to do—but it offers security and a good income. Such decisions are often laden with stress and can cause many a sleepless night for some people.

Predicting Stress from Conflict   The level of stress resulting from any of these conflict situations will be closely related to the individual's personality. Some people tend to worry about decisions more than do others. However, there are also other variables that help us predict stress levels in conflict situations (Weiner et al., 1977). One rule is that the greater the attractiveness of the alternatives, the greater the conflict will be (and, in reverse, the more negative are the negative consequences, the more stressful the conflict will be). A second rule involves the number of alternatives in a decision. Simply put, the greater the number, the greater the conflict. In many of the situations detailed in our discussion above, only one alternative was given. This is not often the case in real life. There are literally hundreds of occupations, or colleges, or lifestyles, or whatever it is you're deciding upon—and the very fact that we have some freedom to make choices for ourselves all adds to the stress or tension we may feel. (Who else can we blame if we make the wrong decision?)

A third general rule in predicting levels of stress is the amount of time available in which to

---

Conflict   The state of being faced with alternatives and having to choose between them. See *approach-approach conflict, approach-avoidance conflict,* and *avoidance-avoidance conflict.*

Approach-approach conflict   A situation in which an individual is faced with two desirable goals or choices and must decide between them.

Approach-avoidance conflict   A situation in which an individual perceives both the positive and negative aspects of a goal or choice.

Avoidance-avoidance conflict   A situation in which an individual is faced with two undesirable goals or choices and must decide between them.

Double approach-avoidance conflict   A situation in which an individual perceives both the positive and negative aspects of two goals or choices and must choose between them.

make a decision. The closer you are to having to make up your mind, the more stress you are likely to feel. Thus, the last few days before choosing a job, or deciding whether to get married, or making virtually any other decision are usually the most difficult.

Pressure

A third factor in stress, *pressure,* is often related to conflict (although it need not be). Pressure refers to the demands from your parents, friends, school, employer, country, and even your own conceptions of what you need to do. These demands influence you to do certain things or act in a certain way, and cause you to feel guilty or uncomfortable if you don't.

Pressure is often external. Some environments place demands upon your body to cope with them. While the exact amount of stress they create is mediated by your own internal state and by your ability to cope with such stimuli, they are stressors in and of themselves. Noise, pollution, heat and cold, and disease all place demands upon your body. So do school work, logistical problems, and changes in your interpersonal environment.

Pressures may be caused by the external environment, but we also often put pressures on ourselves. You may put yourself under pressure to spend more time on an assignment than you need to because you want to get an "A." Or you may pressure yourself to train for a marathon instead of taking running less seriously, or to go into the office on weekends when it's not a necessary part of the job. In any of these cases, you are defining both your limits and your goals, and you are placing extra demands upon yourself to reach those goals.

We may create still another kind of pressure on ourselves, by waiting till the last minute to get things done. If you're due to pick up your date at 5, but don't leave your own home until 4:55, you will experience a harried trip cross-town. The same is true of waiting until the last night before

a final to study, or putting off packing for a trip until a half-hour before you're supposed to depart.

Deprivation

A fourth psychological factor in stress is deprivation. We saw in Chapter 2 that people are motivated to fill certain needs—for food, affiliation, stimulation, and so forth. The term **deprivation** refers to the sense of being without something a person needs. Deprivation brings on stress in that the person recognizes his or her need, and realizes that something must be done about it. The more severe is the perceived deprivation, the greater are the demands to cope with it. The more intense the demand, the more stressful the situation.

Of course, in order for this type of situation to be stressful at all, you must consider yourself deprived. Some people seem to need the company of others constantly, while others don't feel deprived at all if they spend most of their time alone. You may like to have everything organized ahead of time, while your friend prefers to "go with the flow," avoiding advance plans. If this is so, you will feel more stress in a hectic, disorganized situation than she will.

One of the most important needs we have is for security, a sense of stability and belonging in life. We take it for granted most of the time, but being deprived of security creates a great deal of stress. One increasingly common situation that illustrates this is divorce. The literature is filled with studies of the many stresses parents and children experience as a result of divorce proceedings (Gardner, 1976; Wolff, 1969). The divorced person is lonely, and life for a time is very disorganized. There is a need for social supports, which are often supplied through dating and group meetings with other divorced individuals.

Deprivation   A state of extreme need.

After the initial disorganization a new, more stable pattern often emerges.

Divorces are highly stressful for children as well. They are often exposed to many changes in a short period of time. They may be forced to move, to get used to a lower standard of living, and to cope with a one-parent family situation. However, children do cope with these situations, and recent evidence indicates that children's achievement levels drop more during the year before the divorce than the year that follows it (Santrock, 1972). In addition, if a new secure environment can be established and parents spend some extra time with their children, there is no reason why they cannot develop normally and cope with the stresses involved.

All of the elements we have been discussing—life changes, family tension, conflict, job role problems, and more—may have more than just an emotional effect. They also have a physical impact. Exactly what effect they have has been the subject of much theory and research. In the following discussion, we'll explore what we know about physiological patterns of response to stress.

The Body's Reaction to Stress

In moments of crisis my nerves act in the most extraordinary way. When utter disaster seems imminent my whole being is instantaneously braced to avoid it. I size up the situation in a flash, set my teeth, contract my muscles, take a firm grip on myself, and without a tremor, always do the wrong thing. —G. B. Shaw

> **General adaptation syndrome** A three-stage reaction to prolonged stress noted by Hans Selye beginning with *alarm,* continuing to *resistance,* and finally ending in *exhaustion.*
>
> **Alarm** The first stage of the general adaptation syndrome—the body's attempt to cope with stress. A series of physiological changes occur which maximizes the individual's ability to meet the challenge.

George Bernard Shaw's tongue may have been in his cheek when he made this statement, but he provides a good illustration of a few of the ways in which our bodies respond to stress. There are many vernacular or slang expressions to describe physiological responses to stress. "My heart sank," "I had butterflies in my stomach," "my mouth was dry," "my heart pounded in my head" are but a few of these descriptions, and most of us have experienced at least one or two or them. Psychologist Hans Selye has pioneered the study of how our bodies react to stress, and he suggests a much more precise description in his "general adaptation syndrome."

The General Adaptation Syndrome

Our bodies are constructed to react quickly to demands placed on them. They have evolved for rapid action, for survival can depend upon the speed and effectiveness with which we react. When our forefathers saw a bear coming toward them ready for lunch, their reactions had to be quick and certain. Their entire bodies had to mobilize automatically for the life-and-death struggle that would follow. Although having a dead battery, or preparing frantically for an important interview, or getting up to speak before a crowd of people may not be life-and-death situations, they are stressful and they call into play some of the same bodily reactions. Selye has identified a progression of responses to prolonged stress, which he calls the **general adaptation syndrome,** identifying three possible stages: alarm, resistance, and exhaustion (Selye, 1956).

Place yourself for a moment in the shoes (or skins) of our forefathers, just as the bear was coming toward them in the previous paragraph. You perceive the situation, naturally enough, as a threat, and immediately your body gears up for either "fight or flight." This **alarm** stage takes the form of several physiological reactions. Your adrenal glands discharge adrenalin into the body; heart rate increases; body temperature is reduced; and muscle tone increases. Your blood's clotting ability increases, as does the blood sugar level, and the acid level in the stomach rises as well. These changes in body chemistry enable you to put forth a maximum effort to defend yourself or flee, whichever need arises.

Most threats pass quickly, so that your bodily functions can soon return to normal. But what if the demanding situation persists? Perhaps your home life or work presents virtually constant emergencies, or perhaps you bring on your own problems in one way or another. Whatever the reason, there are times when your body is forced to enter the second stage of the general adaptation syndrome, **resistance.**

The glands, especially the pituitary and the adrenals, are called on in this stage to perform a different function. Hormones are diverted from digestion, and greater numbers of antibodies are formed. The metabolic rate rises and the body's sugar resources are consumed. In all, you might say that during the resistance stage the body uses its last reserves in the effort to function, despite the very heavy load placed upon it.

In the final stage of prolonged stress, the body fails in its attempt to adapt, and the state of **exhaustion** is approached. Our bodies were not made to continue in a mobilized state for very long. In fact, stress becomes dangerous when the body reacts after the actual situation has passed (Pelletier, 1977). The results can include a loss of energy, a numb inability to respond to the environment, and a general sense of giving up— scenes familiar to all of us who have watched newscasts showing survivors of tragic fires, earthquakes, or other disasters. The body is also vulnerable at this stage to illness, and the state of exhaustion may express itself in physical breakdown.

Physical Illness and Stress

It is estimated that 50-80 percent of all illnesses have emotional components and are stress-related (Pelletier, 1977). Diseases such as ulcers, colitis, migraine headaches, certain skin rashes, hives,

asthma, and high blood pressure, which often leads to heart disease, may all be related to stress (Lewis & Lewis, 1972). Some authorities believe there may even be an emotional component in cancer, although that is yet to be proven (Young, 1979).

Illnesses that are related to emotions or stress are often called **psychosomatic or psychophysiological disorders.** They all entail real organic damage and should not be confused with hypochondria. (A **hypochondriac** does not have actual tissue damage, but for some psychological reason creates and experiences various symptoms.) Psychophysiological disorders can be debilitating or even deadly. But why does one individual get ulcers while another gets headaches?

There is no simple answer to this question. It has been suggested, however, that stress-related illnesses may actually result from a combination of three components: *a biological predisposition,* or weakness, of one organ or system (for instance, an inherited tendency to produce too much of the

Resistance The second stage in Selye's general adaptation syndrome, in which the body uses its last reserves in an effort to cope.

Exhaustion The last stage of Hans Selye's general adaptation syndrome which describes an individual's response to prolonged stress. In this stage, some structure in the body begins to break down, causing illness and sometimes death.

Psychosomatic or psychophysiological disorders Illnesses that have been caused wholly or in part by psychological factors. Such disorders, which include ulcers and colitis, involve real physical damage to the body.

Hypochondriacal behavior A behavior pattern in which individuals create and experience imaginary symptoms.

Adapting to severe stress takes more coping skills than many untrained persons can muster, at least in the short run.

digestive enzyme pepsinogen might make a peptic ulcer more likely); a *psychological vulnerability,* so that the person may have trouble coping with stress; and the actual *state of being under a great deal of stress,* so that the person is physically vulnerable (Pierloot, 1979). Figure 5.2 shows how this interaction seems to work.

In this theory, stressful events or circumstances act as triggers, and the weakest organs are the first to show signs of stress. The analogy can be made to a chain: it will support pressure or stress only up to a certain point, but then the weakest link will break (Selye, 1979). Such a theory was put to practical use by Dr. Samuel Silver-

man, who made a name for himself by predicting the exact nature of former President Richard Nixon's illness following the Watergate scandal in 1973 (Colligan, 1975). Looking at Nixon's medical history of previous bouts of phlebitis and pneumonia, Silverman predicted the nature, course, and severity of the illness that plagued Nixon after he resigned from the presidency.

In the "weak link" idea, we can easily see how certain physical tendencies—muscle tension, a tic (involuntary muscle spasm), or an overproduction of digestive enzymes, for instance—could act up in response to stress. Another explanation of physical illness and stress explores a different connection: that between personality type and the kind of illness a person is prone to develop.

Stress, Personality, and Illness: The Type A Theory

There is a great deal of evidence that stress is related to some kinds of illness; also, that different people perceive different situations to be stressful. Given these two assumptions, is it possible that some personality types are more prone to illness than others? Or, even further, that certain personality types are prone to certain types of illnesses?

The question is an interesting one, and many theorists have attempted to answer it. Some have suggested, for instance, that the typical migraine headache patient is tense, ambitious, and obsessional, with a tendency to be perfectionistic (Henryk-Butt & Rees, 1973). Again, the stereotyped ulcer patient has been seen as a hard-driving go-getter who probably is not as self-assured and independent as he or she would like to be (Alexander, 1950).

Perhaps the most famous and well-documented examination of the personality-illness thesis is Friedman and Rosenman's research into the connection between personality type and coronary artery disease (1975; 1974). After many years of study, these researchers distinguished two personality types within the population. They labeled these groups "Type A" and "Type B," and they drew conclusions about their vulnerability to coronary disease.

Type A persons lead a hectic lifestyle. Time is a major factor in their lives, and they always seem to be in a hurry. Yet they also tend to overload themselves, taking on more responsibility than they need and imposing high expectations upon themselves. (As the box *Type A Personality and Marriage* suggests, this personality type may also be related to a more stressful home life.) **Type B** persons are calmer and not as time-conscious, and they take things more in stride.

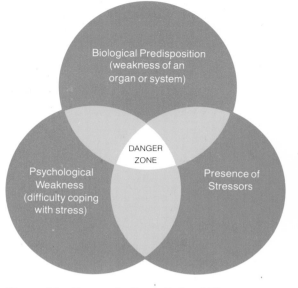

Figure 5.2   Factors in Stress-Related Illness
Source: Pierloot, 1979. Used by permission of Richard Suinn.

The Friedman-Rosenman findings show that Type A persons tend to have more coronaries, and that they have higher cholesterol levels in their blood (Rosenman et al., 1964). This last factor is related to coronary artery disease; exactly how it relates to personality type is not known.

What does it all mean? The research is intriguing—especially the Type A and Type B findings, which have received more corroboration

Type A behavior   A pattern of behavior marked by extreme time consciousness, competitiveness, and impatience. It has been related to a number of illnesses including the increased probability of heart disease.

Type B behavior   A pattern of behavior in which an individual tends to take life in stride, is easy-going, and is not very time conscious. Individuals showing this pattern of behavior are less likely to suffer from heart disease than are Type A individuals.

Up to this point, we have been discussing types of stressors as well as the psychological and physical components of stress. In this overview, we've attempted to understand what stress is and why it occurs. But one important question is still unanswered: What can we do about stress? We'll explore some answers to this question in the remainder of this chapter.

Adapting to Stress

People use many different strategies to cope with stress. Some withdraw; others attack the situation with a vengeance; still others simply surrender to the pressure. Many of us wish we could handle stress better. As testimony to this, literally hundreds of articles have been written in both popular and professional magazines suggesting ways to better handle stress. Many large companies have stress management courses and workshops for their employees, and some colleges offer noncredit courses in handling stress. The National Institute of Mental Health puts out booklets explaining stress and offering suggestions on how to cope with it. One of the recurring themes is the idea that we can control our own stress levels and improve our functioning through a program of self-knowledge, balanced activities, and a careful approach to limiting stress.

"Know Thyself"

A few centuries ago, William Shakespeare put words into Polonius' mouth as he gave advice to his son, who was leaving Hamlet's court: "This above all—to thine own self be true." He wasn't talking about stress reduction, but his words apply here as well. We often take on more than we can handle because we don't really know our priorities or because we don't recognize signs of stress in ourselves. To "know thyself," then, is a first important step in managing stress. It consists of un-

A Type A person in action. Such a lifestyle has been related to coronary artery disease.

than the studies of ulcer, migrane, and other personality types and illness. But a few words of caution are in order, even for the Type A and B findings. First, most people are difficult to categorize as simply one type or another. And second, just because Type A people have more heart attacks, this does not prove that the disease is caused by their personalities. The cause might be their physical make-up, genetic endowment, or perhaps some hidden factor. In all, though, the suggestion that certain patterns of behavior are related to some illnesses might make us look more closely at our own basic lifestyles.

Type A Personality and Marriage

In the past decade there has been a great deal of interest in the Type A personality pattern. Research has shown that the highly competitive, time-conscious workaholic is more likely to have a coronary than the easier-going Type B individual. Some evidence has recently suggested that this deep, total involvement in work may cause problems for the family.

With this in mind, Ronald Burke, Tamara Weir, and Richard DuWors, Jr. decided to examine the possible relationships between a husband's Type A personality characteristics and particular aspects of his marital relationship, including satisfaction.

They found 128 upper-level male administrators and 85 spouses who were willing to volunteer for this study. An assessment instrument specifically designed to measure Type A behavior was administered to the male subjects. Personality attributes specific to this type, such as time urgency, competitiveness, and persistence, were measured.

Wives were sent a questionnaire that contained items aimed at measuring a number of important elements of life, including life satisfaction, social participation, degree of social support in the environment, health habits, coping behavior and self-esteem, and the degree to which they saw their husbands' job as affecting the family. A cover letter asked these wives to fill out the questionnaire independently, informing them that all information would be kept confidential.

Results indicated that the husbands' Type A behavior was related to lower marital satisfaction and a feeling that the husband's job had a negative effect on the family. The wives of Type A men also reported more conflict in their marriage and tendencies to keep their problems to themselves and to experience anxiety and guilt. Wives recognized the husbands' Type A behavior, but they generally saw their husbands as showing more Type A behaviors than their husbands felt they did. It should be noted that not all the correlations were significant. Self-esteem and general life satisfaction were not correlated with the husband's Type A behaviors.

The authors concluded that there is a relationship between husbands' Type A behaviors and some marital and family problems. However, just what it is in this behavior pattern that may affect the marriage is still unanswered. Is it the pressure or loneliness of living with someone who is always at the job (even when he's home)? Is it the isolation caused by the lack of companionship or the feeling of being undervalued? There are probably a number of behaviors that may affect the marriage negatively. Whatever the reason for the problems, the authors of this study believed that Type A males should be made aware of how their behaviors may affect their families, and that their wives be given whatever help and support they require to cope with the stress that arises from their husbands' Type A behavior.

Source: Burke et al., 1979.

derstanding our own priorities, recognizing signals of stress, and understanding our personal responses to stress.

Finding Priorities　People are likely to experience more stress if they don't have a good under-standing of their own priorities. We've seen that both at home and at the workplace, it is easy to become overcommitted. Many companies give their employees more work than they can realistically complete, on the theory that work expands to fill the time allotted to it. Employees who try to complete all their assignments can undergo

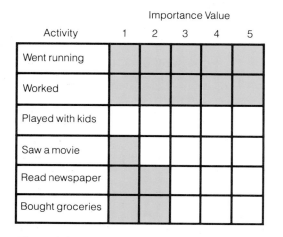

Activity	Importance Value				
	1	2	3	4	5
Went running					
Worked					
Played with kids					
Saw a movie					
Read newspaper					
Bought groceries					

Figure 5.3   Daily Activity List and Priority Rating

prolonged, excessive stress. In such situations, it is important to understand what you can do in the time you have to do it—and not to ask more of yourself than you can realistically expect.

People have other commitments besides those at work, however. Family, studies, friends, sports, or other involvements are all important and meaningful. It isn't hard to feel pulled in several different directions at once. How can people reduce the stress that comes from too many demands?

Figure 5.3 illustrates one exercise for evaluating priorities. After a particularly busy day in which you have felt yourself under a lot of pressure, list the day's activities. Then assign each activity an "importance value" ranging from one through five. Your own evaluations should give you food for thought. Why was one activity given a "3," while another received a "5"? Can you find any themes or patterns running through your choices? For instance, do you consistently value family over work, or vice versa, or is personal pleasure one of the least valued items on the list?

Another revealing part of this exercise is to estimate the relative time you've spent on each activity. Is it congruent with the importance you give to the task? Once you have a better idea of where your own priorities lie, you may be able to organize your day more closely around what is meaningful to you, reducing or eliminating activities that merely take up time.

Recognizing Stress   Another critical area of self-knowledge is to recognize when you are under stress. You might think this is obvious, but people are not always aware that they are experiencing stress. Note that this lack of awareness does *not* mean a person is coping well with stress. It may be building up, but goes unnoticed and unchecked because of prolonged and constant exposure.

Look for environmental stressors, and learn to avoid the avoidable. Noise, pollution, time pressures, lack of privacy and rest can all often be avoided or at least reduced—but only if you are aware of the part they play in your stress. Knowing your own stress level and your own limitations is an important part of any realistic assessment (Holmes & Masuda, 1972).

Watch for warning signs that the situation may be becoming too much for you. For some people, stress shows up in sleepless nights. For others, it shows in an inability to sit still. Other common symptoms are physical or mental fatigue; shortness of temper; vague feelings of depression; anxiety, apathy, or hopelessness; physical symptoms such as stomach aches, nervous tics, headaches, or backaches. Recognizing when you are under stress is a basic first step in taking some action to reduce it.

Knowing How You Interpret Stress   Recognizing stress and knowing your own priorities are important elements in "knowing thyself"; a third factor is understanding your own patterns of response to stress.

As in the relationship between physical illness and stress, people seem to be predisposed to respond to stress in certain ways. Perhaps you know someone who sees every change as a catastrophe and who always seems to be overwhelmed. These people have been labelled **sensitizers** because they are so sensitive to changes; they are likely to overreact to stressors and may develop a number of psychosomatic symptoms. In contrast are the **diminishers**—people who react in just the opposite way, downplaying their troubles and assuming there are virtually no limits to their ability to cope. There are problems associated with both of these types of response. The sensitizers are unable to cope easily with even the most minor levels of stress, while the diminishers bring problems on themselves by taking on more than they can handle.

In understanding your own responses to stress, look for evidence of either pattern. Of course, all of us have moments when we either overreact to stress—after an especially hard day, for instance—or when we bite off more than we can chew. Beyond this, however, you may recognize a tendency to either diminish stress or to be oversensitive to it. Recognizing your own patterns is important in learning to improve your responses to stress.

Taking Steps to Manage Stress

Knowing your own priorities and limits, of course, won't reduce the stress you are undergoing. It is also important to do something about it.

In managing stress, two broad strategies can be helpful. The first is most useful when stress cannot be avoided. It involves finding activities and outlets that can relieve or balance stress. The second strategy involves deciding which stressful circumstances you can change. We'll look at both.

Finding Relief   We all feel like getting away from it all at times. But often, the stressor itself is not something you can change. You may have a young child who is ill and needs care, or a parent who has unreasonable expectations of you despite your efforts to explain your point of view. Or you may be taking a course that is very difficult, yet you need it in order to complete your major requirements. In such cases, you may not be able to eliminate the stressor, but there are things you can do to help relieve your own sense of stress.

One of the most successful strategies for coping with stress is relaxation. We all know people who can't seem to balance work and play. Indeed, this characteristic is a major part of the "Type A" profile we talked about earlier in this chapter. We have also seen that stress tends to accumulate, and that the build-up of stress can cause both physical and psychological problems.

Both meditation and relaxation have been suggested as methods for stress relief; both have the effect of providing a breather and "letting the build-up die down." Goleman (1976) considers meditation an excellent stress reducer, and there are a variety of ways to practice this activity. Some of these are described in Chapter 15. In addition, some relaxation techniques, described in Chapter 6, are very helpful for many people. These procedures all work by counteracting the tension we experience when we are anxious, fearful, or stressed.

You don't need to consciously relax in order to provide yourself a breather from stress. Taking a walk, reading a book, or indulging yourself in a favorite hobby may provide a valuable change of pace; physical exercise is another way of burning off stress and giving yourself a sense of perspective on the emotions you've been experiencing. The degree of exercise, of course, is relative to your own physical condition. The point is that you consider yourself important enough to take some time off and do something for yourself. After a

Sensitizers   A pattern of behavior in which an individual overinterprets and overreacts to changes in the environment. See also the opposite pattern, *diminishers*.

Diminishers   A label describing a pattern of behavior in which an individual reduces the importance of changes in the environment.

"None of us is happy <u>all</u> the time, Farley."
Reproduced by special permission of *Playboy* Magazine. Copyright © 1971 by Playboy.

moderate physical workout, you may find yourself feeling better. In all of these areas, balance is the key. Some work, some exercise, some play, and some rest are essential to dealing with stress.

Talking with someone you trust may also help to reduce your level of stress. If you try to keep all your tensions and worries inside, you may find yourself staggering under the weight of them. Friends or counselors may have another point of view—or they may even have the same problem. Sharing problems or frustrations in this way is often a step toward "getting outside of yourself." Another way of doing this is to discover personally meaningful experiences outside of your own problems. This method of adjusting is often not

listed as a way of reducing stress, but it can be important, and it is emphasized by Selye (1976). Often, people who lose a spouse or other loved one will begin the slow healing process only by giving of themselves to some other person or cause. Giving of yourself not only provides time away from your own problems, it also puts your own stress in perspective.

Another way of reducing your feelings of stress is to adjust your own way of looking at it. Almost any situation can be more stressful than it needs to be, if you let yourself be threatened and overwhelmed. Here, we go back to the cognitive factors noted earlier in the box *Three Questions for Dealing with Frustration.* Instead of telling yourself

Part Two / Safety Needs

that you can't handle a situation, it is helpful to ask yourself how you *can* and to devise your own plan of action for dealing with the stressor. Step-by-step planning is helpful, because it breaks tasks or problems down into small enough parts so that you can control them. Four hundred pages of school work can be seen as 40 pages a week; a major progress report for the office can be broken down into several tasks such as collecting ideas, outlining, drafting, and revising. Such "bite-sized" chunks allow you to see the progress you're making, so that you feel a sense of satisfaction as you edge toward your goal.

Changing the Stressor   So far, the solutions we have discussed have all involved coping with situations that you can't change. There are many cases, however, where the stressor itself can be modified, or even avoided entirely. You may find that the solution to all your problems lies not in taking a relaxation break each day, but in quitting your job, finding another major, moving into a home that is far away from your current roommate—in other words, cutting yourself loose from a situation that you can neither change nor adjust to.

The question, of course, is how you can determine whether *you* need to adjust to the stressors, or whether you can control the situation. The answer is almost never in clear black-or-white terms. In fact, it is quite possible to make a wrong decision even after researching carefully and evaluating all the alternatives. (Have you ever read all the consumer reports on a car or appliance, made your purchase carefully, and still ended up with a lemon?) The truth is, not all the elements in decision making are within our control. A careful, methodical approach to decision making, however—such as that described in the box *A Model for Making Decisions*—can greatly improve the odds that your decision will be right for you.

We have come a long way since we looked in on the young Elvis at the beginning of this chapter. At some points, in fact, we may have seemed to be addressing quite a different topic than the sudden arrival of fame and fortune. But in looking back, virtually all the elements of stress we've explored (with the possible exception of the later stages of Selye's general adaptation syndrome) relate as much to positive as to negative stress. In each case, the individual has to find ways of coping—to regain the safety or security that Maslow identified as the second level in his hierarchy of needs. The same is true of anxiety, guilt, and depression, the emotions we turn to in Chapter 6.

Summary

1. Stress may be studied by at least three approaches. The first involves identifying the stressors that produce stress in an individual. The second involves the psychological and physiological reactions to these stressors, while the third investigates the fit between a person's ability to cope and the demands of the environment. This chapter looked at stress from each of these perspectives.

2. The individual's perception of a situation is an important mediator in determining whether a stress reaction will occur.

3. Stressors include life changes, relationships at home and work, and environmental conditions. Some home and work environments seem to have greater potential for producing stress than others. The structure of a job may bring heightened stress, if factors such as role ambiguity, role conflict, and role overload are present.

4. Situations that are frustrating, cause conflict, or involve feelings of deprivation or pressure are potentially very stressful.

5. The experience of conflict places great demands on the individual. Three types of conflict are approach-approach situations, avoidance-avoidance situations, and approach-avoidance situations. There is a greater potential for stress in conflicts in which the alternatives are either very attractive or unattractive, when there is a large number of alternatives, or if the decision to be made is a very important one.

A Model for Making Decisions

No single, foolproof method exists for making decisions. However, the following model may provide some helpful guidelines. It consists of five steps for decision making.

Step 1: Defining Goals and Limitations

The first step is to examine the nature of your goals and your limitations. You may need to buy a house, for instance. Your goal is plain, but the decision is complicated by utility and economic factors. How many people must live in the house? How many rooms will you need? How large a house can you afford?

In this case, your goal is frankly stated—to buy a house. But the decision might also be between buying a house, buying a condominium, renting an apartment, or living in a mobile home. The greater the number of alternatives, the more difficult the situation will be. Thus, you will first need to analyze your goals and limitations carefully.

Step 2: Generating Alternatives

The second step is to generate as many alternatives as possible. This is not always easy. There is a tendency to feel that if one choice is fairly attractive, there is little need to look for any others (Anderson, 1975). This artificial limitation, however, may narrow our attention and keep us from making the best choice.

One way to counteract this tendency is to *brainstorm*—to write down all the alternatives you can think of, ridiculous or not, without evaluating any of them. The important thing is to think freely and to get the thoughts on paper. This strategy is helpful both in individual and group situations—although it may actually be more important in some group situations, where there is a tendency to conform to the rest of the group. (This tendency is called "groupthink" by Janis (1972), who feels it has influenced many of the critical political decisions of this century.) To avoid this, the group should be reinforcing to those who disagree with others and be tolerant of different ideas.

Beyond brainstorming, another way of generating alternatives is to look outside ourselves to find out how others have handled similar situations. Speaking to people and writing down their options can be an important source of ideas.

Step 3: Evaluating Options

After listing all your options, including radical ideas, you are ready for the third step: evaluating your alternatives. One way to begin is to create a visual display of all your options. Write down each idea you have generated in Step 2, then list the positive and negative aspects of each. (One alternative that should always be on the list is doing nothing. The absence of action is a decision in itself and ought to be listed.) It may be helpful to assign a value to each positive and negative point. Some choices may have five negative aspects, all of which are minor; other options will have only one negative point, but it will be of enormous importance.

Four important questions should be asked during the evaluation process. First, what are the likely consequences of each choice? No one has a crystal ball that can predict the future, but a little bit of research may tell you that a job you're considering doesn't have a future, or that the apartment you want to rent is likely to be sold as a co-op in the next year. A second question is how your decision will affect your own long or short-term goals. Your own sense of direction—what you want to get out of your work days, marriage, or whatever else you're deciding about—is an important element to be considered (Tyler, 1961).

A third question is how much risk your decision involves. If a decision is risky, can it be reversed without great cost? You may not find it easy to change your career path after you've spent eight years at college and graduate school studying only one specialty. If you're not sure of what you want, it may be wise to keep other options open also. A final question is whether you can afford to search for the perfect alternative—the one with no negative consequences. In most cases, this doesn't exist: holding out for it simply makes a difficult decision more arduous.

Step 4: Noting Reappraisal Points

After you have gathered the alternatives and evaluated your options, you should be ready to make your decision. Not only that, but you should be satisfied that you have based your choice on strong grounds. Despite this confidence, though, you will want to be able to evaluate your decision later on. Most decisions are not simply made once and forever. Therefore, it is a good policy to plan ahead for reappraisal points.

Take, for instance, a decision to enter medicine or to buy a business. Before entering medical school or putting an investment into your business, you can stop and evaluate whether you still feel your choice is right; you may also plan a 1-year evaluation point, a 2-year evaluation point, and so forth down the line, where you consider how far you've progressed and whether you still feel as strongly about your decision. By planning such checkpoints ahead of time, you permit yourself the option to adjust both your actions and your goals at a later point.

Step 5: Evaluating Your Decision

Finally, the results of a decision must be examined. This evaluation is an easy and satisfying procedure if the decision has led to the desired goal. If it hasn't, however, this final step is especially important. *Why* wasn't it successful? If there was no realistic way of foreseeing the problems that arose, you know there was no defect in your decision making. Yet, if you find that you could have foreseen the problems, then you will need to evaluate your own decision-making process.

If conflict is a major cause of stress, it stands to reason that adopting realistic and rational decision-making strategies will reduce some of the pressure and stress you are experiencing. It can also provide you with a structure for decision making that will allow maximum flexibility, increasing your ability to make decisions that you can live with.

6. In general, people are physiologically able to react quickly and efficiently to demanding situations. However, the body cannot continue in a mobilized state for long periods of time. The general adaptation syndrome describes three phases in the physiological reaction to prolonged stress: alarm, resistance, and finally exhaustion.

7. Psychosomatic or psychophysiological illnesses are real organic disorders that are related to stress.

8. The relationship between personality, stress, and disease has been investigated. Although there are many exceptions, two personality types have been identified: Type A individuals are time-conscious, hard-driving, and serious; Type B persons are more relaxed. Type A people are at greater risk for developing coronary artery disease.

9. If you feel confident in your ability to cope with a situation, you are less likely to experience stress.

10. Coping with stress involves changing your perceptions of the situation, establishing priorities, and becoming aware of personal signs of stress. Such activities as relaxation, meditation, physical exercise, talking with others, and actively confronting a situation are also helpful.

11. Stress may also be reduced by improving decision making skills. A five-step process includes setting goals, generating alternatives, testing alternatives, making the decision and noting reappraisal points, and evaluating the decision.

Key Terms and Concepts

stress
stressors
role ambiguity
role conflict
role overload
frustration
hydraulic principle
conflict
approach-approach conflict
avoidance-avoidance conflict
approach-avoidance conflict
double approach-avoidance conflict

deprivation
general adaptation syndrome
alarm
resistance
exhaustion
psychosomatic (psycho-physiological) disorders
hypochondria
Type A personality
Type B personality
sensitizers
diminishers

Few of us like to feel anxious, guilty, or depressed. These feelings threaten our sense of well-being, making us feel insecure and ill-at-ease with ourselves and our environment. If we don't learn to cope with these feelings, they may stand in the way of fulfillment and personal happiness.

As unpleasant as these emotions are, however, they are also an unavoidable part of life. Everyone experiences them at one time or another. And while they are unpleasant, each of these emotions can also be seen as a challenge: if we learn to adjust to them, anxiety, guilt, and depression all provide opportunities for personal growth.

Anxiety, Guilt, and Depression

In a sense, you might say that this chapter deals with clouds and with silver linings more than any other chapter in this book. We will explore each of these "cloudy" emotions, investigating the associated feelings and their various causes. But we will also look at the silver linings, as we suggest ideas for coping with anxiety, guilt, and depression in ways that can help bring positive growth. We'll begin with anxiety.

Anxiety

Anxiety is defined as a feeling of foreboding that something negative is going to occur. It is a common emotion. All of us have felt anxious at some point, whether our anxiety is directed toward an upcoming change in life, an exam, or some other, less specific object. In general, anxiety can be distinguished by six qualities:

- The experience is similar to fear, horror, and dread.
- It is unpleasant.
- It is futuristic.
- It is accompanied by subjective feelings of discomfort.
- There are disturbances of bodily functions.
- The threat is not truly definitive—if it does have a specific focus, the emotion is out of proportion to it (Lewis, 1970).

> **Anxiety**   A feeling of foreboding that something unpleasant is going to happen. The object of the anxiety is vague and futuristic. It is differentiated from *fear* in that the object of fear is apparent and more immediate.
>
> **Fear**   An unpleasant feeling very similar to *anxiety*, but usually directed toward a definite object in the present.

Anxiety vs. Fear

Anxiety is very similar to another common emotion, **fear;** and indeed, the two are often confused. Both involve the same sort of emotional response and subjective discomfort, and both are unpleasant. Both are also accompanied by bodily responses. Frequent symptoms include palpitations of the heart, sweating, dizziness, nausea, cramps, trembling and weakness, and the increased urge to urinate (Linn, 1971). Shallowness of breath and a dryness of the throat are also common symptoms of fear as well as of anxiety.

The two emotions are not quite the same, however. While fear is directed toward a specific focus, the object of anxiety is often vague, undifferentiated, and uncertain. (Freud, in fact, had a label for fear that reflected this difference. In a three-part categorization of types of anxiety that we'll discuss shortly, he identified fear as "reality anxiety.")

A second distinction between anxiety and fear is their time orientation. As Figure 6.1 shows, anxiety is directed toward events that haven't yet occurred: it is futuristic. Fear, in contrast, is immediate. Thus, you might be nervous or anxious as you walk alone through the woods at night; you would be afraid if you suddenly hear footsteps coming toward you.

Avoidance and Escape from Anxiety

The sensations we associate with anxiety are almost all unpleasant, and so we try to reduce them as much as we can. We may escape anxiety in many ways. One way is through avoidance. Perhaps you're anxious about calling a friend to break a date: you're nervous about disappointing him, and you don't think you'll handle the situation well. Finally, you watch television and avoid the anxiety by keeping your thoughts focused on the tube—until it's too late to make your call anyway.

Anxiety
Frage

"There are wild animals
in these woods...
What was that noise?...
I wish I wasn't alone."

Figure 6.1 **Fear vs. Anxiety** *While* anxiety *is directed toward events that haven't yet occurred,* fear *is immediate.*

This type of avoidance is one of the most common ways of dealing with anxiety, and it is often so automatic that people may not realize they are doing it. You may elect not to take a class because you feel you won't do well in it, or you may avoid the beach because you don't think you look good in a bathing suit. Avoidance has a way of building up, however. Eventually, you may be avoiding not only the beach, but perhaps even your friends who enjoy going there.

Such a build-up, as we've seen, is typical of anxiety: the emotion is generally out of proportion to the situation that causes it. In some cases, you may actually feel anxious about feeling anxious, if you let yourself—as when you feel your stomach tightening at the very thought of how nervous you get when you speak in front of a group. The more anxious and fearful you become, and the more you tell yourself you'll be nervous, the more likely you are to actually be anxious during the speech.

Avoiding the situation is one way of reducing anxiety; alcohol and drugs are two other methods that some people choose. A person who gets drunk or high each night doesn't have to think about problems such as loneliness or being without a job. These escapes may easily become ways of life, as we shall see in Chapter 15, slowly incapacitating the individual.

One danger of all these "solutions" is that they become self-reinforcing. The person who feels relief each time she stays home instead of

One way of avoiding anxiety. The danger of such avoidance "solutions" is that they become self-reinforcing without ever resolving the problem.

going to the beach, or who consciously avoids any situation where he or she will be asked to speak in public, or who routinely takes a drink to calm the nerves, may actually be strengthening the avoidance response. The more often the situation is avoided, the harder it becomes to confront. This cycle of avoidance bringing on more anxiety may help to explain why the emotion comes to dominate some people's lives. We'll look at several other explanations of anxiety in the following section.

Explaining Anxiety

Larry was raised in a suburban county close to a major city. His parents had always shown a great deal of concern over their physical safety whenever they travelled into the city for a show or dinner. When watching the news on television, they would speak of the possibility that a person could be robbed or even killed in the city without anyone even seeing the assailant. As Larry grew, he began to avoid going to the city—or, for that matter, any out-of-the-way place, especially if he was alone. When he was forced to go for some reason such as a job interview, he would experience a feeling of dread that sometimes would begin days before the scheduled trip. He was constantly frightened at the possibility of being robbed anywhere, at any time. He would have periods in which his legs felt like rubber, his mouth was dry, and he felt faint. He could feel his heart pounding and his breathing become rapid.

Larry's case illustrates extreme anxiety that might even be diagnosed as a phobia, an irrational fear that interferes with a person's everyday functioning. How could Larry's fears and anxieties have developed to such an extent? The three major schools of psychology—the psychoanalytic or Freudian, the behaviorist, and the humanistic—each offer a different explanation for anxiety.

Freud's Theory of Anxiety Freud explained anxieties such as Larry's in symbolic terms. Such anxieties were merely the visible signs of fears or conflicts that are deeply rooted in the unconscious.

One of Freud's very famous cases, in fact, was of a young boy named "Little Hans," who had a phobic fear of horses (Freud, 1909). Freud saw this fear as resulting from an Oedipal complex. Hans feared his father's jealousy, was unconsciously terrified that his father would punish him by castration, and displaced this fear to a fear of being bitten by a horse.

This reasoning may seem convoluted and complex to us, but the symbolic connection can be seen more clearly in some other cases of anxiety. In Larry's instance, for example, it is not hard to see his fear of strange places as a symbolic acting out of the fears that existed in his home during his early years. Some other fears or anxieties may also be interpreted in this way. **Claustrophobia** (a fear of closed spaces), for instance, is often seen as an unconscious terror of being buried alive.

Larry's and Little Hans' anxieties are actually only one of three types of anxiety in Freudian theory: neurotic anxiety, reality anxiety, and moral anxiety (Nye, 1975). **Neurotic anxiety** involves unconscious impulses that we repress or disguise. We may fear that our desires will get out of control, causing us to do something for which we will be punished; or, as in Larry's case, we may fear that someone else will do something to us.

Reality anxiety, unlike neurotic anxiety, is focused on a real, immediate threat. It is close to our conceptualization of fear earlier in this chapter. **Moral anxiety,** the third type of anxiety, is similar to the sense of guilt we describe later in this chapter. Moral anxiety results from a violation of the superego's strictures. (Actually, people don't have to perform an action to feel guilty about it. Sometimes, just thinking about doing something is enough to cause guilt.)

In neurotic, reality, or moral anxiety, Freud recognized the feeling of anxiety as unpleasant. Because of this, he believed that each of us tries to defend ourselves against our unconscious impulses entering our conscious awareness. We do this, he explained, through the use of **defense mechanisms:** specific, usually unconscious adjustive efforts that are used to resolve emotional

Claustrophobia   A phobia involving a fear of closed spaces.

Neurotic anxiety   A Freudian term used to describe anxiety that arises from unconscious impulses that we attempt to repress or disguise.

Reality anxiety   A Freudian term used to describe anxiety that is focused on a real threat.

Moral anxiety   Anxiety that arises from a violation of one's conscience and is experienced as guilt.

Defense mechanisms   Unconscious and automatic adjustive efforts that are used in an attempt to combat emotional conflict and deal with such unpleasant emotions as anxiety.

conflict and free the individual from anxiety (Rowe, 1975). Many specific defense mechanisms have been identified: Laughlin (1970) lists a total of 22 major ones and 26 minor ones. Table 6.1 lists, defines, and illustrates some of the best-known of them.

All of the defense mechanisms have two qualities in common. First, they are unconscious. And second, they are automatically employed. That is, we use them without even realizing we're using them. The question that is often raised by students is whether these mechanisms are normal and healthy, or whether they are themselves signs of weakness or of problems.

Most psychologists consider defense mechanisms to be normal and natural ways of dealing with anxiety, as long as they are used selectively and occasionally. However, when a person continues to use these strategies for minor anxieties, a problem could develop. For example, constantly rationalizing (making up excuses) about why you can't quit smoking will only obstruct any efforts to really quit. And repressing unpleasant experiences won't make them really go away. (As we saw in Little Hans' case, in fact, Freud believed that such repressed ideas could give rise to very serious anxieties.) Thus, defense mechanisms, like so many other things in life, seem to be healthy only when "used in moderation."

The Behaviorist Approach to Anxiety   While the Freudians look to unconscious, hidden conflicts in their effort to explain anxiety, the behaviorists take quite a different approach. These learning theorists see anxiety as an acquired fear, a "learned fear reaction that is highly resistant to extinction and that may be evoked by diverse stimuli similar to those that originally were traumatic" (Mischel, 1976, p. 395). In other words, a learned or conditioned anxiety about one object may be generalized to other sources, just as we saw in Chapter 3 when little Albert's fear of rats spread to furry objects in general.

The learning theory explanation looks directly to conditioning as the cause of anxiety. When an event has had unpleasant consequences in the past, just the thought of its recurring may be enough to cause anxiety. Doing poorly on exams may start a cycle of anxiety, causing poor performance, which causes more anxiety, which causes poorer performance, and so on. This fear of exams is called *test anxiety,* and it is a very common problem. The box *An Explanation for Test Anxiety* looks at some findings that suggest why it might develop.

It is important to note that you don't have to directly experience negative consequences in order to feel anxious. You can also learn anxiety by watching, or by listening to others. This can be seen clearly in the case of Larry, mentioned earlier. After years of observing his parents' anxiety about venturing out to the city, he not only adopted these fears for himself, he also worked himself into such an unpleasant physical and mental state that each outside experience became a sort of self-punishment.

Table 6.1   Some Common Defense Mechanisms

Defense Mechanism	Definition	Example
Rationalization	Ascribing acceptable or worthwhile motives to behaviors, emotions, or thoughts that really have other motives	The fox in Aesop's famous fable, who decided the grapes were probably sour anyway
Displacement	Redirecting an emotion from an original object to a more acceptable substitute	The mother who has a hard day at work then loses her temper with the children at dinner rather than with the client who caused the problem in the first place
Projection	Attributing motives or feelings to other people that are really our own (although we may not recognize them in ourselves)	The feeling that a teacher doesn't like you, when it is really *you* who doesn't like the teacher
Compensation	Unconsciously striving to make up for a perceived or actual deficiency, either directly (in the same area as the deficiency) or indirectly (in a different area)	*Direct compensation:* the underweight adolescent who transforms herself into a stylish model *Indirect compensation:* the same adolescent who becomes a famous physicist
Reaction Formation	Acting in a manner directly contrary to your feelings	The person who feels drawn to drink but instead crusades against the "devil's brew"
Regression	The attempt to return to a more comfortable period of life	The adult who, upon turning 40, suddenly begins acting and dressing like a teenager
Repression	Blocking some event or feeling from awareness, so that it is forgotten	The person who can't seem to remember the name of an acquaintance she doesn't really like
Rechannelization	The energy generated by anxiety or anger is channeled into socially acceptable or creative pursuits	The person who finds a release for aggressive energy in archery or football

Sources: Rowe, 1975 and Laughlin, 1970.

We've seen that the behaviorist and Freudian theories explain anxiety in different ways. Still a third explanation is offered by the third major school of psychology, humanism.

Humanistic Explanations of Anxiety   To the humanistic psychologist, anxiety is a basic condition of human existence. In understanding why we all experience anxiety at one time or another, various theories look at a few universal conditions.

One of these conditions is free will. As you may remember from Chapter 1, humanistic psychologists emphasize the responsibility of each individual to make choices about his or her life. This responsibility is a great one, however, and an awareness of our own freedom and responsibility

An Explanation for Test Anxiety

Very few of us are completely calm, cool, and collected during an exam. It is normal to experience some anxiety, and in fact, some students experience so much *test anxiety* that it injures their performance and affects their grade-point averages. Ralph Culler and Charles Holahan looked at an interesting aspect of this problem: the relationship between test anxiety and study patterns.

Eight hundred freshmen enrolled in an introductory psychology course were rated according to a Test Anxiety Scale, and those scoring in the upper and lower 25th percentiles were noted. The scale was again administered two weeks before the end of the term, and only those students who again scored in the upper or lower quartile were used in the study. (The second administration was needed in order to be certain that these students were really test anxious, and not just reacting to the new situation of being in college for the first time.) During this second administration, students were also asked to complete a study habits scale. The final sample consisted of 65 high test-anxious and 31 low test-anxious subjects. The grade-point average for each subject was obtained at the end of the semester.

As was expected, the grade-point averages of the high test-anxiety group were significantly worse than those of the low-anxiety group. In fact, 29 percent of the high-anxiety group had failing grade-point averages.

How could this difference be explained? Interestingly, there were significant differences in study skills between the two groups. The low test-anxiety group possessed better skills than did the high-anxiety group. Study skills included not only the number of hours spent studying for each course, but the degree of cramming for tests, the number of classes missed, and the number of exams that were either missed or made up late. The high-anxiety group actually spent more hours studying than did the low-anxiety group, and there was a positive relationship between the number of hours studied and grades for this group. Perhaps, as the experimenters reason, high test-anxious students can compensate to some extent for their poor study skills by putting in more study hours. The investigators also argue that the lower scores of the high test-anxiety students in general may be due in large measure to their poorer skills—and not simply to their tendency to "freeze" on tests.

This study does not indicate cause and effect. It does suggest, however, that the differential performance of high and low test-anxiety groups may be due in part to differing preparation for their examinations. It is possible that the high test-anxious student is reacting not only to the pressure of the exam, explain the investigators, but also to the knowledge that he or she did not or does not know how to study. In the light of this study and others in the field, it would seem that the treatment of test anxiety should take the form not only of countering the anxiety itself, but of providing study skill training as well.

Source: Culler & Holahan, 1980.

Existential anxiety   Anxiety that arises from the necessity of dealing with choices that involve unknown consequences.

for our own lives may be a source of anxiety (Corey, 1977).

The anxiety that arises from having to make choices about the unknown is known as **existential anxiety** (Chaplin, 1975). To humanists, existential anxiety is not necessarily negative. On the contrary, it may lead to growth as the individual is propelled toward some type of change. Yet, it is easy to see that many people may have a tendency to avoid this anxiety by trying to create a safe haven. The "safe haven" isn't so safe, however, for two reasons. First, there is no absolute safety or security in life. And second, we narrow our experiences if we try to create the illusion of safety, for we prevent ourselves from growing and experiencing—just as Larry did in the earlier example. As in Larry's case, the very realization that we are limiting ourselves can be a source of anxiety.

Maslow did not discuss anxiety at great length (Arndt, 1974), but his concept of threat relates closely to a second humanistic view of anxiety. According to Maslow (1970), a threat is a danger to one's being needs—needs that involve self-actualization. Other humanists see anxiety as arising from broader sources. According to Rogers (1959), anxiety is caused by our inability to live up to ideals. In this view, there is a vital distinction between our *real self* (the way we actually perceive ourselves) and the *ideal self* (the way we would like to be). The ideal self develops through years of learning. Parents, friends, and society itself give us many "shoulds," which we incorporate into our ideals. The real self involves our subjective day-to-day experiences, and it often occurs that our desires, emotions, and impulses are at odds with our ideal selves. Anxiety results when there is a difference between these two. The greater the difference, the greater the anxiety.

The humanist, the behaviorist, and the Freudian views all recognize that anxiety can be an unpleasant experience, and that it can cause people to function less efficiently than they might otherwise. Is anxiety always a negative emotion, however?

Anxiety and Performance

The boxed discussion on test anxiety explored a common type of experience. Most of us have probably had an experience that is similar. During a test, an athletic competition, an interview, or some other situation in which we want to do our best, anxiety may have caused a poor performance instead.

It is true that anxiety can be responsible for failures. But it is also true that a little bit of anxiety often seems to help. Without some arousal and some challenge, people don't put forth their best efforts in many situations. If you didn't care whether you came in first or last in a race, would you really try as hard as you could? Anxiety is a common form of arousal, and there are few tasks that we can perform well in a state of total relaxation.

If a little anxiety seems to help, but too much anxiety causes problems, an obvious question is raised: How much anxiety is too much anxiety? This question has been the focus of a good deal of research, with the resulting **Yerkes-Dodson Law** (see Figure 6.2). According to this rule, the answer to this question varies with the situation, for each task has its own optimal level of arousal. For simple tasks, relatively high anxiety may be helpful. For example, if you want to improve the performance of an athlete in a sprint, more anxiety may be required. The optimal anxiety level for complicated tasks, in contrast, is relatively low. The more detailed and complex the thinking required by the task, the greater the chance that anxiety will interfere with performance. Complex tasks—such as a multiple choice exam or a calculus test—often require you to choose the required information from a large number of cues. If you are too highly aroused, you may find that you miss some relevant information, and don't do your best (Easterbrook, 1959).

> **Yerkes-Dodson Law** The psychological principle that links arousal with performance. For simple tasks, relatively high levels of arousal are optimal. For complex tasks, far less arousal is required for maximum performance.

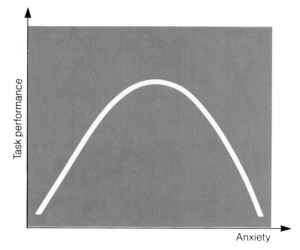

Figure 6.2   Yerkes-Dodson Law

Source: Reprinted by permission from Herbert Selg, Ed. "The Frustration-Aggression Hypothesis," *The Making of Human Aggression* (New York: St. Martin's Press, 1971), Figure 2, p. 26. Copyright © 1971 by Verlag W. Kohlhammer GmbH.

Anxiety can also interfere with learning and studying, especially if the material is new and complex. A little anxiety may be necessary to keep you studying those long hours—but if there is too much anxiety, you may find yourself reading the same passage over and over, unable to truly understand the material. Anxiety can also disrupt interpersonal relationships. If you are afraid to join a conversation, meet someone at a party, or speak out in class, your life is made a bit more difficult and less enjoyable. Bodily symptoms, such as blushing, shaking hands, or a tremulous voice can all add to the anxiety by making it more obvious to other people around you.

Because these kinds of behaviors can stand in the way of your own satisfaction and performance, it is useful to be able to control the tension and anxiety you feel. We'll look next at some ways to cope with anxiety.

Coping with Anxiety

There are many plans and methods for coping with anxiety. As with the stress management techniques discussed in the previous chapter, these strategies cover a broad spectrum, aimed toward both general and specific anxieties. Conditioning (teaching people to relax in response to an anxiety stimulus), meditation, psychoanalysis, group therapy sessions, and assorted plans for overcoming specific problems (such as learning to speak in public, or special training to develop assertiveness) are all included in this grouping.

For reasons of space, we can't explore every method for coping with anxiety. A few basic ideas seem to be especially important, however, and we can examine them from the standpoint of what you can do to ease your own anxiety.

If You Can Think Yourself into It, You Can Think Yourself out of It   Cognitive psychologists look to the role of thought processes in explaining anxiety. And for most of us, personal experience supports the idea that we can think ourselves into a state of anxiety. The more we worry and fret, the more anxious we become (Ellis and Harper, 1975). This process can also work in reverse, for it is possible to learn to use thought patterns that can help you to reduce your own anxiety. Here are a few principles that are basic to this process (Table 6.2 provides a summary).

First, learn to think out your feelings. Albert Ellis noted the importance of this step in a short book about overcoming the fear of flying on airplanes (*How to Master Your Fear of Flying*, 1972). According to Ellis, much anxiety arises from feeling that we ought to worry about anything that is even the slightest bit dangerous. This, of course, leaves the door wide open to anxiety about virtually any experience: crossing the street (you might get hit by a car); taking a more responsible job (you might fail); letting your children start walking to school (they might be kidnapped); and so on.

These worries may sound extreme to an outsider, but most of us have had moments when we've experienced similar anxieties. When this happens, it is helpful to think out the feelings upon which they are based. Are you really worried about being hit by a car, or about something

How much anxiety is too much anxiety? It depends. For complex tasks such as test-taking, high anxiety may interfere more than it does for simpler tasks such as running a race.

else that may happen to you outdoors? What is it that worries you about the new job? Perhaps it is the idea of change that makes you nervous, rather than specific fears about your own abilities. And again, your fears about the children getting kidnapped may actually center around far broader insecurities about their growing up and becoming independent. Recognizing the underlying causes of anxiety will help you find ways to deal with your fears.

A second step in thinking your way out of anxiety is to question the assumptions on which it is based. This process of questioning can take several forms. One is rational argument: is your

Table 6.2   Thinking Yourself out of Anxiety: Three Steps

Step 1	*Think out your feelings.* Does your anxiety have a direct focus, or are you really worried about something else?
Step 2	*Question the assumptions on which your worries are based.* Is your evidence real or imagined? Can you refute your own assumptions?
Step 3	*Prepare for the worst (if necessary).* If your anxieties are well-founded, prepare yourself for the possibility that your fears may materialize. Imagine ways you could still cope under these unfavorable circumstances.

anxiety based on real or imagined evidence? For instance, going back to the examples we just mentioned, what are the actual chances of your being hit by a car, or of your children being kidnapped? (Obviously, you can have some influence over these chances yourself, by looking both ways before you cross the street or by instructing your children how to deal with strangers—but we'll come to this point in a minute.) Again, do you really think that the new job is more than you can handle? If you think this through and realize that you have as many qualifications as anyone else, then your anxiety may automatically diminish. On the other hand, if you truly believe that the job isn't for you, then you may feel justified in deciding against the offer. In either case, a clear knowledge of the facts will help you cope with your anxiety.

Another part of questioning assumptions is called **disputing** (Ellis & Harper, 1975). This

Disputing   A technique used in rational-emotive therapy in which the client is asked to challenge his or her own assumptions that have led to self-defeating actions.

technique consists of taking the assumptions upon which your anxiety is based and arguing yourself out of it. For instance, you may be thinking "If I don't take that job, I'll never make anything of myself." This kind of thought can be the source of considerable anxiety, especially if you dwell on it. But it may also be contrary to the facts. What *will* be the consequences if you don't take the job? Most likely, the answer to this question is simply that another job will come along—and perhaps it will be one you're better qualified for. Much anxiety exists because people react to an inconvenient or unpleasant situation by exaggerating it to life-and-death proportions.

Of course, many of our anxieties are realistic. You may actually be in trouble in school, for instance; or you may have some very good reasons for suspecting that your job is in danger. While cognitive techniques may help ease some symptoms of anxiety, the most effective strategy in this type of situation is to do something about the problem.

Countering Anxiety   There are many times when people can deal with anxiety by resolving a problem or making a decision. As an example, you may want to continue your studies in a certain field, and to do this, you need to go to graduate school. Like applying to colleges, most people find it hard to go through the process of deciding on prospective graduate schools, interviewing, and putting their life goals into words on a written application. From beginning to end, the ordeal is a trying one for almost everyone. How can the anxiety be reduced?

The best way to counter anxiety in this situation illustrates the same strategy that can help to reduce anxiety in many other situations. It is also similar to the problem solving methods discussed in Chapter 5. First, *research* the situation in as many ways as possible. Look into graduate schools, to narrow the choice to those schools that fit your goals best. This way, you won't make the mistake of applying to the wrong schools. At the same time, talk to other people who have been (or are currently) in your situation. It helps to know that others have lived through the same experience—and in addition, they may have some helpful advice.

Once you've gathered your evidence and made your decision, the second step is to *act on it*. Attack the problem: do your best as you prepare your applications, using the information you gathered in your earlier research.

Finally, once you've done all you can, relax. Worrying about the inevitable won't make matters any better, so at this point, the most productive thing you can do is to *not* worry. This isn't always easy, but two techniques that can help are distraction and relaxation. Distraction can take many forms: turn on the TV, visit a friend, focus your attention on another task you have to do. Use whatever activity works best for you. The second strategy, relaxation, is also helpful, especially if you need to calm your nerves before an interview, an exam, or some other situation in which you will need to do your best. A few relaxation techniques are described in the box *Some Ways to Relax*.

In all, there are many different ways to deal with anxiety, and each individual must choose among the research, decision making, and relaxation techniques to find the methods that are personally most effective. You may find that while you do your best research by talking with other people, your friend may gather information by reading; or that the progressive relaxation technique that helps you just doesn't work for some other people you know. One way of finding out what approaches are most successful for you is to go back to some anxiety-provoking situation in the past and ask yourself what you said or did to get yourself through it. If you continually monitor your strategies, and perhaps try new ones, you will be able to develop a set of methods that works especially for you.

One type of anxiety stands out from all the rest as a common feeling all of us experience. It is of special concern to psychologists and deserves to be explored here. This anxiety is the way we feel when we have done something wrong. We call this anxiety **guilt.**

Guilt

What prevents us from lying, stealing, cheating, using other people, or generally disobeying society's rules? The first answer that comes to most people's minds is the fear of being caught. But the answer is more complicated than that. Few of us go through red lights even at three o'clock in the morning when no police are watching. If everyone disobeyed the rules of society, there would be no way society could punish all the offenders.

A more accurate answer is probably that our moral training and our anticipation of guilt feelings "keep us honest." When we do behave contrary to our internalized standards of right and wrong, we feel guilty.

Guilt is a form of anxiety. In fact, as we saw earlier, guilt is sometimes referred to as moral anxiety. You are apt to feel guilty when you violate some accepted standard of behavior. These behavior standards are learned through the same process of socialization that teaches us to dress as we do, sleep in beds instead of on the floor, and to carry our belongings in bags or cases rather than balancing them on our heads in baskets. When we behave in a way contrary to these behavior standards—by hurting someone's feelings or committing some other transgression—the result is often a sense of guilt.

The process of socialization isn't hard to understand, and we've already discussed it in Chapter 3. But how can we explain the sense of worthlessness and self-condemnation that are so characteristic of guilt?

Explaining Guilt

As with anxiety, there are several different ways to explain guilt. Here again, the psychoanalytic

> **Guilt** Feeling of disappointment or sadness due to a real or imagined violation of internal standards of conduct.

Some Ways to Relax

"Calm down." "Take it easy."

These instructions are often easier said than done. Even when we know that worrying will accomplish nothing, most of us find that we can't always relax when we want to. Several techniques have been developed to help people relax; two of the most useful are **progressive relaxation** and **imagery.**

Progressive Relaxation

To practice this form of relaxation, sit in a comfortable chair with your eyes closed. Emery provides instructions:

Take a few deep breaths and begin to feel yourself let go. . . . Now, extending both arms straight out clench your fists more and more tightly. . . [and] count up toward 5, ... 1. . . . . 2. . . . . 3. . . . . 4. . . . . Relax. Just let your arms drop wherever they will and begin to appreciate the difference between the feelings of tension, which you felt a few seconds ago, and the feelings of relaxation in your hands and arms now. . . . (Emery, 1969, p. 270).

This exercise is just a start. Progressive relaxation repeats the same tensing and relaxing pattern in several major muscle groups in the body, from the arms, to the forehead, to the eyes and nose, to the mouth area, to the shoulder muscles, to the back, to the stomach, thighs, and finally the legs. When each muscle group has been tensed (but not to the extent of pain) and relaxed, the subject counts backwards from 5 to 1 and concentrates on the returning feeling of energy. Emery suggests that this exercise, which takes about 13 minutes in all, can be repeated a few times a day. It may be especially helpful right before an anxiety-producing situation.

Imagery

While progressive relaxation is effective, it is not practical in some situations. It may be impossible, for instance, in a crowded elevator or in an exam room. Imagery provides another, less complicated technique that provides a shortcut to relaxation for some people.

To begin, close your eyes and fantasize a scene that makes you feel comfortable. For some people, this may be a beach in July with no one around; for others, a mountain scene in the Rockies. For still others, it may be flying effortlessly through the air (no one said the scene has to be real). Include in your scene as many details as possible—smells, sounds, sensations such as the feeling of the sun on your back—as well as visual details such as the appearance of the waves, birds flying overhead, and so forth.

Now become aware of your breathing. Breathe slowly at a rate of about six to eight breaths per minute. As you do, let your muscles relax and become aware of the feelings of warmth you experience as you imagine the sights, smells, sounds, and feelings of your scene. You should feel more relaxed within a very short time.

The key to both progressive relaxation and imagery is to do what works best for you. If playing soft music helps, use it. If there is a special place in the house where you relax most easily, either go there or try to imagine it. And finally, if you find that relaxation doesn't come easily the first few times you try these techniques, don't give up. Use your own knowledge of the images and sensations that are most comfortable to you to gradually develop your own version of these relaxation techniques.

(Freudian), the behaviorist, and the humanistic explanations each offers a different perspective.

The Freudian View: The Superego and Guilt

We saw earlier that Freudian theory considers guilt to be a form of anxiety—moral anxiety. It results from the workings of the *superego,* which acts to influence the *ego* and counteract the power of the *id* (see Chapter 1).

We aren't born with a superego. Instead, it develops gradually as we incorporate the rules of our parents and our society into our own framework. The do's and don't's come from the superego. The superego also makes us feel guilty if we transgress the rules or standards we have learned.

Learned Avoidance: The Behaviorist Explanation

Learning theorists explain guilt in a different way than do the Freudian theorists. They see guilt in terms of the anticipation of negative appraisals from others (Mowrer, 1960). Throughout our lives, we have learned that certain behaviors are punished. Eventually, we learn to anticipate punishments when we act in these ways, and thus we learn to avoid the punishment. If we go ahead and transgress the rules anyway, we feel that we deserve to be punished.

Behaviorists see guilt, then, as anxiety over anticipated punishment, and many behaviorists even shun the term *guilt.* Instead, they concentrate on investigating behaviors that may be associated with self-punishment or with the avoidance of particular behaviors (Bandura & Walters, 1963).

For example, behaviorists are interested in the effects of punishment on the development of avoidance behavior. In an interesting study, Aronfreed (in Gergen and Gergen, 1981) had a group of boys verbally admonished for touching toys while they were in the act of reaching for them. Boys in another group were punished after they touched them. Aronfreed then placed the boys in a room with toys and instructed them not

to handle the toys. Aronfreed found that the boys that had received the punishment prior to touching the toys were less likely to disobey the experimenter than were the boys that had been punished after touching them. Perhaps these children associated punishment with the first tentative steps toward misbehavior, and the anticipation of punishment served to deter them from even starting to misbehave.

Operant conditioning and social learning theory are used to explain how we incorporate morality into our behavior, through rewards and punishments and through socialization. Of special importance here is observation learning or modeling, for as many childhood lessons about right and wrong come from watching others as from direct operant conditioning.

The Intrinsic Conscience: The Humanistic View

The humanistic view of guilt shares some features with the Freudian view, in that it also sees the conscience as a set of internalized "shoulds" that we learn from those around us. But in the humanistic explanation of Abraham Maslow, this is only half the story. Maslow sees the conscience in even broader terms, and he calls it the **intrinsic conscience.** This he defines as "our conscious and

---

Progressive relaxation A form of relaxation training in which the muscles are slowly tensed, then suddenly relaxed throughout the body.

Imagery A relaxation technique in which the individual fantasizes a scene that makes him or her feel comfortable (for instance, lying in the sun on the beach), while breathing slowly and letting the muscles relax.

Intrinsic conscience A term used by Abraham Maslow to refer to one's own perception of his or her potential or destiny. If an individual does not strive to reach this potential, says Maslow, he or she experiences guilt.

preconscious perception of our own nature, of our own destiny, or our own capacities, or our own 'call' in life" (1968, p. 7).

The intrinsic conscience encompasses not only the behaviors we learn from society, but also our own perception of what we can and should do with our lives. Not living up to your potential can be a source of guilt in a similar way that doing something wrong causes guilt.

This type of guilt is often difficult to understand in the abstract; an example may help. The author knows of a young man whose parents encouraged him in piano study throughout his childhood, and who eventually began writing his own original compositions. When he decided he wanted to study music full time, instead of finding a more secure career, his parents objected until he finally gave up piano and became an engineer. Several years later, he began to feel anxious and depressed and experienced other feelings that he could not explain. After meeting with a counselor, he realized that he still yearned for music, and that this was the source of his depression. He is now back in college part-time, studying music and embarking slowly on a second career: composing.

The anxiety this young man felt illustrates Maslow's broad idea of guilt. But the humanist view, like the Freudian and the behaviorist views, also sees guilt as arising from violation of behavior standards or rules. These values or standards are worth closer inspection, for they vary from person to person and they also change within each of us over the course of development. As a result, each person's conscience is affected by growth and change.

The Challenging and Changing Conscience

"Children should be seen and not heard."
"Children should not talk back."
"Children should say 'please' when they ask for something, and 'thank you' when it is given to them."

We are all acquainted with this list: it goes on (and on) with many variations from one household to the next. It represents a set of ground rules that many families establish in order to impose some sense of order at home. And to one degree or another, most children internalize these rules so that they eventually control their own behavior.

However, we don't expect all the rules we learn in childhood to remain unchanged throughout our lives. As adults, we understand that other phrases can be used besides "please" and "thank you." We also realize that disagreements with other people are inevitable at times, and that you may sometimes need to talk back in order to defend your own position. We still may feel some sense of guilt if we violate some of these childhood codes. That is because our moral system has not been discarded, it has only been modified. But an important part of development has to do with the shift of moral codes and values from external to internal bases.

This pattern of moral development varies from one person to the next. Some people seem to be unable to modify their behavior standards, so that even as adults they feel guilty over even slight transgressions. This overcontrolling conscience can get in the way of experiencing and growing. For other people, a conscience never seems to become established, and this also causes problems. We'll look at both these conditions below.

The Too-Rigid Conscience Having a conscience serves an important function for both individuals and society, for it protects us from harm that we could all inflict upon one another. Although a conscience is a good thing, too strong a conscience is *not* necessarily beneficial. This is true for a few reasons.

For one, excessive worry about whether our actions are right or wrong can keep a person from the experimentation that is necessary for growth and change. People who feel guilty about gratifying even reasonable personal wishes cannot experience very much pleasure in life, and this can cause both personal and relationship problems.

For example, most of us learned during adolescence that it was "wrong" to have sexual relations with a boyfriend or girlfriend. But as people grow older, it's not uncommon to experience at least one relationship in which sex seems to be a natural way of expressing intimacy. The pull between desiring sex and feeling guilty about it presents many people with a classic approach-avoidance conflict. Each of us has to make the personal decision of whether the behavior is "right" or "wrong," and at some point, most people decide to share sexual intimacy. If a person adheres too strictly to the idea that sex is "wrong," however, this behavior may bring a sense of guilt even after marriage. In this case, a too-rigid conscience may not only prevent the person from enjoying sex, it may also cause very deep problems in the relationship.

Another problem that a too-rigid conscience can bring is a general sense of disappointment in oneself. By setting personal standards too high, many individuals stack the cards against themselves. All of us are fallible, but a person who expects to be an exception is bound to feel disappointed and guilty. Feelings of unworthiness may be one cause of depression, as we will discuss in the final section of this chapter.

A third problem associated with an excessive conscience is sometimes called **neurotic guilt** (Knight, 1969). Here, the individual feels guilty simply for thinking bad thoughts, without having actually violated any standards of behavior. A frustrated father may feel overwhelmed with guilt after a momentary impulse to hit a fussy, whining child, for instance; or a student may be mortified to realize that she wanted to flirt with her roommate's boyfriend. The problem in both these situations lies not in realizing that the act would have been wrong, but in equating the thought with the deed. The two are actually quite different; it is important to realize that many momentary impulses are natural, but in the end, it is our self-control that determines how we behave.

Sexual expression is a vital part of love relationships. However, because many people in our culture are taught to believe that sex is "wrong," it is also a frequent source of conflict and guilt.

Neurotic guilt　The guilt an individual experiences when he or she equates forbidden thoughts with forbidden actions. In such cases, a person may feel guilty simply for thinking "bad thoughts."

In all, a rigid, perfectionistic individual who equates intent with action has a great problem in coping with moral anxiety. Rather than aiding growth, too strict a conscience often hinders it. One way to soften this rigid conscience is to look at your standards and the reasons for your "shoulds." Why do you think a particular action is wrong? Why must you be so perfect? The idea is not to eliminate a conscience, but to modify it in order to live a normal life without constantly experiencing unnecessary guilt.

The "Soft" Conscience It seems to be popular today to deal with the too-strict conscience as an obstacle to personal growth. It is also important to note that the other extreme brings problems, too.

People who seem not to profit from experience, have little or no concern for others, show a lack of emotional maturity, and generally seem unreliable have a defect in conscience. In extreme cases, as when an individual experiences no guilt even after committing terrible acts, this person might be called **psychopathic** or **sociopathic.**

Just as there are some techniques for modifying an overly strict conscience, there are some strategies that may help to strengthen a soft conscience in some cases, especially where the individual is still relatively young. The most effective seems to be the use of a **role model.** The individual is encouraged to enter into a uniquely personal relationship with someone he or she respects. This model can sometimes show the desired behaviors, which the client can then imitate. A baseball coach, teacher, boss at work, or a number of community activists may serve as good role models. The model need not be a professional counselor.

Another method is to teach **consequential thinking** to the individual. Often, people with an underdeveloped conscience do not think of the long-term consequences of their activities. For example, what are the consequences of stealing a car? Or, on a smaller scale, of lying to your friends, who may soon stop trusting you? Teaching people to think through their behavior and to delay immediate gratification may be of some help.

Coping with Guilt

When people do something that causes them to feel guilty, there are many ways in which they can cope with their feelings of guilt. Not all of these coping behaviors are equal, however, from the standpoint of personal growth.

As an example, imagine that you have done something that hurt someone else. Perhaps you kept pouring drinks for a friend at a party, and that friend had a crippling car accident on the way home as a result. Or perhaps you had a weekend fling with someone you met at a party, and your partner, whom you love very much, found out. In situations like these, it is impossible to undo the damage that you've done; what's worse, your guilt is compounded by the knowledge that you could have prevented the mistake from happening in the first place. How can you cope with the sense of guilt that you feel?

Defense Mechanisms One common way of coping with guilt is through the use of defense mechanisms. You may unconsciously downplay your role in the deed through rationalization ("Everyone makes mistakes sometimes, and besides, I wasn't myself that night") or displacement ("He was the one who did the drinking—he should have told me he'd had enough") or any of

---

Psychopathic (sociopathic) A term used to describe individuals who experience no sense of guilt about performing antisocial actions.

Role model An individual who serves as an example for another individual to imitate.

Consequential thinking The process by which an individual considers all the consequences or possible results of a behavior before performing that behavior.

---

the other defense mechanisms discussed earlier in this chapter. Defense mechanisms may help you cope as they reduce your sense of unease. However, they don't make the victim feel any better, and they may not prevent the same situation from happening again.

Confession   Some people gain comfort in the act of confession, by talking out their guilt with the person they have hurt or with others. Talking it out and getting things off your chest may help you feel better, both in cases where others know what you did and where nobody else knows. The importance of confession, of course, was recognized long before the field of psychology of adjustment first appeared: many religions ritualize it as a vital step in absolving guilt.

Reparation   A third way of coping with guilt is through reparation, trying to make up for the damage done. You might bring flowers to your partner or buy some other present in an effort to show that you really do care in spite of what you've done. Or if your friend is laid up in the hospital, you might visit every day and also take care of the vacant apartment as a step toward reparation. In some cases where personal injury is involved, of course, reparation is forced upon the guilty party by a lawsuit.

Defense mechanisms, confession, and reparation may all make it easier to live with your guilt becauses they serve to reduce anxiety. Yet none of these behaviors necessarily causes you to grow, nor will they prevent the same thing from happening again. Defense mechanisms merely cover over a mistake. Confession brings a person to own up to a mistake, but goes no further. (The famous Russian novelist Fyodor Dostoevsky, a pathological gambler, lost all of his wife's money several times, confessed contritely each time, and then gambled it away again as soon as they had amassed some more wealth.) Reparation goes a step toward making things easier for the party that has been wronged, but it still doesn't necessarily bring personal growth. A parent who hits a

Confession is one coping strategy that may help the guilty person feel better. But does it prevent the same mistake from happening again?

child, then feels so guilty that she goes out and buys a present to make up for it, is probably no less likely not to do the same thing again.

Introspection: Guilt and Growth   There is another way of coping with guilt. This method is more difficult, but it can actually enhance growth and help prevent the same mistakes from repeating themselves. Coping positively with guilt involves a detailed, introspective look at both your behavior and your value system. Often, we try to avoid this coping behavior, because soul-searching is painful. Yet, if people take the time to integrate their experiences into a step toward growth, they might be able to modify their standards and values. This can serve as a means for changing future behaviors. The box *Growing from Guilt* outlines how this may be possible.

In this chapter, we have considered negative

Growing from Guilt

It is unusual to look at guilt as an opportunity for growth. Most of us see guilt as a negative experience, in which self-punishment or confession can, at most, allow us to return to the self-evaluation we held before we transgressed. In fact, it is possible to deal with guilt in a way that can allow not just a return to our "old selves," but tremendous personal growth. There are three broad steps in this process.

Evaluating Your Standards

The first step involves looking at and evaluating your own personal standards. These standards reflect your beliefs, attitudes, and values, as well as your background. Some people rigidly adhere to narrow moral standards laid down in childhood and never really question them. However, growth requires questioning. Are the rules that you broke necessary? Are your moral standards too strict or too easy? What do *you* want to stand for? Can you accept the fact that you are not perfect?

Taking Responsibility

After you have examined your moral standards, reworking them if necessary, the second step is to take responsibility for your actions. It is a common practice to blame others for an event that you played a part in. You might even blame your parents for teaching you to behave in a certain way or for bringing you up in a poor environment. Taking responsibility for your behavior means accepting the consequences of your actions. It also implies that you have had a choice and will continue to choose your own course.

Changing Your Behavior

The third and most important step is to consider the personal consequences of guilt—that is, the effect that guilt has on your future behavior. If all you do is call yourself names, your situation has not changed: no growth will take place. In order for you to grow, two actions are necessary. The first involves making whatever reparations are necessary, to make things as "right" as possible for the party you have hurt. The second is to change your behavior, so that you won't commit the same action in the future. If your behavior standards are reasonable and moral, and if you act according to these standards, you will be able to function capably, enjoy life, and stand for something all at the same time.

Working through guilt in this manner can lead to positive action, with positive consequences. This three-part process of coping with guilt can help you in becoming a more consistent, happier person, with less guilt and anxiety in your life.

feelings such as anxiety and guilt as signals that something is wrong in the relationship between ourselves and our environment. We've seen that while both anxiety and guilt are unpleasant experiences, each can become a catalyst for personal growth, if we learn to cope positively with these experiences. However, positive change is not easy. If we don't rise to the challenge, stressful experiences such as anxiety and guilt can also have negative consequences. One of the most important of these is depression, which we'll examine in the remainder of this chapter.

Carl was 30 years old when he first visited a therapist. Depressed, lonely, and apathetic, he had reached the end of his rope. He had trouble getting up in the morning, and he would spend entire days in bed, watching television and barely remembering to eat. The longer he remained in this state, the greater his inertia grew and the more depressed he became. Fortunately, a friend pulled Carl out of his depression by making an appointment and driving him to a therapist's office. Had he not made this effort, it is difficult to guess how long Carl might have continued in that state.

Carl's story is not unusual. Each of us has probably experienced some degree of depression, although hopefully not as great as Carl's. We may have lost someone or something, or felt disappointed in our performance on some task, or felt helpless to change something in our environment. Simply stated, **depression** is defined as a "feeling of sadness, loneliness, dejection, or hopelessness" (Rowe, 1975, p. 262). A long list of feelings go hand-in-hand with depression, including sadness, self-blame, apathy, unhappiness, dejection, and listlessness. Other symptoms include reduced hunger and sex drive and sometimes difficulty sleeping. There is an overall lack of motivation, so that the person makes little effort to help lift the depression.

Most of the time, depressions are temporary. Law (1978) estimates that 90 percent of depressions end within 30 days to 6 months. However, for that time, we exist in an unpleasant world that may prevent any positive adjustments toward personal growth. Of course, extreme depression may have even more serious consequences. Approximately 15 percent of severely depressed persons attempt suicide (Arieti, 1959). Of these, 15 percent succeed, with the success rate highest among white males, especially during retirement years. Figure 6.3 illustrates the relationship between race, age, and suicide rates in the United States.

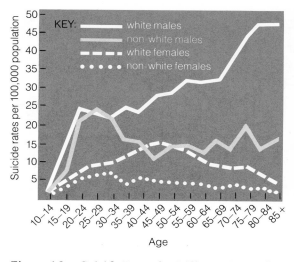

Figure 6.3   Suicide Rates for Different Age and Population Groups

What Causes Depression?

What causes people to become depressed? Many factors seem to be involved, including loss, anger, helplessness, negative self-talk, a lack of pleasant experiences, and even, in some cases, success itself. We'll look briefly at these factors, then at some possible ways of avoiding or relieving depression.

Loss and Separation   Freud emphasized the connection between the loss of a loved one and depression. This observation is fairly well accepted today. The object of the loss, however, does not have to be a person. It can be a material object, such as a home or a car. It may also be less tangible—as when a career or a reputation is lost. Loss can also involve a separation from something

> **Depression**   A feeling of unhappiness, loneliness, or dejection that tends to lead to inactivity.

Each of us experiences some depression at times.

or someone: this is one factor in the depression that sometimes follows a divorce. Homesickness is another example of this. When separated from the people we love, most of us feel a certain amount of unhappiness.

Of course, the nature of the attachment is important. You may be glad to get away from home, or you may miss everything about your home and family. Your reactions will depend considerably upon factors such as your own affiliation needs, your relationship with the person from whom you are separated, and the presence or absence of other friends who can provide support.

Anger Turned Inward   A second factor in depression is known as "anger turned inward." This

> **Learned helplessness**   A condition in which an individual gives up and passively endures some unpleasant situation. Since any action is "futile," the individual gives up trying to make things better.

concept refers to the way people feel when they blame themselves for something. An example is the depression that you might feel after getting a poor grade average. At first, you might feel angry at your teachers, or perhaps at your roommate for interfering with your studies before final exams. But if you realize that your grades are really your own responsibility, you will soon direct your anger inward, toward yourself. This is often a cause of depression.

Self-blame is not always justified. Often, we blame ourselves because we don't know who or what else to blame. Thus, a child may feel responsible for a parent's death, or a parent may take on the full responsibility for a child's involvement with drugs. In cases such as this, depression relates very closely to the sense of guilt discussed earlier in this chapter.

Learned Helplessness   Still another explanation for depression is **learned helplessness:** the belief that any action is futile, so one might as well give up trying to make things better (Seligman, 1975, p. 93). When people believe that it makes no difference how or whether they respond to a situation, they give up. The student who quits studying because she doesn't believe she can pass the course, the business owner resigned to bankruptcy, the mother who feels trapped by her child-rearing responsibilities and stops thinking of ways to find relief are all typical of this kind of self-entrapment. One of the most frustrating elements of this situation is that an escape is often obvious to the outsider. The depressed person, however, refuses to acknowledge it.

According to Seligman, this sense of helplessness can be learned as a result of previous experiences. The box *Learning to Be Helpless: Some Experimental Evidence* shows how this happened in an experiment performed on dogs. The same general effect seems to occur in people—as when a person tries and tries to communicate with an obdurate parent, then finally gives up altogether.

Learned helplessness doesn't always lead to depression, however. In the case above, the per-

Learning to Be Helpless: Some Experimental Evidence

In trying to explain depression, psychologists have noted the frequent role of learned helplessness—the tendency for a person to give up without even trying to escape from a troublesome situation. The effect on humans is discussed in the chapter; an interesting animal experiment sheds even more light on the phenomenon.

Martin Seligman, who first developed the idea of learned helplessness, conducted an early study with psychologist Maier. The two scientists subjected three groups of dogs to electrical shocks. In the first phase of the experiment, the first group of dogs was placed in an apparatus that allowed no escape, then administered shocks. The second group received the same shocks during this phase, but they were permitted to escape. A third group acted as a control, receiving no shocks during this first phase.

In the second phase of the experiment, all three groups were placed in a compartment from which they *could* escape; then a painful shock was administered. The dogs in groups two and three easily learned to escape by jumping to another compartment. However, the first group merely accepted the shock, even though they could also have escaped.

Is there a moral in this for us? According to the researchers, yes. People seem to learn *not* to escape in a similar way as did the dogs in this experiment. Likewise, the feeling that there is "no way out" often seems to be a major contributor to depression. Fortunately, if helplessness can be learned, it can usually be unlearned, also; this chapter discusses some ways this can be done.

Source: Seligman & Maier, 1967.

son who finally gave up on communicating with her parent was probably frustrated and angry as much as depressed. Why? The reason has to do with *attribution*—the cause to which the individual attributes his or her helplessness. This factor, attribution, sets learned helplessness in humans apart from that of the dogs in Seligman's early experiment, as was recognized in a later reformulation of the learned helplessness theory (Abramson, Seligman, & Teasdale, 1978). Humans don't simply give up, as did Seligman's dogs. Instead, they go through relatively complex cognitive processes in the effort to deduce what caused their helplessness.

To explain the relationship of learned helplessness to human depression, these psychologists identified three different dimensions that attribution could take: internal-external, global-specific, and stable-unstable. First, attribution can either be *internal* or *external*. That is, individuals can place blame for a hopeless situation on either themselves (internal attribution) or on an external cause. Internal attribution is more likely to lead to depression than is external attribution. You are likely to be upset that you are failing math despite your hardest efforts, but you'll probably be more depressed if you are the only one having trouble than if 90 percent of the class is also having trouble.

Attribution may also be either *global* or *specific*. This means that individuals may see their problem as either broadly or narrowly related to their efforts or circumstances. A global attribution is more likely to relate to depression than is specific attribution. For instance, you will be more likely to feel depressed about your failing math grade if you see it as evidence that you "can't do anything right." A specific attribution ("I'm not great at math, but I'm good at other things") would be less damaging to your self-esteem and therefore less likely to lead to depression.

A third dimension—*stable* or *unstable* attribution—relates to the individual's perception of the relative permanence of his or her helplessness. To return to the failing math grade, you might attribute your grade to an unstable, or short-lived, cause—for instance, the fact that you were involved in serious marital problems throughout the semester. If you took the course again, you might pass it. On the other hand, you might attribute your helplessness to stable factors: factors that will continue to operate no matter how many times you try to overcome them (for example, the internal factor of your own lack of ability in math).

In all, the way in which people perceive their helplessness is an important contributor to depression. One of the most important elements in understanding depression is the way in which thought patterns mediate between environment and emotions. We'll look next at these thought patterns, or cognitive factors.

Cognitive Factors and Depression   One of the most outstanding characteristics of people who show depression is a self-defeating, pessimistic attitude and thought pattern. If given a compliment, they tend to reject it or shrug it off. If shown "proof" that they are succeeding at a job, they will come back with the one criticism that their supervisor stated a week ago. Instead of seeing the positive, they concentrate on the negative aspects of their lives, overgeneralizing from one less-than-perfect situation to all others (Beck, 1967).

It isn't hard to see how depression can result

from a belief that anything short of total success means abject failure. Indeed, depressed people are often perfectionistic and rigid in defining their success. Naturally, this limits their enjoyment of life and hinders any attempts to feel comfortable and happy.

Absence of Pleasant Events   A fifth factor in depression is noted by many behaviorists. They explain depression in terms of a loss of positive reinforcements in a person's life. Peter Lewinsohn's **pleasant events theory** is representative (Lewinsohn, 1974; Lewinsohn & Graf, 1973; Lewinsohn & Libet, 1972). This theory builds upon the everyday observation that people tend to feel happier when they are doing something they enjoy. It relates people's mood levels to the number of pleasant events or activities they experience.

Table 6.3 ranks the kinds of "pleasant events" that seem to relate most consistently to a happy mood. The events in this list can be grouped according to categories. Thus, a recent study (Lewinsohn & Amenson, 1978) divides pleasant events into five general types of experience: *positive social interactions* (number 1 on the list is an example); *sexual experiences* (number 18); *positive feedback* (number 4); *comfort and competence* (numbers 2, 19); and *passive outdoor experiences* (number 12).

According to behaviorists like Lewinsohn, a person who has few such experiences is likely to be more depressed than is the person who regularly does things he or she enjoys. An absence of pleasant events, in fact, might set in motion a sort of downward spiral in some cases. The fewer pleasant events a person enjoys, the more depressed he or she may feel—and the less inclined to take the initiative in other enjoyable activities. As this kind of pattern continues, it may become very difficult to boost some people out of such a depression.

"Success Depression"   Finally, there is still another, sometimes puzzling, explanation for some cases of depression. Typical of this kind of depression is the person who devotes a great deal of

---

Pleasant events theory   Peter Lewinsohn's theory that people tend to feel happier when they are doing something they enjoy.

---

effort to reaching a goal (for instance, a promotion, a lifetime project, or graduation), then becomes depressed once that goal is reached.

Elkind and Hamsher (1972) call this phenomenon **success depression.** Perhaps it is caused by the end to striving, or the fear that the person isn't "good enough" to take credit for the accomplishment, or even the fear that once the goal has been attained, it won't last.

At any rate, the phenomenon is fairly common. It isn't unusual to find a bit of depression mixed with the joy of graduation, for instance (Lesse, 1968). After years of working toward a degree, graduates find that they are thrust onto the labor market, with new pressures and decisions to be made and without the familiar supports of college life. They must reorient or redirect themselves to new goals.

Normally, success depression passes quickly as new challenges appear and the person adjusts to different goals. However, there are also some instances where the depression hangs on—for instance, when an executive at the peak of his or her career suddenly feels it hasn't been worthwhile and is unable to shake that depression. In these cases, the person needs help in emerging from a depressed state.

The Individual Factor in Depression   In all of the factors we've been discussing, it is important to stress the role of the individual. Loss can be a cause of depression, but only if the person defines that loss as important. Success can also be a factor—but again, only if the person can't adjust to that success. The importance of the individual is perhaps clearest in the cognitive, learned helplessness, and loss of reinforcement factors we've explored. One person may overemphasize even a small failure or respond by giving up, while another maintains a sense of equilibrium despite a series of far greater losses.

All of this suggests that the amount of depression a person experiences is at least partly determined by the individual. In the following section, we'll look at some ways in which people can help themselves deal with depression.

Table 6.3	A Pleasant Events Scale*
Item	Number (Out of 30 Subjects) Who Rated This Item "Good"
1. Being with happy people	12
2. Being relaxed	10
3. Having spare time	9
4. Having people show interest in what you said	8
5. Laughing	8
6. Looking at the sky or clouds	7
7. Saying something clearly	6
8. Talking about philosophy or religion	6
9. Meeting someone new (of the opposite sex)	6
10. Watching attractive women/men	6
11. Reading stories or novels	5
12. Taking a walk	5
13. Seeing beautiful scenery	5
14. Sleeping soundly at night	5
15. Amusing people	5
16. Having coffee or coke with friends	5
17. Having someone agree with you	4
18. Petting	4
19. Being with someone you love	4
20. Traveling	4
21. Breathing clean air	4
22. Having a frank and open conversation	4
23. Having sexual relations with a partner	4
24. Watching people	4

*These items all had a correlation of more than .30 with mood ratings of at least 4 persons in this study.

Source: Lewinsohn, Peter, & Libet, Julian. "Pleasant Events Activity Schedules and Depression," *Journal of Abnormal Psychology,* June 1972, Vol. 79, p. 294. Copyright 1972 by the American Psychological Association. Reprinted by permission of Peter Lewinsohn.

Success depression   The letdown that occurs after one has reached a goal that he or she has sought for a long time.

Overcoming Depression

The last time you were depressed, can you remember what made you feel better? When students are asked this question in class, their answers are rather interesting. Some try to engage in their favorite activity, such as tennis, pool, or playing some music. Others try to analyze why they are depressed and think their way out of it. Still others simply force themselves to go out and try to concentrate on a different aspect of their lives.

The following pages explore a few techniques for alleviating depression. They cover a range of strategies; their effectiveness, of course, varies according to what works best for each individual. If you suffer from prolonged or severe bouts of depression, you should seek professional help. Great strides have been made in the treatment of depression in the past decade or so, and professional help can be very effective.

Thinking Your Way out of Depression   We've seen that the thought patterns of a depressed person tend to be pessimistic, narrow, and self-defeating. By changing these thought patterns, it is often possible to break the cycle of depression. Paul Hauck (1973) believes that self-blame, self-pity, and pitying others leads to depression. According to Hauck, "the major reason we get upset is that we talk ourselves into it" (1973, p. 57).

Hauck advocates using Ellis' method of identifying irrational ideas and disputing them (see "Coping with Anxiety" earlier in this chapter). If you are telling yourself that you are unworthy or that "something must be wrong with me" because of a rejection, for instance, Hauck suggests that you ask yourself whether something is wrong with the other person instead. Depressed people need to begin to value themselves and not merely worry about what others will think.

Noting the Good   One trait of depression is the tendency to see only the negative elements of a situation. If a person can be made to notice the positives, too, that often helps in lifting depression.

To do this, make note of all the positive, enjoyable happenings that take place each day. This is usually difficult at first, for the individual tends not to notice when something good happens. Gradually, however, even small enjoyments—a long morning cup of coffee, or a good conversation at lunch, or a completed assignment—are easier to notice and appreciate. Building upon these positive experiences, it is often possible for a person to open up to even more such pleasures and become less depressed.

UNlearning Helplessness   Once a person has become convinced of his or her helplessness, it is difficult to overcome that feeling. The most effective way of *un*learning helplessness seems to be to force the person to recognize that responding—doing something—*will* have an effect (Seligman, 1975).

One way of doing this is to investigate your feelings of helplessness by comparing your situation with that of others who have suffered the same fate. What have they done? It helps to know that your situation is not unique, and in addition, you might pick up some cues as to effective means of responding.

Another way to overcome learned helplessness is to structure some success into your life. Some people actually seem to structure failure. One student, for instance, was terribly upset because she had done poorly in an advanced creative writing course. It turned out that she hadn't taken basic college English—a fact that greatly increased her chances of failing.

To structure success rather than failure into your life, it is important to set goals that are reasonable. If you have a long-term goal, plan several small steps for reaching it, so that you won't feel overwhelmed. Approaching goals one step at a time, listing what must be done and how long each stage should take, will give you a chance to see your own progress and appreciate small successes.

One way of countering depression is to do something for someone else. Often, simply focusing attention on another's needs can help people forget their own depression.

Reevaluating Goals If constantly failing to live up to your standards is a problem, perhaps you should question those standards. They may be too perfectionistic. If they are, you should alter them. It may be helpful here to compare your own standards with those of others, especially people you respect: you may be using a different yardstick to measure yourself than others.

If your behaviors are not in keeping with your goals, then a change of behavior is required. If you are depressed because you studied little and failed a course, for instance, the answer to depression is to increase your efforts in the next term. Learning from mistakes, provided we put that learning to use, is often an antidote for depression.

Talking It Out For many of us, it is comforting to talk out our feelings with someone who cares. Hopefully, we can receive a bit more than sympathy from loved ones. While it is important to be understood, a depressed person must also be motivated to do something to improve his or her situation. Friends or family can often help provide some motivation. If this fails, a trained therapist may be needed to help a depressed person start to take positive steps.

Doing Something   Perhaps the most insidious aspect of depression is that it leads to inactivity. A depressed person may feel it's hardly worthwhile to make the effort to get out of bed and out of the house each day. Finding and participating in enjoyable activities is one important step in the right direction. These activities may include any of the items listed in Table 6.3, for starters. But each person has special, individual sources of pleasure and enjoyment. Virtually anything that makes *you* feel good may be helpful in lifting depression, as long as it does not hurt anyone else.

Accepting Yourself as Less than Perfect   Finally, accept yourself as less than perfect. Since you are human, you will probably experience failure, rejection, and loss. These are part of life. Although it is easier to talk about than to do, accepting your fallibility is an important step in coping with these experiences.

In all, there are many things you can do to bring yourself out of depression. You do not have to be helpless or constantly unhappy. The power to cope with, master, and finally transcend the rejections and disappointments of life lies within each and every individual. When we accept our humanness and fallibility, we may experience personal growth; we will also spend less time fearing the bumps and pitfalls of life, leaving more time to appreciate its pleasures.

Anxiety, guilt, and depression are not the only negative feelings that threaten our sense of security. Anger is also a negative emotion, and a frequent consequence, aggression, presents a threat not only to the individual but also to other people. The personal and interpersonal consequences of anger and aggression are of great concern to all of us, and it is to these topics that we now turn.

Summary

1.   Physical changes associated with anxiety include increased heart rate, sweating, nausea, trembling, shallowness of breath, and dryness of the throat. The symptoms of fear are very similar; but while fear is immediate and realistic, anxiety is futuristic and often more vague.

2.   According to Freud, people defend themselves from anxiety using defense mechanisms, automatic mental strategies for reducing or eliminating anxiety. Freud described three types of anxiety: reality anxiety, moral anxiety, and neurotic anxiety.

3.   Behaviorists see anxiety in terms of conditioning. Once we learn to anticipate negative experiences in certain circumstances, we feel anxious in each similar situation.

4.   Existential anxiety is the result of the awareness of our responsibility to make our own life decisions.

5.   In small quantities, anxiety may improve performance. However, the optimal amount of anxiety varies with the task. The more complicated the task, the more likely it is that anxiety will interfere with performance.

6.   Reasoning, taking perspective, coming to grips with the problem, and distraction and relaxation are all ways of coping with anxiety.

7.   Freud considered guilt as moral anxiety, a result of a violation of the superego's standards. Behaviorists explain guilt as the anticipation of negative appraisals from significant others. Humanistic psychologists, such as Maslow, believe guilt can also arise from not living up to one's potential.

8.   If a person's conscience is too rigid, he or she may feel perpetually guilty. Individuals whose consciences are too "soft," in contrast, have a different problem. They tend not to think of long-term consequences of their actions and may have difficulty controlling their urges. Both of these conditions can cause problems.

9.   Defense mechanisms, reparation, confession, and introspection are four ways of coping with guilt. Introspection may lead to personal growth if the individual learns from his or her experience.

10. Depression involves feelings of sadness, dejection, and hopelessness. It may be caused by a loss, anger turned inward, or by a lack of reinforcement through pleasant events or experiences. Another possible cause is learned helplessness, especially when the source of helplessness is attributed to global, stable, internal factors.

11. Depressed individuals tend to be self-defeating, pessimistic, inactive, and oriented toward the negative rather than the positive aspects of their lives. Altering these thought patterns can help lift a person out of depression.

12. When we accept our fallibility and humanness, we will tend to be easier on ourselves, accept ourselves, and strive to improve.

Key Terms and Concepts

anxiety
fear
claustrophobia
neurotic anxiety
reality anxiety
moral anxiety
defense mechanisms
existential anxiety
Yerkes-Dodson Law
disputing
progressive relaxation
imagery

guilt
intrinsic conscience
neurotic guilt
psychopathic (sociopathic)
role model
consequential thinking
depression
learned helplessness
pleasant events theory
success depression

Rebecca looked a second time at her brother to make sure she hadn't made a mistake. Sure enough, there he was with her best stuffed animal. And not only that, but it was missing an arm.

She conducted herself as any self-respecting 3-year-old might. She clenched her fists, tightened her body as she readied herself for the attack, then tore at her brother with all her might. Her vocabulary may have failed to express the outrage that she felt, but her physical display more than made up for it.

Anger and Aggression

The temper outburst of a 3-year-old is an example of undisciplined, virtually pure anger. Most of us believe that as adults, we have grown out of such behavior as part of the process of development. In truth, however, our means of expressing anger may have changed, but the emotional experience isn't so different from what Rebecca felt. When a friend loses a favorite sweater he borrowed, we normally don't throw a temper tantrum. We feel angry, but find different ways to express it. We tense up; we mutter something under our breath; we may even kick a chair. No matter what we do with it, our experience of anger is usually unpleasant, and controlling it is vital to our living peacefully in society.

But people don't always control their anger, and sometimes a consequence of this is aggression—behavior directed at hurting someone else. As newspapers, TV shows, and even our own personal experiences attest, acts of aggression present a problem of tremendous proportions in our society.

This chapter looks at anger and aggression, their origins, their consequences, and ways to keep them under control. We also look at assertiveness—behavior that is often confused with aggression. Learning to be assertive is basic to controlling anger and aggression, as we shall see, for assertiveness provides a positive and productive outlet for the frustrations, tensions, and stresses that may otherwise lead to aggression.

Anger

Like frustration, anxiety, and guilt, anger is an emotion that interferes with our sense of security or well-being and forces us to adjust. What causes people to become angry?

Causes of Anger

Anger has many causes. In the late 1930s, a team of psychologists at Yale University formulated the

As adults, we usually express our anger in a more controlled way than does this child. The emotional experience is still very similar, however.

famous **frustration-aggression hypothesis,** which explained anger and aggression as reactions to frustration (Dollard et al., 1939). The fact that frustration sometimes leads to aggression has been validated by much research, as we'll see later in this chapter.

Anger has other sources besides frustration, however. If you think back to your own experiences, you will probably recall several different

Frustration-aggression hypothesis The theory that frustration may lead to aggression. This theory has recently been modified, in recognition of the fact that frustration often does *not* lead to overt aggression.

types of situations that have made you angry. Indignation, annoyance, and physical irritation are subjective experiences that can cause anger. We all experience anger at some point in our lives, but is it always a negative emotion?

Consequences of Anger

Expressions such as "keep your cool" or "don't get so hot under the collar" attest to an underlying, popular belief in our society: it is wrong to feel angry. After our parents and teachers have stopped us countless times from behaving as Rebecca did in our opening example, most of us have not only learned that aggression is wrong—we have also come to equate anger with aggression. Many people in our society feel almost as guilty about their anger as they feel about aggression.

Is anger wrong? As you might expect, the answer to this question is that anger itself isn't wrong. (In many cases, in fact, it is a perfectly reasonable response to an unreasonable situation.) Whether anger is positive or negative depends entirely upon what we do with it. There are three alternatives for this. First, anger may motivate some positive behavior. Second, it may cause a person to act in a negative way. And third, a person may not act on his or her anger at all, attempting to disguise it instead.

Positive Anger   The magazine ad shows a picture of a young child from an underdeveloped country. The child is thin and small for her age, clearly close to starvation. The picture makes you feel sympathetic or angry, for this child and many others like her are the victims of circumstances that are totally incomprehensible to them and to their families. "Will you help this child?" the ad asks. If you experience anger, you might become involved in the organization or demand governmental action.

As this example illustrates, anger sometimes does lead to positive responses. Such signs of our times as sit-ins at nuclear power plants, anti-war demonstrations, and both anti- and pro-abortion movements (both sides are angrily defending the cause that they feel is right) all affirm that anger often does motivate positive action. Where a social issue is involved, anger may cause a person to write a letter to Congress, to donate money or time to an organization, or to take some other positive action to change the source of anger.

There are other ways in which anger may act as a positive force. Have you ever found that when you're angry, you work harder and longer? You may be so bothered that your friend got a better score on the math test that you'll put in extra hours of study this week. Or a football team may be so angry about a critical write-up in the newspaper that they fight like bulldogs through the next game. While there is an optimal level of arousal for each task (see the Yerkes-Dodson law in Chapter 6), there is no doubt that anger can be a positive force as long as it is channeled in a constructive way.

Negative Anger   Although anger sometimes causes people to outdo themselves in a way that gives them pride and satisfaction, it is the negative effects of anger that we most often remember. Like any other form of stress, anger may lead to psychosomatic ailments. Heart conditions, ulcers, high blood pressure, or migraine headaches are all examples of illnesses that may be made worse by the deep and continuous emotional experience of anger.

Finding a release for anger may not improve the situation. We have all indulged, at one time or another, in an outburst that later caused us embarrassment or guilt. Even when we don't aggress against someone directly, activities such as throwing things, yelling, and pounding a fist on a table are likely to be counterproductive. Because of these negative effects, a third common reaction to anger is to try and disguise or hide it.

Disguised Anger   It is surprising how often we disguise our anger. We often feel so guilty about it that we even deny it to ourselves. One man in counseling refused to even consider that he was angry at his father. Banging a clenched fist on the table, he swore to this repeatedly. His emotional state may have been obvious to anyone in the room with him, but he refused to recognize it.

Not only do many individuals hide their anger from their own consciousness, but even our language works to disguise the emotion. Terms such as "disgusted," "sick and tired," "fed up," and "disappointed" are often descriptions of anger. These terms are often used to deny that we are really angry, when either we're not ready to deal with something or we feel that anger is unworthy of us.

At times, people may feel angry (and they may even be aware of this anger), but they may direct their anger toward a substitute focus. This is called *displacement* of anger (Keezer, 1971), and it works in the same way as the displacement we discussed in Chapter 6's list of anxiety defense mechanisms. Displaced anger can be dangerous, as when a parent brings home anger from work and then takes it out on a child. Yet it is a common occurrence.

Another way to disguise anger is through *passive aggression*—indirectly blocking someone else's goals. Examples of passive aggression are the youngster who "accidentally" loses a ballet slipper so that she can't participate in dance class (she never wanted to learn to plié anyway!) or the dissatisfied employee who constantly shows up late for staff meetings, disrupting the entire agenda. The passive-aggressive person generally doesn't recognize his or her own anger. People who deal with their anger in this way may never learn to cope with this basic human feeling.

Dealing with Anger

Disguising anger may make us less aware of it, but it doesn't make it go away. Anger continues to build up, putting emotional pressure on a person until some kind of release or breakdown is unavoidable. For this reason, it is important that people learn to cope with their anger.

This is often easier to say than to do. Many of us are so used to hiding our anger, or to releasing it in negative ways, that we need guidance in order to learn positive ways of dealing with it. It is far easier to deal with someone else's problems than to establish new behaviors for ourselves!

Just how should people deal with their anger? There are many ways of releasing this emotion, and some are healthier than others. Driving recklessly along the highway may be a form of release, but it is hardly a mature adjustment to anger, and it may involve danger to others. The best approach seems to be to recognize the emotion and try to understand its source (see the four-step suggestion in the box *Facing up to Anger*), and then to deal with it in a way that will bring you relief and will—hopefully—correct the situation that makes you angry. It is usually better to deal with the source of the anger, if possible, and the suggestions provided in Chapter 5's box *A Model for Making Decisions* are helpful in doing this. But there are times when a situation is beyond our control. Alcoholics Anonymous perhaps puts it best in its hope that "God grant me the courage to change what can be changed, to accept what cannot be altered, and the wisdom to know the difference." In "accepting what cannot be altered," people need to find ways of releasing anger that will not hurt anyone or anything.

One way to release anger is through sports. This is true of active participation: it feels good to go out and take a run or to have a good, hard game of softball. This process of reducing tensions by acting them out is called **catharsis** (Aronson, 1972). Some people believe that the act of

> **Catharsis**   The process by which fears and problems are acted out or verbally expressed, often resulting in at least a temporary reduction in tension.

Facing up to Anger

There are many ways of working off angry energy, as this chapter discusses. But even before you do this, it helps to understand more about your anger: to face up to it. Dr. Leo Madow (1972) advocates a four-step process for understanding and dealing with anger.

Step 1

First, recognize that you are angry. Many people disguise their anger and may not even be aware of it. Headaches, forgotten responsibilities, or an inability to sleep may all be cues. Becoming aware that you are angry is an important first step in doing something about it. Use introspection, thinking about possible reasons why you might be experiencing such symptoms. It may also be helpful to ask friends for feedback: do they think you've been angry or upset? It may even help to try looking at your own facial gestures in a mirror or to listen to a tape of your own voice. Do your outward expressions match your inward feelings?

Step 2

A second step in facing up to anger is to identify its source. This may not be easy. Some people tend to displace their anger: it is easier at times to blame someone other than the real offender. The source of anger may not be another person at all. It may be one's own inability to change unpleasant circumstances or long-term habits that are bothersome.

Step 3

A third step is to understand the reason for your anger. *Why* does your boss' attitude bother you? Are you really angry at your friend for telling the truth about you, or are you annoyed with yourself because her criticism was valid?

Step 4

The last step is to deal realistically with your anger. According to Madow, this step is not necessarily the most difficult one. Once you have recognized the feeling, identified the source, and have some idea as to why you are angry, the solution may be evident.

Source: Leo Madow, *Anger: How to Recognize and Cope with It,* New York: Scribners, 1972.

---

watching sports may provide some release for pent-up feelings. It is possible that you may feel less hostility or anger after watching two fighters battle it out in the ring or after watching a good football or hockey game. This is not usually the case, however. Sometimes just the opposite event seems to happen—as when fans become so excited that there is a brawl in the stands.

Another way of dealing with anger is through *rechannelization*. As discussed in Chapter 6, this involves channeling an unpleasant emotion (in this case anger) into constructive, socially acceptable pursuits. Examples of rechannelization include drawing, painting, sculpture, playing or listening to music, or even writing a letter (which may never be mailed). Children often manage to

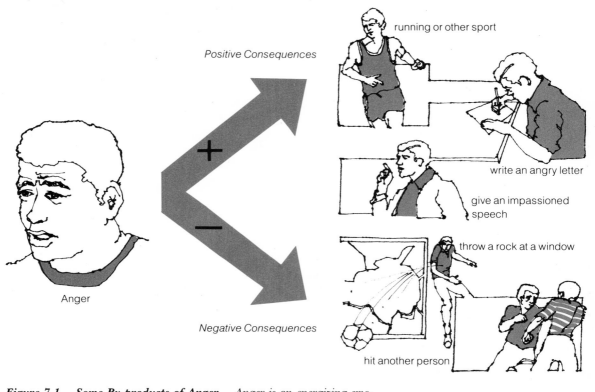

Figure 7.1   Some By-products of Anger   *Anger is an energizing emotion that can lead to either positive or negative actions.*

deal with their anger through play, as they act out the feelings that are bothering them, and such dramatization is helpful for some adults. As with the other stress-reduction methods that we've been discussing in the last two chapters, the kind of release you choose is a matter of individual preference. What works well for one person may not be effective for the next.

In all, anger can be seen as an energizing emotion that can be channeled into constructive activities. As Figure 7.1 shows, however, it is also a powerful emotion that is not always easy to control. When anger flares out of control, it may lead to aggression—a behavior that is a major problem in our society today.

Aggression

According to the Uniform Crime Reports (FBI, 1981), a violent crime is committed every 24 seconds. Someone is murdered every 23 minutes, raped every 6 minutes, assaulted every 49 seconds, and robbed every 55 seconds. But most aggressive activities do not appear in the Uniform Crime Reports. Observe a group of children at play and count how many pushes, shoves, hits, or kicks take place; listen also for verbal aggressions, including insults, name-calling, and threats. This kind of everyday, garden-variety aggression is so common in our society that we often don't think twice about it; it occurs among adults as well as children (although often on a somewhat more subtle level). For instance, it is not unusual at all for a driver to roll down the car window and let loose with a few indelicate expressions if another driver has made a careless mistake.

What Is Aggression?

In the paragraph above, we have referred to several kinds of actions as aggressive acts. That leads us to a question that is somewhat controversial: how can aggression be defined?

Psychologist Patricia Niles Middlebrook (1980) contends that definitions of aggression can follow three directions. The first centers around emotion as the defining element, with aggression defined as the behavior that follows the emotion of anger. This approach makes sense in some obvious cases, as when a person hits someone because she or he is angry. But it presents a simplistic, "tunnel-vision" perspective, for aggression is a far more complex behavior. We have already seen that anger can lead to constructive or socially acceptable behaviors through rechannelization and catharsis. In addition, there is some question as to whether aggression need always be the result of anger.

The second group of definitions looks at intent. Did Rebecca intend to hit her brother in the case at the beginning of this chapter? If she did, we might classify her behavior as an aggressive act. This definition seems to have a firmer foundation than the definition based on emotion, but it still leaves some questions unanswered. For instance, how do we classify Rebecca's act if she swings at her brother, but hits (and hurts) her good friend by mistake? An accident such as this would still seem to be an act of aggression, even if it wasn't intentional.

A third way of defining aggression looks at the behavior itself, and in this way avoids the problems of the emotion and the intention definitions. According to this view, **aggression** is the attempt of one individual to deliver a noxious (unpleasant) stimulus to another person. In other words, aggression is any form of behavior directed toward the goal of hurting or injuring another being who is motivated to avoid such treatment (Baron, 1977). We will use this as a working definition in our discussion.

What Causes Aggression?

By answering the question of "what is aggression," we have been able to establish a working definition. But this definition leaves another, still more important question unanswered. *Why* should someone hurt another person? People are logical, reasonable creatures: why is it so difficult for us to learn to coexist without aggression? This question has fascinated many psychologists, and a number of broad theories attempt to provide an answer. We'll look at three of those answers here: the "death instinct" theory of Freud; the ethologists' theory that aggression is natural to all animals; and the behaviorists' explanation that aggression is learned.

A Death Instinct?   Freud saw aggression as natural and inevitable. He explained it as the result of a strong, inborn urge toward destruction that could be either displaced onto others or turned against oneself (Lundin, 1979). (He called this instinct **Thanatos,** and he contrasted it with an opposite urge: a "life instinct" which he called **Eros.**)

Aggression   The attempt of one individual to deliver an unpleasant stimulus to another.

Thanatos   A term used in Freudian theory to denote the death or aggressive instinct in human beings.

Eros   A term used in Freudian theory to denote the life instinct.

Freud as well as others* believed that anger builds up in an organism, perhaps much as pressure builds up in an active volcano, and that it needs to be periodically released. The longer a person goes without releasing these aggressive urges, the easier it is to trigger aggression. Particular events or objects in the environment—called cues or releasers—act to trigger an aggressive display. This explains why you are likely to lose your temper at even a small annoyance after a day filled with tension.

Are We Aggressive by Nature?   A second theory also sees aggression as an inborn trait, but this explanation is a bit more general than that of Freud. According to the *ethological viewpoint,* we can learn much about human aggression by looking at animals. **Ethology** is a branch of biology concerned with the instincts and action patterns common to all animals (Wrightsman, 1977). Ethologists try to discover behavior patterns that are common to all species, and they speculate as to how these behaviors may be crucial to survival.

Several popular books use an evolutionary or ethological point of view to explain aggression. Robert Ardrey's book, *The Territorial Imperative* (1966), argues that humans have a drive to gain and hold territory. Just like animals, we stake out our own territory, and we protect it by aggressive means. This argument relates clearly to practices such as keeping a handgun in the house in case someone breaks in or even to national policies such as the build-up of nuclear weapons.

Human aggression isn't quite parallel to animal aggression, however. Animals may fight over a potential mate or a territorial stake, but the loser is rarely killed in these battles. According to Lorenz (1966), each species has its own inborn controls that act to inhibit or check aggression before too much damage is done. The stronger animal will prevail, but the weaker one will be permitted to go on its way. In contrast, human aggression is often far more violent, as a look at

* Among them, psychologist Konrad Lorenz (1966).

the newspapers will show any day. What explains the difference?

Ethologists have an answer for this question, too. In purely physical terms, people are poorly equipped for aggression. We lack fangs or claws; we don't have great physical strength or speed; even our hearing and sense of smell are relatively poor. These very weaknesses, say the ethologists, have kept us from developing the natural inhibitory controls found in other animals. And at the same time, our intelligence has allowed us to forge destructive weapons, many of which do not even require face-to-face interaction. The result of all this is that aggression, while it serves a survival function in animals, is often counterproductive in humans.

While ethological viewpoint is interesting, it has also been criticized. Some psychologists question whether we can draw conclusions from lower animals and apply them to humans (Boice, 1976); others have offered specific criticisms. Jonathan Freedman's book, *Crowding and Behavior* (1975), for instance, argues that territoriality and crowding do not necessarily lead to aggression. In addition, there is a great diversity across cultures. Some societies show little territoriality and very low levels of aggression. In all, there seem to be very few generalizations about aggression that are universally true.

The ethological and psychoanalytic theories offer fairly pessimistic outlooks, in that they both see aggression as inevitable. A third explanation views aggression as the product of learning, and it looks for factors that might encourage or inhibit learned aggressive behaviors.

Aggression as a Learned Behavior

From time to time, a movie makes the news because of the behaviors it incites in viewers. In

Ethology   The study of animal behavior in its natural habitat.

1979, a film called *The Warriors* portrayed gang violence in New York City. Many viewers acted in a highly aggressive way after they emerged from the theater. Vandalism and acts of violence occurred, and three people were killed in post-movie brawls. Certainly, only a minority of viewers behaved in this way, but the threat was great enough to cause some theaters to have extra security guards on hand ready to handle any disturbance. This case may be extreme, but it is not alone. Many critics have noted that the violence shown in films and on TV affects the behavior of some people who watch it.

There is little doubt that learning is an important factor in aggression. This is supported by numerous nonscientific observations, as in the example just mentioned; it has also been shown experimentally. Perhaps the most famous of these experiments concerns the social learning or modeling of aggression (Bandura, Ross, & Ross, 1961). In one of these experiments, children were divided into two groups: one group witnessed an adult hitting a Bobo doll; the other group watched an adult model playing peacefully and constructively with some toys. Afterwards, the children were permitted to play with the toys. The results bore out the theory that social learning affects aggression: the group who had watched the aggressive model showed more violence in their play than did the other group. This same tendency is shown in an anecdote told by German psychologist Wilfred Belschner. When an adult "reproached a boy for bullying a smaller one, he was told that since this was precisely what adults did, it was perfectly fair" (1971, p. 92).

If aggression is easily learned by watching others, the learning process is even more effective if reinforcement or reward takes place. Bandura and Walters (1959) found that many parents of aggressive children approved of fighting to solve a problem. One boy speaks in an interview conducted by these researchers:

I'm not trying to be conceited or anything, but I know I can use my feet better than all the guys I hang around with. . . . Like my Dad, he said, "If you know how to fight with your feet, then it's in your hands, you've got it made. . . . You never need be afraid of anybody." (quoted in Belschner, 1971, p. 70)

If children's parents encourage aggression as a way of solving problems, there may seem to be no reason to try any other method.

This kind of learning may occur more commonly in some subgroups than others in our society. Suppose that the people you see each day—both peers and older adults—believe that the best way to settle a dispute is with your fists. You will consistently observe the people you respect behaving violently, and you will see that those who fight are accorded a high social status. In such a cultural group, violence will become a norm—an accepted way of life (Wolfgang & Ferracuti, 1967). This perspective is illustrated in the boxed discussion *Confessions of a Street Criminal,* which tells the story of a small-time hustler who grew up on the streets of Washington, D.C.

Factors That Affect Aggression

If people learn aggression from their families, culture, and everyday experiences, what explains the differences in aggressive responses? Why, for instance, didn't every viewer who emerged from the movie *The Warriors* behave in an unruly manner?

There are certainly great differences in personality and learning from one person to another, and these personal differences help explain why some people act more aggressively than others. As we'll see later in this chapter, people can learn to release anger in productive ways. Here, though, we are interested in some more immediate influences on aggression—factors that help explain why the same person may react aggressively in one situation, but not in another. Psychologists have found a number of factors that have an immediate influence on aggression.

Confessions of a Street Criminal

It seems to me that the kind of neighborhood you come up in may make all the difference in which way you go and where you end up. There was a lot of people in my neighborhood who didn't do much work. . . . Hustling was their thing: number running, bootlegging, selling narcotics, selling stolen goods, prostitution. There's so many things that go on—it's a whole system that operates inside itself. . . .

. . . Somebody was always doing something in each family. If it wasn't the adults, say the mother or father, then it was the son or daughter. I was sticking up; one of my brothers was stealing; one of my sisters was bootlegging; one of my uncles wrote numbers. . . .

. . . The kids, we ran wild, and the adults were wild. It would be nothing for us [as children] to be on the front steps playing hide-and-seek and all of a sudden you hear bang, bang, bang, and people are shooting at each other in the street. And everybody ducking and hiding. This was normal. Eventually you'd be taking all this in. It's just a way of survival. (pp. 1–3)

To what degree is aggression learned? The excerpt above describes street life in the southwest Washington, D.C. ghetto. From the author's words, it seems almost natural for a person raised within this subculture to grow up into a career of theft or narcotics—just as a person raised in some subcultures of our society might expect to be a doctor, teacher, or lawyer. The author, a man named John Allen, was no exception. After a career of crime that began at the age of 8 (an arrest for theft) and continued for the next 20-odd years (charges included rape, narcotics possession, armed robbery, assault with a deadly weapon, and homicide), he is now confined to a wheelchair—the result of a shoot-out with police when he was 35 years old.

Considering John Allen's story as well as other evidence, it is truly amazing that most people who grow up in a ghetto environment become law-abiding citizens—certainly against the odds!

Source: Allen, John, Assault with a Deadly Weapon: The Autobiography of a Street Criminal. New York: Pantheon, 1977. Quotation reprinted by permission of Random House, Inc.

Arousal, Anger, and the Frustration Hypothesis

One factor that helps explain why a person may react violently to a situation is his or her emotional state. Since anger is an energizing force, the amount of anger that a person brings to a situation will affect that person's reaction. Thus, if you were already angry when you entered the theater, a violent film might have a greater effect on you than if you were feeling calm and satisfied.

Environmental stimuli may also affect the amount of aggression shown by a person who is aroused. We have already seen that uncomfortably hot weather may be associated with higher violence, as in the race riots that took place in the summer of 1968. In addition, factors such as noise also make tempers short. Donnerstein and Wilson (1976) found that noise pollution had its greatest effect on previously angered subjects.

A factor that relates closely to such findings is

Frustration, Imitation, and Aggression

There are many paths to violence. Aggression has been linked to frustration as well as the imitation of aggressive models. Children who watch an aggressive model are more likely to show aggressive behavior than children who have not been exposed to such models. It stands to reason, however, that internal and external conditions will determine to what extent violent behavior will be imitated. One of these possible conditions involves frustration, and one research study investigated the effects of frustration on the imitation of aggressive behavior.

Subjects in the study included 30 6- and 7-year-old boys. Half of them were shown a film in which an adult male shook his fist, making angry comments or in some way aggressing toward a clown. The other boys were not exposed to any aggressive model. Some children were then frustrated by being shown a group of toys, told that if they performed well with a partner on a game their chosen toy would be given to them, and then told that their partner had not done well enough and so no toy would be given. At this point one third of the boys was led to believe that the partner who had failed them so miserably was the clown, while another third thought it was another child. The last third was not frustrated at all, nor was any toy offered or game played.

Each subject was then taken to a room and introduced to the clown who stayed perfectly still. A mallet and a toy gun were lying on the floor, and the boy was told that the experimenter had some paper work to do and he was to play here for a while. The behaviors of the subject were recorded for the next five minutes.

The results demonstrate that frustration is indeed an important factor in the imitation of aggressive models. Only those children who had been frustrated actually aggressed against the clown. The investigators note that just viewing the film did not result in more aggression as has been reported in the literature for younger children. Perhaps, the experimenters suggest, as children grow they develop more inhibitions against violence. Thus, an extra cue—in this case frustration—is required for aggressive behaviors to show themselves. It seems clear, then, that frustration can bring out imitative behavior in people and increase the likelihood that imitative aggression will occur.

Source: Hanratty et al., 1972.

the frustration-aggression hypothesis that we mentioned earlier in this chapter. The effects of frustration on aggression have also been supported by research. For example, Barker, Dembo, and Lewin (1941) led two groups of children to rooms in which very attractive toys were displayed. One group was allowed free access to these toys, while the others were frustrated by being made to look at them through a window. When the frustrated group was finally allowed to play with the toys, they were very destructive, much more so than the nonfrustrated group. The box *Frustration, Imitation, and Aggression* describes another experiment in which frustration—this time combined with imitation—led to aggressive behavior.

It seems, then, that the state in which you enter a situation is a crucial variable in determining whether or not you will act aggressively. Returning to our movie, perhaps one reason why

Often, fights like this begin over a minor (or even imagined) disagreement that escalates to far greater proportions.

some viewers became so aggressive was due to their emotional state before the film. If these individuals were already frustrated or angry, they would be more easily aroused to aggression.

Provocation and Escalation   Even if a person is frustrated and angry, aggression usually doesn't take place spontaneously. Instead, some form of provocation acts as a trigger that sets events moving toward an aggressive act; and the **escalation**, or build-up, of angry emotions serves to fuel the fire.

The escalation phase is important, because it helps explain why the final aggressive act is sometimes so wildly out of proportion to the initial

> **Escalation**   The process by which angry actions lead to more angry actions, and emotions build up. The result is often violent aggression.

Does the availability of a weapon encourage violence? This question is central to the gun control controversy. It appears that people are likely to use a weapon if it is on hand.

ment escalates in this manner, people forget just what it was that set things off in the first place.

While escalation rarely leads to homicide, people often feed one another's anger. Aggressive behaviors beget aggressive behaviors (Patterson & Cobb, 1971), so that name-calling leads to shoving, which leads in turn to fist-fighting. The initial triggering event may even be imagined, as when one person interprets another's statement as an insult. Within such a scenario, a small act of violence can be met with devastating and seemingly unnecessary force (Cairns, 1979). One reason for this is that even a minor attack may be symbolic, signifying a need for defense. The amount of aggression may not be as important as the fact that you were attacked (Greenwell & Dengerink, 1973).

Availability of a Weapon   Still another factor in aggression is the center of some controversy in our country today. That is the availability of a weapon. If you were attacked, would you fight back with your fists or would you reach for the gun lying in the drawer? This is a basic question in the issue of gun control. It appears that people will often use whatever weapon is at hand if they are angered and ready to aggress. In fact, the very presence of a weapon may increase the level of aggression.

Berkowitz and LePage (1967) found that stimuli that are usually associated with violence can elicit aggression from those ready to act. Subjects were angered by being exposed to shock. Then they were given the opportunity to shock others. In some cases there was a rifle or a revolver on the table. The very presence of these weapons increased the level of their aggressive responses.

Physical State: Alcohol and Aggression   The physical state of a person can also have some effect on aggression. Drugs such as PCP (sometimes known by the street name "angel dust") have been linked to crime in a number of cases. A more common factor is alcohol. Taylor and Gammon (1975) found that there was a relationship between alco-

provocation. We shake our heads sadly as we wonder how one person could kill another over an argument about what TV show they should watch (a story which, incidentally, appeared in the news not too long ago). The fact is that while the television program served as a trigger, it had little to do with the actual murder. Instead, the choice of a TV show was the source of anger and irritation, but these feelings grew as one person cursed under his breath, then the other reacted with a more inflammatory statement, and the other reacted with even greater emotion. Often, when an argu-

holism and aggression, for instance. And the use of alcohol has been related to many violent crimes, since it tends to reduce inhibitions. A person who may normally be able to keep control of his or her emotions may overreact to provocation after drinking too much.

In all, there are many factors that contribute to violent behavior. Our list here is necessarily an incomplete one, for we couldn't possibly touch on all the influences that play a role in aggression. One factor remains, however, that has received a tremendous amount of attention as a factor in aggression in our society. The boxed discussion *TV Violence: Factor or Scapegoat?* looks at the possible connection between the aggression shown on television and violence in the streets.

Coping with Aggression

Whether or not aggressive behavior is a normal part of our lives, most of us will have to deal with it at times. We see violence on TV; we may worry about it as a neighborhood threat; and we must sometimes cope with our own impulses to let anger get out of control. Two issues in coping with aggression are especially relevant here: learning to deal with aggression in others (especially children's aggressive behaviors) and dealing with our own anger in a positive way.

Dealing with Aggression as Parents

For people who deal regularly with children, either as parents or teachers, the question of how to cope with aggression may be especially important. Should aggression be punished? If so, what type of punishment is most effective? These questions are controversial, but the evidence suggests that punishment (or the realistic threat of punishment) can inhibit aggression, as long as it is also balanced with rewards for positive behaviors (Chasdi & Lawrence, 1955). The type of punishment is important, of course. If parents use aggressive punishment to counter their children's aggression, they serve as role models, as we saw earlier in this chapter. But punishments such as parental disapproval and loss of privileges may be effective.

Punishment, however, is only one way of dealing with aggressive behavior. Another effective method is to change the characteristics of the situation that leads to aggression in the first place. Most parents know what kinds of statements or actions lead to aggression in their homes, and these situations can be limited. For instance, if two siblings always argue over the same TV shows each week night, a system of taking turns can be arranged. It is also helpful to find healthy outlets for anger and frustration (a punching bag may give an active child a legitimate release for aggressive energy, at least until the child learns how to express it in a more socially appropriate manner); to create opportunities for positive actions (such as guiding children in making their own compromises); and to model reasonable, non-aggressive behaviors. Communication is also an important factor. Many people who act aggressively have never learned how to talk their problems out. This can be taught effectively, if children are encouraged to voice their aggressive feelings in a socially acceptable manner (Ginott, 1965).

Finally, aggression can be reduced if its rewards are decreased. Unfortunately, violence is often successful in obtaining short-term goals—albeit at a price both for the individual and others in society. A combination of reinforcements and punishments can be used to control these antisocial behaviors, however, and these may serve to convince aggressive persons to use other, less aggressive means of obtaining their goals.

Assertiveness vs. Aggression

It is useful to know how to help others cope with aggression; but for many people, a more important challenge is to learn to put their own anger or aggressive energy to positive uses. Our soci-

TV Violence: Factor or Scapegoat?

A spectacular and shocking story appeared in the newspapers in 1977. A young man in Florida, accused of murdering his neighbor, claimed an unusual defense. He said that his actions had been the result of TV programs he had been watching.

This line of defense was not successful: the judge ruled that it was impossible to gauge the effect of television on any single individual. Yet the issue itself cannot be dismissed so easily. Although few, if any, cases of violence can be directly linked to television violence, that does not mean that no relationship exists.

Look at the statistics:

- Ninety-five percent of the homes in the United States have at least one television set. Many have two.
- By the time a child enters adolescence, he or she has spent more time in front of the TV than in the classroom (Liebert et al., 1973).
- The average school-aged child spends 15–25 hours each week in front of the television.

While the effects of television viewing on aggression are still a hotly debated issue, it is hard to imagine such a time-consuming activity *not* affecting behavior.

Indeed, the Surgeon General's report in 1972 claimed that a cause-and-effect relationship did exist between television violence and aggression. Other studies—almost 2,000 to date, with thousands more likely to come in the future—have had less clear-cut findings, and some have used qualifiers that weaken the Surgeon General's definitive statement. Although the issue is far from closed, two conclusions are suggested.

First, television violence may not affect all viewers. But for certain people, it does seem to increase the likelihood of aggression. These individuals seem to be brought over the brink by what they see—in the same way, perhaps, that environmental factors such as noise or crowding may lead to aggression in some people but not in others. Television violence, in a sense, is the "straw that breaks the camel's back": it is one additional factor combined with an already flammable situation.

Take, for example, a person who has been raised in a violent subculture, has been exposed to the modeling of aggressive behavior, and enters a specific situation already annoyed or frustrated. Such a person might be easily aroused to violence anyway. Watching it day in and day out might make it an even more attractive alternative to a relatively unexciting existence. In fact, Erich Fromm (1973) has suggested that boredom may be linked to aggressive behavior. Violence has an excitement about it, and this feeling may seem to bring relief to certain individuals.

There is one more possible effect of television violence, and this one may be even more serious than the first. Television may be desensitizing us to violence (Thomas et al., 1977). One commentator puts it this way:

The TV child develops a thick-skinned detachment, a cynical outlook. Constantly exposed to the bloody punch or push, the noise, and the rough language of TV, children learn to accept violence. What is amazing and shameful is the ease with which people accept violence as "OK." (Moody, 1980, p. 91)

When people are shocked by violence, they react against it with a public outcry. But when they accept day-to-day violence, they become apathetic to it and do little about it. Perhaps this acceptance is one of the most dangerous effects of television violence.

ety presents us with such conflicting messages about expressing anger that it is not uncommon for people to feel guilty about standing up for themselves, or to feel that they don't have a right to satisfy their own needs. At the root of this problem, there is often a confusion between the two terms *assertiveness* and *aggressiveness*.

Suppose you are returning something to a store because it doesn't work right. You wait your turn and state in clear, concise terms that the computer game you bought here four days ago is not working properly. The sales clerk says you must be mistaken—perhaps you aren't hooking it up correctly.

At this point, you have a few choices. You may stand five inches from the sales clerk and scream that this lousy product doesn't work, that you want your money back, and that you don't care how much embarrassment you cause them— you are going to make a scene until they have provided you the satisfaction you deserve. Alternatively, you can make your point quietly and politely let the clerk know that you won't be dissuaded and that you know that your complaint is valid. In the first case, you are being *aggressive*— getting your own "needs met but in doing so [stepping] on the rights of others," as Egan describes it (1977, p. 40). In the second case, you are being **assertive,** for you are recognizing others' rights at the same time that you meet your own needs.

Which tactic works better? Many people seem to think that the more noise they make, the more effective they will be. As the old adage goes, "it's the squeaky wheel that gets the grease." However, "squeaking" doesn't necessarily mean being aggressive. A number of students who work in department stores have reported to one of the authors that when their customers act aggressively, they usually respond by giving them a harder time. They allow them to wait; they ask for a sales receipt; they examine it slowly, and the like. They don't like being treated rudely. On the other hand, when an assertive person returns some merchandise, they respond much more willingly and more quickly.

Would you give this man what he wants? Despite the old saying that "it's the squeaky wheel that gets the grease," aggressive behavior is actually less productive than assertive actions.

In sum, assertiveness is productive where aggressive behavior may actually be counterproductive. Thus, it pays to learn assertiveness; and training courses or seminars are being offered all over North America to teach people how to "stand up for yourself without being kicked out, brushed off, put down or shut up" (Dubrow, 1975, p. 40). In the final section of this chapter, we'll look briefly at the points these courses emphasize.

Assertive Acting in a way that will further one's own needs and goals without violating the rights of others.

Assertiveness Training

There is no single, standard procedure used to teach people to be more assertive. However, most seminars follow a fairly similar format.

The **assertiveness training** session generally begins by discussing the problems that brought people to the seminar. Some may feel that their boss takes advantage of them at work. Others may feel depressed about themselves and constantly guilty. Still others may have difficulty turning friends down for money or other favors, or they may not be able to express their needs to a spouse. Some people attend assertiveness training sessions because their aggressive behaviors have been counterproductive. Whatever the problem is, the leader tries to get members to describe it in specific terms. The "why" is not as important as the description of the situation itself.

Once the group members understand the specific types of situations in which they have trouble asserting themselves, they are able to begin trying to change their behaviors. One particularly helpful technique is **role playing.** Perhaps the group leader will play your part while you play the role of the salesperson (or whoever else is giving you trouble). This role playing is combined with behavior rehearsal. You and other members of the group may give advice to the person playing your role, or the leader may model alternative behaviors that you can use to assert yourself and then you are given a chance to rehearse these new behaviors. The leader may also teach you certain rules that can help you become more assertive. One such rule is to repeat your request in the same language if someone is trying to sidestep your demands. You might repeat "I want a refund, please" two or three times as the leader is actively trying to draw you off the track. As all of these strategies are taught and rehearsed, the group takes part in active questioning and discussion.

Other techniques may also be used to help individuals unlearn their old responses while learning new ones. Group members may be taught relaxation techniques, such as those discussed in Chapter 6; or they may be taught to use the cognitive techniques that we explored in Chapter 1's discussion of "The Importance of Talking to Yourself."

The combination of unlearning old behaviors at the same time that new, more effective behaviors are learned is a helpful approach for many people. This very combination, however, makes it difficult to clearly evaluate assertiveness training in general. Is it the role playing or behavior rehearsal that helps, for instance, or is it the relaxation that is most effective? There is no clear-cut answer to this question. However, most of the studies in the field have shown that these programs usually accomplish their purpose and are "a valid and efficient treatment method" (Rimm & Masters, 1974). Of course, assertiveness does not assure that you will always get what you want. You may have to compromise in some situations (Grasha, 1978). This will not be because your strategy isn't effective, though, but because even the most persuasive of us can't change everything.

> **Assertiveness training**   Group workshops using various techniques such as role playing to help the participants act in a more assertive fashion.
>
> **Role playing**   A technique used in assertiveness training, sensitivity groups, and psychotherapy. An individual acts out the role of another person as a way of developing insight into the other person's viewpoint. Role playing also provides an opportunity to practice new behaviors, such as assertiveness.

A Look Back and a Look Ahead

In this chapter and the last two chapters, we have explored a number of personal challenges that may threaten people's sense of safety or security. Stress, anxiety, guilt, and depression, and anger and aggression all put demands on the individual. These states of mind are part of life. They cannot be eliminated. But people can learn to direct these feelings into constructive channels—to control them rather than be controlled by them.

The next four chapters will take us a step further as we turn to the third level of needs. These needs also deal with adjustment challenges, but on a broader plane. The *belongingness* needs involve not just ourselves, but our relationships with others. In Chapters 8, 9, and 10 we will explore the topics of social roles, interpersonal communication, and love relationships; Chapter 11 deals with a related and very important topic, sexual adjustment. Learning to satisfy these needs can help us in our growth toward self-actualization, while failing to find healthy adjustments in this area can prevent us from truly experiencing fulfillment.

Summary

1. Anger is an energizing emotion, and it can have positive as well as negative aspects. Anger is often caused by frustration, as we define it in its broadest sense.

2. Anger is often disguised, in part because many people feel guilty about experiencing it. Anger is sometimes hidden in our language; it may also be directed at inappropriate targets. When a person is angry at one individual, but takes it out on another, this is called displacement.

3. Madow advocates a four-step process in dealing with anger. The first step is recognizing your anger; the second involves identifying the source of anger; the third involves finding the reason for your anger; and the fourth is dealing realistically with anger. Physical activity, hobbies, and expressing yourself verbally in a socially appropriate manner are ways of dealing with anger.

4. Aggression is difficult to define. A good working definition is that aggression is an attempt by one individual to deliver a noxious stimulus to another person.

5. Ethologists approach aggression as a natural phenomenon, as a functional behavior that serves to maintain and support evolution for many species. The Freudians view aggression as a destructive urge that can be turned either toward others or toward oneself.

6. According to the behavioral approach, aggression is simply another learned behavior.

7. Several factors contribute to aggression. When a person is already aroused, aggression is triggered more easily than if that person is in a relaxed state. A series of experiments by Bandura and Walters also showed that aggression can be imitated. A third factor is availability of a weapon—which causes increased likelihood of violent aggression. A fourth factor is alcohol, which may contribute to aggression. Other factors also play a role.

8. Arguments may escalate until they reach a point at which aggression results. Aggression often leads to more aggression. Attack is often symbolic and some people react to mild attacks with unnecessary force.

9. The issue of the relationship of TV to aggression is an important one. Many studies indicate that TV violence can increase the likelihood of violence in some people who have been raised in an aggressive environment. People who watch a great deal of violence on television may tend to accept aggression as a normal and natural part of life.

10. Certain types of punishment may deter aggression, as long as it is swift, moderate, and combined with positive reinforcements for nonviolent behavior. However, punishment is a negative way of dealing with aggression. A more positive method is to provide healthy outlets for anger, as well as nonviolent models, and to reduce the rewards for violence.

11. Assertiveness and aggression are not the same. Aggression implies stepping on the rights of others, whereas assertiveness describes behavior that respects others' rights at the same time one stands up for one's own rights.

12. Role playing, modeling, and behavior rehearsal are often used in assertiveness training seminars. The evidence indicates that such seminars are often successful in encouraging more assertive behavior.

Key Terms and Concepts

frustration-aggression
hypothesis
catharsis
aggression
Thanatos
Eros

ethology
escalation
assertive
assertiveness training
role playing

Belongingness Needs

Psychologist Helen Perlman tells how she first realized the importance of social roles:

"It was a square-dance party, large enough so that some of us were strangers to one another. Within one square was a man who was the despair of us all: he went right when the call was 'left,' he skipped when he was to 'stand,' he bumbled, collided, stood bewildered.... One of us went to our host and asked who this poor soul was. 'Oh, that one!' he said. 'He's X, the famous physicist.' What happened? Attitudes and actions in the whole group somersaulted. This was no dancing imbecile—this was a dancing brain; no dolt, but a genius! Warm

Social Roles and Sex Roles

indulgence ... took the place of annoyance, eager helpfulness rushed in to fill the vacuum of tolerance. But more than this: in his role as dancing partner Mr. X was inept, apologetic, uneasy; but when he was in his major work role of internationally recognized scientist, he was competent, keen, serenely self-confident. Which, I asked myself, is the *real* Mr. X?" (1968, pp. 4-5)*

*Reprinted from *Persona* by Helen Harris Perlman by permission of The University of Chicago Press.

Which indeed? The way we think about other people depends upon their performance of **social roles**—expected patterns of behavior related to a person's position in society. If a person acts like a leader, we think of her or him as a leader. If a person acts shy and insecure, we automatically relate to that person in a way that reflects that judgment. Or, more specifically, if we see a person as a business executive, a teacher, a plumber, a lover, or a world-renowned physicist, we react to that person according to the role we perceive. If we suddenly find that a person is more (or less) than we had imagined, we automatically adjust our relationship with that person. Social roles, in other words, are all-important in defining our relationships with other persons.

Social roles are so important that they even define our self-concepts. This is true both in specific terms and in the very broadest sense. Specifically, we tend to think of ourselves in terms of the social roles that are important to us. You may think of yourself as a student, a mother or father or daughter or son, or a worker, athlete, artist, or "rebel." The way you relate to other people reflects this self-definition. As an athlete, for instance, you might be slightly condescending to others who aren't as disciplined as you. Social roles also affect our self-concepts in a very broad sense. Like Mr. X, we may feel awkward and bumbling in one situation, but competent and comfortable in another. The more our lives are spent in situations in which we feel comfortable, the more positive our self-images will be.

Thus, understanding social roles is basic to understanding the adjustments people make at Maslow's third stage of needs, the belongingness needs. By exploring social roles and their effects on behavior and self-concept in this chapter, we will pave the way for the next three chapters' discussions of communication, love, and sexual relationships. In this chapter we will look broadly at social norms (behavior patterns expected of everyone in a society) and also at social roles and how they change. We will also explore one of the most basic elements of social roles, sex roles, to see whether and how gender makes a difference in our perception of both ourselves and others.

Social Norms and Roles

A number of years ago, a short film entitled *Invisible Walls* was released. The "invisible walls" it explored were walls we don't often think about: the 12–18 inch barrier of space that separates us from the people we talk with each day. While these walls are "invisible," they are real, and we feel uncomfortable if someone violates them. The film documented this well. It showed college students intentionally violating these barriers as they conducted a consumer survey while interviewing subjects in a shopping center. The behavior of the interviewees is fascinating. To maintain the 18-inch barrier, they moved back further and further, almost into the stream of traffic.

The scene is reminiscent of a "Candid Camera" situation in that people are caught off guard, not quite knowing what they are reacting to. In those television episodes from the 60s and 70s a man or woman from the TV show would politely victimize an ordinary person-on-the-street by taking a tire off his car, helping himself to the victim's dinner at a restaurant, and so forth, and the reaction would be secretly recorded on film.

Social Norms: "Invisible" Codes

The film and the television program are similar in that they force into our consciousness something we normally don't think about at all: **social**

Social role An expected pattern of behavior considered appropriate to a person's position in society.

Social norms Shared rules or guidelines that prescribe behavior appropriate in a given situation.

Social norms are often "invisible"—until they are broken, that is! How would you react if this man sat down next to you at a diner?

norms. Social norms are defined as "shared rules or guidelines that prescribe the behavior that is appropriate in a given situation" (Robertson, 1981, p. 67). Norms govern the behavior of everyone in a society, although most of us are unaware of these norms until they are broken. The people interviewed in *Invisible Walls,* for example, were probably not consciously aware of the distance norm until the students violated this tacit agreement. The same is true of many of the episodes on the "Candid Camera" show, as well as countless other everyday situations in which our behaviors are guided by unspoken codes.

A few examples of such common norms are our expectation that we will greet acquaintances with a handshake and a "Hello, nice to meet you" rather than a kiss on the cheek; that we will exchange pleasantries with the store clerk who sells us a new pair of shoes, but won't approach deeper topics such as religion or politics; that we will be reasonably quiet in the library, somber at a funeral, and cheerful at a wedding. The list could go on. At least at the basic level, social norms are rarely called into question. In fact, a person who crosses the "invisible walls" by breaking one of these codes will be met by sanctions—unpleasant consequences that might range from a polite but hasty brush-off (for the person who breaks the "greetings" norms) to being asked to leave (for the person who transgresses the funeral code).

Changing Norms   Although norms govern our behavior, they are not unchanging. For one thing, norms are situationally specific. That is, they may be modified according to the situation. Although you are not normally permitted to embrace a stranger, there are some occasions on which you might do this—on midnight at a New Year's Eve party, for instance, or after you have just escaped from a burning building. Even our strongest norms may be broken in some situations. Thus, while killing is forbidden, it is considered necessary during war or in self-defense.

Just as norms change from one situation to the next, they also vary from time to time, as we saw in Chapter 1's discussion of normal behavior. In ancient Rome, for instance, a father had the right to kill his children if they were disobedient—an idea that would be treated as highly abnormal today (Sinnegen & Boak, 1977). Even in our own society, norms change from one period to another. Not too many years ago, it was unusual for a marriage to end in divorce, and persons who ended a marriage in this way were subject not only to the personal strains that this situation naturally brings, but also to social sanctions. Today, however, divorces are far more common; indeed, divorced women raising young children comprise one of the most rapidly growing segments of the population (Bee, 1978). There are now fewer sanctions against breaking the traditional norm that "marriage is forever."

Norms change for many reasons. Some changes result from a sudden catastrophe or revolution. In wars, many men are killed, and as a result, it is not unusual to find great age disparities in dating and marriage in a country that has recently been involved in such a conflict. Political revolutions are another situation that may result in sweeping changes in norms. This is well illustrated by the communist revolutions that took place during this century. In both the U.S.S.R. and the People's Republic of China, for instance, the social structure was thoroughly revised, as were living arrangements, job structures, education, food distribution, and virtually every other aspect of life. Behaviors that had been commonplace before—such as private ownership of property—were suddenly no longer norms. They were now punished instead. Scientific invention may also change norms. Inventions such as the telephone, automobile, electric light bulb, TV and radio, and now the computer, have clearly affected our lifestyle.

Age Norms   Just as norms change from time to time and from situation to situation, they also vary (to some extent, at least) according to who you are. A clear example of this are **age norms,** culturally based expectations for age-appropriate behaviors. Age norms tell us the age at which a person should finish school, marry, hold a top job position, retire from work, and become a grandparent, as was found in some research by Neugarten et al. (1965). These age norms may be quite specific. For instance, some 80 percent of the middle-aged American men in Neugarten's sample, and 90 percent of the women, thought the best time to marry was between ages 20–25. Both men and women thought the optimum age for retirement was between 60–65.

Age norms govern not only the transition points of life, but also the daily behaviors in which we expect people to engage. For instance, we would hardly expect a child to keep up-to-date with current world events, but we assume that most adults will have at least a basic understanding of what's going on in the world. Again, it wouldn't surprise us to see a 20-year-old at the

---

Age norms   Culturally based expectations for age-appropriate behaviors within a particular society.

local disco, but it probably would surprise us to see that person's parents or grandparents there.

The concept of age norms—of acting in accordance with your age—brings us to the closely related concept of role behavior. While norms shape the behavior of society in general, roles vary from person to person. We'll look more closely at social roles below.

Social Roles

We defined roles earlier as behaviors that are related to a specific position in society. Although roles are based on your own actions or behaviors, it is important to remember that roles are *social* attributes. That is, they usually require an interaction with at least one other individual. There are no teachers without students; no police officers without a population who needs law enforcement; no presidents without organizations.

We can clearly see how roles affect our expectations. You may be willing to talk about something as personal as your sex life with a close friend, but not with your landlord. You may expect a certain degree of knowledgeable expertise from a teacher that you wouldn't expect from the clerk at the supermarket. You expect your parents to react in a certain way if you call and tell them you're out of money again. These role expectations help give our world predictability and security.

While roles provide us with this security, they are neither automatic nor unchanging. We don't grow into roles without some preparation from society; and once we have taken on a role, we may not maintain it forever. Thus, roles have to be learned and relearned throughout our lives.

> **Socialization** The process by which we learn what rules are appropriate in our society.
>
> **Anticipatory socialization** The process by which an individual prepares for a change in role.

Preparing for Roles The process by which we learn what roles are appropriate in our society is called **socialization.** Babies know nothing of what roles they will play later on. Any behaviors, such as crying or sucking, are innate. All this changes radically in the coming years, as young children learn that they are dependent upon their parents; that certain behaviors are expected of them in the home, at school, in other situations; that they should behave in certain ways towards authority figures, and in other ways towards their friends. They come to realize what is considered appropriate for their age and sex, and they begin to understand what life will be like when they become adults.

In fact, we all undergo a rather elaborate process of training for our adult roles as workers, parents, citizens, and the like. We learn from watching others perform these roles, or from helping others carry out a role (as when a child learns about parenting by helping take care of a new baby). We also learn through formal education, at public schools and perhaps later on at a college or a trade school.

We may play many roles during our adult lives, moving from student to husband or wife, to mother or father, to worker to retiree to grandparent (often, these roles overlap). These changes require some preparation. The retiree who has not planned for his or her new financial needs, social changes, and goal orientations, for instance, will feel lost and disappointed in the new unemployed status. With careful planning, however, the retiree may find that this new time of life provides freedom and opportunity. In the same way, the couple who plan to marry need to discuss important questions such as whether they want children, what role expectations they hold for themselves and their partner, and so forth. Planning ahead of time can prevent important misunderstandings; it also can provide partners with long-term goals that provide a sense of direction. When we actively prepare for a new role, this training has a special name. It is called **anticipatory socialization.**

Part of the socialization process occurs as we watch others perform roles we might play as adults.

Anticipatory socialization may require some formal training. For instance, if you plan to live in another country, you might attend language classes or learn what you could about the culture of the country. If you plan a career as a doctor, you would go through the lengthy process of internship as well as medical school. Self-training, through reading or talking to others about their roles, is also an important part of anticipatory socialization. Thus, if you are about to become a parent for the first time, you may very well find that your reading material focuses on your new role and that you are more interested in conversing with other parents of young children.

Not all changes in role are gradual enough to allow us to prepare for them; nor do we always prepare as thoroughly as we might. When too little anticipatory socialization takes place, the results can be unfortunate. For instance, the college athlete from a poor family signs a multi-million dollar basketball contract. All of a sudden, money is plentiful, and the temptation is to spend it quickly. Managing the money is difficult because the youngster has had no experience with large sums; even if he hires a business manager, he doesn't have the knowledge to ascertain whether the money is being invested wisely or not. Stocks, bonds, real estate, and tax write-offs may all be foreign to him. Sadly, many sports figures have been taken, as they neither invested wisely in the present nor planned for a future beyond their sports career.

Adjusting to Roles   Of course, the sudden rise to fame and fortune doesn't always leave time for anticipatory socialization. When one has to learn "on the job," so to speak, without advance preparation, this training has a different name: **resocialization.** Resocialization takes place when you must learn how to cope after you've taken on a new role. It occurs in many situations: through a rise in social status (through marriage, inheritance, or even winning the lottery) and also through a sudden decline in fortune, as when a person is fired from a good-paying job and must suddenly stretch to make ends meet. It involves learning new skills, but it also involves new goals, interests, and attitudes.

Divorce is an increasingly common situation that requires resocialization. It requires several facets of role adjustment, especially when there are children. For one thing, the financial burdens are greater for both ex-spouses, and these pressures are often difficult to adjust to. A second pressure point is the change in status from "married" to "single." Reentry into the "dating game" isn't as easy as it might seem: many newly divorced people are surprised at how ill-at-ease they feel with the rituals of attracting and testing new partners.

A third area of adjustment is the parenting role. The parent who is awarded custody finds that the responsibilities are all the heavier with no

---

Resocialization   The process by which an individual must learn to cope with demands of a new role while occupying that role.

---

other adult in the house; and when the other parent sees the children only occasionally, the relationship may take on an unrealistic or superficial tone, with trips to the zoo, for instance, but little time to talk. Currently, the woman is most often awarded custody, while the man becomes the "weekend parent." Mavis Hetherington and her colleagues studied the effects on both parents (1977). Their findings indicated that at first, mothers discipline more and fathers less, and that the children are given more freedom and the home is generally less organized than before the divorce. This situation peaks at about one year, when both parents settle more comfortably into their new roles and a more systematized lifestyle emerges. Because the problems of adjusting to divorce are serious, therefore, the first year is normally the worst (Trotter, 1976).

Role Conflicts   Socialization, anticipatory socialization, and resocialization help us fit into the separate roles we take during our lives. In this way, they are important processes of adjustment. But while we may learn to adjust to each role we take, the fact is that all of us occupy many different roles at the same time, and sometimes these roles conflict with one another.

For example, the same man may act as a prison guard 30 hours each week; he may also be a father, a husband, the chief household cook, an investor, and a bowling star. Or the same woman may have a full-time career at the same time that she manages the house, the children's routines, and the family finances. Neither of these situations is unusual today, especially as growing numbers of women juggle work and parenthood. Common as they are, however, the question needs to be asked as to how many roles a person can maintain at one time. The father who promised to take his child to a ball game the weekend before an important report is due will experience *role conflict:* whichever role he carries out, it will be to the detriment of the other role. This situation is relatively simple compared to that of the working adult whose own parent becomes gravely ill, but who doesn't want to rely on a nursing home, or to the parent (most often the mother, in our society today) who feels a strong need to further her career but finds that the demands of childrearing make the goal very difficult, at least for the time being.

In the examples mentioned above, the role conflict is felt most painfully as an impossible demand for time; and this dimension of role conflict is one of the most frequently felt. Role conflict can present other problems, however. Take, for example, the worker who is suddenly promoted from the ranks to supervise his or her friends. This person may want to maintain the same warm relationship with fellow workers, but may find that there are inherent conflicts in being both "chum" and "boss" to the same person. Another powerful example of role conflict was presented in the 1981 movie *Chariots of Fire,* in which the Scottish runner Eric Liddell protested that as a Christian he could not run in an Olympic heat on a Sunday. Others told him that his role as a British subject was more important than that of a Christian, but he disagreed.

To this point, we have been talking about roles and role conflict without focusing in on one of the most basic aspects of our role identity: sex roles. Perhaps more than any other roles, sex roles provide us with an underlying sense of who we are in relation to others around us. More than any other area of role identity, too, sex roles have been the center of much research—and also much controversy. We will explore this powerful social role in the remainder of this chapter.

Sex Roles

So they let you dress up like a cowgirl, and when you say, "I'm gonna be a cowgirl when I grow up," they laugh and say, "Ain't she cute." Then one day they tell you, "Look, honey, cowgirls are only play. You can't really be one." And that's when I holler, "Wait a minute! . . . you're screwing around with my personal identity, with my plans for the future. What do you mean I can't be a cowgirl?" When I got the answer, I began to realize there was a lot bigger difference between me and my brother than what I could see in the bathtub. (Robbins, 1976, pp. 129–30)

What is particularly difficult for men is seeking or accepting help from friends. I . . . learned early that dependence was unacceptable. When I was eight, I went to a summer camp I disliked. My parents visited me in the middle of the summer and, when it was time for them to leave, I wanted to go with them. They refused, and I yelled and screamed and was miserably unhappy for the rest of the day. That evening an older camper comforted me, sitting on my bed as I cried, patting me on the back soothingly. . . He was in some ways clumsy or funny-looking, and a few days later I joined a group of kids in cruelly making fun of him, an act which upset me . . . for years. I can only explain it in terms of my feeling, as early as the age of eight, that by needing and accepting his help and comfort I had compromised myself, and took it out on him. (Fasteau, 1974, p. 14)*

These quotations present two very different perspectives. In one case (from *Even Cowgirls Get the Blues* by Tom Robbins), a girl is told that her "when I grow up" dream will never come true; in the other (from Marc Fasteau's *The Male Machine*), a boy is so indoctrinated to avoid seeming dependent that he strikes back at the person who comforted him. Despite these differences, however, the girl and the boy share the same experience. Each felt a great conflict between who they were, as individuals, and who society said they should be, as male or female.

This experience, in one way or another, touches virtually all of us during development; and it is one facet of the influence of sex roles that has received a great deal of attention, both in research and in popular literature. How we conceive of our own sex roles, as well as how others expect us to behave, greatly affects our lives. The development of sex roles and their influence on our behavior are two fascinating areas of study, and we'll explore both of them in the pages that follow.

*Reprinted by permission of McGraw-Hill Book Company.

Two versions of sex-trait ideals. Although we may not aspire to these ideals ourselves, do they affect our perceptions in other ways?

What Are Sex Roles?

Sex roles are social roles. Like the other social roles we have described in this chapter, they are patterns of behavior that are expected of certain groups in society. In our society, for instance, women have traditionally been expected to take on most of the tasks associated with childcare, cooking, and home upkeep, while men's roles have been more centered around breadwinning.

> **Sex roles**   The behaviors expected of individuals within a given society on the basis of whether they are male or female.
>
> **Sex-trait stereotype**   Psychological traits that people in a society believe to be characteristic of either males or females.

Sex-role expectations go far deeper than traditional divisions of labor; for besides being homemakers, breadwinners, and so forth, females and males in our society are also assumed to have certain personality characteristics.

Sex-trait Stereotypes   Best et al. (1977) define **sex-trait stereotypes** as "constellations of psychological characteristics people believe characterize men more or less than women." These stereotypes go far deeper than the half-joking caricatures with which we're all familiar (the nervous woman driver, for instance, or the man who can't find his way around the kitchen). Sex-trait stereotypes make far-reaching assumptions about basic personality characteristics.

Psychologist Inge Broverman and her associates were interested in exploring these assumptions (1972). They compiled a "sex-stereotype questionnaire" listing 122 personality characteristics commonly assumed to be "male" or "female" in our culture and then administered the questionnaire to a large sample. Their series of studies documented not only that these assumptions do exist, but that the male-associated traits (such as dominance, assertiveness, and lack of emotionality) are more likely to be valued by society than are the female sex-trait stereotypes. Table 8.1 summarizes the traits found by the Broverman studies. These qualities are grouped into two "clusters": the *competency cluster* (in which masculine traits are more desirable) and the *warmth-expressiveness cluster* (in which feminine traits are more desirable). The relative size of the two clusters is itself revealing: there are many more highly valued traits in the masculine competency cluster than in the feminine group.

We have all heard these stereotypes ever since we were little. The questions that have intrigued psychologists are whether or not these assumptions are correct and, if not, where these stereotypes have come from. Still a third question is especially important to psychology of adjustment. If these stereotypes are unfair or limiting to individuals, as the quotations from Robbins and Fasteau indicate, what can we do about them?

Evaluating the Stereotypes   It isn't too difficult to take exception to Table 8.1's list. We all know women who are logical, direct, and aggressive; and likewise, men who are gentle, talkative, and unadventurous. Does that prove that the list is wrong, however? After all, the exception often proves the rule. Perhaps there is some truth to these stereotypes.

With that possibility in mind, you may want to evaluate your own beliefs about sex-related traits. The 20 statements in the box *Gender and Personality: Test Your Own Assumptions* provide an opportunity. Read through the list. Place a T, F, or ? in the space to the left of each statement, to indicate whether you agree or disagree with the statement, or whether you think the research is inconclusive.

After you've completed this exercise, you can check your answers against the findings of Maccoby and Jacklin (1974), who reviewed over 1600 studies to see what sex differences, if any, had been consistently supported by research. Their findings may surprise you. Of the statements listed in the box, only the first four sex-related differences received consistent support in the literature: that boys are more aggressive; that girls have greater verbal ability; that boys have greater visual-spatial ability, which "entails the judgment and manipulation of space relationships" (Minton & Schneider, 1980, p. 273); and that boys have greater mathematical ability. The next eight statements (statements 5–12) were shown to be myths and the final eight statements (13–20) are still question marks. Research hasn't verified them, but neither has it demonstrated otherwise.

Maccoby and Jacklin's research is quoted in virtually every psychology text, but we should note that their conclusions are somewhat controversial. Some researchers have criticized Maccoby and Jacklin's methodology, on the grounds that they lumped together studies that used different measurements to evaluate variables (Block, 1976). Others draw different conclusions from the research. For example, Bardwick (1971) argues that the research demonstrates girls to be generally more dependent than boys, a conclusion with which Maccoby and Jacklin disagree.

These differences and disagreements in the field are to be expected. The finding of sex differences is often dependent upon the situation in which the measurements are taken (Maccoby and Jacklin, 1973). In addition, a tremendous amount of overlap exists between the sexes, even where research seems to support sex differences. For example, the experimental finding that girls are superior in verbal ability does not mean that every girl is superior to every boy in this area. In addition, these abilities are not simply either present or absent. Rather, the question is one of degree, with males or females tending to demonstrate more or less of a quality. Where these differences supposedly exist, there remains the question of

Table 8.1 A Listing of Sex-Trait Stereotypes
(Responses from 74 college men and 80 college women)

Competency Cluster: Masculine Pole Is More Desirable

Feminine	Masculine
Not at all aggressive	Very aggressive
Not at all independent	Very independent
Very emotional	Not at all emotional
Does not hide emotions at all	Almost always hides emotions
Very subjective	Very objective
Very easily influenced	Not at all easily influenced
Very submissive	Very dominant
Dislikes math and science very much	Likes math and science very much
Very excitable in a minor crisis	Not at all excitable in a minor crisis
Very passive	Very active
Not at all competitive	Very competitive
Very illogical	Very logical
Very home oriented	Very worldly
Not at all skilled in business	Very skilled in business
Very sneaky	Very direct
Does not know the way of the world	Knows the way of the world
Feelings easily hurt	Feelings not easily hurt
Not at all adventurous	Very adventurous
Has difficulty making decisions	Can make decisions easily
Cries very easily	Never cries
Almost never acts as a leader	Almost always acts as a leader
Not at all self-confident	Very self-confident
Very uncomfortable about being aggressive	Not at all uncomfortable about being aggressive
Not at all ambitious	Very ambitious
Unable to separate feelings from ideas	Easily able to separate feelings from ideas
Very dependent	Not at all dependent
Very conceited about appearance	Never conceited about appearance
Thinks women are always superior to men	Thinks men are always superior to women
Does not talk freely about sex with men	Talks freely about sex with men

Warmth-Expressiveness Cluster: Feminine Pole Is More Desirable

Feminine	Masculine
Doesn't use harsh language at all	Uses very harsh language
Very talkative	Not at all talkative
Very tactful	Very blunt
Very gentle	Very rough
Very aware of feelings of others	Not at all aware of feelings of others
Very religious	Not at all religious
Very interested in own appearance	Not at all interested in own appearance
Very neat in habits	Very sloppy in habits
Very quiet	Very loud
Very strong need for security	Very little need for security
Enjoys art and literature	Does not enjoy art and literature at all
Easily expresses tender feelings	Does not express tender feelings at all easily

Source: Broverman et al., 1972. Reprinted by permission.

whether they are learned or inborn. We'll turn next to that question.

The Question of Causation

Even if we accept Maccoby and Jacklin's conclusions, we still have the knotty problem of explaining sex differences that have been found. Does biological make-up (for instance, hormonal differences) contribute to differences between boys' and girls' behavior? Are males and females simply socialized differently? Or is there a combination between these two factors?

Biological Factors   In trying to explain behavior differences between males and females, you might be tempted to look first to biology. After all, the different appearance of men and women is caused by biology; why shouldn't behavioral differences have the same cause?

The research shows little consistent support for this idea. For instance, one of the most frequent arguments—that women are naturally more nurturant since they were "built" for childbearing—hasn't been documented yet; for as we've seen, the research doesn't clearly support that women are more nurturant than men.

Biology does seem to play a role in a few areas, however. The first of these is the higher rate of aggression found in males. Aggressive behavior may be related to higher levels of the male hormone testosterone; and so this may partly explain behaviors such as the greater incidence of

Gender and Personality: Test Your Own Assumptions

The following 20 statements are based on Maccoby and Jacklin's impressive review of the research on sex differences. Test your own assumptions by reading through the list and marking each statement with a *T, F,* or *?* to show whether you think it is true, false, or has not been substantiated by the research. Maccoby and Jacklin's findings are discussed in the text.

T **1.** Males are more aggressive than females.

T **2.** Girls have greater verbal ability than boys.

F **3.** Boys excel in mathematical ability.

T **4.** Boys have greater visual-spatial ability than girls.

F **5.** Girls are more suggestible than boys.

F **6.** Girls have lower self-esteem than boys.

? **7.** Girls do not have strong achievement motivations.

T **8.** Girls are more social than boys.

F **9.** Girls are better at rote learning and simple tasks, while boys are better at high-level tasks that require creativity.

F **10.** Boys are more analytical thinkers.

F **11.** Girls are more affected by heredity than boys.

T **12.** Girls depend more on their ears; boys on their eyes.

T **13.** Males are more dominant than females.

T **14.** Females are more compliant than males.

___ **15.** Girls are more nurturant than boys.

T **16.** Boys are more sensitive to tactile stimulation.

T **17.** Girls are more fearful, timid, and anxious.

T **18.** Boys are more competitive than girls.

F **19.** Boys are more active than girls.

F **20.** Girls are more passive than boys.

Source: Based on Maccoby & Jacklin, 1974.

---

rough play and fighting among boys. However, this hormonal explanation could only imply a tendency towards aggressive behavior. A person learns to inhibit or allow expression of his impulses as he is socialized into society.

A second possible connection is between boys' visual-spatial abilities and genetics. According to one theory, spatial ability is related to a recessive gene that is carried on the X chromosome.* This genetic explanation is controversial, as some re-

*The female chromosomal configuration is XX, while the male's is XY. Because the trait is recessive, high spatial ability wouldn't appear in a female unless both X chromosomes carried it. In the male, however, it may be expressed (as are other sex-linked traits such as color blindness or hemophilia) when it is carried by the single X chromosome.

cent research casts doubt upon this theory (Vandenberg & Kuse, 1979, in Minton & Schneider, 1980).

A third possible biological link relates to differences in development between girls and boys. According to one theory, society reinforces, and thus exaggerates, subtle differences in development. McGuinness (1979) argues that elementary school-aged boys excel in tasks or games that involve large mass muscle groups, while girls of the same age are more advanced in small muscle coordination tasks (such as writing). McGuinness believes that elementary schools pick up on these differences and reinforce them—and that they discriminate against boys, who may show less patience with academic tasks.

McGuinness' theory is controversial, and some other researchers sharply disagree. The fact remains, however, that we still don't know how rates of development affect behavior; and there are many more questions as to how else biology may affect behavior. The reason for this, of course, is that humans aren't raised in a vacuum. From the time of birth, we are surrounded by cues that tell us how to behave if we are girls and how to behave as boys. The most important of these cues come from parents and from society.

Learning from Parents   As a parent, would you treat your sons and daughters differently? Do you think that boys and girls need different experiences to prepare them for their future roles?

Before answering these questions, think for a minute. If you are like most students, your first reaction is to deny that you would treat your sons and daughters any differently. You might protest that you don't want to view them as having different traits. However, after further thought and some discussion, many students begin to modify their views. Aggression seems to bother them more in females than in males. Beauty may be more important in daughters, while a strong income-earning ability may be less important. They admit to different expectations concerning many things, from the games they will play with their sons to their future hopes for their children.

So despite the initial protests, sex stereotypes still seem to be alive and well among parents of the 80s.

These attitudes and expectations affect children from the very beginning. For example, Jeffrey Rubin and his associates found that parents describe their newborn sons and daughters very differently (1974). While daughters are seen as delicate, beautiful, and weak, sons are strong and robust. Parents are more concerned with the health of their daughters than with that of their sons (Pedersen & Robson, 1969). This is especially interesting since males—the weaker of the two sexes at birth—have higher rates both of infant mortality and of most defects and illnesses (Newman & Newman, 1978).

Parents surround their children with different toys. Boys are likely to have more toys in general, and especially more cars and trucks, while little girls have more household materials to play with or use (Rheingold & Cook, 1975). Boys seem to be fed and held more at very early ages, but then the attention switches to girls at about six months. Both parents give their children independence training, and the evidence on dependence is mixed. At later ages, girls are certainly protected more and receive more praise (along with more criticism) than do their brothers.

One aspect of parenting that seems fairly well established is that mothers and fathers act differently toward their offspring. Although both parents discourage sex-inappropriate behavior in their sons (Fling & Manosevitz, 1972), fathers are much more concerned that their sons show masculine behavior than are mothers. One interesting study found that the opposite-sexed parent was usually the more lenient, that fathers had more concern about sex-typing, and that mothers treated the children more alike than fathers did (Rothbard & Maccoby, 1966). Fathers, however, tended to allow both sons and daughters to be more independent.

Parents' expectations and treatments can't help but have an influence, and children quickly become aware of what roles are in store for them and what traits are valued. Thus, when Green-

"I __am__ thinking of the thrill of being a homemaker, the challenge of being a wife and mother as the years roll by. That's why the answer is 'No!'"

Reproduced by special permission of *Playboy* Magazine; copyright © 1966 by Playboy.

berg and Peck asked 3–6-year-old children to look at photos and tell which person would become a doctor, dentist, teacher, and so forth, the sex stereotypes were already set: the males in the photos would take the traditional male jobs, they said, while the females would take roles such as teacher (cited in Papalia & Olds, 1982).

Interestingly, boys seem to identify with their sex roles earlier than girls do, and with much less flexibility (Rabban, 1950). Boys are less likely to accept a change in sex-typed toys than are girls, for instance. In one study, the researcher encouraged girls to play with trucks and boys to play with dolls, using other girls and boys as models (Wolf, 1973). The change worked better for girls than for boys. It is hard to pinpoint the cause for this difference. Perhaps it is because boys are more rigidly socialized than girls. Parents may be happy to see a daughter playing ball, but they are more likely to be concerned about a son who plays with dolls. Another possible reason why boys are less flexible is the greater value society places on the male role.

Unfortunately, it isn't easy to make sense out of the research findings, for they are full of contradictions. We still don't understand the exact

How Do We Learn Sex Roles? Three Theories

Many different influences contribute to sex-role learning, as this chapter discusses. Despite the vast amount of research on the subject, however, we still don't understand exactly how this learning takes place. Three main theories are proposed by the Freudians, the behaviorists, and the cognitive theorists.

Freud traces sex-role learning to the Oedipal situation during the phallic stage. As we saw in Chapter 4, Freud believed that 3–4-year-old boys have sexual feelings toward their mothers, but are afraid that the father will punish them. The child eventually works through the resulting anxiety by learning to identify with his father and to repress his feelings toward his mother. This identification leads him to imitate male behaviors. The situation is a bit different for girls, but the identification process is similar.

Freud's theory has interesting implications in an era when broken families are so common. What happens if the mother or father isn't present in the house? Perhaps a substitute is available, or the individual may identify with a composite male or female image projected by society. Lately, some writers have argued the importance of the father on the daughter's concept of a heterosexual relationship, in that the father may serve as a model for the daughter to look to in her own relationships. Girls who grow up without a father may sometimes have more difficulty in forming relationships with men (and the reverse is true for boys). Thus, the need for good parental examples may have far-reaching importance for both boys and girls.

In contrast to the Freudians, behaviorists do not believe that the mental gymnastics of the Oedipal situation are necessary in understanding sex-role acquisition. Social reinforcement and imitation are sufficient to explain the phenomenon. The implications of the behavioral approach are sweeping. Change the environment, the models, the rewards and punishments, and you can change the sex-role learning. Good role models are just as important as they were in psychoanalytic theory, but the entire social environment must also be taken into account. Teachers, peers, television, and books cannot be ignored.

A third approach, cognitive theory, emphasizes the importance of thinking and information processing. According to this theory, children learn that they are boys or girls first; then they search the world for information about how they should act as boys and girls. "Since I am a girl, I should do and enjoy girl things."

The implications of this cognitive approach are also interesting, for it sees children not as passive receivers of reinforcements, but as active searchers in the process of identification. Children understand gender differences on their own level, and not only is the information available to them important, but the manner in which it is presented and processed. This means that children of different ages may view the same event in a variety of ways, and that parents should listen to their children to understand the manner in which they are perceiving their environments.

Which of these three views is correct? Each makes a persuasive argument that helps to shed light on a very complicated process in development, and all three can help to explain how children learn sex roles.

process by which sex roles are learned (although there are many theories, as the box *How Do We Learn Sex Roles? Three Theories* discusses). Though we still have many questions, there is little doubt of one thing: that the entire environment must be taken into account. The home, school, friends, siblings, television, books, and the child's teachers all present information concerning appropriate sex traits and roles. We turn next to these broader social influences.

Social Factors   Although parents are a primary influence, the social environment is also powerful. Social influences come from several directions. We can't discuss all of them here, but we'll briefly review two of the most important: television and the schools.

The influence of television seems virtually impossible to escape. Children have already watched a great deal of TV by the time they enter school, and they continue watching throughout childhood. Although some educational shows, such as *Sesame Street,* bend over backwards to avoid social stereotypes, this is not true of most TV fare. In situation comedies, dramas, and cartoons, sex stereotypes are rampant. What is the effect? One interesting study compared the time children spend watching TV with the acquisition of traditional sex-role expectations (Frueh & McGhee, 1975). The findings suggested that the two were related. While this does not prove television was responsible for these stereotypes, it does indicate that it may be one factor.

School is another powerful influence, and here, too, sex stereotypes are likely to be reinforced. Most children's readers, for instance, still tell stories in which boys play more active roles than do girls (Howe, 1971). Not only that, but boys usually excel in physical tasks, in creative activities, in inquiry, achievement, and adventure. There are even more pictures of boys than of girls in most children's books (Guttentag & Bray, 1976). When children learn about occupations at school, they are likely to be presented with images of females as nurses and males as doctors and lawyers.

Fortunately, the school situation is beginning to change. In many junior high schools and high schools, all children (not just girls) take home economics; and likewise, girls as well as boys take metal shop classes. In addition, book publishers in the past few years have become more aware of sexist language and of stereotyped images of males and females, and newly published books make an effort to avoid these images. Finally, new laws forbid certain types of discrimination, especially in physical education programs (where, for instance, girls were once excluded from sports such as soccer or basketball).

Despite these advances, though, changes come slowly. Children's literature still has a long way to go. In high school career guidance, sex stereotypes may exist, so that girls and boys are often counseled to set their sights in different directions. And in many elementary classrooms, it is still the boys who are asked to do the "heavy work" such as lifting chairs or carrying books, while girls keep the sinks orderly. Thus, while changes are being made, the schools still contribute to sex stereotyping.

Sexism and What to Do about It

Whatever sex roles exist, no responsible researcher has claimed that one sex is superior to another, nor that an individual's ability in any job is related to his or her gender. Yet the evidence we've just cited shows that sex roles, and sex stereotypes, are bound to be with us for some time to come. To many people, this is not necessarily a bad thing. Perhaps the fact that males and females tend to choose different occupations is simply a matter of preference, they argue, and sociologists and psychologists should leave it at that.

You have probably heard this argument before. In the authors' opinion, it glosses over a dangerous situation. **Sexism** is a word which is very much in the public eye today. Like racism, it connotes an attitude and a set of behaviors that discriminate on the basis of a physical trait. Discrimination against people because of gender is still prevalent in our society, as Table 8.2 indicates, and sexism exists in both subtle and overt forms. Sexism may not always be easy to label in the real world. For instance, is it sexist to walk a

---

Sexism   Prejudice and discrimination based upon gender. Sexism interferes with the development of an individual's potential and is both limiting and injurious.

---

woman home from the theatre, while a man is left to walk home by himself? Is it sexist to encourage girls to play with trucks and boys to play with dolls? Should women be ensured greater opportunities for jobs and schooling through affirmative action programs and quotas?

Whatever the answers to these questions, there is little doubt that discrimination still exists. Few women are mentioned in history books; most texts are still written from a male-oriented viewpoint; women are underrepresented in the professions and discrimination in hiring is well documented; and sexist language is still commonly used, with terms such as "chairman," "mankind," "policeman," and so forth. Males dominate decision-making positions in the business world, and the economic contributions of women are usually ignored by economists. Even the achievements of women are likely to receive less recognition than those of men, as the box *Was She Skillful—Or Just Lucky?* shows.

Beyond these broad issues, another, more personal effect of sexism is important to us here. That effect takes us back to the two quotes we used to open our discussion of sex roles, and it centers on the way in which sex stereotypes influence personal growth. What is the impact on adjustment when a boy learns that he can't express his feelings because "men aren't emotional," or when a girl learns that she can't be what she wants to be because "girls don't do those things"? Sex stereotypes such as these are actually roadblocks to development, for they prevent individuals from fulfilling their potential, becoming complete in the sense that Maslow envisioned.

In all of these respects, sex stereotypes are alarming. What can be done to counteract them? There are several steps that people can take. Perhaps the best place to start is in the home, and the box *Doing Something about Sexism* provides a brief list of suggestions that we can use to counteract the development of sex stereotypes in others. In addition, many sex-role assumptions have been so deeply ingrained in us that we don't even realize they are there. Thus, another important step is to develop our own awareness as well.

Table 8.2 Median Incomes of Full-Time Women Workers, as a Percent of Men's Earnings (1979)

Major Occupation Group	Percent of Men's Earnings in Comparable Occupation
Professional and technical workers	64.3
Managers and administrators (nonfarm)	53.6
Clerical workers	59.6
Sales workers	52.1
Operatives (including transport)	57.4
Service workers (except private household)	62.7
All occupations	59.6

Source: U. S. Department of Labor, Women's Bureau, 1979.

There may be a need for some consciousness-raising. The only way to truly become aware of your stereotypes and your deeper feelings is through exploration and perhaps discussion with others. All over the country, such consciousness-raising groups attempt to help participants discover their feelings toward sex roles and stereotypes. Hopefully, these groups can avoid the trap of rehashing old ills and condemning the opposite sex. Instead, the purpose should be to explore personal feelings and behaviors as fully as possible, and to become aware of them. There is a need for awareness and understanding in both sexes.

Psychologist Sandra Bem suggests a personal goal that all of us might work toward (1974). She uses the term **androgyny** to describe the combina-

Androgyny The desirable state in which an individual possesses the best of both masculine and feminine traits. Androgynous individuals seem to be more flexible and are not hindered by the stereotyped male and female traits.

Was She Skillful—Or Just Lucky?

What happens when a female succeeds on a male-oriented task? Is she considered skillful and competent—or just plain lucky? This was one of the issues addressed in an interesting study performed by Kay Deaux and Tim Emswiller.

Fifty-five male and seventy-five female undergraduates at Purdue University participated in this study. Subjects were asked to sit in individual cubicles, listen through headphones, and evaluate the performance of another subject on a perceptual motor task. Actually all the subjects were evaluators, for their nonexistent partners were really tape recordings by either males or females responding to questions. The evaluators were given a mimeographed sheet listing the correct answers and told that the test-takers were viewing a series of pictures which had familiar objects camouflaged into the background. The test-taker's task was to answer questions concerning these familiar objects. One group of objects consisted of household objects such as mops and broilers, which were considered female-oriented, while the other group were male-oriented and included such objects as wrenches and tire jacks. Subjects were told that performance on a task might be due to other factors besides skill such as luck. Each subject heard the test-takers correctly answer sixteen out of the twenty-five questions, which they were told was better than average. Each evaluator heard either a male or a female test-taker.

The results of this study clearly showed that despite the fact that the mythical male and female test-takers performed equally well, the sex of the test-taker made a difference in the subject's evaluation of their performance. Male performance on the masculine-oriented task was explained in terms of skill while the tendency was to attribute the same performance by a female to luck. The ratings of male and female test-takers on the feminine task were about the same. Despite the fact that the difficulty level on both tasks was equal, performance on the male-oriented task was perceived as better than the equivalent performance on the female-oriented task. In other words, male accomplishments are viewed as superior both because they are performed by males and because male-oriented tasks themselves are considered better. It is important not to leave the impression that males were rated as skillful and females as completely lucky, for this was not the case. Most of the ratings for the females on the masculine task approached the middle of the scale demonstrating equal luck and skill. When subjects were asked how they thought they would do on the tasks, females expected to do better than the test-takers only on the female task, while males thought they could improve on the test-taker's performance on both the masculine and feminine tasks.

This study demonstrates that when males and females perform the same task equally well, females are apt to be judged as luckier and not as skillful as the male. In addition, although males believe they can do both male and female tasks well, females appear not to have much confidence in their ability to perform male-oriented tasks. It is easy to imagine what effects these feelings have on the motivation and performance of males and females. Women simply do not receive the credit that males do for their successes. As the experimenters state in the title of their study "What is skill for the male is luck for the female"!

Source: Deaux & Emswiller, 1974.

tion of the most desirable personality traits, regardless of gender; and she argues that individuals limit themselves by trying to fit either the male or the female stereotypes. For both men and women, there are times to be assertive and times to be yielding; times to be expressive and times to be silent; times to be dominant and times to let others lead. When individuals can combine these traits, their behavioral repertoires are expanded. Only when people are free to develop according

Doing Something about Sexism

It is easy to shrug your shoulders and claim that sexism is a universal problem, and that there is little an individual can do about it. If everyone did this, however, it is certain that the situation would never change. And in fact, each of us can take certain actions that *can* make a difference. This is especially true for parents of young children. Here are some suggestions:

- Become aware of your own stereotypes (many of us have them without realizing it) and try to avoid passing them on to your children. Encouraging both sexes to clean up, sew, learn to fix things, and enjoy athletic competition is especially important, since these are skills an independent *person* will need, whether that person be male or female. Encouraging only males to cook and only females to climb is sexist in itself, and should be avoided. The key is to encourage each child to develop according to his or her own abilities, regardless of gender.

- Rigid personality stereotypes should be avoided. Teaching a boy that he shouldn't cry, should bear pain stoically, and should not express his emotions may discourage him from finding his own ways of expressing himself. In the same way, telling a girl that competition is not ladylike, that she doesn't need to plan a career, and so forth, is also likely to discourage personal growth. Both tactics simply continue an age-old problem.

- One of the most effective ways to counteract sexism is through modeling in your own home. Whether your family is traditional or not, it is possible for the female of the house to be competent, effective, and practical, just as it is equally important for the male to be warm, expressive, and nurturant. Sound communication, with plenty of opportunity to discuss problems as they arise, can help reinforce the effects of good modeling.

- You can counter the mass media in your own home by making your children aware of the false stereotypes that are portrayed. Textbooks that unfairly stereotype both sexes should be held up for public scrutiny and questioning; and the images of men and women and girls and boys shown on TV can also be brought into the limelight for family discussion.

- You may have your own ideas to add to this list. In all, the general strategy consists of communicating openly about sexism that already exists in society, modeling androgynous behaviors in the home, and providing children plenty of opportunity to develop as fully as possible. The combination provides a highly effective way of doing something about sexism.

to their personal abilities can they control their own lives and destinies, become all they can be, and relate fully and deeply with others.

Summary

1. Norms are culturally based rules that prescribe what behaviors are proper in any given situation. Age norms are the specific behaviors we expect from people of a certain age.

2. The set of behaviors that relate to one's particular position in society is called one's role. Each individual plays many roles, and these roles often conflict with one another.

3. The process of socialization involves learning which roles are appropriate within a given situation. Anticipatory socialization involves anticipating a change in status and taking steps to prepare for it. Resocialization occurs when a person learns to cope while already functioning in a new role.

4. Sex-trait stereotypes are traits and characteristics that people believe characterize one sex more than another. Males, for instance, are seen as being

Androgeny includes the freedom to share even mundane tasks without regard to traditional sex-role stereotypes.

competent, rational, and assertive; while females are considered to be expressive and warm.

5. Like any other stereotypes, sex-trait stereotypes are not accurate, and they injure both males and females. The stereotyped characteristics of females are not as highly valued as those of males. The expectation that a male must be aggressive and ambitious hinders the individual development of many males.

6. Even if a given psychological trait is found more often in one gender than another, the overlap is likely to be very considerable.

7. Maccoby and Jacklin reviewed many studies in the area of sex differences. Their only consistent findings showed males to be more aggressive, females to have greater verbal ability, males to excel in visual-spatial abilities, and males to be more mathematical.

8. We still don't know for sure what causes these differences, but familial, cultural, social, and perhaps biological factors may all play a role.

9. The psychoanalytic approach to the question of how children learn their sex roles revolves around the concept of identification during the Oedipal phase. The behavioral approach stresses learning theory. According to cognitive theory, children first discover their own gender; then they actively search the environment to learn gender-appropriate behaviors.

10. Sexism involves prejudice and discrimination based on a physical trait: gender.

11. The term androgyny refers to a personality that combines the most desirable personality traits of both sexes.

12. People can combat sex stereotypes and sexism by emphasizing the unique abilities of each individual, by avoiding rigid personality stereotyping, by countering stereotypes in the home, and by modeling androgynous behavior. Consciousness-raising is a useful way to become more aware of one's own sex-based assumptions.

Key Terms and Concepts

social role	resocialization
social norms	sex roles
age norms	sex-trait stereotypes
socialization	sexism
anticipatory socialization	androgyny

Adam looked in the mailbox for the fifth day in a row. This time, he saw what he had been waiting for. He reached in and pulled out the letter from the admissions office. It was thick: that was a good sign. He nervously tore open the envelope, unfolded the contents, and scanned the letter quickly. He had been accepted. And not only that, he had been awarded the scholarship he had applied for!

"Hey, Sam!" he called. No answer. Where could his roommate be?

"Sam!" he called again. Still no answer.

Well, this was too exciting to keep

Relationships and Communication

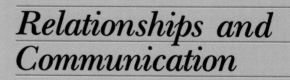

to himself. He had to tell someone. He knocked next door at his neighbors' apartment. He could share his news with them. No one responded, though, so he went home and picked up his phone. As he tried his girlfriend, his parents, his sister, and his friends, all with no luck, his mood began to change. No longer happy and expansive, he became frustrated and even angry. Here he was, experiencing one of the most important moments of his life, but he just couldn't enjoy it because there was no one to share it with.

People gather together to share important life events.

We depend on other people. Like Adam, we look for friends to share our good fortune: without someone else to help celebrate, even the best news seems somehow hollow. We need friends in times of unhappiness, also. Friends and loved ones provide support and stability. When we feel miserable or discouraged, the knowledge that someone else cares, or that someone has faith in us, can provide a tremendous sense of strength. That is why important life events, such as weddings and funerals, are times when people gather together with one another.

Some of the greatest joys in our lives involve the experiences of love, friendship, and companionship. These experiences can also be the source of some of our greatest pain. Anyone who has ever been disappointed by a close friend, experienced the loss of someone close to them, or suffered through an unhappy love affair knows the pain that can come from a deep involvement with someone else. After experiencing such hurt, many people may vow never to become so involved again. Yet after a period of healing, we usually form bonds once more. Memories of the joy of being close to others seem to outweigh the pain.

This chapter is about interpersonal relationships: why we need to be with others; what attracts people to one another; and how we can maintain and improve close relationships so that they may bring us joy and allow both individuals to grow. It is also about the way in which we communicate with one another, both verbally and nonverbally. Communication is the bond that holds relationships together. Many close relationships have been endangered or even fallen apart because partners weren't communicating with one another; poor communication is also a cause of family tensions. Yet communicating is a skill, and like any other skill, it can be learned and improved with practice. We'll be looking at ways in which we can improve communication skills, even during arguments.

A "Social Animal"

As the saying goes, humans are "social animals." We think of ourselves in terms of the roles we play in relationship with other people, as we saw in Chapter 8. We enjoy being with others (at least most of the time). Although we also need time alone, there are clear limits to how much solitude is enjoyable. For most of us, even a day spent without some kind of meaningful communication would be very disturbing. What is the source of this strong need to form relationships?

We saw in Chapter 2 that each person's individual need for affiliation can be considered a learned motive. Yet if we look at our relationship needs in terms of species survival, as an ethologist would, it is also clear that relationships serve a crucial function. Not only do we enjoy being with others, but from the very beginning, we *need* relationships. As infants and young children, we are helpless to care for ourselves. We require someone to feed and protect us in order to survive. One of the greatest fears of young children is abandonment. Thus, our need for contact and interpersonal stimulation may well be innate.

Interpersonal Needs

Of course, survival needs are no longer crucial in our relationships as adults, but there are other needs that interpersonal relationships fulfill. According to Schutz (1966, 1967), each of us has three interpersonal needs, as Figure 9.1 shows. The first is **inclusion,** the need to belong. This need is expressed in our efforts to establish and maintain satisfactory interpersonal relationships. Such relationships enhance our self-images, so that we feel more significant or worthy. The second need, **control,** involves the need to make decisions and hold some power within a relationship. The third need is **affection.** We need varying degrees of affect (emotion) in the relationships we form with other people.

These three interpersonal needs vary greatly from one individual to another, and from one relationship to another. Some people, for instance, show a need to be in complete control of a relationship: they cannot seem to share power with someone else. Others prefer to have the other person make the decisions in the relationship. People have different belonging needs, also. Some need more company than others. Affection needs also vary, with some of us highly emotional and expressive and others much more restrained. While all of us may share these needs to some degree, then, each individual's make-up is also unique.

Satisfying Needs in Healthy Relationships

These personal differences mean that in each friendship or partnership, the individuals involved are likely to have different needs. Some-

> **Inclusion**   The interpersonal need to belong.
>
> **Control**   The interpersonal need to hold some power in a relationship; to influence the decision-making process.
>
> **Affection**   The interpersonal need for tenderness and emotional closeness in a relationship.

Inclusion: The need to belong

Control: The need to make decisions and influence the decision making in a relationship

Affection: The need to share emotional closeness

Figure 9.1   Three Interpersonal Needs

times, these needs complement each other, and the relationship is satisfying and rewarding for each party—but this is not always the case. Have you ever heard people say that their relationship was no good from the beginning? Statements such as "She gave everything; he gave nothing," or "She was always trying to change him" are indicative of unhealthy relationships.

Although there is no consensus as to what differentiates a healthy from an unhealthy relationship, the distinction centers around whether each person's needs are satisfied. This broad criterion can be broken down into four related elements: acceptance, concern, reasonable demands, and communication.

Acceptance   Any friendship or partnership requires some mutual acceptance. It is fruitless to

spend most of your time together trying to change one another. Accepting a person as a separate individual with unique opinions, feelings, and wants is an important aspect of a healthy relationship, but it doesn't always come naturally.

For instance, it isn't unusual to hear someone say "You shouldn't feel that way," or "You can't really believe that." Such statements deny other people's rights to their own feelings or thoughts. A relationship may thrive when each person accepts these differences and is willing to talk about them. A healthy relationship does not necessarily imply a complete agreement on everything.

Concern   Each person in a relationship needs the freedom to maximize his or her potential, and one characteristic of a healthy relationship is a

Did Rhett and Scarlett have a healthy relationship? Hardly, if judged by the four criteria of acceptance, concern, reasonable demands, and communication.

concern with the other's right to grow. Active concern involves not only an acceptance of the other's needs, but also interest and encouragement. Thus, if your friend has just made the gymnastics team, you will probably ask her questions about it, watch her perform, and provide encouragement. You may even learn a great deal about the sport yourself.

Reasonable Demands As we've seen, we seek to satisfy certain needs when we enter a relationship. At the same time, there is an implied responsibility to be responsive and sensitive to the needs of the other person. If you demand more than he or she can possibly give, your relationship will become confining, tense, and strained. For instance, if you have tremendous inclusion needs and demand constant attention, your friend may be forced to give up his or her own needs and goals for yours. Such a demand would show a lack of concern for the other person's need to grow.

Communication   A fourth quality of a healthy relationship is the ability to communicate. Individuals may disagree; they may feel at times that their demands aren't met or that the other person is too demanding; and they may find it hard to accept some things about one another. All of these differences are bound to happen during the course of a relationship. They don't necessarily lead to anger or hostility, however. If people can communicate with one another, it is often possible to work toward a solution. Thus, active communication, which includes both communicator and listener skills, is a vital sign of a healthy relationship. Communication is so important in a relationship that we'll devote the second half of this chapter to these vital skills.

Healthy relationships, then, are marked by acceptance, concern, reasonable demands, and communication. Such relationships give each person "room to grow," enhancing individuality and encouraging personal fulfillment. Whether a relationship will fulfill these qualifications, however, isn't always apparent from the start; and sometimes we wonder how we became involved with someone in the first place. The reason, as any social psychologist might tell you, is that the four qualities above are not necessarily factors in drawing people together. Instead, other elements may be more important in establishing a relationship.

Establishing a Relationship

How We Choose Friends

We come into contact with hundreds of people each day. Yet, we choose to associate closely with only a very few. Researchers have identified five factors that seem important in establishing personal relationships, based on the premise that we normally form relationships with people we like. These factors are attractiveness, closeness, similarity, complementarity, and rewards.

Attractiveness   It is difficult to describe exactly what makes a person attractive; there is a great deal of individual variation. But psychologists have found certain physical as well as personality characteristics that most people consider pleasing.

A few personality traits are likely to draw us to a person. According to Anderson (1968), the three most desirable personality traits include sincerity, honesty, and loyalty. Asch (1946) found that in judging the personality of another person, we cluster our perception around whether that person is "warm" or "cold." When we judge people as warm, we rate them positively according to many other traits as well.

It is more difficult to describe exactly what makes one person "warm" and another "cold." It seems to be the totality of the individual's appearance and behavior. By wearing certain clothing and presenting themselves in a particular manner, some people seem "warm," even before any interaction takes place. There are an infinite number of specific elements that contribute to this image: a pleasant voice, a friendly smile, and a good handshake may be as much a part of it as what a person says to you. Models in magazines or on TV provide an example of some of the kinds of signals that people convey; they are experts at using physical cues such as clothing and facial expression. The same model may appear young and childlike in one pose, and sophisticated and cold in the next.

Although many of us might deny the idea, physical attractiveness is another significant factor in the way we react to people. In fact, physical attractiveness may be the first step in setting the stage for establishing a relationship. This is not only true for male-female relationships, but also, to a somewhat lesser extent, for friendships among people of the same sex. Physical attractiveness is a valued characteristic, and we tend to generalize it to other positive traits (Dion et al., 1972). The person who is physically appealing is more likely to also be considered good, honest, and happy. This tendency to generalize from one positive trait to another is called the "halo effect."

Closeness A second factor in forming relationships is closeness, or proximity. We tend to form relationships with people we see most often. The closer we live or work to any individual, the greater the probability that we will establish a close relationship. Students tend to form relationships with people in their classes or with people who sit next to them (Segal, 1974). In a now classic study, Festinger and his colleagues (1950) found that the distance between homes in a community was a good predictor of friendship patterns. The closer the homes, the greater the chance that these people would form friendships.

Proximity seems to contribute in two ways to relationships. First, it increases the likelihood of our meeting another person in the first place. And second, there is evidence that repeated exposure over a period of time often increases mutual liking, even if we have disagreements with another person (Brockner & Swap, 1976). We may not change our stand on the issues, but repeated contact may give us a better understanding of the other person's position. It may also give us a chance to see another side of the person's character. For example, one couple on an afternoon TV game show told the story of how they first met at the supermarket check-out counter. She thought he was petty when he argued that he was first in line; and he thought she was pushy and rude. After repeated encounters in the neighborhood, however, they began to like one another—and eventually, they married.

Similarity A third element in forming relationships is similarity. In establishing friendships, we tend to seek out people with similar attitudes, values, goals, and interests (Byrne, 1971). This is true not only because conversation is easier when we share a common ground with someone (have you ever tried to make conversation with someone who seemed to share none of your interests?), but also because the opportunities for doing things together increase when you both like the same things.

How can you tell if you have something in common with a person you've just met? Brenton (1974) points out that we don't have to give each new acquaintance an attitude scale to find out about their beliefs or interests. By the very nature of our lifestyle, we tend to come into contact with people with similar interests and backgrounds. Most workers associate with the people they see each day at the same workplace. Parents usually strike up friendships with other parents of same-age children. Our social status and economic level bring us into contact mostly with others who are like ourselves, thus making the weeding process easier. As we get to know people better, we discover more personal similarities or differences, and these help determine how close the relationship will become.

Complementarity Similarity may be a common basis for friendship bonds. But we have all heard the expression "opposites attract," and it is true that people often seem to look for *complementary* qualities in others—qualities, that is, that they themselves lack. If you are a talker, you may strike up a friendship with someone who enjoys listening to you, but is less talkative. If you are a dominant person, you may choose friends who are willing to be led. If you are extremely ambitious, you may select a partner who is less ambitious but who will be able to support you in your quest.

While complementarity is a factor, it is paradoxical in some respects. Certainly, people with opposite qualities may be able to fulfill each others' needs. But it is also true that when people are too different, they often do not get along. What explains the contradiction? The distinction centers around the extent of the differences and the ability to find *some* common ground. A dominant and a very reticent person may enjoy each other's company not only because of their complementarity, but because they also share another quality, such as an interest in jazz or a similar personal history. Being different, in other words, is rarely the only basis for a strong relationship.

Rewards   Finally, we tend to associate with people who reward us. If you know someone who always seems to think your jokes are funny or who gives you compliments (provided you believe they are sincere—see the discussion in the box *Where Will Flattery Get You?*) the chances are that you will feel good with that person, and that you will want to spend more time together. In the same way, if someone always says things that make you feel clumsy or ignorant, you are likely to avoid that person's company. This basic rule of relationships might be stated in a number of ways. But in general, it all boils down to the conditioning principles we discussed in Chapter 3. We tend to establish relationships with people who give us joy rather than pain.

Shyness as an Obstacle

The different qualities we've been discussing—attractiveness, closeness, similarity, complementarity, and rewards—may all be important factors in establishing relationships. But many people have trouble meeting people with whom they might well get along. A large number of people consider themselves to be shy—Zimbardo places the figure at 40 percent (Zimbardo et al., 1977). For these people, meeting others and establishing a rapport is an uncomfortable or even traumatic experience. These individuals are self-conscious, overly concerned with behaving in an acceptable way; and they have difficulty acting assertively. Besides being uncomfortable in a number of social situations, shy people are often lonely and sometimes depressed.

There is a difference between occasional and chronic shyness. Just about everyone is shy at some time in their life, or on some occasion. However, people who are chronically shy are constantly fearful, quiet, and have difficulty making friends and enjoying themselves. Zimbardo offers a composite picture of shy people. They are almost always quiet in the company of strangers. They avoid eye contact and sometimes take steps to keep their distance from other people. They are not action-oriented, and they tend to blend into the background. Three quarters of the shy people Zimbardo questioned did not like being shy. But the large number of shy people he found may mean that being shy is a normal part of many personalities.

There are several ways in which people can help themselves become less shy. The assertiveness training procedures found in Chapter 7 may help, and some counseling services are also available. One promising technique, behavior rehearsal, requires the shy person to strike up a conversation with a counselor who plays the role of a stranger or distant acquaintance. The counselor can respond to the efforts of the shy person, and at the same time model new behaviors that might be more helpful. This allows the individual to develop and improve social skills in an accepting and trusting atmosphere. Another idea is to practice meeting people in places that are comfortable to the shy person. If you are interested in art, for instance, it would probably be easier for you to strike up a conversation with people whom you met at an art show or an art class than in many other settings.

Maintaining Relationships

We've been looking at the kinds of factors that are involved in the initial phase of meeting people and establishing a relationship. Quite another set of factors seems to be involved in keeping a relationship going. These factors center around effort and open communication.

Where Will *Flattery Get You?*

We like to associate with people who reward us. A compliment on losing five pounds, or on doing a good job organizing a meeting, or on being "fun to be with" can give anyone a lift, and we are likely to feel more warmly toward the person who made us feel good. In other words, it looks as if flattery will often "get you somewhere."

But does it? While people often react positively to compliments, it is also true that flattery sometimes backfires, especially if it is insincere. If someone says you look terrific when you know you're 10 pounds overweight and your nose is red from a horrible cold, you are likely to feel offended and irritated rather than warm and friendly. A compliment, then, can be perceived as either false and ingratiating flattery, or as positive and sincere praise. Some research has looked into the factors that determine how people react to praise.

■ Is the praise justified? Flattery will backfire if we don't think it is justified. If you know that your piano playing isn't worth beans, for instance, and someone tells you that it was terrific, you are likely to regard that person with distrust. In contrast, if you feel you've got some talent that deserves to be discovered, you may react by feeling warmly toward the person who praised you.

■ Do you have a positive self-image? Colman (1980) found that people with positive self-images reacted warmly to compliments, but only if they conformed with their own self-image. People with low self-esteem tend to be impervious to flattery, reacting against it by disapproving of the flatterer.

■ What is the status of the person who is praising you? Believe it or not, social status affects our response to praise. If your boss compliments you on your work, you are likely to accept the praise whether or not it conforms to your view; and when someone of higher status compliments you, you are likely to feel more warmly toward that person than you did previously. In contrast, we tend to have different interpretations for the motives of people with lower status. (Why are they trying to butter us up?) Unless you think your boss is about to ask you to work overtime, you are far less likely to be suspicious of praise from those quarters.

In all, compliments must be doled out with care. Flatterers do not always improve their chances of becoming friendly with the person they flatter, unless they are of at least equal status and their compliments sound sincere. The perils of false flattery, however, are probably not that great. Praise that is inconsistent with a person's self-image may create simultaneously positive and negative reactions (so that the flatterer is liked on an emotional level but regarded as insincere on a more rational level). Yet it is unlikely to greatly lower the person's feelings about the flatterer.

Effort

A basic rule of systems analysis states that all systems tend to break down if energy is not directed into them (Bertalanffy, 1966), and this rule also holds true for maintaining interpersonal relationships. Over a period of time, we may begin to take people for granted, to develop unrealistic expectations, or to become overdependent or overcontrolling. It often takes a special effort to continue a relationship over time.

This may not always be obvious when people are involved in a close relationship, but sometimes it becomes more apparent when the normal interaction is interrupted. Many of the closest high school friendships, for instance, go through a gradual dissolution that begins on graduation day. Friends may keep in close touch during the next few years. But eventually, one person usually moves away, or one friend has children while the other doesn't marry, or they become involved in different lines of work, with different interests and different lifestyles. In order to maintain a relationship, these friends would have to invest a great deal of time and concern—an investment that might take too much effort away from more current friendships.

Interacting with someone requires a constant back-and-forth exchange, so that communication might be said to be the glue that holds people together in a relationship. Much of the effort of maintaining a relationship is devoted to keeping lines of communication open; when one or both persons stop trying, the relationship suffers.

Open Communication

Mr. W. and his 15-year-old son came into the office and laid their problem squarely on the table. "We don't communicate," the son said matter-of-factly. "We talk a lot," his father retorted. "Yeah," said the teenager, shaking his head. "We talk but we don't communicate."

Mr. W. and his son shared a common problem: lack of communication. Both talked, but neither of them ever listened to the other. In order to maintain an interpersonal relationship, communication is crucial. In a broad sense, **communication** can be defined as any means by which we influence one another (Ruesch & Bateson, 1968).

> **Communication**   Any means by which we influence one another, both verbally or non-verbally.
>
> **Genuine communication**   Open communication in which each party is able to receive, consider, and respond to the message conveyed by other parties.

It includes verbal messages, but it also includes nonverbal signals—for instance, the icy stare that is described by the expression "if looks could kill." (Nonverbal communication will be discussed in the last part of this chapter.)

Communication is essential to maintaining and improving relationships. It lets us send and receive information about emotions, facts, and experiences. Janis et al. (1969) note that communication skills are learned, and not innate. These skills develop as people mature. Children begin by speaking *at* other children; they do not really listen to what others say. This *egocentric* (self-centered) system makes two-way communication all but impossible: as Janis notes, young children aren't capable of **genuine communication**—the ability to receive, consider, and respond. As children mature, they usually gain some sort of ability to listen. But many people retain an egocentric system that prevents them from really tuning in on what others are saying. This inability to truly communicate acts as a roadblock to close relationships.

We might say that Mr. W. and his son were not sharing genuine communication. Neither showed any understanding of the other's point of view. They spoke at each other, not to each other. Neither showed any desire to improve. Instead, they constantly blamed each other for their problems, demanding that the other change *his* tune. Their case illustrates how poor communication can stand in the way of a rewarding relationship.

How can these kinds of problems be avoided? In any communication, we switch back and forth between two roles: that of the communicator and that of the listener. There are particular skills involved in both of these roles, and these skills can be learned and improved. We'll look at these two roles, as well as the message itself, and see how we can learn to use each of these elements most effectively. Figure 9.2 summarizes the key points.

The Communicator   Imagine that you are moving into an apartment and your new roommate hits you with the rules. "There is to be no noise

Often, nonverbal statements can be just as clear as spoken messages.

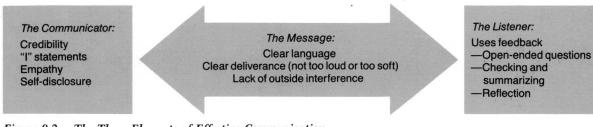

| The Communicator:
Credibility
"I" statements
Empathy
Self-disclosure | The Message:
Clear language
Clear deliverance (not too loud or too soft)
Lack of outside interference | The Listener:
Uses feedback
—Open-ended questions
—Checking and
  summarizing
—Reflection |

Figure 9.2   The Three Elements of Effective Communication

when I'm studying," she says, "and you can't bring dates in to the room. I'll do the cooking but you have the responsibility for the shopping and the cleaning. We'll split the utility bills evenly, unless it looks like you're using up too much electricity. You're going to have to get rid of your cats if you want to stay here. . ."

"What a communicator!" you might think. There's certainly no question of where she stands! But whether she is effective or not is another issue, for while she makes her views known, she has probably done so in a way that makes you feel less than happy about cooperating. In fact, you will probably react with defensive tactics; at the very least, you may decide to spend as little time in her company as you can.

This *hypothetical* (imaginary) example points to a very important fact about the role of communicator: that the goal is not simply to get a message across, but to do it in a way that will have the effect you want on the listener. To be effective as a communicator, you need to be **credible**—a quality that is discussed in the box *Closing the Credibility Gap.* You also need to be able to encourage the other person to want to understand you, and to communicate honestly and openly to you.

What is the difference between stating your mind in a way that puts up the other person's defenses and expressing yourself so that the listener wants to see things your way? A great many factors are involved, but one of the most important centers around the openness you show to further communication from the listener. If you talk "at" someone, stating your views as law, that person is likely to be put on the defensive. If you

express your views simply as one opinion, on the other hand, then you open the door for a response.

An effective way of doing this is through the use of *"I" statements*. The phrases "I feel" or "I think" are good ways of framing your messages, for they present your information as a personal view. Feelings are subjective, and no one can dispute your right to feel as you do. (You may back up your opinion with facts, as you perceive them, but by stating them in terms of how "I feel" or "I think," you invite the listener to explore the point further.) By continually using "I" statements, you are telling the other person that you want to speak on a more personal level and exchange points of view. This helps bring you close to a meeting of the minds—thus, it is instrumental in improving relationships.

Carl Rogers (1951) uses the term *empathy* to describe the idea of understanding something from another person's frame of reference. Empathy is an important goal in any friendly relationship. When you express your feelings and your friend shows he or she understands their true depth, then asks you to explain them more fully, it leads to a positive interchange and to greater acceptance and understanding. It also demonstrates that you are taking responsibility for your own feelings and communications. You are being more open and honest, inviting the listener to communicate on this fuller, deeper level.

Such a step leads to what Jourard has called **self-disclosure** (1959). In general, we feel closer to people who disclose themselves to us.* And when we disclose ourselves to others, we expect them to contribute to the relationship on the same level. Jourard believes that the most powerful determinant of whether another person will disclose personal information is whether the initial communicator did. Normally in the development of a

---

Credibility   The quality of being believable as a communicator. Credibility consists of two components: expertness and trustworthiness.

Self-disclosure   The act by which a person reveals intimate and personal feelings and thoughts to another person.

---

*An exception may be when a person makes disclosures prematurely. People are likely to withdraw from a relationship in which one individual tries to become "too close too quick."

Closing the Credibility Gap

What makes a person effective as a communicator? This chapter discusses several ways in which people can phrase their thoughts so that the listener will feel empathetic toward their point of view. But these qualities deal primarily with personal communications. When we want others to stop and listen to what we have to say, we often have another important goal as communicators: to establish a sense of credibility or believability.

There are two components of communicator credibility: *expertness* and *trustworthiness*. An expert knows the subject matter. If you are communicating your thoughts on the current state of our oil stockpiles, you will only be seen as an expert if you can demonstrate that you have a sound knowledge of the field. (That is why experts often like panel moderators to introduce them by giving the audience a bit of their background, including their credentials.) Trustworthiness involves presenting oneself as fair-minded. The motives of the communicator are vital to this aspect of credibility. For example, if the director of a multinational oil company speaks about the need for higher petroleum prices, we may well recognize his or her expert credentials, but we may doubt the motives behind the message.

The effects of being perceived as either inexpert or nontrustworthy are obvious. The listener simply refuses to listen to the communication or to give it credence. If your friend begins talking about nuclear strategy and you don't think she knows what she's talking about, you may simply shrug your shoulders, listen politely, and forget it. If your parents try to persuade you that the family business will provide the best career for you, you may take their arguments with a grain of salt because you question their motives. (Notice that both expertness and trustworthiness are often contingent upon the subject under discussion. You may respect your friend's opinions about apartment rentals in the neighborhood even though you don't think she knows much about global politics; the same is true for your parents' motivation.)

Whether you are communicating to a group or to another individual, it is important to find out how you are being perceived. In close relationships, your credentials are usually well known to the listener. On the overwhelming majority of issues, we are not experts. In addition, most of our messages concern personal experiences or emotions: these are subjective, and can be phrased as "I" statements that will let the listener know that your statement involves a personal opinion. If you wish to be perceived as trustworthy, it is important to present your facts as facts and your opinions as opinions, and to take responsibility for your own feelings and motives. In this way, credibility gaps can be avoided before they have a chance to develop.

Source: Hovland, Janis, & Kelley, 1953.

---

personal relationship, we disclose material of about the same personal depth. The deeper the relationship, the more personal the material that is communicated. As one person discloses information and accepts disclosures from the other, a cycle is established that leads to a deeper relationship. Credibility, the use of "I" statements, communicating empathy to others, and a willingness to disclose ourselves are four elements

that make us more effective in the role of communicator; and skill in these four areas can be improved through conscious effort. A second part of effective communication is the listener role, and this, too, involves a learned skill.

The Listener   Imagine walking along with your friend and pouring out your heart to him, while he merely looks down at the ground. He doesn't nod his head or grunt, and his eyes never meet yours. After a short time, you will probably begin to feel uncomfortable, then embarrassed, and finally angry.

The lack of listener skills, like the inability to communicate effectively, is a serious obstacle to any relationship. Most of the time, we take these listener skills for granted, assuming that our communications will be met with certain responses (and vice versa). Only when this doesn't occur do we think about these listener skills—and even then, we may react on a more emotional than an analytical level. That is, it's much more common to think "Gee, he doesn't like me" or "I never should have told him this" instead of stopping to consider what kinds of responses would have been appropriate. Since listener skills are so important in the way we interact with others, it is worthwhile to explore a little more carefully the kinds of responses that encourage close communication.

One of the most important listener skills is **feedback,** both verbal and nonverbal. Feedback in interpersonal communication can be defined as any response that lets the person know that you have received his or her message. Your "uh-huh," grunt, or nod all serve to keep a conversation going. They demonstrate comprehension and interest. Such feedback only serves to keep the communicator speaking, however. If you wish the other person to share more feelings, and to alter the level of communication from mere facts to something more personal, a more active form of feedback is necessary. Active feedback may include discreet questioning as well as periodic checking to make certain you understand exactly what has been said.

Discreet questioning helps to demonstrate an interest in what the other person is saying. It also encourages the communicator to be more exact in presenting a message. Responding actively with

---

Feedback In interpersonal communication, any response that lets a communicator know you have received his or her message.

---

questions is more inviting than a simple nod of the head. For instance, imagine the following scene in which your friend begins to tell you what her boyfriend did at a party last night:

Friend: You should have seen what Jerry did last night!

You: Uh-huh.

Friend: He really lost all his inhibitions. I've never seen him that way before.

You: Uh-huh.

Your friend certainly hasn't received much encouragement to carry on with her story, and it is likely that this conversation won't be continued much longer. The picture would be quite different if you had responded with even a simple question indicating that you wanted to know more about what had happened. If she is a close personal friend, your questions might go a step further and explore not simply what happened, but also what she thought about it.

Not all questions are equal in the degree of interest they suggest. Questions that can be answered with a simple "yes" or "no" do not encourage communication much more than does a simple "uh-huh." For instance:

Friend: You should have seen what Jerry did last night!

You: I should have?

Friend: Yes. He really lost all his inhibitions.

You: Did he?

Friend: Yes. . . .

Again, the conversation seems doomed to a fast-approaching dead-end. To avoid this effect, questions should be designed to encourage a slightly deeper reply. Saying "What happened?" asks the communicator to expand on the statement she just made, while a simple yes or no question restricts the conversation to the same level. To be effective, then, questioning should facilitate communication, and not restrict or hinder it.

A second feedback technique that encourages communication is *checking and summarizing*. One of the best ways that you can demonstrate that you've heard the other person is to summarize in your own words what he or she has just said. Responses such as "So you're saying that . . ." or "You feel that . . ." show that you understand the speaker's meaning and indicate how you interpret what has just been said. (Such responses also provide a chance to clarify meaning, in the case of a misunderstanding.) Checking and summarizing is a helpful response for both factual and emotional messages.

Checking and summarizing isn't often used in day-to-day conversation, but it can greatly enrich it. In fact, Carl Rogers, the originator of what is called client-centered therapy (see Chapter 14) uses the term **reflection** to describe a process whereby the counselor mirrors the client's feelings.

This technique, which can open up a discussion to a somewhat deeper, more personal level, can be useful in many situations. During a class, one of the authors made a point of using this type of feedback in a discussion of problems such as prejudice and dependence. Thus, if a student stated that overly dependent people bothered him, the author responded "So you feel a bit uncomfortable with people who are personally demanding." At the end of the class period, two interesting things occurred. First, a number of students had begun to use the same technique, paying more attention to what they heard from other students and responding with accurate summaries. And second, some of the students remarked after class that they had experienced a warm, interested feeling toward the others. They felt closer, and they seemed more tolerant and less judgmental.

Communication skills and listening skills are both essential in developing and maintaining an understanding with another person, but we have not yet looked at the third element in a relationship. The message itself also plays a vital part in any effort to communicate to someone else.

The Message One of the authors has a friend who moved with her family from New York to Massachusetts. Shortly thereafter, she was called to the school because her son had done poorly on a test. Her child had never had any difficulty at school before, so this event was some cause for concern, especially since he was becoming non-communicative at home. When she got to the school and looked at the paper, however, she felt a tremendous relief. Her son and the teacher were completely misunderstanding one another. When the teacher said the word "part" in her best Bostonian accent, the boy thought she was talking about something people cooked with. The boy's poor performance was simply a matter of mixed messages caused by regional differences in accent.

Misunderstandings can easily occur because a message has different meanings for the communicator and the listener. This may happen because of different accents, as in the example above; or it may even occur because the communicator and the receiver have different vocabularies (Ruben & Budd, 1975). During World War II, for instance, there was one episode in which British and American staff members had a long and bitter argument (Lee, 1952). The British general staff stated that they wanted to table an urgent issue, and the Americans retorted that it couldn't be tabled. After considerable wrangling, the two groups realized that they had been in agreement all along—they just hadn't been able to recognize it! "Tabling," to Americans, means putting an issue off until the next meeting, but to the British it means dealing with it immediately.

Reflection A technique developed by Carl Rogers in which the listener (usually the counselor) rephrases the statements of the communicator. Accurate reflection demonstrates empathy and encourages the speaker toward greater understanding of his or her feelings.

Message errors may also take place because a certain word or phrase is ambiguous (that is, has a double meaning). An example is a fight that took place between two junior high school students in the school's music room. One student told the other she was "flat." She took it as a physical evaluation, even though the other person was only referring to the sounds her instrument was making.

In addition to the wording itself, the transmission of the message must also be clear. If the message is delivered in a way that is too loud or soft, it may not have the desired effect. We tend to tune out messages that are too difficult to hear: we consider them nonassertive, and we sometimes become annoyed at the effort we must make to try and comprehend them. Messages that are too loud are also irritating, causing the listener to feel defensive or angry. Even outside interference can make a message ineffective. Too much background noise, or too much hustle and bustle in the surrounding area, can prevent the listener from concentrating or even hearing what is said—just as too much static interferes with a radio transmission. Communication is most effective, then, when the message is clearly phrased and when it is transmitted without outside interference.

As we have explored the communicator role, the listener role, and the message itself, we've seen that people can learn to use each of these three elements to improve their relationships with others. Communicating well does *not* mean never arguing, for whenever two people have any sort of relationship, arguments are bound to take place. However, good communication skills make a difference in the degree to which disagreements affect a relationship.

Arguments and Disagreements

What do people argue about? Perhaps the question should be phrased differently: what *don't* people argue about? Disagreements are inevitable in any relationship, and they may be very destructive.

The nature of arguments often changes with the intensity of the relationship. When a couple begin dating, they may give little thought to issues such as whether or not they want children, or what kind of balance each partner wants between career and home life, or what religious training they would like to provide for a family. As relationships become more serious, however, questions like these may become vital concerns. Roark notes that "As interaction, interdependence, and intimacy increase in a relationship, the potential for conflict also increases. And as the intimacy and intensity of a relationship increase, conflicts are likely to become more emotional, intense, and volatile" (1978, p. 400).

This may occur for a number of reasons. We care more about people with whom we are close, and their decisions seem to affect our own lives more. Whatever the reason, arguments with close friends or partners tend to be emotionally intense and draining. Most people believe that disagreements and arguments *must* be detrimental to their relationships. However, this need not be the case, for there is such a thing as "healthy conflict."

Ground Rules for Healthy Conflict

What would you say to a man who claims he never argues with his wife? Or to a woman who says she and her husband always agree? Your reaction would probably be either that they weren't telling the truth, or that they must live 3000 miles apart and see each other only twice a year. Or perhaps that the relationship is so unbalanced that one person always gives in to the other.

While disagreements can be highly destructive to a relationship, it is neither normal nor particularly healthy to *never* disagree on anything. If disagreements seem almost inevitable, then, it cannot be merely the activity of arguing that endangers relationships. Rather, it is how these differences are handled that will determine whether they enhance or undermine a relationship.

According to Roark (1978), there are three destructive ways of dealing with interpersonal disagreements: using *power*, *smoothing over* the problem, and *avoiding* the issue entirely. None of these methods are productive. People who use power to force the other into some mold often find that they merely receive unwilling compliance, which might not be in either of their best interests. Smoothing over is also ineffective, for it merely covers over the problem without solving it. And avoiding the issue can create new problems. As we saw in Chapter 6, defense mechanisms such as repression require continuous effort. When one deals directly with a problem, that energy is released for other purposes.

Of course, not all problems can be solved, even when the most effective communication techniques are used. However, if people follow certain ground rules in dealing with their conflicts, it may be possible to turn potentially destructive disagreements into opportunities for growth. We'll look at these ground rules below.

Ground Rule #1: No Winners, No Losers   In this corner, wearing Sasson jeans, weighing 110 pounds with blond hair and hazel eyes, we have Martha Wilson. In the opposite corner, wearing Levis, weighing 186 pounds, with brown hair and brown eyes, we present Martin Wilson.

People often see disagreements in terms of a boxing match. One person will win, and the other will lose. Both contestants try to knock each other out, to browbeat one another. They use whatever tactics will be most effective in winning a complete victory over their opponent: staring each other down, intimidating one another, perhaps even bringing in a piece of surprise evidence to clinch the case.

Is this an effective way of resolving disagreements in a relationship? Such tactics may well win the battle, but they will also continue the war. As Bach and Wyden's book *The Intimate Enemy: How to Fight Fair in Love and Marriage* (1968) points out,

there should be no winner or loser. In a boxing match, victory and defeat are appropriate, for the fighters leave the ring and don't need to associate with one another again. If one person tries for absolute superiority in a relationship, however, the result will be quite different. Martha may well let Martin buy the Super-GL-X52 Turbo convertible complete with whitewalls and zebra upholstery, but each month she will find a way to bring up the argument again when the payments are due.

The first ground rule for healthy conflict, then, is to readjust the goals. Instead of a personal victory, the goal should be to maintain the relationship, with no winner and no loser. This can be done by increasing understanding and settling differences in a way that satisfies both parties.

Ground Rule #2: Stay on the Issue   "Remember when you 'borrowed' my mother's savings and then threw it away on that worthless old car?" Helen shot back as Frank attempted to argue that she should get out of her current job and find a career she'd be happier with. Virtually every time they have an argument, Helen dredges up Frank's past mistake and uses it as standard ammunition, no matter how irrelevant it is to the current topic.

This is a common tactic in many family arguments, and it belongs to a *genre*, or general class, of strategies that are based on diverting the argument to another issue. After all, if you can't think of any real objections to the other person's point but you don't want to concede the argument, you can sidetrack the discussion to another point on which you know you've got the advantage.

This may be done by dredging up the past, or it can also be done by picking on the opponent's real or imagined weaknesses—as when one person escalates an argument by accusing the other of "lying about everything" and the other retorts that "all you ever do is sit in front of the tube and drink beer." In his best-seller, *Games People Play* (1964), Eric Berne calls this the game of "uproar," a term that refers to the sudden free-for-all quality the argument takes on.

Of course, such tactics accomplish nothing in terms of solving the problem at hand. If an argument is to have any positive outcome, both parties must resolve to keep on the subject and squarely face the music. The easiest way to do this is to deal with problems as they arise.

Ground Rule #3: Don't "Stockpile" Grievances   It is sometimes easier to ignore a problem than to go through the effort of working out a solution. Unfortunately, however, disagreements don't disappear after they have been swept under the rug—they just pile up and are likely to emerge all at once, the next time an argument occurs. This is an inefficient way of dealing with problems, for today's stored-up grievances are unlikely to get a fair hearing in the heat of next month's (or next year's) fights. It is much more effective to work through differences as they arise, with both parties giving the problem due consideration.

This may not always be possible in the most literal sense. A case in point is one marriage in which the husband complained that his wife wouldn't deal with issues as they arose. She replied that it simply wasn't always possible—and to illustrate her point, she told of the time when their 3-year-old had just become sick to her stomach, yet her husband stood there trying to work out a better way of controlling their credit-card spending. The rule that issues should be dealt with as they come up, like any of the ground rules we've been discussing, needs to be tempered with reality.

Ground Rule #4: Listen to the Other Side   The purpose of any argument is to get your point across to the other person so he or she can see things your way. Of course, the other person has just the same purpose in mind. The only way anything can be accomplished under these circumstances is to listen, understand, and react to what the other person has to say—just as you would like them to do for you.

This may sound simple, but people do not necessarily listen to the other side in an argument. Sometimes partners are so intent on communicating their own point of view that they completely tune out what the other is saying. A husband, for instance, may be trying to encourage his wife to take some time off because she's overworked and tired. But she may assume that he is really trying to tell her she should spend more time taking care of the house.

One way to ensure that the message you are receiving is the same as what the other person is sending is to use the techniques for checking your understanding described earlier in this chapter. Repeating the other person's statements back through checking and summarizing will help you stay on the subject; it will also help you to understand exactly what your friend is trying to say. It may even start a pattern in which the other person becomes more interested in understanding exactly what you have to say.

Ground Rule #5: Be Open to Compromise   The ideal solution to any conflict is to satisfy the needs of both parties (Blake & Mouton, 1970). For instance, if a mother and father both want to go out separately the same evening, the ideal solution would be to hire a babysitter so that neither has to stay home and care for the children.

Ideal solutions are not always possible, however. It may be that no babysitter is available, or that there is no money in the budget to pay for one. Thus, compromise and bargaining are sometimes necessary. **Compromise** involves negotiation to reach some sort of agreement that is mutually acceptable to both parties. In general, a compromise will be most successful when both persons give up something of equal value, and when both have been actively and willingly involved in the decision-making process. Thus, the

---

> **Compromise**   A positive conflict-management technique by which each party agrees to give up some demands and make concessions to the other party.

214

husband and wife may talk over their conflict and agree to take turns going out on alternate weeks; or one may give up an evening out in return for a special favor from the other on a different night.

Not all conflicts can be resolved by compromise. For instance, if you and a friend strongly differ in your political or religious beliefs, it is unlikely that any amount of negotiation will ever bring a meeting of the minds. In such cases, as long as the difference will not intrude too deeply into your relationship, it is usually better to simply agree to disagree. In most practical matters, however, the spirit of compromise is essential to handling conflict productively.

Ground Rule #6: Take Responsibility for What You Say Finally, one of the most basic rules of fighting fair is to take responsibility for what you say—even in anger. Sometimes, people let loose in the heat of an argument and say things that may deeply hurt someone else. Once a word is uttered and heard, it cannot be taken back—and wounds from cruel statements may remain long after an argument has been settled.

These ground rules provide limits that can help keep an argument from going out of bounds, and they may well make the difference between a healthy disagreement and a destructive and bitter fight. In addition to these limits, though, it may be helpful to use a model for negotiating conflicts. Main and Roark (1975) suggest a five-step plan that can serve as an agenda or guideline for airing disagreements. It is summarized in the box *An Agenda for Healthy Conflict.*

As we've explored relationships and communication in the pages above, we have focused on what people say and how they say it. Verbal communication accounts for only part of the messages we send and receive, however. In fact, there is some evidence that nonverbal behaviors may be truer indications of a person's feelings than what that person says (Ekman & Friesen, 1969). Accurately reading body language can give us a great deal of information about how others are feeling or what they are thinking—information that can make us more attuned to the needs of others. We'll learn more about this fascinating area of communication in the remainder of this chapter.

Nonverbal Communication

"My mother was really something when we were young. She could stop us cold with one look. Her face would become so sad. She would then put her arms out with her palms up, as if to say 'you can do what you like, but oh, how it's hurting me.'"

"My mother did it differently. We would be talking and if I said something she didn't care for she'd clam up, shake her head from side to side, and stare at the floor."

"My father never did anything so obvious. He would listen to my explanation of a particular incident and strike a concerned pose—you know, slightly closing one eye, placing his hand on the side of his face and stroking his beard. I would always get nervous—as if a judge were deliberating my fate."

There's an old saying that "actions speak louder than words," and these few examples—taken from a class discussion a few years ago—help to illustrate how effective nonverbal communication can be. When we think about nonverbal behavior or "body language," some of the more obvious gestures come to mind. Shaking a finger at someone is a warning; drumming your fingers usually means you are impatient or bored, for instance. Yet as we communicate with others, we transmit literally hundreds of nonverbal messages. Facial expressions, eye contact, hand movements, postures, as well as the quality of our voices are nonverbal cues that carry messages that are often as clear as or clearer than our verbal statements. Even the way we dress and groom ourselves carries a message: we react differently to a person in a conservative business suit than we would to someone wearing a punk hairdo and skin-tight jeans.

An Agenda for Healthy Conflict

Working through a conflict can take the form of an all-out argument, but it also may be treated as a form of problem solving. Agreements do not just occur. A point must be reached where some agreement is possible. Main and Roark (1975) have suggested a five-step model that may be helpful in setting the stage for some sort of agreement. This model is based on the assumption that it is important for both parties to understand how the other perceives the problem and to establish mutually acceptable goals.

Step 1

Each party describes the situation as they see it, and the other listens until they finish. Sticking to the subject is crucial, and it is important to avoid emotional displays. The goal is to simply provide a framework for later stages by achieving a mutual understanding of the general problem to be solved.

Step 2

Each party makes their feelings known to the other using "I statements." There should be no attempt to blame the other party. Rather, they should be encouraged to take responsibility to communicate accurately their own feelings and needs.

Step 3

Using the understandings from the first two steps, both sides should be able to reach some agreement on a desirable goal. This may require bargaining or compromise at times. Each party should now have some idea of what changes would occur in their life, should the solution go into effect.

Step 4

Each party should agree on what changes they are willing to make. In other words, each side should make it clear how they plan to work toward the solution.

Step 5

In this last stage, a check or some form of evaluation must be built into the system. This might include specific dates for performing necessary changes and for noting how they have worked.

This model may not work in every case. However, even if it does not succeed fully, it may keep the conflict within bounds and reduce the chances that an escalation will occur.

On a more personal level, we learn to "read" the actions of people we are close to, and a sensitivity to these nonverbal cues is important in maintaining close relationships. If your friend is unusually quiet, for instance, this will indicate that something is wrong and will invite you to express your concern. Again, you may recognize certain nervous habits, such as nail biting or fidgeting, that indicate that your friend is uneasy about something (Nierenberg & Calero, 1971). People often don't directly express such feelings. Thus, your awareness of these nonverbal signals can help you be more in tune with your friends' moods and feelings.

We'll look below at two broad types of nonverbal communication. The first, technically known as **kinesics,** is the study of body movements, including gestures, facial expressions, and postures. The second, known as **proxemics,** involves the use of space to signify some sort of meaning. How close you sit to someone on a half-empty bus, your behavior in a crowded elevator, or where you sit at the table when your family has dinner together are all examples of the use of space in everyday life.

Studying nonverbal communication can be a complicated matter. For instance, there are four types of eyebrow behavior: the lifted brow, the knitted brow, the lowered brow, and the single-browed movement (Birdwhistle, 1970). Since it is estimated that the human face is capable of some 20,000 facial expressions, just the study of how people move their eyebrows, noses, or other parts of their faces can be a mammoth task.

Before discussing the details of both body language and the use of space, it is important to note that most of these forms of nonverbal expression are culturally based. That is, your society determines the meaning of most nonverbal behavior. Shaking your head back and forth means "no" to us, but in India it means "yes." Sticking your tongue out is a greeting in Tibet, but it means something quite different here. Again, the English tend to watch the communicator closely and to blink their eyes when they understand a communication, while Americans, who are taught that staring is impolite, communicate understanding by nodding their heads or grunting (Hall, 1966). Personal space is also very much culturally defined: Americans are often very uncomfortable in Middle Eastern marketplaces because of the pushing and shoving that takes place there. The reason is that Arabs have no conception of intrusion into their personal space when they are in a public place. Thus, as we explore nonverbal communications below, we'll keep in mind that these behaviors reflect personal expressions that must be interpreted *in the context of* our own culture.

Body Language

Some "body language" is familiar to almost everyone in our culture. Winking an eye is a way of saying that you were just kidding. Shaking your finger at someone indicates annoyance. The movements of our bodies can accent the meaning of our speech, as when you punch your fist into the open palm of your other hand to emphasize a point (Scheflen & Scheflen, 1972). It can also be used to communicate a specific feeling or state: shrugging your shoulders shows indifference, and burying your face in your hands signifies unhappiness, discomfort, and even despair. The box *Body Talk* illustrates some other common signals in body language. We'll look at a few specific messages below.

Postures and Gestures A story is told of a psychiatrist who was working with a severely depressed client. After one particular session, the psychiatrist found he could not sleep. He couldn't figure out what was bothering him. He specialized in such patients and thought he was making progress with this young man. Then suddenly it hit him. His client had sat differently during this session. He had slumped, holding his shoulders much lower than usual. Evidently, despite his denials, his patient had become more depressed over the week—so he called him and made a special appointment for the next day. During the

---

Kinesics   The study of body movements such as gestures, facial expressions, and postures.

Proxemics   The study of the use of space to signify meaning.

Body Talk

Do actions speak louder than words? Many nonverbal gestures and motions are so clearly understood that no language is needed. A few examples are illustrated in the pictures below.

Left: A symbol of overt censure. The adult is in a dominant position, while the child is in a submissive position.

Left-center: Placing the palm against the chest is a protestation of sincerity.

Right-center: The "thumbs up" sign (or circle with second finger and thumb) means things are fine.

Right: Knitting the eyebrows and looking puzzled while you look at someone usually means you'd like a clearer explanation.

Source: Scheflen, A., and Scheflen, A. *Body Language and Social Order.* Englewood Cliffs, N.J.: Prentice-Hall, 1972.

session the young man admitted to the therapist that he had never felt so low, and he thanked him for taking such an interest in him.

Posture and gestures provide important cues for understanding how another person feels. People indicate strength and determination by standing erect with their shoulders high, while slumped shoulders show sadness. Crossing your arms in front of you is often a defensive stance, indicating that you are closed to everything (Fast, 1970).

Posturing plays a part in daily conversation. When two people are getting along, they tend to lean toward each other as if to decrease the space between them. Their bodies also become less rigid. When one says something that the other disagrees with, they increase the distance and become more rigid, sitting farther back in their chairs and perhaps closing themselves off by folding their arms in front of their chests.

There are many common gestures: some are recognized by virtually all of us while others are highly individualistic. People show readiness by

The Teacher's Glance

In Chapter 4, we looked at an interesting study of how teachers' expectations affect student performance. As you might remember, children who were randomly labeled as "late bloomers" in Rosenthal and Jacobson's study actually showed significantly better academic progress than did the "nonbloomers" at the end of the year. This is an interesting study. But the question remains as to just how the teachers communicated this expectancy to their students. They certainly did not sit down and tell the bloomers that they expected more. Their responses were most probably delivered on the nonverbal level.

To discover the possible nonverbal actions that might result from differential expectations, a group of researchers videotaped 42 undergraduates tutoring 10-year-old students. The undergraduates were told that they were participating in a study on the effects of illumination. After studying the lesson plan for 10 minutes they were given one of three different descriptions of the child to be tutored. All the descriptions stated that the child was highly motivated and got along well with peers. However, one description mentioned that the child was very bright, another made no assessment of abilities, and the third informed the tutor that the student was slow. After the sessions were videotaped, the tutors were asked to fill out a questionnaire concerning their impressions of their student.

Analysis of the tapes indicated a definite difference in the nonverbal signals sent to children thought to be bright and those who were labeled as either neutral or slow. The tutors who were led to believe their students were bright used many kinds of cues to communicate this to their charges. They looked their students in the eye, nodded their heads up and down, smiling and leaning forward more often. The results of the questionnaire indicated that the only difference the tutors perceived in their students related to intelligence.

It seems that when teachers expect students to do well, their nonverbal cues change so that they communicate more approval. It is interesting to note that these effects, which were due to expectancy, were present only in the positive situation. The fact that there were no significant differences between the neutral and slow groups may indicate that the tutors tried not to show their disapproval. (In the real classroom setting, however, in which many more factors operate, this may not be the fact.) In any case, we now have some idea of how teachers signal their acceptance of and expectations for their students.

Source: Chaikin et al., 1974.

---

placing their hands on their hips, with their feet apart. Some other gestures may be mannerisms particular to one individual, such as the person who doodles furiously every time he is disturbed, or the person who tugs on her lower lip when she is deeply concentrating.

Eye Contact   Another important element of body language is eye contact. Of all the parts of the human body that convey meaning, the eyes are perhaps the most expressive. We show atten-

tion by looking at someone. Eye contact demonstrates that the channels of communication are open; looking downward or to the side shows impatience, disinterest, or a desire to end a conversation (Sielski, 1979). The discussion in the box *The Teacher's Glance* shows how eye contact was one signal teachers used to express approval and high expectations for students. Scheflen (1974) notes that Americans do not gaze directly into the eyes of other people in common circumstances. Rather, we tend to focus somewhere between the cheek and the shoulders, just out of range for eye-to-eye gazing.

People use their eyes to express emotion. The gaze of lovers (who do tend to look into each other's eyes) is one example. When the pupils of the eyes dilate, it usually communicates emotion. A wide-eyed look also signals emotion, but in this case it must be interpreted according to the situation. It may indicate fear, surprise, or wonderment, depending on the circumstance.

Facial Expressions   A third basic medium of body language is facial expression. Unlike other nonverbal signals, many facial expressions are universal, meaning the same thing in every culture. As Ekman notes, "If you meet a native in New Guinea or your old boss in a Manhattan bar, you will be able to interpret their facial expressions easily, knowing how they feel—or how they want you to think they feel" (1975, p. 35). Ekman showed pictures of different facial expressions to students in Japan, the U.S., Chile, and Argentina. There was considerable agreement on what emotions were being shown. Ekman presents evidence from other studies performed all over the world to demonstrate that by and large, facial expressions are universal.

Double Messages   While we all recognize most of the nonverbal signals we've been discussing, there are many times when we may not realize we are sending these signals. It is probably true that it is easier to control the content of our speech than our nonverbal behavior. As a result, there are times when people send double messages—as in the case of the man who claimed vehemently that

he loved his wife while he slammed his fist against the table, or the woman who said through clenched teeth "Of course I'm not angry at you" to her child who had just spilled a pitcher of milk. Their words communicate one message, but their body language says something different.

Many people can tell a lie, and some of us have even learned to lie with a straight face, but few of us can fully control our nonverbal behaviors. Desmond Morris describes an experiment that illustrates this fact. Student nurses were asked "to both lie and tell the truth about certain films they had been shown" (1977, p.45). The experiment was filmed, and the body language they used when they were lying was later compared to their gestures when they told the truth. Two differences were found. First, the nurses used fewer hand-only gestures when they were lying. This was probably an attempt to control the most visible type of body language. Secondly, the number of hand-to-face contacts (gestures such as chin-stroking, nose touching, and earlobe-pulling) increased dramatically when the subjects were lying. The most popular of these motions were mouth-covering and nose-touching. These gestures, of course, do not always mean that a person is deceiving you. However, they may sometimes be an indication that someone is trying to hide something.

Personal Space

In addition to the language of gestures, posture, and expression, another kind of nonverbal communication involves the use of space. The study of proxemics explores the significance of the space between people.

Four Distance Zones   Hall (1966) studied personal space and distances, and he found four "distance zones," outlined in Figure 9.3. He calls the first distance zone the **intimate distance zone.** Each of us is surrounded by this protective

---

Intimate distance zone   Hall's name for the distance zone for which the close phase (0–6 inches) is reserved for those with whom we are intimate. The far phase of this zone, 6–18 inches, is reserved for close friends.

"bubble" of space, and we are very selective about whom we permit to enter this space. The close phase of this intimate zone—ranging from touching to six inches—is reserved for those with whom we are intimate. The far phase, 6–18 inches, is reserved for close friends.

Note that there are times when circumstances make it necessary to violate our intimate space. Perhaps you're on a crowded subway or bus, or in a crowded elevator. You may notice that in situations like these, people try to maintain what distance they can. They will stand straight and rigid, and try to avoid touching one another. Normally, there is little conversation between passengers who don't know each other. Felipe and Sommer (1966) found that if strangers stand too close to us, we use a variety of defensive maneuvers including placing our elbows between ourselves and the intruders or simply walking away.

The second distance zone is called the **personal distance zone.** The close phase of this zone, 18–30 inches, is reserved for closer acquaintances. We can shake hands easily from this distance, and this adds a personal touch to conversation. The far zone, 30–48 inches, is used for casual acquaintances. This appears to be a compromise distance, since it allows for personal conversation but still keeps the other person at arm's length.

The third zone is called the **social distance zone,** and it also contains two divisions. The close phase, four to seven feet, is reserved for impersonal transactions. The far phase, 7–12 feet, is used for very formal settings (such as the space between desks in offices).

The fourth zone, the **public distance zone,** is used by public figures such as politicians or lecturers. The distance of 12 or more feet adds a psychological dimension of separateness that is often desirable to accentuate the role of a public speaker.

Behavior on a Bench Although we may not be consciously aware of why we sit where we do, or why we approach another person at a particular

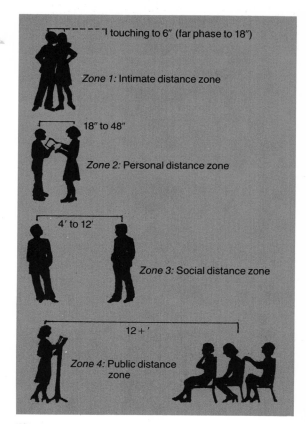

Figure 9.3   Distance Zones in Personal Space
Source: Based on Hall, 1966.

Personal distance zone   The distance between individuals reserved for acquaintances. The close phase, 18–30 inches, is reserved for close acquaintances, while the far zone, 30–48 inches, is for casual acquaintances.

Social distance zone   The distance between individuals reserved for impersonal transactions. The close phase, 4–7 feet, is reserved for nonpersonal interactions; the far phase, 7–12 feet, is used for very formal settings.

Public distance zone   The distance between a public speaker, such as a politician or lecturer, and the audience; 12 feet or more.

distance, these spatial considerations affect our behavior. Suppose you are sitting on a park bench, or on a seat in an almost empty bus, and someone comes along and sits down right next to you. According to social convention, a stranger should choose another seat, or sit on the far side of the bench to maintain a proper distance (unless all other seats are filled). Sommer (1969) found that the newcomer would be considered an intruder if he or she sits right next to you. In reaction, you might strike a defensive posture or simply walk away.

An understanding of both body language and proxemics can be helpful in dealing with other people. First, it is necessary for anyone interacting with people from another culture to be familiar with their spatial conventions. Getting too close may be a problem, since closeness may indicate intimacy. However, in some cultures, remaining too far away may be considered an insult. Secondly, proxemics can be helpful even within our own culture in understanding the use (or misuse) of distance. For instance, people who have a personal history of violence often have a larger "personal bubble," and it might be wiser to be especially careful in keeping your distance from such people (Kinzel, 1971).

Most people already know the meanings of the more common gestures, facial expressions, and posturings. Yet we don't necessarily use this knowledge. Often, people are not consciously aware of the nonverbal signals they see before them. When we become aware of the body language we encounter in everyday life, another dimension is added to our interpersonal world. We can use this knowledge and awareness to actively show sensitivity to the feelings of others, and to communicate active concern by our own behavior.

Summary

1. Our relationships with others offer us great joy but can also result in great pain.

2. Schutz believes that human beings have three interpersonal needs: inclusion, control, and affection. Inclusion relates to the need to belong; control involves the degree to which one dominates the decision-making process in a relationship; and affection is the need for varying degrees of emotion.

3. In a healthy relationship, both individuals are free to develop and maximize their potentials. Important aspects of healthy relationships include making reasonable demands on the other individual, accepting others as they are, and open communication.

4. Attractiveness, closeness (proximity), reward, similarity, and complementarity are important factors in establishing an interpersonal relationship.

5. Flattery can backfire. An individual who desires to flatter you may pretend to share your ideals or emphasize some attractive feature of your personality. If flattery comes from an individual of lower status or who seems to have an ulterior motive, it is usually ineffective. In addition, if the flattery involves a trait that is not rated positively by the individual being flattered, it may not have the desired effect.

6. Shyness is a common problem. Most people are shy in some situations. People who are chronically shy may be fearful and quiet and have difficulty making friends. Assertiveness training procedures can be of help to people who are disturbed by their shyness.

7. Communication is defined as any means by which we influence one another. Communication may be verbal or nonverbal. All communication requires a communicator, a message, and a listener (or receiver). Communication skills are learned. Genuine communication involves the ability to receive, consider, and respond.

8. People are more likely to accept a message if it comes from a communicator who is viewed as credible. Communicator credibility can be divided into two basic components: expertness and trustworthiness.

9. The term *empathy* is used to describe the ability of one individual to understand another person's point of view.

10. Active listening is an important communications skill. Discreet questioning, active feedback,

and periodic checking of one's understanding are important. Reflecting the content or the feelings behind a statement is an effective form of feedback.

11. Conflict is probably inevitable in interpersonal relationships. The use of power, smoothing over, or avoidance are negative ways of dealing with interpersonal conflict. If disputes are handled positively, however, they need not damage a relationship. Fighting fair involves taking responsibility, staying on the issue, and listening carefully to the other person's views. There should be no winner or loser in an argument. Bargaining and compromise are helpful.

12. A helpful approach to conflict management includes five steps: first, describing the situation from both parties' points of view; second, making feelings known without resorting to blame; third, reaching some agreement on the problem; fourth, agreeing on what changes each person is willing to make; and finally, a built-in check or evaluation.

13. Communication also occurs on the nonverbal level. Kinesics is the study of body movements, while proxemics involves the study of how space is used in interpersonal relationships. The specific meaning of most nonverbal communications depends on one's culture.

14. Eye contact is an important part of conveying meaning to other people. Facial expressions are the exception to the rule that nonverbal gestures vary from culture to culture. Many facial expressions appear to be universal.

15. Each of us surrounds ourselves with a protective bubble of space. There are four zones, which Hall labels *intimate, personal, social,* and *public* distance zones, which permit only particular classes of individuals to approach us.

Key Terms and Concepts

inclusion	reflection
control	compromise
affection	kinesics
communication	proxemics
genuine communication	intimate distance zone
credibility	personal distance zone
self-disclosure	social distance zone
feedback	public distance zone

What is love?

As a child, you may have asked this question of someone older and more experienced. If you did, the answer you received may have been something like this: "It can't be described. But when you're in love, you just know it."

This answer probably wasn't much help, and neither are the popular images of love that we see on most movie

Love, Commitment, and Marriage

screens or TV shows. Is it always dramatic, as when Brooke Shields fell in love on a desert isle in the 1981 movie *Blue Lagoon,* or when couples meet and fall head-over-heels on that television cruise ship "Love Boat"? As Joni Mitchell puts it in her song "Both Sides Now": "It's love's illusions I recall. I really don't know love at all." It's not always easy to separate the images from the reality.

For many years, psychologists were of little more help in defining love than are the layperson's answers and images we've just described. They freely admitted that love was an important need and an important and vital force in molding personality. Maslow (1961), for instance, recognized that it could be either a deficiency or a being need, as we'll discuss later; and Harlow's studies of love deprivation in animals (also discussed later) showed that the lack of love could severely affect psychological development. Despite such findings, however, investigations into the nature of love were rare, and they have sometimes even been ridiculed. In 1975, a midwestern senator decried a government grant awarded to a well-respected researcher to study why people fall in love. He argued that people didn't want to scientifically dissect love—that some things are best left a mystery.

There was a widespread outcry against this senator's comments. Since love, marriage, and family life are so closely related, people argued, the subject of love was well worth exploring.

We agree. Learning about love, and learning about the factors that affect relationships with people we love, can only help us to maintain these important relationships. Thus, we will be looking at definitions of love, different types of love, and how love can be measured in the pages that follow. And although love and marriage don't always "go together like a horse and carriage," the two often do. Thus, we will also focus closely on the institution of marriage—the factors that affect its chances for success; the alternatives that are available to marriage; and the ways in which the institution itself is changing. Finally, we will close the chapter by looking at another "institution" that has grown increasingly common in our society: divorce.

What Is Love?

There are many different kinds of love. The love for a pet, a parent, a piece of jewelry, or a lover are all quite different from one another. And though the study of love is normally limited to romantic love, this shouldn't be taken to mean that this is the only type of love worth investigating. However, since *romantic love*—love that leads to intimate relationships, including marriage—plays such an important part in most people's lives, this most commonly researched type of love will be the focus of our attention.

Romantic love is an intense emotion: how can it be described? Most people think they know what it is. Kephart (1967) conducted a study of more than 1,000 college students, and he found that 84 percent of men and 90 percent of women said they knew what love was. Different people do not all describe love in the same terms, however. Some see love as an extreme form of liking, while others describe it in terms of the intense emotions it involves. Some define love as a need, while others focus their attention on the way people act toward one another when they are in love. Which description defines love? We'll explore each of these points in an effort to find out.

Love as an Emotion

Love vs. Liking   Some of the first attempts to define love described this emotion as an intense form of liking (Heider, 1958). Thus, the same explanations for why people like one another were also used to explain love. One such approach, as we saw in Chapter 9, was to predict that lovers, like friends, are drawn together through mutual reinforcement or rewards. We are attracted to people who give us what we need—companionship, interesting conversation, an enjoyable day, lots of laughs, and so forth. If those people continue to reward us, we will interact with them more and more and our feelings will become more intense.

This is certainly true of friendship, for the more time we spend with friends, the deeper our bonds often become. Yet is it also the case for romantic love? According to Berscheid and Walster (1978), it isn't. They distinguish three principal differences between liking and loving.

What Kind of Lover Are You?

Do all people love in the same way? As you might guess, different people have their own individual ways of expressing love, just as they have different personalities and different approaches to any other aspect of life. In a well-known study, John Lee spent more than a decade exploring various types of loving relationships, and he identified six basic patterns or styles of loving:

Eros

Love is very important to the erotic lover, and this person's love has a strongly physical component. This type of love develops rather quickly, with early sexual activity the rule. The erotic lover is not especially jealous or possessive; and although emotions are intense, this lover is not likely to undergo much self-sacrifice in the effort to obtain love.

Ludus

The ludic lover sees love as a game played for fun: deep relationships are avoided, and this individual may juggle a number of partners at the same time. Just the right degree of emotionality is maintained, so that personal commitment never becomes too demanding. To maintain this level, the ludic lover may encourage a partner to see other people.

Storge

The third type of lover, storge, sees love as a slow, steady climb toward commitment. Neither intense emotions nor sexual encounters are central to the relationship. Instead of the roller-coaster ups and downs of a passionate relationship, the storgic lover approaches love as an even sort of relationship based on sharing of activities and interests.

First, there is an unmistakable aspect of *fantasy* in romantic love that is not present in liking. Love may be based upon an idealized view of the other person, so that while rewards are present, they may be intangible, or even unrealistic. We may overlook the weaknesses of our lovers, while their strengths are perceived well out of proportion to reality. Bruno Bettelheim (1975) sees this same idealization process in the fairy tales on which many of us are raised. Although there are always obstacles to happiness, we like to believe that a Prince Charming (or his female equivalent) will come along and help us overcome them. The idealization and fantasy of romantic love do not continue forever; and neither does romantic love, in many cases.

This brings us to a second difference between liking and loving: *the effect of time.* As time goes by, the depth of friendships tends to increase, and the more you interact with a friend, the more you will probably like that person (Homans, 1961). Yet romantic love often tends to cool down after the initial period, which may, incidentally, last for a few years. Time would seem to be the enemy of

Mania

This fourth style of love presents a direct contrast to storge. This lover is obsessed with his or her partner and is jealous and possessive, filled with anxiety that something will happen to ruin the relationship. Such jealousies and insecurities make intimacy a problem.

Pragma

The pragmatic lover is more calculating than the other styles we discuss. This individual knows what he or she wants and goes "shopping" to find a partner with the right interests and goals. The relationship that ensues is not a highly passionate or intense one; rather, it is one that fits into a well-defined pattern.

Agape

Agapic love is pure, patient, kind, altruistic, compassionate—more than the other styles of love, it is given without any conditions and may involve self-sacrifice. This type of love tends not to be intensely emotional, but rather more transcendental and spiritual. If a sexual relationship exists, it is more an act of intimate communication than of pleasure. Lee found no examples of pure agape (pronounced *a-ga-pay*), yet there were some aspects of agape in a number of relationships.

These six styles of loving should be seen as ideal types: very few people fit exactly into one or another of these descriptions. Yet they help us understand why certain people may be incompatible as lovers—for instance, agapic and ludic types would find it hard to build a satisfying relationship. In all, then, Lee's six types are useful in giving us a general picture of how different individuals approach love, and they may provide some insights into our own expressions of love.

Source: Lee, 1974a, 1974b.

romantic love, and many love relationships degenerate with time.

A third distinction between liking and loving is the kind of *feelings* that are involved. It is possible to love someone whom you don't like, or who isn't "good" for you. People in love may prevent each other from growing, or they may even cause suffering in each other—as when a lover is unfaithful or is an alcoholic. John Lee conducted an extensive study of styles of loving and found that some people are highly possessive in the way they show love, that others treat love as a game, and that a range of other feelings are involved in love, according to the individual. The boxed discussion *What Kind of Lover Are You?* looks at the styles of loving he found. In addition to the variations from one person to another, each individual's experience of love often includes ambivalence. Romantic love is not always a totally pleasant experience. The euphoria of passionate love often comes hand-in-hand with doubts, jealousy, and anxiety (Lindzey et al., 1975). Along with the dependence, there may also be a strong wish to be independent.

The ancient Greeks understood this last aspect of love very well. Aphrodite, the goddess of love, was beautiful, beguiling, and sensuous; but she was certainly not portrayed as an heroic figure in mythology. Instead, she and her son Eros (Cupid to the ancient Romans) were malicious, exerting a destructive power from which no mortal could escape. Love has brought humans to the pinnacle of joy, but it has also brought grief to many a person.

In all, Berscheid and Walster's argument seems to be supported: love is distinct from liking. But if being in love isn't the same as enjoying a friendship, how can it be described as a separate emotion?

Problems in Describing Love This question brings us back to the "nondefinition" we mentioned at the beginning of this chapter, that love is so powerful an emotion that it "can't be described." Indeed, it is hard to describe love, for a few reasons.

One problem concerns the language itself. Words are not always a very effective means of communicating feelings, especially when those feelings are very intense. We may verbally transmit our feelings in two ways: by telling a friend about them, describing our experience as best as we can; or by placing a common label on our feelings ("It was 'love'"), and hoping that the other person can understand what that label signifies.

Either way, words often fail us. Describing a situation may be inadequate because we all have different tastes. A movie that you find funny may put your friend to sleep; a situation that frightens you may be exciting to someone else. In the same way, if you try to describe a situation that is highly arousing and romantic to you, you may find that your friend has quite a different reaction to that same situation. The qualities that you find so endearing because they remind you of James Bond, Bo Derek, Han Solo (or whoever you happen to daydream about) may leave another person completely unmoved.

Using the label "love" may not communicate your feelings any better. A blanket statement such as, "It was love at first sight," leaves the interpretation of the word "love" up to the listener— and if he or she has never shared that experience, your meaning won't be clear. In all, labeling our feelings and effectively communicating them to others is a difficult undertaking.

While language gets in the way of defining love, a second problem is presented by the emotion itself. Are the feelings of being in love really so different from other intense emotions? Your first, automatic response might be, "Of course they are different." But there are actually strong similarities between the emotion of love and other emotions.

For instance, there is little doubt that physiological arousal plays a part in our experiencing emotion (Smith et al., 1978). We feel different: our hearts pound, our blood pressure rises, our throats may get dry, and our stomachs may become queasy. Yet these physiological indicators don't seem to be of much help in defining love, for they actually differ very little from what we feel in other strong emotions such as fear, hate, or excitement.

Realizing this, Stanley Schachter has advanced a **cognitive theory of emotion** (1964). When physiological responses occur as we experience deep emotion, Schachter argues, we label them according to their context. If these changes take place at a funeral, we label them as grief; if they take place before a test, we label them as anxiety. If they take place on a moonlit night while taking a slow stroll with a person we've al-

---

Cognitive theory of emotion The theory, suggested by Stanley Schachter, that when we experience physiological responses to emotion, we label them according to the situational context. Thus, sweaty palms may mean fear in one context, but love in another.

Planning a Big Night? Where to Take Your Date

You are met on a swaying bridge that doesn't seem particularly safe by a very attractive person of the opposite sex. That person asks you to answer some questions for a class project—a process that takes a moderate amount of time. Then, as the bridge sways over the chasm, you are thanked and given a phone number. If you are interested in knowing more about the experiment, you are invited to give the interviewer a call.

A bit down the road, another attractive interviewer is doing the same thing on a safe, strong structure. The same type of questions are asked, and then you are invited to call the interviewer later if you wish more information.

This scenario was actually used in a fascinating experiment conducted by Dutton and Aron in order to measure how fear affects romantic attraction. The researchers used male students as subjects, and the interviewers were young women (although the sexes could also be reversed); they measured the level of attraction by the number of males who followed through and called back "for more information." The results? Significantly more students called back under fearful conditions than they did under safe conditions. (When the experiment was performed with a male interviewer approaching other males, there was no difference in the rate of calls from one situation to the other.)

These findings have interesting implications. The fearful situation in the first scenario put subjects in a state of emotional arousal, and this arousal state seems to have affected the way they saw the interviewer. Feelings of having one's heart in one's throat, or being weak-kneed or shaky, may have been caused by the swaying bridge, but they became associated with the attractive woman who was standing on the bridge.

By all this, we don't mean to suggest that you should take your date out on a shaky bridge. But it does seem that under some circumstances, emotions such as excitement, fear, and anxiety might actually heighten feelings of romance. Perhaps this is why suspense movies, throbbing rock concerts, and roller coaster rides are popular choices for dates.

Source: Dutton & Aron, 1974.

---

ways been attracted to, we might label them as love. The box *Planning a Big Night? Where to Take Your Date* describes one interesting experiment that shows just how important context can be.

Love as a Need

Besides being a deeply felt emotional experience, love is also a need. Our language accentuates this—we "hunger for" love or "thirst for" affection—although, of course, the need is not strictly physiological as are hunger or thirst.

How, or why, do we need love? This question is hard to answer, especially regarding romantic love, because people's needs vary so widely. One area of psychology has extensively researched this question, however, and that is the study of child development. Harlow (1959) performed a number of well-known experiments in which he isolated newborn monkeys before they had the experience of being mothered and loved. This love deprivation had a lasting effect on the infant monkeys: they were never able to form bonds with other monkeys, nor were they able to procreate normally. Harlow argued that primates have a need for *contact comfort*—a true need to be touched, fondled, and held.

This kind of research is impossible for human subjects, but studies of institutionally raised children have shown similar effects. One such study found that children who did not receive early love were incapable of forming warm relations with others later on in life (Goldfarb, 1943). Another study linked early maternal deprivation with a number of serious problems, including mental retardation (Spitz, 1945).

Love, then, can be seen as a distinct need, with deprivation of this need leading to a difficulty in learning to love others. From this, it seems to follow that the expression of love is something that we learn. A look at the ways we express love tells us more about what love is, and we'll turn next to those behavior patterns.

Love as a Way of Acting

A woman enters counseling complaining that her husband doesn't show her any love. She has

strong needs for affection that he simply isn't meeting. The husband doesn't understand the problem: after all, he contributes his share to the family income, he is faithful to his wife, and he's a pretty good father, too. He feels that expressions of love are unnecessary, and besides, he has no idea of how to show love in any other manner.

Four Behavioral Components As this case illustrates, love doesn't consist simply of the emotional components and the needs that we explored above. It also involves certain behavior patterns toward the person one loves. Erich Fromm (1956) views love as a group of actions—as something one gives. He also regards love as an art, for it isn't easy to love (or even to be loved, for that matter).

According to Fromm, people are often uncertain about their roles as lover and loved one. They may devise strategies to overcome their doubts. Some use the "window dressing" of acting sexy, powerful, or whatever image is socially acceptable in order to try to attract a person. When this happens, says Fromm, romantic love can become a shopping spree. These images only serve to mask the true nature of a relationship, preventing genuine love from developing. In contrast to this situation, Fromm argues that genuine love contains four separate *behavioral components:*

Knowledge One of Erich Fromm's four components of loving behavior. It relates to the act of learning about the needs, values, and goals of the other individual in the relationship.

Responsibility One of Erich Fromm's four components of loving behavior. It refers to the consideration we give to the way in which our actions may affect the other person, and the extent to which we are willing to take responsibility for our actions.

Respect One of Erich Fromm's four components of loving behavior. It relates to the honor and high esteem in which we hold the other individual in a loving relationship.

Caring One of Erich Fromm's four components of loving behaviors. It relates to a show of concern for the other individual in a loving relationship that promotes the other individual's growth and development.

- ■ **Knowledge.** People need to be aware of one another's needs, values, and goals. Otherwise, they cannot show understanding and help their partner to grow.

- ■ **Responsibility.** It is important that partners act in a manner that will not cause one another shame or hurt. They must take responsibility for their actions, considering how they will affect one another.

- ■ **Respect.** Partners honor and hold one another in high esteem, accepting each other as unique individuals and showing interest in the other's development.

- ■ **Caring.** Lovers show concern for one another, behaving in such a way that their happiness is increased.

Active vs. Passive, or D vs. B Love   These four patterns are encompassed in Jourard's definition of loving behavior, which he sees as "all actions which a person might undertake to promote happiness and growth in the other" (1974, p. 245). In this conception of love, it is *giving* that matters, so that the happiness of the other is a source of joy. This kind of **active love** differs greatly from **passive love,** in which the individual takes but does not give (Stein, 1972). Passive love tends to be selfish, contractual, and limiting, so that one partner may be jealous of the other's growth.

Maslow (1961) also distinguishes between types of love, defining **deficiency love** (*D* love) as separate from **being love** (*B* love). *D* love is based on needs, and therefore it is conditional: when a lover no longer provides what the individual wants, the relationship is dropped. In contrast, *B* love is based on respect for the other individual as he or she is, and each lover considers both partners' personal growth to be important within the relationship.

Some Practical Considerations   How practical are these conceptions of active love or *B* love? To many, they may seem idealistic, but there are some basic ideas that are actually quite useful. We'll look at them briefly:

- First, loving is considered a set of behaviors, not just a personal feeling. Someone may say and believe that they feel love for another person, yet their behavior may be possessive, manipulative, or highly jealous. Although there is an emotional component similar to love, one might question whether this could truly be called love.

- Second, the behaviors involved in love are active, not passive—that is, giving, not taking.

- Third, loving means accepting the individual as he or she is. It doesn't mean trying to change someone else; instead, it hopefully provides a relationship in which both lovers can grow. This point brings up a question that is particularly relevant in our society: for women, hasn't love (and marriage) traditionally meant a foreclosure of identity, rather than an opportunity to grow? Gail Sheehy states this argument in her book *Passages* (1976), as she writes that women are constantly asked to surrender their interests and not think in terms of their own development. Such a foreclosure can lead to eventual dissatisfaction and unhappiness with marriage.

- Finally, Fromm's conception of love leads us to conclude that genuinely loving behaviors involve a deep understanding, respect, and responsibility, as well as a concern that *both* partners continue to flourish in the relationship. There is a wish to involve oneself in the life of a partner, but not to direct it. This combination of qualities involves a fair amount of maturity, and many people have self-doubts about their own ability to love someone else. The box *Can Everybody Love?* looks more closely at the qualities that seem to be most important in a love relationship.

Defining Love

In the preceding discussions, we've seen that love can be viewed as an emotional experience, a need,

---

Active love   Behaviors that aid in the growth of the other person in a loving relationship, as opposed to passive love. Active love involves giving.

Passive love   A type of love that tends to be selfish and limiting. Passive love involves taking rather than giving, and often there is an attempt to change the other person in some fundamental way.

Deficiency love (D love)   Love that is based upon one's unmet needs and lacks. Deficiency love is conditional upon the other individual satisfying some deep need in his or her partner.

Being love (B love)   Love based upon respect for the individual as he or she is and emphasizing the importance of the growth and development of the other individual's potential and abilities.

Can Everybody Love?

It is not unusual for people to doubt their ability to love. After all, the depth of affection, responsibility, dependency, and desire presents a combination of qualities that can be both confusing and frightening. It seems that we desire and fear love at the same time (Blau, 1964).

Certainly, the ability to love demands a certain maturity of a person, and some people are more capable of loving than others. Jourard (1974) identifies six factors that increase an individual's capacity to love. These include:

- *Gratification of Basic Needs.* If a person has a solid identity and no outstanding deficiencies, he or she will be more able to share. In this sense, a person who has a sense of worth is more capable of giving love than is a person with low self-esteem.

- *High Frustration Tolerance.* If love is, in part, considering your lover's needs as at least equal to your own, some frustration is inevitable. A person with high frustration tolerance is better able to deal with a mature love relationship.

- *Self-Love.* In order to love others, you must love yourself. If you are secure and self-accepting, you need not be as jealous or controlling.

- *Reality Contact.* Love requires sensitivity to your partner's needs, moods, and desires. You must be in contact with all of these elements of his or her reality in order to respond within your relationship.

- *Reasonable Ideals.* Perhaps the most difficult task a person can have is to live up to the impossible standards of another person. Although love sometimes brings with it a degree of fantasy, unrealistic expectations usually lead to unhappiness.

- *Emancipation from Parents.* Finally, individuals must be aware of their own needs, wishes, and identity in order to fully enter a love relationship. The need for parental approval (or, for that matter, peer approval) can prevent a relationship from developing fully.

and a pattern of behavioral expression. Which of these aspects of love is most important? Actually, different behavioral scientists disagree on this question, and each quality of love has been emphasized in one definition or another. For instance, love has been defined as an intense absorption in another person (Walster & Walster, 1978), while another definition sees love as a combination of strong interpersonal sexual attraction

> **Love**   In this text, love is defined as an intensely intimate feeling in which the satisfaction of the other's needs are at least as important as one's own and in which one acts in a way to maximize the potential of the other.

and physical arousal in which these feelings are attributed to love (Berscheid & Walster, 1978).

Since we are interested in the behaviors of love as well as the feeling, we will define **love** as an *intense intimate feeling in which the satisfaction of the other's needs is at least as important as one's own, and in which one acts in a way that maximizes the potential of the other.* In this way, we can view love as both an emotional experience and a set of behaviors—a combination that is encompassed in Zick Rubin's three-part analysis of love, outlined in Table 10.1.

Whichever definition is used, love forms a strong bond between people. Most serious romantic relationships, including marriage, seem to be based upon love; and at least in the popular view, love is regarded as an essential ingredient in a successful marriage (Reiss, 1971). Is love the only factor involved in choosing a mate, or in the success of a marriage? We'll turn to that question next.

Choosing a Mate: Is Love Enough?

"Love," says the popular song, "Love will keep us together" no matter what the odds; and this idea is a consistent theme not only in the "bubble gum music" we hear on the radio, but also in movies, poetry, and literature dating back well before Romeo and Juliet.

Although we've been raised with this image, however, many of us may have questioned its accuracy, especially over the long term. Had Romeo and Juliet survived instead of committing suicide, would they really have been happy 15 years after their marriage if their families remained enemies? For the modern-day couple who have radically different religious, economic, or intellectual backgrounds, will Fromm's four qualities of knowledge, responsibility, respect, and care provide life-long happiness?

The question is intriguing, and to test it, one of the authors has conducted classroom surveys to explore students' responses to the "love conquers all" image. The results have demonstrated that the great majority of students think love is necessary for marriage; but they do not think it is a sufficient condition. In other words, most students believe that love must be present, but they also believe that more than love is necessary if a marriage is to succeed. Exactly what factors seem to make a difference between success and failure? We'll examine that question below.

Attraction, Comfort, and Compatibility

Stinnett and Walters (1977) outlined a three-step process that seems to take place in choosing a mate, and in their description we find some clues to the question of what factors are most im-

Table 10.1 Three Aspects of Love

Aspect	Evidenced By
Attachment (strong need for the physical presence of the other person)	Feelings of loneliness when apart; of pleasure when together
Caring (behaviors that show active love)	Showing active concern; placing a lover's needs equal to or above one's own
Intimacy (sharing one's innermost feelings)	Open self-disclosure, as well as an interest in one's partner's disclosures

Source: Rubin, 1970, 1973.

portant. According to these authors, the first phase of a love relationship is *attraction*. We are drawn toward someone, and the basis for this attraction is often a surface characteristic such as physical appearance, personality, or a social trait. Although this attraction may be superficial, or even based on an unrealistic image, we shouldn't minimize the importance of attraction. Surface characteristics, at least initially, take on an important role in forming a relationship.

The second phase in choosing a partner is *comfort,* or *rapport.* In this phase, psychological comfort becomes important. Can I be myself? Does it feel natural to be with this person? If a sense of rapport develops, the relationship may move on to the third phase in which the question of **compatibility** becomes important. Are our interests, values, and goals similar? Can we get along with each other?

The process of commitment is a gradual one which requires answering questions appropriate to each stage; and certainly one factor in the success of a partnership is that lovers allow themselves time to go through all three phases. The marriage that follows three weeks after a couple meets may be a romantic whirlwind, but it may not be destined to succeed because the couple never had a chance to explore important questions about comfort or compatibility.

Who Is Compatible?

The question of compatibility is worth a second look, for it is basic to the success or failure of a marriage. **Compatibility** refers to the fit between partners' values, goals, and lifestyles, and it can involve some very basic issues. For example, listen to the prospective groom and bride:

(The groom): *I want a big house in the suburbs surrounded by a white picket fence. I want three kids, two cars, a good job, and my wife waiting for me when I come home with a beer in one hand and a smile on her face.*

(The bride): *I want an apartment in the city and a full-time career. One child seems OK, but both of us should have equal parenting responsibility.*

If you were asked to rate the probability that this marriage would succeed, what odds would you give? Probably not very high. People who disagree on their basic goals are entering marriage with a great impediment. If a man values his privacy a great deal, and marries a woman for whom togetherness is the most important aspect of marriage, the problems are obvious. If one partner has a strong need for power in the relationship—especially if that partner is the male—this also may cause problems. See the discussion in the box *Power and Love: Do They Mix?*

Compatibility   The fit between partners' (or friends') values, goals, and lifestyles that provides a bond of understanding.

Similarity theory of mate selection   The theory that individuals with similar interests, values, and goals tend to attract one another.

Complementary theory of mate selection   The idea that opposites attract. For instance, a person who needs to be dominant finds someone who will be submissive, or a talkative individual finds a good listener.

Incompatibility can have numerous other causes. In fact, they are too numerous to list here, but we can mention a few, such as differences in religious values, sexual interests, spending habits, intellectual levels, and attitudes about sex roles. Where major differences exist in areas such as these, one partner may be forced to surrender his or her views, and this often leads to unhappiness and dissatisfaction. As a general rule, then, similarity of values tends to lead to happier marriages (Pikunas, 1976).

From the discussion above, it seems that the more different people are, the less likely they are to be compatible. But as we saw in Chapter 9, there are also some cases in which "opposites attract." Indeed, there are two basic theories of compatibility.

The **similarity theory of mate selection** states that we tend to form relationships and marry people who are like us. This seems to be true in a few respects. Schulz and Rodgers (1975) found that people who get married are likely to share similar backgrounds, religious persuasions, educational level, race, interests, and personality characteristics; while Murstein (1971) argues that people who are high in self-esteem tend to marry others with that same quality, and vice versa. Kerkhoff and Davis (1962) suggest that values are another area in which similarity is important, and they find that we tend to marry people who agree with our attitudes about important issues. In addition to these factors, we are more likely to understand another person who is similar to us; and similarity may also lead to shared goals and fewer arguments.

There is another possibility, however. According to Winch's **complementary theory of mate selection** (1958), people who are *complementary opposites* often form deep relationships. A dominant person often finds a submissive spouse; the individual who must be the center of attention finds a spouse who will not compete. Such marriages would seem to satisfy each partner, as long as they are comfortable with the relationship and they also share some common ground.

Power and Love: Do They Mix?

One of the most interesting aspects of any romantic relationship is its power structure. Issues related to control and power are often difficult ones, and they may cause serious problems for a couple.

Researchers Abigail Stewart and Zick Rubin investigated how one partner's need for power affects a relationship. They did this by administering several tests to 63 dating couples in the Boston area. These tests measured a number of factors, including the power motive and perceived future problems. Two years after the first series of tests, the researchers conducted a follow-up study to find out which couples were still dating, which had married, and which had gone their separate ways.

The results were interesting. Male need for power, as measured in the original battery, was found to be inversely related to both partners' satisfaction with the relationship. Men with a great need for power also anticipated many problems with their relationships. They believed that many internal factors, such as different interests and attitudes, would threaten their relationships. It was harder to assess the effect of a female partner's power motive, because few positive correlations were found. There was some tendency for females with a high power need to expect future problems in the relationship, but such feelings were not shared by their boyfriends.

The investigators found that after two years, about one third of the couples had married, one third had separated, and another third were still dating. Fully half of the couples in which the male had a high power need had separated—compared with only 15 percent of couples in which the male had a low power need. In addition, only 9 percent of the high power need males had married the woman they were dating in the original study, compared to 52 percent of the low power-need males.

The investigators argue that a strong male power motive is a source of dissatisfaction in relationships. They explain this by the tendency for high power need males to feel threatened by disagreements. Because of their need to be in control, the researchers felt that these men tended to regard disagreements as potentially serious; and in the long-term, this concern led some men to avoid deep commitments.

Commitment did not seem to be as consistent a problem for females with a high need for power. Perhaps the lack of consistent findings here was due to problems with the measuring instruments. However, the researchers argue that power-motivated women may simply feel more able to resolve conflicts than are power-motivated men. Whatever the reason, it does seem that a strong male power motivation, coupled with an inability to deal with conflict, causes serious relationship problems.

Source: Stewart & Rubin, 1976.

Maturity

Rapport and compatibility are two factors that are important in the success of a marriage; another important factor is maturity. Teenage marriages are not always long-lasting marriages. To the con-trary, men who marry under age 20 and women who marry before turning 18 are twice as likely to divorce as are men and women marrying after these ages (Kelly, 1982). There are several reasons for this. Teenagers may overlook obvious prac-tical problems (for instance, the lack of a job) in their hurry to marry; they may not have the emotional maturity to handle problems that arise; and they may still be trying to develop an identity. The marriage itself may represent a form of rebellion in the effort to build a sense of identity.

A frequent reason for teenage marriages is pregnancy. As might be imagined, such marriages bring a complex array of emotions and responsibilities; and while both young parents may feel tremendous love toward one another and the child, their new roles also require a difficult adjustment. Common problems include jealousy, communication difficulties, and economic hardships (Klemer, 1970). Teenage parents are also likely to cut short their education, hold lower paying jobs, and be less satisfied with their work than the general population (MacDonald, 1979). The young couple has to cope with so much in so short a time that enormous stresses are placed on the marriage. An older age and greater emotional maturity won't guarantee a successful adjustment, but they certainly can help.

Self-Disclosure

Still another factor in the success of a relationship is an open and mutual self-disclosure. At some time or another, most people seek to impress a date by presenting a facade or false image. They may show only one side of themselves because they are afraid their lover will not be able to accept a trait. After a short time, however, they ordinarily come back to themselves. Honest self-disclosure is important in building any serious relationship, not only because it is necessary in building a mutual understanding, but because false images cannot be maintained forever.

Knowledge of another person can never be complete; yet intentionally hiding some characteristic or weakness is a mistake. If we let a future spouse see only a part of us, we are not permitting the relationship to develop along solid ground— nor can the other person experience us as we

really are. In a long-term relationship such as marriage, it will be next to impossible to keep up pretenses. Eventually, the partner will learn that the reality is not equal to the image, and the marriage is likely to sour.

Does Love Change Over Time?

When we began our discussion of what makes a partnership succeed, we noted that one important element is simply allowing time for the gradual development of mutual commitment. This development usually takes place over three phases, as attraction, comfort, and then compatibility are established.

What happens to a relationship once it blossoms into a fully committed partnership, however? Certainly, the story doesn't end once a couple exchanges marriage vows or makes some other commitment. Like everything else in life, relationships don't stop changing; and in fact, studies have explored the course of romantic love after marriage.

The evidence indicates that romantic love decreases with time, beginning to deteriorate almost from the beginning. Perhaps this is due to fantasy giving way to reality: the longer we live with somebody, the more we see of both their positive and negative aspects. Another factor may be the changes that take place when a couple has children. The birth of a first child is usually a happy occasion, but it is also stressful. Less attention is directed toward the spouse because so much is required by the child; as a result, communication may suffer and there may be jealousy. Children grow older, of course, and their growing independence also affects the parents' relationship. Rollins and Feldman (1970) found a steady decline in marital satisfaction—until the children reached school years. Then the curve leveled off and marital satisfaction began to increase again. Figure 10.1 presents a broad outline of this developmental curve for both wives and husbands.

While there is a light at the end of the tunnel,

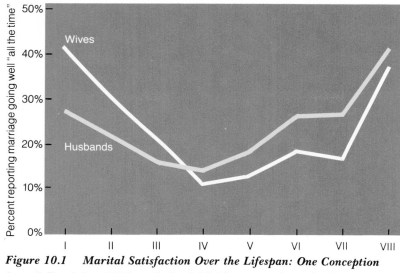

Figure 10.1   Marital Satisfaction Over the Lifespan: One Conception

Source: Rollins, B.C., and Feldman, H. "Marital Satisfaction over the Family Life Cycle," *Journal of Marriage and the Family*, Feb. 1970, p. 25. Copyright 1970 by the National Council on Family Relations. Reprinted by permission.

that light may seem awfully far in the distance to a couple who are in the early stages of this process. Divorce statistics show that many marriages do not last past the initial fading of romantic love, as we'll see at the end of this chapter. There are things that couples can do, though, to stay in love even after the honeymoon is over, and the box *Preventing "Marriage on the Rocks"* provides a few suggestions.

Instead of worrying about saving a marriage after the romance has gone, many people today seem to be wondering whether they should marry in the first place—whether the institution of marriage is itself no longer practical. Our world is changing so fast, and lifestyles have changed so considerably that perhaps marriage no longer fits many people's needs. In addition, modern medicine has increased longevity to such an extent that today's young newlyweds can expect their lifelong commitment to last much longer than it did even a few decades ago. Is marriage dead? We'll examine the evidence.

Is Marriage Dead?

According to Alvin Toffler in his well-known book, *Future Shock* (1970), the institution of marriage is under increasing pressure to adjust to modern society. Toffler admits that some people will certainly continue the normal course of courtship and marriage. But he also predicts an increase in the number of experimental replacements for marriage—including communal arrangements, temporary marriages (perhaps with renewal clauses), and the rearing of children by single parents and homosexuals.

It's been almost a decade and a half since this prediction was made: how does it bear up in the eighties? Newspaper and magazine articles write of the breakup of the family, and changes are certainly taking place. All around us, we see divorce and separation, and there is an increase in people living together without marrying. Such arrangements are not limited to young people who

Preventing "Marriage on the Rocks"

Most couples decide to marry because they are in love. But what happens to the spark once a couple marry? As the chapter discusses, research finds a steady decline in marital satisfaction that begins at the altar and continues until the children hit the teenage years. Many marriages don't make it to this point, of course, as divorce rates have increased tremendously in recent decades.

Is there anything that can be done to prevent this? It seems natural for the fantasy of romantic love to fade with time; but steps can be taken to increase communication and reduce the stress that comes with children and family life. Here are some suggestions:

- *Work on your marriage.* Although they are busy with home, kids, and work, both partners should spend time doing something together and communicating on an intimate level.

- *Don't take your spouse for granted.* Showing interest and noticing changes is important. Such actions show your partner that you care.

- *Allow your spouse to grow.* Each partner has his or her own abilities and potentials, and should be encouraged to develop them.

- *Share parenting responsibilities.* Both partners should actively participate in raising the children, at every age.

- *Allow for "breathing space" in the relationship.* Understand that each partner may require time alone, as well as time to share with the spouse.

- *Be sensitive to changes in your relationship.* Be aware of changes in your communication patterns. If these changes seem harmful to either you or your spouse, take steps to correct them before too much damage is done.

- *Try new things!* Spontaneity is often lost over time when boring, repetitive patterns are established. Try some novel activities if your relationship seems to be in a slump.

Above all, there must be a willingness to improve situations in which one of the partner's needs are not being met. Sensitivity to these needs, and taking steps to fulfill them, is necessary if you are to lessen the deteriorating effects of time on a marriage.

---

are "testing the waters" before making a commitment; indeed, they may involve adults (including older adults who can share Social Security payments) and may last several years.

Living together, or **cohabitation,** is one alternative to marriage that has received a great deal of attention, but there are other alternative lifestyles also. In addition, many people choose to remain single (and even more choose divorce as a way out of an unsatisfying marriage—a topic we'll cover in the final section of this chapter). We'll look at these options below, then explore another question: whether marriage, instead of being replaced by alternatives as some suggest, might itself be adjusting to keep pace with social changes.

Some Nonmarital Lifestyles

Living Together Cohabitation has become an increasingly popular lifestyle in recent years. Ac-

> **Cohabitation** Living together in an intimate, sexual relationship without being married.

cording to one study (Glick and Spanier, 1980) the number of unmarried people of the opposite sex living together doubled in the years from 1970–1978, to an estimated 1.8 percent of all couples (although this estimate is likely to be conservative). Macklin (1978) estimates that 24 percent of college students have cohabited at some time during their college career.

There are many reasons why a couple may choose to live together. According to Karlen (1969), only a small number of cohabiting couples really disagree with the concept of marriage. For some, it is a temporary arrangement that is convenient and satisfies present needs. A significant number of formerly married people choose living together: it provides a satisfying relationship without so great a commitment as another marriage would demand. For still another group, it is a sort of "trial run"—a test of the strength of their relationship prior to making the commitment to marriage.

While it is important not to underestimate the trend toward living together, it is not an alternative to marriage. Few of these arrangements last as long as a marriage would (63 percent of the Glick and Spanier study had lived together for less than two years). And of course, many cohabiting couples eventually do marry. Murstein does not see living together as a threat to marriage. Rather, "for many young people it is a developmental stage on the way to matrimony, a time to love and be loved, to find out more about themselves and their partners before the serious step of marriage" (1971, p. 535).

Staying Single   A second nonmarried lifestyle is simply not to marry. Staying single is a choice that greater numbers of people are making now than in previous years: in 1978, over 27 percent of men ages 25–29 and 18 percent of women of the same age, compared to 20.8 percent and 10.5 percent respectively in 1960 (U.S. Bureau of the Census, 1979).

Despite these increases, there is still a stigma attached to being single. All minorities are stereo-typed as being somehow "different," and the single person is no exception. One study found that many persons associate words like sex, loneliness, swinging, and happiness with the term "single" (Stein, 1976). However, singles do not conform to these images. And in fact, there is no such thing as a "single lifestyle": different single individuals lead lives that are as varied as those of the general population.

Margaret Adams portrayed a positive view of single life in her book, *Single Blessedness* (1976). Adams freely admits that there are problems associated with being single at certain ages. Between 25–30, single people are apt to find themselves in conflict since everyone else seems to be getting married. Acquaintances narrow, as friends start their own families, and the pressure to do the same is great. At older ages there are stresses as well, due to lack of emotional supports. Yet Adams' perspective is one of positive growth and satisfactions. The single person controls his or her own destiny, and most singles have worked out their lives and their problems. It is quite possible, then, to lead a truly meaningful life outside of the marriage/children model.

Other Alternatives   In addition to living together and remaining single, there are other, less common alternatives to marriage (Lamanna and Riedmann, 1981). One lifestyle that some people have chosen is the communal arrangement, in which several adults live together. Two forms of communes are the *group marriage* and the *communal family*. In the **group marriage,** several women and men marry together and share sexual relations among themselves. Usually about six or seven adults are involved, and any children consider all

> **Group marriage**   An arrangement in which a number of adult males and females live together and share sexual relations and child-care responsibilities.

of the adults as their parents. **Communal families** are similar, except that persons share sexual relationships only with one partner, and family units remain distinct.

Another alternative lifestyle is the homosexual marriage. This form of commitment is actually very similar to heterosexual marriage: the couple exchange personal vows, live together, and share a sexual and emotional commitment based on love. There may even be children involved, especially if the couple is *lesbian,* or female homosexual, and one (or both) of the women has custody of her children from a previous union. (It has been very difficult for gay fathers to win custody, although this area is undergoing some change.) The difference between homosexual and heterosexual marriage, of course, is that in the former, the couple are of the same sex. This alternative lifestyle is relatively rare, although it has become much more visible in recent years, especially with cinema coverage in films such as the French movie, *La Cage aux Folles.*

Marriage: Changing to Keep Up with the Times

While many people choose the lifestyles we've described above, marriage itself is still very much alive. According to statistics, 96 to 97 percent of Americans will marry at some time or another in their lives (Carter & Glick, 1970). Although the marriage rate fluctuates somewhat, as Figure 10.2 shows, there is certainly no wholesale desire to avoid marriage. However, there has been an increase in the median age at which people first marry. The median age at which males marry rose from 22.8 to 24.2 during the period between 1960 and 1978, while the age of first marriage increased from 20.3 to 21.8 for women during this same period (Cherlin, 1981). There is, then, a trend toward waiting a bit longer before marrying, but there is no indication of a significant trend away from marriage.

It seems that marriage is not a dying institution, then, despite all the publicity. But the fact that marriage is still vital does not mean that it hasn't undergone some changes. And in fact, its very ability to change with the times may account for the survival of marriage in modern society. We'll look at five areas in which married life has been changing to fit the new needs of people in our fast paced society: attitudes about sex and marriage; the rise of the nuclear family; the decrease in the number of children; the dual-income marriage; and the changes in expectations people hold for marriage.

Marriage and the "Sexual Revolution"   We live in a more permissive atmosphere today, and there is more tolerance and acceptance of sexual activity before marriage (Jersild et al., 1978). This broad change is often labeled the "sexual revolution," as we'll discuss in Chapter 11, and it has had its effect on marriage. For instance, as we saw in the discussion of living together, many more unmarried couples are engaging in sexual relationships, and sexual gratification is no longer as common a motive for marriage as it may have been in the past. At the same time, as some of the past ignorance about sex is being erased, both men and women have higher expectations that their marriage will provide sexual gratification. In this sense, more demands are being placed on the institution than ever before.

The Rise of the Nuclear Family   A second way in which marriage has changed involves the rise of

---

Communal family An arrangement in which groups of adult males and females live together and share childcare responsibilities, although sexual relations are only shared with one partner and the family units tend to remain distinct.

the **nuclear family,** the immediate family consisting only of parents and growing children. Our society today is much more mobile than it was in the past. Few of us live in the same town in which we were born, and it is quite common for families to change location several times over the years. This mobility is one reason why the **extended family,** in which several generations lived together under one roof, has virtually disappeared in our society. It is unusual today to see parents living with, or even near, their grown children.

This change means that many young couples are more isolated from their parents. The older family supports are not as available and they are less likely to receive the emotional and physical support that may be needed in everyday life.

Fewer Children   A third change in modern marriages is that couples tend to have fewer children than they did in the past (Doherty & Jacobson, 1982). There are many reasons why this is true. For one, children are expensive to raise. They are no longer an economic asset, as they were in the days when they could contribute to the family income. Instead, prospective parents today must weigh the heavy costs of medical expenses, food and clothing, and schooling when they consider whether to have children, and how many to have. At the same time that parenthood has become more expensive, many women are maintaining jobs outside of the household. This is causing changes in the traditional role of mothers, and it has been a factor in many families' decisions to have fewer children.

Dual Incomes   The past few decades have seen a fourth change: the tremendous increase in the number and percentage of working women. In 1947, there were 16.7 million women in the work force, while in 1978 the figure was 41.1 million. If this is hard to visualize, percent ratios may be clearer: 28.1 percent of the 1947 labor force were women, compared to 41.7 percent in 1978 (U.S.

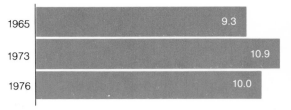

Figure 10.2   Number of Marriages per Thousand Population Over the Past Two Decades
Source: U.S. Bureau of the Census, 1977.

Bureau of the Census, 1979). This figure will probably continue to increase as economic pressures on the lower and middle classes require extra incomes.

Such changes can't help but affect marriage relationships, in terms both of expectations and of actual division of labor at home. Working wives simply don't have enough daytime hours to carry out all the traditional homemaking roles alone, and in many families, husbands are taking on a larger share of these responsibilities. Of course, this change is occurring to a different extent in different families, and there is a certain amount of role confusion that places stress on modern marriages. Still, there is a trend for couples to share in both homemaking and income earning more than in the past.

Increased Expectations   The changes we've been describing help bring marriage more in tune with people's needs today. They have also contributed to a change in people's expectations for marriage. Not only do we expect marriage to fulfill physical and economic functions such as raising a family

Nuclear family   The immediate family, consisting only of husband or wife and children living in a single household.

Extended family   At least three generations of a family, often including aunts and uncles.

A century ago, families were much larger than they normally are today.

and providing economic stability, we also expect the union to help us develop as individuals.*

The rise of the nuclear family means that young couples often do not have parents and relatives close by to help or give them support. The

increased cost of raising a family means that couples are likely to feel economic pressures and, at the same time, have fewer children. The change in our expectations about marriage means that we are no longer satisfied with a comfortable home and the security that someone is there. We want to develop our own capacities and talents and expect the marriage to serve as a vehicle for that development. All of these changes cause stress in modern marriages and they contribute to another major change in marriage patterns in our society: the increasing divorce rate.

*Parsons and Bales (1955) distinguish between the *instrumental* and the *expressive* functions of marriage. (The former relates to functions such as child care and the establishment of a safe, secure home; the latter relates to personal growth and development.) Using their distinction, we would say that the *expressive* function of personal growth has become more important in recent years.

Divorce American Style

Divorce is a costly experience, in terms of emotions and economics. Yet it has become more and more commonplace in recent decades—to the point that some have called it an epidemic. As Figure 10.3 shows, there were 2.6 divorces per 1000 population in 1950, compared to 5.1 per 1000 in 1977; and the total number of divorces has also jumped alarmingly. At the same time, more people seem to be deciding not to remarry after a divorce. The percentage of divorced but not remarried men has risen from 1.8 percent in 1950 to 4.7 percent in 1978, and among women, those figures have shifted from 2.3 percent in 1950 to 6.6 percent in 1978 (U.S. Bureau of the Census, 1979). Today's high divorce rate holds the promise of an even higher one in the future. What are the causes of divorce, and what strategies can people use to adjust after divorce?

Causes of Divorce

Few people enter a marriage with the idea that they will somehow end it if it doesn't work out. Hilsdale (1962) found that four out of five couples entering marriage do not even consider the possibility of divorce. What happens?

In some cases, the cards already seem to be stacked, at least in terms of statistical likelihood. We know, for instance, that couples who marry at a very young age are likely to have more problems, as we saw earlier in this chapter. In addition, both the level of education and income status are linked to the divorce rate. The lower the income and education level, the greater the chances seem to be for a divorce.* Divorce is also more common

---

*This varies among different population groups. Carter and Glick report that for white males, high rates of divorce are linked to lower levels of education and socioeconomic status. For white women, divorce rates increase with higher incomes. For blacks, there is a higher proportion of divorce at both high and low income levels, and a lower one for those in the middle level (Golanty & Harris, 1982).

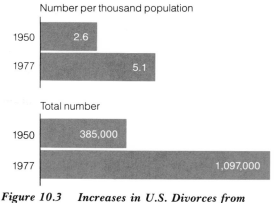

Figure 10.3   Increases in U.S. Divorces from 1950–1977

Source: U.S. Bureau of the Census, 1979.

for people who marry as a means of escape (from their parents, for instance), among children of unhappy or divorced parents, and among couples who married because the bride was expecting a child (Duvall, 1971).

Such factors can make divorce more likely; but more immediate causes are the relationship problems that develop. Landis and Landis (1973) found a number of common problem areas that are most frequently listed as causes of divorce. These relationship problems include finances, communication, sex, children, and in-laws.

Money Problems   One of the most common sources of marital stress is economic problems. A couple who are unable to pay bills or to maintain a comfortable standard of living (an admittedly subjective measure, for each of us has our own ideas about what "comfortable" means) are likely to feel a great deal of pressure, and it is easy to blame one's spouse for not being a good enough provider or for not knowing how to budget what money there is. When economic times are rough—as in our own society today with recent rises in inflation—we can expect to see additional stresses on marriages.

Sexual Problems   A second frequent contributor to divorce is sexual problems. Such problems run the spectrum from an inability to feel satisfied with sexual interactions in the relationship, to a desire for variety that one spouse—no matter who—simply can't provide. Such problems, especially the former, have become more publicized in recent years as a result of the sexual revolution and women's increasing awareness of their own sexual needs. In addition, higher expectations of marriage lead couples to look for more from their spouses, in terms of sexual as well as emotional satisfaction. When one or both partners feel that the couple's sexual needs are not compatible, then the entire relationship can be affected. This is especially true because it is difficult for many people to talk about sex.

Child-Related Problems   A number of marital problems revolve around children. These include jealousy of one spouse's relationship with a child and disagreements on how to raise children. For instance, one parent is often stricter than the other. When this happens, it is not uncommon for the other parent to try to compensate for this, either by being more strict where the other is lax or by giving in more to make up for the first parent's strictness. When a parent reacts in this way, it is easy for the other spouse to feel resentful.

In-law Problems   Our social heritage includes a number of standard in-law jokes, and sometimes not without reason. Meddling in-laws, or excessive loyalty of one spouse to his or her parents, can be a source of considerable stress. The spouse may feel left out, or may feel that the partner cares more about the relationship with the in-laws than the marriage relationship, or may feel that he or she married a whole family, when all that was ever wanted was a spouse. If a partner can't learn to balance loyalties between a spouse and parents, the other partner is put into a difficult position, with marital stress as a result.

Blocked Communication   "We just don't talk to each other any more. There just doesn't seem to be anything to say." Statements such as these are signals of marital problems, no matter whether the immediate problem involves money, sexual compatibility, children, in-laws, or simply a slow erosion of romance as spouses grow apart and have little to share. Even when a couple remain close, there is, after a time, a tendency to expect a spouse to know what we are thinking and to communicate less directly. Assuming that someone else knows how we feel can be a mistake, for people usually don't know things until we tell them. Thus, whether there are immediate problems or not, both partners need to keep making the effort to communicate. This takes time, and sometimes counseling help may be necessary.

"Healthy Divorce"

Any of the problems we've just discussed place stress on a marriage. When such problems reach a severe stage, many couples feel that it is healthier to divorce than to try to remain together. Certainly, the survival of a marriage is not necessarily a good index of the success of a union, for little is healthy about living with someone in a state of mutual hostility. How much stress is too much stress? The question is a difficult one to answer. According to Jourard, a divorce is healthy "when it becomes apparent that the changes necessary to improve the marriage are just not practicable" (1974, p. 261). There is a limit to the degree of change possible even with the help of a competent therapist, for at some point, neither partner is willing to compromise any further.

Although divorce may sometimes be the best solution, this doesn't mean that the divorce process will be any the less trying. Divorce is usually an ordeal, and the divorced individual is likely to feel many conflicting emotions. There is relief that the proceedings are over but also feelings of loneliness, insecurity, and often hostility. If there

A scene from the movie Kramer vs. Kramer. *According to Jourard, it is healthy to dissolve a marriage when the changes necessary to save it are no longer practical.*

are children, another dimension of conflicting emotions is added, for parents try to adjust to their own new lives at the same time that they worry about the effects of divorce on the children. The boxed discussion *Children of Divorce: Minimizing the Hurt* suggests some broad ground rules for helping children through divorce.

Like marriage, divorce marks a change of status and an entrance into a new world. New skills often have to be developed, and older, out-of-practice dating skills need to be sharpened up. In many cases, there is a drastic change in economic status, making it necessary for both ex-partners to adjust to a new lifestyle. The entire life of each individual is disorganized, and every level of functioning is altered.

Since easy rebounds are rare, it may be comforting to know that the first year is usually the worst (Trotter, 1976). After the initial disorientation, regular patterns are slowly established. Divorced people often seek out other people who have shared the same experience; it may be

Children of Divorce: Minimizing the Hurt

Divorce is emotionally draining for all involved, but sometimes the individuals who suffer the most are the children. They may be used as pawns to get further concessions from the other partner; they may be slowly turned against one parent by the other parent. The disorganization, emotional tension, and economic instability in the home all affect the child, and yet the parents may be so wrapped up in their own problems that they may be unable to help the child learn to cope.

We have space here to barely brush over a complex topic, but there are a few things parents can do to help children through a divorce with as few scars as possible.

■ First, as Papalia and Olds (1982) point out, the most important thing a parent can do is to deal with the child's "sensitivities, fears, and anxieties." Both parents should make it clear that the children were not the cause of the split, and that they are still loved by the parents.

■ Second, open communication is especially important. Children should be encouraged to ask questions and express their feelings. At the same time, parents should inform the children of any changes that are taking place, in order to reduce the uncertainty that children are likely to be feeling.

■ Third, a regular routine is important. Parents can help the child adjust if they establish a regular, if different, pattern of contact as soon as possible. Such patterns mean stability to the child.

■ Finally, both parents should refrain from using the children, either financially or psychologically. Berating or "putting down" the other parent in front of the child can only worsen the situation. Instead, talking honestly to the children about the divorce, in a language they can understand, can go a long way in avoiding misunderstandings and unnecessary hurt.

difficult to maintain close relationships with old friends, who may have divided loyalties. Dating becomes important again, not only for the social interaction but for the emotional support it provides. Meeting people, however, is often a bit more difficult than it was before marriage; and it can be unsettling and even frightening to have to start a new social life. Discos, singles bars, or organizations provide atmospheres in which it is easy to meet people in similar situations, and many divorced persons find that such settings help make the transition period easier. Most often, individuals begin to "get back on their feet" within a year or two; and many of them find another partner.

Love and the Second Marriage

Most divorced persons will remarry (Kimmel, 1974). And contrary to popular notion, most people who remarry do not choose a person who is similar to their first spouse (Stinnett & Walters, 1977).

Remarriages are likely to involve another divorced person, and these unions can be complicated by children from the previous marriage. Evidence indicates that stepparents do not tend to be resentful or cruel, as they were depicted in fairy tales such as "Hansel and Gretel" and "Cinderella." Nor do they provide the magical relief desired by the single parent who has lost control of the children and expects the burden to disappear with remarriage. The truth lies somewhere in the middle—between the Brady bunch and the fairy tales. As with any loving relationship, both remarriage and parenting after divorce require active concern, sensitivity, and constant efforts to keep in communication.

In all, it would seem that the modern conception of marriage involves the growth of both individuals. Marriage can be a vehicle for self-actualization when each partner permits and encourages the other to grow and develop. This is likely to happen in an atmosphere in which both partners are mature, responsible, share similar values, have solid identities, and are capable of experiencing intimacy.

Summary

1. Love is hard to define. It is sometimes confused with liking, but there are important differences. First, love includes an idealization not found in liking. Second, liking grows over time, while love often erodes. Third, love is not always pleasant: unlike liking, it sometimes fills us with doubts and anxieties.

2. There are two reasons why love is hard to pinpoint as an emotion. One is language: love is one area in which words often can't convey meaning. Another reason lies in the emotional experience itself. The cognitive theory of emotion states that the physiological arousal of love is not so different from that of other strong emotions and that we interpret these feelings according to environmental cues.

3. There.is extensive evidence that love is a need in young animals and human beings. The way in which we express love is learned.

4. Love can also be viewed as a set of behaviors: Fromm singles out knowledge, responsibility, respect, and care as the four components of love. Active love involves giving, while passive love consists of taking.

5. This text defines love as an intense intimate feeling in which the satisfaction of the other's needs is at least as important as one's own and one acts in a way which maximizes the potential of the other.

6. Lee has identified six styles of loving: eros, ludus, storge, mania, pragma, and agape.

7. There are three steps in choosing a mate: attraction, rapport, and compatibility. Giving a relationship time to progress through all three stages is one important factor in its long-term success; other factors include maturity of the partners and an ability to love actively. Love alone cannot ensure a long-lasting, satisfying relationship unless these qualities are also present.

8. Some writers have suggested that the institution of marriage is dead, and they point to high divorce rates and greater numbers of people choosing other lifestyles—such as living together—as evidence. At this time, however, none of the alternatives to marriage poses a serious threat to marriage. Living single is a viable and satisfying lifestyle, but the overwhelming majority of persons choose marriage, even after a divorce.

9. Marriage itself is undergoing change. There are fewer children per family: nuclear families tend to be more isolated from relatives; more families include a working wife as well as a working husband; and there are higher expectations about sexual expression, self-actualization, and relationship satisfaction in marriage. All of these changes are affecting marriage as an institution.

10. The rise in expectations for marriage may be one reason for the increasing divorce rate. Other, more immediate, reasons include sexual problems, personal finances, in-law problems, and child-related problems. Couples may be able to prevent "marriage on the rocks," however, by making a consistent effort to communicate, show concern for one another, and allow the other a chance to grow.

11. The first year after divorce is often the most difficult. It is important for divorced people to try to stabilize their lives, especially if there are children involved.

12. Marriage can be a vehicle for self-actualization if both partners are mature, responsible, share similar values, have solid identities, and are capable of experiencing intimacy and showing love toward one another.

Key Terms and Concepts

eros

ludus

storge

mania

pragma

agape

cognitive theory of emotion

knowledge

responsibility

respect

caring

active love

passive love

deficiency love

being love

love

compatibility

similarity theory of mate selection

complementary theory of mate selection

cohabitation

group marriage

communal family

nuclear family

extended family

I love my sex, and I've got a wife that loves it just as much as me. . . . Even after twenty years of marriage, it's still about three times a week—and with the kids finally all in school, we've even started up again on that lunch-time business once in a while. . . . Most of the time, naturally, it's in the evening, after the kids are in bed. . . . We'll lay on the couch watching TV and playing around with each other and half forgetting about the show . . . and then go to bed . . . and it's tremendous (Hunt & Hunt, 1975, p. 77)*

Sexual Adjustment

*From *Prime Time*. Copyright © 1975 by Bernice Hunt and Morton Hunt. Reprinted by permission of Stein and Day Publishers.

We chose these words, spoken by a beefy, 54-year-old electrical appliance dealer, to start this chapter because they paint a picture of sexual adjustment. It is certainly not the only possible picture of sexual adjustment. Far from it: individuals need not be middle-aged, heterosexual, married, or to have sex three times a week to be sexually adjusted. They need not be "sexy," according to the popularly accepted use of this term. They simply need to have a sense of satisfaction with their own sexuality and with the ways in which they express this part of themselves.

This chapter appears at the end of Part III's exploration of belongingness needs. That is because sexual relations can form such an intimate bond between two people. Needless to say, sex is not always based on love. Yet a deep, loving relationship is usually expressed sexually, and the quality of this sexual intimacy can have a profound effect on a relationship.

For all its importance in a relationship (or in one's personal sense of well-being), however, sexual adjustment is often complicated by an ambivalence that mirrors our society's mixed messages about sex. Many people harbor feelings of guilt about sex—even though they logically don't think their sexual behaviors are wrong. Such feelings make it difficult for persons to feel free and joyous about their sexuality.

This chapter will look at several factors in the complex area of sexual adjustment. We are all affected by changes that have taken place in sexual attitudes and behaviors in recent decades, and we'll explore the so-called sexual revolution to see how extensive these changes have been. A second topic we'll deal with is sexuality during the life cycle—how it develops in childhood, adolescence, and old age. We'll also look briefly at sexuality in the context of the common question, "Am I normal?" and deal specifically with one controversial area of sexuality: homosexuality. Finally, we'll explore what research has discovered about human sexual response, then look at some specific problems in sexual adjustment. *Sexual dysfunctions*, or

difficulties in having satisfying sexual relations, can have a serious effect on even the closest relationship; and we'll explore some causes and also some common approaches to treating these dysfunctions.

Sexual Attitudes and Behaviors: A "Sexual Revolution"?

Much has been written about the "sexual revolution" in recent years. The term refers to a broad change in sexual attitudes and in patterns of behavior in the past few decades. It encompasses such changes as the development of reliable birth control methods; the increase in premarital sex; the greater concern that sex be a satisfying form of expression for both women and men; and the increasing tolerance of more forms of sexual expression, including homosexual relations and sex between unmarried persons.

How accurate are the reports of a sexual revolution? As we saw in Chapter 10, widely publicized fears that marriage is dead seem to be greatly overblown. In the same way, many people wonder whether the sexual revolution is really as extensive as some writers claim. In order to answer this question, we'll look below at two basic parts of the sexual revolution: sexual attitudes and sexual behaviors.

Attitudes about Sex

There seems little doubt that an important shift has taken place in the way people think about sex (Dreyer, 1982). This is most clear in the "generation gap" that seems to characterize sexual attitudes today. Persons who have reached adolescence since the early 60s tend to view sex differently than do their parents.

Three faces of the "sexual revolution."

The Sexual Double Standard   One area in which this is evident is the traditional **double standard**, which applied different rules to evaluate men's and women's sexuality. For instance, the double standard saw premarital sex as acceptable for males, but unacceptable for women. It also viewed women as having few strong sexual feelings, so that even within marriage, their needs were considered secondary to those of males.

Although these attitudes were pervasive forty years ago, there is evidence that they are gradually disappearing (Shope, 1975). Women's attitudes toward sexuality are changing faster than

Double standard   Different rules that traditionally were applied to the behavior of men and women in our society.

"But darling, the female praying mantis always eats the male during copulation. Any other way would be unnatural!"

men's (Christensen, 1971), probably because their attitudes had so much further to travel to catch up with the liberal, often self-serving attitudes of most men. Although the "revolution" is far from complete, women today are more likely to recognize their own sexual needs than they were in the past.

"Live and Let Live"   Another direction in which sexual attitudes have changed is toward a broader tolerance. The attitude of most adolescents today seems to be "live and let live." Sorenson (1973) found that most of his sample of teens believed that sex outside of marriage was not inherently right or wrong. There seems to be little attempt to condemn another person's sexual behavior, especially if it occurs within a love relationship.

When Sorenson's sample was faced with the statement "Anything two people want to do sexually is moral as long as they both want to do it and it doesn't hurt either one of them," 71 percent of the males and 66 percent of the females agreed. In addition, teens believed that the reactions of both male and female during sex were of equal importance. The old double standard, at least in some respects, seems to be on the way out.

The views of this generation have often been at odds with those of their parents. But this sexual generation gap seems likely to grow smaller as the younger generation become parents themselves (Stassen-Berger, 1980). This is not to argue that the next generation of parents will encourage sexual activity in their children. Yet we may well see a more tolerant and open environment between future parents and children.

Men's and Women's Views of Sex   Despite the fact that the double standard is narrowing, certain gender differences may still remain. Tavris (1973) concluded that women tend to see sex as part of a loving relationship, whereas males are more likely to separate love and sex. These findings should not be overinterpreted. There are certainly women who enjoy sex without love and who would view this conclusion as an extension of the double standard; many men also believe sex is undesirable without emotional involvement. In either case, when lovers have different attitudes about their sexual relationship, those differences can be a serious source of unhappiness, as the boxed discussion *Personal Attitudes about Sex* points out.

Behavior Revolution: Myth or Fact?

If there has been a revolution in some of our attitudes about sex, has this been accompanied by a revolution in sexual behavior? At first, it is tempting to assume that the answer is yes. But the

Personal Attitudes about Sex

What does sex mean to you? Each of us has our own answer to this question. In general, though, there seem to be three main attitudes. The first of these is that sex is primarily for **procreation,** or having offspring. Although this point of view has become less popular in recent decades, it is deeply rooted in certain religious traditions and it still receives some significant support. A second general attitude sees sex primarily as a *pleasurable experience*. There are those who argue that sex need have no other meaning. And finally, there are people who believe that sex is a form of *intimate communication* that should only be experienced within the framework of a loving relationship. These attitudes are highly personal, and they vary not only from person to person but also, for the same person, from one relationship to another. An individual may engage in a very superficial sort of sex with one person, but find that sex takes on a very intimate meaning in a love relationship with someone else.

When two individuals agree with the basic reasons for sex, few problems arise. If neither partner feels much emotional commitment, there is little room for disappointment; the same is true if both partners believe that sex provides an intimate, personal expression. However, where one person considers sex as an intimate communication, and the other merely thinks of it as recreation, someone may well be hurt.

question bears further scrutiny. *Do* we always behave according to our beliefs?

Wicker (1969) reviewed a number of studies and found little correlation between stated attitudes and behavior. He concluded that we usually explain these differences by situational variables. For instance, you may think it is wrong to cheat, but if placed in a situation in which *just* the right answer appeared on your neighbor's desk *just* as you found yourself stymied on an important exam, is it possible that you might bend just a little? Would you rationalize that you are merely checking your answer—not really cheating?

The same thing can happen in the relationship between sexual attitudes and behaviors. Thus, you may believe that premarital sex is wrong, but that belief may not guarantee that you won't get carried away on a particularly romantic date. All things being equal, then, the best conclusion we can draw from attitude studies is that people seem more likely to act in accordance to a stated attitude than against it (Kaplan, 1972).

This conclusion helps to explain some of the findings we'll discuss that indicate behavior changes have not been as revolutionary as attitude changes (Lerner and Spanier, 1980). Still, many changes seem to be taking place, and the best way to understand them is to examine the findings of behavior surveys. Two questions seem especially relevant. First, has there been a dramatic increase in sex before marriage? And second, are young people today having sex with more partners?

Premarital Sex: What the Surveys Show Has there been a revolutionary increase in sex before marriage? Perhaps the best way to begin answering that question is to take a look at sexual behaviors in the past, as shown by Kinsey's data over 30 years ago.

Procreation	The production of offspring.

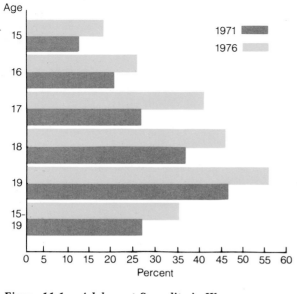

Figure 11.1   Adolescent Sexuality in Women, 1971–1976

Source: Adapted from Zelnik & Kantner, 1977. Reprinted by permission.

Alfred Kinsey and his associates broke new ground in 1948 when they published the results of the most extensive survey of sexual behavior that had ever been conducted. The 1948 study explored male sexuality: 5300 white males, between the ages of 10 and 90, were interviewed extensively (over 300 questions were asked). The findings showed that approximately 27 percent of the sample had experienced sexual intercourse between ages 13–15, and about 63 percent had done so by age 19. In 1953, Kinsey published the results of a companion survey on women. These findings contrasted with those for males, clearly illustrating the existence of the double standard. Only about 3 percent of Kinsey's female sample had experienced intercourse by age 16, and approximately 20 percent had had intercourse by age 19.

How do these findings compare with more recent surveys? Sorenson conducted a survey of adolescent sexuality in 1973, and at least for males, his findings were just a bit higher than those of the Kinsey study. Forty-four percent of the males under 16 had experienced sexual intercourse, while some 72 percent of Sorenson's males had done so by age 19.

Sorenson's findings were quite different for women, however. In contrast to Kinsey's figures, some 30 percent of females had experienced *coitus* (penile-vaginal intercourse) by age 16; and 57 percent had done so by age 19. Other findings have shown the same trend, although the figures may vary somewhat. Zelnik and Kantner conducted two studies of adolescent sexual activity in women, one in 1971 and another in 1976, and they found an increase even in those years, as Figure 11.1 shows. In the late 1970s, some 35 percent of the subjects between ages 15–19 reported having sexual intercourse, compared to 27 percent in the 1971 sample. Christensen and Gregg (1970) reported significantly more young women engaging in sex than Kinsey had found, with the percentage of males remaining about the same. All in all, if one looks at sexual surveys as a whole, the percentage of men experiencing premarital sex seems to fall somewhere in the 50–75 percent range, with the percentage of women lying somewhere around 50 percent—a significant increase from what Kinsey found (Burr, 1976).

How Often and with How Many?   Answering a second question may tell us more about changes in sexual behavior. Are young people today engaging in intercourse more often than in the past, with more partners?

As with the first question regarding the number of teenagers having sex, some behavior trends do show up, but they aren't as striking as some writers claim. More young people (especially women) are experiencing intercourse, but the evidence doesn't suggest that teenagers think of sex as a casual occurrence. Only about 10 percent of Zelnik and Kantner's adolescent subjects reported having sex with as many as six partners. In other research, it seems fairly well established that about half of the young women who have premarital sex do so with only one person—the man they plan to marry (Hunt, 1974).

As to whether teenagers are having sex more frequently than before, the findings don't seem to suggest a "revolution." In Zelnik and Kantner's 1976 survey, only about half of those who had experienced intercourse had done so within the month before being interviewed, and less than 30 percent reported having intercourse as often as three times a month. About 15 percent of adolescent females who had experienced intercourse reported having had sex only once.

In all, then, while there is a general trend for more teenage girls to have sex, these encounters are not taken lightly. "Free sex"—despite what some headlines have claimed—is not so popular as some would have us believe. We might predict that in the future, the differences inherent in the double standard will continue to shrink, and that women will be likely to have more sexual experiences before marriage. Yet there is little reason to assume any sudden, great change in this area. Sex and love—or at least emotional involvement—are still related. What is not as closely related anymore are sex and the institution of marriage.

Sex Research: How Accurate Is It?

In the discussions above, we have cited findings of several well-known studies. While these findings give us an idea of several broad trends, you may have wondered just how reliable they are.

Sex research presents some special challenges to social scientists, and many of the most famous sex surveys have come under criticism. Kinsey's 1948 sample, for instance, has been criticized for being heavily weighted toward an urban, under–50 population. Sorenson's 1973 study is one of the most widely quoted surveys on adolescent sexuality, yet a good portion of Sorenson's original sample could not participate, many because their parents wouldn't let them. We can

only guess what effect this had on the final data, but it seems fair to say that interpreting research in this field is very difficult.

A second caution should be noted in any effort to compare past and current research. We have been comparing recent findings with those of Kinsey, yet these studies aren't always *directly* comparable. Modern investigators usually do not use the exact questions that Kinsey used; nor do they choose their sample in the same manner, and such differences all affect the final outcome of a study.

A third point is that in any study, subjects' responses need to be evaluated carefully. We saw earlier that people do not always behave in accordance with the attitudes they express. Thus, we can guess that no matter how carefully chosen a sample is, survey responses will not always reflect behavior accurately. Indeed, even the physiological responses tested in some experiments may be affected by the experimental conditions. The human mind is tremendously complex, and subjects' expectations can have an important impact on experimental outcomes. See the discussion in the box *Must an Experimenter Deceive the Subject?*

Despite all these cautions, however, sex research does tell us much about past and current attitudes and behaviors. While most of the research to date has looked most closely at the period of life from adolescence to young adulthood, sexuality is important throughout our lives—not only at one stage. It does not begin at puberty and end with marriage. Instead, it begins at birth and lasts through old age.

A Lifespan View of Sexuality

"Childhood sexuality? Infantile sexuality? Come on, now. Sexual feelings don't develop until later, when kids reach adolescence."

At least, that was the traditional reaction to

Must an Experimenter Deceive the Subject?

One of the main features of much of the research described in this text is deception, or deliberately misleading the subjects in an experiment. Investigators argue that without some deception it would be impossible to study many aspects of behavior, for subjects would be on their guard and change their behavior. Others decry the use of such deception, charging that it is unethical and has no place in the behavioral sciences. But, just what would be the effect on the results of telling subjects exactly what is being studied in an experiment? In addition, what if the study is purporting to measure something personal, perhaps even one of the most intimate topics—sexuality?

In order to answer these questions Andrew Barclay randomly assigned 61 male undergraduates to one of two groups. Subjects were asked to void their bladders 30 minutes before the experiment, and then were given an explanation of the purposes of the study. One group was told that they were participating in a study designed to assess the effect of visual sexual stimulation on the production of acid phosphatase (a chemical secreted by the prostate gland during sexual arousal). They were told that half of their group would see a pornographic movie while the other half would view a neutral film. The second group of subjects was told they were participating in a study designed to assess the effects of visual stimulation on imagery. Again, half of this group viewed the sexual film while the others viewed the neutral substitute. Both before and after the film subjects were asked to give urine samples.

As one would expect, all of the subjects who saw the sexual movie reported being aroused. There were differences in their physiological responses, however. Those who had expected to see a pornographic movie showed little physiological response, while those who expected to see less explicit "visual stimulation" secreted quite a bit of acid phosphatase. (Interestingly, members of the first group who saw the neutral film secreted the most phosphatase of all. While the film they were viewing was quite boring, they knew that some of their fellow subjects were seeing an arousing, sexually explicit film. The experimenter believes that they may have allowed their minds to wander during their viewing, thus producing the effect.) The investigator concluded that if an experimenter wants to delve into an area in which there is likely to be strong, defensive reactions, some degree of deception is probably necessary.

This study indicates that expectations about an experiment may change a subject's behavior during the investigation. It seems then, that a certain amount of deception is necessary if researchers are to look into the more personal aspects of life.

Source: Barclay, 1971.

the idea that sexuality began at birth—and there is usually a similar response to the thought of sex in old age. To broadly summarize the stereotype, we might say that most people associate sexuality mostly with the reproductive years. Fortunately, the evidence is contrary to this idea, and we'll explore what we know about lifespan sexuality as we look briefly at childhood, adolescence, adulthood, and old age.

Childhood Sexuality

Is Childhood Sexuality like Adult Sexuality? Viewing sexuality within a developmental perspective presents some definite problems. The same behavior at one age may be considered sexual, while a doubt may exist as to its real meaning at another age. For example, little boys get erections even as infants. Young girls also experience vaginal lubrication, and masturbation is a common childhood activity. How are we to interpret such behaviors?

These behaviors don't seem to be sexual in the adult sense—but, then, maybe "adult" definitions of sexuality are too limiting. As you'll remember from Chapter 4, Freud recognized that even babies experience sexual pleasure, which he defined as a rather general sensuality not necessarily centered in the genitals. Kinsey raised eyebrows when his studies noted more specific sexual behaviors: "Orgasm has been observed in boys of every age from 5 months to adolescence. Orgasm is in our records for a female babe of 4 months" (Kinsey et al., 1948, p. 177).

As children grow older, activities such as playing "doctor," masturbating, and playing at having intercourse are common—although in the last case, children are often ignorant of what really takes place during sexual intercourse. Still, experimentation and exploration are a natural part of childhood sexuality, and it seems that knowledge and self-understanding gained in these ways all contribute to our sense of sexuality as adults. As it happens, though, parents often aren't sure how to react to such behaviors.

"What's a Parent to Do?"   "Doctor, my baby boy seems perfectly healthy, but one behavior troubles me. I always peek in at him during nap time or at night to make sure he's sleeping, and instead of getting his rest, he seems to be spending an inordinate amount of time handling his genitals."

This sort of worry has been heard by many doctors, not just concerning male children but also little girls. Because we've been conditioned by society not to expect sexual behavior from small children, adults are often taken aback by such activities. Most parents are proud to recognize signs that their child is precocious (unusually advanced)—but not so many feel they are ready to deal with *this* kind of precocity!

What's a parent to do? Doctors' responses to reports like the one above have changed a great deal in the last several decades. Around the turn of the century, it was considered dangerous for male infants to touch their genitals, for the activity might develop into perversion at a later age. So, parents were given a sure-fire prescription: tie their baby's hands and feet to the posts of the crib (Winch, 1963).

Today, there is considerably more recognition that these behaviors are normal and healthy. Discovering one's sexuality is part of the developmental process itself: the more punishing the parents' response, the more likely will the child be to grow up with feelings of guilt or ambivalence about sex.

Broderick (1978) believes that three primary conditions in childhood are important for the development of normal heterosexuality. First, the parents must not be too punishing or too weak to allow for a reasonably secure identification. Second, the parent of the opposite sex must not be seductive, punishing, or emotionally unstable, for this can sometimes prevent the child from forming a positive view of the opposite sex. And third, parents must not reject the child's gender, treating their son as a girl or their daughter as a boy.

In addition to parental treatment, still another influence comes from observation. Children learn from watching, as we saw in Chapter 3. If they are exposed to parent models who are brutal and aggressive, or extremely dominant or submissive, they may feel that this is the way males and females are supposed to interact. In the absence of any counteracting influence, this attitude may grow stronger and eventually come to dominate the child's later relationships.

Adolescent Sexuality

While sexuality is present throughout childhood, it takes on new proportions with adolescence. Many well-known physical changes take place in early adolescence, including hormonal increases,

Children learn by watching, and their later attitudes about sex will be influenced by parent models.

Sexually transmitted disease Any disease that is transmitted by sexual contact. Examples are syphillis and genital herpes.

more frequent erections and ejaculation in males, and the enlargement of breasts, menstruation, and hormonal changes in females.

These changes have profound psychological and behavioral effects. While the physiological changes are universal, however, the behavioral and psychological reactions differ according to one's culture, subcultural group, and the individual's past and present environment. In our culture, increased masturbation at this age is usually tinged with guilt. In contrast, there are other cultures, such as that of the Marquesas Islands in French Polynesia, in which children are encouraged to masturbate from a very early age. (In this society, too, adolescents are also encouraged to engage in intercourse [Crooks & Baur, 1983].)

We should stress that there is no single pattern of teenage sexual behavior, even in our society. While some teens have sex quite early, others will not engage in intercourse at all during adolescence. As you might expect, however, there does seem to be a rather predictable sequence. Spanier (1976) found that kissing, light petting, and heavy petting often preceded coitus. Many teens stop the sequence at some point, yet as we saw earlier, ever increasing numbers are experiencing intercourse, and at younger ages than before.

Teenage Sex and Social Problems   These statistics belie some social problems of rather alarming proportions. One teenage problem is **sexually transmitted diseases** (including venereal diseases, such as syphilis, gonorrhea, or genital herpes), which have become epidemic in recent years. An important contributing factor is the fact that young people often don't know how to prevent these diseases or to recognize them if they have them.

Another growing problem is teenage pregnancy. There is a direct relationship between a woman's age and her likelihood of using contraceptives. Thirty-eight percent of 15-year-old girls reported that they never used any contraception, while only 15 percent of 19-year-olds reported the same (Zelnik & Kantner, 1977). (The percentage of adolescents between 15 and 19 who claim that they always use contraceptives is remarkably stable, at about 30 percent.) The younger a woman is when she begins to have sexual intercourse, the less likely she will be to use contraceptives.

These probabilities, when taken together, add up to a dangerous situation in the context of increasing adolescent sex. As more teenage girls experience sex at younger ages, the probability of teenage pregnancy increases tremendously. Indeed, Dreyer (1982) reports that there were about 1 million such pregnancies in 1979, of which some 400,000 ended in abortion.

Explaining the Problem   Why don't more teenagers take a responsible attitude toward sex? Andrea Balis (1981) quotes some teenagers in a group interview that reveals a great deal about the reasons why prevention is lagging so far behind sexual "liberation":

Carol: The first time I had sex, I didn't know ahead of time that I was finally going to do it. . . .

John: I think about sex all the time, but I sure don't think about birth control.

Rose: Well, I don't think about sex all the time, but I never think about birth control. . . .I'm scared I'll turn my boyfriend off if I talk about birth control. It turns me off. (p. 3)

Melanie: I don't like the idea of birth control, because I haven't had sex yet, and I feel funny planning for it. . . .

Rose: And you feel cheap if you carry something around as if you're ready to have sex anytime and with anyone. (p. 5)

From what these teenagers are saying, it is clear that one source of trouble is the feeling that planning ahead is "cheap" or "calculating" or unromantic. Actually having sex, to many teenagers, seems to be more acceptable than the planning that makes it safe. Another problem area is an uneasiness in talking about sex with a partner. Again, it's okay to "do it," but many teenagers still feel uncomfortable discussing it openly. In other words, teenage sex has "arrived" as a statistical reality well before an etiquette of teenage sex has developed to help young people deal with it comfortably (Balis, 1981).

As you might guess, taking steps to alleviate this problem is like opening Pandora's box. Not only are teenage pregnancy and venereal disease highly controversial, but so are any cures that are suggested for these social ills. The evidence seems to indicate, though, that no matter how long we wait, teenagers are unlikely to grow less interested in sex. Under the circumstances, the most effective strategy seems to be to help teenagers learn to deal knowledgeably with their own sexuality. As the discussion in the box *The Birds and the Bees* suggests, sex education may be both controversial and imperfect, but it seems to be a step in the right direction. In addition, an open, honest supportiveness at home is important in reducing guilt and ambivalence.

Is There Sex after Adolescence?

Too often, sexuality is seen as a quality that develops and peaks during adolescence, then declines and disappears in the years after. Teenage and young adult sexuality is certainly the focus of most of the movies and books that capture the public imagination. Bodies are firmer, more beautiful during these years, fitting with the stereotyped image of sexiness; and romance itself is still a new adventure. Yet this perception presents a rather narrow, glossy view—rather like touching up life with an air-brush.

How does this stereotype compare with the facts? We'll look below at two important aspects of adult sexuality: married sex, and sex in old age. Before we start, we should note that our discussion focuses mostly on sex within marriage, simply because the most regular sexual relationships occur within this framework. Later discussions of normality and sexual dysfunctions will look more broadly at adult sexuality.

The Birds and the Bees

Few issues seem to divide public opinion as easily as the question of sex education in the schools. Despite evidence that teenagers are engaging in sex at earlier ages than ever before, there is still widespread disagreement about what to do about it.

The vast majority of today's adults had no formal sex education, from teachers or parents. Instead, they learned about sex from their peers (DeLora et al., 1981). One common argument against sex education is that this system has always worked fine, and that no further sex education is needed. A related argument states that sex education may do more harm than good. Children are innocent: why rush things? Even when children get a little older, sex education may be dangerous because it might put ideas into teenagers' heads (Katchadourian, 1974).

Still a third argument against sex education in the schools looks at the limits of formal education. Many people honestly believe that sex education belongs in the home; and they are concerned about the schools' ability to deal competently with the topic. How well can the schools deal with moral issues, for instance? Libby (1970) found that even among parents who advocated sex education in the schools, there was a strong desire to want their own values to be taught. If parents disagree about values, the schools are left in a difficult spot as they try to determine what they should teach. Yet this subject is one which teenagers want to explore. Hunt's (1970) sample of 13 to 19-year-old girls showed a great interest in the meaning of sexuality and moral values.

Some of these arguments are more difficult to answer than others. It does seem clear, though, that some sort of formal education is necessary. The evidence shows that adolescents are poorly informed about birth control (Osofsky, 1970). Recent findings show that three out of every 10 sexually active adolescent females become pregnant (Vander Zanden, 1981)—a powerful argument against the "I learned from my friends, why shouldn't they?" attitude. And as for objections that children are too young to learn about sex, we should note that such arguments misinterpret the entire notion of *latency* (the period before adolescent sexuality awakens). As our text points out, there is no age at which sexuality is truly latent; thus, there is no time at which sex education is "dangerous" (Gadpaille, 1970).

Most parents do favor some sort of sex education in the schools (Shope, 1975), although the nature and scope of it is controversial. At the same time, there is no guarantee that sex education will decrease the pregnancy or the VD rates among teens. Even though adolescents will know more about sex, they may not all make use of their knowledge. On the whole, however, it is impossible not to conclude that our society has not adequately dealt with teenage sexuality. It seems likely that a well-planned, parent-supported program dealing with values as well as information could only help the situation.

Married Sex: Myth and Fact Here are a few true-and-false statements for you to evaluate:

- There is a sharp drop in sexual activity during the first three years of marriage.

- Married couples are having more sex, and experimenting more with sex, than in previous generations.

- It is normal for a married couple to have sex twice a month.

- It is normal for a married couple to have sex five times or more per week.

- Sexual incompatibility is a frequent factor in divorce.

An explanation of these statements won't tell you everything you ever wanted to know about sex after marriage, but it should provide at least a start. We'll look at them one by one.

Sexual activity declines sharply during the first three years of marriage. True. Although there is a tremendous variation from couple to couple, this statement is often true (Broderick, 1982). Researchers Westoff and Westoff (1971) found a pattern in which sexual activity dropped rather sharply in the first three years, then continued a more gradual decline during subsequent years of marriage. There are many factors that help explain this pattern. For one, there is a parallel decline in romance after the first few years of a love relationship, as we saw in Chapter 10, and it is not hard to see how this would affect a couple's sex life. Another factor is an increase in the stresses of adult life. Once the honeymoon is over, young couples in our society usually have to face up to a range of nitty-gritty responsibilities. Would Casanova ever have earned his reputation as a lover if he had had to deal with building a career, making monthly rent or mortgage payments, and raising children?

Married couples are having more sex, and experimenting more with sex, than in the previous generation. True. Although there is often a decline in the frequency of sex over the course of a marriage, this pattern needs to be seen in perspective. Married people seem to be having more sex than in past generations (Hunt, 1974); and not only that, but they also seem to be quite satisfied with their married sex life. A recent poll (Tavris & Sadd, 1977) found that 33 percent of the population rated sex in their marriages as very good, and another third rated it as good. Twenty-one percent rated sex as fair, while only 12 percent rated it as poor. While such polls should only be taken as a general guideline, they do indicate that most married people appear to be more or less content with their sexual relationship.

Adults are also experimenting more. In an extensive survey, Hunt (1974) found not only that middle-aged couples were engaging in more intercourse than they had in the past, but they were also experimenting more. A 45-year-old woman interviewed by Hunt and Hunt may not be typical, but she illustrates the point:

[*After some years of marriage*] *we felt there was a lot happening that we didn't understand, so I asked my husband if him and I should try to read up on it. So he went out and bought three books, and through them we found all different ways of caressing, and different positions, and it was very nice because we realized that these things weren't dirty. Like I could say to my husband, "Around the world in eighty days!" and he'd laugh and we'd really go at it, relaxed and having fun. . . .* (Hunt & Hunt, 1975, pp. 78–9)*

Statements such as this one point directly toward today's greater availability of information about sex. Modern handbooks, textbooks, and popular books (such as Comfort's *The Joy of Sex* [1972]) have given sexuality an increased visibility as well as respectability that has certainly not gone unnoticed by married couples.

It is normal for a married couple to have sex twice a month. It is normal for a married couple to have sex five times or more per week. Both true. One couple once wrote to an advice columnist that they were 40 years old and only had sex twice a month. Should they see a doctor? They were both satisfied, but they needed the reassurance that they were normal. Today's emphasis on having satisfying sexual relationships means that both partners' needs must be taken into account. Sexual satisfaction is uniquely personal: factors like affiliation needs, physical health, everyday pressures, and the quality of the relationship itself all affect each person's sexuality. If both partners are happy, there is no reason to check the statistics.

Sexual incompatibility is a frequent factor in divorce. This final statement, like the others we've looked at, is true; but we should look at it at two levels. On the first level, we've seen that sexual satisfaction is more important today than it has been in the past. In an age of higher expectations,

*From *Prime Time*. Copyright © 1975 by Bernice Hunt and Morton Hunt. Reprinted by permission of Stein and Day Publishers.

Many healthy adults maintain active lives and satisfying sexual relationships well past middle age.

the reason for these divorces, or did other problems interfere with these couples' sex lives? Sexual problems are often the product of other problems within the marriage (Scanzoni & Scanzoni, 1976). As we'll see later in this chapter, separating one from the other is almost as difficult as determining whether the chicken or the egg came first.

Is There Sex after Middle Age? The De-sexed Generation   We've looked at sexuality during childhood, adolescence, and adulthood. One more important stage of life remains, and that is the years after age 65.

Cameron (1972) questioned three groups of adults divided by age. These groups of young adults (aged 18–25 years), middle-aged individuals (40–55), and elderly people (65–79) were asked to characterize sexuality at different time periods in a person's life. The responses produced a composite impression of each of these three ages and stages of sexuality. Young people were felt to need sex more and to engage in it more often. Middle-aged individuals were considered better lovers, and much more knowledgeable. Older people were considered sexless by many, with little left to offer. These attitudes are rather typical in our society, and they have had the effect of "de-sexing" the older generation. Many people assume that this "de-sexing" occurs naturally, as part of the aging process. That assumption bears closer examination, however.

There can be little doubt that physiology plays a part in the decreased sexual activity with age. In men, levels of the hormone **testosterone** decrease, and there is also a decline in sexual tension. In women, there is a lessening of vaginal lubrication and reduced elasticity of the vaginal cavity; and it may take longer to become aroused.

Yet the aging process itself seems to be relatively less important than other factors. Even menopause does not seem to be a prime factor, despite worries many women experience anticipating problems in this area. Neugarten and her associates (1963) found that following menopause many women experience a feeling of relief since

a disappointing sex life is likely to do more damage to a relationship. In this sense, sexual problems may be a factor in divorce. Indeed, one study showed that 13.8 percent of wives and 20 percent of husbands cited sexual incompatibility as a reason for divorce (Levinger, 1966).

Such statistics need to be examined on a second level, however. Was sexual incompatibility

---

Testosterone   A male sex hormone produced by the testes.

---

they do not have to worry about pregnancy any-more, and some report improvement in their sex lives. The majority of the women sampled felt better following menopause as compared to the time preceding it, reporting that they felt freer to do things for themselves. This is not to say that these women did not experience some negative feelings during this period. However, a sizable number did not report experiencing the period of change as unpleasant. The decline in sexuality, then, cannot be attributed to physical changes such as menopause. The decline in female sexu-ality seems to be slower than for males, and women maintain a high rate of responsiveness until well into middle age and beyond (Kinsey, 1953).

Masters and Johnson (1966) name many other causes that seem to be more directly linked to sexual decline than is the physical aging pro-cess. These factors include monotony, worry, anx-iety, fatigue, alcohol, illness, and even anxieties about decreasing sexual abilities. Young (1975) also argues that reduced sexuality isn't due to the aging process, but more to the emotional and so-cial problems that come with advancing age.

One primary factor seems to be prolonged inactivity. Dr. David Reuben used the slogan "Use it or Lose it" to summarize the point that sexual inactivity often seems related to sexual decline.

The adult sexual histories of males and fe-males differ somewhat. DeLora, Warren, and El-lison (1981) quote research showing that seven out of ten married couples who remain in good health lead active sexual lives. Hendricks and Hendricks (1977) found that men who have had long, relatively uninterrupted sex lives seem to continue an active sex life longer than do those with intermittent periods of inactivity. Women of-ten report that their husbands have lost interest in sex and blame them for the lack of sexual activ-ity. Since women normally outlive their husbands, the chances for sexual fulfillment decline after he dies or becomes seriously ill. Older men, on the other hand, tend to largely determine the course of sexuality within their marital relationship. Af-ter the death of a spouse it is easier for men than for women to find sexual partners, since society shows a greater acceptance of male sexuality and allows men to find somewhat younger partners. The importance of the marital relationship with respect to sexuality for women is shown by the statistics. Feigenbaum (1971) notes that at 60, only 12 percent of widows and divorcees were engaging in sexual relationships, compared to 70 percent in a comparable group of married women.

From such findings, we can conclude that re-duced sexuality with age seems more a psycho-logical than a physical phenomenon. Most im-portantly, sexual satisfaction in middle age and up seems to depend on the will of both partners. This may mean overcoming some physical obstacles, but Hunt and Hunt (1977) believe that couples can call upon their creativity and experience to accomplish this. Perhaps more time should be al-lowed for foreplay and stimulation; or lubricants may need to be used. The couple may need to be more sexually imaginative. Such changes need not dampen sexual interest. In contrast, they may bring a new type of pleasure—perhaps more re-laxed, but still rewarding and enjoyable.

Sexual Adjustment: What Is "Normal"?

In the life cycle discussion above, we have tried to avoid the impression that there is any one pattern of sexual development that is "normal." Some teens experience intercourse, while others don't. Some adults enjoy sex five times a week; others enjoy it—and equally as much—less than once a week. Some people remain sexually active throughout a long life, while others experience little sex after middle age.

Perhaps Kinsey's greatest contribution to our understanding of sexuality may be his finding that many different sexual paths are open to people.

The "average person," he declared, is an abstraction: sex does not take place only within an adult, married, heterosexual context. When he published this fact, many people became less anxious about their own sexuality. For example, many who read Kinsey's material sighed with relief to realize that masturbation past age 20 was not unusual. Another form of sexual expression that has gained greater tolerance in the past decades is homosexuality. Is being gay a form of sexual maladjustment? We'll explore this controversial question below.

Homosexuality

Homosexuality is one of the most difficult topics to approach. Many theories have attempted to explain its causes, as the box *What Causes Homosexuality?* points out, but there still is no clear answer. In addition, the behavior itself is highly controversial. Although most Americans believe that people's sexual behavior is their own business, as long as it is conducted in the privacy of their own homes, a recent survey still shows that 65 percent of the public think homosexuals should not serve as teachers, and 54 percent believe homosexuals should not be allowed in the clergy (Lichtenstein, 1977).

Even the definition of homosexuality is controversial. Is a person considered a homosexual after only one homosexual encounter? If not, what is the cut-off point—two, three, ten experiences? If you use one experience as the criterion, the proportion of homosexual persons in our

population would indeed be high: Kinsey (1948) found that by age 40, some 37 percent of males and 13 percent of females in his sample fell into this category. Yet the percentage of males who engage regularly in homosexual activity in our society is usually considered to be about 2–4 percent while that of females who engage in **lesbian behavior** is around 1–3 percent. For our purposes, we will define **homosexual behavior** as sexual behavior between members of the same sex.

Is Homosexuality an Illness?   Over the years, homosexual individuals have been subject to discrimination and even persecution. Is homosexuality an illness? To answer that question, we can point toward two measures: its official standing in modern psychiatric classification systems, and its relationship to any signs of general lack of adjustment in an individual.

Until just a decade ago, homosexuality was officially classified as a psychiatric disorder in the American Psychiatric Association's *Diagnostic and Statistical Manual* (familiarly known as DSM). Since then, there has been a general turnaround in this psychological classification, however. The second edition, known as DSM II, was published in 1974 and it removed homosexuality from its list of mental disorders. The most recent DSM III (1980) appears to have struck a compromise. Homosexuality itself is not classified as a disorder. However, one form of homosexuality, called **ego dystonic homosexuality**, is considered a disorder. In this case, the individual is disturbed by his or her homosexuality and wishes to have a different sexual orientation.

What of homosexual individuals who are happy with their lifestyle? According to Bell and Weinberg (1978), persons who engage in homosexual activity don't differ very greatly from heterosexual persons. Like any cross-section of the population, they show a great diversity of attitudes and lifestyles, with vocational histories that are similar to those of the heterosexual population. Thompson and associates (1971) compared both men and women who engaged in homosexual behavior to groups of heterosexuals

> **Lesbian behavior**   Sexual activity between females.
>
> **Homosexual behavior**   Sexual behavior between members of the same sex.
>
> **Ego-dystonic homosexuality**   According to DSM III, this is a condition in which an individual practicing homosexual behavior *desires* to change to a heterosexual orientation. (Homosexuality itself is not listed as an emotional disorder.)

What Causes Homosexuality?

There are many theories to explain why some people engage in homosexual behavior and others don't. Unfortunately, no single theory seems to account for this lifestyle. For every promising study that comes along, another one comes to just the opposite conclusion. Over the years, however, three common themes keep reappearing in theories of homosexuality. These revolve around family history, genetic factors, and hormone levels. We'll look briefly at each.

Family History

One theory of homosexuality is based upon Bieber's studies (1962). Irving Bieber researched the personal history of a number of homosexuals in therapy and found some common factors. The typical father was rejecting, cold, detached, and ineffective, while the typical mother was overprotective and dominant. According to Bieber, the individual fails to identify with the proper role model in childhood, and this contributes to later homosexuality.

While Bieber's theory may seem reasonable, it has a serious flaw. Schofield (1965) found no evidence for Bieber's family background characteristics in his study of homosexuals. In fact, the one consistent finding in all the research is that homosexuals tend to come from a vast variety of backgrounds (Hooker, 1969). What explains the difference? Bieber's studies have been criticized since they were conducted on patient populations, and these may not be representative of homosexuals in the general population.

Genetic Theories

If family background doesn't explain homosexuality, perhaps genetics does. This theory was suggested years ago by Kallman (1952), who based his argument on studies of identical twins. Kallman examined a sample of twins and found a high concordance rate. That is, if one twin became homosexual, so did the other—even if they were raised in different homes. But Kallman's study, like Bieber's, has not been supported by subsequent research. Thus, at least for the present, it remains merely a possibility.

Hormones and Homosexuality

A third line of reasoning is that sexual preference may be related to hormone levels. Like the other theories, the logic behind this argument sounds reasonable; and indeed, some studies have shown that homosexuals have lower levels of the male hormone testosterone in their systems (Evans, 1972). However, other studies have found no difference to exist (Tourney et al., 1975). Thus, the evidence concerning this theory is just as confused—if not more so—as that for the other two theories. This led Martin (1977) to conclude that the connection between hormone level and homosexuality has not been adequately demonstrated.

How can homosexuality be explained? At this point, the question remains unanswered. All we can do is to await further research and hope that more significant evidence is uncovered in the future.

---

who were matched for age, sex, and education. The heterosexual and homosexual groups showed no significant differences in personal adjustment, with some minor exceptions. The male homosexual sample was less self-confident and less defensive, while the female homosexual sample was more self-confident than was the heterosexual control group.

There has been much less research on lesbianism than on male homosexuality. Findings do show one interesting difference between the two, however: that lesbians tend to have more lasting relationships than do male homosexuals (Mileski & Black, 1972). "One-night stands" tend to be less characteristic, and in general, these relationships seem to be more stable.

In general, it seems that homosexuality itself is not an illness. Homosexual personalities show no significant adjustment problems compared to the population at large. However, these individuals must cope with the rejection that they often find in the world around them, as well as some unique family problems. These are often the types of problems that homosexual persons come to therapy to solve. Only recently, in the wake of the political activism of the 60s, have homosexuals begun to try another tactic: to group together in the gay rights movement in order to put an end to discrimination.

Gay Rights   The gay rights movement has done something unique in the history of humanity: it has brought homosexuality, for centuries the object of discrimination and persecution, into the limelight as a political issue. Persons in favor of gay rights, both gays and heterosexuals, claim that gays are being discriminated against for no rational reason, and that they require the protection of the law. They point to the fact that homosexuals may indeed be found in all stations of life, that homosexuals are no less (or more) competent than the rest of the population, and that there is no evidence that this group presents any threat to the general population.

On the other side of the issue, many persons are against the open sanction of homosexuality, especially in jobs such as teaching. There is a fear that an overt homosexual role model would have an unwanted effect on a classroom full of children. Other objections to legislating gay rights are based on moral and religious grounds. For instance, some religious doctrines state that sex that is not intended for procreation is wrong.

As local gay rights bills attempt to eliminate discrimination on the grounds of sexual prefer-ence, it is unfortunate that so much ignorance still surrounds homosexuality. Hopefully, future debate on this issue will be based on facts and research rather than myth and innuendo.

Sexual Problems and Adjustments

Whether a person be homosexual or heterosexual, young or old, the importance of sexuality varies enormously from one individual to another. Some persons find sexual expression one of the great satisfactions in life; for others, it plays only a minor role. We have noted during this chapter that two individuals who have a deep relationship, as in marriage, must find their own adjustment to the different needs and requirements of their partner.

The sexual synchrony of a relationship must be seen in terms of the couple rather than simply the individual. Sexual intercourse involves two people, both of whose needs must be met. The box *Human Sexual Response* outlines the four stages of sexual response noted by researchers Masters and Johnson in their observations of approximately 10,000 male and female orgasms. An awareness of this sexual response pattern and its variations, as outlined in the figure, helps in understanding the origins of some sexual problems. For example, if one partner comes to climax quickly, leaving the other unsatisfied, there is a problem whether the first partner is aware of it or not.

Clearly, open communication could help a couple avoid or solve a problem such as this one. But sexual needs are difficult for many people, even married couples, to discuss frankly. The subject is a delicate one: most of us have been socialized *not* to be open about discussing what we like or don't like. Indeed, many people—especially women in our society who have been trained to respond rather than to initiate sexual behavior—may not be truly aware of their own sexual needs as separate from those of their partner. It is not

With the gay rights movement, homosexuality has become recognized as a social and political issue.

surprising how many married couples still do not communicate with each other about this most intimate subject (Hite, 1976).

Unfortunately, many small sexual problems become larger and larger because of a couple's inability to communicate. Sexual problems may have other sources, however, besides communication, and partners often are not able to solve such problems alone, no matter how openly they talk about them. The help of a professional therapist may be necessary, and some problems may not be solved even with professional help. In the remaining pages, we'll look briefly at some common sexual problems or dysfunctions that affect men and women, then at one prominent means of therapy.

Human Sexual Response

Sex research is often controversial, and the uniquely personal nature of the activity makes scientific study difficult at best. That is why many people are startled when they read about Masters and Johnson's landmark studies of human sexuality. After 12 years of study, in which they observed 270 married couples and 142 unmarried males and females ranging in age from 18–89, Masters and Johnson were well able to compile the most thorough picture ever of human sexual response. What they found were four distinct stages that occur in both women and men: arousal, plateau, orgasm, and resolution. As the illustrations suggest, these four phases vary greatly from one individual to another, with the sexual response pattern being far more variable among women.

Arousal

The first stage of arousal or excitement is characterized by a number of responses. Most obviously, a man's penis becomes erect and a woman experiences increased vaginal secretions. Other changes may also take place: the nipples may become erect in both sexes, there may be a quickening of the heart beat and an increase in muscle tension throughout the body, and the body may become flushed.

Plateau

During the plateau stage, the penis is fully erect and the vagina well-lubricated. Structural changes take place. The uterus becomes elevated in the woman, for instance, and in the man, the testicles become enlarged and elevated. The plateau phase may last only a few seconds before orgasm takes place, or it may be more extended.

Orgasm

Orgasm is a pulsating release of sexual tensions. The female orgasm usually consists of 5–12 involuntary contractions of the vagina, uterus, and related structures. In the male, the orgasm first involves rhythmic contractions of the muscle at the base of the penis, then ejaculation of semen, the fluid containing sperm.

Resolution

The last period, called resolution, involves the restoration of the body to its normal, unaroused state. Genital organs, which have become engorged with blood, return to the pre-excitement phase. At the same time, muscles relax, heartbeat slows to normal, and any overall body flush subsides.

In men, the resolution stage is usually followed by a period of relative inactivity called the **refractory period.** Further genital activity is not possible during this time if the male has experienced orgasm and ejaculated. The length of this period varies tremendously, and it seems to be associated with age: the younger male usually requires less time between orgasms than does the older man.

Source: Masters & Johnson, 1966.

Female Sexual Response Cycle   *As is shown above, female sexual response patterns are far more variable than is the male sexual response pattern. The chart shows three different female response patterns: (A) resembles the male pattern except for the absence of a refractory period; (B) has an extended plateau phase but no definite orgasm; and (C) is characterized by a rapid rise to orgasm, followed by a quick resolution. Other patterns may also occur.*

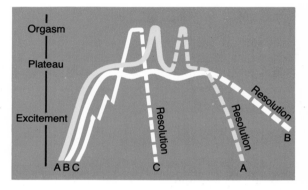

Male Sexual Response Cycle   *Masters and Johnson identify only one male sexual response pattern. The excitement phase builds to plateau, then there is orgasm and resolution. A refractory period distinguishes this pattern from the female response pattern. A second orgasm does not occur until after this refractory period has passed.*
Source: Masters & Johnson, 1966. Used by permission.

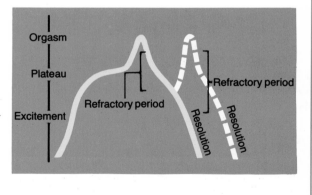

Problems That Affect Men

Primary Erectile Dysfunction   **Primary erectile dysfunction** (sometimes called impotence) is a condition in which a man has never been capable of maintaining an erection long enough to complete coitus.*

Primary erectile dysfunction has many causes, most often psychological. These include extremely strict religious beliefs in which sex is thought of as sinful, as well as a personal history which includes a troublesome event or relationship. Occasionally, for instance, the problem traces to the man's first sexual experience, in which he was so traumatized at not being able to "perform" that the same reaction occurred at each subsequent attempt. Sometimes, too, erectile dysfunction is related to an anxiety-ridden childhood seduction—as when a boy has been seduced by his mother.

Secondary Erectile Dysfunction   **Secondary erectile dysfunction** is a condition in which a man has

---

*Erectile dysfunction is a very different problem from sterility. Sterility relates only to a person's inability to have children; it has nothing to do with the frequency, quality, or desire to engage in intercourse.

Primary erectile dysfunction (primary impotence)   A sexual problem in which a male has never been able to maintain an erection for long enough to complete coitus.

Secondary erectile dysfunction (secondary impotence)   A sexual problem in which a man has failed to gain or maintain an erection 25 percent of the time during sexual encounters.

Premature ejaculation   A sexual dysfunction in which the male cannot delay or control ejaculation for long enough to satisfy his partner at least 50 percent of the times they engage in coitus.

---

difficulty in either having an erection or maintaining one, even though he once had no difficulty. (To be a bit more scientific, Masters and Johnson [1970] define secondary erectile dysfunction as being unable to gain or maintain an erection 25 percent of the time in encounters in which the man wants to have intercourse.)

As with primary erectile dysfunction, this problem usually has psychological causes. Many of Masters and Johnson's patients have shown histories of premature ejaculation (discussed below), alcohol problems, significant life stresses, or dominant, punishing parents. A variety of physical disorders might also be involved (many illnesses may be associated with a temporary inability to have an erection). The physical disorder itself is usually not the direct cause of a lingering problem, though. Instead, it is more often due to the man's doubts that he will be able to return to normal functioning. In erectile dysfunction as well as the overwhelming majority of sexual problems, anxiety is the prime cause; and the greater the anxiety, the greater is the chance of failure.

Premature Ejaculation   One of the most misunderstood of all the sexual problems catalogued by Masters and Johnson is premature ejaculation. Many times, it has been defined in terms of time— so that a male might be considered a premature ejaculator if he were unable to wait a certain period of time before orgasm.

This definition is rather arbitrary, however, for it fails to consider both partners. What if the man can control his response for ten minutes, but it doesn't satisfy his partner? Since we regard sexual expression as a mutual act that brings joy and satisfaction to both partners, we will avoid any "time" definitions in this text. Instead, we'll use the definition established by Masters and Johnson, that **premature ejaculation** is an inability to control ejaculation "for a sufficient length of time during vaginal containment to satisfy [one's] partner in at least fifty percent of their coital connections" (1970, p. 92). This definition is interesting in that it is couple specific. Since each sexual relationship is unique, it is entirely possible for a man to have difficulty with one partner but not with another.

Premature ejaculation may exist by itself, or it may lead to secondary erectile dysfunction. However, Masters and Johnson believe that most men with this condition do not develop erectile problems; and premature ejaculation often occurs among men with active sex lives. Many men react to the problem by concentrating on something else during intercourse, in order to block out sensory stimuli. This approach brings its own problems, however, for it forces a psychological withdrawal from the partner. We'll look at some more successful therapy techniques later, after a discussion of some sexual dysfunctions that women experience.

Problems That Affect Women

As with men, most sexual problems in women have psychological causes. This is not to say that these problems are any less serious than if they had underlying physiological causes. It is worth taking a moment to look a little more closely at how socialization relates to female dysfunctions.

Society has a rather complicated ambivalence toward female sexuality. On the one hand, women and girls are often treated as sex symbols in movies, men's magazines, and also in advertising aimed toward the female market. On the other hand, women have traditionally been socialized to have only a limited understanding of their own sexuality. This training relates closely to many female dysfunctions. We'll look at two of the most common dysfunctions below.

Primary Sexual Dysfunction   Women who have never reached orgasm by any form of stimulation are said to have a **primary sexual dysfunction**. The causes most often involve psychological fac-

tors. For instance, overly strict upbringing, or a harsh training in which sex was equated with sin, are sometimes part of the woman's background. According to Belliveau and Richter, the major cause is the woman's "inability to identify with her partner" (1970, p. 165)—if, for instance, she is disappointed with him as an intellectual partner or as a provider, or if he seems a social failure. Another common factor is a sexual problem on the part of the man. For instance, a woman with primary sexual dysfunction may be married to a partner who is a premature ejaculator.

Situational Orgasmic Dysfunction   The term **situational orgasmic dysfunction** is used to denote a number of different problems, all involving the inability to experience orgasm in the course of normal sexual relations. Some may only achieve orgasm through masturbation or only in a special situation (such as during a vacation). Again, background figures prominently in these cases.

In both primary and situational orgasmic dysfunction, the male's sexual patterns can have a profound effect on the woman. If the man is inadequate as a lover, or if he has an arrogant personality, it may be impossible for the woman to respond during coitus, at least without help. If the man doesn't understand that the woman requires more time during the first phase of sexual response, it will be more difficult for her to reach climax. In addition, if she is uncommunicative, resentful, or disappointed in her lover, this can also either cause or worsen a dysfunction.

> **Primary sexual dysfunction**   A sexual problem of women in which females do not reach orgasm by any method of stimulation.
>
> **Situational orgasmic dysfunction**   A sexual problem of females in which a woman can experience orgasm only under particular conditions, or in which a female who once attained orgasm finds that she is currently unable to do so.

Treating Sexual Problems

Problems such as those we've been discussing can be extremely troublesome—a veritable "black cloud" over a relationship. One reason is that dysfunctions may be misinterpreted: the partner of a man with erectile difficulty may worry that he doesn't find her attractive anymore; or the man who tries and tries to bring his partner to orgasm may feel frustrated and even deeply hurt when she fails to respond. Such problems often become exaggerated with time, as partners feel more and more anxious, and more and more pressured to "succeed." It is not hard to see why professional counseling is often necessary to try to reverse the cycle. The therapy techniques used by modern counselors are revealing. Although we wouldn't recommend trying "home cures" from the brief summary we'll provide here, much can be learned from an overview of some of the strategies they use. We'll outline three central concepts used by modern counselors, including eliminating the pressure to perform; improving couple communication; and improving couple awareness.

Eliminating Orgasm as a Goal   One of the most essential points made by most therapists is that sex cannot be equated with orgasm. There is more to sex and love than coming to climax; and holding this achievement up as a goal that *must* be reached creates a tremendous achievement pressure. Since anxiety is so basic to most sexual dysfunctions, such a goal orientation is counterproductive. Sometimes, couples feel in a rush to reach sexual harmony and feel discouraged when this goal isn't met early in a relationship. As in any other part of marriage, sexual adjustment takes time (Klemer, 1970); and for women especially, it may take time, experience, and communication with a partner before orgasms are achieved regularly (Kaplan, 1974).

How do therapists help couples who do want to experience orgasm, but who seem to be unable to? One of the most effective treatments is to take away the goal of orgasm during intercourse. Couples may be told to do anything in bed, but not to have intercourse. This often reduces the pressure to perform; and in this more relaxed setting, the couple can often make progress.

Improving Couple Communication   Faulty communication is one of the most frequent factors in sexual dysfunction; and as a result, improving communication is a primary strategy in therapy. To do this, counseling is often done jointly by two co-therapists, one male and the other female. Trust in the therapist is vital, and one partner often relates more closely to one therapist than to the other. Sexual dysfunctions can fill an individual with self-doubt, and if the couple don't respect and trust the therapists, they will be less able to accept constructive criticism. Having two therapists offers one other advantage besides encouraging greater trust, for one therapist is usually free to observe how the couple reacts while the other therapist is interacting with them. In addition, if one is a male and the other female there is a greater opportunity to understand and relate to each client.

The co-therapists try to help the couple reach a deeper level of sexual communication than had been possible before the treatment sessions. For example, a man may never have been able to admit to his wife that he is worried he can't satisfy her, or a woman may never have been able to discuss her specific sexual desires with her husband.

Increasing Awareness   Many individuals are unaware of their own and their partners' feelings, and a third therapy strategy aims at increasing this awareness. One technique often used is called **sensate focus.** Here, both partners become more

> **Sensate focus**   A technique used in sex therapies in which both partners stimulate the other in order to learn what each enjoys, then talk freely and openly about their feelings and experiences.

aware of the physical experiences of both themselves and the mate during sex. Exploration, touching, and caressing are used to increase the individual's awareness of feelings. Since sexual intercourse and orgasm are not the main objective, partners can focus more attentively on other sensations.

Many techniques are used to increase awareness of sexual feeling and to become more sensitive to a partner's needs. Often, these involve exercises and direct instructions from the therapist. The emphasis is on enjoyment, intimacy, communication, naturalness, and sensuality. Each individual is encouraged to become actively involved in lovemaking and to be honest and open with the other partner.

How Effective Is Sex Therapy? Remembering that the goals of the therapy are limited to improving sexual functioning, Masters and Johnson's methods have proven quite successful. According to Belliveau and Richter (1970), only four clients did not report improvement out of a total of 186 men treated for premature ejaculation at the Masters and Johnson clinic. The therapy for primary erectile dysfunction in males is 59.4 percent successful. Masters and Johnson report a 73.8 percent success rate with secondary erectile dysfunction. Also, 83.4 percent of those individuals treated for primary orgasmic dysfunction and 77.2 percent of those treated for situational orgasmic dysfunction have been successfully able to achieve sexual climax.

Masters and Johnson's methods serve as the foundation for many systems of sex therapies. There are many other well-trained sex therapists. However, as in every other field of professional services, it is important to check each professional's credentials before undergoing treatment. As a consumer of professional services, you are entitled to ask searching questions concerning method, philosophy, fee, and background. The therapy for sexual dysfunction requires a level of skill and training that may take years to develop. Caution in choosing a therapist is definitely in order.

Summary

1. There has been a revolutionary change in sexual attitudes in the past few generations. Both male and female attitudes seem to be converging, with women's attitudes changing more rapidly than those of men. In addition, there is a greater tolerance for sexual behaviors, especially in the context of a loving relationship. Most teenagers today believe that what two consenting people do in privacy is their own business.

2. Although there has been a steady evolution towards both earlier and more sex, especially on the part of females, there is no evidence that most youngsters view sex as a casual act. In fact, about one-half of the women who have premarital sex do so with only one person, the man they plan to marry (although this proportion seems to be falling).

3. It is difficult to interpret sexual research because it is so personal and the outcome so dependent on the wording of questions. In addition, a person's sexual behaviors may not always be in accordance with that person's stated attitudes.

4. We are sexual beings throughout our lives. Childhood sexuality is normal as children explore their own bodies and learn from the models they observe.

5. There is no one, single pattern of adolescent sexual behavior, but teenagers in general tend to have sex earlier than before. Because younger women are less likely to use contraceptives than are older women, this change has meant a tremendous increase in teenage pregnancies. Sexually transmitted diseases have also become a serious social problem.

6. Although many parents approve of sex education in the schools, they want their own values stressed. Most teens favor some sort of sex education, but they want to discuss values as well as biology. Some parents who oppose sex education in the schools believe it should be done in the home. Others may worry that their children aren't yet ready to learn about such issues.

7. Sexual activity diminishes with age. However, this decline would seem due more to psychological factors than to physiology. In elderly persons, continued sexual activity seems important to sustained interest and functioning in old age.

8. Kinsey found that there were many sexual paths open to people. As long as both individuals are satisfied, there appears to be little reason to check the statistics to make certain they are "normal."

9. Homosexuality is defined as male or female sexual behavior with a member of the same sex. It is highly controversial, in many respects. Its causes are still unknown. In addition, there is an ongoing debate as to whether homosexuality is an illness, and whether certain jobs should be closed to persons who are self-described gays. Research has demonstrated that persons who engage in homosexual activity come from many backgrounds and are no less adjusted than the population as a whole. The term *ego dystonic homosexuality* is used to describe a condition in which the person is unhappy and wants to change his or her sexual orientation.

10. Masters and Johnson discovered four stages in human sexual response: excitement, plateau, orgasm, and resolution. These stages are similar in both women and men.

11. One common factor in sexual problems is a couple's inability to synchronize their sexual response patterns; but the problem is not just physical. Communication is often involved, both in the origins of some problems and in their development.

12. Three common sexual dysfunctions in males are primary erectile dysfunction, secondary erectile dysfunction, and premature ejaculation. Two common dysfunctions in women are primary sexual and situational orgasmic dysfunction. In all of these conditions, psychological factors (such as rigid training that sex is sinful, anxiety about performance, or an inability to accept one's own sexual needs) are usually deeply involved.

13. Only recently have nonthreatening therapy techniques been developed to help people deal with sexual problems. Sexual therapy involves helping the couple eliminate "performance pressure" to reach orgasm; helping partners learn to communicate openly with one another; and increasing awareness of both the individual's needs and those of the partner. Therapy often involves the use of co-therapists with whom the couple can relate on a more complete level.

14. Studies indicate that sexual therapies are reasonably effective in helping people deal with sexual problems.

Key Terms and Concepts

double standard	resolution
procreation	refractory period
sexually transmitted disease	primary erectile dysfunction
testosterone	secondary erectile dysfunction
lesbian behavior	
homosexual behavior	premature ejaculation
ego dystonic homosexuality	primary sexual dysfunction
arousal	situational orgasmic dysfunction
plateau	sensate focus
orgasm	

Esteem Needs

A little girl was busy playing alone in her backyard very early one morning when a neighbor happened to notice her. After watching the child play happily for a few moments, he walked over to her and asked where her parents and brother were. "Oh, they're still sleeping," the child answered without looking up from her play. "Well, aren't you lonely?" asked the neighbor. "Oh, no," the girl replied. "I like me."

The Self

As is so often the case, the simple utterances of a child contain a great deal of wisdom. This child thought of herself in positive terms and was comfortable with who she was. There was no need for long explanations or idle talk. She liked herself.

Each of us has a picture of ourselves that we call our **self-concept**. We may see ourselves as warm or cold, good or bad, friendly or shy, a success or a failure. We may even see ourselves as warm *and* cold, and friendly *and* shy, depending on the situation: such inconsistencies are also a part of our self-concepts. Overall, these self-images affect many aspects of our functioning—the way we present ourselves to others, our goals, and even the way in which we interpret what others do.

Closely related to the notion of the self-concept is another notion: **self-esteem**. While your self-concept is the picture you have of yourself, your self-esteem is the value you place on yourself: your own sense of worth. If you possess a negative view of yourself, every failure is likely to be interpreted as a total failure and the actions of others are likely to be seen as criticisms. If your self-esteem is high, you will be more able to isolate a failure in one area from the rest of your life (Stein, 1970).

In this chapter, we will lay the foundation for Part IV's discussion of the self, self-definition, and self-esteem. In the pages that follow, we will be exploring this relationship between self-concept and adjustment. In Chapter 13, we will look at one important area that relates closely to most people's sense of esteem: vocational choice. The chapter will explore the kinds of vocational choices people make—either by active selection or by default—and the ways in which this relates to the self-concept, to the esteem of others, and to life satisfaction. Finally, Chapter 14 looks at therapy, both as a vehicle of healing problems and as a vehicle for personal growth. Several forms of therapy will be discussed, as well as the human potentials movement.

Some Questions about Your Self

- "I don't know what I'm doing in school. I don't even know whether I'd be better off going out into the world and seeing life instead of staying here."

- "I feel myself trapped both in body and soul. If I do the things I feel like doing I feel guilty, if I don't I feel angry and frustrated. My parents and upbringing drag me in one direction while my friends pull me in the other."

- "I've always thought I wanted to get married and settle down. But recently, I don't know, I feel that I want to do something else, but I don't really know what yet. My mother is sure worried."

- "I guess I've gone from cause to cause seeking to believe in something. My parents had no real religion; they just raised me to know right from wrong. There must be something else in this world besides me."

These four statements were all made by teenagers who were asked to discuss their feelings about their lives. Each shows a yearning for direction and, to some extent, a search for self-identity.

What is your "self"? As we saw in Chapter 4, Erik Erikson saw the search for identity as the central question of adolescence. According to Erikson (1968), adolescents cannot simply accept their childhood attitudes, beliefs, and feelings, but must form an **identity** of their own. Ruittenbeck (1964) sees questions such as "Who am I?",

> **Self-concept** The way in which individuals perceive themselves.
>
> **Self-esteem** The value individuals place on their own worth.
>
> **Identity** The sense of knowing who you are. Identity is often attained only after extensive searching and experiencing.

Identity and Intimacy

The search for an identity is a primary task of adolescence. According to Erik Erikson's theory of lifelong development, this challenge must be met if a person is to become self-actualized as an adult. Is a relatively stable identity also necessary if a person is to develop the kind of deep, intimate relationships that are characteristic of young adulthood? This question was investigated by three researchers as part of a larger study of identity development.

The subjects of this study were 53 junior and senior male university students, all volunteers. The researchers evaluated the subjects by first administering questionnaires, then, within a few weeks, conducting interviews to measure factors relating to identity and intimacy.

On the basis of the questionnaires and interviews, the researchers were able to divide the subjects into four groups, supporting the notion that there is a link between a mature identity and the ability to share intimacy. The first of these groups, called *identity achievers* by the researchers, had made some commitment to philosophical or vocational choices, and most of them had also developed mature and successful intimate relationships. The second group, termed *moratorium subjects*, were experiencing conflict about their identities. They showed a great interest in others and lacked defensiveness, and many had close friendships with other males; but they were hesitant to take the risk of an intimate relationship with a female. A third group were called *foreclosure subjects*. These students had made commitments to occupational or philosophical choices, but these choices had actually been made by their parents or other authority figures. Most of these subjects had experienced only "formal dating"; few had formed a deep, close partnership with a woman. Finally, a fourth group called *diffusion subjects* were confused and uncommitted about their identities. They often didn't date at all, and they had few close friends.

These findings seem to illustrate a definite relationship between a mature identity and an ability to share intimacy—although the investigators note that a number of technical issues still bear further study. Looking at this data, one wonders whether the very high divorce rates among teenage marriages may be due in part to the lack of developed identity, a factor that seems to stand in the way of attaining true intimacy.

Source: Orlofsky et al., 1973.

"Where am I going?", and "Do I belong?" as basic to the adolescent's preparation for the new role of adult. As the box *Identity and Intimacy* discusses, such questions are also related to people's ability to form intimate relationships.

Working through these questions is a long and arduous process: most people don't suddenly wake up one morning with all the answers. In fact, while the search for the self is associated most closely with adolescence, it certainly doesn't end there. Many of these same questions may not be easy to answer even as adults, for several reasons. First, the "self" itself is a rather broad concept, made up of many elements that change from situation to situation and that sometimes seem to contradict one another. Your name and your appearance may remain the same from day to day, but somehow, your self-concept is not so consistent. Secondly, we change over time, during the course of the life cycle. It's a good bet that the "you" of 10 or 15 years ago is not quite the same person as your current self; nor will you be quite the same several years in the future. Finally, we each project images of who we would like to be, and we identify with others who seem to reflect our ideals. At times, it may be hard to separate our real selves from these images. These three qualities of the self—its many dimensions, its changeability, and

Each of us has many "selves," all of which contribute to an overall sense of esteem.

the way we project it through images and ideals—will form a basic structure for this chapter. (We'll end the chapter with a look at some ways of improving our self-concepts.)

One Person; Many "Selves"

How do you see yourself? An interesting exercise may provide some insight. On a sheet of paper, try writing 20 statements beginning with the words "I am." It may be difficult, but give yourself free range—you may include statements about your physical self, your personality, roles, beliefs, status, characteristic feelings, group identification, or virtually anything else, so long as it is accurate.

The list may seem to contain a jumble of qualities that don't necessarily go together. But it can tell you something about your self-concept. Kuhn and McPartland (1954) created a simple scheme for organizing your self-statements by dividing them into four categories. The first category relates to your physical self: your gender, height, weight, race, and general evaluations of your physique. The second category involves your identification with the roles you play, such as being a student, a parent, a member of a specific group, and so forth. The third category includes your perceptions of characteristic moods and feelings. The fourth category contains abstractions, such as "I am me, a human, a conscious being."

If you organize your statements according to these categories, you may begin to understand how you see yourself.* We can look more closely

*A related exercise is to ask someone who knows you well to complete 20 statements beginning with "You are," and see how closely this list relates to your own list. The odds are that the lists will be quite similar. Videbeck (1960) found a significant link between our own self-concepts and the ratings of others in our environment. If you see yourself as happy-go-lucky, there is a good chance that your friends will regard you in the same way.

at these four kinds of "selves"—your physical self, the roles you play, your personality, and the abstract self—then examine a question that still causes some controversy among psychologists: Does each of us have one identity, or do we have many?

Four Elements of the Self

The Physical Self   Some of the most common self-statements revolve around your physical self. In recent years, people seem to have become more and more interested in their bodies. Physical fitness is "in": jogging is a national passion, and tennis, skiing, aerobic exercises, biking—and certainly dieting—are common practices. The mass media continually remind us of our physical condition; and many products are on the market to help us change our appearance to be more in keeping with society's image of competency and fitness. We fight aging every step of the way, through creams, lotions, carefully chosen clothing, and exercises that can keep us feeling and looking young. Is all this effort really worthwhile—is physical appearance really so important to our self-concepts?

In general, the answer to this question is "yes," although it varies from person to person. The way we look has quite a bit to do with the way we feel about ourselves. As you might expect, this is generally most true during adolescence; and it seems to have at least some effect on the development of the self-image. One study compared early and late maturing youths (Mussen & Jones, 1957). It found that early-maturing boys both rated themselves and were rated by others more positively than late-maturing boys. They saw themselves superior on just about every personality and physical attribute. The evidence for early maturation for females is less clear, but it seems to indicate that they stood out in elementary school and that they were not especially happy about it. Upon entering junior high school, though, the

For many people, physical fitness is an important part of a healthy self-concept.

situation changed and they found their early development to be an asset.

Although sooner or later their friends caught up with these early developers, the experiences of both the early and the late groups seem to have some lasting effect. Follow-up studies have found that 30 years later, late-maturing males were still different, although these differences weren't necessarily negative. The early maturers were more relaxed and conforming and they could still be found in leadership roles, while the late maturers were more talkative and assertive (Jones, 1957).

Our physical self is an important part of our self-images in other ways besides early or late development. Many of us set our sights on a physical goal—usually an ideal "10" such as actress Bo Derek in the film of that name, or perhaps an Arnold Schwarzenegger or an O. J. Simpson—then slowly realize that the odds are against our ever achieving that goal. In some cases, feelings of inadequacy can have long-term effects on our self-concepts. Even when our appearance is satisfactory, nagging doubts often remain. Three-quarters of the high school girls questioned by

The "ideal woman," c. 1607. Clearly, physical ideals are determined more by culture than by medical considerations.

The great majority of us, however, do eventually accept ourselves even though we may not live up to our physical ideals (Stein, 1970). We try to make the most of what we have. In addition, we may adjust our ideals to bring them a little closer to reality. Most women decide that there is more to life than being a ravishing beauty; most men decide that they don't have to look like movie heroes. And both men and women usually learn to deal with the gradual changes in appearance and in physical well-being that come with age. A much more difficult adjustment is required when a sudden physical loss takes place as a result of an accident or an illness. The effect on a person's self-concept can be quite far-reaching, as is discussed in the box *Physical Disability: What Happens to the Self-concept?* One reason why physical impairment can have such a staggering effect is that it often prevents a person from carrying out social roles that are themselves important to the self-concept.

Social Roles and the Self A second important part of the self-concept consists of social roles. As we saw in Chapter 8, we think of ourselves in terms of the roles we play. Consequently, your status as a student, an athlete, a parent or child, an employee, and so forth, not only influences your behavior (you behave differently as a student than you would as a teacher, for instance) but is also basic to your self-definition.

Roles are highly changeable, however. You outgrow certain roles and take on new ones over the course of a lifetime, as you move away from your parents and set up a household of your own, and as you take on the responsibilities of work or parenthood, or both. You may even play several roles at the same time. For instance, you may be both a parent and a student; or a student, an employee, and an apartment house manager. These roles are not always compatible with one another, and as we saw in Chapter 8, wearing too many "hats" can be very stressful. The solution is usually to downplay one of the most expendable

DeJong (1977, cited in Middlebrook, 1980) felt they needed to lose weight even though the vast majority were of normal stature. In the 1960s when the thin British model, Twiggy, was popular, many women who were already thin went on diets to lose those five "extra" pounds. Our physical ideals, then, seem to be determined more by social factors than by medical considerations, as the photographs illustrate.

Physical Disability: What Happens to the Self-concept?

Our society has rigid standards for physical appearance. If a slight deviation such as a too-long nose or too-large hips bother us, what are the consequences when a person loses a leg, is scarred for life, or suddenly becomes disabled?

It's hard to generalize an answer to this question, since disability affects individuals differently. However, Wright (1960) believes that two factors influence the extent to which a disability may affect the self-concept. First, the higher the value of the disability to society, the greater the effect on the self-concept. (Society values certain physical attributes more than others, so that paralysis of the legs usually has a greater effect than the loss of an arm.) Secondly, the closer the connection between the disability and the core of the self-concept, the more dramatic the effects will be. For instance, if you think of yourself as a musician, losing the ability to play an instrument would probably be more devastating than would the loss of a leg.

We'll look first at the reactions of society. If we accept the argument that people internalize how others see them (see the discussion of "the looking glass self" in this chapter), the consequences of society's rejection can be severe. Attitudes toward the disabled are often negative (Siller, 1976). Therefore, if disabled persons simply mirrored these feelings, each of these individuals would have a negative self-concept.

The issue is more complex than that, however. The second factor we mentioned above was the degree to which a disability interferes with the person's established self-concept. Some research by Shelsky (1957, cited in Wright, 1960) is interesting here. In his study, Shelsky interviewed both amputees and tuberculosis victims six months after the onset of their disabilities. Presumably, the first shock had worn off and the results of the study reflect a more lasting view of themselves. As you might expect, these people did view themselves as changed from what they had been before; but their perceptions of the changes were quite realistic. The amputees felt that they had been more active before the disability, and the tuberculosis victims felt they had been healthier. However, Shelsky found little or no change in their self-concepts as measured by some 300 possible personality traits. This was especially true of traits that were not directly related to the disability.

It would seem that after the initial shock, each individual can react to a disability in a variety of ways. If the person feels he or she can cope with the new circumstances, there may be little or no long-term damage to the self-concept. However, if the disability directly affects a person's self-definition, if the public reacts negatively to the individual, and if the person is unable to function well with the disability, then we can predict a negative change in the self-concept.

This has some practical implications, for it points toward an important conclusion. It is important to limit the extent to which any specific disability affects other areas of a person's functioning. Physical barriers—such as high curbs that deny access to wheelchairs, or public buildings with steps but not ramps, or media that is inaccessible to persons with hearing or sight impairments—serve to limit the opportunities of people with disabilities. By removing such physical barriers, we may find that these individuals are able to function effectively in society, and we may reduce the amount of damage to the self-concept that these individuals might otherwise experience (Rusalem, 1976).

roles—for instance, to cut down your course-load or give up the apartment manager job so that you can carry out your other roles more comfortably.

Roles may also be a source of stress if they require you to behave in a way that is inconsistent with your self-concept. Suppose you see yourself as joyful, warm, and loving, but your job requires you to behave in another manner. Perhaps you must lay off an employee, or apprehend shop-lifters in a department store. Playing the "heavy" conflicts with your view of yourself. Which person are you: the efficient, cool authority figure, or the sympathetic, friendly human being? Perhaps you are both—one reason why the self-concept is sometimes hard to pinpoint!

Personality and the Self   Your physical person and the roles you play are not the only important elements of your self-concept. In fact, you may have considered these to be relatively *unimportant* in your list of self-statements, compared to personal descriptive qualities such as "serious," "fun-loving," "compassionate," "moody," "intelligent," and so forth. Such qualities describe your personality, a very important part of your self-concept.

How consistent is personality? Most of us assume that we are the same person in every situation. Yet our self-concept may consist of a wide range of attitudes, behaviors, and feelings. Not even the most happy-go-lucky person is happy every minute of the day; nor is the most self-confident person always certain that he or she is doing the right thing. British author H. G. Wells put it succinctly:

Every one of these hundreds of millions of human beings is . . . [neither] altogether noble nor altogether trust-worthy nor altogether consistent; and not one is altogether vile" (in Sheehy, 1981, p. 54).

The exercise in the box *Two Sides of the Self* may help you be more aware of the seemingly contradictory qualities that exist side-by-side in each of us. If it disturbs you to acknowledge that you—of all people!—are sometimes mean, or cold, or dishonest, remember that being aware of these qualities is not the same thing as approving of them. Your self-concept is not a unified single construct that you either accept or reject completely. If you are like most people, you'll be more comfortable with some parts of your self than with other parts.

This point was supported in an experiment by Akeret (1959). Students were asked to describe themselves in terms of four constructs: their academic values, interpersonal relations, sexual adjustments, and emotional adjustment. The responses showed some wide variations. Students who felt they were well adjusted in one area of their lives often felt quite differently about another area of functioning. For example, a high academic self-acceptance did not correlate exceptionally well with interpersonal self-acceptance. In other words, the self-concept does not seem to be a unified whole; people value and accept certain parts of themselves more than others. An awareness of the bad as well as the good can help you to see more clearly which areas of your self you would like to change. We'll look further at both the inconsistencies in our self-concepts and at ways to bring about change later on in this chapter.

The Abstract Self   A fourth group of self-statements are more broad and abstract. Statements such as "I am a human being," or "I am a being created for a purpose" are relatively impersonal compared to the other elements of the self-concept we've been discussing. That is, they focus less directly on you as an individual than does a statement about your personality, roles, or physical state. But this element may also be a part of your self-concept, to a varying extent. Even the least philosophical of us sometimes define ourselves in more abstract terms, perhaps during religious moments or as we think about our small place in the evolution of humankind. It is likely, however, that these abstract self-definitions comprise a smaller part of your self-concept than do the other three categories we've discussed above.

Two Sides of the Self

Below are 10 pairs of opposite adjectives. Next to each, note how it fits into your self-concept. At what times have you acted in one way; at what times might you act in the other way? Can you accept yourself as behaving in both ways?

_____ Kind	Mean _____	
_____ Active	Passive _____	
_____ Warm	Cold _____	
_____ Beautiful	Ugly _____	
_____ Obedient	Rebellious _____	
_____ Generous	Stingy _____	
_____ Honest	Dishonest _____	
_____ Mature	Immature _____	
_____ Silent	Talkative _____	

One Identity, or Many?

It should be clear from the discussion above that there are many ways of defining the self. Does this mean that there is no such thing as a coherent, consistent identity? This question can be answered in two ways, and there are psychologists who will argue for each side.

According to one school of thought, each of us has a consistent self-concept, a unified sense of who we are. Perhaps we can illustrate this best by looking at others. Most of us know of people, usually family members or friends, who have had a certain personality trait since childhood—such as an offbeat sense of humor, or a stubbornness, or a sensitivity to others. We see the same kinds of consistent threads in ourselves, so that our self-concepts remain basically the same throughout most of our lives. In the view of some psychol-

ogists, this consistency is important to our mental health (Kimmel, 1974).

It's certainly true that some parts of our personality are fairly stable. However, we also recognize changes in ourselves, both over time and from situation to situation. Some psychologists, most notably Gergen (1972), have questioned the assumption that the self is a unified whole and that inconsistency causes problems. According to this point of view, people's self-concepts are rather flexible, changing easily with situational differences; and there is some experimental support for this argument.

In one experiment, 18 women college students were asked about their backgrounds (Gergen, 1972). They were divided into three groups: in one, the interviewers were careful to provide highly positive feedback; in another, they provided negative reinforcement; and in a third, neither positive nor negative feedback was provided. An interesting pattern emerged in the first group, in which the students' positive self-statements were all reinforced through some subtle response such as a nod or a smile. Gergen reports that the students' self-evaluations became more and more positive as the reinforcements were provided. Were the students putting on a show for the interviewers? Apparently not—for even when they were questioned privately and assured that the interviewers would not see their self-ratings, their self-evaluations were higher than those of students who had received either negative or no reinforcement.

Such findings seem to indicate that the self-concept is rather flexible, and that it can change according to the environment. This does not mean that we change *completely* from one situation to the next. Indeed, radical personality changes of the Dr. Jekyll and Mr. Hyde nature would be just as unhealthy as would a total inability to grow or change. Under some extraordinary circumstances, of course, people sometimes do undergo rather remarkable changes in identity, as is discussed in the box *Will the Real Patty Hearst Please Stand Up? Some True-Life and Experimental Evidence on the Changing Self.* Fortunately, such experiences are unlikely to happen to most of us. We do, however, undergo less sudden changes during the course of development.

The Self: Changes over Time

Have you ever wondered how you got to be you—whether you might have been a different person

had you grown up with more opportunities, or had you had a different family life? Most of us have, and the question has been studied by many psychologists who don't always agree on the answers. We'll present a broad overview.

How Did You Get to Be You? Two Views

We begin to develop a self-concept as soon as we can tell the difference between ourselves and the environment (Rogers, 1951); and this self-concept changes tremendously as we develop. Some theorists believe that humans develop self-awareness in a manner that parallels the growth process. Nixon, for instance, identifies five stages in the development of the self-concept, and as Figure 12.1 outlines, these stages reflect the child's readiness for new experiences. We won't dwell on the specific stages here, as Chapter 4 has already discussed development in detail. What does interest us, though, is the broader process. Is the self a reflection of what others tell us about ourselves over the years, or do we develop a self-concept on our own? We'll look at how different psychologists answer this question.

The "Good-Me, Bad-Me"   An American psychiatrist named Harry Stack Sullivan saw the self-concept as a reflection of how others see you. If your parents, teachers, and friends gave you generally positive feedback as you were growing up, said Sullivan, your self-concept will likely be positive. If, in turn, you were always being told that you were a sneak, or lazy, or not very smart, you would probably incorporate these negative evaluations into your self-concept.

According to Sullivan, each of us internalizes such **"good-me, bad-me"** evaluations, beginning in infancy and continuing through adolescence. In infancy, our evaluations result from nonverbal types of parent-infant interaction (Chapman,

"Good me, bad me"   Harry Stack Sullivan's explanation for the way in which people develop positive ("good me") or negative ("bad me") self-appraisals. In this view, both these self-concepts reflect the feedback people receive from others.

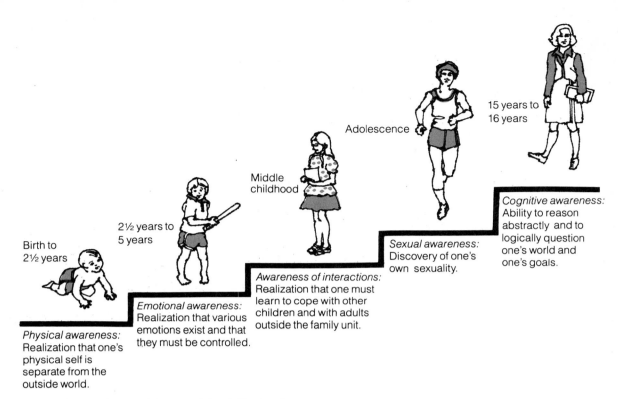

Figure 12.1   The Development of the Self: Five Stages
Source: Based on Nixon, 1962.

Birth to
2½ years

Physical awareness:
Realization that one's
physical self is
separate from the
outside world.

2½ years to
5 years

Emotional awareness:
Realization that various
emotions exist and that
they must be controlled.

Middle
childhood

Awareness of interactions:
Realization that one must
learn to cope with other
children and with adults
outside the family unit.

Adolescence

Sexual awareness:
Discovery of one's
own sexuality.

15 years to
16 years

Cognitive awareness:
Ability to reason
abstractly and to
logically question
one's world and
one's goals.

1976). A parent who always acts angry or frustrated around a fussy baby, for instance, may not be providing the infant with a warm and positive sense of being loved, and the infant may react by being less responsive. As children grow, their language abilities expand, and so do the number and type of evaluations they receive. Not just parents, but friends, teachers, and other authority figures become important, and their opinions are valued. If we receive positive evaluations, we develop a sense of the "good-me." On the other hand, a person who is constantly reminded of his or her failings develops a "bad-me" image (Elkind, 1972). The individual with a bad-me image is likely to feel anxious and rejected, and may combat these feelings by forming protective mech-

anisms such as the defense mechanisms we discussed in Chapter 6.*

Whether or not these good-me or bad-me evaluations are accurate, they are hard to shake. It's likely that you will be doubtful if someone tells you that you're not the person you think you are. For instance, if you were always at the top of your class in high school, but in college you're no longer a "star," you may find it very hard to adjust your self-concept.

*Another reaction to the "bad-me" image might be labelled *creative incompetence*. Here, the individual develops a way of using a negative quality to his or her advantage. An example of this is the man who believes he has no mechanical ability, and points to this every time some repairs need to be done around the home.

Will the Real Patty Hearst Please Stand Up?
Some True-Life and Experimental Evidence
on the Changing Self

I was led [blindfolded] up some stairs, down some hallways. . . .We came to a stop and . . . I
could sense that they were opening some kind of door. A stale, dirty smell assaulted my
nose. . . .I remembered in a flash the news story of a girl who had been kidnapped and buried
in a box for days, with only an air pump keeping her alive.

I don't know how long I fought. Probably for not more than a few seconds, but it seemed
like forever before I was subdued. Then they slammed the door shut. I groped around and
found that it was a closet, a padded, empty closet. (Hearst & Moscow, 1982, pp. 46, 59)

Thus began the extraordinary saga of newspaper heiress Patricia Hearst. Wealthy and privi-
leged, Hearst had led a sheltered life until she was kidnapped by the radical Symbionese Liberation Army in February, 1974. By the time of her capture in September, 1975, Hearst had
become Tania, a self-avowed soldier of the SLA who had declared the ruling class, including
her own family, to be "clowns" and "pigs." She was wanted for possession of firearms and for
armed robbery.

Hearst's case offers a remarkable illustration that people's self-concepts can change radically under some extraordinary situations. (Her case is no less remarkable when we consider
that less than 7 years later, at the time of her book's publication, she had reverted to a peace-
ful, secure life—this time as a new mother.) From both her own account and those of others
who witnessed her kidnapping and the early months of her capture, she was subjected to
classic brainwashing techniques, remaining blindfolded for weeks in a solitude that was interrupted only by propaganda lectures from her captors.

Would most people react as Patty did, and undergo a change in personality under these
circumstances? We can't provide a definite answer, but we can offer some experimental evidence. The findings of a classic "mock prison" experiment (Zimbardo et al., 1973) have been
cited often as evidence that severe conditions can radically alter people. in this experiment,
student volunteers were chosen to play the role of either guard or inmate. The situation was
made as realistic as possible: "prisoners" were brought to the mock prison in a police car,
fingerprinted, and treated as any prisoners would be. The "guards" were instructed to maintain
order. They were told that they were the law, and they had rigid rules to enforce. For instance,
prisoners were allowed to address each other by their numbers only, and they were not permitted to visit the toilet facilities without special permission.

The experiment was supposed to last for two weeks, but it had to be abandoned after
one. The reason: Even though the subjects knew they were participating in an experiment, the
situation had become too real. Behavior patterns that had been established over a lifetime suddenly changed. The guards viewed the prisoners as less than human, flaunting their authority in

In the same way, it may be difficult to up-
grade your self-image. What if you've always
known that you're not very artistic? In all the years
of grade school and high school, you never won a
prize in an art competition and your teachers
never had a word of praise for your pictures.

When you take a class in college, however, your
teacher tells you that you have tremendous creative talent. "Who, me?" may be your reaction.
"You must be mistaken."

We don't always believe these new evaluations, especially if they are contrary to the self-

Patty Hearst, and Patty Hearst.

a highly aggressive fashion. The prisoners thought only of escape, or of influencing the guards to give them small privileges. The emotional cost was great: some of the prisoners developed psychosomatic problems and began suffering from anxiety and depression, while some of the guards became abusive.

After a lifetime of building an identity, most of us feel reasonably secure in our self-concepts. However, both the Zimbardo experiment and the Hearst case raise disturbing questions. Under severe circumstances, how many of us would change our own ground rules of conduct? It is impossible to answer that question in the abstract. Judging from the evidence, though, it's hard not to conclude that the "self" may not be as immutable as we often assume it is.

concept we've developed over a lifetime. In fact, we often dismiss them. The greater the disparity between your self-concept and the new evaluation, the more likely we are to reject the new information—*unless* it comes from a reliable source. As a general rule, you will be more likely to reassess your self-concept if the source of the new opinion is credible. In order to be credible, that source must be trustworthy and have a degree of expertise (Hovland et al., 1953).

If we accept this point of view, it can have some practical implications for changing someone else's self-concept. Assuming that you want to give someone a more positive self-image, it is best to take a two-pronged approach. First, the person must be led to show a different behavior than in the past, so that your praise won't sound like idle flattery. A child who has trouble finishing assignments in class can be given very short, easy-to-complete projects to help her realize that she *can* get her work done. Secondly, compliments (or criticisms) that run counter to the self-image should be moderate if they are to have any effect. Moderate praise and criticisms cause less anxiety; thus, the individual is less likely to respond by using defense mechanisms.

Other theorists have expressed views about the development of the self-concept that are similar to that of Sullivan. Sociologist Charles Cooley (1902) also believed that we see ourselves in the manner that others see us; and he coined the term **looking glass self** to describe this phenomenon. Another sociologist, George Herbert Mead (1934), went a step further and expanded Cooley's ideas by including values and attitudes that we get from others in the environment. The totality of the self-concept, according to Mead, is determined by the expectations, appraisals, and attitudes of others that we internalize.

It's hard to deny that people's self-concepts reflect the evaluations of others. However, Sullivan's theory has been questioned by other psychologists. Is the development of the self-concept really such a passive process? Don't our own skills, feelings, and competencies play a role in what we think about ourselves?

The Experiencing Self   Suppose you're 25 years old and you've always thought of yourself as fairly clumsy and unathletic. Lately, though, you have

---

Looking glass self   The way in which people see themselves through the behaviors and reactions of others.

---

developed an interest in running: you find that it gives you a welcome change of pace each day, and it helps keep your weight down. After a few months, you find that you're spending more and more time at it. You enter a race, and do well; and soon you enter competitions regularly. If you accept your objective experience, you no longer think of yourself as clumsy and awkward. Instead, you're an athlete.

People often learn about themselves in an active process of self-discovery that is different from the ones described by Sullivan or Cooley. This kind of process is emphasized by Carl Rogers (1951), who sees the development of the self-concept as an active process rather than a passive reflection. Rogers does not deny that we internalize many of the views of others. But he sees this process as an active evaluation, by which we also learn directly from our own experiences.

Rogers would agree with Sullivan that people find it hard to accept messages that are inconsistent with their self-concept. But Rogers recognizes that these messages may be internal as well as external. For instance, if you think of yourself as a calm, even-tempered person, you may find it hard to admit how angry you are at the cute 3-year-old who just spilled soda all over the back seat of your car. You might deny these feelings, or even project them onto someone else (the child's parents, perhaps, or even the manufacturer—for making the stuff so darn sticky!).

Rogers also recognizes that the process by which we form our own opinions and values involves both personal experience and the views of others. That is, we don't always accept what others tell us; and if someone else's views are forced upon you, problems may result.

For instance, suppose that, as a child, you simply detested your cousin. Everything about her, from her ignorance to her whiny behavior, sets your teeth on edge; and whenever she came to visit, you tried your best to be otherwise occupied. Your parents refused to understand, reacting by telling you that you had to love your family, that your cousin was really a nice girl, and that anyway, it was your duty to be a good host. Instead of respecting your point of view, they punished you for expressing it.

Under such circumstances, a person is likely to go through some sort of change. If you had thought of yourself as a basically good person, your parents' strong reaction may have persuaded you that you weren't as good as you thought. Or, you may have decided that you must have been wrong about your cousin. If your parents thought she was wonderful, maybe she wasn't so bad after all. Either way, you were likely to feel confused and lost, out of touch with your own feelings. If you went the first route, you probably ended up feeling guilty; if you went the second route, you were denying feelings that were truly your own, and this cover-up probably caused you anxiety.

While Rogers recognizes that this problem can occur, he offers a practical way of avoiding it. Parents might accept their children's negative feelings, but at the same time reason with the children and show them how their behaviors might affect others. To some extent, this approach was adopted by a leading child psychologist of the late 60s and early 70s, Haim Ginott (1965). Ginott argued that *behaviors* are separate from *feelings*, and that parents can deal with one without necessarily trying to change the other. For instance, your parents might have told you that you had a right to your own opinions about your cousin—but that you still had to be polite to her. In other words, aggressive feelings should be voiced and accepted, but hostile acts need to be controlled.

As you have seen, Rogers emphasizes each person's active role in determining his or her own self-concept, stressing the importance of being aware of one's own feelings. Yet in everyday life, we are not necessarily honest in our dealings with others. We may sometimes project an image to others and we may act, feel, and think more in relationship to our roles than to our selves. We'll look next at these images, and at the way they help to shape our self-concepts.

Masks and Ideals: Their Role in Who You Are

Around election time we are bombarded by commercials seeking to communicate something about each candidate to the electorate. We are never quite certain how much of these messages we can believe, because professional public relations people continue to create images for candidates. Millions of dollars are spent on campaign commercials in which you are treated to a glimpse of the candidate in action. She may want you to see her as dynamic, so you are presented with a scene of her demanding justice. Another candidate may want to be seen as the friend of the working person, so the film clip shows him shaking hands with construction workers and vowing more money for building projects.

You and Your Persona

Few of us will ever have professional image makers working for us, but we all send out messages that convey an image to others. The man in the conservative gray suit carrying his heavy briefcase is saying something about himself by his appearance; so is the student with chronically rumpled shirts and torn blue jeans.

Each of us projects a special image to the world, through the way we dress, our facial expressions, our manner of speaking, and our interpersonal actions, among other means. This mask we show others is called a **persona** (Campbell, 1973). The persona is a person's public self. It is an attempt to cover up feelings to some extent, and to project the image we feel will influence others. Most people present an image that changes little from day to day, keeping the real

Persona A person's "public self"; the image we project to others.

A candidate projecting an image. Most of us don't have professional image-makers working for us, but we all send out messages that convey an image to others.

self for those with whom they are more intimate. In this sense, the persona serves a valuable social function. Imagine how you would feel if your psychology teacher moped through the class on days he was in a bad mood, and jumped around excitedly whenever he felt cheerful. Before long, you'd probably resent his inconsistencies, and wish he'd stick to business.

While the persona serves a purpose, it can also get in the way if it's taken too seriously. Occasionally, people identify so closely with their image that they lose touch with their inner feelings.

If you become too wrapped up in being a perpetually efficient, professional rising star at the office, it can interfere disastrously with your family life at home, for instance. It may also lead to personal confusion as you become alienated from your inner feelings. Another problem may occur if you use your persona as a protective mask. The teacher who is afraid to admit she doesn't know everything, or the parent who can't let his child know that he's made a mistake, often have problems in showing themselves even in situations where there's no longer a need for such an act. Taking off the mask becomes more difficult as the individual identifies more closely with the image.

Think of your own image for a minute. Are you aware of your persona? Try to think of situations in which you hide behind a mask or try to project an image to others. Do you use your public self when it isn't necessary? What would happen if you gave up the mask in some of these situations?

A Second Kind of "Mask": The Cult Phenomenon

A related process should be mentioned as we talk about forming self-identities through images, and that is what Erich Fromm calls *escape from freedom* (1965). In his book by that name, he argues that the challenge of forging our own identities is a frightening one—so frightening that some people try to escape from it. Many of us yearn for someone else to tell us what to do, give us direction, and take the decision-making responsibility off of our shoulders. We look for the strong leader, and we often worship power although we may also fear it. We are willing to give up our freedom, which has isolated us to some extent from others, and become part of a larger, conforming body.

Some individuals do indeed give up this freedom. The cult phenomenon may be one example of this. One way to avoid the difficult decisions involved in figuring out who we are, what goals we want in life, and so forth, is to completely identify with a cause and allow its dictates or its leadership

A mass wedding of Sun Yung Moon's Unification Church on July 1, 1982 in New York's Madison Square Garden saw 2,075 couples wed. How would a psychologist explain this phenomenon?

to provide all the answers for us. In the past few decades, some of the most radical of these cults have hit the headlines: Charles Manson's band of followers and Jim Jones' People's Church, whose members committed mass suicide a few years back in Guyana, are two of the most notorious examples.

These groups were exceptional in the degree to which their followers gave up responsibility for their own actions; but their characteristics are broadly typical of fanatic or radical political or religious groups. These groups are usually much stricter than the environment of the person's original family. Thus, most cults are very dogmatic and depend a great deal on the reinforcements of other group members. Many have charismatic leaders who rule with an iron hand. They provide an identity for their members, who no longer need to make their own decisions. This total submergence of the individual's identity into the group short-circuits the identity process, forming another mask to hide behind.

Virtually all of us belong to some group, of course, and our sense of belonging plays a part in our self-concept. Church membership, or belonging in a family, school, sports club, and so forth, can be considered to represent a related sense of security to that offered by cult membership. The difference—and it is a significant one—is that there isn't a total submergence of identity in these ordinary social institutions.* There is, however, a sense of support, belonging, and identification with group ideals or goals.

Both the persona and group identification, then, affect the self-concept and are, in turn, affected by the self-concept. A third important element is also significant. That is the ideal self: the person you would like to be.

You and Your Ideal Self

Meet Walter Mitty, the famous hero of James Thurber's short story,[†] who imagines he's commanding an 8-engined navy hydroplane while he's driving his wife to her hairdresser appointment ("Not so fast, [dear]! . . . What on earth are you driving so fast for?"); who imagines he's a world-famous surgeon performing a rare operation for "obstreosis of the ductal tract"(!) as

he parks his car in a public lot ("Back it up, Mac! Look out for that Buick!"); who can't take a drag on a cigarette while he stands waiting for his wife to finish her errands without transforming himself into a proud, undaunted hero facing the firing squad.

There is probably at least a little bit of Walter Mitty in each of us. Although most of us lead a somewhat more restrained fantasy life, we have our own ideals of the kind of person we would like to be. You may wish you were an A-student, or that you were always the life of the party, or that you had the kind of personality that made people immediately stop, take notice, and listen to what you had to say with respect.

This image of who we would like to be is often called the **ideal self,** while the actual perception of ourselves is called the **real self**. In and of itself, the ideal self can be a positive force providing us with standards and goals. For instance, if your ideal self is honest in the face of dishonesty, it may serve to raise your standards of conduct, and thus become a positive force. Yet people's ideal selves are often unrealistic and perfectionistic, and this can lead to problems. If your ideal self is never angry, you'll find that it's impossible to live up to this standard. If your ideal self manages the home in a neat and organized fashion, you'll be disappointed and anxious if your work, parenting, and schooling activities take up so much time that you can't keep the house in order. While your ideal self *can* give you some direction, then, it can also be rigid and unforgiving.

Most psychologists are well aware of the negative consequences that result when your ideal self and your real self are too far apart. People whose ideal selves are not so impossible seem to be more comfortable with themselves (Burns, 1979). There is much experimental evidence demonstrating the importance of self-acceptance. Brophy (1959) found that people were happier in their jobs if the difference between their real and ideal selves wasn't too great. Turner and Vanderlippe (1958) found that college students whose ideal selves were close to their real selves were likely to participate in extracurricular activities

*As you might expect, there comes a point where it is difficult to draw the line. For instance, military groups are not considered to be "fringe" organizations, but at times of war they may inspire members to at least momentarily submerge their own values and ideals. A much-publicized example from the Vietnam War was the My Lai massacre, in which a number of American soldiers opened fire on the villagers of My Lai, indiscriminately killing both adults and children. Would any of these Americans have committed such an act on his own, under other circumstances?

[†] "The Secret Life of Walter Mitty," James Thurber, in *The Greatest American Short Stories* (New York: McGraw-Hill, 1953), pp. 302–307.

> **Ideal self** The image people have of what they would like to be.
>
> **Real self** The way in which an individual perceives himself or herself at a particular point in time.

Evaluating Your Ideal Self

Complete the statements below by listing five personal goals in whatever order they come to mind:

1. I would like to be _____

2. I would like to be _____

3. I would like to be _____

4. I would like to be _____

5. I would like to be _____

Now read through your statements, and try to identify those areas in which your real and ideal self most closely match. In which areas are they farthest apart? In general, we feel the most self-acceptance when our ideals are not unrealistic or impossible. Thus, one step toward feeling happy with your self-concept may be to adjust your ideals to make them more realistic. If your ideals are reasonable, on the other hand, then some change of behavior on your part may be necessary.

and to have higher scholastic averages. They were also given higher interpersonal ratings by other students, and were better adjusted according to a standardized psychological inventory. It would seem that the closer a person comes to his or her ideal, the higher will be that person's evaluations by both their self and their peers.

Self-acceptance

According to the psychological literature, self-acceptance is a highly desirable quality. Accepting ourselves leads to less anxiety, and it also leads to greater tolerance for others. This was supported by Suinn (1961), who found a relationship between self-acceptance and accepting others. It was also shown by Medinnus and Curtis (1963), who discovered a relationship between a mother's accepting herself and her acceptance of her own children.

This isn't to say that complete self-acceptance is the same as complete fulfillment and adjustment. The person who leans back and sighs "I've arrived—I'm perfect just the way I am!" is ducking reality just as surely as Walter Mitty was. If we don't recognize any areas in which we'd like to improve ourselves, we won't have any motivation to keep on learning and growing.

Yet there is much to say for a good fit between your ideal and real selves. A great deal depends upon whether your ideal self is reasonable. Some ideals can be impossible, and trying to live up to them leads to inevitable unhappiness. However, if your ideal self is an attainable goal toward which you can strive, it can function as a motivating force in your life. The boxed exercise *Evaluating Your Ideal Self* provides you with a way of identifying those areas in which your real and ideal selves most closely match, and it may help you to readjust your sights—if need be— to a more helpful level.

Changing Your Own Self-concept

By now you should have a better understanding of your self-concept, how it has been shaped, and what you like and dislike about it than you had when you started reading this chapter. None of us is completely happy with ourselves as we are; and we've made a few suggestions here and there in this chapter that may help you to change those elements of your self-concept that you dislike. In these closing paragraphs, we'll try to present some more coherent guidelines.

First, in order to change your self-concept you must identify the areas that cause you the most difficulty. Is it your physical self? Your academic or vocational self? Your way of getting along with other people? These different aspects of your self are certainly interrelated, but they are not identical. A problem with your physical self—feeling you are unattractive, for example—may prevent you from interacting effectively with others, but it is important to identify which problem is the main one.

Second, look at the disparity between your real and your ideal self, and consider some tough questions. Are you trying to live up to someone else's ideals? Where is the disparity? Are your expectations for yourself unreasonable? If, after analyzing the situation, you find your ideal self is too perfectionistic, try the technique of refutation discussed in Chapter 6. If your ideal self is a realistic goal, try to approach it! Some of the behavioral and cognitive techniques discussed previously (see, for instance, Chapter 2's box *A Weight Program That Works*) can be helpful in altering your behavior or planning some effective strategy.

This second step may be difficult if you aren't fully aware of your real self. According to Sidney Jourard (1959), when we identify too closely with our roles or images, we run the risk of losing contact with ourselves. How can you evaluate yourself accurately? One way is through some of the introspective ("looking inward") exercises described in this chapter. Another is to talk with close friends or family members. They know you well, and you have disclosed your feelings to them. A third way of understanding yourself is through understanding others. Developing empathy, a sensitivity to others' feelings and motivations, takes practice, but it is rewarding. Not only does it bring you closer to others, but it can make you more attuned to your own feelings and behaviors.

A *third*, final step is to act in accordance with your feelings. This last point may require a little explanation. Students often wonder if it means telling your date that he or she looks awful tonight, or bursting into tears because a friend has hurt your feelings. This is not necessarily what is meant by reacting honestly. You can behave according to your feelings without being brutal or overemotional, just as we saw in Chapter 7 that you can be assertive without being aggressive. For instance, you can decide whether or not a comment needs to be made about your date's appearance (if it does, it can be phrased as a polite suggestion). And you can politely tell a friend that your feelings have been hurt, without creating a scene. Some theorists have argued that the consequences of being honest are far more positive than those that result from hiding or disguising your feelings. Indeed, others have a better understanding of how you feel if you take the time to explain yourself; and they will be more likely to share your feelings if they understand you.

One last word on the self-concept is in order. Often, people dwell on those parts of the self that they consider their weakest points. They may become obsessed with some problem, failing to see anything good within themselves. It is important that we emphasize our good points as well as the parts of ourselves we don't like. Liking and accepting ourselves make it easier to like and accept others; when we are cynical and harshly self-critical, we tend to be more critical of others. A positive self-concept and a sense of identity are important if we are to make personally meaningful choices. It is important to be able to say, as did the little girl at the beginning of this chapter, "I like me."

Summary

1. The picture we hold of ourselves is called the self-concept.

2. The self-concept affects the way in which people present themselves in everyday life, as well as their interactions with others. People with poor self-concepts usually generalize failure in one facet of their lives, so that they are discouraged about their total selves. People with positive self-concepts can isolate failures and accept success.

3. Our self-concepts are usually neither totally positive nor totally negative. Instead, they are composed of conflicting and opposing feelings, beliefs, and traits that are partly determined by the current situation. However, there is also some degree of consistency in the self.

4. Four elements of the self are discussed in this chapter: the physical self, social roles, the personality, and the abstract self.

5. Both the rate of physical development and physical attributes themselves can affect the self-concept. Early-developing teenagers, both boys and girls, tend to see themselves differently than do late developers. The physical self can have a profound effect on the self-concept in cases where an accident or illness causes a disability, especially if it interferes with an important aspect of functioning.

6. Nixon sees five stages in the development of self-awareness. Physical awareness occurs in infancy; emotional awareness between ages $2\frac{1}{2}$–5; social awareness during the school years; sexual awareness during early adolescence; and cognitive awareness during middle adolescence (ages 15–16).

7. Psychologists disagree about how the self-concept is shaped. Sullivan believed that it arises from the evaluations we receive from others throughout our lives. Basically positive evaluations lead to a "good-me" image, while negative judgments lead to a "bad-me" image. In contrast, Rogers sees the development of the self as a more active process involving subjective experience and interactions. Awareness of one's feelings is very important.

8. The mask one wears in public is called the *persona*. An individual who fully identifies with the persona may lose contact with his or her real self. Some individuals may also lose touch with their selves by joining cults, as they avoid the challenge of making their own decisions about goals and values.

9. The ideal self is who you would like to be. When the ideal self and real self approach one another, self-acceptance is increased. A reasonable ideal self may spur an individual to action, while ideals that are too perfect may be a source of discouragement and frustration.

10. Most psychologists consider one's identity as a coherent whole that is rather consistent. However, Gergen argues that a person's sense of self is flexible and situationally determined.

11. It is possible to act in a manner consistent with your true feelings without hurting other people. You may become more aware of your real self through introspection, self-disclosure, and empathy with others.

12. People tend to dwell on the parts of their selves that are weakest. It is important to emphasize the positive aspects of the self as well.

Key Terms and Concepts

self-concept	looking glass self
self-esteem	persona
identity	real self
"good-me, bad-me"	ideal self

Dr. John R. Coleman, president of Haverford College, took an unusual sabbatical during the early months of 1973. He worked at menial jobs. In one instance, he was fired as a porter-dishwasher. "I'd never been fired and I'd never been unemployed. For three days I walked the streets. Though I had a bank account, though my children's tuition was paid, though I

Work and Leisure

had a salary and a job waiting for me back in Haverford, I was demoralized. I had an inkling of how professionals my age feel when they lose their job and their confidence begins to sink." (*New York Times*, June 10, 1973)*

*From Studs Terkel, *Working* (New York: Pantheon, 1974), p. xviii. Reprinted by permission of Random House, Inc.

According to the popular song, "workin' 9 to 5" is just a way of "tryin' to make a living," but Dr. Coleman's story illustrates another perspective. For most of us, there is far more to work than simply bringing home paychecks. Work dominates our thinking and our daily existence. It may bring us joy and prestige, or boredom and frustration; and whichever reaction it brings, it will affect the way we feel not just from 9 to 5 but throughout our waking—perhaps even our sleeping—hours.

This chapter is about work: what it means to us; how we choose vocations and what factors should be considered in making a job decision; how women's and men's vocational patterns differ and how they are changing; and how leisure time acts as a balance for working hours. These elements are all important to Part IV's discussions of self-concept and esteem. Not only is a great proportion of our lives spent working (one estimate sees the average man as working 80,000 hours or about 30 percent of his total life [Miller, 1964]); but work also affects our self-concepts and our very identities (Kennedy, 1978). In the pages that follow, we'll see how this is so.

Some Perspectives on Work

"What do you want to be when you grow up?"

Children take it for granted that adults work. Adults do, too. We expect to spend most of our hours during the most productive years of our lives at work—and we expect other adults to do the same. During those years, many people feel their jobs (or careers—there is a distinction, as the box *Jobs vs. Careers* points out) take up so much of their time and energy that there's little left for anything else in their lives.

For such an important part of our lives, it is worth exploring some facts about work and establishing a sense of perspective before we go on. We'll look below at the functions of work, at people's attitudes about work, and at changing job markets today.

Work Serves Many Functions

Work fulfills many functions. The most obvious of these is the satisfaction of material needs. Some kinds of work provide far more financial reward than do others. A financier or an attorney earns a different salary than does a factory worker or a gardener. The degree to which work satisfies these needs affects many other areas of life—where you live, where you go on vacation, what schools your children attend, even what kind of recognition and respect you have in your community.

While financial reward is usually an important reason for working, work may also provide personal satisfaction. The individual with a need to help others may find fulfillment in a job as a physical therapist; the person with a need to create may be happy as an artist. Some psychologists argue that there may even be an element of sublimation (the defense mechanism discussed in Chapter 6) in work. According to Brill (1949), the butcher is finding an outlet for a desire to cut, while the police officer and drill sergeant have an inner need to become authority figures. While many authorities might not go this far, it is clear that work provides a means of satisfying deep personal needs.

Work does not always bring very much financial reward or personal satisfaction, however. For many people, work is seen simply as a way of scraping together a living. It may even be a source of frustration and resentment. But even in these cases, work may provide some basic functions as it satisfies people's needs to be occupied, have status, be independent, and feel worthwhile.

Finally, work fulfills an important function for society. It provides an occupational structure

Jobs vs. Careers

Many laypersons use the terms "job" and "career" interchangeably, but the two are not the same. According to Whitely and Resnikoff (1972), a **career** is a sequence of occupations, jobs, and positions that are occupied during the course of a person's working life. A career implies a number of pathways along which one can move, but these pathways all tend to follow an upward direction, toward greater responsibility and increased income. In other words, a career can be seen as a series of vertical steps that follow one another.

Like a career, a **job** provides work. But the similarity ends there, for a job offers little hope of advancement. While a management trainee may aspire to become an assistant manager, then a manager, and then perhaps a district supervisor and regional manager, there is no such orderly sequence of steps toward which the factory assembler can aim.

---

that makes a tremendous range of goods and services available to its members. Life would certainly be different if we all had to build our own houses, grow our own food, make our clothing, and construct and repair our own cars! Work is a social necessity, then, for each person's specialized skills contribute to the support structure upon which we all depend.

Because work is so important to society, most of us are socialized according to the **work ethic**— the doctrine that hard work, thrift, and productivity are the measure of a person's worth. This doctrine has a profound effect upon our attitudes

about work, as Chapter 16 discusses. Yet the traditional work ethic seems to be declining as people put new emphasis on both job satisfaction and leisure-time fulfillment. How does this changing outlook affect our own perspectives about work?

Changing Attitudes about Work

The work ethic has underscored many traditional values in our society. Examples are the ideas that money and status are measures of achievement; that employees owe loyalty to the employer; and that as long as a job is decent and provides a living, it is sufficient. The evidence indicates that some of these values are giving way, however, and that new values and attitudes are taking their place (Albanese & Van Fleet, 1983).

An Emphasis on Leisure　One change is a greater emphasis on personal goals and satisfactions that people can find outside their jobs (Yankelovich, 1978). Hobbies, athletic training, reading, community participation, and many other leisure activities are examples of some of the ways in which

> **Career**　A sequence of occupations, jobs, and positions in an individual's working life. Unlike a job, career pathways usually involve the possibility of upward mobility.
>
> **Job**　Work that a person performs with income as a primary purpose. A job is distinguished from a *career:* the latter term implies a sequence of vocational steps in an upward direction.
>
> **Work ethic**　A group of values emphasizing the importance of hard work, achievement through one's own efforts, and success.

What's my line? For many people, work is not just a way of making a living, but an integral part of the self-concept.

people fulfill needs during their hours away from work. The modern interest in the "pursuit of leisure" is actually fairly recent in our history—primarily because leisure time itself is quite recent. The 12-hour workday and 6-day work week may be exceptional today, but only 50 years ago it was the rule. Today, the average work week is about 39 hours, as opposed to 60 hours in 1870 (Havighurst, 1982). Our increasing emphasis on leisure today doesn't mean that the modern worker is uninterested in working hard, but rather that people want more of a balance between work and leisure. We'll explore this topic more at the end of this chapter.

Highly repetitious jobs such as this are unlikely to produce a sense of satisfaction and achievement.

Table 13.1   Common Sources of Job Satisfaction and Dissatisfaction

Job Satisfaction	Job Dissatisfaction
Recognition and appreciation	Company procedures
Responsibility	Supervision
Feelings of achievement	Salary
	Working conditions

Source: Adapted from Herzberg et al., 1959.

Increasing Importance of Satisfaction   A third shift in attitudes about work is a greater demand for jobs that are interesting. In the past, money and prestige were sufficient to allow a person to overlook the negative, boring aspects of a job. Today, though, these rewards may not be enough. Many people were shocked in 1962 when automobile assemblers struck over boredom on the job. Their plant was brand new, and the workers were well paid. The repetitive, non-meaningful, mechanical aspects of their jobs were their chief complaints. Workers who are uninterested in their jobs or do not feel they are doing anything meaningful are likely to become dissatisfied no matter what the pay. Table 13.1 outlines the most common sources of job satisfaction and dissatisfaction. It's interesting that the sources of satisfaction tend to be intrinsic (related to the worker's sense of worth), while sources of dissatisfaction are more related to external factors (Wernimont, 1966).

Actually, most workers today are satisfied with their jobs (Quinn, et al., 1973). According to most studies performed over the last two or three decades, the percentage of dissatisfied workers is only about 10 percent. This doesn't mean that most workers have no complaints about their jobs, however. Organizational problems are a common complaint, even among people who enjoy their work; and poor relationships with supervisors is another (Fournet, et al., 1966). Poor management is one problem that psychologists have studied in

Declining Company Loyalty   Another change in attitudes is a decline in company loyalty (Renwick & Lawler, 1978). Most workers today feel little commitment or responsibility toward their employer. If they are dissatisfied with a job, there is no feeling that they owe anything to the company, even if they have been with it for many years or undergone extensive training at the company's expense. They seek new pastures.

Waiting for the Training to "Take"

Hundreds of major industrial firms around the country have instituted **human relations training programs** in an effort to help managers become more effective. These programs have involved considerable time, money, and effort. How effective are they? Many studies have sought to find out, but they have suffered from technical problems. Some have used measures that are not meaningful within the factory or organizational framework, while others have found no improvement.

This lack of clear findings was puzzling, until a study by Herbert Hand and John Slocum developed a slightly different approach. This study set out to measure the effect of a human relations training program on managerial attitudes and performance. The subjects were 21 line and staff managers from a steel plant in Central Pennsylvania. (Another 21 received no training, acting as a control group.) The program consisted of 18 weeks of weekly meetings, arranged in three phases. Phase I consisted of a group discussion of various types of leadership and managerial styles. Phase 2 involved group exercises, with both individual and group feedback. Phase 3 involved an exposure to various theories of motivation, including that of Abraham Maslow.

The managers were measured on their change of attitude (especially their self-awareness and sensitivity to others), as well as leadership style and initiation of structure. Their actual behavior on the job was also rated. The results, at first, were not impressive. An evaluation performed 90 days after the conclusion of the training program failed to show any significant changes in either attitude or behavior.

Had this study used the same approach as previous research, it would have stopped here, concluding that the training program was ineffective. However, Hand and Slocum continued their investigation, conducting a second round of testing after 18 months. This follow-up study found significant change. "Graduates" of the program were significantly more aware of themselves and were more sensitive to others. Their subordinates said they had established better rapport and communication with them. These subjects also attained superior scores on a test that measured managerial behavior. Trainees also showed improvement in a number of other areas, including initiation of structure. There seems no doubt that both attitude and behavior had improved over the long term. (The control group also changed over the long term, but in the opposite direction. There were rated as less sensitive and less effective—changes that may have been related to their confusion about what was happening around them.)

These findings seem to indicate that human relations training can improve both the attitudes and the performance of managers. They also present a practical lesson concerning time. This study shows that change sometimes takes time, more time than is often allotted by researchers. To evaluate the true effects of human relations training programs, it seems that investigators must wait, perhaps for as long as 18 months or two years, to give the training a chance to "take."

Source: Hand & Slocum, 1972.

recent years, and many companies have instituted human relations training programs to improve management attitudes and performance. The box *Waiting for the Training to "Take"* describes the interesting outcome of one of these programs.

Human relations training programs A general term used to describe seminars in which people learn to deal more effectively with others in an organizational or industrial setting.

In all, people's attitudes toward their jobs are different than they were in the past, and we can conclude that the "work ethic" has indeed changed. Today, many people have a broader attitude toward work as they place more emphasis on leisure-time satisfactions. People are also less likely to feel loyalty to one particular employer. And finally, job satisfaction has grown more important—and in response, some employers have instituted programs to increase management's sensitivity.

The changes we've just described show one important facet of the world of work, and understanding these changes provides us with a sense of perspective. Another area of change has a great deal of practical significance: the shifting job market. We'll turn next to that topic.

Changes in the Job Market

What do these six occupations have in common: computer systems analyst, doctor, health service administrator, geologist, engineer, dentist?

Now, what do these six occupations have in common: teacher, military officer, newspaper reporter, public relations manager, lawyer, architect?

According to a *Money* magazine survey (1980), the first six occupations are expected to grow substantially during the eighties, while the second six careers have less rosy futures (see Table 13.2). For a variety of reasons, the careers in this last group are victims of too little demand and too much supply in a changing job market.

Today, it is not enough to simply graduate from college with a skill. A person who is well qualified to be an architect may be unable to find a suitable position; a lawyer fresh out of law school may be disappointed in his or her starting salary. This presents a sharp contrast to the past, when specific training in almost any professional field meant guaranteed employment. A college graduate who wanted to be a teacher would have been virtually assured success in finding a job during the late sixties, but such jobs are scarce now.

These changes in demand represent but one facet of a broad shift in the job market. A second trend involves technological change. In general, job opportunities for unskilled jobs are decreasing, while an increasing proportion of jobs require specific training. This doesn't mean that any job with training will be in demand. As we've just seen, certain fields seem to be on the decline. And in addition, as Alvin Toffler argues in his book *Future Shock* (1970), training may not be enough to ensure employment. Technological changes are occurring so rapidly that the skills required by many jobs are constantly changing. Without retraining, even highly trained workers may find themselves with obsolete skills. Medical doctors are now required in certain states to take periodic refresher courses; and certainly, fast-moving fields such as computer technology require virtually constant updating.

In addition to changes in demand and technological change, a third important shift in the job market is organizational change. These changes are affecting established fields as well as new fields. Many job titles did not exist before the present individual occupied the position. Positions seem to be created overnight; and they disappear just as suddenly. Toffler, for instance, argued that the occupation of flight engineer hit its peak and began to die out within a span of 15 years. Sudden organizational changes like these are now a fact of life, and they add both insecurity and a transitory nature to the world of work.

In the face of these changes in the work environment, it's not hard to understand why many people feel confused and frustrated about choosing a vocation. Yet in many ways, our options are already limited by a number of personal factors such as experience, interest, and skills. We'll look next at some of the factors that affect vocational choices.

Table 13.2   Outlooks for Selected Occupations

Occupation (1978 Employment)	Estimated Growth in Jobs to 1990	Prospects for Job Seekers	Starting Salary	Mid-career Salary
The Sunniest				
Computer systems analyst (182,000)	37%	Excellent	$16,500	$34,000
Doctor (405,000)	38%	Good	$45,000	$82,000
Health service administrator (180,000)	57%	Good	$18,000	$37,500
Geologist (31,000)	36%	Good	$17,600	$31,000
Engineer (1,136,000)	27%	Good	$19,200	$35,000
Dentist (120,000)	29%	Good	$27,000	$53,000
The Variables				
Dietitian (35,000)	43%	Good	$14,000	$25,000
Economist (130,000)	39%	Good	$14,500	$45,000
Banker (330,000)	55%	Good	$12,500	$27,000
Accountant (985,000)	29%	Good	$14,000	$31,000
Personnel administrator (405,000)	17%	Good	$12,500	$29,500
Physicist (44,000)	9%	Good	$16,000	$30,400
The Cloudiest				
Teacher (2,409,000)	2%	Poor	$11,000	$17,000
Military officer (272,530)	1%	Good	$10,000	$22,000
Newspaper reporter (45,000)	20%	Poor	$12,500	$25,000
Public relations manager (131,000)	24%	Poor	$12,000	$32,000
Lawyer (487,000)	25%	Poor	$18,000	$50,000
Architect (54,000)	43%	Poor	$12,000	$28,700

Source: Reprinted from *Money* magazine, May, 1980, p.76, by special permission. © 1980, Time Inc. All rights reserved.

Factors Affecting Vocational Choice

We still don't completely understand all the factors that affect people's job decisions. However, it's clear that certain people are drawn to certain occupations. It's also clear that some other people seem not to be able to make up their minds what to do. We'll look at a few theories that may help to explain these differences, then at some personal factors that narrow people's choices about jobs.

What Determines Job Choice? Three Theories

Many theories have tried to explain why some people are drawn to certain occupations, and three in particular are worth noting here. One centers on personality types, another on development, and a third on needs.

Holland's theory matches the individual's personality and problem-solving orientation to six different work environments (Holland, 1973). Table 13.3 outlines these six orientations: the *investigative,* the *social,* the *conventional,* the *artistic,* the *enterprising,* and the *realistic;* and one common

Super's theory of vocational development Donald Super's theory views occupational choice in terms of the totality of an individual's experiences with the world of work, beginning in early childhood and continuing throughout life.

Vocational maturity A term coined by Donald Super, referring to an individual's particular level of vocational development.

vocational interest measurement known as the Strong-Campbell Interest Blank uses these six categories. If you look at the table and consider your own vocational orientation, remember that not everyone fits into only one category. Many people may see themselves as fitting into two or even three categories.

Not all theories see vocational choice in terms of matching personality to occupational group. A second theory, Donald Super's **theory of vocational development** sees vocational choice as a developmental process beginning in early childhood and continuing throughout life. The child explores the occupational world through play and fantasy. Thus, the 6-year-old playing firefighter is, in effect, involved in vocational development at a very low level. The adolescent between ages 14–18 becomes aware of the need for self-evaluation, in the effort to discover strengths and weaknesses that will narrow his or her options. By ages 18–21, young adults can usually tell which field they want to enter.

Super evaluates people's development along these stages through the concept of **vocational maturity**—the congruence between an individual's actual vocational behavior and the expected vocational behavior at that age (Osipow, 1968, p. 123). For example, we would expect the average 12-year-old to be concerned with getting to know his or her own abilities and strengths, and that the average 20-year-old would be well on the way toward making a vocational decision. In his landmark study, Super found that the level of vocational maturity attained by most 9th-grade boys strongly suggested that they were not yet ready, in terms of knowledge and experience, to make sound career choices. We might conclude from this that early decision making is probably *not* in the best interests of most young teens.

While Holland sees vocational choice in terms of personality orientation and Super takes a developmental perspective, a third theory approaches vocational decisions from still a different perspective. Roe (1957) views occupational choice

Table 13.3 Six Vocational Types

Vocational Type	Characteristics	Vocations
Investigative	Task-oriented, thoughtful; prefers to work independently	Scientific vocations, such as chemistry or zoology
Social	Popular, oriented toward other people; expresses self well	Clinical psychologist, teacher
Conventional	Controlled, stable; likes to know exactly what responsibilities are	Bank teller, bookkeeper, accountant
Artistic	Independent, unconventional, expressive	Composer, dramatist, conductor
Enterprising	Confident, dominant, enthusiastic	Business executives, some sales people
Realistic	Practical, strong, rugged	Mechanics, agricultural workers, technicians

Source: Adapted from Holland, 1973.

in terms of **need satisfaction**. Vocational choices can often be traced back to early childhood needs and childrearing practices. For instance, if you were raised in an overprotective, loving environment, you might have developed a need to be with people, and this need causes you to be interested in service occupations.

Roe also accepts Maslow's concept of a need hierarchy, and she applies portions of his theory to vocational choice. Thus, if a person's basic needs for food and clothing are not easily met, they may become the dominant force in a vocational choice. Only after these needs are clearly satisfied can other needs—such as those for an interesting job, a long-term career, and personal fulfillment—become serious considerations.

The theories of Holland, Super, and Roe are but three of many theories that try to explain people's occupational choices. We know that accident and error account for some decisions (Caplow, 1954): some people "fall into" a job by being at the right place at the right time. We also know that we can pinpoint many influences, such as experience, abilities, and family background, that directly affect vocational choices. We'll look at some of these factors next.

Personal Background

Who you are affects the vocational choice you will make. Five personal factors stand out as especially influential. These are socioeconomic status, gender, family environment, intelligence and academic background, and personal abilities or problems.

Socioeconomic Status As we've seen, socioeconomic status affects many areas of life. Low socioeconomic status increases the pressure to find a job; but it is also influential in more pervasive ways. It decreases exposure to high-paying jobs: a child from a poor family is less likely to have contact with professionals with whom he or she can relate.

> **Roe's theory of need satisfaction** The theory developed by Roe in which occupational choice is viewed in the context of an individual's needs. For example, a person with high affiliation needs would choose work with high interpersonal contact.

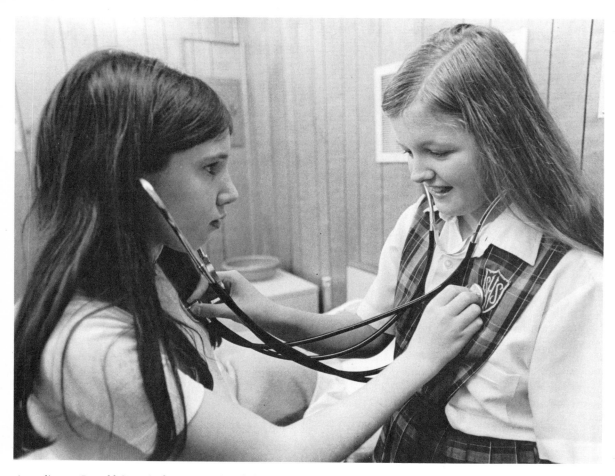

According to Donald Super's theory, vocational choice is a developmental process that begins in childhood with games such as this one.

Low socioeconomic status also affects academic training and achievement. Even when they do attend college, there are often significant differences between students from lower socioeconomic backgrounds and their middle-class peers. In a two-year study, Gottlieb (1975) found that low-income students are more likely to be found in the colleges that have the fewest academic offerings, and to enter programs that terminate with a bachelor's degree. If these students are able to complete their college educations, Gottlieb concludes, "their access to higher status occupations and higher salaries is not equal to that of more affluent students" (p. 117). They may face the reality of discrimination in hiring, and they may also be confronted with the unpleasant realization that still more advanced degrees are necessary for promotion.

Gender   A second factor that shapes people's vocational choices is gender (Vondracek & Lerner, 1982). We'll discuss this issue later in the chapter, but one central point needs to be mentioned here. From early in life, children acquire stereotypes of women's and men's work that narrow their own vocational development: women appear in stories, textbooks, and television as secretaries, mothers, clerical workers, and teachers (Howe, 1971). Few are shown doing creative, self-directed work. One study reported that of 140 characters portrayed on evening television shows, 43 were women. Thirty of these women were employed, mostly in stereotyped female occupations, while 13 were housewives (Kaniuga et al., 1974).

Such portrayals have influenced people's work expectations. It's true that more women today are entering male-dominated professions, yet the majority still choose areas such as social welfare and education. A woman who is a brilliant math student may choose engineering as a profession, for instance. But the odds are that the decision will not be easy, and that she will face a certain amount of pressure to become a math teacher instead. At the same time, many stereotypes still limit people's acceptance of men studying to enter "female occupations," such as nursing or secretarial work (Schlossberg & Goodman, 1972). For both women and men, there is evidence that the vocational stereotypes acquired in childhood may remain throughout life in the absence of some form of active intervention (Harris, 1974).

Family Background   A third factor that influences vocational choice is family background. This is important in several ways. As we've seen, theorists such as Roe (1957) believe that vocational choice is based on needs that arise during childhood. Parents or other relatives act as models, providing exposure to certain types of work but not to others. Children who grow up in a family in which the father stays home while the mother spends her working days at a laboratory

may well have different expectations than they would if only the father held a paying job. Parents may be influential in another way, by giving active encouragement or discouragement toward one or another vocation (Stassen-Berger, 1980)—as when your parents want you to become a lawyer but you want to open a flower shop.

Intelligence and Achievement   A fourth factor is intelligence and academic achievement. No one would seriously expect a student with a 70 percent scholastic average to become a nuclear physicist, nor a person with an IQ of 80 to become a physician. Research does show a relationship between intelligence and occupation. Although there is considerable overlapping, workers with higher intelligence scores tend to be found in higher status positions.

A sizeable correlation has been shown between intelligence and academic achievement. In general, people who score higher on intelligence tests get better grades and enter professional training. Cromback (1970) found that the average IQ of high school graduates is 110, of college graduates is 120, and of Ph.D.'s is 130. Such data shouldn't be overinterpreted, however. Intelligence testing itself is suspect, for a variety of reasons (Kaplan, 1977). In addition, other factors such as motivation are important in academic achievement, and these personal qualities can sometimes cause a person to perform above or below the level that might be predicted from intelligence measures.

Personal Strengths and Weaknesses   A fifth factor influencing vocational choices is personal limitations—physical problems or abilities, personality characteristics and interests, as well as emotional makeup. A person whose total mechanical ability is expended in the act of replacing a light bulb, for instance, is unlikely to choose to become an automotive mechanic; nor would a person with little athletic ability be likely to choose sports as a career.

Family background is often highly influential in job choice, through factors such as exposure, expectations, and parental encouragement. The family of Joseph P. Kennedy, which included John Kennedy, Robert Kennedy, and Ted Kennedy, is a striking example.

Job Goals

It's hard to overestimate the influence of personal background on the kind of jobs people take. Another factor is equally important, however, and that is job goals: what a person wants from a job. When students are asked what the most important factors are in a career choice, most of their responses can be grouped into four areas: interest, money, lifestyle, and job setting and structure.

Interest is probably the most important job goal: most students seem to want their future positions to be interesting; and as we saw earlier in the discussion of job satisfaction, interest is indeed important in determining whether a person will be happy in a job. Unfortunately, it isn't always easy to predict whether a job will be interesting or not. The job market is changing so rapidly, and relatively few young people have the opportunity to observe people in different occupations. However, as Holland points out, we all feel drawn toward certain types of work: "[T]he most efficient way to predict vocational choice is simply to ask the person what he wants to be . . ." (in Bolles, 1978, p. 91).

A second important factor is money. While many students do not place money at the top of the list of what they want from a job, they often mention that they want to live "comfortably." It would be a mistake to downplay the importance of financial reward, for as we've seen, economic need or comfort affects so many other factors of life.

Lifestyle is a third consideration in choosing a job. Your choice of occupation affects your hours, your amount of vacation time, and the flexibility of your daily schedule. With the increased demand for leisure has come a demand that jobs have more flexible schedules. The desire for job flexibility may mean sacrificing something else. For instance, teachers have more vacation time than the average business executive, but they also have lower salaries.

Finally, a fourth factor in choosing an occupation is the setting and structure of the job. Do you prefer indoor or outdoor work; do you prefer to set your own pace or work under someone else's direction; do you like to work with others, or by yourself? Considerations such as these are often overlooked, but they are important.

All of the factors we've been discussing combine to make each of us different from everyone else, in terms of job qualifications, interests, needs, and goals. They form the basis for our job search, but to truly understand vocational choice we must look at the decision-making process itself.

Vocational Choice: Making the Decision

When people ask you what you're doing and you say stewardess, you're really proud, and you think it's great . . . I have five older sisters and they were all married before they were twenty. The minute they got out of high school, they would end up getting married . . . When I told my parents I was going to the airlines, they got excited. They were so happy that one of the girls could go out and see the world and spend some time being single . . . . (Terkel, 1974, p. 4l. Used by permission).

The first thing that happens at work: when the arms start moving, the brain stops . . . . I put on my hard hat,

change into my safety shoes, put on my safety glasses, go to the bonderizer. It's the thing I work on. They rake the metal . . . dip it in a paint solution, and we take it off. Put it on, take it off, put it on, take it off, put it on, take it off . . . . When I come home, know what I do for the first twenty minutes? Fake it. I put on a smile. If I feel bad, I can't take it out on the kids . . . . This is why you go to a tavern . . . . What does an actor do when he's got a bad movie? I got a bad movie every day. (Terkel, 1974, pp. xxxiv-xxxv. Used by permission.)

Work provides different levels of satisfaction for different people. In the first quote above, taken from Studs Terkel's famous book *Working,* work is a source of personal satisfaction and pride. In the second, spoken by a steelworker, it is something so painful that it needs to be blotted out each evening by a trip to the tavern on the way home. The gulf between these two people's feelings about their jobs points squarely to one fact: that vocational decisions are among the most important decisions people can make.

What can you do to make sure the vocation you choose isn't like being in a "bad movie every day"? In the next few pages, we'll look at the decision-making process in an effort to see what people can do to match their own abilities and goals to the choices available in the job market.

When Is a Choice Not a Choice?

The term "vocational choice" is often a misnomer. It implies that most people sit down and thoughtfully choose a career, based on a careful survey of their own interests and the available options.

This rarely occurs. Many people don't know exactly what they want. Although few of us use a Ouija board to make our job choices, it would be a mistake to think that most people carefully weigh all the alternatives. There is good evidence that vocational choice may be rather haphazard (Janis & Wheeler, 1978). Students today may be more conscious of the importance of their vocational decisions (Lidz, 1976), but this consciousness does not necessarily translate into action. And even after people decide on a line of work, they often shift to another.

Taking all of this evidence together, we can discard the old stereotype of the person who wanted to be a lawyer ever since the age of two, when she first opened her mouth to cross-examine her mother. While this may be the case for a few people, it doesn't happen often. In fact, there are many different approaches to making (or avoiding) vocational decisions. The box *How Do You Make Career Decisions?* lets you evaluate your own style according to Janis and Wheeler's four categories.

For most of us, vocational choice is fraught with indecision and anxiety. In fact, Super and Hyde (1978) report that at the age of 25, one fourth of all adults are still uncertain about their vocational choice. How can the process be made more effective? Almost every authority in the field of vocational guidance stresses two essential factors: a realistic understanding of the world of work, and the importance of knowing what you want.

Understanding the World of Work

There are over 22,000 separate occupations listed in the *Dictionary of Occupational Titles* (U.S. Dept. of Labor, 1978), a reference work sometimes used by professional counselors. Considering the rapid changes that are taking place in the job market, how can young people gain enough understanding to let them make intelligent decisions about the right job or career?

It isn't easy. There is a great deal of information available on various occupations, but comparatively little is unbiased. Nor are the vocational resources that are available to students necessarily used or interpreted correctly. Guidance counselors tend to spend more time with students who plan to go to college than with those who don't plan to continue their education (Shertzer & Stone, 1974)—probably in good part because aca-

demically oriented students often relate better to counselors who have themselves gone through academic training. In addition, vocational choice is often a process by which people rule out alternatives. Most people have a better idea of what they don't want to do than what they really want (Housely, 1973).

These obstacles can be overcome, however, and there are basically two methods for weeding out alternatives. The first is to search your own experience for information about different vocations. You have been exposed to a number of occupations, in one way or another. Perhaps you know a programmer who is bored with her job, or a translator who is able to earn a nice supplementary income while working at home. Or you may have a friend who knows someone in a line of work that interests you. If you can make connections with people in the occupations that seem interesting to you—perhaps spend a day or even a few hours with them to observe what they do—you can gain some information that may be of help.

Secondly, you may gain occupational information from books. There are a number of sources available. Various organizations publish recruitment literature that seeks to acquaint the public with its functions. Of course, such literature tends to be highly favorable and optimistic about that particular organization, but it is a source of information. Another source of broader, impartial information is the *Occupational Outlook Quarterly Magazine,* published four times each year by the Department of Labor. These publications, along with their yearly compilations, provide objective information about the outlook of a particular field for the 80s, the training that is required, the average earnings, and a number of other important facts. Almost every library has at least one copy. Finally, there are several popular manuals for job-hunting (Bolles' *What Color Is Your Parachute?* is one of these, and we'll present some of its recommendations shortly). These practical resources are available at libraries and at most bookstores.

How Do You Make Career Decisions?

We all have characteristic approaches to making decisions about work. According to researchers Janis and Wheeler, there are four styles of vocational decisionmaking. Can you recognize yourself in any of these categories? As you might guess, the vigilant mode of decisionmaking is the most effective.

The Complacent Style

This type of person has a passive, wait-and-see attitude. He or she shows a nonchalant attitude about job decisions, and is willing to take whatever comes rather than making career plans.

The Defensive-Avoidance Style

These people are afraid of making the wrong decision, so they rationalize and make up excuses to explain their lack of action.

The Hypervigilant Style

These people panic at making a decision. They search here and there without planning, and pile up hundreds of pamphlets without getting anywhere. Despite the mass of papers they may accumulate, they often miss important facts within their chosen area. They are very time conscious, and may make their choices under stressful conditions.

The Vigilant Style

This individual evaluates information in an unbiased manner, looking at both the positive and negative aspects of each choice. A balance sheet may be used to weigh the possible gains against the possible losses of each alternative. When a decision is finally made, it is based on a clear understanding of the alternatives.

Source: Janis & Wheeler, 1978.

Knowing What You Want

If understanding the world of work is important to making the right job decision, a second crucial factor is to know what *you* want. This is not as easy as it may seem. You may want to earn a six-digit salary, but you may also want to work only one day a week—a condition that would hamper your money-making potential. It is important to understand your own priorities. Which is more important: money or lifestyle? You may have to sacrifice one for the other. Again, suppose you want to own your own business. The money and independence are both attractive, but the hours are long and there is no security. What type of lifestyle will you be experiencing? What will you get, and what will you have to give up?

Each vocation has its pros and cons, and the importance of each will be determined by your own needs. There is no substitute for self-knowledge. Exploring your own aptitudes and interests normally involves searching your experiences, academic records, and perhaps taking a **vocational interest inventory.** These tests can't tell you what you should be; they won't even tell you about your aptitudes. Most inventories simply compare your responses to the answers given by people who work in different fields and are happy at their jobs.* The theory is that if your interests are close to those of workers who are happy in those jobs, there will be a higher probability that the field will be appropriate for you (Brown, 1983). To this degree, such tests are worthwhile. If you do take interest inventory tests such as the Strong-Campbell Interest Blank or the Kuder Preference Test, however, you should remember that such tests only suggest areas for you to investigate: they do not tell you what specific job will be "right" for you.

Before you seek professional help by taking an inventory test or talking to a vocational counselor, there's a lot to be said for doing some soul-searching on your own. The more you learn about yourself, the better equipped you'll be to know what you want. The box *What Kind of Job Do You Want?* is adapted from Richard Bolles' book *What Color is Your Parachute?* (1978), and it provides a brief series of exercises for helping you assess your own vocational needs.

*In contrast, an **aptitude test** attempts to predict how a person will perform in a certain area (when given training), by exploring and measuring skills and inclinations. Still a third type of test, the **achievement test,** attempts to evaluate an individual's present skills or learning.

> **Vocational interest inventory** A measuring instrument designed to discover the extent to which the test-taker's interests coincide with workers in particular occupational groups.
>
> **Aptitude test** A measuring instrument designed to predict how well an individual will perform in a particular task, if given training in that area.
>
> **Achievement test** A test that measures the skill or knowledge an individual possesses at a certain point in development.

Career Development: Theme and Variations

After people choose an occupation and prepare for it, the next step is to find an entry-level position. This involves a commitment of sorts, although the degree of commitment varies considerably, and it may develop slowly. Most people entering a line of work are hoping to gain competence and experience, and to advance up the occupational ladder.

Vocational development is gradual. It is part of the adult developmental cycle. As such, psychologists have been interested in it. They have traced "typical" patterns of career development, especially in the traditional stages through which many men travel as they pursue success. Variations on these typical patterns have also been the subject of much study, particularly the vocational patterns of women in our society. We will look at both of these—the theme and the variations.

The Theme

In his book *The Seasons of a Man's Life* (1978), Daniel Levinson has mapped out a broad view of adult development.† A primary task is to find a balance between job satisfaction and a sense of perspective and accomplishment in the person's life outside of work, and he divides this task into three basic stages.

In the first stage, persons between the ages of 20–40 establish themselves in a stable occupation and work their way up through the ranks. In their early 20s, people are at the top of their form physically, and are very receptive to learning new skills on the job. In early adulthood, Levinson sees strength, quickness, endurance, and output as dominant qualities.

†Levinson looked at male development, which he saw as inextricably tied to career patterns. This same pattern also exists for growing numbers of women.

By the late 30s or early 40s, many people enter what is often called a *mid-life transition*. This is a stock-taking time when people look at what they have accomplished and evaluate it against their youthful dreams. The result may be a more cautious use of one's past experience; it may also be a doubtfulness about the value of one's strivings. The job may take on different meaning, as in the case of an advertising executive who became dissatisfied with what he had been doing, reduced his working hours, and spent more time and energy on community and family affairs. Instead of finding a new balance between work and outside life, a person may quit a job completely and start all over again, as in one case, known by one of the authors, of a stockbroker who decided to become a secondary school teacher. A third alternative may also occur, and the individual may neither take stock nor readjust goals and lifestyle. In some cases, this can have disastrous effects on a person's private life, as in the story presented in the box *I Gave My Life to the Company, or "Hey, Where Did Everybody Go?"*

As a person ages, a third stage revolves around finding a balance between the self and involvement with society. In looking toward retirement, it is not easy to admit that a new generation is taking over. Coping with this transition is not easy, and many people never do come to grips with these problems. Especially for people who have devoted their whole lives to work, the vacuum created by retirement often leaves a sense of being lost, unwanted, and unfulfilled. It is not unusual for retired men and women to take part- or even full-time jobs—not just for financial reasons, but to keep busy. One man who had worked in college admissions opened a business doing odd jobs around the house; others may enter real estate, community work, politics, and a host of other fields.

These three stages represent one pattern of career development that is descriptive of many women as well as men. However, women's traditional roles as well as their expectations have not always been geared toward the same occupational goals as men. Partly as a result of this, and partly because of society's stereotypes and hiring practices, women's vocational development can often be described as a variation on the theme that Levinson described above.

Variations on a Theme: Women at Work

Women have always worked in our society. However, the sheer numbers of women entering the job market, and their slow but steady entrance into jobs that were originally considered to be men's work—including everything from bank presidencies to chairpersons of the board to truckdrivers—have brought permanent changes in both the nature of women's work and the numbers of working women. We'll look briefly at this changing scene before exploring its potentials and consequences.

Women in the Job Market　As of mid-1978, one half of all women aged 16 and over (an estimated 42 million women) were either working or actively seeking employment. The statistic represents the highest number yet of women in the labor force and also the greatest percentage of women in the work force, as Figure 13.1 shows. To a degree, their growing numbers reflect many aspects of the women's movement, for many women are not only waiting longer to marry, but they are also pursuing careers within marriage and parenthood to a greater degree than before. Their numbers also reflect a shaky economy and increased cost of living: many families find it hard to make ends meet with just one breadwinner.

More significantly, the figures represent a change in women's work patterns. Years ago, working mothers usually quit their jobs to care for their young children, then perhaps went back to work. The unmistakable modern trend is for married women to work while they raise their families, or often to decide not to raise a family at all. The

What Kind of Job Do You Want? Three Exercises to Help You Find Out

Making decisions about jobs is not easy. There are so many fields to choose from, and so many kinds of work, that it is often difficult to tell just where you fit in. In his job-hunting manual, *What Color Is Your Parachute?*, Richard Bolles suggests several exercises that can help to narrow the choice. The three we've adapted below are based on three frames of reference suggested by Bolles: your *past* experience, your *present* feelings, and your *future* goals. Each can be used to help determine what kind of job you want.

Using Your Past

You can learn more about what kind of job you want by becoming aware of the experiences that have been most satisfying in the past.

Here is an exercise that can help you "raise your consciousness." First, write a brief "diary" of your life, your talents, and your accomplishments. Discuss your skills and the ways in which you have used them in your spare time, as well as in various tasks. Include both the experiences you've enjoyed and those you have disliked.

Now, read through your diary and group these experiences and skills according to whether you want them or don't want them to play a role in your future career. Make your lists as long as you like:

Things I want to have or use in my future career(s)	*Things I want to avoid in my future career(s)*
1. _____	1. _____
2. _____	2. _____
3. _____	3. _____

Finally, take the most important of the items in the first list and rank them in order of importance. The result will provide you with a general idea of the opportunities you'd like your job to provide, while the second list helps define what you don't want in a job.

Using Your Present

A second direction to take in deciding what kind of job you want is to look into your current feelings.

One short exercise can help you discover some of your own natural tendencies. Ask yourself what kinds of things make you unhappy. Then divide your answers to this last question according to whether they are within your power to change, or beyond your control. (Your own lists will probably be longer than the spaces provided below.)

What kinds of things make me unhappy?

	Things that lie within my own control		*Things that are beyond my control*
Things I can change through changing the environment:	Things I can change through changing me:		
1. _____	_____	_____

2. _____ _____ _____

3. _____ _____ _____

These three lists can help you narrow the field considerably. You can probably eliminate most jobs that have the qualities found in the third column, but carefully consider the items in the first two columns. Column I tells you what you don't want in your environment. If these qualities are important to you—for instance, if you're unhappy in indoors settings—then you should choose a work setting that suits your needs. Column 2 tells you what you can change within yourself. If you're unhappy typing letters for someone else, it may well be within your power to obtain the training that will let *you* dictate letters to someone else.

Using Your Future

The first two exercises should have provided you with a fairly specific idea of what you want and don't want in a job. Bolles suggests a third exercise that uses your future—your goals and visions—to help define how your job can help bring you closer to those goals.

What *are* your goals? Many people never stop to think about this question, yet knowing what you want out of life can provide direction for your job search. To find out, write an essay entitled "Before I Die, I Want To . . . " Make your list as thorough as possible, omitting nothing.

When you're finished, read through your essay and list those goals you haven't yet accomplished. Organize them in order of importance. Then, next to the most important items on that list, write a second list of the steps needed to accomplish each goal. Your lists will vary in length: you may have five goals that relate in some way to your job search, while another reader may list ten relevant goals.

Goals yet to be accomplished

1. _____

Steps needed to accomplish each goal

a. _____

b. _____

c. _____

2. _____

a. _____

b. _____

c. _____

When you've completed these exercises, you may not yet know precisely what job is for you. If you have been honest and thorough in your answers, however, you probably have a good picture of the general types of work you can perform, as well as what will be most fulfilling—and equally important, you should have specific ideas of what work will be least satisfying to you. With this sense of direction, you'll be able to make informed decisions about where you fit into the job market. Good luck!

Source: Adapted by permission from Richard Nelson Bolles, *What Color Is Your Parachute?* (Berkeley, Ca.: Ten Speed Press, 1983), pp. 83–99. Available from Ten Speed Press, Box 7123, Berkeley, CA 94707.

I Gave My Life to the Company
—or—
"Hey, Where Did Everybody Go?"

Robert H. was always a hard-driving individual who opened his own import store at the age of 28. A private business requires many hours and family sacrifices, and Sandy, his wife, worked as bookkeeper to help keep things running smoothly. And run smoothly they did: by the age of 37, Robert had 7 stores. Since the operation was now so complicated, Sandy was no longer able to keep the records. Besides, they now had three children, and someone had to stay home and care for them.

As for Robert, he had made it. But there was no time to sit back and relax. There was always one more store to open, and something to check at each store. He worried constantly about business, and despite a good income, he found he could not relax. Sandy tried to warn him several times that there was no longer much communication in their marriage, but with little effect. Finally, after 22 years, they were divorced.

Unlike the Hollywood scripts that are so often written, Robert neither saw nor understood the cause of this marital breakdown. He attributes it to a brief affair he had had the year before the divorce. He is still a bit bewildered by his wife's attitude and his children's coolness. He still puts every waking moment into the business, and he is under medication for periodic depression. To this day, he does not understand why he feels the way he does or what went wrong with his family life.

The moral of the story? In simple terms, too much of a good thing is no longer a good thing. Many men in our society are trained to equate occupational success with a happy and successful life. According to Kaye (1974), people sometimes become so concerned with their jobs that they miss much of the beauty and joy that is present in other areas of life—from their families, from hobbies, from community activities. If they succeed in their jobs, they may find that they have gained money and prestige—but that they are no longer in touch with themselves or their families. Many times, "workaholics" become the victims of stress-related problems, and prime among these is heart trouble (another common ending to stories such as Robert's is an early death from a heart attack). In all, while we aim for vocational success, it is also important not to lose sight of the other parts of life.

birth rate has declined—from 19.4 births per thousand population in 1965 to 14.7 in 1978—with the result that families are smaller and the childrearing years shorter. While many mothers wait for their children to enter school before returning to work, some take only a few months off before they find alternative care for their children. There is evidence for these trends in recent statistics: by 1978, 63 percent of women aged 25–44 were in the labor market, including 44 percent of women with preschool children (U. S. Department of Labor, 1978).

Many of the women in the labor force are heads of households: divorced, widowed, or single. The number of one-parent families has increased 80 percent since 1970. In 1978, 8.2 million households were headed by women. Ross and Sawhill (1975) estimate that one out of every seven children are being raised in a one-parent household; some other estimates are even higher.* Most of these families are living with

* Schlessinger's 1975 figure is closer to one out of every six children.

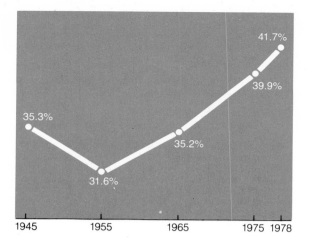

Figure 13.1   Women as a Proportion of the Labor Force, 1945–1978

Source: Women in the Labor Force: Some New Data (Report #575) Washington D.C.: U.S. Department of Labor, 1979.

insufficient alimony and child support; all face the rising cost of living. Some 61 percent of female heads-of-households are working.

These statistics together point to several significant conclusions about women and work:

■ First, most women will work sometime in their lives. More will continue to work throughout their married lives, and we can expect to see many families in which both husband and wife work.

■ Second, there will be an increasing demand for daycare services, and more pressure on government to provide such services for a reasonable cost, especially to poor women.

■ Third, if the rate of divorce continues (or increases), we may also see an increase in the number of families headed by women, many of whom will be sole providers.

■ Fourth, as increasing numbers of women pursue lifetime careers, we can expect women to gain easier access to traditionally male-dominated lines of work, with more equal pay structures.

Social and Psychological Barriers   Despite the fact that more women are working than ever before, a persistent fact stands out. Even when a woman is well educated, the odds are against her getting a top-paying job. Women are still heavily overrepresented in traditional female, "pink-collar" occupations: 79 percent of clerical positions, and a full 59 percent of service positions, are held by women. While there has been an increase in the percentage of women holding professional jobs, this growth has been slow, not in keeping with the increase of women in the work force. Why has the progress been so slow?

One reason concerns the attitudes of both men and women. Most women find it harder to achieve without the active support of the men in their lives, and this support is not always present. Most male students today still expect their own careers to take priority over their wives, according to an informal poll conducted by one of the authors each term. (At the same time, most of these same men deny that it would bother them if their wives earned more than they did.) As for women, some research by Hawley (1972) is revealing. Hawley questioned some 136 women who planned to enter male-oriented occupations, and found that only 10 percent would continue if their husbands objected. Ashburn (1977) points out that in order to succeed in a male-dominated occupation, a woman must have the necessary values and a solid identity.

Ashburn emphasizes the importance of role models as well as the encouragement of the woman's father and husband. Certainly, the lack of adequate role models can be considered a second barrier to women's achievement in top jobs. There are relatively few women scientists and engineers available to serve as role models. And even in cases where parents make sure that their children are exposed to these vocational role models, social stereotypes are surprisingly persistent. As an example, one of the authors has always brought his children to female pediatricians, in part to counteract the stereotype that doctors are men. Despite this experience, though, his

8-year-old daughter recently declared that she wants to be a nurse when she grows up—because women are nurses and men are doctors. Sometimes, the stereotypes and models provided by society are even more powerful than personal experience.

Still another factor is the lack of encouragement or reward from society. Even correcting for such factors as experience or training, Treiman and Terrell (1975) still found that women in the same professions as men earn less than men. A recent three-year study by the Carnegie Corporation found that the median weekly income of women in professional technical jobs was 73 percent of that earned by men—and the figures were even more glum for clerical jobs (64 percent of men's incomes) and sales jobs (45 percent) (Reidmann & Lamanna, 1982).

Finally, there is the sense of conflict between family needs and job goals and responsibilities. This conflict is felt both physically, in terms of practical logistics and energy drain, and emotionally, as psychological stress. The physical load of most working mothers is clearly seen. Ideally, when both partners work, there should be a fifty-fifty split of childrearing and housekeeping tasks; but in reality women almost always take on more of both duties (Stevens-Long, 1979). The result is an overload, which is compounded by many logistical problems. Where can the children go until the parents come home from work? What happens when they are sick? When can groceries be bought, dishes be washed, laundry be done? Husbands are taking on a greater share of these tasks than they did in the past, but it is still true that in most families, even when the husband helps, it is usually the woman who takes ultimate responsibility for these tasks.

The psychological conflict between home and family is also great. As we discussed earlier, most women in our society are raised to take care of family needs first, and the stereotype of the mother who stays home to raise the children is still prevalent. We saw in Chapter 2 that there is evidence that some women are motivated to avoid success, especially in male-dominated occupations (Horner, 1972), and it may be true that males limit their choices and refuse to consider female-dominated occupations. As a result of this socialization toward family nurturing and away from job success for women, the mother who leaves the children to go to work is apt to feel anxiety, ambivalence, and even guilt.

Many women are forced to choose between their achievement and affiliation needs (Bardwick et al., 1970). If they choose one, they feel guilty about the other; if they choose the other, they feel unfulfilled. Either way, working mothers may feel vulnerable to criticism, and they may also feel guilty about their inability to give their children "complete" attention. Guilt may be especially severe if the woman is working mostly for her own fulfillment rather than financial hardship (Beckman, 1978). There is a fine line here: many, perhaps most, women work for both. And either way, excessive guilt can have a negative effect.

The guilt and worries that many working mothers feel is worth a second look, for it results in an underlying ambivalence. Do the children suffer when Mother gets a full-time job? The question has been explored by recent research.

Does Working Affect the Children? Charlotte is the mother of two young boys, ages 4 and 12. She was divorced about two years ago, and her husband has remarried and moved to another state. He pays alimony and child support—occasionally, that is, when he has the money. He sees the boys mostly during the summer, and he has started a new family and a new life.

Charlotte lives in a small apartment in a nice urban neighborhood. She really never wanted to work while the children were young, but she has no choice now. After dipping into a small inheritance and using up the money she received from the sale of the house she and her husband had lived in, Charlotte found a reasonably good position with a credit card company, and she now works full-time.

She is not without worries, however. It was a problem to find adequate care for her 4-year-old, and it is still hard to keep tabs on her eldest child, since he comes home from school two hours before she returns from work. Both of these problems have contributed to a sense of inadequacy. Although Charlotte had no choice but to work, she still feels guilty. She is concerned about the effect of her absence on both children. She is also tired when she gets home from work, and feels she no longer has the patience she had in the past to deal with the boys.

Charlotte's sense of guilt and inadequacy is not uncommon (Beckman, 1978). It is experienced not only by single mothers but also by married mothers who work. How realistic are Charlotte's fears? Two factors seem especially important. The first is the quality of the daycare available to the child; and the second is the mother's feelings about going to work or staying home.

Daycare Quality   In general, as long as daycare arrangements are chosen carefully, there seems to be little need to worry about its detrimental effects on children. (Leaving older children unattended as Charlotte did, however, might well be more damaging, and some supervision might be recommended depending on the age and responsibility of the child.) Most research studies have failed to find any negative effects from daycare (Etaugh, 1980). Some have even reported some benefits, depending on the kind of care the child received before entering daycare. For instance, a mother who is unhappy and dissatisfied is likely to have a negative effect on the children (Etaugh, 1974); and in such a case, a good daycare set-up might well be an improvement.

In evaluating research on daycare, however, we should note an important caveat. Most of the research to date has studied better daycare centers, many of which are attached to universities. This has undoubtedly affected their findings. There are also some centers that have a high child-to-caretaker ratio, no real program, poor nutritional guidance, and broken toys. Doubtless, the research would uncover some negative findings here—but such centers rarely allow investigators to study their programs.

Attitudes about Working   A second important issue involves the mother's feelings about her job. Many women find fulfillment, status, and satisfaction in their work, so that their jobs can be said to add a positive dimension to their lives. But many jobs are dull and repetitive. If a woman finds her job a drudgery and resents the fact that she can't stay at home, her anger might spill over in her dealings with her children. In addition, in a one-parent family, there may be no one to come home and complain to except the kids. One therapist found that her client came home from work complaining to her 10-year-old how boring, repetitive, and tiring her job was. The result was that her daughter felt guilty about her mother's working!

In conclusion, working mothers need not become overly concerned about the effects of their working on the children (Hoffman & Ney, 1974). Important factors, of course, are her own happiness at her job, as well as the way she and her family adjust to the increased family pressure; and a great deal depends upon what happens when she returns home from work. For employed women—just as for unemployed women—the quality of the time a mother spends with her children is the most vital factor in determining the success of childrearing.

Rethinking Some Old Traditions

Working is an important part of people's lives, yet many traditional elements of both women's and men's work require rethinking.

Women and Working   In the case of women, as we've just seen, attitudes, interest, and the need to work have all changed radically over the past two decades. More and more women are coming of age who have had working mothers or other women as role models. These women will be seeking professional jobs in many areas. Childrearing patterns at home need to be changed to reflect this division of labor, and so does occupational training. It is urgent to rewrite curricula and vocational education literature, and many professionals are now advocating a change in counseling strategies for women.

Judith Worrell (1980) argues that all counseling should take into consideration the changes that have occurred in the past decade and a half, to provide women with what she calls "feminist counseling." She argues that counselors must encourage women to develop multiple skills in order to increase women's competence and productivity. She also advocates consciousness-raising "as a means of enabling women to define themselves apart from their relationships to men, children and home" (1980, p. 480). Such counseling would aim to encourage women to consider many different lifestyles, and to increase the number of choices available to them.

It is important, however, not to leave the impression that every homemaker is dying to go out into the business world and compete. The stereotype of the unhappy, depressed housewife is as inaccurate as the traditional view of the woman who wants only to raise a healthy, happy family. Different women have different goals.

Tavris (1976) quotes a study by Fidell and Prather that has criticized much of the research in this field. According to this study, most research tends to divide married women into two groups: those who have jobs and those who don't. The researchers argue that if a third category is added—women who desire to enter the job market but can't or don't—the results are radically changed. Instead of one group of employed women who are happy and a second group of unemployed women who are dissatisfied, there is also a significant group who are happy about being full-time homemakers. If any of these groups fits the stereotype of the unhappy housewife, it is the middle group. Generalizations must be made with care, however, for many women with young children are not interested in finding jobs.

Men and Working Although most men don't share the same problems as women, their traditional place in the world of work also needs some rethinking. Unlike women, most men in our society are trained from childhood to be breadwinners; they are less likely to feel ambivalence about being successful. Traits such as aggression, non-nurturance, courage, and ambition are often drummed into them because these traits are valued in a competitive work setting (Fasteau, 1974). This socialization gives men a head start, launching them in the direction of a successful career (Freize et al., 1978).

Men's certainty about career goals is not without costs, however. A man who feels he does not live up to his goals—if he is unemployed, or even retired—may experience a terrible blow to his self-image. As one teenager who was out of work put it:

The worst time is when I'm looking at myself and I feel lousy, so lousy I want to smash the window. If I had a job I wouldn't be standing there, staring at myself in the first place. (Coles, 1978, p. 226)

If there are dangers to failing in the job market, there are also dangers to success, or to the singleminded pursuit of success. Robert's case, presented earlier in the box *I Gave My Life to the Company,* illustrates the common problem of marital breakdown, and the prevalence of stress-related illnesses among men in our society is another. We mentioned heart ailments; other problems may include ulcers, tension headaches and hypertension, and alcoholism, which we discuss in Chapter 15.

There are no easy recommendations for helping men (or women) who define themselves primarily in terms of their occupational identity. We should remember, however, that the total definition of a person must be more than merely a statement of what he or she does for a living and the amount of income that person earns. We are individuals who hold life goals, relationships, challenges, and pleasures that are completely separate from what we do at work; and fulfillment or self-actualization requires the development of

Leisure-time satisfaction is significant to adjustment, just as is vocational satisfaction.

these parts of our identity. In the last few pages of this chapter, we'll look at leisure time and its importance in people's sense of satisfaction with their lives.

Leisure

As important as work may be, it is not the primary source of satisfaction for most people. Yankelovich (1978) reports that when work and leisure were compared as sources of satisfaction, only 21 percent of respondents said work was more satisfying. Most told the investigator that

although they liked their work, it was not their major source of satisfaction. Instead, it was leisure time.

Troll (1975) defines **leisure time** as discretionary time utilized for self-fulfillment. This is relatively new in human history, however. Most people had little leisure in centuries past, and thus, few decisions to make about how to best use their free time.

> **Leisure** Time that is free from work, in which an individual may indulge in a number of activities chosen for personal satisfaction.

Work and Leisure

There has been a steady decline in the number of hours an employee works per week (Schultz, 1978). Nothing is holy about the 40-hour, 5-day-a-week work schedule, and some firms have experimented with varying these time schedules, either by staggering work hours (so that different employees arrive and leave at different times of day) or by permitting two employees to share a work-week. **Flextime,** in which employees are expected to be in the office during a certain "core" period (say, 10 to 3), but may choose to schedule the rest of their working hours according to their own needs, has helped to make jobs more liveable and has also reduced traffic congestion in many areas (Maier & Verser, 1982). Some corporations have begun implementing a four-day work week in which each day is extended two hours.

Even with the standard 40-hour week, people have more leisure today than ever before. Unfortunately, though, we have not been educated to make the most of this time. Especially when people are tired from a day at work, it is far easier to drink a 6-pack and watch television than to read or exercise.

Using Leisure Time

These habits may be changing, however. Within the past decade, a significant change in attitudes seems to be taking place. Participatory sports as well as activities such as jogging, biking, and exercising have gained popularity, as people have become more interested in developing themselves. The 1970s produced what has been called the "me generation"—a generation bent on developing itself. The only danger in this involves its lack of emphasis on giving to others. Becoming involved

> **Flextime** A schedule in which the hours an individual spends at a job are specially suited to that person's personal and familial responsibilities.

only in one's own development can be just as narrow as not using your leisure time for self-development at all.

In choosing leisure-time activities for yourself, Jourard (1974) suggests that people take their normal activities into consideration. For instance, if your job requires you to stay at a desk all day, you might try a more active leisure activity that will provide you with some regular form of exercise. Even a daily walk may be helpful, and many people feel it helps "clear the cobwebs." Again, people who work all day with others might enjoy a solitary pursuit—although this is not always true. As with vocational choices, people shouldn't feel constricted by sex stereotypes in choosing ways of using leisure time. One of the authors knows a male dentist who knits, and a female office manager who enjoys carpentry.

Leisure-time avocations or hobbies serve another purpose besides development in your spare time. Sometimes they become important later in life, especially in retirement. A stamp collector or coin collector may become a dealer after retiring from a 9-to-5 job; a person who always enjoyed travelling may open a travel agency. In sum, then, leisure-time satisfaction is significant to adjustment, just as is vocational satisfaction.

Summary

1. For most people, work is more than a 9-to-5 effort to make a living. It affects people's self-concept and often dominates their way of thinking.

2. Work serves many functions, by providing people with an income, with personal satisfaction, and by organizing their lives. It serves an indispensable social function by providing goods and services for society.

3. The traditional work ethic is changing as new values take its place. There is a new emphasis on leisure, a decline in company loyalty, and an increased emphasis on satisfaction from work.

4. The job market is changing rapidly, as skills need to change to keep pace with technology and as new fields and even positions appear and disappear rapidly.

5. Several theories have tried to explain how people choose different jobs. Three of the most important theories tie job choice to personality, to development, and to needs. There is also a cause-and-effect relationship between several factors in each individual's personal background, including socioeconomic status, gender, family experiences, intelligence and achievement, and personal strengths and weaknesses.

6. Making job decisions isn't easy, and many people don't actively make the choice at all. Instead, they take what comes. Janis and Wheeler found four general ways of making vocational choices: the complacent, the hypervigilant, the defensive-avoidance, and the vigilant.

7. In making the best job decision you can for yourself, most experts stress two points. First, you should understand what is "out there" in the job market. And second, know what you want.

8. We can look at career development patterns in terms of a theme and variations. Levinson outlines one theme in his study of male adult development. The first stage is one of establishing oneself in a vocation; the second, a mid-life transition, is a stock-taking stage; and the third is a preparation for retirement and for phasing out of the work force.

9. Women's work patterns have traditionally been different, although more women now have full-time careers and fit Levinson's pattern.

10. Women face many social and psychological barriers to career success, including lack of male support, lack of role models, lower reward from society (women are hired less often for white-collar jobs, and even when they are, they usually earn less than men), and a sense of conflict between family roles and work roles.

11. Much of this conflict centers around worries about the children in daycare. Most studies reveal, however, that as long as the daycare center is of good quality, and the woman feels good about working and spends "quality time" with her children, the mother's working will not negatively affect the child. It may even have positive effects in some cases.

12. Both men's and women's work patterns require rethinking. For women, better counseling, more equal hiring practices, and (if they have children) increased availability of daycare and more support from other family members are all essential. For men (and for women who share the same career pattern), it is important to be able to devote more energy to family and leisure time: the "workaholic" syndrome has many inherent dangers.

13. Our society is beginning to recognize the value of leisure time. Not only do we have more leisure time than we did in the past, but people are learning to use it. Leisure should provide a healthy balance to work: activities such as jogging, hobbies, reading, carpentry, or educational classes all allow people to develop other parts of themselves, and they may pave the way for a more satisfying retirement.

Key Terms and Concepts

career

job

work ethic

human relations training program

Super's theory of vocational development

vocational maturity

Roe's theory of need satisfaction

complacent style

defensive-avoidance style

hypervigilant style

vigilant style

vocational interest inventory

aptitude test

achievement test

leisure

flextime

Paul was annoyed. Painting the garage was a boring job and, as he muttered, he tried to concentrate on finishing the job. His 4-year-old daughter was "helping."

As he continued working feverishly, he suddenly noticed that his daughter had stopped painting and was looking at a beautiful Long Island sunset. Birds were crossing in front of the clouds, which radiated various colors as the sun put on a spectacular display. As he stood watching for a moment, Paul realized that if it hadn't been for his daughter, he would hardly have stopped to enjoy it. His daughter had no thoughts of returning

Therapy and the Human Potentials Movement

to work before she had fully experienced the moment. She seemed to know intuitively that the work would still be there—but the scene would last only a moment.

At times like this, we realize how often the rush to get things done keeps us from sensing and enjoying special moments. The stresses that put pressure on us may cause us to bog down in problems that we can't seem to untangle. And the daily routine that governs our lives can make us less aware of the joys of life. We are more likely to reserve those joys for weekends. But, as one wise person pointed out, however, five-sevenths of our lives is spent on weekdays. Sometimes, we need help in finding how to make the most of ourselves during these times.

In Part IV's exploration of esteem needs, we've looked at the self-concept. We've also seen how work can be one of the most important ingredients of people's self-definition and esteem. In this chapter, we'll look at one further aspect of this topic. That is the use of professional help both to heal problems and to help healthy individuals grow to discover even more of their potentials and to experience greater satisfaction.

Therapy: What It Is

The word *therapy* (or *psychotherapy*) often confuses people. Traditionally, people have sought therapy for mental problems, such as anxiety attacks, depression, or nervous habits. Such reasons are still the most common causes for seeking treatment. According to one definition, **psychotherapy** is "any form of treatment for mental illness, behavioral maladaptation, and/or other emotional problems . . . in which a trained person deliberately establishes a professional relationship with a patient for the purpose of removing, modifying, or retarding existing symptoms . . . and of promoting positive personality growth" (Hinsie & Campbell, 1970). This definition is long, but it can be simplified into three essential parts, as outlined in Figure 14.1 The first is a *professional therapist* who is trained to help the *client* and is accepted as

an expert by the client. The second is the *client* who desires some sort of emotional or behavioral change. And the third is the series of *regular contacts* that takes place between the client and therapist for the purpose of producing changes in the client (Frank, 1973).

You may have noticed in the definition above that therapy is also used for positive personality growth. Today, in fact, more and more basically healthy persons are undergoing therapy—in order to understand themselves better and to function on a higher level. This desire to work through feelings and to continue growing is a part of the *human potentials movement,* and it can be seen in phenomena such as encounter groups, which we'll discuss below. It is also seen in the many self-help books available at bookstores. There are so many of these, in fact, that most people don't know which advice to believe. The box *So You Want to Buy a Self-help Book, but You Don't Know Which One to Choose . . .* provides some consumer guidelines.

There are many different approaches to therapy—over 130, according to one count (Parloff, 1976). Each one makes promises to help people, and each has its own devoted following of people who have been helped by it. Of this rather incredible range, a handful stand out as major schools of therapy. These are psychoanalytic (Freudian) therapy, behavior therapy, humanistic therapy, and cognitive therapy. In addition, therapy may take place individually or in a group setting. We'll look at each of these as well as the related human potentials movement; then we'll turn to some practical advice for finding professional help.

> **Psychotherapy** Any form of treatment in which a trained professional therapist has regular contact with a client for the purpose of producing some sort of emotional or behavioral change.

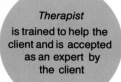

Figure 14.1   The Three Elements of a Therapeutic Relationship

Psychoanalysis

For many people, **psychoanalysis** is synonymous with psychotherapy. This is due to the pervading influence of Freud. Actually, the chances that you will ever be treated by an orthodox Freudian psychoanalyst are quite small: relatively few therapists remain completely faithful to Freud's teachings (Garfield, 1981). However, many have adopted at least some of his goals and still use a

> **Psychoanalysis**   The method of psychotherapy based upon the writings of Sigmund Freud, psychoanalysis attempts to treat disturbances by providing clients with insights into their often unconscious sources. Techniques such as free association and dream analysis are used.
>
> **Psychodynamic**   A term used to describe therapies that are extensions of the thoughts and techniques of Freud and other therapists who have stressed the importance of insight.
>
> **Insight therapies**   A group of therapies that aim at increasing the client's understanding of his or her unconscious processes.
>
> **Free association**   A therapeutic technique used in psychoanalysis in which a client relates everything that enters his or her consciousness.

number of his techniques. These therapists describe themselves as **psychodynamic** rather than psychoanalytic.

All therapies have a characteristic way of looking at the cause and nature of emotional problems, and psychoanalysis is no exception. Freud's view was that psychological problems were caused chiefly by the strain between people's unconscious drives and society's prohibitions. People unconsciously want things—the big house on the outskirts of town, or a neighbor's spouse, for instance—that society says they can't have. Most of these drives and forbidden impulses remain hidden, even from themselves, and any disturbed behavior is simply an outward symptom of this deeper conflict.

Discovering the Unconscious

According to psychoanalytic theory, the only way to solve psychological problems is to get at their unconscious roots. For this reason, psychoanalytic therapies are sometimes called **insight therapies.** Once the therapist has uncovered deep-seated conflicts, the client can use this insight to deal with the problem. There are several ways of discovering hidden wishes or conflicts; we'll look briefly at some of the best-known of these techniques.

Free Association   One of the most important avenues to the unconscious is through **free association.** In this technique, clients are instructed to

Freud's office in Vienna. Patients were made as comfortable as possible in order to encourage free association of thoughts.

say whatever enters their minds, holding nothing back. Most of us are accustomed to blocking or filtering a large proportion of our thoughts, stopping them from entering our conscious awareness. When the client begins expressing every thought (a practice that can be very difficult for some people), some important clues may find their way into the individual's speech.

Dreams   Dreams are another source of information about the unconscious. According to Freud in his classic book *On Dreams,* dreams are the workings of the unconscious portion of the mind. The mind attempts to discharge its tension by expressing its hidden conflicts and wishes during dreams (Hall & Lindzey, 1957). But even in dreams, the true meaning of some conflicts may be hidden. For instance, a 13-year-old girl dreamed she was being held down by a man whose face was always in the shadows. The identity of the man would be an important clue to the dream, yet the girl would awaken each time the shadows began to disappear. Freud felt that dreams contained a great deal of symbolism. He

So You Want to Buy a Self-help Book, but You Don't Know Which One to Choose . . .

Walk into any bookstore, and you'll see shelves of books devoted to self-improvement. They range from combating your fear of flying to acting more assertively to managing your time more effectively. For virtually any of these books, there is a reader—somewhere—who claims that the book has changed his or her life. Yet many professionals express doubt. Some claim that the books give easy answers to difficult problems, and may actually prevent some people who need therapy from getting it. Some criticize the *psychobabble* found in many of these books—that is, the psychological jargon that sounds impressive but carries little substantial meaning (Rosen, 1975). And some point to the contradictions that appear from one book to the next. A behaviorist may write that reinforcements must be used to lose weight, while the book next to it on the shelf, written by a Freudian, may say that deep conflicts must first be resolved.

Despite these drawbacks, self-help books will continue to be popular; and some will be helpful, especially to readers who are already functioning well. Some therapists have even recommended certain books as adjuncts to counseling, since some of these books are now written by respected experts in the field (Dilley, 1978).

But which ones are worth reading? Unfortunately, self-help books aren't regularly evaluated by professional organizations such as APA (American Psychological Association), so the average reader such as you must often judge these books by their covers. There are no established criteria that can assure the right choice, but a few guiding questions may help steer you in the right direction.

1. Who wrote it?

It takes many years of work to become an expert in a field. Unfortunately, it isn't so hard to publish advice. The story is told, for instance, of a woman who wrote a newspaper column advising parents how to raise their children. She had no training other than being a mother and a writer, and her own child was badly in need of therapy. It makes sense to read the "About the Author" section before buying the book. This doesn't mean that only the giants in the field should write for the public. However, if you recognize an author's name from your course work, or if the author has good credentials, then the book stands a better chance of being worth your while.

2. What promises are made?

Some books promise the world—eternal happiness, sexual bliss, or the complete elimination of guilt. They are, to say the least, impossible promises to keep, and potential readers shouldn't be taken in by them.

3. Are the suggestions reasonable?

Forget your troubles! Live for today! Become the life of the party in 120 easy pages!

Can it be done? The odds are against it. Not only is it impossible to expect radical changes to come so easily, but the advice offered by such books is difficult to translate into action. It is important to note that just reading these books will *not* necessarily mean that you will be able to follow their advice or practice the techniques they offer. If the goals are too far out of reach, you can bet that the book won't be much practical help.

4. Does the book represent a fad?

Many self-help books use the words *new* or *proven* in their advertising. If you thumb through the pages, though, you may find little that is new, nor any controlled research to substantiate the claims of being "proven." Instead, there may be page after page of testimonials from satisfied readers.

Just as in every other field, psychology has its share of fads. In the absence of scientific evidence, it may be best to wait than to throw yourself into something that may be potentially hazardous.

5. What is the author's theoretical orientation?

Now that you have some background in psychology, you are aware of the various theoretical schools of psychology. If a book is written by someone who claims to be a behaviorist, you know you can expect an approach that will include reinforcements for the desired behaviors and reliance on learning theory in solving problems. If the author is a cognitive psychologist, then thought processes will be the key to change. Discovering the author's orientation can give you some clue as to the techniques you can expect to read about.

There is no doubt that self-help books have something to offer for people who wish to improve some aspect of their lives. They may give a person a hint as to how to experience life more fully, add new dimensions of awareness, or give valuable examples about how others have coped with problems. However, these books need to be evaluated critically and carefully; and they should *not* be seen as a substitute for psychotherapy.

distinguished between **manifest content**—the content that is visible in dreams—and **latent content**—the underlying meanings.

Slips of the Tongue   As we saw in Chapter 1, slips of the tongue (or of the pen) also reveal the unconscious in action. What is actually happening is an unintentional breakdown of normal filtering mechanisms, so that we are truly saying what we mean, even though we may not intend to. Thus, the friend who politely issues a family invitation to "bring the brats—er, I mean the kids" is only being honest, albeit more honest than she wants to be. As with dreams and free association, slips such as this can give both the psychoanalyst and the client insight into unconscious processes.

Resistance   It is not only what people say or dream that reveals what's going on in the unconscious. A fourth clue to unconscious processes is a person's behavior. For instance, if you are consistently late for your therapy session it might show what Freudians call resistance. **Resistance** refers to "a characteristic of the client's defense system which opposed the purposes of counseling or therapy" (Brammer & Shostrom, 1968, p. 255). Perhaps you unconsciously do not want to deal with the issues that are deeply troubling you, or you are angry at the therapist for some reason. The interpretation of these unconscious feelings is basic to Freudian therapy. At the right moment,

the therapist would help you become aware of your unconscious resistance and your repressed feelings.

Transference   A final factor that gives psychoanalysts a clue to unconscious conflicts or needs is **transference.** Transference is a process by which a client projects feelings toward significant others—for instance, parents—onto the therapist. A client may act irritated every time the therapist makes a suggestion just as he did with his mother when he was a child; or he may expect the therapist to make all the decisions. Such attitudes serve as graphic indications of underlying needs and feelings.

Evaluating Psychoanalysis

How effective is psychoanalysis? The question is not easy to answer. Processes such as resistance and transference are so difficult to measure that it is hard to evaluate psychoanalysis. In addition, only a few therapists use purely psychoanalytic methods—so that the results may be due to the therapist's individual method more than to Freudian techniques.

In spite of these complications, however, some findings do support some of Freud's teachings. Recently, research has validated the notion that some mental disorders are related to unconscious wishes, at least in certain instances (Silverman, 1976); and there is also some evidence that insight therapies work. Feldman (1968) believes that case studies have shown insight therapy to be valuable, and other experimental studies also suggest that they help people to deal consciously with their problems. Some critics have contended that problems seem to improve with time even without any therapy (Eysenck, 1961), but most evidence suggests that psychotherapy works, and that insight therapy can be effective. One interesting study divided patients into three groups: one received Freudian therapy; another behavioral; and

---

Manifest content   The content of the dream as viewed and reported by the dreamer.

Latent content   A Freudian term describing the unconscious meanings behind people's dreams.

Transference   In psychoanalysis, the client's transfer to the therapist of feelings he or she held towards significant others in the past.

a third, no treatment (Sloane et al., 1975). The results showed more improvement in both of the therapy groups than in the control group.

This doesn't mean that Freudian psychoanalysis is for everyone. It is a lengthy process, taking years for some people, and thus it is expensive. In addition, many individuals are not willing or able to express all their feelings. However, the goal of insight into one's problems, as well as the idea that you can cope with problems once you are aware of their causes, are both concepts that are used by many non-Freudian therapists.

Behavior Therapy

Why am I afraid of dogs? unable to concentrate on my work? frustrated in my attempt to lose weight? While Freudian therapists might look for the answers to these questions hidden in the unconscious, behavior therapists would argue that the questions themselves were misstated.

What difference does it make why you have a problem, behaviorists argue, if it can be solved without understanding the original cause? If you are afraid of dogs, the "cure" would be to master that fear; if you can't concentrate, increasing your concentration skills is the answer; if you have trouble losing weight, the solution is to find a successful dieting strategy.

For many years, behavior therapists have been arguing that the root cause of the problem may be very interesting to the therapist, but relatively unimportant to the therapy. **Behavior therapists** believe that since problems are learned, then learning processes such as those discussed in Chapter 3 may also be used to alleviate them. Their emphasis is on observable behavior change and relief of the person's distress. There are several techniques for the unlearning and relearning processes involved in behavior therapy, and we'll look at them below.

HERMAN

"It's a real treat to talk to someone who doesn't keep laughing."

Behavior Therapy Techniques

Systematic Desensitization   Perhaps the most impressive behavioral technique is **systematic desensitization,** a programmed means of reducing

---

Behavior therapy   Therapy that is based on the principles of learning and focuses on producing a change in overt behavior rather than dealing with the unconscious or inner workings of the mind.

Systematic desensitization   A technique used in behavior therapy to reduce or eliminate anxiety. The client is placed into a state of deep relaxation and small amounts of the anxiety-producing stimulus are presented until he or she gradually learns to tolerate the stimulus.

---

anxiety toward a particular focus. We can use an example to show how this technique works.

Suppose you are so afraid of spiders that every time you see one, you freeze. You refuse to go camping for fear you'll meet a big fuzzy brown one. You can't enter an old garage or an attic for the same reason, and even walking around the house in the dark gives you the shivers. In general, your fears are making your life miserable. If you visited a behavior therapist, the desensitization procedure would probably follow several steps:

- First, the therapist might learn the details of your problem: when you get anxious, what you do about it, and so forth.

- Next, you would be asked to subjectively rate a list of various anxiety-provoking and neutral situations on a scale from 0 to 100. (For instance, when a spider is 20 feet away, how much anxiety do you feel? How much do you feel when you see a picture of a spider?)

- The therapist next teaches you how to relax, since deep muscle relaxation inhibits the development of anxiety. The procedures are similar to those described in Chapter 6.

- Now the therapist will ask you to relax, then imagine a particular scene that is low on your anxiety rating list. If you don't feel any anxiety, this means that the relaxation has inhibited your anxiety toward this source (or *desensitized* you); and the therapist will proceed to the next higher scene on the list. If you do feel some queasiness, the therapist will return to a previous scene that no longer makes you anxious.

Eventually, the client and therapist work themselves up the list until the client is no longer afraid of even the items at the top of the list. Some

---

Aversive conditioning A form of conditioning used in behavior therapy, in which a behavior is paired with an unpleasant stimulus in order to reduce or eliminate undesirable behavior.

---

therapists prefer to use real situations, perhaps placing a spider in a jar at various distances from the client. While some researchers consider this so-called *in vivo* desensitization to be more effective, both the imaginary and the realistic procedures have been successful. Desensitization has been used for many varied anxieties, including fear of speaking up in class, performing on stage, or taking tests.* It has even been used to reduce stuttering (Boudreau & Jeffrey, 1973).

Positive Reinforcement   A second behavior therapy technique is *positive reinforcement,* or reward for a desired behavior, as we discussed in Chapter 3. Positive reinforcement may be delivered by the therapist, by parents, or even by the client. Scoresby (1969) describes a case in which a client used self-reinforcement, under the steady direction of a counselor, to improve study habits. The reward—a 10-minute phone call or time out with a friend—was administered each time the client completed a certain prescribed amount of studying. As you probably remember from Chapter 3, a great many behaviors can be modified by use of positive reinforcement. The technique is sometimes combined with punishment, so that the desired behavior is strengthened while the unwanted one is discouraged.

Aversive Conditioning   Reinforcing yourself for studying or meeting new people seems like an easy enough application of behavior therapy; but punishment, or **aversive conditioning,** is another matter. Since few of us have the will to burn a five-dollar bill each time we leave homework till the last minute, we might need a therapist to carry out the punishment for us. This opens the door to a number of ethical questions—such as the issue of informed consent. If a client is a child, an incompetent adult, or an individual who is institu-

---

*To make the therapy more realistic in such cases, the desensitization would be performed in the place where the behavior change needs to take place. For instance, the client might sit in the classroom or stand on a stage.

tionalized, he or she may not be able to avoid unfair punishment (Stolz et al., 1975). Despite instances such as these, however, there are also many cases in which punishment has been shown to be effective.

As one example, Feldman (1966) describes his work with homosexuals who wished to change their sexual orientation.* He administered an electrical shock each time the client saw a picture of homosexual behavior, creating a negative association between the homosexual behavior and the client's emotional experience. The procedure had a high rate of success. When clients were also reinforced for reacting pleasurably toward heterosexual stimuli, the therapy was even more effective.

Shock is only one of several aversive stimuli that have been used to condition clients. Suspension of privileges is also used (for instance, when you were a child your parents may have punished you by not letting you play with friends), as are a number of other negative stimuli. Morganstern (1974) used cigarette smoke as an aversive stimulus for treating compulsive eaters. Most aversive techniques are more effective if, along with punishment for the incorrect response, there is also a reward for the desired behavior.

Coverant Control While aversive conditioning uses a direct punishment to discourage a behavior, the negative stimulus need not be so overt or obvious. **Coverant control** uses less direct negative conditioning to produce the same effect. For instance, in one technique to discourage smoking, a chain smoker was taught a series of thoughts (cognitions) such as "smoking is ugly, smoking is dangerous, smoking causes cancer." He was in-

structed to think of one of these sayings each time he lit up; and he kept a log of when, where, and under what conditions he smoked (Homme, 1965). In another use of coverant control, a client was taught to think of an extremely overweight person or to visualize a scene of someone throwing up each time she wanted to eat something fattening (Elliott & Denney, 1975).

Coverant control is somewhat effective in the short-term, especially when it is combined with positive reinforcement for the desired behavior. Long-term effects have not yet been shown to be so impressive, however. Further research is required in this area.

Extinction Still another learning theory technique is to let the unwanted behavior extinguish without necessarily using direct punishment. For example, if your child whines or throws temper tantrums, an effective treatment might be to ignore the tantrums while providing rewards for calm behavior. Williams (1959) instructed parents of a child who howled after being put to bed to ignore the cries. The tantrums disappeared within a very short time. (Parents should check with their pediatrician before using this technique, especially with very young children.) A combination of extinction and positive reinforcement for desired behavior is especially effective when the subject's environment can also be controlled—one reason why this technique is so often used by parents of young children.

Flooding Finally, **flooding** is a very different approach to treating some types of unwanted behaviors, such as hoarding. Most often used in institutional settings, it involves overloading a person

Flooding A behavior therapy technique that is effective for some unwanted behaviors, such as hoarding. The client is overloaded with the stimulus that is the object of the compulsion, until he or she becomes sick of it.

with the object of the desire until he or she is sick of it.

An example is a family in which five siblings were salami fanatics. They simply refused to eat anything else but salami. They ate it at breakfast, at lunch, and at dinner. The parents tried to stop them by restricting the salami, but the children simply bought their own. Another approach was more successful. They bought a 20-pound salami and hung it from the kitchen ceiling. It was gone in a few days, with the consequent stomach aches, and the parents immediately replaced it with another. This second salami lasted a full week. The third one had to be cut down: no one was interested in eating it. Flooding is not a technique to use without professional help, for it can be dangerous. In addition, it is not useful for every problem (for instance, it would be impractical as a means for treating a Cadillac fanatic). However, there are times when it can be used effectively.

Evaluating Behavior Therapy

When behavior therapies such as desensitization are first explained to students, they often wonder how they can be effective: isn't treating the symptoms of an emotional problem the same as treating pneumonia with a cough suppressant?

The problem with this analogy is that it assumes a *medical* or *disease model* for psychological problems. In a medical disease, the virus or bacteria must be eliminated if the patient is to recover. However, behaviorists argue that emotional and behavioral problems are different: they are learned, while diseases such as pneumonia are caught. While it can be effective to treat underlying causes of a problem, they believe that this is

> **Client-centered therapy** A type of therapy developed by Carl Rogers, more recently called the *person-centered* approach. Two elements are critical in this type of therapy: the warm personal relationship between client and therapist, and the belief in the client's ability to help himself or herself.

both unnecessary and time-consuming.*

Indeed, many studies show that behavioral techniques are successful for several problems (Rimm & Masters, 1974). Wolpe's classic works on desensitization reported that out of 210 clients treated, 90 percent were improved or had their symptoms completely eliminated. Other therapists agree that desensitization is quite successful in treating anxiety (Paul, 1967). Other problems, from nailbiting, to aggression, to shoplifting, to a fear of meeting new people have all been treated by behavior therapy methods.

While there is no question that behavior therapy is valuable, it requires a solid, measurable goal in order to succeed. It isn't difficult to place behaviors such as overeating or stealing into this kind of perspective, but not all problems are so well-defined. Imagine a person with an identity problem or one who is confused about the meaning of life. In these cases forming behavioral objectives is much more difficult. In addition, the behaviorist's emphasis on the task rather than the person may be disconcerting to many; and ethical issues must also be considered, especially when behavior therapy is used in a coercive setting. In all, behavior therapy is certainly effective in many cases, but it does not answer everyone's needs.

Humanistic Therapy

In the behavioral scheme, the relationship between the client and the therapist is not considered as crucial to the success of the therapy as are the techniques that are used. In psychoanalysis, too, the client's personal relationship with the analyst is not as essential to the treatment as is the process of uncovering unconscious processes.

All this is reversed in the best known of the humanistic therapies, **client-centered** or *Rogerian*

*There is some contention over this point. According to the psychoanalytic school, merely dealing with the symptoms will cause other symptoms to crop up instead. This *symptom substitution* may occur in some instances, but it is quite rare (Rimm & Masters, 1974) and behaviorists argue that it isn't a factor in most cases.

therapy, or as it is more recently called, the *person-centered approach* (Rogers, 1980). In this approach, developed by Carl Rogers, two elements are seen as crucial to the success of therapy. The first is the warm, personal relationship between the therapist and the client; the second is the belief that clients can help themselves.

Client-Centered Therapy

The Client-Centered Therapist Rogers (1967) believes that the therapist's personality and attitudes are the most important predictors of successful counseling. The ideal therapist, according to Rogers, shows genuine understanding, interest, and positive regard for the client, and is willing to listen without judging the client's actions. He or she is open, honest, and willing to see the situation from the client's point of view. The counselor tries to see everything from the client's point of view (this is called the **phenomenological viewpoint**), demonstrating a deep empathy or understanding.

In such a setting, most clients feel safe in disclosing themselves, and little by little, they are able to listen to their own feelings. They realize that they do feel jealous or angry. As such feelings are expressed, the therapist accepts them, showing clients that they can accept their own feelings, too. In this way, clients move toward what Rogers calls congruence, accepting and acting in accordance with their true feelings. They become able to change, grow, and act more naturally in all situations.

The behavior and attitude changes that take place in Rogerian therapy don't result from the counselor's delving into the clients' past; nor are they the product of reinforcement procedures. Instead, they come from the client's own inner growth, as they learn to solve their own difficulties within the framework of the counselor relationship. The responsibility for this growth rests squarely on the clients' shoulders. The counselors are not miracle workers, but rather are individuals who can provide an atmosphere conducive to an honest, open exploration of the clients' perceptions of their own innermost feelings.

Reflection and Clarification Although client-centered counseling does not rely on specific techniques as much as do most other therapeutic approaches, two procedures are particularly valuable: reflection and clarification.

Reflection, as we saw in Chapter 9, involves mirroring or repeating the feelings that the client is expressing. For instance, if a woman was troubled because she couldn't decide whether or not to postpone law school in order to marry, a Rogerian therapist wouldn't give advice. Indeed, such a response would be seen as narrow and stultifying, since it wouldn't encourage her to explore her own feelings. A more appropriate response would be to reflect what she has expressed—for instance, "You seem desperate to make the right decision"—in order to encourage her to work out her own feelings.

As she expresses more of what she feels, the therapist might ask her to clarify her statements by asking questions whenever her statements weren't clear ("Do you mean that you think you aren't ready for marriage?"). **Clarification**—asking the client to rephrase statements so the counselor can better understand them—is important because it helps the client define her own feelings. She might find that fear, anger, insecurity, or jealousy are behind her inability to make a decision. After she has explored her present feelings and become aware of them, perhaps she will be able to accept them and finally make her own decision.

Phenomenological viewpoint The humanistic view that stresses the importance of an individual's subjective experiences. In counseling, the therapist attempts to perceive the world from the client's point of view.

Clarification A technique used in client-centered therapy in which the counselor asks the client to rephrase statements so they can be better understood.

Compared to techniques such as systematic desensitization or dream analysis, reflection and clarification may seem rather undramatic. However, if you try the techniques yourself, you may find that after a bit of practice you are more sensitive to the feelings of others. You may also notice, when you discuss your own problems with friends, how infrequently people reflect your feelings.

Evaluating Client-Centered Therapy

Carl Rogers was always very interested in evaluating his client-centered approach. He was the first to tape sessions and to insist on evaluations, and those evaluations have been rather positive. Rogers (1967) found that treatments worked best when therapists had empathic personalities, when clients were verbal, and when both clients and therapists came from similar backgrounds (a factor that probably aids in empathizing).

The most common positive outcome seems to be in the direction of an improved self-concept (Rogers & Dymond, 1954), and these changes in self-concept have been shown to be related to improved personal functioning (Rubin, 1967). In other words, the results of client-centered therapy are an improved self-concept, greater self-acceptance, and an increased awareness of one's true feelings (Burns, 1979).

Cognitive Therapy

Psychoanalysis uncovers unconscious processes, behavior therapies aim at symptoms, and human-

> **Rational-emotive therapy** A type of cognitive therapy developed by Albert Ellis, which stresses the importance of an individual's beliefs, thoughts, and self-statements. It focuses on changing a person's thought patterns in order to alter feelings and behavior.

istic therapy works toward personal growth and self-acceptance. Still another approach, *cognitive* or **rational-emotive therapy,** tries to bring about change by modifying thought processes.

According to this view, as expressed by Albert Ellis (Ellis & Harper, 1975), it is not events that cause us to feel depressed, unhappy, apathetic, or angry; it is our perceptions of those events instead. For instance, if you feel that being fired or rejected is the end of the world, then you will likely be deeply depressed if you are fired. On the other hand, if the prospect of being fired is merely annoying, then your reaction will be more positive. Compare the two series below:

Activating Event: You're fired.

Belief: "It's the end of the world."

Consequence: Depression, inactivity.

Activating Event: You're fired.

Belief: "It's too bad, but I'll get by. Other people have been fired and survived."

Consequence: Sadness, but capacity for enjoying other areas of life. Job-seeking behaviors can follow.

Modifying Thought Processes

Since Ellis sees thought patterns as the source of many problems, the key to his rational emotive therapy is to modify thought processes, or self-statements. Two techniques for doing this are disputing and rational-emotive imagery.

Disputing As we saw in Chapter 6, *disputing* involves teaching clients to argue against their own thoughts. For instance, the therapist may instruct the client to write down all the reasons why being fired is awful, and then to refute each one in turn. Basically, the goal is for the client to realize that what happened (or what might happen, as when someone is worried she won't get hired for the job she wants) isn't pleasant, but also to realize that there is much more to life. Individuals are encouraged to use refutation whenever their thoughts produce emotions that impair their functioning.

Rational-Emotive Imagery In **rational-emotive imagery,** clients learn to use their imaginations to change their emotions. For instance, a therapist might tell you to imagine you've just been fired, and to feel exactly how you would feel, then to say something to yourself that will make you feel better. In this way, clients learn what kinds of self-statements they can use to change their own emotions. According to therapists of this school, this prepares clients to cope with problems when they do occur, and to combat emotional distress.

Once a person learns to react to failures or rejections in a rational manner the next step is to provide the client with a new set of cognitions that can serve as motivation to improve the situation. Solid behavioral steps are then taken. For instance, the key to changing behavior patterns may simply lie in trying something new that you were always afraid to try. Perhaps you've always felt you can't dance, and so you end up sitting in the corner at party after party. After refuting your worries (would people really laugh at you? and if they did, would it make any difference?), the next step would be to go ahead and dance, to see what the consequences really are. In most cases, they are not as bad as you had expected; and you'll find that people are far too busy looking after their own lives to be concerned with your behavior. Even if they do notice, the client has learned a number of positive self-statements that can help.

Evaluating Rational-Emotive Therapy

Although rational-emotive therapy is a relatively new approach, some outcome studies suggest it can be effective (DiGiuseppe et al., 1977). Therapy does not stop when the client walks out the counselor's door. It often involves clients in "homework"—practicing techniques such as refutation in their daily lives.

While many people see rational-emotive therapy as an interesting and valuable approach, the research to date still isn't conclusive. The central hypothesis, that people can learn to adjust positively by changing their thought patterns, still hasn't been proven (Mahoney, 1977). For now, perhaps the best conclusion would be that rational-emotive therapy is an interesting new approach, whose potential still has to be explored.

The Human Potentials Movement

In recent years, a new movement aimed at improving the functioning of essentially healthy people has arisen. This has been loosely termed the **human potentials movement,** and its aim is to help people grow personally and interpersonally, through increased awareness. In this aim, we should note, there is some overlap with the forms of therapy we've been discussing. But this movement's emphasis is on self-improvement. Perhaps the most notable outgrowth of this movement are training groups, or *T-groups*.

The Group Format

Today, the terms *T-groups, sensitivity groups,* and *encounter groups* are common everyday words. T-

> **Rational-emotive imagery** A therapeutic technique used in rational-emotive therapy in which the client is asked to imagine himself or herself feeling a certain way, then taught how to counter that feeling through the use of self-statements.
>
> **Human potentials movement** A humanistic movement devoted to the development and maximization of the unique qualities and abilities of human beings.

groups or **sensitivity groups** may be run in factories, schools, churches, and jails, among other places. Basically, the goal of these groups is to facilitate personal and interpersonal growth. Sensitivity groups began as a means of training people to be more sensitive in their interpersonal relations. Using various exercises, with plenty of verbal feedback from other members, group members become more sensitive to their own and others' opinions, attitudes, and beliefs. This honest feedback allows group participants to assess their own communication skills more accurately, and to change their behavior where the need exists.

Encounter groups began on the West Coast, and they involve more interpersonal confrontation than do the sensitivity sessions. Their aim, in general, is personal growth, with goals that are usually very broad. Feedback tends to be very frank and honest. Differences between encounter and sensitivity are relatively minor, however, since each has adopted techniques from the other.

Techniques

Although a variety of techniques are used in group sessions, there are three basic types of techniques: verbal, nonverbal, and physical. In each of these categories, the techniques may be mild, causing little trauma to group members, or harsh,

> **Sensitivity groups**   Short-term groups conducted by a leader, in which the participants interact in a way that facilitates personal and interpersonal growth. Members increase their awareness of how they affect others and how others affect them through a variety of verbal and nonverbal techniques.
>
> **Encounter groups**   Small groups that meet in an effort to promote personal growth and change through a variety of verbal and nonverbal techniques.

challenging the individual's powers of growth and honesty.

An example of a *verbal* technique might be to ask each group member to disclose a personal secret to the rest of the group. This often leads to a discussion of trust; at the same time, it enables members to react to one another. Another verbal technique is role playing. If you have always found it hard to relate to your boss, you might be asked to play the role of your boss as someone else plays you. There are many other verbal techniques.

Nonverbal techniques vary widely. One common nonverbal technique is to eliminate speaking entirely. Group members are instructed to communicate only with gestures or eye contact; and as you can imagine, this opens up a new dimension of sensitivity to others within the group. Eye contact and gestures are an important source of information, and through such training, members may gain insight into themselves and others in the group.

The physical techniques are often employed as ice breakers, or as a way of creating a shared group experience. In *blind milling,* members walk around the room with their eyes closed and when they meet another person they communicate only through touching the shoulders, hands, face, or hair. They then find a nonverbal way of saying good-bye and continue to mill around until they find someone else (Lewis & Streitfeld, 1972). In the *trust fall,* a member is asked to fall backwards into the arms of other members, who catch the individual before he or she hits the ground.

Each group leader has his or her own favorite techniques, which vary from group to group. Some are simple, such as having everyone choose a new name for themselves, wear masks, or disclose something personal about themselves; others are more difficult. For instance, touching has intimate connotations in our society, and some group members find it very difficult to enter into such activities. Again, group members may be asked to be completely honest to one another; and sometimes this can be painful.

A Three-Stage Process

Encounter groups seem to have a never-ending repertory of exercises such as those we've just described; and in the hands of a competent leader, they can be powerful tools for personal growth. A question that students often ask is how that growth takes place. Generalizations are impossible, for each group has a personality and a chemistry of its own. In addition, participants often see themselves as achieving something, then regressing, instead of steadily progressing (Lakin, 1972). However, most groups seem to go through a three-stage process.

The Trust Stage   The first goal of the group leader is to establish a sense of trust, both among members and between members and the leader. This doesn't come automatically, for it's natural for new members to be nervous and to have second thoughts about being in the group.

Most participants, especially if they have never been in a group before, expect the leader to begin things. This does not always happen, however. Some leaders do use warm-up exercises, but often they simply wait for someone to start things. A member will usually ask, "O.K. What do we do now?" To this, the most common answer is, "What would you like to do?" This is usually followed by some discussion of what people are doing there, as well as some hostility toward the leader for not giving more direction. The questions "Why should I start saying something personal?" and "How do I know I can trust you?" are often asked.

These questions need to be answered during the **trust stage.** At this stage, two things occur. First, group members learn that they are largely responsible for the success or failure of the group. And secondly, the questions of trust are raised, and hopefully solved. Since very personal material may come out, the question is in the back of everyone's mind. Suspicions, fears, and anxieties are expressed. To help resolve these issues, the leader may suggest some exercises. In one, the *trust walk,* members walk blindfolded assisted by

Sensitivity and encounter groups use many methods—verbal, nonverbal, and physical.

another member whom they do not know. The trust fall, as we saw earlier, also involves putting one's safety in the hands of someone else in the group.

If group members begin to trust each other, they may move to the second stage. If not, this

> **Trust stage**   The first stage of an encounter group, in which the participants work out personal issues relating to the consequences of trusting the other members of the group.

Encounter Groups: Does the Leader Make a Difference?

How extensively does an encounter or sensitivity group affect its group members? As this chapter points out, the answer to that question depends to a great extent upon the experience and training of the leader. A number of studies have indicated that properly led groups have indeed been beneficial to their participants by improving sensitivity to others, increasing self-confidence, and helping individuals function better at their jobs. But little research has explored the effect of encounter group experiences on an interesting variable called **locus of control.**

For years, psychologists have known that people differ on how they perceive the cause of events that affect their lives. People with an *external* locus of control believe that they are at the mercy of fate or luck. On the other hand, those with *internal* control believe that they control most of the things that happen in their lives. Most psychological studies have found that internal people tend to be better adjusted, more self-confident and trusting, and tend to work on their own personal problems more often. If there is a shift from external to internal locus of control due to the encounter group experience, this change could be of significant value to the participants.

Michael Diamond and Jerrold Shapiro designed a study to evaluate how an encounter group experience affected locus of control. Thirty-one volunteer graduate students from the University of Hawaii were randomly assigned to three treatment groups led by expert leaders who used different approaches to conduct their encounter groups. Each subject was given a test that measured locus of control at the beginning and at the end of the group sessions. In a parallel study, six rather inexperienced group leaders conducted groups using a similar format. As the investigators expected, the expertly led groups showed dramatic changes in locus of control. Subjects who had participated in the group sessions developed an internal orientation whereas the control subjects did not. Those groups led by the inexperienced student leaders also showed these changes—but they were not as pronounced as in the groups led by the experts.

Two important conclusions come directly from this data. First, the encounter group experience can lead to a shift from an external locus of control to a more internal focus. And secondly, if you want to get the most out of an encounter group, look into the credentials and experience of the leader. The better the leader, the greater chance of a successful and satisfying outcome.

Source: Diamond & Shapiro, 1973.

question will remain unresolved, and the group will progress very little beyond this first stage. As the box *Encounter Groups: Does the Leader Make a Difference?* documents, one of the most important variables determining the progress of a group is the training and ability of its leader. Even if a group remains at the trust stage, however, the experience can still be valuable because of the questions of responsibility and trust that it raises.

Locus of control   An individual's belief that his or her actions are controlled by either external or internal factors.

The Attack Stage   The second stage is qualitatively different from the trust stage. "Now that we can trust each other," the thinking goes, "I can be totally honest for the first time—and I've got a few things to say to you!"

The first emotions to be honestly expressed are often hostility and anger, and during the **attack stage,** as it is often called, members use their newfound freedom to criticize others. Perhaps the woman next to you has been acting like a little girl. In your daily life, you would simply ignore her. But since you're encouraged to be frank in the group, you may feel called upon to bend over backwards to be honest—if brutally so—and tell her just what you think.

The leader must provide extremely careful guidance at this stage, allowing members to express enough so that each person understands the others' perceptions, yet protecting the more vulnerable members from situations they can't handle. This is one of the most important skills a leader can possess. Attack, hostility, and confrontation, unless they are handled properly, can cause damage rather than growth. Thus, the third stage is necessary as the culmination of a successful group process.

The Embracement Stage The third stage is known as the **embracement stage.** At this point, the group is past the point of expressing anger, and members are willing to support each other's growth. They are supportive, often encouraging an individual to take exciting new steps. Successes and failures are often discussed openly, without fear of disapproval or censure. The entire group has a positive feeling. Indeed, membership in such a group can be a positive experience, leading to new methods of coping with interpersonal situations and a more sensitive understanding of others.

Evaluating Group Experiences

Group growth sessions like those we've described have become very popular; but do they work? A number of studies have looked into the effectiveness of sensitivity groups and encounter groups in bringing about changes in attitudes or behaviors. So far, their findings have been far from unanimous.

Certainly, some potential problems exist. For instance, the growth that takes place within the group may not always transfer to the outside world (Houts & Serber, 1972). What works in the group might not work when you tell your boss or spouse the honest truth. Another potential problem lies in the fact that some people are simply not comfortable interacting in groups. One study found that out of every nine participants, one has a negative experience in encounter groups (Lieberman et al., 1973).*

Individuals who have serious problems in coping with group situations are often called **casualties.** A variety of causes seem to be involved in casualties. Sometimes it is the failure of the leader

---

*Other studies have shown a wide variation in the rate of negative experiences, from less than 1 percent to almost 50 percent (Hartley et al., 1976). The huge variation is probably due to a combination of problems, including a lack of agreement as to criteria and measurement difficulties. Perhaps a reasonable figure is between 7 and 14 percent.

Attack stage Often the second stage in an encounter group, in which participants may feel free enough to be very frank and honest in focusing on the negative qualities of other group members. It follows the trust stage and precedes the embracement stage. This stage has the potential for being destructive unless the leader has the skills necessary to help the group through it.

Embracement stage The third and final stage of an encounter group, in which the group supports the individual's attempt to change, often through experimentation with new modes of behavior.

Casualties Those individuals injured psychologically due to their participation in an encounter group.

to cope with the participants' anxieties (Gottschan, 1966); other times, a certain technique—such as a physical contact—bothers certain members (Ross et al., 1971).

Despite these problems, however, many people still report positive changes within encounter group experiences. For example, Miles (1965) asked co-workers to rate participants who had gone through sensitivity training together, and found that these workers were rated as more sensitive, relaxed, and better able to communicate. Another study (Rubin, 1967) linked group experiences with increased self-acceptance and decreases in prejudicial attitudes. With results such as these, it is fair to say that the human potentials movement will probably continue to grow, and perhaps to expand. You may well have some experience with a group yourself at some time in your life (if you haven't already). The box *Checking Out T-Groups* should give you some ideas about what to expect as well as what you might consider if you're thinking of joining a T-group.

The discussions above have tried to give you a broad understanding of the different approaches to therapy and the nature of the human potentials movement. If you think that therapy might help you, though, you'll need more than this general knowledge. Many practical questions will need to be answered, and we'll turn to these next.

Some Practical Questions

Suppose you have a problem that you can't seem to solve on your own. It may be a big emotional or psychological problem; or it may be relatively

> **Developmental counseling** Counseling in which the main focus is on aiding the client to deal more effectively with the normal problems and tasks arising at a particular time in life.

"minor"—something that doesn't interfere with your happiness all of the time, but which keeps on coming back to bother you. After much soul-searching, you decide to seek professional help.

What next? If you think you (or someone close to you) can be helped by a therapist, the next step may be full of questions. Who visits therapists? Where can you find help? What kinds of credentials are important in a trained therapist? How much will you have to pay? And finally, what should you do if you're not satisfied with your therapist, or if you don't think you need to continue treatment? Most of us have had little practical consumer advice about psychotherapy—much less so than for regular medical care. Yet without answers to questions like these, decisions can be very difficult indeed. We'll provide some brief answers below.

Who Visits Therapists?

There is no single reason for visiting a counselor or therapist. After all, there are considerable differences between the person who seeks help from a $75-per-hour psychoanalyst, a student who visits a counselor in a college setting, and a middle-aged person seeking help in a community mental health clinic.

A few generalizations are possible, though. As we saw in Chapter 4, people's needs change somewhat over the course of development, and certain differences also seem to be associated with particular age groups. For example, school-aged children might have achievement or discipline problems, while adolescents might have difficulty with identity and vocational choice. Depression may be relatively more common during middle age, while problems in later age are more likely to center around the need to cope with both declining health and the inevitability of death (Atchley, 1977). Therapists trained in **developmental counseling** place emphasis on the normal challenges appropriate for a client's age group.

Checking Out T-Groups

With the nation-wide popularity of groups, it's a sure thing that some will be more helpful to you than others. Some groups will have goals or methods that don't meet your own needs. And unfortunately, there are some leaders who are willing to exploit unwary individuals by running groups that accomplish nothing and may even cause more harm than good. If you're thinking of joining a T-group, therefore, it pays to do some detective work first to find out if it is going to provide the service you need. The following questions may help minimize the chances that your own experience will be a negative one.

1. Would your goals be better realized in private treatment with a competent therapist?

If you can answer that question to your own satisfaction (and to that of the group leader, if there is a regular screening procedure), then the questions that follow can help you protect yourself from choosing the wrong group.

2. What are the leader's credentials?

When you read about the three stages of therapy, you might have been impressed with the subtle skills required by the leader. Vehement feelings are often expressed in groups, and without the right guidance by a leader with credentials and training, the group experience may actually be harmful to some people.

3. What are the leader's methods?

If possible, you should meet the leader and try to evaluate not only experience and credentials but also the methods that will be used. If getting physical bothers you, you'll want to know if the group uses such techniques. If long hours will interfere with your own schedule, you should check into this point as well. Some groups may become *marathons,* going on for days at a time with little or no break. This supposedly helps to break down members' barriers and defenses; but it may also wreak havoc with your private life. In general, the more you know about what to expect, the less likely you'll be to end up as a "casualty."

4. What rules will be in effect, and what goals will the group have?

Usually, group members agree to certain rules—for instance, that they will remain in the group for a certain time, that no physical violence will be allowed, and that no one will be forced to deal with material they do not wish to explore. Rules differ from group to group, however, and some groups have no rules that are specifically stated. Goals vary from group to group also; and it's wise to check first to make sure that the leader's goals are similar to your own.

5. Who else will be in the group? How will they be chosen?

Is there a screening procedure to make certain that seriously disturbed people will not be included in the group? The composition of the group can be an important factor, for one person's serious problems can prevent the rest of the group from making progress.

These questions may seem overly dramatic to you. However, the truth is that, as in all therapeutic services, the final responsibility lies with you. *Caveat emptor* (let the buyer beware) is still an important consideration in choosing a group (Hartley & Strupp, 1978).

Psychological problems are also related to work setting. A therapist who works on a submarine base may be continually confronted with wives who are depressed because of their husbands' prolonged absences at sea. In a dense inner-city area, therapists may see a high proportion of people troubled by anxiety and alienation. People who have worked in human service jobs—as welfare workers or dentists, for instance—are especially prone to an overwhelming sense of apathy known as **burnout.**

In predicting whether you or someone else needs help, the nature of the problem may not be as important as whether the person feels he or she can cope with it (Frank, 1973). For instance, John and Frank may both get hives whenever they speak before a group. If John isn't particularly bothered by hives, he probably won't think he needs a therapist. If Frank finds that they cause him so much worry that he's completely miserable, then he will probably seek help. If you've wondered whether you should seek help, therefore, some of the most important cues will come from your own feelings about the way in which you are coping.

How Do You Find the Right Therapist?

Once individuals decide they need professional help, the next question is how to find the *right* sort of help. Notice the emphasis on the word "right": all sorts of therapists are in practice, but not all will be right for any one person.

Resources for Getting in Touch　Most people have a family physician and know where the hos-

pital emergency room is in their community. However, relatively few laypersons know where to find psychological help. Several resources can be helpful in starting people off in the right direction.

Most colleges offer psychological services. Some have counseling centers right on campus, while others specialize in crisis work and then refer students to a resource list of community agencies that can help for less urgent problems. One advantage of this type of referral service is that the college may have checked out these centers, can arrange your first appointment, and can make certain the charges do not exceed your budget.

Other resources include local professional organizations. Here, you can find a list of certified specialists. Still another resource may be your family physician, who probably knows of mental health professionals practicing in your area. Clergy may also be able to act as a resource. Finally, many people use personal referrals from friends who have had psychological help. This is a frequent way to find help, but it is risky. A counselor may have been able to help your friend, but this is no assurance that the same treatment will be right for you. Several other criteria should be considered in determining whether a professional can give you the help you need.

Criteria for Choosing a Therapist　If you were looking for a therapist, which would be most important to you: the therapist's techniques, experience, credentials, or personality?

The answer will vary from one person to another, but it helps to know what you're looking for. *Techniques* are one factor that might be considered. We've seen earlier that there are four major approaches to therapy; and in your reading, you may have felt that one of these schools seemed especially appropriate or inappropriate to you. For instance, the behaviorist approach may have seemed too impersonal—or, on the other hand, it may have seemed highly efficient to you. It's possible, of course, that you have had no such

---

Burnout　An overwhelming sense of apathy that sometimes affects persons working in human service jobs.

Table 14.1 Who's Who in the Mental Health Profession

Psychiatrist	A psychiatrist is a medical doctor who has specialized in psychiatry. Psychiatrists can prescribe medication while the other professionals listed here cannot. In private practice, however, their fees tend to be rather expensive.
Psychologist	A psychologist has a Ph.D. in psychology. Not all psychologists can provide therapy. However, clinical and counseling psychologists are usually proficient in one or more techniques of therapy. Many psychologists have close working relationships with medical specialists who prescribe medication if needed.
Guidance counselor	Guidance counselors have training in guidance and counseling. They may have masters or doctorate degrees. In some states they are *licensed,* that is, certified by the state as having completed the appropriate course of study.
Social worker	Social workers have a degree in social work and are normally licensed by the state.

leanings, either toward or away from an approach. If you have, however, these feelings should certainly be a factor in your choice.

A second and probably more important factor is the therapist's *experience* and *credentials.* Since you will be putting your problems in the therapist's hands, it's worth doing a little research to find out what kinds of qualifications he or she has. In many states, the terms "therapist," "counselor", or even "psychotherapist" are not protected titles; anyone can use them. Thus, the therapist's credentials should be available for inspection by any potential client. Table 14.1 lists the differences between a **psychiatrist**, a **psychologist**, a **guidance counselor**, and a **social worker**—just a few of the many titles that are used by mental health professionals. Their jurisdictions overlap greatly, and it's impossible to generalize about which professional would be more helpful for which type of problem.

A third factor is also important in choosing an individual therapist, and that is *personality.* As we saw earlier, Carl Rogers felt that the most important determinant of the success of a client-therapist relationship was the therapist's personality, and this is a very important factor in most forms of therapy. A person may be eminently qualified to provide treatment, but you may find that you're not comfortable working with that therapist.

What if You Aren't Satisfied with Your Therapist?

Even though you've made your choice carefully and considered all the factors above, it's possible that you may be disappointed with your therapist. Like any other consumer service, you may find you need to switch from one counselor to another to find the help you need.

Unlike other consumer services, however, it may be very difficult to tell whether your reason for changing is valid. For instance, you may worry that your terrible desire to get out of therapy may be *your* fault, not the therapist's. It is not unusual for clients to want to escape sessions if you and your counselor are dealing with emotionally charged material. How can you tell the difference?

You may be able to recognize the symptoms yourself. One sign that you may need to find a new therapist is a feeling that you can't seem to establish a good working relationship. If you discover you aren't accomplishing anything during your sessions, your best course is to discuss your doubts with your therapist. It may be that he or she has taken you as far as is possible in your relationship. No counselor succeeds with every client, and therapists need to accept this themselves. If your therapist is unwilling to discuss these doubts, it may mean that he or she is not very confident.

There are other more obvious symptoms. If your counselor seems always to be discussing his or her personal problems rather than yours, or if you find each of you continually blaming the other for a lack of progress, the relationship is unlikely to provide you with the help you need. In all, the important point is that you become aware of your reasons for changing: is it to avoid dealing with a problem, or is it because of your relationship with the therapist? (Ehrenberg & Ehrenberg, 1975).

How Expensive Is Therapy?

Still another question in many people's minds is the cost of therapy. Psychological help has the reputation for being expensive, and there is no doubt that it can be. However, some techniques tend to be more expensive than others. In psychoanalysis, it may take a longer time to find the unconscious roots of a problem. Other forms of treatment may take less time, and consequently less money; but the question of whether they are better is a matter for personal judgment. It is possible to find counselors who work on sliding scales (that is, they take your financial status into consideration when setting their fee), or who are available at a community health center a few times a week. Also, group therapy may be available at a lower cost. While this offers less one-to-one interaction between the client and therapist, it does provide feedback from other patients, and this can be helpful in some cases.

Even when psychological help is costly, those expenses should be kept in perspective. A counselor may earn $35 per session. But remember that you are getting a full 50 minutes from him or her. When was the last time you received such

attention from a physician? If the cost is considered on an hour-to-hour basis, it is not so excessive after all.

What Determines Success?

Perhaps the most difficult question to answer is what type of therapy is best for you. After all, there are so many different approaches. There is little clear-cut evidence that any one therapy is better than the others (Smith & Glass, 1977). In fact, the authors don't know of a single case in which a practicing group of therapists disbanded because their approach was found to be less effective than another.

This may be due to the many difficulties in determining outcome of therapy. Do you measure success according to what the client reports, or by behavior changes that can be observed? A client may claim to be no better, but may show tremendous improvement in daily functioning. Again, the problem is complicated by the many technical difficulties in assessing different goals and techniques of the various approaches.

Yet there are certain factors that seem to be most important to successful counseling. According to one study (Luborsky & Spence, 1971), the most important indicator of success is a healthy, intelligent, highly motivated client. Also important is the therapist's experience, attitude, and his or her ability to convey empathy. The counselor's approach and techniques are a third factor—but these are often hard to evaluate. The longer a therapist practices, the more *eclectic* he or she is likely to be. That is, many psychologists may begin their practice concentrating on one method, but as the years go on, they may modify that approach by borrowing techniques from other schools of thought.

In all, the experience of therapy is a unique one. If you are thinking of seeing a therapist, you'll want to consider many factors. Both therapy and sensitivity groups may help you move toward increased self-awareness and behavior changes. Psychotherapy is used to treat many problems ranging from mild to quite severe, and there is evidence that it can effectively improve functioning (Tramontana, 1980; Garfield, 1981). Psychotherapy is also used more and more for helping people actualize their potentials.

Our responsibility to ourselves is to grow; to be a little better today than we were yesterday—and hopefully, a little better tomorrow than we were today. These are basic elements in the esteem needs, and for some people, therapy can be an important aid in reaching these goals. In the next and final section of this text, we'll look even further at how people can reach their potentials as we explore Maslow's final level of self-actualization needs.

Summary

1. The most important factor determining whether individuals seek therapy is whether they feel they need help.

2. The key elements in any psychotherapy include a person who desires some change, a professional therapist, and a trusting relationship between the therapist and client that leads to insight or some behavioral change.

3. Psychoanalysts try to find the root cause of the client's problem. Freud believed that problems were caused by the tension between unconscious drives and the prohibitions of society. Techniques such as free association, dream analysis, interpretation of slips of the tongue, resistance, and transference are used to uncover such conflicts. When the problem is understood, the client and therapist are better able to deal with it.

4. Behavior therapists do not look for the underlying causes of a problem. Assuming that the behavior is learned, they use various techniques to help the client learn new behaviors that will be more useful. These techniques include systematic desensitization, positive reinforcement, aversive conditioning, coverant control, extinction, and flooding, as well as a number of other methods.

5. There are many humanistic therapies. Client-centered psychotherapy was developed by Carl Rogers, and it centers around the accepting atmosphere provided by the therapist. Reflection and clarification are used to encourage clients to deal with their feelings.

6. In rational-emotive therapy, the client is made aware of irrational thought patterns and learns to dispute illogical beliefs. In RET, it is your belief about a particular event, not the event itself, that is of great importance. Rational-emotive therapists help clients to change self-defeating thought patterns and try out new behaviors.

7. T-groups, encounter groups, and sensitivity groups are all part of the human potentials movement, which aims at increasing self-awareness and sensitivity to others. The techniques used by these groups vary greatly. Some involve physical contact, while others stress verbal interaction. Encounter groups are not meant as substitutes for therapy.

8. Encounter groups ideally go through a three-stage process including trust, attack, and embracement.

9. The most important factor influencing the success of a group is the experience and skill of the leader. About 7–14% of all people entering encounter groups have severe problems coping with the group situation.

10. The vast majority of studies concerned with the effectiveness of psychotherapy have demonstrated that all the major schools are effective in helping their clients, and no one approach can claim it is more effective than the others with every problem.

11. People who are interested in entering therapy can be more sure of getting the help they need if they consider certain guidelines. Caveat emptor (let the buyer beware) applies to therapy just as it does to any other consumer service. Clients need to take

responsibility for their own success in therapy not only by working with the therapist, but by choosing help carefully in the first place.

12. There are many types of mental health professionals. Psychiatrists have medical degrees and can prescribe medication, while psychologists have Ph.D. degrees in psychology. Guidance counselors and social workers are among many other titles of trained professionals that may provide guidance. In many states, the titles *counselor* or *therapist* are not protected by law.

13. Although psychotherapy can be expensive, free or inexpensive help can often be found through college counseling centers, community agencies, or by contacting local professional agencies.

14. The experience, personality, and attitudes of the counselor, as well as the therapist's ability to convey understanding of the problem, seem to be the most important factors in a successful therapeutic outcome. The counselor's school of thought is relatively less important. Clients who are basically healthy, intelligent, and highly motivated tend to improve most in counseling.

Key Terms and Concepts

psychotherapy

psychoanalysis

psychodynamic

insight therapies

free association

manifest content

latent content

resistance

transference

behavior therapy

systematic desensitization

aversive conditioning

flooding

client-centered therapy

phenomenological viewpoint

clarification

rational-emotive therapy

rational-emotive imagery

human potentials movement

sensitivity groups

encounter groups

trust stage

attack stage

embracement stage

locus of control

casualties

developmental counseling

burnout

Self-Actualization

The story is told of a man trying to sell a beautiful rug. "Who will give me 100 pieces of gold for this rug?" he called out. After the sale was concluded, a friend asked him why he did not ask more than that for the priceless merchandise. "Is there any number higher than 100?" asked the seller.

Robert Ornstein (1972), one of the leading psychologists in the study of consciousness, compares the rug seller to ourselves. It is easy to accept the limits imposed on us by our everyday consciousness. It is much harder to break through those limits and explore

Consciousness

our inner selves by altering our consciousness. Yet inner knowledge can raise our awareness to a different level, offering new avenues for us to explore. It may help not only to overcome stress and anxiety, but also to fulfill our own potential.

Throughout this text, we have discussed many concepts and presented some tools for adjustment. We hope that these concepts and tools have challenged you to become more aware of both your external and internal feelings and experiences. All of these elements are involved in laying the foundations for adjustment. In Part V, however, we'll try to extend our discussion a bit more and look at some ways of developing our inner selves and transcending our day-to-day situations, as we explore consciousness in this chapter and as we look at value systems in Chapter 16.

Why Study Consciousness?

Consciousness is very much in the news today. Newspapers constantly carry stories concerning hypnosis, dreams, and meditation. However, the topic of consciousness has not always been a favorite with Western psychologists. Before about 1910, conscious experience was considered an important area of study. However, in the early portion of the twentieth century John Watson, the famous behaviorist, argued that psychology should shun such subjective areas as conscious experience and concentrate on the more scientific and objective study of observable actions (Jaynes, 1976).

The behaviorist approach provides answers to many questions about why people act as they do. Processes like conditioning and modeling explain a great deal about behavior. However, the approach of Watson (and of later learning theorists) still leaves questions unanswered about what is going on within the mind. For instance, someone might step on your toe—an experience that, if repeated, might condition you to change your own behaviors (if only to flinch when you saw the stimulus coming again). This process takes place under normal conditions, but not always. If you've had a lot to drink, or if your thoughts are totally absorbed by last night's date, or if the poison ivy on your arm is driving you

crazy, you might not even notice the pain in your toe. It seems clear that to explain some behaviors, we have to look deeper than "what comes in" and "what must go out." Things also happen in between, and these internal processes prevent our behavior from being perfectly predictable.

We still don't understand just how our minds function to control our actions. But the more we learn, the more fascinating the mind becomes. For instance, if you've ever wondered what your dreams are telling you about yourself, you probably have an inkling of how much we still have to learn about conscious and unconscious processes. The box *To Sleep, Perchance to Dream* might help you make some headway in understanding this altered state of consciousness.

In the past few decades, science has begun to look more closely not only at dreams, but at other states of consciousness and their effect on behavior. Modern instruments let us monitor blood pressure, brain waves, and other bodily functions, so we can see that these functions change at various levels of consciousness. As Figure 2.1 showed, EEG readings have measured changes in brain waves during several levels of sleep; and other types of measurements have also documented the relationship between other body functions and states of consciousness.

If consciousness is related to body functions, does it follow that we might be able to control some body functions through controlling our consciousness? As we'll see in this chapter, this seems to be possible—in some cases, at least. For instance, people have been shown to be able to control their own brain waves, heart beat, and blood pressure. Influences from the East—Yogis, master teachers of meditation, and philosophers—have popularized the idea that people can alter their own consciousness to reach new plateaus of awareness.

Learning to control your own heartbeat won't make you self-actualized. Nor will an ability to reach altered states through meditation. Yet a greater understanding of human consciousness does hold promises. In Albert Rosenfeld's words,

To Sleep, Perchance to Dream

All of us have dreams—and many of us have awakened after a vivid or bothersome dream, wondering what it meant. Dream interpretation is as old as human history. Even in the Bible, Joseph interpreted the Pharoah's dream to predict seven years of plenty followed by seven years of famine; and in the ancient world people would visit oracles or soothsayers to find meaning in their dreams. There is still a great interest in interpreting dreams, and there are many approaches. To Freud, dreams were representations of repressed conflicts or wishes; to the Gestalt psychologist Fritz Perls, they are statements of each person's own meaning—if only the individual can learn to recognize them for what they are.

Most people go to neither a Freudian nor a Gestalt psychologist for help in understanding dreams. Instead, we are more likely to muse over them for a short time (if we remember them at all), then put them out of our consciousness. Perhaps we're missing something, though, for understanding our dreams is one possible route to greater self-awareness.

If you are puzzled or troubled by your own dreams, or frustrated that you can't remember them, here are some tips that may help:

If you can't remember your dreams . . .

This can be highly frustrating. People are more likely to remember a dream if they awaken during the dream (Webb & Kersey, 1967) . . . but even then, they may forget it all by morning.

While there is little anyone can do about complete absence of dream memory, many people find that they have fleeting memories that are quickly lost. To remember more of your dreams, lie passively for a few minutes before writing down what you remember (Chetwynd, 1972). If you try not to let your daytime cares interrupt this process, you may find that your last dream may stay in your mind, and that you may be able to remember it in striking detail.

If you don't know how to interpret your dreams . . .

Dream interpretation is far from simple. If you are trying to discern the meaning of your dreams, you can expect to encounter some frustration. It will help to look for recurring dreams and for

---

there is a "great chasm between what we are and what we could be" (1977). The way to actualize your potential lies not through changing yourself to fit other people's ideas of what you should be, but through discovering what lies within yourself. Learning more about your own consciousness is one way of doing this.

In the following pages, we'll look first at consciousness and then at some of the avenues people use to approach a heightened or altered consciousness, through drugs, meditation, biofeedback, and hypnosis. These approaches have

had varied success as we'll see. In all of the altered states of consciousness that we'll be exploring, the most impressive fact is how little we still understand. The clues we have uncovered, however, hold fascinating potential.

What Is Consciousness?

What do we mean when we say that the victim of an accident is conscious? When a man "has his

repetition in dream content. If you're still stuck, you may need to visit an expert consultant or perhaps a therapist. These people have special training and can help you recognize hidden meanings.

If you're having bothersome dreams . . .

In our culture, we don't seem to be able to control our dreams. But as with some of the other altered states of consciousness discussed in this chapter, we can take some cues from other cultures.

People of the Senoi culture on the Malay Peninsula work with their dreams and seem to be able to influence them (Stewart, 1969). From childhood, they learn techniques for entering into the dream world and actively confronting their content. If children have bothersome dreams they are taught that the dreams have a purpose and that they can learn from them. If they dream of a terrifying episode with a jungle animal, they are taught that it is *their* animal: they can make peace with it. Since people's dreams belong to them, they learn that they can control them so that they end happily.

Is it possible for us to program our dreams? In order to use any of the Senoi's techniques, we would have to relinquish our Western belief that dreams are beyond our control. As yet, we haven't been able to do that. But there have been some pilot studies that indicate we might have some control over what we dream. In one study, subjects repeated to themselves right before retiring a statement about a quality they would like to change in themselves (Cartwright, 1978)—and more often than not, that target quality appeared in their dreams. There was little success in actually changing that quality, as the Senoi might be able to. But perhaps with more study we will be able to approach that goal, and use our own dreams not only to understand ourselves better but to improve our own functioning.

consciousness raised" and learns to think differently about the effect of sex-role stereotypes on his life? When a person who practices meditation speaks about an "internal consciousness"?

The term *conscious* usually describes an everyday waking state of awareness. But just how aware are we of our environment? We tend to see what we are used to seeing, as Bruner and Postman demonstrated in the experiment shown in Figure 15.1. It may have been raining for an hour, but you were so engrossed in a book that you didn't even notice. Such is also the case with our internal environment: how often are you aware of your breathing or digestive processes, except when they prove troublesome?

In other words, there is no single, simple definition of **consciousness.** For our purposes, however, we can use as a working definition a

> **Consciousness**   A process of awareness that requires an individual to focus attention upon a variety of internal and/or external stimuli.

Figure 15.1   Effects of Expectations on Consciousness
Bruner and Postman flashed pictures of playing cards quickly onto a screen.
Some of these cards had their color reversed, such as a red two of spades.
Many subjects reported seeing a black two of spades or a red two of hearts.

Source: Adapted from Bruner & Postman, 1949.

process of awareness that requires a person to focus attention on various external and/or internal stimuli. The term **altered states of consciousness** refers to the focusing of attention on different stimuli, so that the person becomes aware of material (again, internal or external) that

> **Altered state of consciousness**   A state of awareness in which a person becomes conscious of internal or external material that had been hidden from view before.

had been hidden from view before. Perhaps the most common means people use in trying to reach an altered state of consciousness is through drugs.

Drugs and Consciousness

Chris Farasopoulos was one of the leading punt return specialists in the National Football League during the early 70s. His career with the New York Jets was prematurely shortened by a knee injury, which may have been related to use of drugs. Before the game in which he was injured, he had been awake on cocaine for three solid days, getting some sleep only the Saturday night before the game. "I wouldn't have been that weak from no sleep when I tried to split tacklers on a punt return. . . . I was running back a punt when two guys hit me, and the world was like in slow motion" (D. Anderson, Aug. 31, 1980).

Farasopoulos wasn't completely incapacitated from this first injury. He subsequently spent a year with another NFL team, but then was let go. Farasopoulos drank and used drugs, especially amphetamines. Why did he do it, even though it was harmful to his career? "I had everybody fooled. . . . I had been raised to be friendly and polite, but inside I was lonely, empty. I had to drink to come out of my shell. I had a hidden, deep down problem of wanting to be liked by other people" (ibid.).

Drugs: As American as Apple Pie?

Farasopoulos' story is not unique. Similar stories have become all too commonplace in all professional sports. A **drug** is defined as "a chemical substance other than food that alters physical and/or psychological functioning" (Altrocchi, 1980, p. 671). The use of drugs by athletes has been heavily publicized. Since they supposedly act as role models for youth, these athletes have come under heavy fire.

However, drug taking can be seen as a predictable spin-off of Western society. We take Valium and other tranquilizers to calm down; we have a drink-or-two-or-three to loosen up at a cocktail party or to relax after a rough day; we use sleeping pills to get to sleep, caffeine in our coffee to wake up, and amphetamines (in diet pills) to lose weight. Most of us have learned that drugs "do things" for us—and many of those drugs (an estimated 300,000) are available over the counter (Hughes & Brewin, 1979). Here are some brief figures on the use of some of the more common drugs in our society:

- *amphetamines:* 12 billion doses consumed each year (Coon, 1980).
- *tranquilizers:* 4 billion doses consumed in 1977. This includes 3.2 billion pills of Valium, the most popular tranquilizer (Hughes & Brewin, 1979).
- *marijuana:* Estimates for its use among high school and college students run as high as 56 percent (Johnston et al., 1977), with perhaps 25 percent of college students smoking it once a week (Page, 1975).
- *alcohol:* Two-thirds of adults drink occasionally, and there are approximately 9 million alcoholics in the United States (Goode, 1972). It is estimated that between 5 and 10 percent of the workforce suffers from alcoholism (Quayle, 1983).

It is difficult to gauge the extent of drug use among adult Americans, but according to one estimate (Quayle, 1983), some 3 to 7 percent of the employed population use some form of illicit drug, ranging from marijuana to heroin, on a daily basis. In all, you might say that drugs have become as American as apple pie.

Drugs and Behavior

Despite the widespread use of drugs in our society, we still have much to learn about their effects on human behavior.

At first glance, this statement may seem puzzling. Alcohol, marijuana, and a variety of other drugs have been around for centuries. Some have been the target of considerable research. Yet, for many drugs, the effect on personality and behavior is still a matter of debate and confusion.

> **Drug** Any chemical substance except food that alters one's psychological and/or physical functioning.

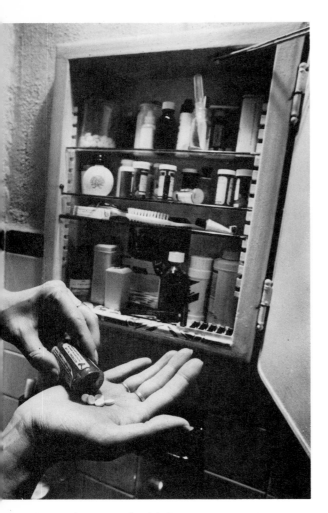

As American as apple pie? Drugs are a common household item in Western society.

Organismic variables The term used in drug research to describe such user-related factors as weight, age, and personality that must be taken into account when studying the effect of any drug on behavior.

An important reason for this is that we can go only so far in studying the effects of drugs. If you wanted to find out how marijuana affects motivation, for instance, your research strategies would be limited by some very practical constraints. It would be unethical to experimentally test a random sample of the population. Thus, you would have to find volunteers—and these volunteers might not be representative of the population in general. In addition, other questions would complicate your research. How much should the subjects smoke, and over what period of time? What does heavy usage really mean? Do the subjects also use other drugs, and if they do, does this affect their level of ambition? Finally, if your results are positive, one significant question still remains. Does your group of subjects lack motivation because they smoke pot, or do they smoke pot because they lack motivation?

Again, the question of how alcohol affects behavior may *seem* easy to answer: simply observe someone under its influence, and carefully record the subject's behavior. The answer isn't so easy, however, for different people respond differently to alcohol—and the same is true for other drugs as well. Even aspirin may be effective in reducing pain for some people but not for others. In general, there are three main factors that influence how an individual responds to a drug: organismic variables, drug variables, and environmental variables.*

Organismic Variables Imagine you're attending a party at which each person drinks exactly two glasses of champagne. Do you think everyone will be affected in the same way?

If your answer is no, you're right. There are a variety of user variables, or **organismic variables**—such as age, weight, and genetic

---

*A fourth factor, called *task variables,* involves the study of activities before and after drug taking that may influence the drug's effect. Since this variable has been researched chiefly in animals, it is beyond the scope of this chapter.

endowment—that affect each person's response to drugs. A person who weighs 250 pounds is less likely, all else being equal, to show the effects of a drink or two than is a 110-pound person.

One of the most interesting organismic variables is personality. For instance, some people "hold their liquor" while others are quickly affected by alcohol. Some individuals seem to become addicted to drugs more easily than do others; some tolerate drugs better than others. Some research by Frostad helps illustrate one aspect of the relationship between personality and drugs (Leavitt, 1974). Subjects were grouped according to whether they were action-oriented or not, and also whether they showed high or low-anxiety tendencies; then they were given an anti-anxiety drug called *diazepam*. The groups were found to react differently, with the nonaction-oriented, low-anxiety group benefiting most (but also showing the most side-effects) and the action-oriented, low-anxiety group responding least.

Environmental Variables **Environmental variables** are a second factor that influences the effects of drugs. There is some evidence that factors such as crowding and temperature can make a difference; so can the behavior of other people in the environment. For instance, if you see other people become affectionate and giggly after taking a drug, you are more likely to respond in a similar manner. Likewise, if you are told a drug will make you anxious, you will be more likely to feel anxious after you take it.

Drug Variables A third important factor is **drug variables**—the way in which the drug is taken. One element in this is the dosage of the drug, or the amount taken. For example, very small doses of strychnine can improve learning in laboratory animals, while larger doses cause death. Repeated doses may also influence the effect of a drug. We know that people tend to build up a **tolerance** to many drugs, so that higher and higher amounts

are required to produce the same effects. There may be other long-term effects, too. For instance, years of heavy alcohol use are often linked to liver damage. In many cases, though, we aren't sure exactly how a drug will affect personality and bodily functions over the long term.

Another aspect of drug variables involves drug interactions. A drug may have one effect when taken alone, but an entirely different effect when combined with another drug. One highly damaging combination is alcohol and barbiturates. A person may come home from a party slightly drunk, then take a few doses of sleeping pills to help get to sleep. Although neither the alcohol nor the pills may be taken in high enough doses to cause harm alone, the combination of the two can cause brain damage or even death.

The most important drug variable, of course, is the drug itself. Different drugs have different effects. We don't have space to discuss the effects of most of the common drugs in our society, but we will look at two of the most widely used drugs, alcohol and marijuana. Table 15.1 summarizes the effects of a few other commonly used drugs, including barbiturates, amphetamines, LSD, and cocaine.

Environmental variables The term used in drug research to describe variables in the environment which must be taken into account when studying the effect of any drug. Crowding, temperature, behavior of other people, and a user's expectations of the drug's effect are some of the factors that may be pertinent.

Drug variables The term used in drug research to describe such drug-related factors as dosage, one drug's interaction with other drugs, and duration of usage. These factors must be taken into account when studying the effect of any drug.

Tolerance The state at which a user requires greater and greater amounts of a drug in order to attain the same effects.

Table 15.1   Some Common Drugs: Their Uses and Effects

Drugs	Often Prescribed Brand Names	Medical Uses	Dependence Potential (Physical and Psychological)	Usual Methods of Administration	Possible Effects	Effects of Overdose
Narcotics						
Opium	Dover's Powder, Paregoric	Analgesic, anti-diarrheal	High	Oral; smoked	Euphoria, drowsiness, respiratory depression, nausea, constricted pupils	Slow, shallow breathing; clammy skin; convulsions; coma; possible death
Morphine	Morphine	Analgesic	High	Injected; smoked		
Codeine	Codeine	Analgesic, antitussive	Moderate	Oral; injected		
Heroin	None	None	High	Injected; sniffed		
Depressants						
Barbiturates	Amytal, Pheno-barbital, Seconal, etc.	Anesthetic, anticonvulsant, sedation, sleep	High	Oral; injected	Slurred speech, disorientation, seemingly "drunken" behavior	Shallow breathing; cold, clammy skin; weak and rapid pulse; dilated pupils; coma; possible death
Metha-qualone	Optimil, Quaalude, Somnafac, Sopor, etc.	Sedation, sleep	High	Oral		
Tranquil-izers	Equanil, Librium, Miltown, Valium, etc.	Anti-anxiety, muscle relaxant, sedation	Moderate	Oral		
Stimulants						
Cocaine[a]	Cocaine	Local anesthetic	Possible physical; high psychological	Sniffed; injected	Increased alertness; excitation; euphoria; dilated pupils; increased pulse rate and blood pressure; insomnia; loss of appetite	Agitation; increase in body temperature; hallucinations; convulsions; possible death
Amphet-amines	Benzedrine, Biphetamine, Desoxyn, Dexedrine	Weight control; treatment of hyperkinesis and narcolepsy	Possible physical; high psychological	Oral; injected		
Other stimulants	Bacarate, Cylert, Didrex, Lonamin, Sanurex, etc.	Weight control	Possible	Oral		

Drugs	*Often Prescribed Brand Names*	*Medical Uses*	*Dependence Potential (Physical and Psychological)*	*Usual Methods of Administration*	*Possible Effects*	*Effects of Overdose*
Hallucinogens						
LSD	None	None	No physical; unknown psychological	Oral	Illusions and hallucinations; poor perception of time and distance	Longer, more intense "trip" episodes; psychosis; possible death
Mescaline	None	None	No physical; unknown psychological	Oral; injected		
Psilocybin-psitocyn	None	None	No physical; unknown psychological	Oral		
PCP[b]	Semylan	Veterinary anesthetic	No physical; unknown psychological	Oral; injected; smoked		
Cannabis						
Marijuana, hashish	None	None	Unknown physical; moderate psychological	Oral; smoked	Euphoria; relaxed inhibitions; increased appetite; disoriented behavior	Fatigue; paranoia; possible psychosis

[a] Designated a narcotic under the Controlled Substances Act.
[b] Designated a depressant under the Controlled Substances Act.
Source: Adapted from "Controlled Substances: Uses and Effects," in *Drugs of Abuse*, 3rd edition, Drug Enforcement Administration, U. S. Department of Justice, 1978.

"That's what I tell my kid. 'Hey, Charley!' I tell him. 'Look at me, Charley. I don't need drugs, Charley,' I tell him. 'Just plain living turns me on.' Right? Just plain living."

Reproduced by special permission of *Playboy* Magazine. Copyright © 1972 by Playboy.

Alcoholism   A condition marked by dependence on alcohol. The dividing line between problem drinking and alcoholism is fine, but signs of the latter include frequent drinking to intoxication, blackouts, a steady increase in alcohol consumed, and increased conflict with family and friends over drinking.

Problem drinking   This condition is generally distinguished from *alcoholism*, which involves a dependence on alcohol. It is hard to draw the line, but signs of problem drinking include intoxication when driving, intoxication four times within a year, or the feeling that one "must" have a drink in order to perform certain functions.

Alcohol

John was a ninth grader when his teachers first called his alcohol problem to the guidance counselor's notice. He was acting in a peculiar fashion, they said, and he smelled of alcohol. The counselor called John's mother and they arranged for a meeting.

When John's mother arrived, her concern was obvious. Trying to soften the blow, the counselor talked for a while before coming to her conclusion: "I'm sorry to say that John seems to have a drinking problem."

John's mother's reaction took the counselor by surprise. She sighed with relief and her face brightened. "What a relief," she blurted out. "I thought he was on drugs."

"C'mon, Have a Drink": An Institution, a Social Problem, or Both?   John's mother's attitude is not unlike that of many other parents. They are upset to the point of despair to find that their child smokes marijuana, but they feel relieved if the problem is "only" drinking.

Alcohol consumption is accepted in our society. It is even institutionalized. The business luncheon, the drink before dinner, the beer bash at the fraternity party, the wine taken as part of a religious ceremony, the bar scene, and the cocktail party are all widely accepted functions. The invitation, "C'mon, have a drink," is usually seen as a simple extension of courtesy, like offering a friend a bite to eat.

As with anything else, however, drinking can be overdone—and it often is. As we saw earlier, there are approximately 9 million alcoholics in the United States. According to the National Institute on Alcohol Abuse and Alcoholism (NIAAA), alcoholism is the third most serious health problem in this country (after heart disease and cancer) and the most important mental health problem. It is our society's number one drug problem. The definition of **alcoholism** is often confused, however, and it is hard to draw the appropriate lines between **problem drinking** and alcoholism.

There is no one definition of alcoholism, but the box *When Does Drinking Become a Problem?* points out some of the most important distinctions.

The use of alcohol has reached rather striking proportions among teenagers also, as John's story illustrates. Alcohol is very much the drug of choice, with 85 percent of adolescents using it at some time or another according to a survey of over 7,000 New York State high school students (Yancy et al., 1972). It is estimated that anywhere between 2 and 6 percent of the entire adolescent population can be classified as problem drinkers (Braucht et al., 1973).

Why Do People Drink?   It's clear to see that alcohol is an American institution. What may not be so obvious are the reasons why drinking becomes a problem for so many people.

To understand this, we need to look at drinking from two levels. At the first level is the glossy image of drinking that has become popularized, mostly by advertisers. Magazine ads, commercials, billboards, and many TV shows or movies show glamorous adults having a drink to celebrate one thing or another. This sophisticated image is particularly appealing, especially to teenagers who are trying to act "adult." When this heavy promotion is coupled with the general availability of alcohol at most social occasions, it is easy to see why alcohol use is so widespread.

There are more personal reasons why people may drink to excess, although even the user may not always be aware of these reasons. Chafetz (1970), one of the leading researchers in the field, believes there are four main reasons why people drink: because of *social pressures,* to *combat depression,* to *reduce inhibitions,* or as *an excuse to express their feelings.*

The first three of these reasons are fairly clear. The pressures to drink at a party or luncheon can be great, and alcohol's ability to reduce inhibitions and to change one's psychological state is well known. But most students are surprised to hear that alcohol is also used as an excuse for

Drinking has become institutionalized in our society.

acting out feelings or behaving in a certain way. Think, however, of the person who drinks too much, then lets loose with a bitter tirade at her partner. Was it the drink talking, or the person's real feelings? The same may also be true of people who overindulge, then have one-night stands with someone other than their spouse. Blaming such behaviors on alcohol may allow people to assuage their guilt—but perhaps they should look more closely at the feelings that underlie such behaviors.

When Does Drinking Become a Problem?

Most people with drinking problems (and a good number of people without) have misconceptions about alcoholism. One involves the difference between *problem drinking* and *alcoholism*. Although there is no definite dividing line between the two, there is a difference.

Chafetz has listed seven criteria for determining whether a person has a drinking problem (Chafetz et al., 1970). A problem drinker, according to those criteria, is:

1. Anyone who, by personal definition or by definition of those with him or her, has been intoxicated four times within a year.
2. Anyone who goes to work intoxicated.
3. Anyone who must drink in order to get to work and perform at work.
4. Anyone who is intoxicated when driving a car.
5. Anyone who sustains bodily injury requiring medical treatment as a result of being intoxicated.
6. Anyone who comes into conflict with the law as a result of an intoxicated state.
7. Anyone who, under the influence of alcohol, does something he or she wouldn't do without alcohol—or at least that is the person's contention.

These symptoms indicate a serious problem, but not necessarily the addiction that characterizes alcoholism. (**Addiction** can be defined as a "physiological dependence on a drug . . . characterized by withdrawal symptoms and increased tolerance" [Mears & Gatchel, 1979, p. 481]). It's difficult to say exactly at what point problem drinking becomes alcoholism; but the NIAAA (1972) give a few criteria that suggest a person is crossing the dividing line:

1. Frequent drinking to intoxication
2. A steady increase in the amount a person drinks
3. Not getting to work on Monday mornings
4. Denying that one drinks
5. Family quarrels about the drinking problem
6. The incidence of blackouts, after which a person may be unable to remember what he or she did after drinking

Some recent research suggests that men and women may have typically different reasons for drinking. According to David McClelland and his

Addiction   Physiological dependence on a drug, characterized by tolerance to the drug and by withdrawal symptoms when the drug is removed.

associates (1972), men drink to enhance their sense of power—and the more a man drinks, the greater seems to be his concern for the personal power and ambition our society values in men. Interestingly, Wilsnack found a parallel motivation in women, who also drink to ease doubts about their sex role. Women questioned by Wilsnack did not drink to feel powerful, as did men in McClelland's study. Instead, they described their feelings after a couple of drinks as "warm, loving, considerate, expressive, open, pretty, affectionate, sexy, and feminine" (1973, p. 40)—all adjectives that are associated with a sense of "enhanced womanliness."

The Effects of Alcohol   The actual effects of alcohol, as you might guess, are not always what the drinker imagines. Alcohol is a consciousness-changing drug (Jones & Parsons, 1975) and it acts as a central nervous system depressant.

Alcohol takes effect quickly. About 20 percent of a drink is absorbed directly into the bloodstream from the stomach, while the other 80 percent is quickly processed by the small intestine. After a very short time, alcohol is present in every tissue of the body.

In small amounts, alcohol seems to act on the upper centers of the brain, which control learned behaviors and self-control (NIAAA, 1972). Its initial effects may be a sense of relaxation and euphoria; inhibitions may be loosened and the individual may behave in patterns that aren't normal for that person. As the box *Alcohol and Aggression* indicates, it may make a person more aggressive, under some circumstances. When drinking continues, brain activity is further depressed, impairing memory, coordination, and balance. A bit more alcohol consumption brings marked loss in judgment and sensory processing. Continuing to drink produces toxic effects, which can include "staggering, lack of coordination, incoherent speech, vomiting, and even unconsciousness" (Jones & Parsons, 1975, p. 54). Drinking beyond this point may result in coma or even death—but fortunately, by now even raising a glass to the mouth may be far too difficult a task.

Treating Alcohol Problems   As unpleasant as the description above sounds, alcohol is habit-forming and such experiences may be repeated again and again. Stopping isn't easy. The success of any treatment program depends on the person admitting that a problem exists in the first place.

Alcohol is the drug of choice among adolescents, with some 2% to 6% of the teenage population classified as problem drinkers.

This may be difficult, for a primary psychological defense used by problem drinkers is denial.

Effective treatment generally has two distinct targets. That is because alcohol problems themselves affect two separate groups: problem drinkers themselves, and their families and close friends. Several methods of treatment are available for problem drinkers. There are drugs that make the consumption of alcohol very unpleasant. There are hospitalization and detoxification

Alcohol and Aggression

Almost everyone has heard of the term "belligerent drunk." But like some other catch-phrases in our language, the term can provide *too* neat a description, and it tends to be overused.

Do people actually become more aggressive after they've had too much to drink? The question has been a controversial one. Many people involved in law enforcement and family crisis counseling will tell you that there is a positive relationship between alcohol and aggression. Yet over the years, many studies have failed to find the link.

Recently, however, a group of investigators reviewed the research that had been done on the subject, and arrived at a hypothesis that they believed explained the connection. According to Taylor, Gammon, and Capasso, the link between alcohol and aggression is *perceived threat.* The investigators argue that it is possible that people under the influence of alcohol act more aggressively only in conditions in which they perceive threat, and they tested their hypothesis at Kent State University.

Forty male undergraduate students participated in the study, which they were told involved the influence of alcohol on perceptual-motor skills. Subjects were assigned randomly to one of four conditions: *alcohol–threat; alcohol–no threat; threat–no alcohol;* and *no threat–no alcohol.* Each subject in the two alcohol groups drank two drinks (which were measured using the formula of 1.5 ounces of 100-proof vodka per 40 pounds of body weight), while the subjects in the nonalcohol groups were given two drinks that tasted the same as the alcoholic drinks, but without a significant amount of alcohol.

A half hour after the second drink, each subject was led into a small cubicle in which the perceptual-motor task was to be given. A shock electrode was attached to the left wrist, and the experimenter then presumably went to attach the same to another subject who would serve as his opponent. All the subjects overheard the opponent tell the experimenter that the shock was quite unpleasant. Then, they listened to tape-recorded instructions telling them that they were competing in a reaction time experiment, and that each time they won a trial they were to administer a shock to their opponent. If they lost, of course, their opponent would deliver a shock to them. Each subject was asked to select the intensity of the shock he wanted to deliver to his opponent if he won. The choice ranged from mild to more severe.

At this point, subjects were asked if there were any questions. Those in the no-threat groups heard their opponent make a statement about his "strong convictions against hurting other people," while those in the perceived threat group heard their opponent say "no questions"—indicating that their opponents were ready and willing to deliver a shock. Each subject won half the trials, and the experimenters determined not only which trials they would win but also the amount of shock they would experience.

The results confirmed the researchers' hypothesis. There were no significant differences in the shock levels set by the intoxicated and the nonintoxicated subjects when there was no perceived threat. However, the findings were quite different under the threatening condition. Here, the subjects who had been drinking set clearly higher levels of shock than did the subjects in the no-alcohol group. The researchers believe that alcohol somehow disrupted the perceptual and cognitive processes, causing subjects who had been drinking to misinterpret the degree of threat.

Whatever the explanation, it appears wise not to provoke people who have been drinking heavily. It is difficult to predict how your behaviors will be interpreted. If the findings of this experiment are any indication, however, intoxicated persons seem more likely to perceive threat in a situation, and to react more aggressively than they would if they were sober.

Source: Taylor et al., 1976.

programs. Some major corporations, in an effort to help employees with alcohol problems, have begun programs to help discover and treat both alcoholics and potential problem drinkers. And psychotherapy is sometimes helpful.

The best known approach to treatment has been that of **Alcoholics Anonymous** (AA). This organization, founded in 1935, bases its treatment on the belief that only complete abstinence is a successful cure. The program involves frequent group meetings, support from sponsors, and fellowship among members. Both alcoholics and ex-alcoholics provide support and counseling for problem drinkers, and the members follow the twelve steps to recovery shown in Table 15.2. Alcoholics Anonymous seems to be successful in treating alcoholics who are strongly motivated to stop drinking (Leavitt, 1974): by its claims, over 1 million people are currently members of the organization.

The AA program is not successful with everyone, however, and recently other approaches have been developed based on very different premises. One such approach (Pattison, Sobell & Sobell, 1977) permits alcoholics to drink moderate amounts socially without getting drunk. It does this by conditioning people to avoid inappropriate drinking behaviors (such as gulping drinks too quickly or not waiting between drinks), and teaching them appropriate behaviors instead. At the present time this treatment is still somewhat controversial.

The second focus of treatment involves not the individuals with drinking problems, but family members and close friends. Although these individuals do not drink too much, their lives are profoundly affected by problems such as marital strain, financial insecurity, and abusive behavior that may be associated with drinking. Support and counseling are necessary for these people also, for they are likely to feel confused, frustrated, and unsure about what to do. In addition, if they know what kind of support to provide, concerned friends or family may themselves be able to help minimize some effects of the problem, at least in

Table 15.2 Alcoholics Anonymous' Twelve Steps to Recovery

1. Belief that the individual is powerless to control his or her drinking.
2. Belief in a power greater than ourselves.
3. Decision to entrust our "will" and our lives to God, as we understand Him.
4. Completion of a searching, frank moral inventory of ourselves.
5. Ability to admit to God, ourselves, and at least one other person the exact nature of our wrongs.
6. Willingness and readiness to allow God to remove our defects in character.
7. Ability to humbly request that God remove our shortcomings.
8. Completion of a list of all persons we have harmed; willingness to make amends to them all.
9. Implementation of plans to make these amends directly whenever possible, unless those plans would injure that person or others.
10. Constantly taking account of ourselves, and admitting promptly when we are wrong.
11. Using prayer and meditation to improve our conscious contact with God, to obtain knowledge of His will for us and the power to carry out that will.
12. Attempting to carry this message of AA to other alcoholics and to practice AA principles in all our affairs.

some cases. Table 15.3 provides some tips for what to do and what not to do if you know of someone who drinks too much.

While the suggestions in Table 15.3 may help in managing the problem, they are unlikely to provide a cure. The best advice is still to seek advice from one or more of the many trained

Alcoholics Anonymous An organization of alcoholics and former alcoholics whose purpose is to help alcoholics or problem drinkers quit drinking. The program, which aims for complete abstinence, involves group meetings, sponsor support, and fellowship.

Table 15.3   Some Do's and Don't's for Friends of Problem Drinkers

Do	Don't
Try to remain calm and factually honest in speaking with the problem drinker about his or her behavior	Attempt to punish, bribe, threaten, preach—or try to be a martyr.
Let the problem drinker know that you are learning about alcoholism, attending meetings of Al-Anon or other groups.	Make excuses or cover up for the problem drinker, or shield him or her from the consequences of the drinking behavior.
Seek help. Discuss the situation with someone you trust—clergy, friend, or someone who has experienced alcoholism, either firsthand or as a family member.	Take over the person's responsibilities. This not only shields consequences, but it diminishes his or her sense of dignity.
Establish and maintain a healthy home atmosphere, including the problem drinker in family life. Encourage him or her to see old friends and to participate in favorite leisure-time activities.	Hide or dump bottles or shelter the problem drinker from situations where alcohol is present.
Refuse to ride with the problem drinker if he or she insists on drinking and driving.	Argue with the problem drinker after he or she has had too much to drink. Do not try to drink along with the person.
Be patient and live one day at a time. Alcohol problems generally take a long time to develop, and recovery seldom occurs rapidly and without some setbacks.	Above all, do not accept guilt for another's behavior.

Source: U. S. Department of HEW, 1975.

professionals who can provide guidance. Groups such as Al-Anon and Alateen (for families of teenage alcoholics) work with friends and families of problem drinkers and are usually listed in telephone directories. Many other resources are available in most communities, including clergy, family physicians, local offices of the National Council on Alcoholism, alcoholism clinics or referral centers, Veteran's Administration services, and community mental health centers. Information about local resources can be obtained through local county public health offices, or by writing to the National Clearinghouse for Alcohol Information.*

As popular as alcohol is, marijuana is the drug of choice of many people. As one college student claimed, "It's not fattening, it doesn't give you bad breath, and you won't get a hangover the next morning." We'll look next at what effects marijuana *does* have—those we know, at least.

Marijuana

Of the following statements, which do you believe are supported by scientific research?

■ Marijuana usage decreases an individual's achievement motivation, *or,*

■ Marijuana does not affect a person's achievement motivation.

■ Marijuana usage leads to sexual problems, *or,*

■ Marijuana usage does not lead to sexual problems.

■ Marijuana usage has been definitely related to brain damage, *or,*

*The address of the National Clearinghouse for Alcohol Information is: Box 2345, Dept. 10, Rockville, Maryland. We have based our discussion on a very helpful bulletin entitled *Someone Close to You Drinks Too Much* (U.S. Department of Health, Education, and Welfare, 1975).

- Marijuana usage has not been definitely related to brain damage.

- Marijuana usage seems to reduce people's ability to fight disease, *or,*

- There is no clear link between marijuana usage and damage to the immunological system.

- Marijuana usage can lead to chromosomal damage, *or,*

- It is a myth that marijuana leads to chromosomal damage.

All finished? Actually, we have to admit that we've led you on. No matter which of these options you selected, you could find scientific evidence to support your viewpoint.

We chose this series of statements to illustrate just how little we know about the effects of **marijuana.** The evidence is controversial, conflicting, and open to all kinds of interpretation. The findings vary according to highly personal characteristics of the user. Factors such as personality, expectations, past experiences with marijuana and other drugs, emotional state, social and environmental setting, and the amount and purity of the drug all have a critical influence on its effects (Tart, 1970). Needless to say, few studies have been controlled for all these variables. Add to this the fact that many studies have been poorly controlled or performed by persons with biases, and the result is confusion, hysterics, and misinformation.

Effects of Marijuana   Despite the controversy over marijuana and its effects, we do know quite a lot about the nature of marijuana—a.k.a. pot, grass, weed, and many other street names—and how it affects the body.

The active ingredient in marijuana is *tetrahydrocannabinol,* or THC. It may be smoked, drunk, or eaten: any way it's taken, its immediate effects are in great measure determined by its purity, dosage, and the user's experience. When

Tetrahydrocannabinol, a.k.a. marijuana, is widely used in our society. Its long-term effects, however, are still controversial.

pot is inhaled, there is an increase in the heart rate, reduced muscle coordination, redness of the eyes, dryness of the nose and throat, and an increased appetite. It may be hard to tell how much time has passed. It is difficult to concentrate, and smokers may have trouble expressing themselves or thinking abstractly. Reaction time is slowed—

Marijuana   A drug used to bring on feelings of euphoria, dreaminess, or relaxation. Its effects differ with its strength, the user's past experiences with the drug, the user's emotional state, and a number of other variables.

Some Facts about Marijuana

Readers who are old enough to have seen the famous *Dragnet* series on television may remember detective Joe Friday finding a joint in a teenager's home and telling the boy's stunned parents that he was one step away from becoming a full-fledged addict. This conclusion is but one of many myths about the use of marijuana. There are many more, as they say, where that one came from! Despite marijuana's broad usage in our society, we sometimes seem to have more questions than answers about its effects. However, we can summarize a few conclusions here.

■ First, marijuana is an intoxicant. It can cause temporary loss of control over physical and mental powers, just as alcohol can.

■ Second, because it is an intoxicant, it is dangerous to drive after smoking marijuana. It increases braking time and detracts from the user's ability to pay attention and concentrate on the task of driving (Fourth Report to Congress on Marijuana and Health, 1974).

■ Third, most marijuana smokers use the drug only occasionally (Johnston et al., 1977). As it is smoked in the U.S. and Canada, it does not seem to create a tolerance that would cause a user to go to heavier and heavier doses to get the same feeling (Leavitt, 1974). However, it may become more and more important to the user, causing some people to direct quite a bit of attention and energy to drug usage.

■ And finally, Joe Friday was wrong. Marijuana users seem to be more likely to use other drugs (Brecher, 1972); and the younger smokers are when they start to use marijuana, the more likely they seem to be to experiment with other drugs (Kandel, 1974). Despite these facts, there is no evidence at all that heroin addiction is the next step up from pot.

one reason why it is dangerous to drive under the influence of marijuana, as is pointed out in the box *Some Facts about Marijuana.* A short-term memory deficit may also occur (Finkleberg et al., 1970).

Subjective reports of users indicate a variety of reactions. In general, relatively small doses bring changes in mood. Individuals often feel euphoric (Hollister, 1971). There is sometimes a dreamy feeling, and the user may report feelings

of relaxation. The drug may also bring on panic and anxiety, however. Sensory experiences include a vividness of vision, touch, and smell (Tart, 1970). In larger doses, marijuana can act as a **hallucinogen,** producing unreal images, and it may also result in sensory distortions (Gazzaniga, 1980).

Other effects have also been reported that are less documented but certainly far more disturbing. These include findings of chromosomal damage, birth defects, brain damage, sexual problems, and a reduced resistance to disease (Maugh, 1974a, 1974b). Although such charges are highly controversial, it would be incorrect to conclude that marijuana is a harmless drug. In fact, drawing virtually any foreign substance into one's lungs cannot be considered a healthy activity.

Hallucinogen Any of a number of drugs that tend to cause the user to experience imaginary sensations that have no relationship to the individual's real external environment.

Although the number of marijuana cigarettes smoked by the average user does not approach that of the tobacco smoker, the risk of respiratory problems is still present.

The Amotivational Syndrome   One other possible effect of marijuana has received a great deal of publicity. Most of us have known heavy users of marijuana who have little motivation to get anything done, or who talk about plans but never seem to accomplish them. These traits are collectively known as the **amotivational syndrome.**

Is there a direct connection between smoking marijuana and the amotivational syndrome? The evidence, as with that on many other possible effects of the drug, is contradictory. One report noted that heavy marijuana smoking reduces work output—although this report cautioned that there is a complex relationship between motivation and work output, and that more experimentation is needed (Fourth Annual Report to the U.S. Congress on Marijuana and Health, 1974). Other research has suggested that marijuana users have a false sense of achievement, and they tend to postpone decisions (Bakwin & Bakwin, 1972).

However, findings such as these remind us of the classic chicken-or-egg situation: which came first? It's possible that these characteristics were present in one form or another before the user began to smoke. It is also possible that some troubled individuals turn to the drug, which then increases these characteristics because it allows these persons to escape from problems. In all, the amotivational syndrome is quite controversial, and any conclusion needs to concede that personality variables are important.

Other Drugs   Several other substances besides alcohol and marijuana are used as a means of altering consciousness. Table 15.1 provides an overview of the major drug families, listed according to the effect they have on the person who takes them, as well as several common drugs in each group. Many of these drugs, including hallucinogens such as LSD, are taken primarily for their "mind expanding" qualities, although with this and any other drug, the danger exists that the drug will have far less pleasant effects than the individual expects.

Perhaps more notable in the table is the number of drugs that have legitimate medical uses. Depressants (drugs that act to depress central nervous system activity) such as **tranquilizers** and highly addictive **barbiturates** may be prescribed to induce sleep, as well as to reduce tension. Librium and Valium are two tranquilizers that are so commonly used that they are household words in our society. Again, stimulants (drugs that act to stimulate central nervous system activity) such as **amphetamines** may have legitimate uses. Curiously, one use of amphetamines has been in controlling *hyperkinesis,* or hyperactivity, in some children (Kavale, 1982). Although these drugs and many others may all be prescribed to treat a condition, they are far from safe. Problems may develop later because the user eventually builds up a tolerance to some drugs, requiring greater amounts or even combining it with other drugs to produce the desired effect. Carol's case, described

---

Amotivational syndrome   A condition, sometimes linked to heavy marijuana use, in which an individual displays a lack of drive or ambition and shows little or no desire to work.

Tranquilizers   Any of a number of drugs that depress central nervous system functioning, reduce anxiety, and have a calming effect on agitated individuals.

Barbiturates   A class of drugs that depress the central nervous system and are highly addictive.

Amphetamines   A group of drugs that act as stimulants on the central nervous system. The excitement effect is often followed by feelings of depression and irritability.

A Prescription Junkie

Carol was reborn at St. Vincent's Hospital in New York City at the age of 30. She was brought there by ambulance after her roommate found her unconscious with a bottle of Valium (a prescription tranquilizer) next to her. She could not wake her. Carol was a prescription junkie, one of thousands of people living on literally tens of pills a day.

It had all begun honestly and innocently. The pressures of her job as a flight attendant, along with her inability to sleep, motivated her to seek medical advice. The doctor prescribed Librium. At the beginning she took the pills only when needed. They made her feel "that the world around me had turned all warm and mellow. . . . I felt like I had been wrapped up in a wonderfully protective coating of foam rubber that insulated me from the dirt and grime, the madness and noise of New York" (p. 5).

Her use of Librium began to increase. She'd take them to handle social situations such as dates, as well as to cope with tension on the job. After six months, however, Librium no longer worked and she found herself taking two pills instead of one. After another appointment with the doctor, she began taking Valium also. As with Librium, it was a success at first. But soon she was taking more and more until she could not even tell how many she took a day.

At this point, things started to change. She began to develop gaps in her memory. She would drop trays, and her responses slowed. She began to take another drug to help her get to sleep; then more prescription drugs followed, including Tofranil, an antidepressant. When things worsened even more, she started supplementing her regular prescriptions with pills she obtained from street connections. She would take pills in bunches, and she began to shake when she did not have them. "My work deteriorated. I was always getting to the airport late or not at all. I became surly and started to neglect my appearance. My social life withered away to almost nothing but the television set, the pills and me" (p. 7). Only after the overdose and a stay at the rehabilitation center did Carol come back to life and learn to live without pills again.

Source: Adapted from *The Tranquilizing of America,* copyright © 1979 by Richard Hughes and Robert Brewin and reprinted by permisison of Harcourt Brace Jovanovich, Inc. and Harold Matson Company, Inc.

in the box *A Prescription Junkie,* provides a chilling example of how medical drug use can turn into drug dependence. The drug use figures we described earlier in this chapter must be understood from this perspective.

While drugs may be one avenue to expanding consciousness, other practices have also been used to produce a similar effect—and without the side-effects of drugs. In the following sections, we'll explore some of these drugless approaches to altering consciousness, including meditation, biofeedback, and hypnosis.

Meditation

Sri Ramanand Yogi is a man in his forties who will be presented with a unique task. He will spend the next several hours in an airtight box in a research laboratory. He will be given an escape buzzer. No air can get in, and he must contend not only with a shortage of oxygen, but also with the buildup of carbon dioxide. Heart rate, blood pressure, and physiological indicators will be used to monitor his progress. Simply stated, the Yogi's mind will be called on to master the bare needs of his body.

Sri Ramanand Yogi spent 10 hours in the laboratory box. He was able to decrease his oxygen intake substantially, using only 70 percent of what is considered to be the minimum necessary for a man of his age and size. During one period, his body used only half of that amount (Anand, 1961; NET, 1970).

This experiment is one of many that have documented some of the effects of **meditation,** a process by which individuals voluntarily produce an altered state of consciousness. The practice is an ancient one in the East, but it is still being studied with wonder in North America. Other masters of meditation have been carefully observed in laboratories, with findings that continue to fascinate both researchers and the public. Swami Rama is reported to have been able to control the blood flow to his hands, changing the temperature of his right palm by 10° Fahrenheit. He was also able to put his heart into fibrillation, a state in which the heart flutters but doesn't pump blood (Green et al., 1972).

Ways to Practice Meditation

Findings such as these are fascinating, but it is easy to dismiss them as imports from a foreign culture—too foreign to our way of life to be useful to us. What use are they to the Western layperson? The last few decades have seen the development of several meditation strategies that do not require years of training with a master teacher; and many of these fit nicely into the lifestyles of most Westerners. One researcher in the field, Herbert Benson, has written a popular book entitled *The Relaxation Response* (1976), in which he describes a simple and seemingly effective method for meditating without referring to the mysteries of the East. The most popular form of meditation in the West is probably **transcendental meditation,** or *TM*. TM was popularized by the

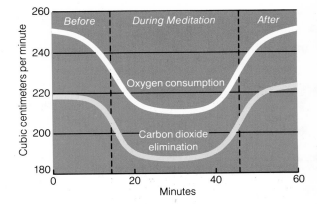

Figure 15.2   The Effects of Transcendental Meditation on Oxygen Consumption and Carbon Dioxide Elimination

Source: Reprinted by permission from Wallace, Robert K., and Benson, Herbert, "The physiology of meditation." *Scientific American,* Feb. 1972. Copyright © 1972 by Scientific American, Inc. All rights reserved.

Maharishi Mahesh Yogi, and it is taught at various centers throughout the world. As Figure 15.2 illustrates, it is accompanied by physical side-effects similar to those documented for Sri Ramanand Yogi. In addition to these two methods of meditation, there are also many others.

In general, all of these forms of meditation share a common feature, and that is the focusing of attention on one point—be it the meditator's breathing pattern, a sound, a picture, or some

---

Meditation   The process by which one focuses attention on a narrow objective (breathing, a particular sound, etc.) in order to reach a higher plane of consciousness.

Transcendental meditation (TM)   A type of meditation popularized by the Maharishi Mahesh Yogi. In this form of meditation, the individual usually reaches an altered state of consciousness through focusing on a Sanskrit sound called a *mantra.*

Meditation has become a popular method to produce an altered state of consciousness.

tually, the meditator is aware only of the breathing pattern: the external world seems nonexistent. In transcendental meditation, the focal point of concentration is a Sanskrit sound, such as the sound "OM," called a *mantra*. Each mantra is personalized by a master and is supposed to be kept secret. Whenever meditators find their attention is wandering, they simply repeat the mantra until they are eventually aware of nothing else. As Forem describes it, TM is "a way of allowing the attention to go from the gross, surface level of ordinary thought to increasingly subtle levels until finally the subtlest level is reached and then transcended" (1973, p. 27).

The relaxation response described by Benson (1976) provides another approach, perhaps less exotic to most Westerners . Meditators sit quietly in a comfortable position, with eyes closed, relaxing as completely as possible. They breathe in and out while quietly repeating the word "one" as they focus their attention on the sound. Although this strategy may lack the mysteries of some Eastern meditational practices, it is beneficial for many people.

Claims and Uses of Meditation

Experiments such as that of Sri Ramanand Yogi remind us of stories we've heard of Indian fakirs, who walk through hot coals or sleep on a bed of nails. Such stories seem so exotic to many of us that it may be hard to visualize how we can use meditation to help ourselves.

Meditation has many practical uses, however. It has been successful in combating anxiety and stress, as school children relax before a test, or busy executives gain renewed strength during a harried day. The effects are both physiological and psychological.

Several physiological effects have been documented. These include a reduced heart rate and lowered rate of oxygen consumption (Wallace, 1970). (A decrease in carbon dioxide discharge

other focal point. The objective of this focus is to narrow the content of awareness to a fine point. By clearing the mind of everything else, the meditator may eventually break through to a higher, more intense plane of consciousness.

The focus of concentration varies from one form of meditation to another. Rahula (1959) describes the technique in which the person concentrates on the normal breathing pattern. Even-

also takes place.) Levels of lactic acid, a chemical associated with anxiety, are also decreased in the blood (Wallace & Benson, 1972). There is an increased production of alpha waves, the brain waves associated with states of alert relaxation.

Psychological changes are also reported. Goleman (1966) reported that meditators show a greater initial arousal to stressful conditions, but a faster recovery to a normal state. People who have learned to meditate report feeling relaxed, renewed, and at peace afterwards. They find that they are able to go about their business after meditating, and they claim to perform better at their jobs and at school. Some individuals find that meditation gives them a "drugless high" (Campbell, 1974). There is some evidence that meditation may be useful in work with some drug users (Benson & Wallace, 1972).

If meditation is starting to sound like the answer to everyone's problems, we should note that the evidence needs to be evaluated carefully. Meditation may not be helpful for everyone. Indeed, everyone who begins meditation lessons won't finish them. Otis (1974) points out that while many studies document physical and psychological results from meditation, most of these studies use only the successful "graduates" of such lessons. These subjects are probably more motivated than the average person, with higher expectations.

In addition, it's possible that meditation may have negative effects for some people. Ornstein warns of taking meditation to an extreme. As he points out, an "obsessive overindulgence in these exercises may lead to a permanent withdrawal from life, a regression and a devaluation of intellectuality" (1972, p. 105). As with anything else, one should never forget the purpose and become overly involved in the procedures.

While meditation relies on ancient Eastern traditions as a means of altering consciousness, another technique has recently been developed that seems radically different—at first glance, at least. We'll look next at this newer strategy, known as biofeedback.

Biofeedback

"Lie still, relax, and try to keep the tone on," the researcher tells the subject, who is hooked up to a machine that monitors his blood pressure. The subject's task is to lower his blood pressure, using his powers of mind. As his blood pressure drops below a certain point, a tone is sounded, telling him he is succeeding (Jonas, 1972).

The researcher is Neal Miller, a pioneer in the field of biofeedback. **Biofeedback** can be defined as the "use of monitoring instruments (usually electrical) to detect and amplify internal physiological processes, such as heart rate and blood pressure, in order to make this internal information available to the individual—literally to feed it back to the person" (Altrocchi, 1980, p. 181).

How Biofeedback Works

The most important element of biofeedback is the continuous and immediate feedback of information about the function the person wants to control. As we discussed in Chapter 3, feedback is important in all learning; only through it can a person learn to control specific functions. In our daily lives, we receive a constant stream of visual and auditory feedback from the environment. Yet we receive virtually no feedback about normal body functions. Biofeedback provides this kind of information, by connecting a person to a machine that not only monitors an internal process, but tells the subject when and how it is changing.

> **Biofeedback** The use of instruments to monitor some internal process, amplify the measurement, and feed it back to the individual. Attempts to gain control over one's heart rate, brain waves, or blood pressure are examples of the use of biofeedback.

Table 15.4   Brain Waves and Associated Levels of Consciousness

Alpha waves	Relaxed awareness
Beta waves	Everyday concentration
Delta waves	Sleep
Theta waves	Exact nature unknown; perhaps associated with creativity

Through using the machine, subjects learn to control specific functions to the degree that eventually, they can take control even without the machine. The potential uses of this ability are impressive, as we'll see below.

Potential Uses of Biofeedback

Self-control of Brain Waves   The brain produces four types of waves, as outlined in Table 15.4. Of these, **alpha waves** are associated with a state of mind that is perhaps best summarized as relaxed awareness, in some ways similar to meditation. Since an abundance of alpha-wave activity produces a state of relaxation, it has been used successfully in reducing tension in many individuals. People who have been taught to produce alpha waves at will describe themselves as being more relaxed and aware, more capable of meeting new challenges. "It's akin to the good feeling that comes from taking a massage or a sauna bath—a relaxed, put together sort of feeling" is one way the results have been described (Pines, 1973, p. 63). As a practical routine, executives can take alpha breaks, and students can mentally prepare for a test by consciously producing such waves.

> **Alpha waves**   Brain waves that are associated with a state of relaxed awareness.

The technique for producing alpha waves is similar to other biofeedback procedures we'll be describing. Subjects relax in a comfortable chair, in this case with a pair of electrodes attached to their heads (Brown, 1974). The electrodes are attached to a machine that causes a light to appear whenever alpha waves are being produced. Subjects watch for the light and try to make it appear.

The technique works for many people. In one research study, a number of subjects succeeded in producing alpha waves in the very first session, and by its end, the average subject "had more than doubled the amount of alpha in his EEG" (Brown, 1974, p. 105). Once people learn to control their brain waves through biofeedback, they are often able to duplicate the results on their own, without the machine.

Alpha wave production isn't successful for everyone. Some people find the whole process extremely frustrating. Yet for those who do succeed, the technique can be highly useful as a way of relaxing at will.

Headache Control   Biofeedback has other uses besides helping people learn to relax. Researchers and doctors are beginning to recognize its potential for medical treatment. One promising use is for the control of headaches associated with muscle tension.

In this technique, the feedback device is called an *electromyograph,* or EMG (Budzynski et al., 1970). The EMG is attached to the subject's forehead and monitors the activity in the frontalis muscle (Qualls & Sheehan, 1981). It sounds a low-pitched tone whenever the muscle is relaxed and increasingly higher tones as muscle tension increases. The subject is told to keep the tone as low as possible.

As with the alpha wave biofeedback technique, some subjects report success. One patient, a playwright, had been incapacitated by headaches that occurred as often as three or four times a week. After 15 sessions and many hours of practice away from the machine (to keep him from becoming too dependent on the EMG), he learned to relieve his own symptoms and even to prevent headaches from coming on. Another case involved a 22-year old woman who suffered from intense fears, or phobias. EMG training enabled her to enter a relaxed state when she needed to, so that she could be successfully treated for her phobias.

Regulation of Heartbeats Still another use of biofeedback has been to teach subjects to control their own heartbeats.

Weiss and Engle (1971) used biofeedback to treat eight patients who suffered from *premature ventricular contractions* (PVCs), a disorder associated with sudden death. The patients were hooked up to a machine that monitored their heartbeat, showing a red, green, or yellow light to indicate how fast the heart was beating. They were instructed to slow their heartbeat when the red light came on, and to speed it up if the green light appeared. Their goal was to keep their heartbeat in the safe yellow zone.

The results were interesting. All the patients learned to control their heart rate to some degree. Five were actually able to decrease the frequency of premature ventricular contractions. The results were monitored again over a year and a half later. Unlike some of the other studies in biofeedback, the subjects could still control their heart rate. Most of them couldn't explain to the researchers just how they did it, except that they were responding to indescribable internal cues that they had learned to recognize.

Evaluating Biofeedback

The feats we've just described are fascinating, but how have they been received by medical and psychological experts? So far, reviews have been mixed but hopeful. Certainly, biofeedback is no cure-all. Many authorities warn against accepting easy solutions for difficult problems, stressing the need for more research. As Gary Schwartz, a leading researcher in the field, states, "Unfortunately, research on biofeedback and on related cognitive self-regulation procedures such as meditation is tainted by simplistic and at times wild speculation by scientists and journalists alike" (1975, p. 261). Schwartz doesn't deny that some of these practices may have tremendous potential for some individuals; he simply believes that there has been too much publicity over too small a number of cases.

Other critics agree. There are no well controlled studies demonstrating that biofeedback can cure any important physical problems, as Shapiro and Surwit (1976) point out. Many of the studies that do exist have been poorly controlled. In addition, there is a tendency for positive results to be short-lived: many times, long term follow-ups show that subjects' control has diminished (Blanchard & Young, 1973). Still, the weight of the evidence shows biofeedback to be potentially valuable as a tool in medicine and psychotherapy and as an aid for people in their daily functioning. The next few years will certainly bring more findings on the subject.

Hypnosis

One of the most controversial of all the altered states of consciousness is hypnosis. Modern psychologists still argue over such fundamental questions as what it is, and whether it is a separate state at all. As we've seen, we have reliable indicators that meditation and relaxation (and sleep also, if you'll remember from Chapter 2) bring about recognizable physiological changes that can be measured on an EEG. However, this is not the case with hypnosis: there is no clear change from the waking state. For this reason, some psychologists suggest that hypnosis is not really a special state of consciousness at all (Barber, 1970).

What Is Hypnosis?

If there are no physical states unique to hypnosis, then what is it? **Hypnosis** is usually defined as a "state of heightened awareness in which attention is focused intensely on the suggestions of the hypnotist" (Hilgard, 1974, p. 128). Both those who argue that hypnosis is a separate state and those who argue that it isn't agree on two points. First, the subject must cooperate if he or she is to respond to the hypnotist's suggestion. And second, there has to be a shift in the way the subject thinks (Spanos & Barber, 1974). The person under hypnosis must focus so closely on the hypnotist's suggestions that he or she disregards any information that isn't consistent with them.

Under hypnosis, individuals suspend their own judgment about what kinds of feats they can perform (Ferguson, 1975). For example, you may not normally believe that you can lie rigid, with your feet and head supported but with no support for your back. Since you believe it's impossible, you won't be able to do it. Under hypnosis, however, your attitude would change if the hypnotist told you you *could* suspend yourself in this way. By believing you could do it, you'd find that you were able to perform the task.

The power of suggestion seems to be basic to people's increased abilities under hypnosis. When people are encouraged to feel they can do something, experiments have demonstrated that they may sometimes be able to perform even very difficult tasks. Theodore Barber claims that when he encouraged male subjects in an experimental group by telling them "you can do it," almost every one of them was able to support another person on his chest (Barber, 1970). Barber believes that the power of suggestion is an important area of research; it certainly seems to be the key to the success of hypnosis as a form of treatment for some medical or personal problems.

Uses of Hypnosis

Hypnosis has been put to use to help treat several conditions. It has been helpful in reducing the pain of childbirth, curing migraine headaches, for instance. It has also been used to help people cope with pain, quit smoking, or lose weight (Wolberg, 1972).

Another possible use of hypnosis is to help a person recapture lost experiences or feelings, as an aid to psychotherapy (Ferguson, 1975). For instance, a therapist may wish to uncover a deep-seated conflict that has its roots in the past. The patient is hypnotized, then asked to relive the original crisis. The therapist can gain valuable information from this kind of process, uncovering long-forgotten feelings and helping the patient work through them (Hilgard, 1974). The same kind of process can be used for reproducing unconscious dreams or fantasies.

One of the most interesting applications of hypnosis is the use of **post-hypnotic suggestion.** While under hypnosis, the subject is given instructions to be acted out after he or she comes out of the hypnotic state. For instance, subjects may be told that they will feel no pain in an arm, that they will suddenly feel very hungry, or that they will feel nauseous when they pick up a cigarette. Subjects may also be told that they will not remember the suggestion at all. They are then brought out of the trance, and they usually perform as expected.

How Suggestible Are We?

Of course, hypnotism isn't always used to treat problems or to help people expand their abilities. We've all heard of instances in which hypnotism

Hypnosis A state of heightened awareness in which attention is focused intensely on the suggestions of the hypnotist.

Post-hypnotic suggestion Instructions given by a hypnotist to an individual, to be carried out after he or she emerges from the hypnotic state.

has been used for entertainment—when the subject is told to act like a chicken or like a 3-year-old whose ice cream has just fallen off the cone. Such procedures raise an interesting question: will people do things under hypnosis that they wouldn't do otherwise?

A story that is told about the great French neurologist, Philippe Charcot, may help to answer that question. Charcot (who, by the way, was one of Freud's instructors) was demonstrating hypnosis on an 18-year-old girl when he was called away. He asked one of his young assistants to take over. This young man promptly told the young lady to take off her clothing. She immediately awakened from her trance, slapped the assistant's face, and walked out of the room (Eysenck, 1957).

Most of the research demonstrates that people will not accept all suggestions, even when under a hypnotic trance. Subjects will not harm a person they love, or jump in front of a moving car, or do anything else that would contradict deeply rooted values. However, if a situation can be engineered in which an action *seems* appropriate, then a person may do some things that would not normally be done in public. Even in these circumstances, though, people will usually go only so far in performing acts they wouldn't perform in a normal waking state.*

Consciousness and Adjustment: Conclusions

When most people think of altering consciousness as a means of changing aspects of functioning, the method that comes first to mind is drug use. Yet

*We should remember, too, that even without being hypnotized, people can be manipulated and encouraged to perform in uncharacteristic ways. Suppose, for instance, that someone convinced you that a faithful friend had been double-timing you. You might take counter-measures and perhaps even break off the relationship, acting on the suggestion even though you weren't under hypnosis.

there are many other practices, including meditation, biofeedback, and hypnosis, that use altered consciousness to heighten some aspect of functioning. While these means are less known in our society, they are beginning to be explored by Western scientists and they seem to hold potential value. Ironically, drug use—the method of choice in our society—is the one means of altering consciousness that is potentially harmful as it is commonly practiced.

In this chapter, we have explored several problems associated with drug use and abuse, looking at some ways of recognizing and avoiding those problems. But the topics of consciousness and adjustment are also related in more positive ways. In looking at meditation, biofeedback, and hypnosis, we have tried to suggest some ways by which altered consciousness might, for some people, be helpful as one possible tool for adjustment. The potential of resources such as meditation and biofeedback is still not well understood. It shouldn't be overestimated. However, as Robert Ornstein pointed out at the beginning of this chapter, we shouldn't set limits on possible avenues for awareness and adjustment simply because we've never experienced them.

Summary

1. The term *consciousness* may be used in many ways. In the text, consciousness describes a process of awareness that requires the focusing of attention on various internal and/or external stimuli.

2. People sometimes use drugs as a means of altering consciousness. The same drug may affect people in different ways. In drug research, three important variables—organismic or user variables, environmental variables, and drug variables—must all be taken into consideration.

3. Alcohol consumption is our society's number one drug problem. Alcohol is a nervous system depressant that loosens inhibitions.

4. People drink for many reasons. Chafetz names social pressures, depression, a wish to reduce inhibitions, and an excuse for expressing feelings as common reasons why people drink. There is some evidence that men drink to enhance their sense of power while women may drink to assuage doubts about their femininity. A problem drinker is not necessarily an alcoholic.

5. The best known treatment for alcoholism has been the Alcoholics Anonymous program, which calls for complete abstention. Recently, however, some other controversial treatments have been developed that center on training the alcoholic to be able to drink in moderation.

6. Much of the evidence surrounding the effects of marijuana on achievement motivation, chromosomes, and so forth is controversial; but a few facts seem clear. Marijuana is an intoxicant; it makes driving dangerous because it slows reaction times; and finally, as it is used in our society, it does not seem to cause users to build up a tolerance.

7. Other commonly used drugs include tranquilizers and barbiturates, both of which are depressants; amphetamines, which stimulate the central nervous system and are often taken to alleviate fatigue (these and tranquilizers and barbiturates all have the potential of causing dependence in some cases); cocaine, a stimulant which may cause psychological dependence; and hallucinogens such as LSD.

8. Meditation offers another avenue to altered consciousness. It involves narrowing your awareness to focus attention totally on a sound or on an experience such as breathing, until you are aware of nothing else. At this point, you may be able to break through to another plane of consciousness.

9. Meditation brings physiological changes, including increased alpha wave production, a reduction in heart rate and oxygen usage, as well as a decreased carbon dioxide production. People who meditate report feeling refreshed and renewed, so that they perform better at their jobs and at school.

10. While some meditation techniques require skill and training, there are some others, such as Benson's relaxation response, that do not.

11. Biofeedback uses monitoring instruments to measure and amplify a physiological process such as heart rate and feed it back to the person.

12. Many experiments point to the fact that with practice, people can learn to control various internal processes once thought to be completely involuntary, such as blood pressure and even brain waves.

13. The production of alpha waves is associated with a feeling of relaxed awareness. In alpha wave training, an individual receives feedback when he or she produces alpha waves.

14. Hypnosis is defined as a state of heightened awareness in which attention is focused intensely on the suggestions of the hypnotist. There is some controversy over whether hypnosis is a separate state of consciousness, since it brings no identifiable change in brain wave patterns.

15. Hypnosis may be effective in reducing pain and aiding a person in reliving some past event. If a post-hypnotic suggestion is implanted, an individual may perform an act desired by the hypnotist after he or she is brought out of a trance.

16. The attainment of altered states, through biofeedback, meditation, and hypnosis as well as the greater understanding of our dreams opens up new possibilities for personal discovery and increased awareness.

Key Terms and Concepts

consciousness	hallucinogen
altered state of consciousness	amotivational syndrome
drug	tranquilizer
organismic variables	barbiturate
environmental variables	amphetamine
drug variables	meditation
tolerance	transcendental meditation
alcoholism	biofeedback
problem drinking	alpha waves
addiction	hypnosis
Alcoholics Anonymous	post-hypnotic suggestion
marijuana	

Pavel Morozov is a hero of the Soviet Union. During the forced collectivization of the 1930s, he informed on his father for storing extra grain against government policy. The town's people, in anger, dispatched Pavel to his eternal reward a short time later. Yet Pavel's memory lives on—not as an unfaithful son who dishonored his father, but as a martyr. Pavel's tomb is decked with flowers brought by school children, and his story is repeated over and over again in Russian schools (Smith, 1976).

Values, Attitudes, and Moral Behavior

*Have American values changed? Certainly, few families today follow the strict, hardworking lifestyle that this image conveys (*American Gothic *by Grant Wood); yet some values have remained remarkably stable.*

Values Enduring beliefs that guide behavior. Specifically, they are beliefs that a specific behavior or end state is better than the opposite behavior or end state.

Attitudes Perceptual sets or predispositions to respond to particular people, objects, or events in a certain manner. Attitudes contain affective, cognitive, and behavioral components.

Many Americans find such stories odd or even shocking. Pavel's values seem strange to us: why should a person be considered a hero for informing on his own father? There are other traditions or folk tales that do make us feel more at home, for they illustrate our own values. Examples are the tale of George Washington, who confessed that he had chopped down the cherry tree because he couldn't tell a lie (the value of honesty); or stories of Abraham Lincoln trekking five miles through the wilderness to get to school (the value of diligence). In the late 1800s, Horatio Alger wrote a number of success stories in which an office boy, typically, would start out shining doorknobs to the president's suite, then finally become president himself through his diligence. Such stories strike a chord in our culture. At one time or another, each has been tremendously popular because it exemplifies a traditional American value.

Values, attitudes, and the behaviors they guide are the topic of this chapter. We have waited until the close of the book to discuss these highly personal guidelines and behaviors for a good reason. Different individuals achieve differing levels of values; and in an important sense, this development relates directly to each person's growth toward self-actualization.

We should define the terms *value* and *attitude* at the outset of this chapter, for the two words are often confused. **Values** are enduring beliefs that guide behavior in the direction of certain goals rather than others. In Rokeach's words, values are beliefs that "a specific mode of conduct or end state of existence is personally or socially preferable to an opposite or converse mode of conduct or end state of existence" (1973, p. 5). Examples of values include courage, comfort, cooperation, peace, equality, achievement, individuality, liberty, and justice.

Values are the underlying component of **attitudes,** which are defined as "perceptual sets to respond to persons, things and events" (Hollander, 1976, p. 139). If you value courage, you may show a positive attitude toward bravery in battle. Values are more abstract than attitudes, and they often serve as guiding principles for our behavior (Wrightsman, 1972). A person may have literally thousands of attitudes, but only a few dozen values (Rokeach, 1968).

As we look below first at values, then at attitudes, and finally at moral behavior, keep in mind a few questions about yourself. What values do you live by? Are you aware of the attitudes that underlie your behaviors? How do you put your own system of values into action, and in what situations might you be likely to stray from your values?

Values

What Has Happened to American Values?

"What has happened to people's values?" is a question many of us have heard, especially from people who have been around long enough to remember what things used to be like. Such critics point to the demise of the Puritan ethic of hard work, thrift, and competition (how seriously would people take Horatio Alger nowadays?); to the increased dependence on the central government to provide services and assistance; to the rise of the charge card and decline of the savings account; to the increased crime rates. . . . The list could go on.

Some critics have noted a significant change in Americans' attitudes over the past half-century (Pei, 1969). They decry the loss of individualism and liberty and the tendency to look to the central government to assume people's individual burdens. Americans, may no longer be the rugged individualists they once were.

How accurate are such critics? Have our values really changed? The answer seems to be a qualified "yes." Two points are important to re-member, however. First, there are some values that may very well need to change, as many critics argue. Within the last few decades, for instance, it was considered practically un-American to conserve fuel. Time-honored traditions such as the American-made "gas hog," inefficient heating and cooling systems, and the waste of natural resources all serve to underscore this point. And secondly, it should be noted that even in the past, many people simply paid lip service to values such as individualism and liberty. Corruption and laziness certainly did not originate in this decade. Yet many observers have seen a shift in values, and their observations are worth noting.

Shifting Values   According to David Riesman (1950), we have changed from an **inner-directed** society to an **other-directed** one. In the past, argued Riesman, Americans defined themselves in terms of individual values while in modern American society we look to others to define our priorities. Thus, individuality and tradition have fallen to some degree, and have been replaced by more social values.

Thrift is another value that has certainly changed. Per capita savings are very low in our country today, and credit card use is very high (Spencer, 1980). With high inflation rates, it isn't hard to see the reason for the change: people often buy today for fear that they won't be able to afford the purchase tomorrow.

Inner-directed   A term coined by David Riesman, referring to an orientation in which individuals are directed by their own personal attitudes and goals rather than what is socially acceptable.

Other-directed   A term coined by David Riesman that refers to an orientation in which an individual is directed by attitudes and goals that have first been checked for social acceptability.

"Looks to me like the breakdown of respect for authority is working its way up to other age groups."

Reproduced by special permission of *Playboy* Magazine, Copyright © 1968 by Playboy.

A value that seems to be growing more important is comfort. One interesting study found that 9-and 10-year-old Finnish children were far more competitive than American children, but that comfort and pleasure were more important to the American children (Britton et al., 1969). Does this signify a radical change in our values? Have we become a comfort-laden people unwilling to work hard or compete for the things we want out of life?

Happily, this does not seem to be the case. There is evidence that our values have not changed so radically, as is discussed in the box *American Values: Still Home, Mother, and Apple Pie?* Another explanation is that at least in some cases, we are learning the same values as we did in the past, but through different channels. This is seen most clearly in the changing place of formal religion in our society.

Religious Values, Today and Tomorrow   When people express concern over declining values in America today, one piece of evidence that is often cited is dwindling church and synagogue attendance. Even a generation ago, congregations were far larger than they are today. Since many of our values are so closely tied to the teachings of religion, does this signal a moral decline?

To answer this question, we should first consider the functions of religion. According to Nelson and Torrey (1973), three of religion's most important functions—enrichment of social life,

American Values: Still Home, Mother, and Apple Pie?

We hear many complaints that the old values are changing—that people just don't seem to care any more about the things that used to be important in life. In some senses, this may be true, as the chapter discusses. Yet many of our traditional values seem to be as strong 'among the new generation of college-aged adults as they were in past generations. This is shown by an extensive nationwide survey conducted by the University of Michigan's Institute for Social Research (Bachman and Johnston, 1979). Some 17,000 high school seniors were questioned about their values. These students were basically pessimistic about the state of their country, but they were quite optimistic about their own personal futures.

What values did they express? The most often expressed goal was "having a good marriage and family life." A full 79 percent of college-bound young people and 76 percent of non-college adolescents rated this goal as extremely important. A second frequent goal was "having strong friendships." Over two-thirds of the sample listed this goal as important. In contrast, only 16 percent of college students and 19 percent of noncollege students rated "having lots of money" as important, while only 10 percent of college freshmen and 4 percent of non-college youngsters thought it important to "be a leader in my community."

The authors concluded that this sample seems to show that the generation of young adults today seem to value marriage, parenthood, friendships, and meaningful work above money. Whether time and experiences will change these values is open to question, of course. However, it seems that these young people hold values fairly similar to those of their parents and their parents before them.

explanation of the unknown, and provision of a solid set of values—can be at least partially provided by other sources. Both psychology and the physical sciences have begun to explain many phenomena that were once great mysteries (take, for instance, the scientific view of evolution that has challenged the Biblical version of the creation); and many secular institutions enrich people's social lives. In addition, the schools have now begun to teach value clarification courses, encouraging students to explore and discuss values (Fiske, 1976). Of course, a fourth function is the highly personal religious experience. To some people, this is one quality of religion that can *not* be transferred to a secular source.

Perhaps the most important religious training involves value education. An obvious example of this is the Ten Commandments, stressed in both Christianity and Judaism. But even though such precepts are taught in both church and temple, how much effect does religion have on an individual's values? Actually, it is difficult to say, since so many other variables enter the picture. The examples set by parents, the personalities of religious teachers, and the situations in which individuals find themselves all play important roles. It has been argued that religious training itself may not be essential if a person has the opportunity to learn from other sources such as school and parents.

If secular institutions are at least partially taking over the functions of organized religion, does

Despite the fact that the majority of people do not regularly attend religious services, most believe in the existence of a Supreme Being.

this mean that religious beliefs are on the decline? Not so, if we can believe the results of a survey of 40,000 *Psychology Today* readers* (Wuthnow & Glock, 1974). A full 75 percent of respondents stated that they believed in some form of the su-

---

*We should note that the readership of *Psychology Today* differs somewhat from the mainstream population in that they tend to be better educated and more affluent than the average person. There is even further self-selection in that the sample of respondents consisted of persons who were motivated to fill out and mail in their responses to a lengthy questionnaire. Perhaps these readers felt more strongly than did some of those who didn't take the trouble.

pernatural, and, as Figure 16.1 indicates, slightly more than half believed in the philosophy of a major religious group (Eastern or Western)—even though only 21 percent attended religious meetings regularly. The authors concluded that "more and more Americans have come to regard formal religion with skepticism and disinterest" (p. 136). However, they noted that there is still a tremendous religious sentiment, and that most people believe in the existence of a Supreme Being of some sort.

So it seems that even among the young people we might expect to be the most skeptical, there

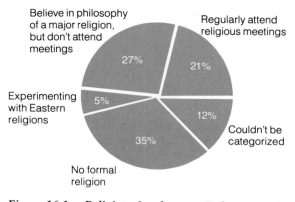

Figure 16.1 Religious Involvement Today, According to a Psychology Today Survey

Source: Wuthnow & Glock, 1974.

exists a motivation to believe in something spiritual. Religious feeling is still strong and, although organized religion is being challenged by many secular institutions, its spiritual functions still seem to be important to many people. Religion and its values make it a force to be reckoned with in attempting to understand human behavior.

How Constant Are Values?

Although the values of society seem to shift gradually over time, most of us think of our *own* values as consistent, remaining stable from one situation to the next. We like to believe that an honest person will probably be consistently honest, and that people who believe in values such as courage, altruism, and responsibility will act according to these values. As we saw in Chapter 12, however, people do not always act according to their beliefs. Indeed, studies of individual values seem to indicate that for many people, values vary according to the situation.

An extensive study performed in the late 1920s is a case in point. Hartshorne and May (1928, 1930) observed literally thousands of children in a variety of situations in which they had the opportunity to cheat or lie . The findings: the value of honesty was not always consistent. Among many children, it came and went with the situation. A later re-evaluation of the same data used statistical techniques that had been unavailable to Hartshorne and May (Burton, 1963). It showed a weak carryover for the trait of honesty from one situation to another. In other words, some children seem to be more honest than others, but few are honest all of the time.

These experiments dealt with children—but might we expect adults to be more consistent? Your own experience may well provide an answer. We'll assume that the same value, honesty, is important to you. Among your friends, or in close relationships, or in parenting if you have children, you may consider it very important to tell the truth and be open about your feelings. Yet there may be times when it is counterproductive to be honest, or situations in which is it difficult to tell the truth.

For instance, imagine you were alone in the room with your 3-year-old's Halloween candy. Just after temptation overcame you, the child walked in and asked for the chocolate bar you just ate. Telling the truth is certain to spoil your image, and in addition, you'd be acting as a poor role model. And besides, the child is still young enough to believe virtually any story you invent. ("Gee, I don't know. Maybe the dog ate it.") It takes real courage to admit an act of theft under such circumstances!

Value Conflict

In the example above and in similar situations, one common reason why people may waver from their values may be a **value conflict.**

> **Value conflict**   A situation in which two or more values are at odds, so that an individual is forced to make a choice.

A value conflict is a situation in which two or more values are at odds. For instance, you and your best friend might be stranded in the desert, with only your friend's flask of water (you've already finished yours). There is no chance that both of you could survive in the baking sun if you were to share the flask. If only one of you drinks, though, that person might make it. What do you do—let your friend have all the water, share even though you know it's useless, or take the flask for yourself?

The first reaction to a moral dilemma such as this is usually to seek ways around it. When these are ruled out, the next step is often to state that until you are in the situation yourself, it is impossible to tell what you would do. This is true, of course, but it is also an attempt to delay consideration of the values that are at stake. What personal value do you place on your own survival? Is it more important than other values, such as friendship and fair play? What if you were placed in the same situation with your own child, or spouse, or sister or brother instead of your best friend? Would that make a difference?

We are constantly placed in situations in which our values are in conflict. Take the example of the Halloween candy theft we discussed above. If you decide not to tell the whole truth to your child, the reason will probably be because your desire to be a good model is more important under these circumstances than your value of honesty. It seems, then, that if you are aware of which values are most important to you, you might be able to predict how you will respond in a given situation.

Terminal values Values related to end states that are positively viewed by society and/or an individual, such as freedom, happiness, or salvation.

Instrumental values Values related to modes of behavior such as cleanliness, cheerfulness, and courage.

Value Ranking and Personality

Each of us has a hierarchy of values that helps us set personal guidelines; and for each of us, some values are more important than others. For instance, you may feel that achievement is more important than honesty, or that security is more important than achievement. Few of us take the time to stop and consider what our values are and how we would rank them in order of importance. Yet these values are basic to our self-concepts and our behaviors. If you consider achievement to be more important than honesty, for instance, it's clear that both your goals and your methods will be quite different from those of a person who values integrity above all else. If you develop a relationship—either a business partnership or a romantic alliance—with someone whose value structure is very different from your own, certain problems can probably be predicted on the basis of those differences. Thus, it is helpful to have at least a basic understanding of your own value priorities. We'll look below at two different methods for assessing values.

Terminal and Instrumental Values Psychologist Milton Rokeach (1973) has developed a scale designed to help people rank their own values. The box *Rank Your Own Values* offers you the opportunity to try this kind of self-assessment. The scale distinguishes between two types of values, *terminal* and *instrumental*. **Terminal values** relate to end states, which are either self-centered or interpersonal. For instance, salvation and self-respect are self-centered terminal values, while friendship and social recognition are interpersonal. **Instrumental values** relate to modes of conduct, such as honesty, courage, and obedience. Take some time to rank your own values and recheck your answers. Are your values reflected in your behavior and in your judgments? Do most of your best friends have similar values? In what ways are your values similar to those of the rest of your family, and in what ways are they different?

A Value Inventory Rokeach's scale provides quite a detailed ranking of two main types of values; still another analysis takes a broader perspective, looking at six categories in less detail. According to Allport, Vernon, and Lindzey's inventory (1970), any one person's value orientation may be defined by one of any of six categories: theoretical, economic, aesthetic, social, political, or religious.

At least in theory, the authors argue, you can view an individual's personality best by looking at that person's values. Thus, if your values lie in the *economic* sphere, you are primarily interested in what is useful and materially satisfying. People with a *theoretical* orientation would be more interested in abstractions and philosophy—in finding truth, for instance. The *aesthetic* person sets great store in harmony and form. This person is not necessarily a creative artist, but he or she finds meaning in qualities such as beauty, grace, and fitness. Persons with *social* values are altruistic (doing things for others without thought of reward), prizing relationships with other people. In contrast, the *political* person is power-oriented, valuing competition and challenge. Finally, the *religious* person is mystical, and is likely to view himself or herself in relation to some sort of universal plan.

The value inventory grouping designed by Allport, Vernon, and Lindzey gives us a helpful overview of the ways in which different people's values may vary. However, very few of us can be said to belong squarely in one category. Instead, we usually lean toward one value orientation more than others; and even then, our values may not be completely consistent. We are even less consistent in our reactions to specific elements in our environment. These responses comprise our attitudes, and we'll examine them next.

Attitudes

Attitudes are more specific than the global values we have been discussing. Attitudes are internal predispositions to evaluate actions, events, or circumstances in a certain way, and to behave accordingly.

Three Components of Attitudes

Psychologists have found it useful to analyze attitudes in terms of three components (Zimbardo et al., 1977). The **cognitive component** consists of your knowledge of the item or the facts that support your evaluation. The **affective component** consists of your emotional response to the object. The **behavioral component** refers to your observable behavior toward the object of your attitude.

We can see these three components more clearly if we use an example—for instance, your attitude about dogs that wander about the neighborhood unleashed. The cognitive component of your attitude consists of the mental notes you have stored in your mind regarding this topic. You've seen a few large dogs roaming through your neighborhood, and you've noticed not only that this phenomenon has had an effect on your yard (not for the better!), but also that your own dog is in danger of being attacked when you take her out on her leash. The affective component of your attitude consists of your emotional response to this situation. In this case, you're angry. The behavioral component of your attitude is what you do about the feelings you experience. If you

---

Cognitive component of attitudes The portion of an attitude that consists of an individual's knowledge of an object or idea and the facts that support that evaluation.

Affective component of attitudes The portion of an attitude that consists of a person's emotional response to an object or idea.

Behavioral component of attitudes The observable actions of an individual toward another individual or object, as a reflection of that person's attitudes.

Rank Your Own Values

What values are most important in your life? Which values are less important? Most of us know what our values are, but people don't always stop to prioritize them. If we are aware of which values are most important, however, we may be able to predict our own behaviors and to feel more sure of ourselves if faced with a value conflict.

Psychologist Milton Rokeach has developed a scale for ranking personal values, which he groups into two categories. *Terminal values,* in the first list, are values that relate to end-states or goals, while *instrumental values,* in the second list, relate to modes of conduct. Try ranking each list according to your own order of importance, then go back and consider how well this hierarchy is reflected in your own behavior and judgments.

Terminal Values

_____   A comfortable life (a prosperous life)

_____   An exciting life (a stimulating, active life)

_____   A sense of accomplishment (lasting contribution)

_____   A world at peace (free of war and conflict)

_____   A world of beauty (beauty of nature and the arts)

_____   Equality (brotherhood, equal opportunity for all)

_____   Family security (taking care of loved ones)

_____   Freedom (independence, free choice)

_____   Happiness (contentedness)

_____   Inner harmony (freedom from inner conflict)

_____   Mature love (sexual and spiritual intimacy)

_____   National security (protection from attack)

_____   Pleasure (an enjoyable, leisurely life)

_____   Salvation (saved, eternal life)

_____   Self-respect (self-esteem)

_____   Social recognition (respect, admiration)

_____ True friendship (close companionship)

_____ Wisdom (a mature understanding of life)

Instrumental Values

_____ Ambitious (hard-working, aspiring)

_____ Broadminded (open-minded)

_____ Capable (competent, effective)

_____ Cheerful (lighthearted, joyful)

_____ Clean (neat, tidy)

_____ Courageous (standing up for your beliefs)

_____ Forgiving (willing to pardon others)

_____ Helpful (working for the welfare of others)

_____ Honest (sincere, truthful)

_____ Imaginative (daring, creative)

_____ Independent (self-reliant, self-sufficient)

_____ Intellectual (intelligent, reflective)

_____ Logical (consistent, rational)

_____ Loving (affectionate, tender)

_____ Obedient (dutiful, respectful)

_____ Polite (courteous, well-mannered)

_____ Responsible (dependable, reliable)

_____ Self-controlled (restrained, self-disciplined)

Source: Based on Rokeach, 1973, pp. 358–61. Value scales © 1967. Used by permission of Halgren Tests, Sunnyvale CA 94087.

feel strongly about the nuisance created by these dogs, for instance, you may call up the pound next time you see them.

As we've noted several times, of course, the correlation between one's feelings and one's behavior is not always very high. This was demonstrated in a now classic study by LaPiere (1934), summarized in the box *What Did You Say Was Your Policy?* The correlation does seem to be higher regarding normal, everyday, nonemergency situations than it is for less ordinary circumstances. For instance, you may routinely recycle your aluminum cans because you believe in doing what you can to preserve natural resources. But when an environmental group asks you to join a sit-in that's taking place at a new local power plant, you find the time neither to join the sit-in yourself nor to send a donation to the group, even though you believe in the cause.

In addition, although attitudes are usually rather stable (Zimbardo et al., 1977), they can be changed either gradually or rather suddenly. New information or changes in the opinion of your group may cause us to change even some long-standing attitudes. This was demonstrated in a classic study of changes in college students' attitudes.

Attitude Formation and Change

Bennington College is a small college in Vermont with a traditionally liberal faculty. In a classic study, Newcomb (1943) decided to see whether the liberal atmosphere of this school would affect the attitudes of its women students. Newcomb selected a group of students from wealthy, conservative families, tracing their attitudes as they progressed from their freshman years on up through college. Many of the students became quite liberal, and in most cases, this change was permanent, as a follow-up study more than two decades later showed (Newcomb et al., 1967). In explaining the permanence of this attitude change, Newcomb saw it as a function of these women's social environments after college. Those students who had become liberal tended to marry liberal partners and also to choose friends who held similar views.

The Bennington study points toward the conclusion that our environment plays an important role in attitude formation and change. When the Bennington students were exposed to new ideas, many were affected by these ideas, and indeed adopted them for themselves. Without this exposure, their attitudes and values would likely have remained similar to those they had learned from their parents.

Parents, of course, form the most important part of the child's environment during the early years, and many of our attitudes and values reflect what we learn from them. Some theorists explain the formation of attitudes through a combination of operant conditioning and imitation. Parents are the sources of primary rewards from infancy, providing food, comfort, and warmth. Since parents' approval is linked with these reinforcements, this approval takes on a value of its own. Such a process by which something becomes linked with a primary reinforcement is often called *secondary reinforcement* (Rachlin, 1976), and it can be one way of explaining the similarity of attitudes between children and parents. Since children want their parents' approval, they internalize the values of their parents (Mowrer, 1950).

There are many other influences on attitude besides parents, and such sources as the peer group and teachers become more important as each year passes. Normally, however, we associate with people who do not differ too greatly in terms of background and experience (Ringness, 1975). (We even choose TV shows, movies, and books that make us feel comfortable.) Thus, peer groups often reinforce many of the attitudes already held. Peer groups are important to us, especially during the teenage years; and they may present quite a contrast to our parents, at least with respect to surface values and attitudes (for example, in the area of fashion and speech patterns). Yet in the absence of experiences such as those of the

What Did You Say Was Your Policy?

As we have mentioned many times in this text, the correlation between attitudes and behavior is not always very high. This was demonstrated in a study by LaPiere conducted in 1934. At this time, anti-Chinese sentiment was very high in the country, and discriminatory treatment was recognized to be fairly common in hotels and restaurants.

To test the consistency between attitudes and behavior, LaPiere took a Chinese couple on a tour of the United States, stopping at literally hundreds of eating places and hotels. Only once during the entire tour did anti-Chinese attitudes surface. All of the other times, the couple were treated courteously and with respect. After the tour was concluded, LaPiere wrote to all the restaurants and hotels they had visited, asking them whether they would serve Chinese customers. The great majority of proprietors wrote back that they were against serving Chinese—even though they had just done so! It seems that even when people openly express attitudes, they may not always carry them through in their behavior.

Source: LaPiere, 1934.

Bennington students, our deeper values and attitudes often tend to reflect those of our parents. This tendency to hold on to attitudes we've already formed is one reason why prejudice is so difficult to eradicate.

Prejudice: Who, Why, and What to Do About It

In 1971, the United States Supreme Court ruled that busing of students could be ordered to integrate schools. Since then, countless local showdowns have occurred as families have protested their children's forced commutes to distant schools.

Have the results justified all the battles? From the perspective of almost a decade and a half later, the answer certainly isn't completely clear. While there have been some successes, there have also been many instances where students emerge from integrated classes with exactly the same racial prejudices they arrived with. Even in integrated schools, there may be relatively few interracial contacts (Shaw, 1973), and preference for one's own group may remain strong.

The term **prejudice** refers to a negative attitude toward an individual: "a rejection . . . solely because of his or her membership in a particular group" (Zimbardo et al., 1977, p. 163). This attitude affects the perceiver's view of another individual before they even begin to interact—as when an interviewer decides not to even consider hiring a job applicant because of that person's religion, sex, or ethnic background. When this prejudicial attitude shapes a person's behavior we call it **discrimination:** the acceptance or rejection of an individual on the basis of group membership (Wrightsman, 1977). Prejudice often

> **Prejudice** A negative attitude about an individual based on his or her membership in a particular group.
>
> **Discrimination** In social psychology, the acceptance or rejection of an individual, based on some group identification.

Hard Times and Scapegoating: Are They Related?

Some years back, Hovland and Sears (1940) conducted an intriguing study of the relationship between displaced aggression and prejudice. They studied the price of cotton in the years between 1882 and 1930, and found an inverse relationship between the number of blacks who were lynched in the South and the price of cotton.

Their explanation: scapegoating seemed to be related to economic frustration. When the price of cotton was low, economic times in the South were hard. It was impossible for southern farmers to vent their anger fully at northern buyers, so they may have sought other outlets. Southern blacks were a large but relatively powerless minority group, certainly highly visible and none to popular among whites in the wake of the Civil War. In Hovland and Sears' view, the lynchings might be partly explained as a venting of economic frustrations on a handy target.

This line of reasoning is a fascinating one, and the relationship between scapegoating and levels of frustration is certainly food for thought. Numerous examples might be cited to illustrate this kind of behavior—as, for instance, when a majority group member feels frustrated and angry when a minority group member gets the job she wanted, and pins the blame on the group rather than the particular qualifications of the job—or when the opposite event takes place.

As the economic situation in your community changes for better or worse, it would be interesting to note the pattern of anti-minority acts. Do they show the historical pattern of scapegoating described above?

leads to **scapegoating,** displacing anger and aggression from the source of a problem to a minority group. Whether scapegoating becomes more common when there is more anger to displace is an interesting question. Some controversial research is discussed in the box *Hard Times and Scapegoating: Are They Related?*

While it's easy to state in the abstract that all people are essentially alike, no matter what their race, religion, or ethnic group, the fact remains that prejudice seems to be a persistent factor throughout human history. What causes one group to single out another group, and how can we deal with this social problem?

Two questions stand out as we try to explain prejudice. The first is what causes people to be prejudiced; the second is why a particular group is singled out as the object of prejudice rather than another group. We'll try to answer both questions.

What Causes Prejudice?   In explaining why prejudice occurs, it is helpful to take a minute and look at the process of **stereotyping,** the holding of "a set of beliefs about a group of people based on inadequate instances of information gathering" (Ringness, 1975, p. 109).

Stereotyping is but one form of a normal human attribute—the tendency to categorize the

> **Scapegoating**   The displacement of anger and aggression from the source of a problem onto an individual or a group.
>
> **Stereotypes**   A set of beliefs and attitudes towards a group of people that is based upon inadequate information, almost always an overgeneralization.

things around us. We group our environment into flowers and trees, flatlands and hills, dormitories and apartments and houses, and so forth; and we group people as males or females, friends or acquaintances or strangers. The problem in stereotyping lies not in the activity of categorizing, but in the evaluations of the attributes that are associated with a group (Brown, 1965). For instance, categorizing a person as a woman is fair enough (so long as she is one). When you proceed to make certain judgments about her mechanical abilities or her cooking skills on the basis of her being a woman, however, you may run into trouble—for these personal evaluations have no basis in the direct experience of the individual.

Most or all of us make at least some assumptions about people because of their group membership. However, it also seems to be true that some personality types are more likely to make judgments based on stereotypes. When we think of the "prejudiced personality"—the kind of personality that is likely to hold prejudices—the TV character Archie Bunker is likely to come to mind. We laugh at his ignorant stereotypes and outlandish prejudices: everyone who is not a member of his own "true-blue" American group is suspect, but Archie can't always tell *why* they're suspect! Archie's character, made famous in the enormously popular series *All in the Family*, has become such an institution that his armchair was placed on display in the Smithsonian Institution.

Archie might be called the stereotype of the stereotyp*er*. His popularity comes from the fact that he reminds many of us of people we have met—people who are rigid, who see the world in simple "them vs. us" terms, and who are intolerant of anyone who is different. Adorno and a team of associates (Adorno et al., 1950), in a brilliant study, found that this personality type was related to prejudiced attitudes. In fact, Adorno's study originally dealt with anti-Semitic prejudices, but it was soon found that these people didn't particularly like any other minority group, either. From these studies, Adorno identified a personality pattern called the **authoritarian personality,**

Archie Bunker's popularity is probably based in the fact that he reminds us, in a nonthreatening way, of people many of us have had to deal with.

and people with this personality type tended to be prejudiced. Interestingly enough, these individuals also tend to see Archie Bunker himself more positively than people who score low on authoritarian personality scales (Chapko & Lewis, 1975).

Authoritarian personality A group of attitudes that often characterize prejudiced individuals. Authoritarian personalities are rigid, moralistic, authority-oriented, conforming, and ethnocentric.

It seems, then, that certain people are more likely to be prejudiced than are others, by the nature of their personalities. We can add to this the fact that prejudice may be learned, much in the same manner as any other attitude. Prejudiced parents tend to have children who reflect these attitudes (Epstein & Komorita, 1966). Given both of these factors, it isn't hard to see how prejudice might remain as a rather consistent condition in generation after generation of society.

Why Does a Group Become a Target?   A second question in explaining prejudice has to do with the target group itself. What determines which groups will be singled out as the object of prejudice? There are a number of answers to this question. Berkowitz (1962) notes four factors that seem especially important:

- First, if a group is powerless, prejudiced individuals can feel safe in venting their frustrations upon the group.

- Second, a group that is highly visible and easily identifiable in terms of physical traits is easy to single out, avoid, and shun. Thus, this characteristic, too, can make a group a prime candidate for prejudice.

- Third, groups whose traditions cause them to act differently are also the victims of such attitudes. Not only are they visible in terms of behavior, but the strangeness of their customs seems foreign and may arouse suspicion.

- Finally, if one group has had a prior history of disliking a certain group, the cycle may continue in the absence of any experiences to the contrary.

Another, more controversial explanation centers on value differences. According to Rokeach and his associates (1960), people tend to be prejudiced when they perceive others as having values that are different from their own. This theory helps explain the prejudice that exists between different economic classes. For instance, if a low-income apartment complex is planned for a racially mixed middle class neighborhood, the op-

position will be equally strong among black and white residents.

A series of studies have explored this issue. Usually, subjects are given a description of a hypothetical individual, then asked whether they think they would like or dislike such a person. Racial and attitudinal traits are controlled in the description, so that the experimenters can tell which of these characteristics would be more important. In the words of one group of researchers, "the typical, although not unanimous, finding was that similarity of attitudes was more important in determining liking than was belonging to the same racial group" (Freedman et.al., 1970, p. 87).

Doing Something about Prejudice   Whether it be based on race, ethnic group membership, perceived value differences, or any of countless other qualities, prejudice is a difficult problem to combat. Just as no one reason accounts for prejudice, it also seems reasonable that no one solution exists for the problem. However, certain basic guidelines are effective, when they can be put into practice.

First, it is very difficult to overcome prejudice unless groups are brought together. This is one basic reason for movements to integrate schools. High school and college are often the first places in which students from different backgrounds and racial groups are brought together, and indeed there is some data to suggest that such integration can help to decrease racial prejudice (Silverman & Shaw, 1973; Caffrey et al., 1969). Yet, from a psychological viewpoint, we have not seen the tremendous decrease in prejudice we might have hoped for. True, there is some evidence that college students are a bit less prejudiced today than they have been in the past, but stereotypes of minority groups are still present and prejudice remains a problem (Fisher, 1982). It seems that simply increasing contact among students is not sufficient.

Gordon Allport (1954) first noted this, when he suggested that just throwing various groups together may not work. Allport argued that con-

One significant factor in reducing prejudice is sharing a common goal. In racially mixed infantry companies, for instance, racial groups who fought together learned to trust one another.

tacts need to be planned to fulfill three characteristics. First, the groups must have equal status. Second, they should share a common goal. And third, they should engage in activities that are supported by authority figures. Group projects or sports activities are examples of teamwork that can help bring different groups together in working toward a common goal.

A number of studies have supported Allport's theory. Perhaps the most significant involved the assignment of black platoons to all-white infantry companies (Star et al., 1965). After fighting side-by-side for a time, the initial racial prejudice on the part of the whites declined sharply. The reasons: soldiers were forced to cooperate and rely on one another; they all shared the same purpose. Once the two groups worked together, they developed a mutual respect based on their abilities to perform their jobs. These same factors have been shown over and over again to be vital to the success of any program intended to reduce racial prejudice.

Before moving on, an interesting sideline to these findings is worth noting. It concerns the progress we've made in reducing prejudice toward another group: mentally handicapped persons. Interestingly, although most of the developments on this front have occurred only in the last decade (since Public Law 94-142 was enacted in 1975), we appear to be repeating the same mistakes that hindered so many racial integration programs. One of the most visible effects of this act has been "mainstreaming"—the placement of handicapped students in regular classrooms whenever possible. One of the hopes behind this practice was that daily contact in the schools would reduce the negative attitudes of non-handicapped children toward handicapped students and increase social interaction.

In a recent review, however, Gresham (1982) found that mainstreaming has not been an unblemished success. As in so many instances of racial integration, relatively little interaction has occurred between the two groups of students. In fact, there is little evidence that handicapped students are now more accepted by their non-handicapped peers. Again, we seem to have evidence that the mere physical presence of a minority group will not alone reduce prejudice. Using Allport's suggestions and the findings of researchers such as Star's group, we might suggest that in addition to correcting myths about the handicapped through education, policymakers and teachers should structure more social interaction between the two groups of students, encouraging communication and shared responsibilities wherever possible.

In the discussions above, we've been looking at the values and attitudes people hold, but we've said relatively little about the ways in which people act upon these values. When we consider the values or attitudes of others, however, people's actions are usually as important as their cog-

nitions. Thus it is impossible to do justice to the topic of values without exploring moral behavior. We'll turn next to that topic.

Moral Behavior

Imagine yourself in the following position. Your husband (or wife) needs very expensive medication to live, but you don't have the money to pay for it and have no legal way of obtaining the money. Under such circumstances, would it be wrong for you to steal the money you need?

The moral dilemma is very similar to one that psychologist Lawrence Kohlberg put to his subjects (1964, 1969), and it points to the fact that the value systems we have been discussing are important. We put them to use in making moral decisions and in acting upon our values. Kohlberg suggested a scenario similar to that described above because he was fascinated by the process of moral reasoning behind the actions people take. As we'll see below, some other psychologists place more emphasis upon the final behavior than the reasoning behind it. From either perspective, the topic of *moral behavior*—acting according to a set of values—is especially relevant to the study of adjustment, for the greater the difference between our values and our behaviors, the less satisfied we are likely to be with ourselves.

It's the Thought That Counts . . . or Is It?

According to Kohlberg, an understanding of moral behavior must look at the process of **moral reasoning**—the reasoning process behind moral decisions. In the hypothetical case we just mentioned, Kohlberg wasn't interested in the final decisions made by his subjects. He was interested in the reasoning process—the *way* in which they arrived at their decision.

Three Levels of Reasoning   Kohlberg proposed a famous theory that links people's moral reasoning directly to their cognitive abilities. After much research, Kohlberg proposed three levels of moral reasoning. These levels, he stated, are culturally universal, involving developmental changes in people's abilities to reason (Kohlberg, 1975). The three levels are the preconventional level, the conventional level, and the postconventional level (see Table 16.1).

Individuals in the **preconventional level** make moral decisions based upon a simple hedonistic (pleasure-centered) principle: how can I avoid punishment and satisfy myself? This preconventional level is illustrated by a child's decision not to cheat because she might get caught, or your decision to report that you received duplicate pay checks because you fear your employer might find out.

The second, **conventional level** involves approval and conformity. Here, the reasoning process is oriented toward an external authority, such as the law. But a police officer doesn't need to be present in order for moral reasoning to occur. For instance, an individual at this level may not cheat because it is against the rules, or may stop at a red light at 3 o'clock in the morning because he or she has been taught that this is the rule of the road.

The last and highest level of moral reasoning, called the **postconventional level,** involves moral reasoning based on personal values in which the individual believes, and which have been developed through experience. While persons at the preconventional level might not shoplift because they feared being caught and while those at the conventional level would behave in the same way because shoplifting is against the law, the postconventional person would not shoplift because he or she believes it is wrong to be dishonest. Kohlberg's highest concept of moral reasoning involves the formation of universal, ethical principles that revolve around the value of human life and the dignity of human labor.

Kohlberg's theory has gained considerable attention, and it is useful to look at the reasoning behind moral decisions. Yet, many psychologists have criticized Kohlberg's approach. Some take issue with his research methodology (Kutines & Grief, 1974). Others feel that Kohlberg's theory has a middle-class bias and doubt that his levels of morality are universal (Gibbs, 1977). In addition, there are cultures in which postconventional morality simply doesn't seem to exist. Some studies performed in poor villages in Turkey, Taiwan, and Mexico have failed to find any individual who has reached postconventional morality (Hetherington & Parke, 1979). Thus, Kohlberg's stages may not be as universal as claimed.

Table 16.1   Kohlberg's Three Levels of Moral Reasoning

Preconventional level	Moral decisions are based on achieving pleasure and avoiding pain.
Conventional level	Moral reasoning is oriented toward external laws or authority.
Postconventional level	Moral reasoning is based on personal rather than external values.

Preconventional level of moral reasoning   The first and lowest level of moral reasoning in Kohlberg's theory, in which decisions are based on achieving pleasure and avoiding pain.

Conventional level of moral reasoning   The second level of moral reasoning in Kohlberg's theory. Here, decisions are based upon gaining or holding the approval of others.

Postconventional level of moral reasoning   The third and highest level of moral reasoning in Kohlberg's theory, in which moral decisions are motivated by internal personal principles.

Is value-oriented behavior always explained by moral reasoning? According to Haan, the group in this sit-in probably contained a good number of demonstrators who were functioning at a preconventional level of reasoning.

Looking at Behavior Instead of Reasoning A much more deep-seated objection to Kohlberg's theory comes from the behaviorist school. According to their argument, moral reasoning does not always lead to moral behavior (Evans & Mc-Candless, 1978). Therefore, why not just study the behavior itself?

Most behaviorists would refuse to label a behavior as moral or immoral. Like Kohlberg, they are interested in such behaviors as sharing, steal-ing, killing, cheating, and so forth. But unlike Kohlberg, they feel that factors such as the situational variables that cause the person to act in such a way, or the individual's personal history, are as relevant as is the reasoning process that leads to a specific action.

The problems involved in trying to explain behavior solely on the basis of moral reasoning are aptly demonstrated by a study performed by Norma Haan and her colleagues (1968). The researchers interviewed a large number of college students in order to determine their level of moral reasoning according to Kohlberg's scale. Some of these students had demonstrated for free speech on the university campus while others had not. As it turned out the vast majority of students at the postconventional stage of morality participated in the demonstrations. A much lower number of those on the conventional level participated. So far, this is exactly what we would expect. However, 60 percent of the males and 33 percent of the females who were judged preconventional in their moral reasoning also joined the protestors, but for different reasons. The preconventional protestors tended to see the situation as a power conflict in which they could better their own status. The postconventional protestors saw the issue in terms of civil rights. People, then, can engage in the same behaviors, but for very different reasons.

Thus, instead of looking at the reasoning process, behavioral researchers look at the relationship between the situation and the behavior, or between the person's past experience and the present actions. This doesn't mean that these researchers rule out the idea that a person can be consistently honest or generous (or any other value) from one situation to others, especially if these situations are similar. However, they feel that *in many cases,* people will not act consistently with their stated values.

Some behaviorists also see moral behavior as a product of socialization. Thus, one study found that children tended to develop strong consciences if they were praised for good behavior and deprived of love for misbehavior (Sears et al., 1957). If individuals learn that doing good deeds pays off with attention or other rewards, they are likely to develop attitudes that produce such behaviors (Skinner, 1971); and the reverse also seems to be true. Another study found that if a child expects punishment—say, for getting caught stealing cookies—but doesn't receive it, its very absence can be considered a reward and the behavior will be more likely to be repeated (Walters & Parke, 1964). And since people learn from watching others, the child's siblings may follow the example if they know that someone else got away with it.

In all, both the behaviorist view and Kohlberg's moral reasoning view make some valid points. It is true that the reasoning process by which we reach moral decisions is important, and certainly, understanding moral reasoning can help us understand moral behavior. Yet at the same time, both attitudes and moral behaviors can be viewed according to a learning model, for most of us do not behave consistently with our stated values in *all* situations. This inconsistency is perhaps best shown in the related behaviors of obedience and conformity, in which people may go against their own judgment because of pressure from others.

Obedience and Conformity: What Happens to Personal Values?

To Obey, or Not to Obey   Perhaps no situations demonstrate the possible conflict between a person's value system and outside pressure more than those in which persons are asked to do something they believe is wrong.

Obedience can be defined as doing something that someone else tells you to do (Milgram, 1968). Obedience doesn't always create a problem. In fact, living with others would be very difficult if no one bothered to obey the rules. As children, we were all taught to obey, and no matter how strongly we believe in the value of independence, it's a safe bet that most of us who have children will teach them to obey.

At the same time, obedience involves giving up a certain amount of autonomy (independence) to the person you are obeying, and this can lead to

> **Obedience**   Doing something that someone else tells you to do; compliance with the request or order of another individual.

trouble if the obedient individual gives up responsibility for his or her actions. Wrightsman (1974) points out that when people believe they are operating as agents for someone else's wishes, their own consciences are less likely to operate. There are countless examples of wartime atrocities that illustrate this point—for instance, as World War II Nazis tortured and exterminated "undesirables" in the name of the state or in more recent times, as many Vietnamese civilians were killed by American soldiers.

Such instances are extraordinary, of course, and most of us assume that we could never obey orders that would actually harm someone else. Or could we? Some experiments by Milgram provide some rather unnerving evidence. Milgram (1974, 1968) found that most people would inflict what they considered to be severe and painful shocks to helpless individuals, if they were obeying someone else's orders. He began by telling subjects they were participating in an experiment on learning and memory. In one set of experiments, subjects were told to read a list of word pairs to a "learner" who was supposedly hooked up to a shock apparatus. Then the "learner" was to be tested on the material. For each incorrect response, the subject was instructed to deliver a shock, which would begin at a mild 15 volt level and be increased with each error until it reached a maximum of 450 volts. If subjects were hesitant to deliver the shocks they would be chided by the experimenter to continue. No shocks were actually inflicted, of course, but there were plenty of realistic noises, such as grunting, moaning, banging on the walls, and finally, an ominous silence.

The results of Milgram's experiment shocked many, including a group of psychiatrists whom Milgram had asked to predict the outcome. Even these psychiatrists had expected that very few subjects would actually obey the experimenter, yet

over 60 percent followed through with the experiment to its conclusion and inflicted the maximum of 450 volts.* Shocking or not, the results suggest that values may be quite flexible under external pressure to obey. Conformity is another form of external pressure which may be less direct, but it also can bring about rather surprising changes in behavior.

Conformity: Going Along with the Crowd   Imagine you are a subject in a simple experiment. You and four other people are asked to look at a line, then compare it to three other lines, as shown in Figure 16.2, to judge which of the three is closest in length to the sample. For the first two comparisons, all goes well. The lengths of the lines are easy to judge, and you and the other subjects are in agreement. In the third comparison, though, something odd happens. Although it is clear to you that line 2 is closest in length to the sample, each of the other subjects names line 1. When they have all indicated their choices, it's your turn. What do you say—line 1 or line 2?

Solomon Asch performed an experiment that put subjects in exactly this situation, using a number of confederates who would unanimously provide the wrong answer (1956, 1955). He wanted to test the power of **conformity**—the change in behavior or attitudes of an individual due to real or imagined group pressure (Worchel & Cooper, 1979). He found that conformity is a powerful force indeed: even in the absence of any overt pressure, Asch found that his subjects went against their own judgment about a third of the time and answered line 1.

Why did people change their answers even though they knew they were right? The subjects were interviewed after the experiment, and their

---

Conformity   The change in behavior or attitudes of an individual, due to real or imagined pressure from a group.

---

*One criticism of Milgram's experiment was that its original setting at Yale University, with all the trimmings of academic superiority, had influenced the results. However, even when the setting was moved to a commercial building in downtown Bridgeport, Connecticut, almost half—48 percent—of the subjects completed the experiment (Milgram, 1965).

answers were interesting. Many claimed that they knew they were uttering an incorrect answer, but they didn't want to go against the group. Others stated that the group made them feel unsure of their own perceptions, so they changed their answers.

Asch's experiment tested a clear-cut issue. When we compare this experiment to many real-life situations, where people are often much less sure of their own judgments, it is easy to see how difficult it can be to go against the group. In addition, in real life there may often be sanctions against nonconformity. This was illustrated by another experiment.

To test the consequences of nonconformity, Stanley Schachter (1951) presented a small group of students with a case history of a terribly mixed-up boy who had been in trouble with the law, and asked them to come to an agreement as to what should be done with the boy. The students didn't realize it, but one member of their group was a confederate of the experimenter. While all the students advocated a disciplined but loving treatment for the boy, this confederate spoke up for a far harsher punishment. The group tried to convert him, but when he refused they took a strong stand against him. At this point, the experimenter stepped in, stated that the group was too large, and asked the members to decide which one should be eliminated from the group. As you might expect, the nonconformer was rejected: it seemed that no one wanted him in the same group with them.

It is this type of experience that is likely to make us think twice before splitting from a group on any issue, and there are many real-life examples that show the same kind of consequence for nonconformity. One example that was mentioned in an earlier chapter is what Janis calls **groupthink.** According to Janis (1972), groups seem to develop a momentum of their own, rejecting or ridiculing dissenting opinions. Janis blames groupthink for some historical crises, including the Bay of Pigs invasion and the Vietnam War. To combat this tendency, it is suggested that group

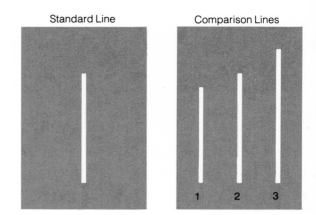

Figure 16.2   Asch's Standard and Comparison Lines   *Although line 2 is clearly closest in length to the standard line, the group unanimously chooses line 1. Would your answer be line 2, or would you change it to line 1?*

members be encouraged to play the "devil's advocate"—to look for opposing views and try to come up with alternatives.

Understanding Obedience and Conformity   Milgram's, Schachter's, and Asch's experiments, as well as Janis' criticisms of "groupthink" all provide food for thought. After spending most of this chapter discussing the values and attitudes that we hold, these examples all remind us how easily we can compromise our own sense of right and wrong.

Yet we do not always give in to others. In fact, there are many situations in which people stand up for their own views, sometimes against impressive pressure. In understanding conformity

Groupthink   A term coined by Irving Janis to describe the decisionmaking process in small, cohesive groups, in which the attempt to retain group solidarity interferes with critical thinking.

"Well, heck! If all you smart cookies agree, who am I to dissent?"
Drawing by Handelsman; Copyright 1972 The New Yorker Magazine, Inc.

and obedience, a few factors seem to be important in determining how great will be the group's influence on the individual.

First, *the group* itself is a factor in determining conformity. Asch noted in his experiment group unanimity was very important in determining whether a person would conform. If even one other subject went against the rest of the group in judging the length of the lines, the level of conformity was greatly reduced. Another quality of the group that affects conformity is its perceived trustworthiness or expertise. If you have a personal theory about preventing common colds, you'll be far more likely to yield to a group of doctors than to a group of student friends who disagreed with you.

A second factor that is important in determining conformity is *the individual*. If you are

confident of your own judgments and opinions, you are less likely to change them than if you lack self-confidence (Krech et al., 1962). Another factor may be your past involvement with an issue. If you once took a public stand on a certain question (for instance, if you petitioned fellow students on an environmental issue), you may feel reluctant to change your attitudes even though you now have second thoughts. The power of previous commitments can be great, as is discussed in the box *The Foot-in-the-Door Technique: Why It Works.*

A third factor affecting conformity is *the situation* itself. Not all situations produce the same degree of conformity. If the consequences of nonconforming seem great, you are likely to think twice before you go against the group. Again, if the situation is novel, frightening, dangerous, or threatening, you might seek the protection of the

The Foot-in-the-Door Technique: Why It Works

Experienced salespeople have long known about the so-called "foot-in-the-door" technique. This strategy involves getting the customer to do something small, then encouraging him or her to do "just a little bit more," and then more again. Eventually, the "victim" has done things that he or she would never have agreed to under normal circumstances.

How does this technique work? Researchers Mark Snyder and Michael Cunningham decided to find out in an interesting experiment. They selected 78 female and 14 male subjects at random out of the Minneapolis phone directory, and assigned them to one of two groups. The first group was asked to answer eight questions, while the second group was asked to answer 50 questions for a nonexistent public service organization. Subjects who agreed to participate in the survey were told that the interviewer was simply lining up people for the survey, and that they would be contacted again at a later date.

Two days later, they were contacted again. In this second contact the subjects were asked whether they would agree to answer another 30 questions for a different service organization at a later time. At this time also, a third group who had not been contacted before was asked if they would answer a 30-item questionnaire.

The results showed that the technique works. Just over half of the group who were first asked to answer only 8 questions agreed to participate in a second, 30-question survey, compared to only about 33 percent of the third group, who were asked to answer the 30-question survey. The difference was even more striking for the second group, who were initially asked to answer 50 questions. Only one-fifth of these subjects agreed to continue with the 30-question survey.

Why is the foot-in-the-door strategy so successful? Perhaps individuals who comply with a small request change their attitudes about getting involved. They begin to change their self-perceptions, also. Once they see themselves as the type of person who is willing to respond to a survey (or anything else), their likelihood of responding again is increased. The initial step is easiest if it is a small one.

There is a practical lesson to be learned from this study. If you want to get someone to do something that he or she would not ordinarily agree to, the best approach might be to start by asking for something small. It also stands to reason that you should be on the lookout for others who may use this technique to enlist your help. There's no harm in agreeing to small favors if you have the time, but be fully aware of exactly how involved you want to become. Don't be led on by the foot-in-the-door technique!

Source: Snyder & Cunningham, 1975.

group, even if it meant acting in a way you normally wouldn't consider.

In order to understand conformity and obedience we must look at all three of these elements. We should also consider that under many circumstances, conformity serves a purpose, both for society and the individual. People's willingness to "go with the flow" helps us get along with one another. It also permits society to be organized in a reasonably predictable manner.

Toward Independent Values

Throughout this chapter, a few points have been underscored again and again. One is that our values and attitudes are important in determining our behaviors, and that some of our values are more important than others. Another point is that situational variables may also affect behaviors, sometimes to an alarming degree. As the Milgram experiment pointed out, it seems possible under some conditions to commit acts that compromise even some of our most important values, especially when we are acting under pressure, or as an agent for someone else. Few of us rest easily with that thought, but what can be done to strengthen our values? A few points can be noted in closing.

First, a knowledge of your own values is important. If you know what is important to you, and have a sense of the priorities you place on different values, it will be easier to make decisions when your values are placed in conflict. Second, a healthy self-concept, as discussed in Chapter 12, provides an independence that enables you to feel secure in asserting your own values, even where there is pressure to conform or to obey someone else.

If you are concerned about teaching values to others, such as children, it should be remembered that telling the story of George Washington and the cherry tree can only go so far. There are many processes by which values are learned. Operant conditioning—the rewarding of desirable behaviors—seems to be important, but modeling is also important, as when a child watches a parent's honesty or generosity. The more the child identifies with the adult, the more likely it is that the parents' values will remain an important influence (Kagan, 1958).

A new approach is to present children with hypothetical moral dilemmas and allow them to develop their own solutions from a number of viewpoints. In fact, many schools are beginning to offer value clarification courses (Fiske, 1976).

These courses encourage students to discuss and explore values, and they seem to be influenced strongly by Kohlberg's emphasis on moral reasoning. Parents may use a similar approach by discussing moral questions with their children and encouraging them to see all sides of an issue.

A Last Word

This chapter began by asking you to examine the values you live by. In order to become more aware of them, it was necessary to examine the nature of values, attitudes, obedience, and conformity.

No one ever said that acting in accordance with self-selected values was easy. As you have seen, our values can conflict with each other, forcing us to choose between them in rather difficult situations. However, in order to make such decisions, you must have an understanding of just what your values are, as well as some idea of your life goals and purposes. Only then can you truly take charge of your own life, and take responsibility for your own choices and behaviors.

Summary

1. Values are enduring beliefs that one specific mode of conduct or end-state of existence is personally or socially preferable to others. Values direct behavior, set priorities, and prescribe what is right and wrong. Attitudes, which are based on values, are perceptual sets to respond to persons, things, and events.

2. Values are shaped by society. Some values, such as thrift, appear to be changing. However, our society's values do not appear to be changing radically. Although many critics worry about the decline in modern values, some changes, like the increased concern for preserving the environment, have been praised by many.

3. Religion can be seen as both an experience and a set of values and principles. Organized religion faces many new challenges in our complex technological society. However, most people still believe in one supernatural being.

4. Values are at least in part situationally determined. Sometimes, our values are in conflict with one another. To a certain degree, we can predict how we will respond to value conflicts if we are aware of our own value hierarchies. Two assessments, Rokeach's survey of instrumental and terminal values, and Allport, Vernon, and Lindzey's value orientations grouping, may help us to understand our own value systems.

5. Attitudes have cognitive, affective, and behavioral components. The cognitive component relates to one's knowledge of facts. The affective component involves the emotions of the individual, while the behavioral component relates to the person's responses in relation to the attitude.

6. Prejudice is a negative attitude toward an individual because of group membership. A group that is powerless, identifiable, and whose traditions are different is often the victim of prejudice. If one group has a history of disliking another, the vicious cycle may continue. Scapegoating involves the displacement of anger from one source to a minority group. Discrimination is the behavioral byproduct of prejudice.

7. When a set of beliefs (positive or negative) about a group is based upon inadequate information, it is called stereotyping. A certain degree of categorization is probably inevitable. The key questions in stereotyping involve the nature and evaluations of these attributes.

8. Prejudice may be reduced through organized contacts between groups, so long as these contacts are carefully structured. Integration is most effective when groups receive equal status, when they share common goals and interests, and when activities are supported by authority figures.

9. Moral reasoning involves the process by which a moral decision is made. Moral behavior relates to the action itself. The correlation between moral reasoning and moral behavior is far from perfect.

10. Lawrence Kohlberg has developed a theory that describes moral reasoning in three stages or levels: the preconventional, the conventional, and the postconventional. Most people do not reach the postconventional level of moral reasoning.

11. Behaviorally oriented psychologists focus on the behavior itself rather than the reasoning behind it, and they look at the characteristics of the situation and the past learning of the individual.

12. Both obedience and conformity can involve conflict in values. Stanley Milgram, for instance, found that most people obeyed even when they were requested to give what they thought were potentially harmful shocks. Conformity is defined as a change in behavior or attitudes of an individual toward a group due to real or imagined group pressure. People who do not conform are often rejected by the group.

13. Many schools are now beginning to explore values in courses influenced by Kohlberg's theory of moral reasoning. These courses often involve presenting moral dilemmas to students and encouraging them to analyze them from many different viewpoints.

Key Terms and Concepts

values

attitudes

inner-directed

other-directed

value conflict

terminal values

instrumental values

cognitive component of attitudes

affective component of attitudes

behavioral component of attitudes

prejudice

discrimination

scapegoating

stereotyping

authoritarian personality

preconventional level of moral reasoning

conventional level of moral reasoning

postconventional level of moral reasoning

obedience

conformity

groupthink

BIBLIOGRAPHY

A

Abramson, L. Y.; Seligman, M. E. P.; & Teasdale, J. D. Learned helplessness in humans: Critique and reformulation. *Journal of Abnormal Psychology*, 1978, *87*, 49–74.

Adams, M. *Single blessedness: Observations on the single status in married society*. New York: Basic Books, 1976.

Adorno, T.; Frenkel-Brunswik, E.; Levinson, D.; & Sanford, N. *The authoritarian personality*. New York: Harper & Row, 1950.

Akeret, R. U. Interrelationships among various dimensions of the self concept. *Journal of Counseling Psychology*, 1959, *6*, 99–202.

Albanese, R., & Van Fleet, D. D. *Organizational behavior: A managerial viewpoint*. Chicago: Dryden Press, 1983.

Alcoholics Anonymous. *Twelve steps and twelve traditions*. New York: Alcoholics Anonymous World Services, Inc., 1974.

Alexander, F. *Psychosomatic medicine*. New York: Norton, 1950.

Allen, J. *Assault with a deadly weapon: The autobiography of a street criminal*. New York: Pantheon, 1977.

Allport, G. W. *Pattern and growth in personality*. New York: Holt, Rinehart & Winston, 1961.

Allport, G. W. *The nature of prejudice*. Garden City, New York: Doubleday, 1954.

Allport, G. W.; Vernon P. E.; & Lindzey, G. *A study of values*. Boston: Houghton Mifflin, 1970.

Altrocchi, J. *Abnormal psychology*. New York: Harcourt, Brace, Jovanovich, 1980.

American Psychiatric Association. *Diagnostic and statistical manual of mental disorders* (3rd ed.). Washington, D.C.: American Psychiatric Association, 1980.

Anand, B. K.; China, G. S.; & Singh, B. Studies on Sri Romanand Yogi during his stay in an air tight box, 1961, cited in Bloomfield H. H.; Cain M. P.; & Jaffe, D. T. *TM: Discovering inner energy and overcoming stress*. New York: Delacorte, 1975.

Anastasi, A. *Psychological testing* (4th ed.). New York: Macmillan, 1976.

Anastasi, A. Heredity, environment and the question "how?" *Psychological Review*, 1958, *65*, 197–208.

Anderson, B. F. *Cognitive psychology: The study of knowing, learning and thinking*. New York: Academic Press, 1975.

Anderson, D. Former Jet speaks out on his life of drugs. *New York Times*. August 31, 1980, Section 5, 1; 9.

Anderson, N. H. Likableness ratings of 555 personality-trait words. *Journal of Personality and Social Psychology*, 1968, *9*, 272–279.

Anderson, R. C., & Faust, G. W. *Educational psychology: The science of instruction and learning*. New York: Dodd, Mead & Co., 1973.

Ardrey, R. *The territorial imperative*. New York: Atheneum, 1966.

Arehart-Treichel, J. Mental patterns of disease. *Human Behavior*, January 1976, *5*, 40-43.

Arieti, S. Manic depressive psychoses. In S. Arieti (ed.), *American handbook of psychiatry*. New York: Basic Books, 1959.

Arndt, W. B., Jr. *Theories of personality*. New York: Macmillan, 1974.

Aronfreed, J. *Conduct and conscience: The socialization of internalized control over behavior*. New York: Academic Press, 1968.

Aronson, E. *The social animal*. San Francisco: Freeman, 1972.

Asch, S. E. Studies of independence and conformity: A minority of one against a unanimous majority. *Psychological Monographs*, 1956, *70*, Whole No. 416.

Asch, S. E. Opinions and social pressure. *Scientific American*, November 1955, *193*, 31–35.

Asch, S. E. Forming impressions of personality. *Journal of Abnormal and Social Psychology*, 1946, *41*, 258–290.

Aserinsky, E., & Kleitman, N. Regularly occurring patterns of eye motility and concomitant phenomena during sleep. *Science*, 1953, *118*, 273–274.

Ashburn, E. *Motivation, personality and work-related characteristics of women in male-dominated professions*. Washington, D.C.: National Association for Women Deans, Administrators and Counselors, 1977.

Atchley, R. C. *The social forces in later life*, (2nd ed.). Belmont, Calif.: Wadsworth, 1977.

Atkinson, J. W. *An introduction to motivation*. Princeton, N. J.: Van Nostrand Reinhold, 1964.

Ayllon, T., & Azrin, N. H. *Token economy: A motivational system for therapy and rehabilitation*. New York: Appleton-Century-Crofts, 1968.

B

Bach, G., & Wyden, P. *The intimate enemy: How to fight fair in love and marriage.* New York: William Morrow, 1968.

Bachman, J. G., & L. D. Johnson. The freshmen. *Psychology Today*, September 1979, 78–87.

Bakwin, H., & R. M. Bakwin. *Behavior disorders in children.* Philadelphia: Saunders, 1972.

Balis, A. *What are you using? A birth control guide for teenagers.* New York: The Dial Press, 1981.

Bandura, A. *Social learning theory.* Englewood Cliffs, N. J.: Prentice-Hall, 1977.

Bandura, A. *Aggression: A social learning analysis.* Englewood Cliffs, N. J.: Prentice-Hall, 1973.

Bandura, A.; Ross, D.; & Ross, S. A. Transmission of aggression through imitation of aggressive models. *Journal of Abnormal and Social Psychology*, 1961, *63*, 575–582.

Bandura, A., & Walters, R. H. *Social learning and personality development.* New York: Holt, Rinehart & Winston, 1963.

Bandura, A., & Walters, R. H. *Adolescent aggression.* New York: Ronald Press, 1959.

Barber, T. X. Who believes in hypnosis. *Psychology Today*, July 1970, 4, 20–28, 84.

Barclay, A. M. Information as a defensive control of sexual behavior. *Journal of Personality and Social Psychology*, 1971, *17*, 244–249.

Bardwick, J. M. *Psychology of women.* New York: Harper & Row, 1971.

Bardwick, J.; Douvan E.; Horner, M. S.; & Gutman, D. *Feminine development and conflict.* Belmont, Calif.: Brooks/Cole, 1970.

Barker, R. G.; Dembo, T.; & Lewin, K. *Frustration and regression: A study of young children.* University of Iowa Studies in Child Welfare, 1941, *18*, No. 1.

Baron, R. A. *Human aggression.* New York: Plenum Press, 1977.

Baumrind, D. Current patterns of parental authority. *Developmental Psychology Monographs*, 1971, *1*, 1–103.

Baumrind, D. Child-care practices anteceding three patterns of preschool behavior. *Genetic Psychology Monographs*, 1967, *75*, 43–88.

Beck, A. T. *Depression: Clinical experimental and theoretical aspects.* New York: Harper & Row, 1967.

Beckman, L. J. The relative rewards and costs of parenthood and employment for employed women. *Psychology of Women Quarterly*, 1978, *21*, 215–234.

Bee, H. *Social issues in developmental psychology* (2nd ed.). New York: Harper & Row, 1978.

Bell, A. P., & Weinberg, M. S. *Homosexualities: A study of diversity among men and women.* New York: Simon & Schuster, 1978.

Belliveau, F., & Richter, L. *Understanding human sexual inadequacy.* Boston: Little, Brown, & Co., 1970.

Belschner, W. Learning and aggression. In H. Selg (ed.), *The making of human aggression.* New York: St. Martin's Press, 1971, 61-106.

Bem, S. The measurement of psychological androgyny. *Journal of Consulting and Clinical Psychology*, 1974, *42*, 155–162.

Benson, H. *The relaxation response.* New York: William Morrow, 1976.

Benson, H., & Wallace K. Decreased drug abuse with Transcendental Meditation—A study of 1862 subjects. In C. Zarafonetis (ed.), *Proceedings of the International Symposium on Drug Abuse.* Philadelphia: Lea & Febiger, 1972, 369–376.

Bergan, J. R., & Henderson, R. W. *Child development.* Columbus, Ohio: Charles E. Merrill, 1979.

Berkowitz, L. *Aggression—A social psychological analysis.* New York: McGraw-Hill, 1962.

Berkowitz, L., & Green, R. G. Film violence and the cue properties of available targets. *Journal of Personality and Social Psychology*, 1966, *3*, 525–530.

Berkowitz, L., & LePage, A. Weapons as aggression-eliciting stimuli. *Journal of Personality and Social Psychology*, 1967, *7*, 202–207.

Berne, E. *Games people play.* New York: Grove Press, 1964.

Berscheid, E., & Walster, E. *Interpersonal attraction.* Reading, Mass.: Addison-Wesley, 1978.

Bertalanffy, L. V. *General system theory.* New York: McGraw-Hill, 1968.

Best, D.; Williams, J. E.; Cloud J. M.; Davis, S. W.; Robertson, L. S.; Edwards, J. E.; Giles, H.; & Fowles, T. Development of sex-trait stereotypes among young children in the U.S., England and Ireland. *Child Development*, 1977, *48*, 1375–1384.

Bettelheim, B. *The uses of enchantment.* New York: Knopf, 1975.

Bieber, I.; Dain, H. J.; Dince, P. R.; Drellich, M. G.; Gundlach, R. H.; Kremer, M. W.; Rifkin, A. H.; Wilbur, C. B.; & Bieber, T. B. *Homosexuality: A psychological study.* New York: Basic Books, 1962.

Birdwhistle, R. C. *Kinesics and context.* Philadelphia: University of Pennsylvania Press, 1970.

Birney, R. C. Research on the achievement motive. In E. F. Borgatta & W. W. Lambert (eds.), *Handbook of personality theory and research.* Chicago: Rand McNally & Company, 1968, 857–890.

Bischof, L. T. *Adult psychology* (2nd ed.). New York: Harper & Row, 1976.

Blake, R., & Mouton, J. The fifth achievement. *Journal of Applied Behavioral Science*, 1970, *6*, 413–426.

Blanchard, E. B., & Young, L. D. Clinical applications of

biofeedback training: A review of evidence. *Archives of General Psychiatry,* 1973, *30,* 573–589.

Blau, P. M. *Exchange and power in social life.* New York: Wiley, 1964.

Block. J. H. Issues, problems, and pitfalls in assessing sex differences: A critique of the psychology of sex differences. *Merrill-Palmer Quarterly,* 1976, *22,* 283–308.

Bloomfield, H. H.; Cain, M. P.; & Jaffe, D. T. *TM: Discovering inner energies and overcoming stress.* New York: Delacorte, 1975.

Boice, R. In the shadow of Darwin. In R. G. Green & E. C. O'Neal (eds.), *Perspectives on aging.* New York: Academic Press, 1976.

Bolles, R. *What color is your parachute?* Berkeley, Calif.: Ten Speed Press, 1978.

Bonime, W. *The clinical use of dreams.* New York: Basic Books, 1962.

Borow, H. Career development in adolescence. In J. F. Adams (ed.), *Understanding adolescence* (2nd ed.). Boston: Allyn & Bacon, 1973.

Boudreau, L. A., & Jeffrey, C. J. Stuttering treated by desensitization. *Journal of Behavior Therapy and Experimental Psychiatry,* 1973, *4,* 209–212.

Bowlby, J. Separation anxiety. *International Journal of Psychoanalysis,* 1960, *41,* 89–113.

Brammer, L. M., & Shostrom, E. L. *Therapeutic psychology* (2nd ed.). Englewood Cliffs, N.J.: Prentice-Hall, 1968.

Bransford, J. D. *Human cognition.* Belmont, Calif.: Wadsworth, 1979.

Braucht, G. N.; Brakarsh, D.; Follingstad, D.; & Berry, K. L. Deviant drug use in adolescence: A review of psychosocial correlates. *Psychological Bulletin,* 1973, *79,* 92–106.

Brayfield, A. H., & Crockett, W. A. Employee attitudes and employee performance. *Psychological Bulletin,* 1955, *52,* 346–424.

Brecher, E. M. and the Editors of Consumer Reports. *Licit and illicit drugs.* Boston: Little, Brown & Co., 1972.

Brenton, M. *Friendship,* New York: Stone & Day, 1974.

Brieland, D.; Costin, L. B.; & Atherton, C. R. *Contemporary social work.* New York: McGraw-Hill, 1975.

Brill, A. A. *Basic principles of psychoanalysis.* New York: Doubleday, 1949.

Britton, J. H.; Britton, J. O.; & Fisher, C. F. Perception of children's moral and emotional behavior: A comparison of Finnish and American children. *Human Development,* 1969, *12,* 5–63.

Brockner, J., & Swap W. Effects of repeated exposure and attitudinal similarity on self disclosure and interpersonal attraction. *Journal of Personality and Social Psychology,* 1976, *33,* 531–540.

Broderick C. B. Sexuality and the life cycle: A broad concept of sexuality. Cited in L. A. Kirkendall and I.

Rubin (eds.), *Readings in psychology.* Guilford, Conn.: The Dushkin Press, 1978, 217–223.

Broderick, C. B. Adult sexual development. In B. B. Wolman (ed), *Handbook of developmental psychology.* Englewood Cliffs, N. J.: Prentice-Hall, 1982, 726–733.

Brophy, A. L. Self, role and satisfaction. *Genetic Psychology Monographs,* 1959, *54,* 263–308.

Broverman, I. K.; Vogel, S. R.; Broverman, D. M.; Clarkson, F. E.; & Rosenkrantz, P. S. Sex role stereotypes: A current appraisal. *Journal of Social Issues,* 1972, *28,* 59–78.

Brown, B. B. Biofeedback: An exercise in "self control." *Saturday Review.* February 22, 1975, 22–27.

Brown, B. B. *New mind, new body biofeedback: New directions for the mind.* New York: Harper & Row, 1974.

Brown, F. G. *Principles of educational and psychological testing.* New York: Holt, Rinehart, & Winston, 1983.

Brown, R. *Social psychology.* New York: The Free Press, 1965.

Bruch, H. Transformation of oral impulses in eating disorders: A conceptual approach. *Psychiatry Quarterly,* 1961, 458–481.

Bruner, J., & Postman, L. On the perception of incongruity: A paradigm. *Journal of Personality,* 1949, *18,* 206–223.

Budzynski, T. H.; Stoyva, J. S.; & Adler, C. Feedback-induced muscle relaxation application to tension headaches. *Journal of Behavior Therapy and Experimental Psychiatry,* 1970, *1,* 205–211.

Burka, J. M., & Yuen, L. M. Mind games procrastinators play. *Psychology Today,* 1982, *1,* 32–37.

Burke, R. J.; Weir, T. W.; & DuWors, R. E., Jr. Type A behavior of administrators and wives' reports of marital satisfaction. *Journal of Applied Psychology,* 1979, *64,* 57–65.

Burns, R. B. *The self concept: Theory, measurement, development and behaviour.* London: Longman, 1979.

Burr, W. R. *Successful marriage: A principles approach.* Homewood, Ill.: The Dorsey Press, 1976.

Burton, R. V. Generality of honesty reconsidered. *Psychological Review,* 1963, *70,* 481–499.

Byrne, D. Sexual changes in society and science. In D. Byrne & L. Byrne, (eds.), *Exploring human sexuality.* New York: Thomas Crowell Co., 1977.

Byrne, D. *The attraction paradigm.* New York: Academic Press, 1971.

C

Caffrey, B.; Anderson, S.; & Garrison, S. Changes in racial attitudes of white southerners after exposure to the atmosphere of a southern university. *Psychological Reports,* 1969, *25,* 555–558.

Cairns, R. B. *Social development: The origins and plasticity of interchanges.* San Francisco: Freeman, 1979.

Cameron, P. The generation gap: Beliefs about sexuality and self-reported sexuality. In W. R. Looft (ed.), *Developmental psychology: A book of readings.* New York: Holt, Rinehart & Winston, 1972.

Campbell, C. Transcendence is as American as Ralph Waldo Emerson. *Psychology Today,* 1974, *7,* 37–38.

Campbell, J. (ed.). *The portable Jung.* New York: Viking Press, 1973.

Cant, G. Valiumania. *New York Times Sunday Magazine,* February 1, 1976, 34–48.

Caplow, T. *The sociology of work.* Minneapolis: The University of Minnesota Press, 1954.

Carrington, P. Dreams and schizophrenia. *Archives of General Psychiatry,* 1972, *26,* 343–350.

Carroll, H. A. *Mental hygiene: The dynamics of adjustment* (4th ed.). Englewood Cliffs, N. J.: Prentice-Hall, 1964.

Carroll, L. *Alice in Wonderland.* New York: Grossett & Dunlap, 1980.

Carter, H., & Glick, P. C. *Marriage and development: A social and economic study.* Cambridge, Mass.: Harvard University Press, 1970.

Cartwright, D. S., & Cartwright, C. I. *Psychological adjustment.* Chicago: Rand-McNally, 1971.

Cartwright, R. D. Happy ending for our dreams. *Psychology Today,* December 1978, *12,* 66–78.

Chafetz, M. E.; Blane, H. R.; & Hill, M. J. *Frontiers of alcoholism.* New York: Science House, 1970.

Chaikin, A. L.; Sigler, E.; & Derlega, V. J. Nonverbal mediators of teacher expectancy effects. *Journal of Personality and Social Psychology,* 1974, *30,* 144–149.

Chapko, M., & Lewis, M. Authoritarianism: All in the family. *Journal of Psychology,* 1975, *90,* 245–248.

Chaplin, J. P. *Dictionary of psychology* (rev. ed.). New York: Dell Publishing Co., 1975.

Chapman, A. H. *Harry Stack Sullivan: His life and his work.* New York: G. P. Putnam, 1976.

Chapman, A. H. *Management of emotional problems in children and adolescents.* Philadelphia: Lippincott, 1965.

Chasdi, E. H., & Lawrence, M. S. Some antecedents of aggression and effects of frustration in doll play. In D. McClelland (ed.), *Studies in motivation,* New York: Appleton-Century-Crofts, 1955.

Cherlin, A. *Marriage, divorce, and remarriage.* Cambridge, Mass.: Harvard University Press, 1981.

Chetwynd, T. *How to interpret your own dreams.* New York: Wyden, 1972.

Chilman, C. S. *Adolescent sexuality in a changing American society.* Washington, D. C.: Department of Health, Education and Welfare, 1979.

Christensen, H. T. Scandinavian versus American sex patterns. *Sexual Behavior,* December 1971, *1,* 4–10.

Christensen, H. T., & Gregg, C. F. Changing sex norms in America and Scandinavia. *Journal of Marriage and the Family,* 1970, *32,* 616–627.

Cirese, S. *Quest: A search for self.* New York: Harper & Row, 1977.

Clarke, A. M., & Clarke, A. D. B. *Early experience: Myth and fact.* New York: The Free Press, 1976.

Cohen, D. B., & Cox, D. Neuroticism in sleep laboratory: Implications for representational and adaptive properties of dreaming. *Journal of Abnormal Psychology,* 1975, *84,* 91–108.

Coles, R. Work and self respect. In E. H. Erikson (ed.), *Adulthood.* New York: Norton, 1978.

Coles, R. What can you expect? *New Yorker,* April 19, 1969, 69–177.

Colligan, D. That helpless feeling: The dangers of stress. *New York Magazine,* July 14, 1975, 28–32.

Colman, A. Flattery won't get you everywhere. *Psychology Today,* May 1980, *13,* 80–84.

Comfort, A. *The joy of sex.* New York: Simon & Schuster, 1972.

Cooley, C. H. *Human nature and the social order* (rev. ed.). New York: Scribner, 1922. (Originally published, 1902.)

Coon, D. *Introduction to psychology: Exploration and application.* Minneapolis: West Publishing Co., 1980.

Coopersmith, S. *The antecedents of self esteem.* San Francisco: Freeman, 1967.

Corey, G. *Theory and practice of counseling and psychotherapy.* Monterey, Calif.: Brooks/Cole, 1977.

Corter, C., & Bow, T. The mother's response to separation as a function of her infant's sex and vocal distress. *Child Development,* 1976, *47,* 72–76.

Cox, T. *Stress.* Baltimore: University Park Press, 1978.

Cronbach, L. J. *Essentials of psychological testing* (3rd ed.). New York: Harper & Row, 1970.

Crooks, R., & Baur, K. *Our sexuality* (2nd ed.). Menlo Park, Calif.: Benjamin/Cummings, 1983.

Culler, R. E., & Holahan, C. J. Test anxiety and academic performance: The effects of study related behaviors. *Journal of Educational Psychology,* 1980, *72,* 16–20.

D

Darley, J. M.; Glucksberg, S.; Kamin. L. J.; & Konchla, R. A. *Psychology.* Englewood Cliffs, N. J.: Prentice-Hall, 1981.

Davis, J. A. *Great aspirations,* Vol. 1. Chicago: National Opinion Research Center, University of Chicago, 1963.

Deaux, K., & Emswiller, T. Explanations of successful performance on sex-linked tasks: What is skill for the male is luck for the female. *Journal of Personality and Social Psychology,* 1974, *29,* 80–85.

DeJong, W. The stigma of obesity: The consequences of

naive assumptions concerning the causes of physical deviance. In P. N. Middlebrook, *Social psychology and modern life*, (2nd ed.). New York: Knopf, 1980.

Dekker, E., & Groen, J. Reproducible psychogenic attacks of asthma. *Journal of Psychosomatic Research*, 1956, *1*, 58–67.

DeLora, J. S.; Warren, C. A. B.; & Ellison, C. R. *Understanding sexual interaction* (2nd ed.). Boston: Houghton Mifflin, 1981.

Dement, W. C. *Some must watch while others must sleep*. San Francisco: Freeman, 1974.

Dement, W. C. The effect of dream deprivation. *Science*, 1960, *131*, 1705–1707.

Deutsch, J. A., & Deutsch, D. *Physiological psychology* (rev. ed.). Homewood, Ill.: The Dorsey Press, 1973.

Diamond, M. J., & Shapiro, J. L. Changes in locus of control as a function of encounter group experiences. *Journal of Abnormal Psychology*, 1973, *82*, 514–518.

DiGiuseppe, R. A.; Miller, N. J.; & Trexler, L. D. A review of rational-emotive psychotherapy outcome studies. *The Counseling Psychologist*, 1977, *7*, 57–64.

Dilley, J. Self-help literature: Don't knock it till you try it. *The Personnel and Guidance Journal*, 1978, *56*, 293–295.

Dion, K. K.; Berscheid, E.; & Walster, E. What is beautiful is good. *Journal of Personality and Social Psychology*, 1972, *24*, 285–290.

Dobzhansky, T. Differences are not deficits. *Psychology Today*, December 1973, 97–101.

Dodd, D. H., & White, R. M., Jr. *Cognition: Mental structures and processes*. Boston: Allyn & Bacon, 1980.

Doherty, W. J., and Jacobson, J. S. Marriage and the family. In B. B. Wolman, (ed.), *Handbook of developmental psychology*. Englewood Cliffs, N. J.: Prentice-Hall, 1982, 667–680.

Dollard, J.; Doob, L. W.; Miller, N. E.; Mowrer, O. H.; & Sears, R. R. *Frustration and aggression*. New Haven: Yale University Press, 1939.

Donnerstein, E., & Wilson, D. W. Effects of noise and perceived control on ongoing and subsequent aggressive behavior. *Journal of Personality and Social Psychology*, 1976, *34*, 774–781.

Dreyer, P. H. Sexuality during adolescence. In B. B. Wolman (ed.), *Handbook of developmental psychology*. Englewood Cliffs, N. J.: Prentice-Hall, 1982, 559–601.

Dubrow, M. Female assertiveness: How a pussycat can learn to be a panther. *New York Magazine*, July 28, 1975, 40–45.

Dutton, D. G., & Aron, A. P. Some evidence for heightened sexual attraction under conditions of high anxiety. *Journal of Personality and Social Psychology*, 1974, *30*, 510–517.

Duvall, E. M. *Marriage and family development* (5th ed.). Philadelphia: Lippincott, 1971.

Dworkin, R. H.; Burke, B. W.; Maher, B. A.; & Gottesman, I. I. A longitudinal study on genetics and personality. *Journal of Personality and Social Psychology*, 1976, *34*, 510–518.

E

Easterbrook, J. A. The effect of emotion on cue utilization and the organization of behavior. *Psychological Review*, 1959, *66*, 183–201.

Egan, G. *You and me: The skills of communication and relating to others*. Monterey, Calif.: Brooks/Cole, 1977.

Ehrenberg, O., & Ehrenberg M. How, when and why to fire your shrink. *New York Magazine*, May 17, 1975.

Eidelberg, L. E. (ed.). *Encyclopedia of psychoanalysis*. New York: The Free Press, 1968.

Eisdorfer, C., & Wilkie, F. Stress, disease, aging and behavior. In J. E. Birren & K. W. Schaie (eds.), *Handbook of the Psychology of Aging*. New York: Van Nostrand, 1977.

Ekman, P. The universal smile: Face muscles talk every language. *Psychology Today*, September 1975, *4*, 35–39.

Ekman, P., & Friesen W. V. Nonverbal leakage and clues to deception. *Psychiatry*, 1969, *32*, 88–106.

Elias, M. F.; Elias, P. K.; & Elias, J. W. *Basic processes in adult psychology*. St. Louis, Mo.: C. V. Mosby, 1977.

Elkind, D. Good me or bad me: The Sullivan approach to personality. *New York Times Magazine*, September 24, 1972, 18.

Elkind, D., & Hamsher, J. H. The anatomy of melancholia. *Saturday Review*, September 30, 1972, *55*, 54–61.

Elliott, C. H., & Denney D. R. Weight control through covert sensitization and false feedback. *Journal of Consulting and Clinical Psychology*, 1975, *43*, 842–850.

Ellis, A. Rational-emotive therapy: Research data that support the clinical and personality hypotheses of RET and other modes of cognitive-behavioral therapy. *The Counseling Psychologist*, 1977, *7*, 2–43.

Ellis, A. *Humanistic psychotherapy*. New York: McGraw-Hill, 1974.

Ellis, A. *How to master your fear of flying*. New York: Wyden, 1972.

Ellis, A., & Harper, R. *A new guide to rational living*. (rev. ed.). Hollywood: Wilshire Books, 1975.

Ellis, H. C. *Fundamentals of human learning and cognition*. Dubuque, Iowa: Wm. C. Brown, 1972.

Emery, J. B. Systematic desensitization: Reducing test anxiety. In J. D. Krumboltz & C. E. Thoresen (eds.), *Behavioral counseling*. New York: Holt, Rinehart & Winston, 1969.

Endler, N. S.; Boulton, L. R.; & Osser, H. (eds.). *Contemporary issues in developmental psychology* (2nd ed.). New York: Holt, Rinehart & Winston, 1976, 1–31.

Ephron, H. S., & Carrington, P. Rapid eye movement

sleep and cortical homeostasis. *Psychological Review*, 1966, *73*, 500–526.

Epstein, R., & Komorita, S. S. Childhood prejudice as a function of parental ethnocentrism, punitiveness and outgroup characteristics. *Journal of Personality and Social Psychology*, 1966, *3*, 259–264.

Erikson, E. H. Reflections on Dr. Borg's life cycle. In E. Erikson (ed.), *Adulthood*. New York: Norton, 1978.

Erikson, E. H. *Identity: Youth and crisis*. New York: Norton, 1968.

Etaugh, C. Effects of nonmaternal care for children: Research evidence and popular views. *American Psychologist*, 1980, *35*, 309–319.

Etaugh, C. Effects of maternal employment on children: A review of recent research. *Merrill-Palmer Quarterly*, 1974, *20*, 71–98.

Evans, E. D., & McCandless, B. R. *Children and youth: Psychosocial development*. New York: Holt, Rinehart & Winston, 1978.

Evans, R. B. Physical and biochemical characteristics of homosexual men. *Journal of Consulting and Clinical Psychology*, 1972, *39*, 140–147.

Ewing, D. W. Discovering your problem-solving style. *Psychology Today*, December 1977, *7*, 69–75.

Eysenck, H. J. The effects of psychotherapy. In H. J. Eysenck (ed.), *Handbook of abnormal psychology*. New York: Basic Books, 1961.

Eysenck, H. J. *Sense and nonsense in psychology*. Baltimore: Penguin Books, 1957.

F

Farley, J. *Women going back to work: preliminary problems*. New York: State School of Industrial and Labor Relations, #358, 1970.

Fast, J. *Body language*. New York: Evans, 1970.

Fasteau, M. *The male machine*. New York: McGraw-Hill, 1974.

Federal Bureau of Investigation. *Uniform crime reports: Crime in the U.S.* Washington, D.C.: U.S. Government Printing Office, 1981.

Feigenbaum, E. M. Sexual behavior in the later years (1971). In R. A. Kalish (ed.), *The later years: Social applications of gerontology*. Monterey, Calif.: Brooks/Cole, 1977.

Feldman, F. Results of psychoanalysis in clinic case assignments. *Journal of the American Psychoanalytic Association*, 1968, *16*, 274–300.

Feldman, M. P. Aversion therapy for sexual deviations: A critical review. *Psychological Bulletin*, 1966, *63*, 65–79.

Felipe N., & Sommer, R. Invasions of personal space. *Social Problems*, 1966, *14*, 206–214.

Ferguson, M. *The brain revolution*. New York: Bantam Books, 1975.

Ferree, M. The confused American housewife. *Psychology Today*, 1976, *10*, 76–80.

Feshbach, S., & Weiner, B. *Personality*. Lexington, Mass.: D. C. Heath, 1982.

Festinger, L. Informal social communication. *Psychological Review*, 1950, *57*, 271–282.

Festinger, L.; Schachter, S.; & Back, K. *Social pressures in informal groups: A study of human factors in housing*. New York: Harper & Row, 1950.

Fine, R. *The development of Freud's thought*. New York: Jason Aronson, 1973.

Finkelberg, J. R.; Melges, F. T.; Hollister, L. E.; & Gillespie, H. K. Marijuana and immediate memory. *Nature*, 1970, *20*, 226–33.

Fisher, R. J. *Social psychology: An applied approach*. New York: St. Martin's Press, 1982.

Fiske, E. B. New techniques help pupils develop values. *New York Times*, April 30, 1976.

Fitch, S. K. *Insights into human behavior*. Boston: Holbrook. 1970.

Fling, S., & Manosevitz, M. Sex typing in nursery school: Children's play interests. *Developmental Psychology*, 1972, *7*, 146–152.

Forem, J. *Transcendental meditation: Maharish Mahesh Yogi and the science of creative intelligence*. New York: Bantam Books, 1973.

Foulkes, D. Dreams of innocence. *Psychology Today*, December 1978, *12*, 78–88.

Fournet, G. P.; Distefano, M. K., Jr.; & Pryer, M. G. Job satisfaction: Issues and problems. *Personnel Psychology*, 1966, *19*, 165–183.

Frank, J. D. *Persuasion and healing* (rev. ed.). Baltimore, Md.: The John Hopkins University Press, 1973.

Frank, J. D. The bewildering world of psychotherapy. *Journal of Social Issues*, 1972, *22*, 27–43.

Frank, J. The demoralized mind. *Psychology Today*, April 1973, *6*, 22.

Freedman, J. L. *Crowding and behavior*. San Francisco: Freeman, 1975.

Freedman, J. L.; Carlsmith, J. M.; & Sears, D. O. *Social psychology* (3rd ed.). Englewood Cliffs, N. J.: Prentice-Hall, 1978.

Freedman, J. L.; Carlsmith, J. M., & Sears, D. O. *Social psychology*. Englewood Cliffs, N. J.: Prentice-Hall, 1970.

Freize, I. H.; Parsons, J. E.; Johnson, P. B.; Roble, D. N.; & Zellman, G. L. *Women and sex roles: A social psychological perspective*. New York: Norton, 1978.

Freud, S. *On dreams*. J. Strachey (trans.). New York: Norton, 1953.

Freud, S. Analysis of a phobia in a five-year-old boy. In A. Strachey & J. Strachey (trans.), *Collected papers*, Vol. 3. New York: Basic Books, 1959.

Friedman, M., & Rosenman, R. H. *Type A behavior and your heart,* Greenwich, Conn.: Fawcett, 1975.

Friedman, M., & Rosenman, R. H. *Type A behavior and your heart* New York: Random House, 1974.

Fromm, E. *Escape from freedom,* New York: Avon, 1965, (originally published, 1941.)

Fromm, E. *The art of loving.* New York: Harper & Row, 1956.

Fromm, E. *The anatomy of human destructiveness,* New York: Holt, Rinehart & Winston, 1973.

Frueh, T., & McGhee, P. E. Sex role development and amount of time spent watching television. *Developmental Psychology,* 1975, *11,* 109.

G

Gadpaille, W. Is there a too soon? *Today's Health,* 1970, *48,* 34–54.

Gardner, H. *Developmental psychology.* Boston: Little, Brown, 1978.

Gardner, R. A. *Psychotherapy with children of divorce.* New York: Jason Aronson, 1976.

Garfield, S. L. Psychotherapy: A 40-year appraisal. *American Psychologist,* 1981, *36,* 174–83.

Garmezy, N. Vulnerable and invulnerable children: Theory, research and intervention, 1976, cited in K. Stassen-Berger, *The developing person,* New York: Worth Publishers, 1980.

Gazzaniga, M. *Psychology.* San Francisco: Harper & Row, 1980.

Gergen, K. J. Multiple identity: The healthy and happy human being wears many masks. *Psychology Today,* May 1972, 31–35, 64–66.

Gergen, K. J., & Gergen, M. M. *Social psychology.* New York: Harcourt, Brace, Jovanovich, 1981.

Gibbs, J. C. Kohlberg's stages of moral judgment: A constructive critique. Cambridge, Mass.: *Harvard Educational Review,* 1977, *47,* 43–61.

Giffin, K., & Patton, B. R. (eds.). *Basic readings in interpersonal communication.* New York: Harper & Row, 1971.

Ginott, H. G. *Between parent and child.* New York: Avon, 1965.

Ginsberg, L. J., & Greenley, J. R. Competing theories of marijuana use: A longitudinal study. *Journal of Humanistic and Social Behavior,* 1978, *19,* 22–36.

Ginzberg, E. *Career Guidance.* New York: McGraw-Hill, 1971.

Glick, P. C., & Spanier, G. Married and unmarried cohabitation in the United States. *Journal of Marriage and the Family,* February, 1980, *42,* 19–30.

Goertzel U., & Goertzel M. G. *Cradles of eminence.* Boston: Little, Brown, 1962.

Golanty, E., & Harris, B. B. *Marriage and family life.* Boston: Houghton Mifflin, 1982.

Goldberg, R., & Pearlman, C. Delirium tremens and dream deprivation, 1964, cited in H. A. Witkin & H. B Lewis *Experimental studies of dreaming.* New York: Random House, 1967.

Goldfarb, W. The effect of early institutional care on adult personality. *Journal of Experimental Education,* 1943, *12,* 106–129.

Goldman, A. *Elvis.* New York: McGraw-Hill, 1981.

Goleman, P. Meditation helps break the stress spiral. *Psychology Today,* February 1976, *9,* 82–86.

Goode, E. *Drugs in American society.* New York: Knopf, 1972.

Gottesman, I. I. Personality and natural selection. In S. G. Vandenberg (ed.), *Methods and goals in human behavioral genetics.* New York: Academic Press, 1965, 63–80.

Gottlieb, D. College youth and the meaning of work. *Vocational Guidance Quarterly,* December 1975, *24,* 116–125.

Gottschan, L. A. Psychoanalytic notes on T-groups at the human relations laboratory, Bethel, Maine. *Comprehensive Psychiatry,* 1966, *74,* 72–87.

Graham, D. *Moral learning and development.* New York: Wiley, 1972.

Grasha, A. F. *Practical applications of psychology.* Cambridge, Mass.: Winthrop, 1978.

Gray, F. with Graubard, P. S., & Rosenberg, H. Little brother is changing you. *Psychology Today,* March 1974, 41–46

Green, E; Green, A.; & Walters, E. Voluntary control of internal states: Psychological and physiological. *Journal of Transpersonal Psychology,* 1972, *2,* 1–26.

Greenberg, R., & Pearlman, L. REM sleep and the analytic process: A psychological bridge. *Psychological Quarterly,* 1975, *44,* 392–403.

Greenberg, S., & Peck, L., 1974, cited in D. E. Papalia & S. W. Olds, *A Child's World* (2nd ed.). New York: McGraw-Hill, 1979.

Greenwell, J. & Dengerink, H. A. The role of perceived versus actual attack in human physical aggression. *Journal of Personality and Social Psychology,* 1973, *26,* 66–71.

Gresham, F. M. Misguided mainstreaming: The case for social skills training with handicapped children. *Exceptional Children,* 1982, *48,* 422–33.

Gribbon, A. Prisoners of Fear. *The National Observer,* January 17, 1976.

Grovevant, H. D.; Scarr, S.; & Weinberg, R. A. Are career interests inheritable? *Psychology Today,* 1978, *11,* 88–90.

Gustavson, C. R.; Garcia, J.; Hawkins, W. G.; &

Rusiniak, K. W. Coyote predation control by aversive conditioning. *Science,* 1974, *184,* 581–583.

Guttentag, M., & Bray, H. *Undoing sex stereotypes: Research and resources for educators.* New York: McGraw-Hill, 1976.

H

Haan, H.; Smith, M. B.; & Block, J. Moral reasoning of young adults: Political-social behavior, family background and personality correlates. *Journal of Personality and Social Psychology,* 1968, *10,* 183–201.

Hall, C., & Van De Castle, R. *The content analysis of dreams.* New York: Appleton-Century-Crofts, 1966.

Hall, E. T. *The hidden dimension.* New York: Doubleday, 1966.

Hall, C. S., & Lindzey, G. *Theories of personality.* New York: Wiley, 1957.

Hamblin, R.; Buckholdt, D.; Bushell, D.; Ellis, D.; & Ferritoon, D. Changing the game from "get the teacher" to learn, 1969. In S. Hochman, P. Kaplan, & D. Hazan, (eds.). *Readings in psychology: A soft approach.* Dubuque, Iowa: Kendall-Hunt, 1974, 77–84.

Hamilton, E. M., & Whitney, E. *Nutrition: Concepts and controversies.* St. Paul: West Publishing Co., 1979.

Hand, H. H., & Slocum, J. W. A longitudinal study of the effects of a human relations training program on managerial effectiveness. *Journal of Applied Psychology,* 1972, *56,* 412–417.

Hanratty, M. A.; O'Neal, E.; & Sulzer, J. L. Effect of frustration upon imitation of aggression. *Journal of Personality and Social Psychology,* 1972, *21,* 30–34.

Harlow, H. *Learning to love.* New York: Ballantine Books, 1973.

Harlow, H. Love in infant monkeys. *Scientific American,* June 1959, 68–74.

Harlow, H. The Nature of Love. *American Psychologist,* 1958, *13,* 673–685.

Harris, B. Whatever happened to little Albert? *American Psychologist,* 1979, *34,* 151–60.

Harris, S. R. Sex typing in girls' career choices: A challenge to counselors. *The Vocational Guidance Quarterly.* December 1974, *2,* 128–134.

Harris, T. G. Why pros meditate. *Psychology Today,* October 1975, *9,* 4.

Hartley, D.; Roback, H. B.; & Abramowitz, C. I. Deterioration effects in encounter groups. *American Psychologist,* 1976, *31,* 247–255.

Hartley, D. D., & Strupp, H. N. The new psychotherapies: Caveat emptor. *New York University Education Quarterly,* 1978, *9, 17*–23.

Hartmann, E. L. *The functions of sleep.* New Haven, Conn.: Yale University Press, 1973.

Hartmann, E. L. The D. state: A review and discussion of states on the physiological state concomitant with

dreaming. *International Journal of Psychiatry,* 1966, *2,* 11–31.

Hartshorne, H., & May, M. A. *Studies in the nature of character* (Vol. 1, 1928 & Vol. 3, 1930). New York: Macmillan, 1928 & 1930.

Hauck, P. A. *Overcoming depression.* Philadelphia: The Westminster Press, 1973.

Havemann, E. Alternatives to analysis. *Playboy,* November 1969, *16,* 133–134.

Havighurst, R. J. *Developmental tasks and education* (3rd ed.) New York: David McKay, 1972.

Havighurst, R. J. *Developmental tasks and education.* New York: Longmans, 1953.

Havighurst, R. J. The world of work. In B. B. Wolman (ed.), *Handbook of developmental psychology.* Englewood Cliffs, N. J.: Prentice-Hall, 1982, 771–787.

Hawley, P. Perceptions of male models of feminity related to career choice. *Journal of Counseling Psychology,* 1972, *19,* 308–313.

Hearst, P., & Moscow, A. "Patty Hearst," an exerpt from *Every secret thing,* published in *People,* February 1, 1982, *17,* 44–67.

Heider, F. *The psychology of interpersonal relations.* New York: Wiley, 1958.

Heilman, A. W. *Principles and practices of teaching reading.* Columbus, Ohio: Charles E. Merrill, 1967.

Hendricks, J., & Hendricks, C. D. *Aging in mass society: Myths and realities.* Cambridge,: Winthrop Press, 1977.

Henryk-Butt, R., & Rees, W. L. Psychological aspects of migraines. *Journal of Psychosomatic Research.* March 1973, *17,* 142–153.

Heron, W. The pathology of boredom. *Scientific American,* 1957, *196,* 52–56.

Herzberg, F.; Masusner, B.; & Snyderman, G. *The motivation to work.* New York: Wiley, 1959.

Hetherington, E. M., & Parke, R. *Child psychology: A contemporary viewpoint* (2nd ed.). New York: McGraw-Hill, 1979.

Hetherington, E. M.; Cox, M.; & Cox, R. Beyond father absense: Conceptualization of effects of divorce. In E. C. Smart & M. S. Smart (eds.). *Readings in child development and relationships.* New York: Macmillan, 1977, 195–204.

Hill, O. T.; Rubin, Z.; & Peplau, L. A. Breakups before marriage: The end of 103 affairs. *Journal of Social Issues,* 1976, *32,* 147–168.

Hilgard, E. R. Hypnosis is no mirage. *Psychology Today,* November 1974, 120–128.

Hilsdale, P. Marriage as personal existential commitment. *Marriage and Family Life,* 1962, *24,* 137–143.

Hinsie, L. E., & Campbell, R. B. *Psychiatric Dictionary* (4th ed.). New York: Oxford University Press, 1970.

Hite, S. *The Hite report.* New York: Dell, 1976.

Hjelle, L. A., & Ziegler, D. J. *Personality Theories: Basic assumptions, research and applications.* New York: McGraw-Hill, 1976.

Hoffman, L. W., & Ney, F. I. *Working mothers.* San Francisco: Jossey-Bass, 1974.

Holland, J. *Making vocational choices.* Englewood Cliffs, N. J.: Prentice-Hall, 1973.

Hollander, E. P. Independence, conformity and civil liberties: Some implications for social psychological research. *Journal of Social Issues,* 1975, *31,* 55–67.

Hollander, E. P. *Social psychology* (3rd ed.). New York: Oxford University Press, 1976.

Hollister, L. E. Marijuana in man: Three years later. *Science,* 1971, *172,* 21–29.

Holmes, T. H., & Masuda, M. Psychosomatic syndrome. *Psychology Today,* April 1972, 71–72.

Holmes, T. H., & Rahe, R. H. The social readjustment rating scale. *Journal of Psychosomatic Research,* 1967, *11,* 213–218.

Homans, G. C. *Social behavior: Its elementary forms.* New York: Harcourt, Brace, 1961.

Homme, L. E. Control of coverants, the operants of the mind: Perspectives in psychology. *Psychological Reports,* 1965, *15,* 501–511.

Hooker, E. *Final report of the Task Force on Homosexuality.* Bethesda, Md.: National Institute of Mental health, 1969.

Hopkins, J. R. Sexual behavior in adolescence. *Journal of Social Issues,* 1977, *33,* 67–86.

Horner, M. S. Toward an understanding of achievement related to conflict in women. *Journal of Social Issues,* 1972, *28,* 157–176.

Horner, M. S. Fail: Bright women. *Psychology Today,* 1969, 36–38.

Horney, K. *Our inner conflicts.* New York: Norton, 1945.

Housely, W. F. Vocational decision making: A function of rejecting attitudes. *The Vocational Guidance Quarterly,* June 1973, *21,* 288–293.

Houts, P. S., & Serber, M. (eds.). *After the turn-on, what? Learning perspectives on humanistic groups.* Champaigne, Ill.: Research Press, 1972.

Hovland, C. I.; Janis, I. L.; & Kelley, H. H. *Communication and persuasion.* New Haven: Yale University Press, 1953.

Hovland, C. I., & Sears, R. R. Minor studies of aggression: Correlations of lynchings with economic indices. *Journal of Psychology,* 1940, *9,* 301–310

Howe, F. Sexual stereotypes start early. *Saturday Review,* October 16, 1971, *54,* 76–94.

Hughes, R., & Brewin, R. *The tranquilizing of America.* New York: Harcourt, Brace, Jovanovich, 1979.

Hunt, B., & Hunt, M. *Prime time: A guide to the pleasures and opportunities of the new middle age.* New York: Stein & Day, 1975.

Hunt, M. *Sexual behavior in the 1970's.* Chicago: Playboy Press, 1974.

Hunt, M. Special sex education survey. *Seventeen,* July 1970, 94–97.

Hunt, M. *The world of the formerly married.* New York: McGraw-Hill, 1966.

Hunt, M., & Hunt, B. *The divorce experience.* New York: McGraw-Hill, 1977.

Hurlock, E. *Child development* (6th ed.). New York: McGraw-Hill, 1978.

J

Jaffe, J. H. Drug addiction and drug abuse. In L. S. Goodman & A. Gilman (eds.), *The pharmacological basis of therapeutics.* New York: Macmillan, 1965.

Janis, I. L. *Victims of groupthink.* Boston: Houghton Mifflin, 1972.

Janis, I. L.; Mahl, G. F.; Kagan J.; & Holt, R. R. *Personality: Dynamics, development and assessment.* New York: Harcourt, Brace & World, 1969.

Janis, I. L., & Wheeler, D. Thinking clearly about career choices. *Psychology Today,* May 1978, *11,* 66–78.

Jarvik, L. F.; Klodin, V.; & Matsuyama, S. S. Human aggression and the extra Y chromosome: Fact or fantasy? *American Psychologist,* 1973, *28,* 674–682.

Jaynes, J. *The origins of consciousness in the breakdown of the bicameral mind.* Boston: Houghton Mifflin, 1976.

Jersild, A. T.; Brook, J. S.; & Brook, D. W. *The psychology of adolescence* (2nd ed.). New York: Macmillan, 1978.

Johnston, L. D.; Bachman, J. G.; & O'Malley, P. M. *Drug use among American high school students 1975–1977.* Rockville, Md.: National Institute on Drug Abuse. DHEW Pub #78619, 1977.

Jonas, G. Visceral learning, 1972. In I. S. Cohen (ed.), *Perspectives on psychology.* New York: Praeger, 1975, 112–131.

Jones, B. M., & Parsons, O. A. Alcohol and consciousness: Getting high, coming down. *Psychology Today,* 1975, *8,* 53–61.

Jones, M. C. The later careers of boys who are early- and late maturers. *Child Development,* 1957, *28,* 113–128.

Jones, R. Human effects. In R. C. Petersen (ed.), *Marijuana research findings: 1976.* Rockville, Md.: National Institute on Drug Abuse, 1977.

Jourard, S. M. *Healthy personality.* New York: Macmillan, 1974.

Jourard, S. M. The healthy personality and self disclosure, 1959. In S. Hochman & P. S. Kaplan (eds.), *Readings in psychology: A soft approach* (rev. ed.). Lexington, Mass.: Ginn, 1979, 34–40.

Jourard, S. M., & Landsman, T. *Healthy personality* (4th ed.). New York: Macmillan, 1980.

K

Kagan, J. The concept of identification. *Psychological Review*, 1958, *65*, 296–305.

Kahn, R. L., & Quinn, R. P. *Role stress: A framework for analysis*. Ann Arbor, Mich.: University of Michigan Press, 1969.

Kahn, R. L.; Wolfe, D. M.; Quinn, A. P.; Snoek, J. D.; Diedrich, J.; & Rosenthal, R. A. *Organizational stress*. New York: Wiley, 1964.

Kales, A., & Kales, J. Recent advances in the diagnosis and treatment of sleep disorders. In G. Usdin (ed.), *Sleep research and clinical practice*. New York: Brunner Mazel, 1973.

Kallman, F. J. Comparative twin study in the genetic aspects of male homosexuality. *Journal of Nervous and Mental Disorders*, 1952, *115*, 283–298.

Kandel, D. B. Inter and intra generational influences on adolescent marijuana use. *Journal of Social Issues*, 1974, *30*, 107–135.

Kaniuga, N.; Scott, T.; & Gade, E. Working women portrayed on evening television programs. *Vocational Guidance Quarterly*, December 1974, *23*, 134–138.

Kaplan, H. S. *The new sex therapy*. New York: Brunner Mazel, 1974.

Kaplan, P. S. It's the group I.Q. tests that flunk. *New York Times*, March 13, 1977, 26.

Kaplan, P. S. *The effects of information giving on the semantic meaning of the concept counselor*. Unpublished doctoral dissertation, New York University, 1972.

Karen, R. L. *An introduction to behavior theory and its applications*. New York: Harper & Row, 1974.

Karlen, A. The unmarried couples on campus. *New York Times Magazine*, January 26, 1969, *29*, 77–80.

Kastenbaum, R. *Humans developing: A lifespan perspective*. Boston: Allyn & Bacon, 1979.

Katchadourian, H. *Human sexuality: Sense and nonsense*. San Francisco: Freeman, 1974.

Kavale, K. The efficacy of stimulant drug treatment for hyperactivity: A meta-analysis. *Journal of Learning Disabilities*, 1982, 15, 280–289.

Kaye, E. *The crisis in middle management*, New York: AMA Com., 1974.

Keezer, W. S. *Mental health and human behavior* (3rd ed.). Dubuque, Iowa: Wm. C. Brown, 1971.

Kell, B. L., & Burow, J. M. *Developmental counseling and therapy*. Boston: Houghton Mifflin, 1970.

Kellogg, R. *Analyzing children's art*. Palo Alto, Calif.: Mayfield, 1970.

Kelly, J. B. Divorce: The adult perspective. In B. B. Wolman (ed.), *Handbook of developmental psychology*. Englewood Cliffs, N. J.: Prentice-Hall, 1982, 734–750.

Kennedy, C. E. *Human development: The adult years and aging*. New York.: Macmillan, 1978.

Kennedy, J. F. *Profiles in courage*. New York: Harper & Row, 1956.

Kephart, W. M. Some correlates of romantic love. *Journal of Marriage and the Family*, August 1967, 470–474.

Kephart, W. M. Cited in W. M. Kephart, *The family, society, and the individual* (3rd ed.). Boston: Houghton Mifflin, 1972.

Kerkhoff, A. C., & Davis, R. E. Value consensus and need complimentarity in mate selection. *American Sociological Review*, 1962, *27*, 295–303.

Kimmel, D. C. *Adulthood and aging*. New York: Wiley, 1974.

Kinsey, A. C.; Pomeroy, W. B.; & Martin C. E. *Sexual behavior in the human male*. Philadelphia: Saunders, 1948.

Kinsey, A. C.; Pomeroy, W. B.; & Gebhard, P. H. *Sexual behavior in the human female*. Philadelphia: Saunders, 1953.

Kinzel, A. F. Body buffer zones in violent prisoners. *New Society*, January 28, 1971, 149–158.

Klemer, R. H. *Marriage and family relations*. New York: Harper & Row, 1970.

Knight, J. A. *Conscience and guilt*. New York: Appleton-Century-Crofts, 1969.

Knittle, J. L. Obesity in childhood: A problem of adipose tissue cellular development. *Journal of pediatrics*, 1972, *81*, 1048–1059.

Kohlberg, L. The cognitive developmental approach to moral education. *Phi Delta Kappan*, 1975, *56*, 670–677.

Kohlberg, L. Continuities in childhood and adult moral development revisited. In B. Baltes and K. W. Schaie (eds.), *Life span developmental psychology*. New York: Academic Press, 1973.

Kohlberg, L. Stage and sequence: The cognitive developmental approach to socialization. In D. A. Goslin (ed.), *Handbook of socialization theory and research*. Chicago: Rand McNally, 1969.

Kohlberg, L. Development of moral character and moral ideology. In M. L. Hoffman and L. W. Hoffman (eds.), *Child development research* (Vol. 1). New York: Russell Sage Foundation, 1964.

Knight, J. A. *Conscience and guilt*. New York: Appleton-Century-Crofts, 1969.

Krech, D.; Crutchfield, R. S.; & Baliachey, E. L. *Individual in society: A textbook of social psychology*. New York: McGraw-Hill, 1962.

Krippner, S., & Hughes, W. Dreams and human potential. *Journal of Humanistic Psychology*, 1970, *10*, 1–20.

Kuhn, M. H., & McPartland, T. S. An empirical investigation of self attitudes. *American Sociological Review*, 1954, *19*, 68–76.

Kutines, W., & Grief E. B. The development of moral thought: Review and evaluation of Kohlberg's approach. *Psychological Bulletin*, 1974, *81*, 453–470.

L

Lakin, M. *Interpersonal encounter: Theory and practice in sensitivity groups.* New York: McGraw-Hill, 1972.

Lamanna, M. A., & Riedmann, A. *Marriages and families: Making choices throughout the life cycle.* Belmont, Calif.: Wadsworth, 1981.

Landis, J. T. *Making the most of marriage* (4th ed.). New York: Appleton-Century-Crofts, 1970.

Landis, J. T. A comparison of children from divorced and non-divorced unhappy marriages. *Family Life Coordinator,* 1962, *21,* 61–65.

Landis, J. T., & Landis, M. G. *Building a successful marriage* (6th ed.). Englewood Cliffs, N. J.: Prentice-Hall, 1973.

La Piere, R. T. Attitudes and actions. *Social Forces,* 1934, *13,* 230–237.

Laughlin, H. P. *The ego and its defenses.* New York: Appleton-Century-Crofts, 1970.

Law, C. E. A darkness at noon. *Science Forum,* July/August 1978, 32–38.

Lazarus, R. S. A cognitively oriented psychologist looks at biofeedback. *American Psychologist,* May 1975, *30,* 533–562.

Lazarus, R. S. *Psychological stress and the coping process.* New York: McGraw-Hill, 1966.

Lazarus, R. S., & Goleman, D. Positive denial: The case for not facing reality. *Psychology Today,* November 1979, *13,* 44–60.

Leavitt, F. *Drugs and behavior.* Philadelphia: Saunders, 1974.

LeFrancois, G. R. *Psychology.* Belmont, Calif.: Wadsworth, 1980.

Lee, J. A. The styles of loving. *Psychology Today,* October 1974a, 44–51.

Lee, J. A. *Colours of love.* Toronto: New Press, 1974b.

Lee, I. J. *How to talk with people: A program for preventing trouble that comes when people talk together.* New York: Harper & Row, 1952.

Leff, H. L. *Experience, environment and human potentials.* New York: Oxford University Press, 1978.

Lentini, J. R. *Vice and narcotics control.* Beverly Hills, Calif.: Glencoe Press, 1977.

Lerner, R. M., & Spanier, G. B. *Adolescent development.* New York: McGraw-Hill, 1980.

Lesse, S. The multivariant masks of depression. *Depression,* Supplement to the *American Journal of Psychiatry,* May 1968, *124,* 35–40.

Levinger, G. Sources of marital dissatisfaction among applicants for divorce. *American Journal of Orthopsychiatry,* 1966, *36,* 803–807.

Levinson, D. J. *The seasons of a man's life.* New York: Knopf, 1978.

Lewin, K. *Field theory in social science.* New York: Harper & Row, 1951.

Lewinsohn, P. M. A behavioral approach to depression. In R. J. Friedman & M. M. Katz (eds.), *The psychology of depression: Contemporary theory and research.* Washington, D.C.: Winston-Wiley, 1974.

Lewinsohn, P. M., & Amenson, C. S. Pleasant and unpleasant mood-related events and depression. *Journal of Abnormal Psychology,* 1978, *87,* 644–54.

Lewinsohn, P. M., & Graf, M. Pleasant activities and depression. *Journal of Consulting and Clinical Psychology,* 1973, *41,* 261–68.

Lewinsohn, P. M., & Libet, J. Pleasant events, activity schedules, and depression. *Journal of Abnormal Psychology,* 1972, *79,* 294.

Lewis, A. The ambiguous word "anxiety". In *International Journal of Psychiatry* (Vol. 9). New York: Science House, 1970, 62–79.

Lewis, H. R., & Lewis, M. E. *Psychosomatics.* New York: Viking, 1972.

Lewis, H. R., & Streitfield, H. S. *Growth games.* New York: Bantam, 1972.

Libby, R. Parental attitudes towards high school sex education programs. *The Family Coordinator,* 1970, *19,* 234–247.

Lichtenstein, G. Homosexuals are moving towards open ways of life as tolerance rises among the general population. *New York Times,* July 17, 1977, 34.

Lidz, T. *The person: His and her development throughout the life cycle* (rev. ed.). New York: Basic Books, 1976.

Lieberman, M. A.; Yalom, I. D.; & Miles, M. Encounter: The leader makes the difference. *Psychology Today,* March 1973, *6,* 69–78.

Liebert, R. M.; Neale, J. M.; & Davidson. E. S. *The early window: Effects of television on children and youth.* New York: Pergamon Press, 1973.

Lindzey, G.; Hall, C.; & Thompson, R. F. *Psychology.* New York: Worth, 1975.

Linn, L. Physical characteristics and attitudes towards legitimate use of psychotherapeutic drugs. *Journal of Health and Social Behavior,* 1971, *12,* 132–140.

Lorenz, K. *On aggression.* New York: Harcourt, Brace & World, 1966.

Lowenthal, M., & Weiss, L. Intimacy and crisis in adulthood. *The Counseling Psychologist,* 1976, *6,* 10–15.

Luborsky, L., & Spence, D. P. Quantitative research on psychoanalytic therapy. In A. E. Bergin & S. L. Garfield (eds.), *Handbook of psychotherapy and behavior change: An empirical analysis.* New York: Wiley, 1971.

Luce, G., & Peper, E. Mind over body, mind over mind. In S. Hochman & P. S. Kaplan (eds.), *Readings in psychology: A soft approach* (rev. ed). Lexington, Mass.: Ginn, 1979.

Lundin, R. W. *Theories and systems of psychology* (2nd ed.). Lexington, Mass.: D. H. Heath, 1979.

Lundin, R. W. *Personality: A behavioral analysis* (2nd ed.). New York: Macmillan, 1974.

M

McClearn, G. E. Genetic influences on behavior and development. In P. Mussen (ed.), *Carmichael's manual of child psychology*. New York: Wiley, 1970.

McClelland, D. C.; Atkinson, J. W.; Clark, R. A.; & Lowell, E. L. *The achievement motive*. New York: Appleton-Century-Crofts, 1953.

McClelland, D. C.; Davis, W. N.; Kalen, R.; & Warner, E. *The drinking man*. New York: The Free Press, 1972.

Maccoby, E. E., & Jacklin, C. N. *The psychology of sex differences*. Stanford, Calif.: Stanford University Press, 1974.

Maccoby, E. E. & Jacklin, C. N. Myth, reality, and shades of gray: What we know and don't know about sex differences. *Psychology Today*, December 1974, *8*, 109–116.

Maccoby, E. E. & Jacklin, C. N. Stress, activity and proximity seeking in the one-year-old child. *Child Development*, 1973, *44*, 34–42.

MacDonald, C. The stunted world of teen parents, *Human Behavior*, 1979, *8*, 52–55.

McGuinness, D. How schools discriminate against boys. In S. Hochman & P. S. Kaplan (eds.), *Readings in psychology: A soft approach* (rev. ed.). Lexington, Mass.: Ginn, 1979, 74–79.

McKee, M., & Robertson, I. *Social problems*. New York: Random House, 1975.

McKinney, F. cited in Evans, I. M. & Murdoff, R. *Psychology for a changing world* (2nd ed.). New York: Wiley, 1978.

Macklin, E. D. Nonmarital heterosexual cohabitation. *Marriage and Family Review*. 1978, *1*, 1–12.

McWhirter, N. *Guinness book of world records*. New York: Sterling Publishing Co., 1981.

Madow, L. *Anger—How to recognize and cope with it*. New York: Scribner's, 1972.

Mahoney, M. J. Reflections on the cognitive learning trend in psychotherapy. *American Psychologist*, 1977a, *32*, 5–12.

Mahoney, M. J. A critical analysis of rational-emotive theory and therapy. *The Counseling Psychologist*, 1977b, *7*, 44–46.

Maier, N.R.F. *Psychology in industrial organizations* (4th ed.). Boston: Houghton Mifflin, 1978.

Maier, N.R.F., Verser, G. C. *Psychology in industrial organizations* (5th ed.). Boston: Houghton Mifflin, 1982.

Main, A. P. & Roark, A. E. A consensus method to reduce conflict. *Personnel and Guidance Journal*, 1975, *53*, 754–759.

Malinowski, B. *The sexual life of savages in northwestern Melanesia* (2 vols.). New York: Harcourt, Brace & World, 1929.

Mandell, C. J., & Fiscus, E. *Understanding exceptional people*. St. Paul, Minn.: West, 1981.

Margolis, B. L., & Kroes, W. H. Work and the health of man. In V. J. Darlega & L. H. Janda (eds.), *Personal adjustment: Selected readings*. Glenview, Ill.: Scott, Foresman & Co., 1979.

Marijuana and Health—Fourth annual report to Congress from the Secretary of HEW. Washington, D.C.: U.S. Government Printing Office, 1974.

Martin, B. *Abnormal psychology: Clinical and scientific perspectives*. New York: Harper & Row, 1977.

Marx, M. H. & Bunch, M. E. *Fundamentals and applications of learning*. New York: Macmillan, 1977.

Maslow, A. H. *Motivation and personality*. New York: Harper & Row, 1970.

Maslow, A. H. *Toward a psychology of being* (2nd ed.). New York: Van Nostrand, 1968.

Maslow, A. H. Health as transcendence of environment. *Journal of Humanistic Psychology*, Spring 1961.

Masters, W. H., & Johnson, V. E. *Human sexual inadequacy*. Boston: Little, Brown, 1970.

Masters, W. H., & Johnson, V. E. *Human sexual response*. Boston: Little, Brown, 1966.

Matson, F. W. Humanistic theory: The third revolution in psychology. *The Humanist*, March/April, 1971, *31*, 7–11.

Maugh, T. H. Marijuana: Does it damage the brain? *Science*, 1974a, *185*, 775–776.

Maugh, T. H. Marijuana: The grass may no longer be greener. *Science*, 1974b, *185*, 683–685.

Mead, G. H. *Mind, self and society*. Chicago: University of Chicago Press, 1934.

Mead, M. *Coming of age in Samoa*. New York: William Morrow, 1928.

Mears, F., & Gatchel, R. J. *Fundamentals of abnormal psychology*. Chicago: Rand McNally, 1979.

Medinnus, G. R., & Curtis, F. J. The relation between maternal self-acceptance and child acceptance. *Journal of Counseling Psychology* 1963, *27*, 524–544.

Meichenbaum, D. H., & Goodman, J. Training impulsive children to talk to themselves: A means of developing self-control. *Journal of Abnormal Psychology*, 1971, *77*, 115–126.

Menning, A. J., & Whittmayer, C. M. Administrative and program provision for undecided students. *Vocational Guidance Quarterly*, 1979, *28*, 175–81.

Middlebrook, P. N. *Social psychology and modern life* (2nd ed.). New York: Knopf, 1980.

Miles, M. Changes during and following laboratory training: A clinical experimental study. *Journal of Applied Behavioral Science*, 1965, *1*, 215–242.

Mileski, M., & Black, D. J. The social organization of homosexuals. *Urban Life and Culture*, 1972, *1*, 187–199.

Milgram, S. *Obedience to authority*. New York: Harper & Row, 1974.

Milgram, S. Some conditions of obedience and disobedience to authority (1968). In R. Flacks (ed.), *Conformity, resistance and self-determination: The individual and authority.* Boston: Little, Brown, 1973, 225–39.

Milgram, S. Some conditions of obedience and disobedience to authority. *Human Relations,* 1965, *18,* 57–76.

Miller, D. C. *Industry and the worker.* In H. Borow (ed.), *Man in a world at work.* Boston: Houghton Mifflin, 1964.

Miller, W., & Seligman, M.E.P. Depression and the perception of reinforcement. *Journal of Abnormal Psychology,* 1973, *82,* 62–73.

Millman, M. *Such a pretty face: Being fat in America.* New York: Norton, 1980.

Minton, H. L., & Schneider, F. W. *Differential psychology.* Monterey, Calif.: Brooks/Cole, 1980.

Mischel, W. *Introduction to personality* (2nd ed.). New York: Holt, Rinehart & Winston, 1976.

Mischel, W. Continuity and change in personality. *American Psychologist,* 1969, *27,* 1012–1018.

Mischel, W. *Personality and assessment.* New York: Wiley, 1968.

Money Magazine. Special report: The right stuff for careers in the eighties. *Money Magazine,* May 1980, 68–72.

Moody, K. *Growing up on television: The TV effect.* New York: Times Books, 1980.

Moore, R. S., & Moore D. N. How early should they go to school? In B. B. Glanville & A. Gilpin (eds.), *Readings in human development.* Guilford, Conn.: Dushkin Press, 1978.

Morganstern, K. P. Cigarette smoke as a noxious stimulus in self-managed aversion therapy for compulsive eaters. *Behavior Therapy,* 1974, *5,* 255–260.

Morris, C. G. *Psychology: An introduction* (4th ed.). Englewood Cliffs, N. J.: Prentice-Hall, 1982.

Morris, D. Non-verbal leakage: How you can tell if someone's lying. *New York Magazine,* October 17, 1977, 43–46.

Morse, D. R., & Furst, M. L. *Stress for success: A holistic approach to stress and its management.* New York: Van Nostrand Reinhold, 1979.

Mowrer, O. H. *Learning theory and symbolic processes.* New York: Wiley, 1960.

Mowrer, O. H. *Learning theory and personality dynamics.* New York: The Ronald Press, 1950.

Mullahy, P. *Psychoanalysis and interpersonal psychiatry: The contributions of Harry Stack Sullivan.* New York: Science House, 1970.

Mullahy, P. *Oedipus: Myth and complex.* New York: Grove Press, 1948.

Murray, H. A. *Explorations in personality: A clinical and experimental study of fifty men of college age.* New York: Oxford Press, 1938.

Murstein, B. I. *Theories of attraction and love.* New York: Springer, 1971.

Mussen, P. H.; Conger, J. J.; & Kagan, J. *Child development and personality* (5th ed.). New York: Harper & Row, 1979.

Mussen, P. H., & Jones, M. C. Self-conceptions, motivations and interpersonal attitudes of late and early maturing boys. *Child Development,* 1957, *28,* 243–256.

Mussen, P., & Rosenzweig, M. R. *Psychology: An introduction.* Lexington, Mass.: D. H. Heath, 1973.

N

National Commission on Marijuana and Drug Abuse. *Drug use in America: Problems in perspective.* Washington, D.C.: U.S. Government Printing Office, 1973.

National Educational Television. *The Mind of Man.* 1970.

National Institute of Mental Health. *Plain talk about stress.* Rockville, Md.: Department of Health, Education and Welfare, 1977 and 1980, Pub No. 80–502.

National Institute on Alcohol Abuse and Alcoholism. *Alcohol: Some questions and answers.* Rockville, Md.: U.S. Government Printing Office, DHEW 72–9153, 1972.

Natsoulas, T. Consciousness. *American Psychologist,* 1978, *33,* 906–915.

Nelson, S. H., & Torrey, E. F. The religious function of psychiatry. *American Journal of Orthopsychiatry,* 1973, *43,* 362–368.

Neugarten, B. L. (ed.). *Personality in middle and late life.* New York: Atherton, 1964.

Neugarten, B. L.; Moore, J. W.; & Lowe, J. C. Age norms, age constraints and adult socialization. *American Journal of Sociology,* 1965, *70,* 710–717.

Neugarten, B. L.; Wood, V.; Kraines, R. J.; & Loomis, B. Women's attitudes toward the menopause. *Human Development,* 1963, *6,* 140–151.

Newcomb, T. M.; Koenig, K. E.; Flacks, R.; & Wardwick, D. P. *Persistence and change: Bennington College and its students after 25 years.* New York: Wiley, 1967.

Newcomb, T. M. *Personality and social change.* New York: Holt, Rinehart & Winston, 1943.

Newman, B. M., & Newman, P. R. *Infancy and childhood: Development and its contexts.* New York: Wiley, 1978.

Nielsen Television Index Audience Estimates, *National audience demographic report.* November, 1980.

Nierenberg, G., & Calero, H. *How to read a person like a book.* New York: Hawthorn Books, 1971.

Nisbett, R. E. Hunger, obesity and the ventromedial hypothalamus. *Psychological Review,* 1972, *79,* 433–453.

Nixon, R. E. *The art of growing.* New York: Random House, 1962.

Nordby, V. J., & Hall, C. S. *A guide to psychologists and their concepts.* San Francisco: Freeman, 1974.

Nye, R. D. *Three views of man.* Monterey, Calif.: Brooks/Cole, 1975.

O

Orlofsky, J. L.; Marcia, J. E.; & Lesser, I. M. Ego identity status and the intimacy versus isolation crisis of young adulthood. *Journal of Personality and Social Psychology,* 1973, *27,* 211–219.

Ornstein, R. E. *The psychology of consciousness.* San Francisco: W. H. Freeman, 1972.

Osipow, S. H. *Theories of career development.* Englewood Cliffs, N. J.: Prentice-Hall, 1968.

Osofsky, H. J. Teenage out of wedlock pregnancy: Some preventive considerations. *Adolescence,* 1970, *5,* 151–170.

Otis, L. S. The facts on transcendental meditation: If well-integrated but anxious try T.M. *Psychology Today,* April 1974, *7,* 45–46.

P

Page, J. D. *Psychopathology: The science of understanding deviance* (2nd ed.). Chicago: Aldine, 1975.

Papalia, D. F., & Olds S. W. *A child's world* (3rd ed.). New York: McGraw-Hill, 1982.

Papanek, H. Alfred Adler. In A. M. Freedman & H. I. Kaplan (eds.), *Personality: A survey of 20th century views.* New York: Athenium, 1971, 117–131.

Packard, V. *The sexual wilderness: The contemporary upheaval in male-female relationships.* New York: Pocket Books, 1970.

Parloff, M. B. Shopping for the right therapy. *Saturday Evening Post,* February 21, 1976, 1–20.

Parsons, T., & Bales, R. F. *Family socialization and interaction process,* Glencoe, Ill.: The Free Press, 1955.

Patterson, C. R., & Cobb, A. A. A dyadic analysis of "aggressive" behavior. In J. P. Hill (ed.), *Minnesota Symposium on Child Psychology* (Vol. 5). Minneapolis: University of Minnesota Press, 1971.

Pattison, E. M.; Sobell, M. B.; & Sobell, D. C. Emerging Concepts of Alcohol Dependence. New York: Springer, 1977.

Paul, G. L. Insight versus desensitization in psychology two years after termination. *Journal of Consulting Psychology,* 1967, *37,* 333–348.

Pedersen, F. A., & Robson, K. S. Father participation in infancy. *American Journal of Orthopsychiatry,* 1969, *39,* 466–472.

Pei, M. *The America we lost.* New York: Signet, 1969.

Pelletier, K. R. Mind as healer, mind as slayer. *Psychology Today,* 1977, *10,* 35+.

Perlman, H. H. *Persona: Social role and personality.* Chicago: University of Chicago Press, 1968.

Pearlman, C. Cited in Smith, R. E.; Sarason, I. G.; &

Sarason, B. R. *Psychology: The frontiers of behavior.* New York: Harper & Row, 1978.

Perls, F. *Gestalt therapy verbatim.* Lafayette, Calif.: Real People Press, 1969.

Peter, L. J. *The Peter plan.* New York: Morrow, 1975.

Peter, L. J. *The Peter prescription.* New York: Morrow, 1972.

Petersen, R. C. Summary, marijuana research findings: 1976. In R. C. Petersen (ed.), *Marijuana research findings: 1976,* Rockville, Md: National Institute on Drug Abuse, 1977.

Petersen, R. C., & Stillman, R. C. *Cocaine 1977.* Washington, D.C.: U.S. Government Printing Office. NIDA Monograph No. 13, 1977.

Pettigrew, T. F. Racially separate or together. *Journal of Social Issues,* 1969, *25,* 43–69.

Phillips, J. L. *The origins of intellect: Piaget's theory.* San Francisco: Freeman, 1975.

Piaget, J. On the development of memory and identity (Vol. 2). In *1967 Heinz Werner Lecture Series.* Worcester, Mass.: Clark University Press, 1968.

Pierloot, R. A. Psychogenesis of somatic disorders. An overview. *Psychotherapy and Psychosomatics,* 1979, *32,* (1–4), 27–40.

Pikunas, J. *Human development: An emergent science* (3rd ed.). New York: McGraw Hill, 1976.

Pines, M. Superkids. *Psychology Today,* January 1979, *12,* 53–61.

Pines, M. In praise of invulnerables. *APA Monitor,* December 1975.

Pines, M. Head, Head Start. *New York Times Magazine,* October 26, 1975, 14.

Pines, M. *The brain changers: Scientists and the new mind control.* New York: Harcourt, Brace, Jovanovich, 1973.

Porter, L. W., & Steers, R. M. Organizational, work and personal factors in employee turnover and absenteeism. *Psychological Bulletin,* 1973, *80,* 151–176.

Poulton, E. C. Skilled performance and stress. In P. Warr (ed.), *Psychology at work.* Baltimore, Md.: Penguin, 1971, 55–75.

Pressey, S. L., & Kublen, R. G. *Psychological development through the life span.* New York: Harper & Row, 1957.

Q

Qualls, P. J. and Sheehan, P. W. Electromyograph biofeedback as a relaxation technique: A critical appraisal and reassessment. *Psychological Bulletin,* 1981, *90,* 21–42.

Quayle, D. American productivity: The devastating effect of alcoholism and drug abuse. *American Psychologist,* 1983, *38,* 454–458.

Quinn, R. P.; Staines, G.; & McCullough, M. Job satisfaction in the 1970's: Recent history and a look to the future. *Manpower Monographs,* 1973.

R

Rabban, M. Sex role identity in young children in two diverse social groups. *Genetic Psychology Monographs,* 1950, *42,* 81–158.

Rachlin, H. *Introduction to modern behaviorism* (2nd ed.). San Francisco: Freeman, 1976.

Rahula, W. *What the Buddha taught.* New York: Grove, 1959.

Raths, L. E.; Harmin, M.; & Simon, S. B. *Values and Teaching.* Columbus, Ohio: Merrill, 1966.

Reiss, I. L. *The family system in America.* New York: Harper & Row, 1971.

Renwick, P. A., & Lawler, E. E. What do you really want from a job? *Psychology Today,* May 1978, *11,* 53–65.

Rheingold, H. L., & Cook, K. V. The contents of boys' and girls' rooms as an index of parents' behavior. *Child Development* 1975, *46,* 459–463.

Richardson, S. Ecology of malnutrition: Non-nutritional factors influence intellectual and behavioral development, 1972, cited in H. L. Bee & S. K. Mitchell, *The developing person.* San Francisco: Harper & Row, 1980.

Riesman, D. *The lonely crowd.* New Haven: Yale University Press, 1950.

Rimm, D. C., & Masters, J. C. *Behavior therapy: Techniques and empirical findings.* New York; Academic Press, 1974.

Ringness, T. A. *The affective domain in education.* Boston: Little, Brown, 1975.

Roark, A. E. Interpersonal conflict management. *Personnel and Guidance Journal,* March 1978, *56,* 400–406.

Robbins, T. *Even cowgirls get the blues.* New York: Bantam, 1976.

Robertson, I. *Sociology.* New York: Worth Publishers, 1981.

Rodin, J. Current status of the internal-external hypothesis for obesity: What went wrong? *American Psychologist,* 1981, *36,* 361–372.

Roe, A. *The psychology of occupations.* New York: Wiley, 1957.

Roffwarg, H. P.; Muzio, J. N.; & Dement, W. C. Ontogenic development of the human sleep-dream cycle. *Science,* 1966, *152,* 604–619.

Rogers, C. R. *A way of being.* Boston: Houghton Mifflin, 1980.

Rogers, C. R. *Becoming partners: Marriage and its alternatives.* New York: Delacorte, 1971.

Rogers, C. R. The conditions of change from a client-centered viewpoint. In B. Berenson and R. Carkhuff (eds.), *Sources of gain in counseling and psychotherapy.* New York: Holt, Rinehart & Winston, 1967.

Rogers, C. R. A theory of personality, 1959, in T. Mellon (ed.), *Theories of psychopathology and personality* (2nd ed.). Philadelphia: Saunders, 1973, 217–223.

Rogers, C. R. *Client-centered therapy.* Boston: Houghton Mifflin, 1951.

Rogers, C. R., & Dymond, R. *Psychotherapy and personality change.* Chicago: University of Chicago Press, 1954.

Rokeach, M. *The nature of human values.* New York: The Free Press, 1973.

Rokeach, M. A theory of organization and change within value-attitudinal systems. *Journal of Social Issues,* 1968, *24,* 14–16.

Rokeach, M. *The open and closed mind.* New York: Basic Books, 1960.

Rollins, B. C., & Feldman, H. Marital satisfaction over the family life span. *Journal of Marriage and the Family,* 1970, *32,* 20–28.

Rosen, G. M. The development and use of non-prescription behavior therapies. *American Psychologist,* 1976, *31,* 139–142.

Rosen, R. D. Psychobabble. *New Times,* October 31, 1975, *5,* 44–49.

Rosenfeld, A. (ed.). *Mind and supermind.* New York: Holt, Rinehart, & Winston, 1977.

Rosenman, R. H.; Friedman, M.; Strauss, R.; Wurm, M.; Kositchok, R.; Hahn, W.; & Werthessen, N. T. A predictive study of coronary heart disease: The western collaborative group study. *Journal of the American Medical Association,* 1964, *189,* 15–22.

Rosenthal, D. *Genetic theory and abnormal behavior.* New York: McGraw-Hill, 1970.

Rosenthal, R.; Darcher, M. R.; Matteo, D. I.; Hall, J.; Koivumaki, L.; & Rogers, D. L. Body talk and tone of voice: To laugh without words. *Psychology Today,* September 1974, *8,* 64–72.

Rosenthal, R., & Jacobson, L. *Pygmalion in the classroom: Teacher expectation and pupils' intellectual development.* New York: Holt, Rinehart & Winston, 1968.

Ross, H. L., & Sawhill, I. V. *Time of transition: The growth of families headed by women.* Washington, D.C.: The Urban Institute, 1975.

Ross, W. D.; Kligfeld, M.; & Whitman, R. W. Psychiatry, participants and sensitivity groups. *Archives of General Psychiatry,* 1971, *25,* 178–180.

Rossi. A. S. Women in science: Why so few? *Science,* 1965, *148,* 1196–1202.

Rothbard, M. K., & Maccoby, E. E. Parents' differential reactions to sons and daughters. *Journal of Personality and Social Psychology,* 1966, *4,* 237–243.

Rowe, C. J. *An outline of psychiatry* (6th ed.). Dubuque, Iowa: W. C. Brown, 1975.

Ruben, B. D., & Budd, R. W. *Human communication handbook.* Rochelle Park, New York: Hayden Book Co., 1975.

Rubin, I. M. Increased self-acceptance: A means of reducing prejudice. *Journal of Personality and Social Psychology*, 1967, *5*, 233–238.

Rubin, J.; Provenzano, F.; & Luria, Z. The eye of the beholder: Parents' views on sex of newborns. *American Journal of Orthopsychiatry*, 1974, *44*, 512–519.

Rubin, Z. *Liking and loving*. New York: Holt, Rinehart & Winston, 1973.

Rubin, Z. Measurement of romantic love. *Journal of Personality and Social Psychology*, 1970, *62*, 65–73.

Rubinstein, E. A. Television and the young viewer. In B. B. Glanville & A. Gilpin (eds.), *Human development*. Guilford, Conn.: Dushkin, 1979, 187–196.

Ruesch, J., & Bateson, G. *Communication: The social matrix of psychiatry*. New York: Norton, 1968.

Ruittenbeck, H. M. *The individual and the crowd: A study of identity in America*. New York: The New American Library, 1964.

Rusalem, H. Ecological approaches to counseling the physically disabled. In H. Rusalem & D. Malikin (eds.), *Contemporary vocational rehabilitation*. New York: New York University Press, 1976, 175–191.

Rutter, M. Protective factors in children's response to stress and disadvantage, cited in Stassen-Berger, K. *The Developing Person*, New York: Worth Publishing Co., 1980.

S

Salkind, N. J. *Theories of human development*. New York: Van Nostrand, 1981.

Santrock, J. W. Relation of type and onset of father absense to child development. *Child Development*, 1972, *43*, 455–469.

Sarafino, E. P., & Armstrong, J. W. *Child and adolescent development*. Glenview, Ill.: Scott, Foresman, 1980.

Sarason, I. G., & Sarason, B. R. *Abnormal psychology* (3rd ed.). Englewood Cliffs, N. J.: Prentice-Hall, 1980.

Sarnoff, I. *Testing Freudian concepts: An experimental social approach*. New York: Springer, 1971.

Scanzoni, L., & Scanzoni, J. *Men, women and change*. New York: McGraw-Hill, 1976.

Scarf, M. Oh! For a decent night's sleep. *New York Times*, October 21, 1973, 36.

Schachter, S. Deviation, rejection and communication. *Journal of Abnormal and Social Psychology*, 1951, *46*, 190–207.

Schachter, S. The interaction of cognitive and physical determinants of emotional state. In L. Berkowitz (ed.), *Advances in experimental social psychology* (Vol. 1). New York: Academic Press, 1964, 49–80.

Schachter, S. *The psychology of affiliation: Experimental studies of the sources of gregariousness*. Stanford, Calif.: Stanford University Press, 1959.

Schachter, S.; Goldman, R.; & Gordon, A. Effects of fear, food deprivation and obesity on eating. *Journal of Personality and Social Psychology*, 1968, *10*, 91–97.

Schachter, S., & Grose, L. P. Manipulated time and eating behavior. *Journal of Personality and Social Psychology*, 1968, *10*, 98–106.

Schachter, S., & Singer, J. Cognitive, social and physiological determinants of emotional state. *Psychological Review*, 1962, *69*, 379–399.

Scheflen, A. E. *How behavior means*. New York: Aronson, 1974.

Scheflen, A. E., & Scheflen. *Body language and social order*. Englewood Cliffs, N. J.: Prentice-Hall, 1972.

Schlessinger, B. *The one-parent family: Perspectives and annotated bibliography* (3rd ed.). Toronto: University of Toronto Press, 1975.

Schlossberg, W. K., & Goodman, J. A. Woman's place: Children's sex stereotyping of occupations. *Vocational Guidance Quarterly*, 1972, *20*, 266–270.

Schofield, M. *Sociological aspects of homosexuality*. Boston: Little, Brown, 1965.

Schroeder, H. E., & Rich, A. R. The Process of fear reduction through systematic desensitization. *Journal of Consulting and Clinical Psychology*, 1976, *44*, 191–199.

Schulz, D. A., & Rodgers, S. F. *Marriage, the family, and personal fulfillment*. Englewood Cliffs, N. J.: Prentice-Hall, 1975.

Schutz, W. C. *Joy*. New York: Grove Press, 1967.

Schutz, W. C. The postulates of interpersonal needs: Descriptions, 1966. In K. Giffin & B. R. Patton (eds.), *Basic readings in interpersonal communication*. New York: Harper & Row, 1971, 65–93.

Schultz, D. P. *Psychology and industry today* (2nd ed.). New York: Macmillan, 1978.

Schultz, D. P. *Psychology and industry today*. New York: Macmillan, 1973.

Schwartz, B. *The psychology of learning and behavior*. New York: Norton, 1978.

Schwartz, G. E. Biofeedback, self-regulation and the patterning of physiological processes, 1975. In I. L. Janis (ed.), *Current trends in psychology*. San Francisco: Freeman, 1977, 261–271.

Schwartz, G. E., & Shapiro, D. Biofeedback and essential hypertension: Current findings and theoretical concerns. *Seminars in Psychiatry*, 1973, *5*, 493–503.

Scoresby, A. L. Improving academic performance. In J. D. Krumboltz & C. F. Thoreson (eds.), *Behavioral counseling: Cases and techniques*. New York: Harper & Row, 1969.

Sears, R.; Maccoby, E.; & Levin, H. *Patterns of child rearing*. Evanston, Ill.: Row, Peterson, 1957.

Segal, M. W. Alphabet and attraction: An unobstrusive measure of the effect of propinquity in a field setting. *Journal of Personality and Social Psychology*, 1974, *30*, 654–657.

Selg, H. The frustration-aggression hypothesis. In H. Selg (ed.), *The making of human aggression.* New York: St. Martin's Press, 1971.

Seligman, M.E.P. *Helplessness: On depression, development and death.* San Francisco: Freeman, 1975.

Seligman, M. E., & Maier, S. F. Failure to escape from traumatic shock. *Journal of Experimental Psychology*, 1967, *74*, 1–9.

Selye, H. *The stress of my life: A scientist's memoirs* (2nd ed.). New York: Van Nostrand Reinhold, 1979.

Selye, H. *Stress without distress.* New York: Signet, 1976.

Selye, H. *The stress of life.* New York: McGraw-Hill, 1956.

Shapiro, D. & Surwit, R. S. Learned control of physiological function and disease. In H. Leitenberg (ed.), *Handbook of behavior modification and behavior therapy.* Englewood Cliffs, N. J.: Prentice-Hall, 1976.

Shattuck, R. *The forbidden experiment: The story of the wild boy of Aveyron.* New York: Farrar Straus Giroux, 1980.

Shaw, M. E. Changes in sociometric choices following forced integration of an elementary school. *Journal of Social Issues*, 1973, *29*, 143–158.

Sheehy, G. *Pathfinders.* New York; William Morrow, 1981.

Sheehy, G. *Passages.* New York: E. P. Dutton, 1976.

Shelsky, I. The effect of disability on self-concept. Unpublished doctoral dissertation, Columbia University, 1957, cited in B. A. Wright, *Physical disability: A psychological approach.* New York: Harper & Row, 1960.

Shertzer, B., & Stone S. C. *Fundamentals of counseling* (2nd ed.). Boston: Houghton Mifflin, 1974.

Shaffer, L. F., & Shoben E. J., Jr. *The psychology of adjustment* (2nd ed.). Boston: Houghton Mifflin, 1956.

Shirer, W. L. *The rise and fall of the Third Reich.* New York: Simon & Schuster, 1960.

Shope, D. F. *Interpersonal sexuality.* Philadelphia: Saunders, 1975.

Shore, M. F. Legislation, advocacy and the rights of children and youth. *American Psychologist*, 1979, *34*, 1017–1020.

Sielski, L. M. Understanding body language. *Personnel and Guidance Journal*, 1979, *57*, 238–244.

Siller, J. Attitudes towards disability. In H. Rusalem & D. Malikin (eds.), *Contemporary vocational rehabilitation.* New York: New York University Press, 1976.

Silverman, I., & Shaw, M. E. Effects of sudden mass school desegregation on interracial interaction and attitudes in one southern city. *Journal of Social Issues*, 1973, *29*, 133–142.

Silverman, L. H. Psychoanalytic theory: The reports of my death are greatly exaggerated. *American Psychologist*, 1976, *31*, 621–638.

Silverstein, S. "Melinda Mae." In S. Silverstein, *Where the sidewalk ends.* New York: Harper & Row, 1974.

Sinnegen, W. G., & Boak, A. R. *A history of Rome* (6th ed.). New York: Macmillan, 1977.

Skinner, B. F. *About behaviorism.* New York: Knopf, 1974.

Skinner, B. F. *Beyond freedom and dignity.* New York: Bantam, 1971.

Sloane, R. B.; Staples, F. R.; Yorkston, W.; Cristol, A.; & Whipple, K. *Behavior therapy versus psychotherapy.* Cambridge: Harvard University Press, 1975.

Smith, H. *The Russians.* New York: Ballantine, 1976.

Smith, M. L., & Glass, B. V. Meta-analysis of psychotherapy outcome studies. *American Psychologist*, 1977, *32*, 752–760.

Smith, R. E.; Sarason, I. G.; & Sarason, B. R. *Psychology: The frontiers of behavior.* New York: Harper & Row, 1978.

Snyder, M. & Cunningham, M. R. To comply or not to comply: Testing the self-perception explanation of the "foot-in-the-door" phenomenon. *Journal of Personality and Social Psychology*, 1975, *31*, 64–67.

Snyder, S. H. The true speed trip-schizophrenia. *Psychology Today*, January 1972, *5*, 42–46; 74–75.

Sommer, R. *Personal space: The behavioral basis of design.* Englewood Cliffs, N. J.: Prentice-Hall, 1969.

Sorenson, R. C. *Adolescent sexuality in contemporary America.* New York: World, 1973.

Spanier, G. Formal and informal sex education as determinants of premarital sexual behavior. *Archives of Sexual Behavior*, 1976, *5*, 39–67.

Spanos, N. P., & Barber, T. X. Toward a convergence in hypnosis research. *American Psychologist*, 1974, *29*, 500–512.

Spencer, M. H. *Contemporary economics.* New York: Worth, 1980.

Spitz, R. A. Hospitalism: An inquiry into the genesis of psychiatric conditions in early childhood (Part 1). *Psychoanalytic Studies of the Child*, 1945, *1*, 53–74.

Star, S. A.; Williams, R. M., Jr.; & Stouffer, S. A. Negro infantry platoons in white companies. Cited in Middlebrook, P. N., *Social psychology and modern life* (2nd ed.) New York: Knopf, 1980.

Stassen-Berger, K. *The developing person.* New York: Worth, 1980.

Stechler, G., & Halton, A. Prenatal influences on human development. In B. B. Wolman (ed.), *Handbook of developmental psychology.* Englewood Clifss, N. J.: Prentice-Hall, 1982, 175–89.

Stein, A., & Bailey, M. The socialization of achievement orientation in females. *Psychology Bulletin*, 1973, *80*, 345–366.

Stein, J. *Effective personality: A humanistic approach.* Belmont, Calif.: Brooks/Cole, 1972.

Stein, J. *Neurosis in contemporary society: Process and treatment.* Belmont, Calif.: Brooks/Cole, 1970.

Stein, P. *Single.* Englewood Cliffs, N. J.: Prentice-Hall, 1976.

Stern, W. C., & Morgane, P. J. Theoretical view of REM sleep function: Maintenance of catecholamine systems in the central nervous system. *Behavioral Biology,* 1974, *11,* 1–32.

Stevens-Long, J. *Adult life.* Palo Alto, Calif: Mayfield, 1979.

Stewart, A. J. & Rubin, Z. The power motive in the dating couple. *Journal of Personality and Social Psychology,* 1976, *34,* 305–309.

Stewart, K. Dream theory in Malaya. In C. T. Tart (ed.), *Altered states of consciousness.* New York: Wiley, 1969.

Stinnett, N. & Walters, J. *Relationships in marriage and family.* New York: Macmillan, 1977.

Stolz, S. B.; Wienckowdki, L. A.; & Brown, B. S. Behavior modification: A perspective on critical issues. *American Psychologist,* 1975, *30,* 1027–1048.

Stone, L. J., & Church, J. *Childhood and adolescence* (4th ed.). New York: Random House, 1979.

Stroup, A. L. *Marriage and the family: A developmental approach.* New York: Appleton-Century-Crofts, 1966.

Strupp, H. H., & Hadley. S. X. Specific versus non-specific factors in psychotherapy: A controlled study of outcomes. *Archives of General Psychiatry, 36,* 1125–1136.

Stuart, R. B. A three-dimensional program for the treatment of obesity. *Behavior Research and Therapy,* 1971, *9,* 177–186.

Stunkard, A. J. Eating patterns and obesity. *Psychiatric Quarterly,* 1959, *33,* 284–295.

Suinn, R. M. *Abnormal psychology* (rev. ed.), unpublished manuscript, 1982.

Suinn, R. M. The relationship between self-acceptance and acceptance of others: A learning theory analysis. *Journal of Abnormal and Social Psychology,* 1961, *63,* 37–42.

Super, D. E. *The psychology of careers.* New York: Harper & Row, 1957.

Super, D. L., & Hyde, D. T. Career development: Exploration and planning. *Annual Review of Psychology,* 1978, *29,* 333–372.

Surgeon General's Scientific Advisory Committee. *Television and growing up: The impact of televised violence.* Rockville, Md.: U.S. Public Health Service, Department of HEW, Pub. No. HSM 72-9090, 1972.

T

Tart, C. T. Marijuana intoxication: Common experiences. *Nature,* 1970, *226,* 701–704.

Tavris, C. Women: Work isn't always the answer. *Psychology Today,* September, 1976, *10,* 78.

Tavris, C. Woman and man: Results of a questionaire. In C. Tavris (ed.), *The female experience.* Del Mar, Calif: Communications Research, Inc., 1973.

Tavris, C., & Sadd, S. The Redbook report on female sexuality. New York: Delacorte, 1977.

Taylor, S. T., & Gammon, C. B. Effects of type and dose of alcohol on human physical aggression. *Journal of Personality and Social Psychology,* 1975, *32,* 169–175.

Taylor, S. T.; Gammon, C. B.; & Capasso, D. R. Aggression as a function of the interaction of alcohol and threat. *Journal of Personality and Social Psychology,* 1976, *33,* 938–941.

Teevan, R. C., & McGhee, P. E. Childhood development of fear of failure motivation. *Journal of Personality and Social Psychology,* 1972, *21,* 345–348.

Terkel, S. *Working.* New York: Pantheon, 1974.

Thomas, M.; Horton, R.: Lippincott, E.; & Drabman, R. Desensitization to portrayals of real life aggression as a function of exposure to televised violence. *Journal of Personality and Social Psychology,* 1977, *35,* 450–458.

Thompson, N. L., Jr.; McCandless, B. R.; & Strickland, B. R. Personal adjustment of male and female homosexuals and heterosexuals. *Journal of Abnormal Psychology,* 1971, *78,* 237–240.

Thurber, J. The secret life of Walter Mitty. In A. G. Day (ed.), *The greatest American short stories.* New York: McGraw-Hill, 1953, 301–307.

Time Magazine. Alcoholism: New victims, new treatment. April 22, 1974, 75–81.

Toffler, A. *Future shock.* New York: Random House, 1970.

Toland, J. *The rising sun: The decline and fall of the Japanese Empire.* New York: Random House, 1970.

Tourney, G.; Petrilli, A. J.; & Hartfield, L. M. Hormonal relationships in homosexual men. *American Journal of Psychiatry,* 1975, *32,* 288–290.

Tramontana, M. G. Critical review of research on psychotherapy outcome with adolescents: 1967–77. *Psychological Bulletin,* 1980, *88,* 429–50.

Treiman, D., & Terrell, K. Sex and the process of status attainment: A comparison of working women and men. *American Sociological Review,* 1975, *40,* 174–200.

Troll, E. *Early and middle adulthood.* Monterey, Calif.: Brooks/Cole, 1975.

Trotter, R. J. Divorce: The first two years are the worst. *Science News,* Oct. 9, 1976, *110,* 237–238.

Turner, R. T., & Vanderlippe, R. H. Self-ideal congruence as an index of adjustment. *Journal of Abnormal and Social Psychology,* 1958, *57.*

Tyler, L. E. *The work of the counselor.* New York: Appleton-Century-Crofts, 1961.

U

Ubell, E. How to save your life: The behavior-control diet, 1973. In S. Hochman & P. S. Kaplan (eds.), *Readings in psychology: A soft approach* (rev. ed.). Lexington, Mass.: Ginn, 1979, 10–17.

Underwood, B. J. Forgetting. *Scientific American*, March 1964, *210*, 91–100.

U.S. Bureau of the Census. *Statistical abstract of the United States*, Washington, D.C.: U.S. Department of Commerce, 1977.

U.S. Bureau of the Census. *Statistical abstract of the United States*, Washington, D.C.: U.S. Department of Commerce, 1979.

U.S. Department of Health, Education, and Welfare, Public Health Service. *Someone close to you drinks too much.* Rockville, Maryland: National Institute on Alcohol Abuse and Alcoholism, 1975.

U.S. Department of Justice, Drug Enforcement Administration. Controlled substances: Uses and effects. In *Drugs of abuse* (3rd ed.). Washington, D.C.: U.S. Government Printing Office, 1978.

U.S. Department of Labor, Employment and Training Administration. *Dictionary of occupational titles* (4th ed.). Washington, D.C.: U.S. Government Printing Office, 1977.

U.S. Department of Labor. *Women in the labor force: Some new data.* Washington, D.C.: U.S. Department of Labor (Report No. 575), 1979.

U.S. Department of Labor. *Employment in perspective: Working women.* Washington D.C.: Bureau of Labor Statistics, June 1978.

V

Vandenberg, S. Heredity factors in normal personality traits. In J. Wortis (ed.), *Recent Advances in Biological Psychiatry* (Vol. 9). New York: Plenum, 1967.

Vander Zanden, J. W. *Human development* (2nd ed.). New York: Knopf, 1981.

Vander Zanden, J. W. *Social psychology.* New York: Random House, 1977.

Verville, E. *Behavior problems of children.* Philadelphia: Saunders, 1967.

Videbeck, R. Self-conception and the reactions of others. *Sociometry*, 1960, *23*, 351–359.

Vondracek, F. W., & Lerner, R. M. Vocational role development in adolescence. In B. B. Wolman (ed.), *Handbook of developmental psychology.* Englewood Cliffs, N. J.: Prentice-Hall, 1982.

W

Wallace, K. Physiological effects of TM. *Science*, 1970, *167*, 1751–1754.

Wallace, K., & Benson, H. The physiology of meditation. *Scientific American*, February 1972, *226*, 85–90.

Walster, E., & Walster, G. W. *A new look at love.* Reading, Mass.: Addison-Wesley, 1978.

Walters, R. H., & Parke, R. D. Influence of response consequences to a social model on resistance to deviation. *Journal of Experimental Child Psychology*, 1964, *1*, 269–280.

Watson, J. B. *Psychological care of the infant and child.* New York: Norton, 1928.

Watson, J. B. Psychology as the behaviorist views it. *Psychological Review*, 1913, *20*, 158–177.

Watson, J. B., & Raynor, R. Conditioned emotional reactions. *Journal of Experimental Psychology*, 1920, *3*, 1–14.

Webb, W. B. *Sleep: The gentle tyrant.* Englewood Cliffs, N. J.: Prentice-Hall, 1975.

Webb, W. B., & Kersey, J. Recall of dreams and probability of stage 1-REM sleep. *Perceptual and Motor Skills*, 1967, *24*, 627–631.

Weiss, T., & Engle, B. T. Operant conditioning of heart rate in patients with premature ventricular contractions. *Psychosomatic Medicine*, 1971, *33*, 301–322.

Weiner, B.; Renquist, P.; Ravon, B. H.; Meyer, W. J.; Leiman, A.; Kutscher, C. L.; Kleinmuntz, B.; & Haber, R. N. *Discovering psychology.* Chicago: SRA, 1977.

Werner, H. The concept of development from a comparative and organismic point of view. In D. Harris (ed.), *The concept of development.* Minneapolis: University of Minnesota Press, 1957.

Wernimont, P. F. Intrinsic and extrinsic factors in job satisfaction. *Journal of Applied Psychology*, 1966, *50*, 41–50.

Westoff, L. A., & Westoff, C. F. *From now to zero.* Boston: Little, Brown, 1971.

Whitaker, C. A., & Miller, M. H. A reevaluation of "psychiatric help" when divorce impends. *American Journal of Psychiatry*, cited in Gardner, R. A. *Psychotherapy with children of divorce.* New York: Jason Aronson, 1976.

Whitely, J. M., & Resnikoff, A. *Perspective on vocational development.* Washington, D.C.: American Personnel and Guidance Association, 1972.

Wicker, A. W. Attitudes versus actions: The relation of verbal and overt behavioral responses to attitudinal objects. *Journal of Social Issues*, 1969, *25*, 41–78.

Williams, C. D. The elimination of tantrum behavior by extinction procedures. *Journal of Abnormal and Social Psychology*, 1959, *59*, 260–269.

Williams, J. H. *Psychology of women: Behavior in a biosocial context.* New York: Norton, 1977.

Williams, T. R. *Introduction to socialization: Human culture transmitted.* St. Louis: C. V. Mosby, 1972.

Wilsnack, S. C. Femininity by the bottle. *Psychology Today*, April 1973, *6*, 39–45.

Winch, R. F. *Mate selection: A study of complementary needs.* New York: Harper & Row, 1958.

Winch, R. F. Rearing by the book. In M. B. Sussman (ed.), *Sourcebook in marriage and the family* (3rd ed.). Boston: Houghton Mifflin, 1968, 333–344.

Winick, M.; Meyer, K. K.; & Harris, R. C. Malnutrition and environmental enrichment by early adoption: Development of adopted Korean children differing greatly in early nutritional status is examined. *Science,* 1975, *190,* 1173–1175.

Wolberg, L. R. *Hypnosis, is it for you?* New York: Harcourt, Brace, Jovanovich, 1972.

Wolf, T. M. Effects of live modeled sex-inappropriate play behavior in a naturalistic setting. *Developmental Psychology,* 1973, *9,* 120–123.

Wolff, S. *Children under stress.* Baltimore, Md.: Penguin Press, 1969.

Wolfgang, M. F., & Ferracuti, F. *The subculture of violence: Towards an integrated theory in criminology.* New York: Barnes & Noble, 1967.

Wolpe, J. The systematic desensitization treatment of neuroses. *Journal of Nervous and Mental Disorders,* 1961, *132,* 189–263.

Wolpe, J. *Psychotherapy by reciprocal inhibition.* Stanford Calif.: Stanford University Press, 1958.

Worchel, S., & Cooper, J. *Understanding social psychology* (rev. ed.). Homewood, Ill.: The Dorsey Press, 1979.

Worrell, J. New directions in counseling women. *Personnel and Guidance Journal,* March 1980, *58,* 477–485.

Wright, B. *Physical disability: A psychological approach.* New York: Harper & Row, 1960.

Wrightsman, L. S. *Social psychology* (2nd ed.). Monterey, Calif.: Brooks/Cole, 1977.

Wrightsman, L. S. The most important social psychological research in this generation? A review of Milgram's obedience to authority. *Contemporary Psychology,* 1974, *19,* 803–5.

Wrightsman, L. S. *Social psychology.* Monterey, Calif.: Brooks/Cole, 1972.

Wuthnow, R., & Glock, C. Y. The shifting focus of faith: A survey report, God in the gut. *Psychology Today,* November 1974, *8,* 131–136.

Wykert, J. Why sleeping pills are keeping you awake. *New York Magazine,* May 24, 1976, 33–38.

Y

Yancy, W. S.; Nader, P. R.; & Burnham, K. L. Drug use and attitudes of high school students. *Pediatrics,* 1972, *50,* 739–45.

Yankelovich, D. The new psychological contracts at work. *Psychology Today,* May 1978, 46–50.

Yankelovich, D. New rules in American life: Searching for self-fulfillment in a world turned upside down. *Psychology Today,* April 1981, 35+.

Young, P. For a zestier life . . . Rx: Sex over sixty. *The National Observer,* February 1, 1975, 35–41.

Young, P. Cancer and personality: Can they be connected? In G. E. Schwartz (ed.), *Readings in personality and adjustment.* Guilford, Conn.: Dushkin, 1979.

Z

Zelie, K.; Stone, C. I.; & Lehr, E. Cognitive-behavioral intervention in school discipline: A preliminary study. *Personnel and Guidance Journal,* 1980, *59,* 80–84.

Zelnik, M., & Kantner, J. F. Sexual and contraceptive experience of young unmarried women in the U.S.: 1976 and 1971. *Family Planning Perspective,* 1977, *9,* 55–71.

Zimbardo, P. G. *Shyness: What is it, what to do about it?* Reading, Mass.: Addison-Wesley, 1977.

Zimbardo, P. G.; Ebberson, E. B.; & Maslach, C. *Influencing attitudes and changing behavior* (2nd ed.). Reading, Mass.: Addison-Wesley, 1977.

Zimbardo, P. G.; Haney, C.; & Banks W. C. A Pirandellian prison. *New York Times Magazine,* April 8, 1973, 38–40.

PHOTO CREDITS

O

Olds, S.W. 190, 246
Orlofsky, J.L. 278
Ornstein, R.E. 352, 375
Osipow, S.H. 306
Osofsky, H.J. 260
Otis, L.S. 375

P

Page, J.D. 357
Papalia, D.F. 190, 246
Papanek, H. 15
Parke, R.D. 92, 399, 401
Parloff, M.B. 327
Parsons, O.A. 365
Parsons, T. 242
Patterson, C.R. 168
Pattison, E.M. 367
Paul, G.L. 336
Pei, M. 383
Pikunas, J. 234
Peck, L. 190
Pedersen, F.A. 189
Pelletier, K.R. 115
Perlman, H.H. 176
Piaget, J. 68, 88
Picasso, P. 88
Pierloot, R.A. 116
Pines, M. 94, 95
Postman, L. 355, 356
Poulton, E.C. 106
Prather, J. 322
Presley, E. 101-2

Q

Qualls, P.J. 372
Quayle, D. 357
Quinn, R.P. 106, 302

R

Rabban, M. 191
Rachlin, H. 392
Rahe, R.H. 103, 104
Raynor, R. 53
Rees, W.L. 113
Reidmann, A. 320
Renwick, P.A. 302
Resnikoff, A. 300
Reuben, D. 263
Rheingold, H.L. 189
Richardson, S. 94
Reiss, I.L. 233
Rich, A.R. 334
Richter, L. 271, 273
Riedmann, A. 239

Rimm, D.C. 172, 336
Ringness, T.A. 392, 394
Roark, A.E. 212, 213, 215
Robbins, T. 183
Robertson, I. 178
Rodgers, S.F. 234
Rodin, J. 35
Roe, A. 306-7, 309
Rogers, C. 24-25, 135, 268, 286, 290-1, 337-38, 347
Rokeach, M. 382, 383, 388-89, 390-1, 396
Rollins, B.C. 236, 237
Roosevelt, T. 15
Rosen, R.D. 330
Rosenfeld, A. 353-54
Rahula, W. 374
Robson, K.S. 189
Rosenman, R.H. 117
Rosenthal, D. 89
Rosenthal, R. 89, 93
Rosenzweig, M.R. 67
Ross, D. 18, 164
Ross, H.L. 318
Ross, S.A. 18, 164
Ross, W.D. 344
Rothbard, M.K. 189
Rowe, C.J. 132, 147
Ruben, B.D. 211
Ruben, I.M. 344
Rubin, J. 189
Rubin, Z. 189, 232, 233, 235
Ruesch, J. 206
Ruittenbeck, H.M. 277
Rusalem, H. 283

S

Sadd, S. 261
Salkind, N.J. 18
Santrock, J.W. 114
Sarafino, E.P. 56
Sarason, B.R. 53
Sarason, I.G. 53
Sawhill, I.V. 318
Scanzoni, J. 262
Scanzoni, L. 262
Schachter, S. 34, 48, 228, 407
Scheflen, A.E. 217, 219
Schlessinger, B. 318
Schlossberg, W.K. 309
Schneider, F.W. 185
Schofield, M. 265
Schroeder, H.E. 334
Schwartz, G.E. 377
Schultz, D.P. 324
Schutz, W.C. 199
Schulz, D.A. 234
Scoresby, A.L. 334

Sears, R. 394, 401
Segal, M.W. 203
Selg, H. 136
Seligman, M.E.P. 148-49
Selye, H. 114-15, 122, 123
Serber, M. 343
Shakespeare, W. 118
Shapiro, D. 377
Shapiro, J.L. 342
Shattuck, R. 51
Shaw, G.B. 114
Shaw, M.E. 393, 396
Sheehy, G. 231, 284
Shehan, P.W. 277
Shelsky, I. 283
Shertzer, B. 312
Shope, D.P. 251, 260
Shore, M.F. 94
Shostrom, E.L. 332
Sielski, L.M. 219
Siller, J. 283
Silverman, L.H. 332, 396
Silverman, S. 116
Sinnegan, W.G. 179
Skinner, B.F. 16-17, 401
Sloan, R.B. 337
Slocum, J.W. 303
Smith, H. 381
Smith, M.L. 348
Smith, R.E. 37, 228
Snyder, M. 405
Sobell, L.C. 367
Sobell, M.B. 367
Sommer, R. 221, 222
Sorenson, R.C. 252, 254, 255
Spanier, G.B. 239, 253, 258
Spanos, N.P. 378
Spence, D.P. 348
Spencer, M.H. 383
Spitz, R. 93, 230
Star, S.A. 397, 398
Stassen-Berger, K. 87, 252, 309
Stechler, G. 94
Stein, J. 231, 277, 282
Stein, P. 239
Stern, W.C. 38
Stevens-Long, J. 320
Stewart, A.J. 235
Stewart, K. 355
Stinnett, N. 233, 241
Stolz, S.B. 335
Stone, S.C. 312
Strupp, H.N. 345
Stunkard, A.J. 34
Suinn, R.M. 295
Sullivan, H.S. 286-87
Super, D.L. 306, 312
Surwit, R.S. 377
Swap, W. 263

Key terms and concepts, which are boldface when they first appear in the text and are listed at the end of each chapter, are set in color and defined again in this subject index.

behavioral 132–33
humanistic 133–35
psychoanalytic 131–32

Approach-approach conflict A situation in which an individual is faced with two desirable goals or choices and must decide between them.111

Approach-avoidance conflict A situation in which an individual perceives both the positive and negative aspects of a goal or choice.112

Aptitude test A measuring instrument designed to predict how well an individual will perform in a particular task, if given training in that area. 314

Arguments and disagreements 212–16
destructive techniques 213
healthy techniques 213–15

Arousal stage of sexual response The first stage of human sexual response, in which the penis becomes erect in men and an increase in vaginal secretions is found in women. 268

Assertive Acting in a way that will further one's own needs and goals without violating the rights of others. 169–72

Assertiveness training Group workshops using various techniques such as role playing to help the participants act in a more assertive fashion. 172

Attack stage Often the second stage in an encounter group, in which the participants may feel free enough to be very frank and honest in focusing on the negative qualities of other group members.
attack as cause of aggression 342–43

Attitudes Perceptual sets or predispositions to respond to particular people, objects, or events in a certain manner.253, 382–83, 389, 392–98, 405
attitude change 392–93, 405
correlation with behavior 253, 392, 393
definition 382–83
formation of 392
(*see also* Prejudice and Discrimination)

Authoritarian personality A group of attitudes that often characterize prejudiced individuals. Authoritarian personalities are rigid, moralistic, authority-oriented, conforming, and ethnocentric.394–95

Authoritarian style of childrearing A style of childrearing in which parents establish absolute standards for conduct, prize obedience, use punishment liberally, and provide little opportunity for children to question.84

Authoritative style of childrearing A style of childrearing in which parents guide their children's activities but give them freedom to act within limits. Verbal discussions are common and feelings are often expressed.84

Autism (infantile) A condition involving a lack of responsiveness to others, impairments of communication, and bizarre responses to the environment. It develops before the age of 30 months.60–61

Autonomy versus doubt The second of Erik Erikson's eight psychological stages, this one occurring between the ages of about one-and-a-half and three.81

Aversive conditioning A form of conditioning used in behavior therapy, in which a behavior is paired with an unpleasant stimulus in order to reduce or eliminate undesirable behavior.334–35

Avoidance-avoidance conflict A situation in which an individual is faced with two undesirable goals or choices and must decide between them. 111–12

B

Barbiturates A class of drugs that depress the central nervous system and are highly addictive.359, 371

Behavior modification The use of the principles of learning in order to change behavior.58, 62

Behavior therapy Therapy that is based on the principles of learning. 333–36
ethical problems involved 334–35
evaluation of 336

Behavioral component of attitudes The observable actions of an individual toward another individual or object, as a reflection of that person's attitudes.389–90

Behaviorism A school of psychology that rejects the study of consciousness and internal phenomena in favor of techniques that measure overt, observable behavior patterns.16, 353

Being love (B love) Love based upon respect for the individual as he or she is and emphasizing the importance of the growth and development of the other individual's potential and abilities.231

Being needs (B-needs) or metaneeds A group of needs that involve a striving after the attainment of a higher goal associated with the development of one's potential.22

Belongingness needs The third level of needs in Maslow's need hierarchy, involving a striving for love, interpersonal intimacy, and a feeling of belonging.23

Biofeedback The use of instruments to monitor some internal process, amplify the measurement, and feed it back to the individual.375–77
evaluation of 377
process 375–76
uses for 376–77

Birth control (*see* Contraception)
Birth order 17

Blind milling A technique used in sensitivity training, in which people mill around a room with their eyes closed and when meeting must communicate by touching.340

Blood pressure 375

Boredom A feeling of weariness due to constant repetition or exposure to monotonous stimuli.42–43, 44

Burnout An overwhelming sense of apathy that sometimes affects persons working in human service jobs. 346

C

Career A sequence of occupations, jobs, and positions in an individual's working life.300, 313
(*see also* Vocational choice and Work)

Caring One of Erich Fromm's four components of loving behaviors. It relates to a show of concern for the other individual in a loving relationship that promotes the other individual's growth and development. 230–31

Casualties Those individuals injured psychologically due to their participation in an encounter group.343–44

Catharsis The process by which fears and problems are acted out or verbally expressed, often resulting in at least a temporary reduction in tension.159–60, 162

Children's Rights 94–95

Clarification A technique used in

client-centered therapy in which the counselor asks the client to rephrase statements so they can be better understood. 337–38

Classical conditioning A learning process in which a neutral stimulus is paired with a stimulus that elicits a response until the originally neutral stimulus itself produces the response. 18, 52–55

Claustrophobia A phobia involving a fear of closed spaces. 131

Client-centered therapy A type of therapy developed by Carl Rogers, more recently called the *person-centered* approach. 336–38
    techniques 336–37
    evaluation 338

Cognitive-behavioral approach The modification of the learning or behavioral model to include such cognitive factors as the state of the organism, expectations, beliefs, and thought patterns. 19

Cognitive component of attitudes The portion of an attitude that consists of an individual's knowledge of an object and the facts that support that evaluation. 389

Cognitive theory of emotion The theory suggested by Stanley Schachter, that when we experience physiological responses to emotion, we label them according to the situational context. 228

Cohabitation Living together in an intimate, sexual relationship without being married. 238–39

Communal family An arrangement in which groups of adult males and females live together and share child-care responsibilities, although sexual relations are only shared with one partner and the family units tend to remain distinct. 240

Communication Any means by which we influence one another, both verbally or nonverbally. 206–21
    definition 206
    disputes 212–15
    listener 209–210
    message 207, 211–212
        model for 206–212
        communicator 206–209
        credibility 208
        trustworthiness 209
        expertness 209
    nonverbal 215–21
    skills 206–11

Compatibility The fit between partners' (or friends') values, goals, and lifestyles that provides a bond of understanding. 233–34

Compensation A defense mechanism in which an individual makes up for a perceived or an actual deficiency. (*See also* Direct compensation and Indirect compensation.) 133

Complementary theory of mate selection The idea that opposites attract. 203–4, 234

Compromise A positive conflict-management technique by which each party agrees to give up some demands and make concessions to the other party. 214

Confession 145

Conflict The state of being faced with alternatives and having to choose between them. (*See* Approach-approach conflict, Approach-avoidance conflict, and Avoidance-avoidance conflict.) 111–13
    approach-approach 111
    approach-avoidance 112
    avoidance-avoidance 111
    multiple approach-avoidance 112

Conformity The change in behavior or attitudes of an individual, due to real or imagined pressure from a group. 402–4
    factors affecting 404

Congruence Accepting one's true feelings and acting in accordance with them. 337

Conscience 142–44
    problems from "too soft" 144
    problems of rigidity 142–43
    (*see also* Superego)

Conscious A Freudian term used to denote the thoughts and emotions that any individual is aware of at a particular moment. 11

Consciousness A process of awareness that requires an individual to focus attention upon a variety of internal and/or external stimuli. 352–79
    biofeedback and 377–79
    definition 353–55
    dreams 355–56
    drugs and 357–72
    Freud's conception of 11–14
    hypnosis and 377–79
    meditation and 372–75

Consequential thinking The process by which an individual considers all the consequences or possible results of a behavior before performing that behavior. 144

Continuous reinforcement A reinforcement schedule that involves rewarding each instance of the desired behavior. See, by contrast, *partial reinforcement*. 57–58

Contraceptive use 258–59

Control The interpersonal need to hold some power in a relationship; to influence the decision-making process. 199

Conventional level of moral reasoning The second level of moral reasoning in Kohlberg's theory. Here, decisions are based upon gaining or holding the approval of others. 399

Covenant control A technique in which behavior is modified by teaching the client to associate particular thoughts with certain activities. For example, a person may be taught to think of a very overweight individual whenever considering fattening food. 335

Credibility The quality of being believable as a communicator. 108–9

Cults 292–93

Culture 91

D

Day care 321

Decision making 124–25

Defense mechanisms Unconscious and automatic adjustive efforts that are used in an attempt to combat emotional conflict and deal with such unpleasant emotions as anxiety. 131, 133, 144–45
    types of 133

Deficiency love (D love) Love that is based upon one's unmet needs and lacks. 231

Deficiency needs (D-needs) Needs such as food, air, security, and even possibly love, whose absence motivates the individual to search relentlessly until they are satisfied. See also *B-needs*. 21

Denial 133, 365

Depression A feeling of unhappiness, loneliness, or dejection that tends to lead to inactivity. 147–54
    causes of 147–51
    definition of 147
    overcoming 151–54

Deprivation A state of extreme need. 113

Developmental counseling Counseling in which the main focus is on aiding the client to deal more effectively with the normal problems and tasks arising at a particular time in life. 344, 346

Developmental psychology The branch of psychology that studies how organisms change qualitatively and quantitatively over time. 77–96

Developmental tasks Specific tasks that individuals in a particular society are expected to master at a certain stage in their lives. 78–79

Developmental trends 77–79
external to internal 78
involuntary to voluntary control 77
mass to specific 78

Dieting 335

Diminishers A label describing a pattern of behavior in which an individual reduces the importance of changes in the environment. 121

Direct compensation A form of compensation in which an individual attempts to overcome or make up for real or imagined deficiency or failure by achieving in this area. 15

Discipline styles 84

Discrimination In learning theory, the process by which an individual learns to differentiate between stimuli. 18–19

Discrimination In social psychology, the acceptance or rejection of an individual, based on some group identification. 393

Displacement The defense mechanism in which an emotion is redirected from an original object to a more acceptable substitute. 133, 159

Disputing A technique used in rational-emotive therapy in which the client is asked to challenge his or her own assumptions that have led to self-defeating actions. 338

Divorce 243–47
causes of 243–44
"healthy divorce 244–45
minimizing effects on children 246–47

Double approach-avoidance conflict A situation in which an individual perceives both the positive and negative aspects of two goals or choices and must choose between them. 112

Double standard Different rules that traditionally were applied to the behavior of men and women in our society. 251–52

Dream analysis 329, 332

Dreams 353, 354–55

Drive A state of arousal within an organism that leads to behaviors that will satisfy a need. 29, 30

Drugs Any chemical substances except food that alter one's psycho-

logical and/or physical functioning. 356–72
and behavior 357–62
definition of 357
extent of usage 357

Drug variables The term used in drug research to describe such drug-related factors as dosage, one drug's interaction with other drugs, and durations of usage. (These factors must be taken into account when studying the effect of any drug.) 357

E

Early experience (question of importance of) 12, 92–97

Eclectic Choosing aspects of many different theories as opposed to embracing the principles or techniques from only one. 25, 348

Educational influences on development 92

Ego The term used to describe the partially conscious portion of the mind in psychoanalytic thought. The ego mediates between the individual's wishes and desires and the realities of the environment. 14, 141

Ego-dystonic homosexuality According to DSM III, this is a condition in which an individual practicing homosexual behavior *desires* to change to a heterosexual orientation. (Homosexuality itself is not listed as an emotional disorder.) 264, 335

Electroencephalograph A machine that measures and records electrical impulses in the brain. 38, 377

Electromyograph A machine to measure muscle tension. 376–77

Embracement stage The third and final stage of an encounter group, in which the group supports the individual's attempt to change, often through experimentation with new modes of behavior. 343

Empathy 208, 337, 338

Encoding The process by which new information is initially stored for memory in the brain. 66, 68

Encounter groups Small groups that meet in an effort to promote personal growth and change through a variety of verbal and non-verbal techniques. *See* Human potentials movement. 339–44

Environmental influences on development 91–92

Environmental variables The term used in drug research to describe

variables in the environment which must be taken into account when studying the effect of any drug. 359

Eros A term used in Freudian theory to denote the life instinct. 102

Eros (type of love) A type of fast-developing love containing a strong physical component. Although emotions are intense, there is little self-sacrifice. 226

Escalation The process by which angry actions lead to more angry actions, and emotions build up. The result is sometimes aggression. 167

Esteem 327, 349

Esteem needs The fourth level of Maslow's need hierarchy, involving such needs as recognition and praise for one's achievements. 23

Ethology The study of animal behavior in its natural habitat. 163

Exhaustion The last stage of Hans Selye's general adaptation syndrome which describes an individual's response to prolonged stress. In this stage, some structure in the body begins to break down, causing illness and sometimes death. 115

Existential anxiety Anxiety that arises from the necessity of dealing with choices that involve unknown consequences. 134–35

Extended family At least three generations of a family, often including aunts and uncles. 241

Extinction The gradual decrease in a response that occurs due to a lack of reinforcement. 55, 335

F

Fading of the memory trace An explanation that views forgetting as a result of lack of use of certain information or knowhow. The theory has recently been deemphasized. 71

Family influences on development 91

Fat cells 35

Fear An unpleasant feeling very similar to *anxiety,* but usually directed toward a definite object in the present. 128–29

Fear of failure One of the important elements in achievement motivation. Individuals with a need to achieve but a high fear of failure tend to avoid challenging problems, opting for very easy or almost impossibly difficult ones. Individuals with a high need for achievement and a low fear of failure tend to choose challenging tasks, since the possibility of failure does not bother them as much. 45–46, 47

Fear of success Matina Horner's explanation for some women's seeming hesitancy to achieve. 46–47

Feedback Information that is received concerning one's behavior or the behavior of others. In learning, feedback is used to guide and correct behavior. 66

Feedback In interpersonal communication, any response that lets a communicator know you have received his or her message. 210–11, 375

    techniques of 210–11

Fitt's Law A rule stating that the more an individual knows about a particular subject or the better someone is in performing a behavior, the more difficult it will be to show improvement. 67

Fixation A behavior pattern that results from the over- or under-gratification of the needs of an individual during a particular psychosexual stage, according to Freudian theory. 80

Fixed-interval reinforcement A schedule in which reinforcement is delivered after a fixed time interval, providing the correct response is given. 57–59

Fixed-ratio reinforcement A schedule in which reinforcement is delivered according to a fixed number of correct responses. For instance, you may receive a pat on the back from your boss every second time you sell your quota of suits. 57–59

Fixity A term used in problem solving to describe an individual's tendency to approach a problem in the same way. 73

Flattery 205

Flextime A schedule in which the hours an individual spends at a job are specially suited to that person's personal and familial responsibilities. 324

Flooding A behavior therapy technique that is effective for some unwanted behaviors, such as hoarding. The client is overloaded with the stimulus that is the object of the compulsion, until he or she becomes sick of it. 335–36

Foot-in-the-door-technique 405

Forgetting 71

Four-step process for social learning In order for imitation, or modeling, to occur, four separate steps are necessary: attention, memory, behavioral reproduction, and reinforcement. 64

Free association A therapeutic technique used in psychoanalysis in which a client relates everything that enters his or her consciousness. 328–29

Friendship 202–3

Frustration Any interference with, or blocking of, the attainment of a goal. 108–10

    and imitation 166

Frustration-aggression hypothesis The theory that frustration may lead to aggression. 157–58, 165

Frustration tolerance The ability to continue to function competently during times of frustration. 109

G

General adaptation syndrome A three-stage reaction to prolonged stress noted by Hans Selye beginning with *alarm*, continuing to *resistance*, and finally ending in *exhaustion*. 114–17

Genetic influences on development 88–90

Generativity versus self-absorption Erik Erikson's description of the psychosocial crisis of middle age. 86

Generalization A term used in learning theory to denote an individual's response to stimuli that resemble the originally conditioned stimulus. (*See also* Stimulus generalization.) 18–19

Genital stage The final psychosexual stage, beginning at puberty, in which an individual attains adult sexuality. 80

Genuine communication Open communication in which each party is able to receive, consider, and respond to the message conveyed by other parties. 206

Gestalt theory of problem solving An explanation of one process by which people solve problems. 72–73

"Good me, bad me" Harry Stack Sullivan's explanation for the way in which people develop positive ("good me") or negative ("bad me") self-appraisals. 286–87

Group marriage An arrangement in which a number of adult males and

females live together and share sexual relations and childcare responsibilities. 239

Group therapy 348

Groupthink A term coined by Irving Janis to describe the decisionmaking process in small, cohesive groups, in which the attempt to retain group solidarity interferes with critical thinking. 403

Guidance counselors 347

Guilt Feeling of disappointment or sadness due to a real or imagined violation of internal standards of conduct. 139–46

    coping with 144–46
    definition of 139, 141
    views of guilt 141–43
        behavioral view 141–42
        Freudian view 141
        humanistic 142–43

H

Hallucinogen Any of a number of drugs that tend to cause the user to experience imaginary sensations that have no relationship to the individual's real external environment. 370, 371

Headaches 376–77

Healthy adjustment 4–7

Hierarchy of needs 21–24

Holism An approach to studying behavior whose central position is that human beings can only be understood by looking at the whole individual rather than one specific element. 21

Homosexual behavior Sexual behavior between members of the same sex. 264–66

Human relations training programs A general term used to describe seminars in which people learn to deal more effectively with others in an organizational or industrial setting. 303

Human potentials movement A humanistic movement devoted to the development and maximization of the unique qualities and abilities of human beings. 327, 339, 340–45

    encounter and sensitivity groups, 340
    evaluation of 343–44
    group leader 342
    process of 341
    techniques of 340

Humanistic psychology The branch

of psychology focusing upon the basic qualities and inner nature of human beings in order to understand how they may reach their potential. 19–25

Hunger drive 33–34

Hypnogogic sleep A term used to describe the boundary between sleep and wakefulness. 38

Hydraulic principle A principle that states that frustrations and pressure build up until they finally reach a point at which the individual must release them through anger. 110

Hyperkinesis A condition in which an individual shows hyperactivity and distractibility. 371

Hypnosis A state of heightened awareness in which attention is focused intensely on the suggestions of the hypnotist. 377–79

Hypochondriacal behavior A behavior pattern in which individuals create and experience imaginary symptoms. 115–16

I

Id The construct of the mind that Freud viewed as the focus of all the instinctual wishes and needs. 14

Ideal self The image people have of what they would like to be. 294–95

Identity The sense of knowing who you are. 85–86, 277–78, 285–86, 336, 344
    identity achievers 278
    identity diffusion 278
    identity foreclosure 278
    identity moratorium 278

Identity versus role confusion The positive and negative outcomes of adolescence, according to Erik Erikson. 85–86
    single vs. multiple 285–86

Imagery A relaxation technique in which the individual fantasizes a scene that makes him or her feel comfortable (for instance, lying in the sun on the beach), while breathing slowly and letting the muscles relax. 140

Imitation (*see* Social learning theory)

Inclusion The interpersonal need to belong. 199

Indirect compensation A form of compensation in which an individual attempts to overcome a real or imagined deficiency by achieving in another unrelated area. 16

Industry versus inferiority The fourth stage in Erik Erikson's theory of psychosocial development, this one takes place around ages 7–12. 82–84

Informed consent 334–35

Initiative versus guilt The third stage in Erik Erikson's theory of psychosocial development, this one encompasses much of early childhood. 82

Inner-directed A term coined by David Riesman, referring to an orientation in which individuals are directed by their own personal attitudes and goals rather than what is socially acceptable. 383

Insight therapies A group of therapies that aim at increasing the client's understanding of his or her unconscious processes. (*See also* psychoanalytic therapy.) 328

Insomnia A general term used to describe the inability to get to sleep, stay asleep, or wake up refreshed in the morning. 38–39, 40

Instrumental values Values related to modes of behavior such as cleanliness, cheerfulness, and courage. 388

Interference theory of forgetting The theory that forgetting occurs because one bit of information learned either at an earlier or a later time interferes with the information already stored. 71

Interpersonal needs 199

Interpersonal relationships 202–6
    establishment 202–4
    maintenance 204–6

Integrity versus despair The positive and negative outcomes of later maturity, according to Erik Erikson. 86

Intimacy versus isolation The fifth developmental conflict in Erik Erikson's theory, this one typical of early adulthood. 86

Intimate distance zone Hall's name for the distance zone (0–6 inches) reserved for those with whom we are intimate. The far phase of this zone, 6–18 inches, is reserved for close friends. 220–21

Intrinsic conscience A term used by Abraham Maslow to refer to one's own perception of his or her potential or destiny. 141–42

Introspection 145–46

Invulnerables A term used to describe children who are raised in very bad environments and yet show little or no emotional disturbance. 95–96

J

Job Work that a person performs with income as a primary purpose. A job is distinguished from a *career:* the latter term implies a sequence of vocational steps in an upward direction. (*See also* Work and Vocational choice.) 300

K

Kinesics The study of body movements such as gestures, facial expressions, and postures. 217–20
    double messages 220
    eye contact 219
    facial expressions 220
    postures and gestures 217–19

Knowledge One of Erich Fromm's four components of loving behavior. It relates to the act of learning about the needs, values, and goals of the other individual in the relationship. 230

L

Latency stage The psychosexual period during middle childhood, in which sexuality is largely hidden. 80

Latent content A Freudian term describing the unconscious meanings behind people's dreams. 332

Learned helplessness A condition in which an individual gives up and passively endures some unpleasant situation. 148–50

Learned motives Motives such as achievement which are not innate but are based upon learning. 43–49

Learning Relatively permanent changes in behavior due to experiences. 16–19, 51–97
    factors affecting 65–66
        attention 65
        feedback 66
        meaningfulness 65
        motivation 65
        practice 66
    plateau 67
    theory 16–19
    (*See also* Operant conditioning, Classical conditioning, and Social learning theory)

Leisure Time that is free from work, in which an individual may indulge in a number of activities chosen for personal satisfaction. 300–1

Lesbian behavior Sexual activity between females. 264, 265–66

Libido Freud's term for sexual energy. As an individual develops, the libido attaches itself to different parts of the body in a sequence of stages Freud called *psychosexual*. 80

Librium A commonly prescribed tranquilizer. 372

Life changes and stress 103

Life events scale 103

Locus of control An orientation involving attributing behavior to either external or internal factors. 342

Long-term memory Memory storage that is relatively resistant to forgetting. Long-term memory includes all the information we retain for long periods of time, perhaps throughout our life-span. 70

Looking glass self The way in which people see themselves through the behaviors and reactions of others. 290

Loss and separation 147

Love In this text, love is defined as an intensely intimate feeling in which the satisfaction of the other's needs are at least as important as one's own and in which one acts in a way to maximize the potential of the other. 224–37

  as an emotion 228

  as a need 229–30

  as a set of behaviors 230–31

  definition of 232

  effects of time on 236–37

  styles of love 226–27

LSD A potent hallucinogen. 361, 371

Ludus (style of loving) The ludic lover avoids deep relationships and sees love as a game. 226

M

Mainstreaming A process by which handicapped and disabled individuals are integrated as much as possible into regular classes and the normal school routine. 398

Malnutrition 94–96

Mania (style of loving) A type of love in which an individual is obsessed with his/her partner and is very jealous and very insecure. 227

Manifest content The content of the dream as viewed and reported by the dreamer. 332

Marijuana A drug used to bring on feelings of euphoria, dreaminess, or relaxation. 358, 362, 368–71

  and the amotivational syndrome 371

  effects on body 369–70

Marriage 233–47

  attitudes toward 238–41

  changing instution 241–43

  divorce and 244–45

  mate selection 233–37

  power and 235

  prevent marital problems 238

Mate selection 233–37

Maternal employment 320–21

Maturity 235–36

"Me" generation 324

Medical or disease model 336

Meditation The process by which one focuses attention on a narrow objective (breathing, a particular sound, etc.) in order to reach a higher plane of consciousness. 372–75

  methods of 373–74

  uses of 374–75

Memory (*see also* Encoding, storage and retrieval)

Men

  premarital sex 253–54

  sex trait stereotypes 184–85, 186–87

  sexual problems 270

  socialization 189

  view of sex 252

  work patterns 314–15

Menopause 202–3

Mnemonic device Any device that facilitates memorization. 68, 69

Moral anxiety Anxiety that arises from a violation of one's conscience and is experienced as guilt. 131

Moral behavior 398, 400–1

Moral reasoning 398–99

Motivation An inferred condition that arouses behavior directed towards some goal. 29–50

  defined 29

  drive theory and 29–30

  learned (secondary) motives 43–49

  primary motives 33–39

  stimulus motives 39–43

  value/expectancy theory 30–31

Motive Any force, internal or external, that is involved in the instigation, direction, or termination of behavior. 32

Motor learning One of the most persistent forms of learning, motor learning involves the acquisition of such skills as riding a bike or roller skating. These abilities tend to stay with us virtually throughout out lives, even if we make little use of them. 65

Moving toward, away, or against Karen Horney described three possible reactions to problems that one encounters beginning with early parent-child conflicts. 4

N

Need A specific deficit that when satisfied, improves the welfare of the individual. 21–23, 29

  Maslow's hierarchy 21–23

Neo-Freudian Literally, "new Freudian." Psychologists of this orientation tend to downplay Freud's original emphasis on sexuality and the unconscious, emphasizing the ego's functioning and the influence of sociocultural factors. 15–16

Neurotic anxiety A Freudian term used to describe anxiety that arises from unconscious impulses that we attempt to repress of disguise. 131

Neurotic guilt The guilt an individual experiences when he or she equates forbidden thoughts with forbidden actions. 143

Nonverbal communication 215–22

Normality A broad range of the usual or accepted behaviors within a particular society. 6

Norms (developmental) Standard societal rules that govern appropriate behavior in any particular situation. 87–88

Nuclear family The immediate family, consisting only of husband or wife and children living in a single household. 241

O

Obedience Doing something that someone else tells you to do; compliance with the request or order of another individual. 401–2

Obesity 34–35

Oedipal situation According to Freud, during the phallic stage the male child develops a sexual attraction towards his mother and wishes to do away with his father. (In females, a similar conflict arises called the Electra situation, in which the girl develops a sexual attraction toward the father.) 80

Open communication 206

Operant conditioning The learning process in which behavior is altered because of the consequences it has on the environment. 18, 55–63, 401, 406

Oral stage The first psychosexual stage, in which the life energy is focused on the oral cavity and such activities as sucking and biting. 80

Organismic variables The term used in drug research to describe such user-related factors as weight, age, and personality that must be taken into account when studying the effect of any drug on behavior. 358–59

Orgasm The third stage of human sexual response, involving a pulsating release of sexual tensions. 268, 272

Orthogenetic principle Heinz Werner's concept that development is directional, proceeding from an undifferentiated and global state to a more integrated and differentiated one. 77

Other-directed A term coined by David Riesman that refers to an orientation in which an individual is directed by attitudes and goals that have first been checked for social acceptability. 383

Overlearning Continuous practice of a skill even after it has been performed correctly. 66

P

Partial reinforcement Reinforcement that is not delivered on a continuous one-to-one, behavior-reinforcement basis. If partial reinforcement is used, only a portion of the desired responses will receive reinforcement. 77–79

Passive love A type of love that tends to be selfish and limiting. Passive love involves taking rather than giving, and often there is an attempt to change the other person in some fundamental way. 231

Peer influences on development 92

Permissive style of discipline A style in which parents make few demands on their offspring and depend upon the children to control their own behavior. 84

Person-centered therapy (*see* Client-centered therapy)

Persona A person's "public self"; the image we project to others. 291–92

Personal distance zone The distance between individuals reserved for acquaintances. The close phase, 18–30 inches, is reserved for close acquaintances, while the far zone, 30–48 inches, is for casual acquaintances. 221

Personality An individual's distinctive behavior patterns that may include thoughts, attitudes, feelings, and values. 7, 8, 10–25
  adjustment and 25–26
  definition 7
  stability of 8–9
  theories of 10–25
    cognitive-learning view 19–20
    Freudian view 10–15
    humanistic view 20–25
    learning theory view 16–19
    Neo-Freudian view 15–16

Phallic stage The third psychosexual stage, occurring during early childhood, in which focus of the child's sexuality is on his/her genital organs. During this period the Oedipal situation develops. *See* Oedipal situation. 80

Phenomenological viewpoint The humanistic view that stresses the importance of an individual's subjective experiences. In counseling, the therapist attempts to perceive the world from the client's point of view. 337

Phobia A fear that is either irrational or out of proportion to the danger presented by a particular object or situation. 53

Physiological needs Those needs that arise from tissue deficiencies, such as needs for food, pain reduction, and warmth. 22

Plateau stage in sexual response The second stage in human sexual response, in which structural changes take place. 268

Pleasant events theory Peter Lewinsohn's theory that people tend to feel happier when they are doing something they enjoy. 150

Positive reinforcement 334

Postconventional level of moral reasoning The third and highest level of moral reasoning in Kohlberg's theory, in which moral decisions are motivated by internal personal principles. 399

Post-hypnotic suggestion Instructions given by a hypnotist to an individual, to be carried out after he or she emerges from the hypnotic state. 378–79

Pragma (style of loving) The pragmatic lover is calculating and goes shopping to find a partner with the right interests and goals. The relationship is neither passionate nor intense. 227

Preconventional level of moral reasoning The first and lowest level of moral reasoning in Kohlberg's theory, in which decisions are based on achieving pleasure and avoiding pain. 399

Preconscious (foreconscious) A Freudian concept describing the construct of the mind that contains memories and feelings that can easily be brought into the consciousness if the individual focuses upon the material. 13

Prejudice A negative attitude about an individual based on his or her membership in a particular group. 393–98
  contact and 396–97
  definition 393
  economic conditions and 394
  handicapped and 398
  methods of reducing 396–98

Premack Principle A principle of learning that states that a common behavior can be used to reinforce a less-common behavior. 62, 63

Premarital sex 253–55

Premature ejaculation A sexual dysfunction in which the male cannot delay or control ejaculation for long enough to satisfy his partner at least 50 percent of the times they engage in coitus. 270–71

Pressure 113

Primary drives Drives that occur in every human being and are based upon innate biological needs. 32–33

Primary erectile dysfunction (primary impotence) A sexual problem in which a male has never been able to maintain an erection for long enough to complete coitus. 270

Primary sexual dysfunction A sexual problem of women in which females do not reach orgasm by any method of stimulation. 271

Privacy 48

Problem drinking This condition is generally distinguished from *alcoholism,* which involves a dependence on alcohol. It is hard to draw the line, but signs of problem drinking include intoxication when driving, intoxication four times within a year, or the feeling that one "must" have a drink in order to perform certain functions. 362, 368

Problem solving 71–73

Procreation The production of off-spring. 253

Progressive relaxation A form of relaxation training in which the muscles are slowly tensed, then suddenly relaxed throughout the body. 140

Projection A defense mechanism in which unacceptable motives or feelings are attributed to others. 133

Proxemics The study of the use of space to signify meaning. 217, 220–23

Psychiatrist A medical doctor who has specialized in psychiatry. A psychiatrist may prescribe medication. 347

Psychoanalysis The method of psychotherapy based upon the writings of Sigmund Freud. Psychoanalysis attempts to treat disturbances by providing clients with insights into their often unconscious sources. 328–29, 332–33
  evaluation of 332–33
  techniques used in 328–29

Psychoanalytic theory The theoretical position of Sigmund Freud and his followers. Psychoanalytic theory looks to the unconscious forces within the mind to explain personality and motivation. 10–15
  constructs of the mind 14–15
  levels of consciousness 11–13

Psychobabble Psychological jargon that sounds impressive but is devoid of any real meaning. 330

Psychodynamic A term used to describe therapies that are extensions of the thoughts and techniques of Freud and other therapists who have stressed the importance of insight. 318

Psychologist A professional usually possessing a Ph. D in psychology. 347

Psychology The study of human and animal behavior. 3

Psychopathic (sociopathic) A term used to describe individuals who experience no sense of guilt about performing antisocial actions. 144

Psychophysiological disorders 115–17

Psychosexual development 80

Psychosocial theory Erik Erikson's theory of psychological development within a cultural or social framework.

Each individual, says Erikson, travels through eight stages beginning at birth and ending in old age. Each stage has its positive as well as its negative outcomes. 79–88

Psychosomatic or psychophysiological disorders Illnesses that have been caused wholly or in part by psychological factors. Such disorders, which include ulcers and colitis, involve real physical damage to the body. 115–17

Psychotherapy Any form of treatment in which a trained professional therapist has regular contact with a client for the purpose of producing some sort of emotional or behavioral change. 327–49
  defined 327
  practical questions concerning 344, 346–49
  schools of 328–39
    behavior therapy 333–36
    cognitive therapy 338–39
    humanistic therapies 336–38
    psychoanalysis 328–29, 332–33
  self-help literature and 330–31

Public distance zone The distance between a public speaker, such as a politician or lecturer, and the audience; 12 feet or more. 226

Punishment Any event following a behavior that reduces the probability of the behavior reoccurring. Punishment is used to reduce or eliminate an undesirable behavior. 61, 63, 141

R

Rapid Eye Movement (REMs) Eye movements during sleep that are indicative of dreaming. 38

Rational-emotive imagery A therapeutic technique used in rational-emotive therapy in which the client is asked to imagine himself or herself feeling a certain way, then taught how to counter that feeling through the use of self-statements. 338

Rational-emotive therapy A type of cognitive therapy developed by Albert Ellis, which stresses the importance of an individual's beliefs, thoughts, and self-statements. It focuses on changing a person's thought patterns in order to alter feelings and behavior. 338–39
  evaluation 339

Rationalization A defense mechanism in which worthwhile motives

are ascribed to behaviors that really have other motives. 133

Reaction formation A defense mechanism in which an individual acts in the manner directly contrary to his or her actual feelings. 133

Readiness A developmental state in which an individual has the psychological and physical abilities to cope with a particular task. 90

Real self The way in which an individual perceives himself or herself at a particular point in time. 294–95

Reality anxiety A Freudian term used to describe anxiety that is focused on a real threat. 131

Rechannelization A defense mechanism in which the energy generated by anxiety or anger is channeled into socially acceptable pursuits. 133, 160

Recall The process of remembering something when few if any meaningful cues are provided. 70

Recognition A measurement of memory in which an individual is asked to identify information to which he or she has been exposed in the past. Recognition is tested in multiple-choice examinations. 70

Reflection A technique developed by Carl Rogers in which the listener (usually the counselor) demonstrates understanding of the feelings that underlie the client's statements by rephrasing them in a way that mirrors the client's feelings. 211, 337–38

Regression A defense mechanism in which an individual attempts to return to a more comfortable period of life. 133

Reinforcement Any event that increases the likelihood that the event preceding it will reoccur. 18, 56–58

Relaxation (see also Progressive relaxation) 140, 334, 375

Religious values and experiences 384–87

Reparation 145

Repression A defense mechanism by which unacceptable or anxiety-producing impulses, thoughts, or feelings are not allowed to enter consciousness. 14, 71, 133

Resistance (in psychoanalysis) Efforts on the part of the client in psychotherapy to avoid dealing with painful or anxiety-provoking material. For instance, a client may arrive late or simply refuse to discuss certain subjects. 332

Resistance stage of general adaptation syndrome The second stage of Selye's general adaptation syndrome, in which the body appears to return to its normal stage but in reality important glandular changes are taking place. 114–15

Resocialization The process by which an individual must learn to cope with demands of a new role while occupying that role. 180, 182

Resolution phase of sexual response The last stage of human sexual response, which involves the restoration of the body to its normal, unaroused state. 268

Respect One of Erich Fromm's four components of loving behavior. It relates to the honor and high esteem in which we hold the other individual in a loving relationship. 230

Responsibility One of Erich Fromm's four components of loving behavior. It refers to the consideration we give to the way in which our actions may affect the other person, and the extent to which we are willing to take responsibility for our actions. 230

Retirement 315

Retrieval 70

Roe's theory of need satisfaction The theory developed by Roe in which occupational choice is viewed in the context of an individual's needs. 307

Role ambiguity Work situations in which workers are uncertain of the exact nature of their responsibilities. 106

Role conflict A situation in which the demands of two or more roles assumed by an individual are to some extent contradictory. In the workplace, role conflict may refer to a situation in which two or more supervisors expect different, inconsistent, and incompatible behaviors from a worker. 107, 182–83

Role model An individual who serves as an example for another individual to imitate. (See also Social learning theory.) 144

Role overload A situation in which individuals cannot accomplish everything expected of them and thus must assign priorities to various tasks. 107

Role playing A technique used in assertiveness training, sensitivity groups, and psychotherapy. An individual acts out the role of another person as a way of developing insight into the other person's viewpoint. Role playing also provides an opportunity to practice new behaviors, such as assertiveness. 172

S

Safety needs (see also Security needs) 23

Scapegoating The displacement of anger and aggression from the source of a problem onto an individual or a group. 394

Schizophrenia A serious mental disorder often marked by hallucinations, delusions, and disorders in thinking. 89, 95

Second marriages 246–47

Secondary erectile dysfunction (secondary impotence) A sexual problem in which a man has failed to gain or maintain an erection 25 percent of the time during sexual encounters. 170

Secondary (learned) motive A motive, such as achievement or power, which is determined largely by the culture and is acquired through the various processes of learning. 32

Security needs The second level of needs in Maslow's hierarchy, involving the need for safety and order. 23

Self 24–25
  Rogers concept of 24–25
Self acceptance 294, 295–96

Self-actualization The fifth and highest level of needs in Maslow's need hierarchy, involving the full development of one's abilities and the reaching of one's potential. 24
  characteristics of self-actualized people 24

Self-concept The way in which individuals perceive themselves. 277–96, 406
  abstract self 285
  changes over time 286
  changing one's 289–91
  definition 277
  effects of disability on 283
  formation of 286–93
  ideal self 294–95
  personality and 284
  physical self 280–82
  real self 294–95
  social roles and 282–84

Self-disclosure The act by which a person reveals intimate and personal feelings and thoughts to another person. 208, 236, 337

Self-esteem The value individuals place on their own worth. 271

Self-fulfilling prophecy The concept that one's expectations concerning some event affect the probability of its occurrence. 93, 219

Self-help literature 327, 330–31

Self-monitoring One of the important steps to be taken in an attempt to alter one's own behavior. Individuals note the extent to which they indulge in a particular behavior, as well as the circumstances that surround it. This material is then used as a basis for a program of behavior change. 62–63

Self-reinforcement (See also Behavior modification, Learning, and Behavior therapy) 392

Sensate focus A technique used in sex therapies in which both partners stimulate the other in order to learn what each enjoys, then talk freely and openly about their feelings and experiences. 272–73

Sensitivity groups Short-term groups conducted by a leader, in which the participants interact in a way that facilitates personal and interpersonal growth. (see also Human potentials movement) 339–44

Sensitizers A pattern of behavior in which an individual overinterprets and overreacts to changes in the environment. See also the opposite pattern, *diminishers*. 121

Sex education 259–60

Sex roles The behaviors expected of individuals within a given society on the basis of whether they are male or female. 183–95
  definition 184
  formation of 187–92
    biological factors 187–89
    learning 189–92
  stereotypes of 184–87
  theoretical views of 191
Sex therapy 272–73

Sex-trait stereotype Psychological traits that people in a society believe to be characteristic of either males or females. 184–87

Sexism Prejudice and discrimination based upon gender. 192–95.

Sexual adjustment 249–73
  attitudes 250–52

in operant conditioning in which an individual receives a token for performing some desired behavior and may either save the tokens and combine them with others or redeem them for some object or privilege. 60

Tolerance The state at which a user requires greater and greater amounts of a drug in order ro attain the same effects. 339

Tranquilizers Any of a number of drugs that depress the central nervous system functioning, reduce anxiety, and have a calming effect on agitated individuals. 371

Transcendental meditation (TM) A type of meditation popularized by the Maharishi Mahesh Yogi. 373

Transference In psychoanalysis, the client's transfer to the therapist of feelings he or she held towards significant others in the past. 332

Trial-and-error An approach to problem solving in which a number of alternatives are tried until one succeeds. 73

Trust stage The first stage of an encounter group, in which the participants work out personal issues relating to the consequences of trusting the other members of the group. 341

Trust versus mistrust The first of Erik Erikson's eight psychosocial stages, this one occurring from birth to about eighteen months. 81

Type A behavior A pattern of behavior marked by extreme time consciousness, competitiveness, and impatience. 117–18
  and marriage 119

Type B behavior A pattern of behavior in which an individual tends to take life in stride, is easy-going, and is not very time conscious. 117–18

U

Unconscious One of Freud's three levels of conscious awareness; consists of the thoughts, impulses, and feelings of which an individual is not aware. 13, 328

V

Valium A commonly prescribed tranquilizer. 357, 372

Values Enduring beliefs that guide behavior. Specifically, they are beliefs that a specific behavior or end state is better than the opposite behavior or end state. 382, 383–89, 106
  changing 383–84
  conflict of 387–88
  constancy of 387
  definition 382
  differences and prejudice 396
  instrumental 388–89
  religious 384–85
  strength of personal 406
  terminal 388–89

Value clarification courses Courses, often based upon Kohlberg's theory, which entail presenting dilemmas to students and encouraging them to reason them out, taking into consideration many points of view. 385, 406

Value conflict A situation in which two or more values are at odds, so that an individual is forced to make a choice. 387–88

Variable interval reinforcement A schedule in which reinforcement is delivered when a correct response occurs after various lengths of time. 57–59

Variable ratio reinforcement A schedule in which reinforcement is delivered in response to a variable number of correct responses. 57–59

Verbal learning One form of learning (as opposed to *motor learning*), verbal learning involves the information we gain through the medium of language, as we read or hear about things from others. 65

Vocational choice 306–15, 344
  decision making and 311–15
  factors affecting 307–8
    family background 309

gender 309
intelligence 309
personal strengths and weaknesses 309–10
socioeconomic 307–8
theories of 306–7
  Holland 306
  Roe 306–7
  Super 306

Vocational interest inventory A measuring instrument designed to discover the extent to which the test-taker's interests coincide with workers in particular occupational groups. 314

Vocational maturity A term coined by Donald Super, referring to an individual's particular level of vocational development. 306

Vocational life patterns 314–19
  men's life patterns 314–15
  women's life patterns 315, 316–19, 321–22

W

Weight control programs 36
Wild boy of Aveyron 51–52
Women
  attitudes towards sex 252
  employment and 241, 315, 318–20
  fear of success 46
  premarital sex 254
  sex roles 185, 186–90
  sex trait stereotypes 184, 186–7
  sexual problems 271–72
Work 298–23
  changes in job market 304–5
  functions of 299–300
  life styles and 314–22
  vocational choice 306–15

Work ethic A group of values emphasizing the importance of hard work, achievement through one's own efforts, and success. 300–4

Y

Yerkes-Dodson Law The psychological principle that links arousal with performance. 135